INTRODUCTION TO CRIMINOLOGY

Eighth Edition

INTRODUCTION TO CRIMINOLOGY

Hugh D. Barlow

Southern Illinois University Edwardsville

David Kauzlarich

Southern Illinois University Edwardsville

Prentice Hall

UPPER SADDLE RIVER, NEW JERSEY 07458

Library of Congress Cataloging-in-Publication Data

Barlow, Hugh D.
    Introduction to criminology/Hugh D. Barlow, David Kauzlarich—8th ed.
      p. cm.
    Includes bibliographical references and index.
    ISBN 0-13-085124-8
      1. Criminology.   2. Criminal Justice, Administration of.   I. Kauzlarich, David.   II. Title.

HV6025.B29 2001
364—dc21
                                                2001036034

VP, Editorial director: Laura Pearson
AVP, Publisher: Nancy Roberts
Senior acquisitions editor: Christopher DeJohn
Editorial assistant: Christina Scalia
Editorial/production supervision: Kari Callaghan Mazzola
Prepress and manufacturing buyer: Mary Ann Gloriande
Electronic page makeup: Kari Callaghan Mazzola and John P. Mazzola
Interior design: John P. Mazzola
Director, Image Resource Center: Melinda Reo
Manager, Rights and Permissions: Kay Dellosa
Interior image specialist: Beth Boyd
Photo researcher: Melinda Alexander
Image permissions coordinator: Charles Morris
Cover design: Ximena Tamvakopoulos
Cover art: Teofolio Olivieri/Images.com

This book was set in 10/12 Meridien by Big Sky Composition
and was printed and bound by Courier Companies, Inc.
The cover was printed by Phoenix Color Corp.

© 2002 by Pearson Education, Inc.
Upper Saddle River, New Jersey 07458

Printed in the United States of America
10 9 8 7 6 5 4 3 2 1

ISBN 0-13-085124-8

Pearson Education LTD., London
Pearson Education Australia PTY, Limited, Sydney
Pearson Education Singapore, Pte. Ltd
Pearson Education North Asia Ltd, Hong Kong
Pearson Education Canada, Ltd., Toronto
Pearson Educación de Mexico, S.A. de C.V.
Pearson Education—Japan, Tokyo
Pearson Education Malaysia, Pte. Ltd
Pearson Education, Upper Saddle River, New Jersey

To our wives, Karen and Sandy

CONTENTS

CHAPTER 4

VIOLENCE AGAINST WOMEN AND CHILDREN   68

CHAPTER 11

CRIME AND SOCIAL STRUCTURE   240

PREFACE

This eighth edition of *Introduction to Criminology* makes a significant departure from earlier editions: Dave Kauzlarich has joined Hugh D. Barlow as coauthor of the text. This change has brought new vitality to the writing and new coverage that reflects Dave's special expertise. We believe that users of earlier editions will find that this change has resulted in a better book.

We have saved those features of previous editions that made it a unique introduction to criminology. For example, many chapters still frame their subject matter within a historical context. Learning about history helps students understand how present-day conditions and events came about, and it suggests prospects for the future as well. Crime has a past, and what students learn today may come to influence crime's future.

The book also continues to embrace a social constructionist/labeling approach. This perspective takes nothing for granted, and includes an emphasis on reactions to crime and criminals. Indeed, criminology is not just about studying those who violate laws; it is also about how laws and rules are made and who is subject to them. Thus, many chapters include a discussion of the official and unofficial reactions to crimes.

The chapters continue to be organized in a way that we feel best introduces the student to the field of criminology. After an introduction to basic concepts and definitions, we discuss how information about crime is produced and the major scientific methods used to study it. We then describe and illustrate varieties of crime and criminality. Finally, we delve into the complex business of explanation. Such an inductive approach, it seems to us, helps students at both the front and back ends of the learning process. Only when students have a broad knowledge of the nature and varieties of crime are they ready to contemplate theories to explain it. The number of chapters on theory remains unchanged from the seventh edition, but there is now more on the explanation of white-collar crime. The last chapter, on general theories of crime, continues to be unique, and now includes Tittle's control balance theory.

In addition to the usual updating of crime statistics, tests of theory, and important studies, several other changes have been made. There are now fourteen chapters rather than eighteen chapters; we believe this makes the book more manageable for the typical course. We have collapsed the former robbery chapter into a new chapter on violence that also covers school violence, gangs, and hate crimes. We now discuss public order crimes in one, rather than two, chapters. Domestic violence is now in a new chapter that focuses on violence against women and that also includes discussion of sexual assault. Perhaps most notably, we have dropped the separate police, courts, and corrections chapters in favor of one chapter that focuses on the relationship between criminology and criminal justice. We have learned that many instructors never assigned the original chapters on police, courts, and corrections, preferring to spend more time discussing the nature of crime and its explanation. We therefore decided to concentrate on the criminology of criminal justice, including the nature and consequences of discretion, the crime prevention function of the police, and the relationship between crime and punishment.

We have added more information in Chapter 2 on research methods in criminology, including a revised section on research ethics. A new review of lesser-known research methods such as ethnography and case study approaches adds balance to the chapter. We have reorganized and rewritten the chapter on white-collar crime to more clearly distinguish occupational from organizational crime. In doing so, we have drawn upon Dave Kauzlarich's special expertise—state crime. We now include sections on human rights violations, economic terrorism, and crimes of the nuclear weapons industry.

Chapter 10 now reads as a stand-alone chapter on metatheory. It explains the nature, form, and history of criminological theory, including issues such as causality, ideology, level of analysis, paradigmatic assumptions, and the scope and breadth of theory. The second section of the chapter discusses the philosophical, scientific, and classical sociological influences on the development of criminology and criminological theory.

Finally, we have attempted to make the writing more accessible to undergraduates without sacrificing quality or oversimplifying a complicated field. We now provide boldfaced key terms within the text, as well as the following end-of-chapter sections: Key Terms, Recommended Readings, and Recommended Web Sites.

SUPPLEMENTS

The supplementary materials that accompany *Introduction to Criminology* have been carefully created to enhance the topics being discussed. Please contact your school's Prentice Hall representative for more information or to order copies for classroom use upon adoption.

Test Item File

This carefully prepared resource, available in both print and computerized form, includes 470 questions—approximately 34 per chapter—in multiple choice, true/false, and essay formats. The answers to all questions are page-referenced to the text. Prentice Hall Test Manager is a computerized test generator designed to allow the creation of personalized exams. It is available in Windows and Macintosh formats. Users of this text can also obtain a test preparation service by calling Prentice Hall's toll-free 800 number.

Prentice Hall Criminology PowerPoint Slides

Created by Steve Glennon, this PowerPoint slide set combines graphics and text in a colorful format to help convey criminological principles in a new and exciting way. Created in PowerPoint, an easy-to-use, widely available software program, this set contains over 200 content slides keyed to topics within the text.

ABC News/Prentice Hall Video Library for Sociology

Prentice Hall and ABC News are working together to bring you the best and most comprehensive video ancillaries available for your introductory course. Selected video segments from award-winning ABC News programs such as Nightline, ABC World News Tonight, and 20/20 accompany topics featured in each chapter. In addition, an instructor's guide to the videos includes a synopsis of video and discussion questions to help students focus on how concepts and theories apply to real-life situations. (Volume for Criminology: 0-13-375163-5.)

Criminology Companion Website™

In tandem with the text, students and professors can take full advantage of the World Wide Web to enrich the learning process in criminology. Features of the Web site include chapter objectives, chapter summaries, and quizzes, as well as hundreds of links to interesting material and information from other sites on the Web that can reinforce and enhance the content of each chapter. The address is **www.prenhall.com/barlow**

Sociology on the Internet: Evaluating Online Resources, 2001

This guide provides a brief introduction to navigating the Internet, along with references related specifically to the discipline of sociology and information on how to use the *Companion Website*™ for *Introduction to Criminology, Eighth Edition*. This supplementary book is free to students when shrinkwrapped as a package with *Introduction to Criminology, Eighth Edition*.

ACKNOWLEDGMENTS

The authors have many people to thank. At Prentice Hall, John Chillingworth, Wayne Spohr, Chris DeJohn, and Christina Scalia welcomed the project and gave important symbolic and material support. Kari Callaghan Mazzola of Big Sky Composition made the production process go smoothly—we appreciate her hard work. The Department of Sociology at Southern Illinois University, Edwardsville, gave us support and encouragement, and special thanks go to professor John Farley and to Barbara Hickman, department secretary, for their valuable support. Thanks also go to the following graduate assistants for their help on this project: Kate Marchioro, Karen Rieser, and Robin Peterson. In particular, Kate made this book easier to write by providing extensive literature reviews, insightful substantive feedback, and sound editorial advice.

The authors are indebted to the critical insights of colleagues around the country. These include professors who have used previous editions, as well as the following reviewers of the new edition: Keith Crew, University of Northern Iowa; Thomas Petee, Auburn University; Ronald Burns, Texas Christian University; Fred Markowitz, Northern Illinois University; Frank Steyn, Kettering College of Medical Arts; and Bernadette Jones Palombo, Louisiana State University at Shreveport. We would also like to acknowledge reviewers of previous editions of this text: Jay Corzine, University of Nebraska–Lincoln; Patrick Donnelly, University of Dayton; Pat Dorman, Boise State University;

Kevin Early, Oakland University; C. Randall Eastep, Brevard Community College; Jawad Fatayer, West Texas A&M University; David Horton, St. Edwards University; Michael Milakovitch, University of Miami; Robert L. Robinson, Lincoln University; and Javier Trevino, Marquette University.

Since this is Dave Kauzlarich's first involvement with the book—and his first experience as a textbook author—he wishes to thank the following people for their influence on his work as a criminologist: Ronald C. Kramer, Steven A. Egger, Robert K. Moore Jr., Gerald E. Markle, Rick A. Matthews, Paul C. Friday, Eric O. Johnson, Brian B. Smith, Raymond J. Michalowski, Regan Smith, David O. Friedrichs, Larry Golden, Bill Chambliss, and Claire M. Renzetti. Finally, Dave thanks Hugh Barlow for the invitation to join him as coauthor; he promises not to beat him at golf anymore.

We both wish to thank our families. Hugh is indebted to—and grateful for the love and understanding of—his wife, Karen, and his children, Alison, Melissa, Eric, Colin, Chelsea, and Kelsey. Dave wishes to express his deepest gratitude to his wife, Sandy, for over a decade of patience, love, and support, and to his children, Elaina and Jake, for helping him become more centered and appreciative of the smaller things.

The experience of writing this book has been memorable. Many days were spent hunched over the computer, side by side, slurping coffee and rifling through books and papers. Intense periods of work and intellectual discourse were thankfully interrupted by absolutely back-breaking laughter, witty retorts, spontaneous debates, ribbing about each other's golf games, and even, in a few instances, the pleas of our office neighbors to "keep it down." We suspect that we are among the few members of a lonely club: "Textbook coauthors who had a great time writing their book."

Hugh D. Barlow
David Kauzlarich

ABOUT THE AUTHORS

Hugh D. Barlow (left) and David Kauzlarich (right).

Hugh D. Barlow, Ph.D., is professor of sociology and chair of the Department of Sociology at Southern Illinois University, Edwardsville.

Dr. Barlow received his M.A. and Ph.D. degrees from the University of Texas at Austin. At SIUE he has developed a variety of courses in crime and delinquency, victimology, and criminal justice; in 1997 he designed a new undergraduate major in criminal justice. Students have nominated Dr. Barlow for teaching awards on numerous occasions, and in 1995 he received the SIUE Teaching Recognition Award.

Dr. Barlow has published articles on homicide and assaults, the spatial aspects of crime, and white-collar crime. He is also the author of *Criminal Justice in America*. He is coauthor with Theodore N. Ferdinand of *Understanding Delinquency*, and editor of *Crime and Public Policy: Putting Theory to Work*. The journal *Federal Probation* rated this book one of the top ten published works of 1995.

In addition to teaching and research, Dr. Barlow has been active in applied areas and in service to the profession. From January 1986 to December 1989 Dr. Barlow was Editor of *The Criminologist*, published by the American Society of Criminology. In 1993 he received the Herbert A. Bloch Award from the ASC for "outstanding service contributions to the American Society of Criminology and to the professional interests of criminology."

On a less serious level, Dr. Barlow enjoys driving, golfing, snow skiing, and playing poker.

David Kauzlarich, Ph.D., is an assistant professor of sociology at Southern Illinois University, Edwardsville. In 1989 he received his undergraduate degree in Social Justice Professions from the University of Illinois–Springfield. He received both his M.A. (1991) and Ph.D. (1994) in sociology from Western Michigan University. From 1994 to 1997 Dr. Kauzlarich was a member of the Sociology and Criminal Justice faculty at St. Joseph's University, where he also directed the Graduate Criminal Justice Program.

Dr. Kauzlarich particularly enjoys teaching introductory criminology. As a graduate student teacher at Western Michigan, he was awarded the "Excellence in Teaching Award" three consecutive times. His most challenging but rewarding teaching experience was in the Florence Crane Prison, a medium-security prison for women in Michigan.

He is indebted to those students, for he learned from them important lessons about criminal stereotypes and the role of education in preventing traditional forms of crime and criminality.

Dr. Kauzlarich has authored or coauthored over a dozen scholarly articles and one other book, with Ron Kramer, *Crimes of the American Nuclear State: At Home and Abroad*. He has published on the topics of state and corporate crime, including problems such as environmental crime, human rights abuses, and nuclear weapons experiments. He has also written on theoretical explanations of white-collar crime.

Dr. Kauzlarich enjoys writing and playing music, golf, fishing, and camping. Even more, he enjoys clowning around with his children, Elaina and Jake.

INTRODUCTION
TO CRIMINOLOGY

CRIME AND CRIMINALITY

Most Americans are touched by crime at some point in their lives. If they are not directly victimized themselves, they see or hear of others being victimized. Despite the fact that crime surrounds us, it is often misunderstood. In large measure this has to with how the media portrays the crime "problem" (Best 1999). Open almost any newspaper and you will find at least one article about crime. However, big city papers do not bother to report petty thefts and vandalism, or even most robberies, assaults, and burglaries, while small-town papers often make them headline news. Big-city newspapers seldom give front page coverage even to rape or murder unless there is a sensational angle to it. The arrest and prosecution of O. J. Simpson, the Unabomber (Ted Kaczynski), the bombers of the Oklahoma City Federal Building (Timothy McVeigh and Terry Nichols), and the investigation of the death of JonBenet Ramsey are prime examples. All of these cases involved murder, which represents less than 0.1 percent of all crimes committed in the United States each year. The cases were front page news for many days, and the JonBenet case is still a hot topic. Even so, most murder stories do not stay on the front page for long, and many are forgotten by the time the trial (if there is one) begins.

If newspapers were the sole source of information about crime and criminals, the picture would be highly distorted. For example, newspapers report violent crimes much more often than property crimes, but the real frequency of these phenomena is the reverse: The vast majority of crimes are property offenses. Newspaper editors weigh the information they receive according to its newsworthiness and then report it selectively. Furthermore, conjecture and opinion are presented as news and "experts" are used whose views fit the particular version of the story being told (Kappeler, Blumberg, and Potter 2000). The resulting "reality" is generally far from the truth. The reality of crime reported by the press is one of exceptionally violent, exceptionally greedy, or exceptionally corrupt people picking on exceptionally vulnerable victims. In addition, the coverage is often racially biased (especially against African-American males), as Barlow, Barlow, and Chiricos (1995a) have found from their content analysis of *Time* magazine.

The image portrayed on TV and movie screens is even more distorted. Consider shows such as *NYPD Blue*, *Crime and Punishment*, and *Law and Order*, along with *COPS* and *The True Stories of the Highway Patrol*. Crime and criminal justice are even the subjects of science fiction-fantasy television shows like the *X Files*, where FBI agents are charged with saving the world from aliens or supernatural serial murderers. The images of crime on television are often sensational, and the criminals are brought to justice because of exceptionally talented police, exceptionally tenacious lawyers, or exceptionally wily private eyes (Barak 1994; Lichter & Lichter 1983). In short, "ordinary crime is not news" (Chermak 1994, 99), nor is there much entertainment value in it.

UNCOVERING THE "TRUE" STORY OF CRIME

Criminologists try to uncover the "true" story of crime, but the truth is socially constructed. What we know about the world of crime is a product of how people—particularly those in power—define, interpret, and react to crime (Chambliss 1999). What "officially" counts as crime depends on, among other things: what behaviors legislators declare as punishable; whether or not a victim decides to report an incident to the police; how the police exercise discretion in making a stop, search, or arrest; what specific charges the prosecutor's office decides on and whether they drop the case or continue with it; and what the courts declare as fair and reasonable evidence. So, when people speak of the nature, extent, and distribution of crime, it is important to consider the source upon which those claims are based.

In sum, when we speak of "crime" or "criminals" our images and ideas are influenced by the people and institutions that regulate human behavior, and by those who sell the images to us. Even self-report and victimization surveys of crime (discussed in Chapter 2) are based on socially constructed images. One person's experience and understanding of crime may not be the same as another's, even though the objective facts are the same. Simply put: "There is no such thing as a pure fact innocent of interpretation" (Zinn 1999, 658).

Criminology is, nevertheless, interested in seeking out the facts about crime. Exposure to these facts is sometimes painful and often surprising. As you read through the fourteen chapters of this text, you will learn that the most likely victims of crime are the poor; you will learn that crime is like a huge iceberg of which only the tip is reported to and by the police; you will learn that most criminals are not punished for their crimes. You will also learn that the most likely place where women and children are assaulted is the home, and the numbers are staggering—as many as four million women and three million children are abused by other family members in the United States each year. You will learn that gang violence and drug use are widespread—but also that many youth gangs spend most of their time doing other things. You will learn that American jails and prisons are full of young males, half of them African-American, and most of them from city neighborhoods where joblessness, overcrowding, and physical deterioration are commonplace. You will learn that even though the costs of corporate and state crime far exceed those of traditional street crimes such as robbery, burglary, and auto theft combined, white-collar criminals are less likely than others to be arrested and prosecuted, and, if convicted, less likely to go to jail or prison. Box 1.1 (at top of page 4) provides some other well-known facts about crime.

One of the goals of criminology is to separate fact from myth. Sometimes the reality may contradict not only media representations but our own personal beliefs as well. For example, many students we talk to believe that the crime rate has been growing in recent years. However, the reality is that all available measures show a decrease in nearly all forms of traditional street crime. Figures 1.1 and 1.2 (at the bottom of page 4) show a measure of crime based on victimization rates—in this case the number of households per 1,000 experiencing a crime against one or more household members from 1993 to 1999. Studies recently conducted in Canada, Australia, and the United States reveal that, most of the time, the public believes that violent crime rates are much higher than they actually are (Roberts and Stalans 1997). In fact, a recent Gallup poll showed that despite falling crime rates, half or more of the U.S. respondents believed that the crime rate grew in each of the past several years (The Gallup Organization 2000).

While every science tries to distinguish between myth and reality, the task is especially difficult in criminology because students often come to the study of crime with preexisting assumptions and conclusions. Some students have strong opinions about the causes of crime and what to do with people convicted of crimes. However, rarely does someone walk into an introductory biology class with a strong moral or political opinion on zygotes or photosynthesis. The challenge of understanding crime demands the ability to suspend final judgment until our conclusions are based on valid and reliable information. Most people, however, simply have not had the opportunity to study crime in detail. This text is designed to provide readers with this opportunity.

BOX 1.1   SOME FACTS ABOUT "STREET" CRIME

"Street" crime is a term that identifies common crimes such as burglary, assault, drug possession and sales, robbery, rape, and many less serious offenses involving theft or destruction of property. It excludes corporate crime, state crime, tax evasion, embezzlement, and a variety of other offenses committed in connection to work.

The text mentions various facts about crime that challenge conventional wisdom and illuminate the limitations of media portrayals of crime and justice in America. Here are some facts about street crime that are true in America as well as in many other countries.

- Crime is committed disproportionately by males.
- Crime is committed disproportionately by 15–25-year-olds.
- Crime is committed disproportionately by people living in large cities.
- Crime is committed disproportionately by those who live in areas of high residential mobility.
- Young people who are strongly attached to their school are less likely to engage in crime.
- Young people who have high educational and occupational aspirations are less likely to engage in crime.
- Young people who do poorly in school are more likely to engage in crime.
- Young people who are strongly attached to their parents are less likely to engage in crime.
- Young people who have friendships with criminals are more likely to engage in crime themselves.

Source: John Braithwaite, *Crime, Shame, and Reintegration* (Cambridge, Eng.: Cambridge University Press, 1989), 44–46.

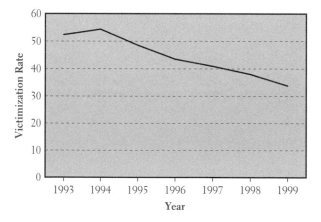

▲ FIGURE 1.1
Violent Crime Victimization Rates per 1,000 Households, 1993–1999
Source: Bureau of Justice Statistics, *Criminal Victimization, 1999* (Washington, D.C.: U.S. Department of Justice, 2000), 10.

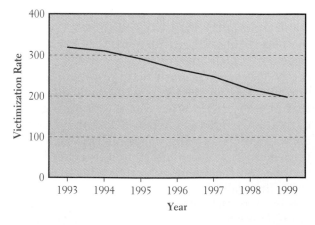

▲ FIGURE 1.2
Property Crime Victimization Rates per 1,000 Households, 1993–1999
Source: Bureau of Justice Statistics, *Criminal Victimization, 1999* (Washington, D.C.: U.S. Department of Justice, 2000), 10.

WHAT IS CRIMINOLOGY?

Criminology can be defined in any number of ways, but Sutherland and Cressey's (1974) conceptualization is the clearest: **Criminology** is the study of lawmaking, lawbreaking, and the reactions to crime. There are many specialties in criminology, and Table 1.1 provides a list of some of the major ones.

Lawmaking

The first part of the definition of criminology is the study of *lawmaking*, which focuses on political, economic, and cultural factors that help shape laws and criminal justice policies: Why and how are certain behaviors crimes? Why has there been an historic lack of effective laws protecting women and children from abuse in the home? Why and how were early laws prohibiting theft developed? Why and how were "three strikes and you're out" policies created, and why are they supported? The criminological study of lawmaking, sometimes called the sociology of law, has shown that law and policy reflect the interests of those in power. For example, the history of rape laws has largely been the history of males exercising power over females. This is discussed in more detail in Chapter 11.

Crime and victimization rates are highest in inner cities and lowest in rural areas. What is it about "place" that explains this difference? Is it poverty? Unemployment? Lack of social cohesion? Or something else? The complex relationship between place, class, and crime is an important focus of criminology.

TABLE 1.1   **Some Major Subject Areas in Criminology**

Age and Crime
Alcohol, Drugs, and Crime
Biology and Crime
Comparative Criminology
Crime and Public Policy
Crime and the Media
Criminological Theory
Economic Class and Crime
Environmental Criminology
Fear of Crime
Gender and Crime
Guns and Crime
Hate Crime
Juvenile Delinquency
Race, Ethnicity, and Crime
Research Methods
Social Control Institutions (Police, Courts, and Corrections)
Victimology
Violence against Women
White Collar Crime (Including State and Corporate Crime)

Lawbreaking

The second major part of the definition of criminology is the study of *lawbreaking*. Criminologists are interested in how and why people commit crime. Criminologists might study the causes and correlates of juvenile delinquency, drug and alcohol use, violent crime, property crime, hate crime, violence against women, or literally dozens of other types of crime. They might also focus on what specific things draw people toward or away from crime, such as family relationships, peers, neighborhood, social class, gender, race, and employment status.

One example of how some criminologists have addressed the question of lawbreaking can be shown in the area of race and crime. Although the risk of being a victim of most street crimes has remained relatively stable or even declined during the past fifteen years, the risks are not borne equally: African-Americans have higher rates of victimization than whites for many offenses, including rape, robbery, aggravated assault, and motor vehicle theft (see Figure 1.3). Most of this crime is young black males victimizing other blacks. When explaining this fact, it has become fashionable in some circles to downplay the dehumanizing and disruptive setting in which many urban blacks spend their lives, as if their behavior is somehow unaffected by the environment and they are personally responsible for (or deserve) the ills that confront them.

A good place to begin studying the plight of America's underclass from a sociological perspective is by reading William Julius Wilson (1987) and Elijah Anderson (1990, 1994, 1999). These scholars have documented the life experiences of young inner-city black males, and the picture is grim. On the issue of violence, for example, Anderson (1994, 81) has this to say:

> The inclination to violence stems from circumstances of life among ghetto poor—the lack of jobs that pay a living wage, the stigma of race, the fallout from rampant drug use and drug trafficking, and the resulting alienation and lack of hope for the future.

While this is only one view on the complicated topic of race and crime, much criminological theory and research supports this interpretation, as will become evident in later chapters of the text.

Reactions to Crime

The third major area of inquiry within criminology is the study of the *reactions to crime*. This includes the study of the state's reaction (e.g., the police, courts, and correctional institutions) as well as the analysis of various other criminal justice policies and practices (e.g., capital punishment). Criminologists also study the public's reaction to crime. One well-researched topic in this area is the fear of crime.

FEAR OF CRIME   Public opinion surveys conducted by the National Opinion Research Center show that over 40 percent of those polled are afraid to walk alone at night in their own neighborhoods (Maguire and Pastore 1999, Table 2.37). A major study conducted in 1995 revealed that 45 percent of the respondents feared that their homes would be burglarized and 38 percent feared that they themselves or members of their family would become victims of sexual assault (Haghighi and Sorensen 1996).

Fear of crime is greater for some groups of people than for others. For example, women are almost three times more likely than men to feel unsafe in their own neighborhoods at night. Some other findings are that African-Americans are more fearful than whites, and that fear tends to go up as income goes down. Over the years since 1971, these national levels and differences in fear have not changed in any meaningful way.

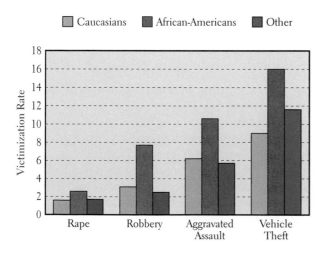

▲ FIGURE 1.3
Race and Criminal Victimization, 1999, Self-Reported Victimization per 1,000 Households

Source: Bureau of Justice Statistics, *Criminal Victimization, 1999* (Washington, D.C.: U.S. Department of Justice, 2000), 6, 9.

> People living in inner-city slums like Harlem show the effects of fear in ways that would be unimaginable in middle-class neighborhoods: In any Harlem building, ... every door has at least three locks on it. Nobody opens a door without first finding out who's there.... If you live in Harlem, USA, you don't park your automobile two blocks from your apartment house because that gives potential muggers an opportunity to get a fix on you. You'd better find a parking space within a block of your house, because if you have to walk two blocks you're not going to make it. (Claude Brown, cited in Moore and Trojanowicz 1988, 2)

Conventional wisdom holds that the people most afraid of crime are those who have been personally victimized by it. While this is true to some extent, the relationship between experiencing crime and fearing crime is not simple. Elderly women, for example, are most afraid yet least often victimized, and young men are least afraid yet most often victimized (Skogan and Maxfield 1981; Bureau of Justice Statistics 1993a; Haghighi and Sorensen 1996). Those who have experienced crime themselves are no more likely to be afraid than people who have merely heard about other people's victimization. In fact, one researcher discovered that actual criminal victimization is less important as a cause of fear than the physical and social environments in which people live (Skogan 1986). So-called "social and physical incivilities" in a neighborhood such as unkempt lots, graffiti, homeless people, drunks, and trash may raise levels of fear among both residents and visitors by affecting people's *perceptions* of the risk of being victimized (LaGrange, Ferraro, and Supancic 1992). Finally, there is recent evidence that television news broadcasts have a strong impact on people's fear of crime, regardless of their victimization experiences or local crime rates (Chiricos, Padgett, and Gertz 2000).

The remaining sections of this chapter discuss some of the important concepts and ideas that define the subject matter of criminology. What is crime? Who is the criminal? Where does law come in? What is the connection between crime and public policy?

WHAT IS CRIME?

The legal or *legalistic* definition of crime is a departure point for considering the subject matter of criminology. The definition simply states, "Crime is a human act that violates the criminal law."

This definition has two important components. First, crime involves behavior: Someone has to perform some act. Second, this behavior is identified in terms of a body of substantive law. According to that law, a number of specific criteria must normally be met for an act to be considered a crime and the perpetrator a criminal. First, there must be conduct, or *actus reus* (mere thoughts, no

matter how terrible, are not crimes). Second, the conduct must constitute a social harm; that is, the conduct must be injurious to the state (or "the people"). Third, the conduct must be prohibited by law. Fourth, the conduct must be performed voluntarily. Fifth, the conduct usually must be performed intentionally (the issue here is criminal intent, expressed in the concept of *mens rea*, meaning guilty mind); however, unintentional acts of negligence or omission may qualify as crimes in some cases. Sixth, the harm must be causally related to the conduct; that is, the act must produce the harm. Finally, the conduct must be punishable by law (in fact, the punishment must be specified in advance of the conduct).

The legalistic definition of crime is popular among both criminologists and the general public; however it has not gone without challenge (see Box 1.2 on page 8 for examples). Many years ago Thorsten Sellin (1938) argued for a more universally applicable definition that would encompass any violation of what he called *conduct norms*. Sellin believed that the legal criteria used in legal definitions of crime are at best artificial and arbitrary and at worst ignore other actions that conflict with the "general social interest." In Sellin's view, criminologists should study all conduct that violates group norms.

Around the same time, Edwin H. Sutherland (1945) argued that crime should be defined not only in terms of traditional criminal law, but also in terms of regulatory law—for example, restraint of trade, antitrust, and unfair labor practices, rules, and regulations. Sutherland, who coined the term "white-collar" crime, argued that criminologists who only study robbery, burglary, or theft are biased because they neglect the crimes of the more powerful members of society. Sutherland's viewpoint was very influential and it gave rise to the study of white-collar crime, an important subfield of criminology that is the subject matter of Chapter 6.

Other critics of the legalistic approach to the definition of crime include Jeffrey Reiman and Herman and Julia Schwendinger. Reiman (2001) lists a variety of acts and conditions that are similar to crime in terms of their consequences, for example, loss of life, physical injury, or property loss: "The workplace, the medical profession, the air we breathe, and the poverty we refuse to rectify lead

Box 1.2   THREE CHALLENGES TO THE LEGALISTIC DEFINITION OF CRIME

The legalistic definition of crime is popular for its simplicity, but has been challenged for various reasons, as discussed in the text. The following quotes illustrate three different positions on the definition of crime.

(The) argument for limiting criminological inquiry to the specifications of the law overlooks the fact that the law itself reflects a set of subjectively held values, and limiting investigation within its boundaries reflects a no more inherently "scientific" choice than expanding inquiry beyond the law.... Right and wrong are moral concepts. The criminal law is essentially a politically enforced definition of right and wrong. Therefore, neither those who support a criminology that goes beyond the law's definition of right and wrong nor those who wish to keep it within these limits are making morally neutral choices. Any moral choice, even those about "scientific" data, will reflect the individual's values. (Raymond J. Michalowski, *Order, Law and Crime* [New York: Random House, 1985], 317)

Criminologists often complain that they do not control their own dependent variable, that the definition of crime is decided by political-legal acts rather than by scientific procedures. The state, not the scientist, determines the nature or definition of crime. This book breaks with this tradition of passive compliance and attempts to construct a definition of crime consistent with the phenomenon itself and with the best available theory of criminal behavior.... [C]rimes [are] acts of force or fraud undertaken in pursuit of self-interest." (Michael R. Gottfredson and Travis Hirschi, *A General Theory of Crime* [Stanford, CA: Stanford University Press, 1990], 3, 15)

Only those are criminals who have been adjudicated as such by the courts. Crime is an intentional act in violation of the criminal law.... Criminology ... cannot tolerate a nomenclature of such loose and variable usage [by anti-legalists]. (Paul Tappan, "Who is the Criminal," *American Sociological Review* 12 [1947]: 100)

It should be remembered that all legal systems are contextual in that they reflect the particular cultural and political characteristics of the times and places in which they were created or modified. This means that the legalistic elements of a crime may not be the same over time or in different jurisdictions.

to more human suffering, far more death and disability, and take more dollars from our pockets than the murders, aggravated assaults, and thefts reported annually by the FBI" (Reiman 2001, 98). Reiman believes that the legal definition of crime does not encompass all or even the most socially injurious acts.

The Schwendingers argue that the definition of crime does not have to be associated with law. They propose that criminologists can and should study things such as imperialism, racism, sexism, and other violations of human rights:

Our disagreement with such social scientists as Thorsten Sellin and Edwin Sutherland ... is not over the independent character of criminal behavior. Instead, the issue at hand is whether social scientists have been fully justified in regarding the legalistic definitions of the behavior under study as the only justifiable definitions of what can be treated as crime. (1970, 73)

Other criminologists argue that crimes include violations of international law, such as the Declaration of Human Rights, the Nuremberg Principles, and the Geneva Conventions (Kauzlarich and Kramer 1998).

A quite different approach is taken by Michael Gottfredson and Travis Hirschi (1990), although they too believe that the subject matter of criminology should not be restricted to strictly legal categories of crime. They believe that many acts are similar to common crimes, from smoking cigarettes and eating between meals to gambling and speeding. Just like robbery, murder, rape, employee theft, and drug use, these acts are easy to commit, require little or no planning or skill, and are exciting, risky, or thrilling.

Finally, the so-called **labeling perspective** argues that crimes are distinguished from other acts precisely because they have been defined as crimes by people whose reactions matter. In other words, the social significance of a given act is in the reactions it calls forth. As Howard Becker (1963, 9) has observed:

> ... deviance is not a quality of the act the person commits, but rather a consequence of the application by others of rules and sanctions to an 'offender.' The deviant is one to whom the label has been successfully applied; deviant behavior is behavior that people so label.

Pursuing this reasoning, what makes behavior distinctive is the kinds of reactions it calls forth. The distinctive aspect of criminal behavior is that the behavior in question has been labeled crime (Hartjen 1974, 5–8). When labeled as crime, behavior is transformed into criminal behavior, and the actor may be transformed into a criminal. This transformation is called **criminalization**. The opposite process—when the label criminal is removed from an action, event, or person—is called **decriminalization**. The labeling perspective views crime as status rather than as behavior. Bearing these points in mind, an alternative definition of crime might be stated as follows: Crime is a label that is attached to behavior and events by those who create and administer the criminal law (Barlow 1996, 10).

While sensitive to the complex issues surrounding definitions of crime, in the end many criminologists use the legalistic definition. Even though most of the activities and events called crime in this text fall under the legalistic definition, we prefer a definition that treats crimes as both a behavior and a status. In this text, therefore, we define **crime** as

> actions and/or labels that represent violation of criminal laws and other regulations designed to protect individuals and groups from victimization.

Consistent with this definition, a **criminal** is

> a person whose actions violate the criminal law and/or have been called crimes.

VICTIMS OF CRIME

Victims are arguably the forgotten people in the crime scene. The primary reason is historical: The development of modern criminal law and the corresponding decline of primitive law (discussed in the next section) left victims no formal role in the criminal process. Historically, the word *victim* did not even appear in many statute books, nor were individuals thought of as victims—the "state" or the "people" were the victimized by any crime. This is why criminal cases are usually titled "The People" or "The State of X" versus a defendant.

A secondary reason relates to the orientation of science and public policy in criminal matters, which has traditionally focused on how to explain and deal with the behavior of criminals. Little attention has been paid to victims, and when they are brought in it is either as contributing causes of crime (especially common in discussions of assault, rape, and murder), in debates over whether some crimes are victimless (consensual sex offenses and drug use, for example), or as people who can help convict the offender.

But this picture has been changing dramatically in recent years. An international effort is underway to study the victimizing effects of crime (and other social ills) and to bring the real victim back into the picture. Much of this effort has been directed at changing criminal justice policy and practice to accommodate a more active role for victims.

For years, victims have been "twice victimized," first by the criminal and then by the system to which they have turned for help. Women who have been raped are particularly at risk for this type of multiple victimization. Treated as nonentities, victims have been shuffled around, kept in the dark, had their property taken and not returned; worse still, they have been subjected to abuse and ridicule in court.

A variety of constructive responses are now being directed to the needs of crime victims. Some of these responses seek to reduce the probability of victimization and in that sense are part of crime prevention efforts. Neighborhood crime watch programs and "Operation Identification" are examples. Other responses seek to improve the treatment of victims by the judicial process, and others seek to redress the grievance occasioned by crime. The latter are generally divided into two kinds of support: *restitution*, where victims are compensated for their loss by the offender either through fines or work, and *compensation*, where the state provides resources to help victims deal with the monetary loss resulting from crime. Today, all fifty states and the District of Columbia have compensation programs, and judges in most states are permitted to include some form of restitution in their sentencing options (Barlow 2000, 497–500). Many jurisdictions have also established formal organizations, such as "Victims Advocate Offices," specifically to help victims of a variety of crimes. As of April, 2000, thirty-three states now have constitutional amendments listing victims' rights (www.nvcan.org). A federal constitutional amendment, similar to those in many states, stalled in Congress in May, 2000, but may by now have been reintroduced. The majority of these amendments require that victims be treated with "fairness, dignity and respect." More specifically, they are entitled to the right to be informed, present, and heard at significant criminal justice proceedings. Approximately half of the states give victims the right to notice of the release of the offender. About one-third of the states require a speedy resolution of the case and reasonable protection from the accused (The National Center for Victims of Crime 1996).

The impact of crime on victims can be devastating. Horror stories abound about victims who were horribly mutilated, killed, driven insane, or made penniless by crime. Every time gruesome murders come to light—Jeffrey Dahmer's atrocities, the bombing of the Oklahoma City Federal Building, the "Manson family" murders—our sympathies go out to the families and friends of the victims. But on a much more mundane level, millions of crime victims—many not even realizing they are victims—suffer unsensationally and find that few seem to care about their plight. Criminologists agree that the people most likely to be victimized by crime are the very same people who are least equipped to deal with it and least able to change their social situation: the poor, African-Americans, people living in public housing, the divorced, and single-parent families. We also know that "previous victimization is a significant predictor of future victimization" (Wittebrood and Nieuwbeerta 2000, 92).

There are some critics who fear that the victim movement has been co-opted and manipulated by politicians and criminal justice officials whose real agenda is to secure more resources and public support for cracking down on criminals rather than reducing the pains of victimization (Elias 1993; Mawby and Walklate 1994). The true picture is probably somewhere in between: Victims *are* more significant players than they used to be, and they *are* receiving more services and support than they used to; however, the reforms have been piecemeal, and the social injustices that underlie much victimization—and which victimization makes worse—have not really been addressed.

SOCIAL CONTROL AND LAW

Crime and law are intertwined. As a type of law, criminal law is generally regarded as a relatively recent development. Although no specific date of origin can be identified, criminal law in the Western world developed 2000 years ago from already existing systems of law and began to take shape in the later years of the Roman Empire. In considering the development of criminal law, an examination of the nature of law in general is desirable.

In any social group, efforts are made to ensure that members behave predictably and in accordance with the expectations and evaluations of others. These efforts are at the heart of social control, and their success is thought to be indispensable to orderly group life. It is difficult to imagine how group life could endure if members simply acted impulsively or in continued violation of the expectations of others.

Social control may be informal or formal. It may appear in facial expressions, gestures, gossip, or ostracism. It may consist largely of unwritten rules passed on by word of mouth or by example. Or it may take the form of written rules backed by force. Sometimes conformity is promoted through the use of rewards (positive sanctions), and sometimes through the use of penalties (negative sanctions).

The effect of all these measures may be to create a sense of guilt and shame, which becomes an internal control.

Law is a type of formal social control, which "is characterized by (1) explicit rules of conduct, (2) planned use of sanctions to support the rules, and (3) designated officials to interpret and enforce the rules, and often to make them" (Davis 1962, 43).

Origins and Development of Criminal Law

Much of what is known about the origins and development of criminal law has come through the efforts of legal historians and cultural anthropologists. Classic historical works such as *Ancient Law* by Sir Henry Sumner Maine (1905) and *The Growth of Criminal Law in Ancient Greece* by George Calhoun (1927) provide important interpretative accounts of early law. Twentieth-century anthropologists have added to the store of knowledge through their studies of primitive societies. Works by A. R. Radcliffe-Brown (1948), Bronislaw Malinowski (1926), E. Adamson Hoebel (1941), and E. E. Evans-Pritchard (1940) are among the best-known studies.

THE DECLINE OF PRIMITIVE LAW   It is generally agreed that *primitive law*—the system of rules and obligations in preliterate and semiliterate societies—represents the foundation on which modern legal systems were built. Primitive law contains three important features: (1) Acts that injured or wronged others were considered "private wrongs"; that is, injuries to particular individuals rather than the group or tribe as a whole. (Exceptions to this were acts deemed harmful to the entire community, for example, aiding an enemy or witchcraft.) (2) The injured party or family typically took personal action against the wrongdoer, a kind of self-help justice. (3) This self-help justice usually amounted to retaliation in kind. Blood feuds were not uncommon under this system of primitive justice.

Strongly held customs and traditions, the relative independence of the family, the similarities among people and their activities, and other features of primitive life changed as technological progress and a growing division of labor moved society toward the modern era. Growing differences in wealth, prestige, and power were associated with new patterns of authority and decision making. The rise of chieftains and kings and the centralization of political authority set the stage for the emergence of the civil state. The handling of disputes slowly moved out of the hands of the family and into the hands of the sovereign and the state. Eventually, the creation of legal rules was claimed by heads of state in the name of the people.

These changes did not happen overnight. Today's criminal law is a product of centuries of change. The earliest known code of written law dates back to the twenty-first century B.C. This is the code of Ur-Nammu, the Sumerian king who founded the Third Dynasty of Ur. The famous Code of Hammurabi was discovered in 1901 in Susa, near the Persian Gulf. This code dates from around 1750 B.C. Other ancient codes of law include the Twelve Tables of Rome, the Mosaic code, the laws of ancient Greece, and the laws of Tacitus. All these codes show strong ties with the self-help justice typical of more primitive eras. As Maine (1905, 341–342) notes, early penal law was primarily the law of torts (or private wrongs). The Twelve Tables treated theft, assault, and violent robbery as *delicta* (private wrongs), along with trespass, libel, and slander. The person, not the state or the public, was the injured party.

The maturing legal systems of ancient Greece and Rome moved steadily toward the formulation of offenses against the state (public wrongs, or *crimena*) and the establishment of machinery for administration and enforcement. According to Maine, the legislative establishment of permanent criminal tribunals around the first century B.C. represented a crucial step in the emergence of true criminal law.

One of the most interesting features of these early codes is the number of activities they cover. The Code of Hammurabi is particularly wide-ranging. The laws covered such diverse areas as kidnapping, unsolved crimes, price-fixing, rights of military personnel, the sale of liquor, marriage and the family, inheritance. and slavery (Gordon 1957). The contents of these early codes suggest three observations: (1) Some laws articulate long-established customs and traditions and can be thought of as formal restatements of existing mores; (2) some laws reflect efforts to regulate and coordinate increasingly complex social relations and activities; and (3) some laws articulate prevailing moral standards and show close ties to religion.

At the top of an ancient pillar (c. 1760 B.C.) is the image of Hammurabi, King of Babylonia, confronting the Sun God. Hammurabi authored one of the most extensive of the early legal codes.

MALA PROHIBITA AND MALA IN SE   In the minds of some people, law is based on moral beliefs, and criminal codes are a sort of catalog of sins. But others have argued that there is much in criminal codes that bears no obvious connection with ethics or morality. In what sense, for example, are laws prohibiting certain forms of drug use or certain kinds of business activities matters of sin?

Laws were once indistinguishable from the general code governing social conduct. As primitive societies became more complex, law and justice were identified as concepts that regulated the moral aspects of social conduct. Even the extensive legal

codes of Greece and Rome fused morality with law. In some languages (Hungarian, for example) the word for crime means not only an act that is illegal but also one that is evil or sinful (Schafer 1969). In time, criminal codes expanded and laws were passed to regulate activities in business, politics, the family, social services, and even people's intimate private lives. The connection between law and morality became less clear, and people categorized crimes as **mala prohibita** (meaning bad or evil because they are forbidden) or **mala in se** (meaning bad or evil in themselves). *Mala prohibita* crimes include drug offenses, traffic violations, and embezzlement; examples of *mala in se* crimes include incest, murder, arson, and robbery.

INTERESTS AND THE DEVELOPMENT OF LAW   Studies of the history of criminal law have documented the role that interests play in the creation, content, and enforcement of legal rules. Interests are simply the things that people value, and different people sometimes value different things.

One of the first systematic discussions of interests in the formulation of law was by Roscoe Pound. According to Pound (1943, 39), law helps to adjust and harmonize conflicting individual and group interests:

> Looked at functionally, the law is an attempt to satisfy, to reconcile, to harmonize, to adjust these overlapping and often conflicting claims and demands, either through securing them directly and immediately, or through securing certain individual interests, or through delimitations or compromises of individual interests, so as to give effect to the greatest total of interests, or to the interests that weigh the most in our civilization, with the least sacrifice of the scheme of interests as a whole.

The **functionalist theory** of sociological jurisprudence offered by Pound has been attacked for its emphasis on compromise and harmony and for its suggestion that there will be consensus where important social interests are concerned. Some scholars believe a **conflict perspective** better reflects the real workings of societal institutions. According to Richard Quinney (1970, 35),

> society is characterized by diversity, conflict, coercion, and change, rather than by consensus and stability. Second, law is a result of the operation of

interests, rather than an instrument that functions outside of particular interests. Though law may control interests, it is in the first place created by interests. Third, law incorporates the interests of specific persons and groups; it is seldom the product of the whole society. Law is made by men, representing special interests, who have the power to translate their interests into public policy. Unlike the pluralistic conception of politics, law does not represent a compromise of the diverse interests in society, but supports some interests at the expense of others.

Historically, those low in status or power have been labeled criminals most often and punished most severely for their crimes (see Chambliss 1973). Early legal codes specified different reactions according to distinctions of status. The most powerful were the most privileged. Conflict and power help explain why some activities are not crimes. This is especially evident in matters relating to business and government but also applies to laws regarding sexual assault. Still today, women and poor people find it hard to protect their interests through law. In part this is because the state must support not only certain economic relationships, but also other social relationships and institutions that can and oftentimes do reflect social inequality (Chambliss 1988). The relationship between law and *patriarchy*, a social condition in which men have disproportionate power and privilege over women in a society, is one such example. Gender bias not only exists in law but also in official data-gathering processes by the state, and in formal social control institutions, such as the police and courts. For example, until very recently there were few states that considered it criminal for a man to rape his wife (Caulfield and Wonders 1993). Laws, criminal justice institutions, and actors within those institutions, have gradually become more sensitive to issues such as violence against women. As long as a society is structurally and culturally organized around patriarchy, however, there will continue to be relationships and institutions within criminal justice that reflect and sometimes promote gender inequality.

Another example of how law does not necessarily reflect the interests of the majority can be illustrated by a relationship between a multinational corporation and Third World mothers. Some years ago the Nestle Company launched an international campaign to promote its infant formula. Ads proclaiming "Give your baby love and Lactogen" were used to promote the product in less-developed countries, where families are typically large. However, the promotion discouraged mothers from breast feeding and encouraged practices that were more expensive, irreversible, and, because of contaminated water supplies, potentially harmful. Many babies became ill, and some died. But Nestle's had committed no crime, legally speaking, nor were any sanctions imposed on the company. In effect, the law both here and abroad protected the company, and had it not been for publicity surrounding the efforts of social activists in England and America, the company doubtless would have continued its legal but ultimately victimizing practices (Post and Baer 1978). U.S. corporations operating internationally can often engage in practices that would be illegal in the United States, but which are not illegal in the host country (Kramer and Michalowski 1987, 1999).

The advantages enjoyed by corporations in matters of crime also extend to situations in which corporations are the victims of crime: "The form and content of criminal justice in modern capitalistic societies supports and legitimates the use of criminal law for the protection of corporate property against individuals. That is ... the modern criminal justice system better serves corporate than individual interests" (Hagan 1982, 1019). These issues are examined in detail in Chapter 6, but they are discussed from time to time throughout the text.

ANGLO-AMERICAN CRIMINAL LAW Criminal law in the United States draws mainly from Greek, Mosaic, and Roman law via English law. The common law of England can be traced to the reign of Henry II (1154–1189). For centuries, English law had been a system of tribal justice, the primitive law of private wrongs and self-help retaliation. As feudalism took hold in the eighth and ninth centuries, Anglo-Saxon society underwent important changes. The family lost its autonomy; kings and kingdoms emerged; and the blood feud was replaced by a system of material compensation (usually money), directed by individuals with special status—by king, lord, or bishop. Equally important, political unification was underway, as territorial acquisitions by the new kings transformed a patchwork of small kin-dominated domains into fewer, larger kingdoms. With the Norman conquest of 1066, complete political unification was but a short step away.

The Normans centralized their administrative machinery, including that of law. During the reign of Henry II, new legal procedures emerged, including a court of "common law." Those with complaints against others could bring them to traveling courts, and justice dispensed there became a body of precedent to guide future judgments. During this period certain acts were identified as offenses against king and country ("Breaches of the King's Peace"), and these are the bones of modern criminal law. The Puritans brought English criminal law to the New World. Over the next 400 years, English common law was slowly "Americanized."

The rules embodied in American criminal law come from four sources: (1) federal and state constitutions; (2) decisions by courts (common law or case law), including decisions of precedent and Supreme Court rulings; (3) administrative regulations—those policy decisions employed by agencies on the federal, state, and local levels as they carry out their legal duties; and (4) statutory enactments by legislatures.

A distinction is made between **procedural rules** and **substantive law**. This distinction draws attention to two basic issues: (1) how the authorities handle lawbreaking and lawbreakers—the question of procedure, and (2) the content of the specific rules making up the body of criminal law—the question of substance. Thus substantive criminal law spells out the nature of criminal acts and the punishments associated with them.

Procedural rules govern the way lawbreaking and lawbreakers are handled by the criminal justice system. They are applicable at all stages of the legal process. Procedural rules shape the administration of criminal justice and help determine whether given acts and individuals will be officially identified as criminal, how offenders will be "processed," and what will happen to them if they are found guilty of a crime. Procedural aspects of criminal law set the tone for the process of criminalization and provide insights into criminal law in action. Together with the substance of criminal prohibitions, procedural rules reflect and reinforce

The U.S. Supreme Court. Seated from left: Antonin Scalia, John Paul Stevens, Chief Justice William Rehnquist, Sandra Day O'Connor, Anthony M. Kennedy. Standing from left: Ruth Bader Ginsberg, David Souter, Clarence Thomas, Stephen Breyer.

public policy and the ideology that underlies it. The following section deals with the important topic of public policy.

CRIME AND PUBLIC POLICY

Public policy impinges on all aspects of the crime scene. Its impact begins with official decisions about what and whom to identify as criminal, and continues through all phases of the criminal process. Policy influences arrest, prosecution, trial, and sentencing. It also influences penalties and how punishment is carried out.

Many things shape public policy, whether on crime or anything else. The attitudes, beliefs, ideas, and assumptions about crime held by people in power comprise the ideological underpinnings of policy and shape the positions taken on specific issues. These positions are often uncritically adopted by the public. This is called the *hegemonic effect* of ideology. The particular ideology underlying public policy is not always obvious, but it is there nonetheless and actual policy decisions cannot be divorced from it. As noted thirty years ago, "ideology is the permanent hidden agenda of criminal justice" (Miller 1973, 142).

The same ideology is not, of course, shared by everyone, or even by those who work in the criminal justice system. For example, a study of attitudes among criminal justice practitioners found that prosecutors and judges were less likely than probation officers and defense attorneys (1) to agree among themselves, and (2) to advocate alternatives to prison as punishment for crime (Lein, Richard, and Fabelo 1992).

Nor does a particular ideology necessarily retain its influence over time. Policies will change as time passes. Different assumptions and beliefs about criminal matters have achieved prominence at different times. The underlying ideology sometimes stimulates policy changes and sometimes reinforces existing policies. Whether or not a particular ideology influences policy depends on many things, and the power and influence of those subscribing to it matter most.

Samuel Walker (2001) claims that both liberals and conservatives are guilty of "peddling nonsense" about crime. Most people, Walker notes, base their ideas about crime and justice on "faith" rather than facts. This faith serves to undermine the sensible and successful implementation of criminal justice policy. This echoes the theme we began this chapter with—perceptions about crime are often biased.

Despite the obvious importance of ideology, there have been few attempts to identify and classify beliefs and assumptions about crime. Thirty years ago, Walter Miller (1973) developed one of the most detailed statements on major ideological positions; it is still relevant today. Miller analyzed public statements on criminal matters made by a variety of Americans, including novelists, sociologists, journalists, government officials, lawyers, police, clergy, historians, and labor leaders. Though one does not hear so much these days from the radical left, the distinctions that Miller presents provide a useful starting point in thinking about ideology and public policy on crime.

Miller placed the different ideological positions he was able to identify on a one-dimensional scale:

LEFTIST					CENTRIST					RIGHTIST
5	4	3	2	1	0	1	2	3	4	5
RADICAL										CONSERVATIVE

The most extreme ideological positions were given the value 5. More moderate ones ranged between the extreme left and extreme right positions. The ideological position left 3 is more leftist than position left 1 but less leftist than position left 5. Each ideological position Miller identified concerns a specific crime issue and is made up of assumptions and beliefs about that issue.

For example, left 5 opinions on the causes of crime include assertions that the behavior called crime by the ruling elite "is an inevitable product of a fundamentally corrupt and unjust society. True crime is the behavior of those who perpetuate, control, and profit from an exploitative and brutalizing system ..." (Miller 1973, 155). This, of course, is a radical conflict perspective.

In contrast, right 5 views on the causes of crime include assertions that "crime and violence are a direct product of a massive conspiracy by highly organized and well-financed radical forces deliberately seeking to overthrow the society ... [through an] ... unrelenting attack on the fundamental moral values of the society..." (Miller 1973, 156).

More moderate views are reflected in left 3 and right 3 positions. Left 3 views place the responsibility for crime on the shoulders of public officials who allocate "pitifully inadequate resources to criminal justice agencies" and on the shoulders of "damaging social conditions": poverty, urban collapse, lack of jobs and educational opportunities, and race/ethnic segregation (Miller 1973, 156–157). This may be called the classic liberal position on crime (see Walker 1998) Right 3 views include this sort of statement: "The root cause of crime is a massive erosion of the fundamental values which traditionally have served to deter criminality, and a concomitant flouting of the established authority that has traditionally served to constrain it. The most extreme manifestations of this phenomenon are found among ... the young, minorities, and the poor" (Miller 1973, 157). This view underlies the classic conservative policy position, summarized by Messner and Rosenfeld (1994, 94) as follows:

> The police will act swiftly to remove criminals from the streets; prosecutors will vigorously bring their cases to court without plea-bargaining them to charges carrying lesser penalties; judges and juries will have less discretion in determining the penalties imposed; and more criminals will serve longer sentences for their crimes.

People's views about the proper ways to deal with criminals and the proper operating policies of criminal justice agencies are consistent with their views about the causes of crime. In Miller's study, more radical opinions stressed the brutalizing and militaristic strategies of government crime control, while more conservative views stressed the dangerousness of offenders and the need for swift, certain, and severe punishment.

Left 1 and right 1 opinions show that the moderate left and right converge on policy matters: Moderate liberals stress a holistic approach to crime in which the criminal justice apparatus is coordinated with other agencies that serve the general welfare of the community, and where the role of the federal government is to finance and oversee reform of the criminal justice system. Moderate conservatives also stress system reform, but put more emphasis on increasing criminal justice efficiency through modern management and information processing techniques.

Miller believes that both left and right can be reduced to basic governing principles or values and that few Americans would quarrel with them, since they are "intrinsic aspects of our national ideals":

> For the right, the paramount value is order—an ordered society based on a pervasive and binding morality—and the paramount danger is disorder—social, moral and political. For the left, the paramount value is justice—a just society based on a fair and equitable distribution of power, wealth, prestige, and privilege—and the paramount evil is injustice—the concentration of valued social resources in the hands of a privileged minority.... Stripped of the passion of ideological conflict, the issue between the two sides could be viewed as a disagreement over the relative priority of two valuable conditions: whether order with justice, or justice with order should be the guiding principle of the criminal justice enterprise. (Miller 1973, 148)

While Miller"s research is valuable, liberals and conservatives probably have more in common when it comes to crime control policy than anything else. Former U.S. President Bill Clinton, for example, who was considered fairly liberal in some ways, often supported very conservative crime control measures, such as limiting death penalty appeals and advocating longer prison terms (Kramer and Michalowski 1995). While some of the policies Clinton supported were closer to classic liberal thinking, such as his support of community policing and certain rehabilitation programs, the traditional conservative ideology appears to have influenced liberals more than liberal ideology has influenced conservatives.

The expectation that ideology influences public policy is based on the assumption that views or theories about an issue largely determine how people deal with it (Barlow 1995). In the past hundred years or so, public policy on criminal matters has indeed incorporated competing crime strategies. Two "ideal type" models of organized reactions to crime and criminals have been identified. One rests heavily on *order* with justice, the other on *justice* with order. Although neither model exactly reproduces the real world, both are drawn from criminal justice in action and emphasize what are thought to be fundamental divergences in assumptions and beliefs about the correct way to deal with criminals. The models were first suggested by Herbert L. Packer (1964, 1968), who calls them the *crime control model* and the *due process model*.

Order with Justice: The Crime Control Model

According to Packer (1968, 158), the ideology underlying the **crime control model** emphasizes repression of criminal behavior as the most important function of the criminal process:

> The failure of law enforcement to bring criminal conduct under tight control is viewed as leading to the breakdown of public order and thence to the disappearance of an important condition of human freedom. If the laws go unenforced—which is to say, if it is perceived that there is a high percentage of failure to apprehend and convict in the criminal process—a general disregard for legal controls tends to develop. The law-abiding citizen then becomes the victim of all sorts of unjustifiable invasions of his interests. His security of person and property is sharply diminished, and, therefore, so is his liberty to function as a member of society. The claim ultimately is that the criminal process is a positive guarantor of social freedom.

To support this ideology the crime control model pays the most attention to the capacity of the criminal justice system to catch, prosecute, convict, and dispose of a high proportion of criminal offenders. With its emphasis on a high rate of apprehension and conviction, and given limited resources, the crime control model places a premium on speed and finality. Speed is enhanced when cases can be processed informally and when procedure is uniform or standardized; finality is secured when the occasions for challenge are minimized. To ensure that challenges are kept to a minimum, those who work in criminal justice presume that the apprehended are in fact guilty. This places heavy emphasis on the quality of administrative fact-finding and the coordination of agency tasks and role responsibilities. Success is gauged by how expeditiously nonoffenders are screened out of the process and whether offenders are passed through to final disposition. Packer likens the crime control model to a conveyer belt, down which flows an endless stream of cases processed by workers who perform routine tasks.

Justice with Order: The Due Process Model

Whereas the crime control model resembles an assembly line, Packer (1968, 163) visualizes the **due process model** as an obstacle course: "Each of its successive stages is designed to present formidable obstacles to carrying the accused any further along in the process."

The due process model sees the crime control function as subordinate to ideals of justice. This model emphasizes ensuring that the facts about the accused are subjected to formal scrutiny; ensuring that the accused is afforded an impartial hearing under adversary procedures; ensuring that coercive and stigmatizing powers are not abused by those in an official position to exercise them; maintaining the presumption of innocence until guilt is legally proven; ensuring that all defendants are given equal protection under the law, including the chance to defend themselves adequately; and ensuring that suspects and convicted offenders are accorded the kind of treatment that supports their dignity and autonomy as human beings. The emphasis, then, is on justice first.

U.S. Crime Policy: Due Process or Crime Control?

American public policy on crime appears to be dominated by the ideology and practices of the crime control model. Through the years there has been a proliferation of public and private police forces whose primary goal is the detection and apprehension of criminals and the defense of order. There have been continued efforts to create and enforce laws dealing with moral questions and essentially private behavior. There have been increasing efforts to unite and coordinate crime control at the federal, state, and local levels. There has been a growing emphasis on informality in the criminal process, best exemplified in the extensive use of plea bargaining. There have been continued efforts to promote efficiency, productivity, and professionalism in the activities and personnel of law enforcement agencies. There have been, conversely, a paucity of judicial decisions supporting due process values and few serious efforts to organize and fund programs to ensure equal protection under the law and to guarantee the dignity and autonomy of either victims or offenders.

American public opinion also appears to be leaning toward crime control. While the majority of Americans believe that we need to attack social problems that give rise to crime (e.g., poverty, neighborhood disintegration), a recent Gallup poll found that 70 percent of the respondents believed that the criminal justice system is not "tough enough" in its handling of crime (The Gallup Organization 2000). Not surprisingly, and also representing the popularity of the crime control model, 67 percent of respondents felt the system was more fair than unfair in dealing with persons accused of criminal conduct (The Gallup Organization 2000).

Historically, important congressional support for the crime control model came in 1968 when Congress passed the Omnibus Crime Control and Safe Streets Act. Under Title 1 of the act, Congress established the Law Enforcement Assistance Administration (LEAA) under the Department of Justice. Through this move, Congress extended federal involvement in the enforcement activities of state and local governments, and helped establish what were to become the primary crime strategies throughout the nation. Although the Constitution specifically places the major responsibility for criminal matters in the hands of the states, the federal government was able to assume considerable power and influence in such matters.

To help the LEAA carry out its mandate, Congress allocated just over $60 million for operation in 1969. Over the next few years, the LEAA was one of the fast-growing federal agencies; its annual budget quickly reached half a billion dollars (in 1971), then climbed to over $800 million, and by 1976 it stood at $1.015 billion (U.S. Department of Justice 1976, 42).

As a result of numerous criticisms of agency practices during the 1970s, however, Congress voted the LEAA only $486 million for 1980 and then scrapped the agency altogether. The Justice System Improvement Act of 1979 established as its successor agency the Office of Justice Assistance, Research and Statistics (OJARS). Its budget for fiscal 1981 was $144,397,000 and, after a couple of leaner years, grew to $197.3 million in 1984 (McGarrell and Flanagan 1985, 25). In 1984, Congress created the Office of Justice Programs (OJP) as successor to OJARS, and the OJP budget for 1990 was $762 million (Maguire and Flanagan 1991, 15).

Most of the federal money goes to police agencies. In 1988, for example, just under half of all federal expenditures on criminal justice went to police protection (Maguire and Flanagan 1991, 2). From 1980 to 1993, per capita expenditure on police protection rose 143 percent (Bureau of Justice

Statistics 1997). Funds are used to purchase new and sophisticated police equipment (from weapons and ammunition to vehicles, computers, and bulletproof clothing); to train officers and to reorganize police departments; to finance management training programs and operations research; to fund scientific and technological research; and to plan future policy throughout the various levels of the legal process. Furthermore, the police are becoming more militarized, even those in relatively small towns. A study of local police agencies serving populations of 25,000–50,000 people found that over 80 percent of them had "… MP5 submachine guns, tactical semiautomatic shotguns, night vision equipment, sniper rifles, flash-bag grenades, tactical shields, battle dress uniforms, and specialized dynamic entry tools" (Kraska and Cubellis 1997, 612). Fifty percent of these small-town policing agencies had "electronic surveillance equipment, tactical helmets, tactical communication headsets, and a … SWAT van." Prisons, jails, and various correctional programs have also experienced a boom in funding. From 1980 to 1993, local, state, and federal expenditures rose 253 percent (Bureau of Justice Statistics 1997).

The crime control approach is also reflected in current "three strikes and you're out" policies and the passage of the 1994 Crime Act. Besides authorizing the use of capital punishment for some sixty offenses, specific Crime Act provisions included: $10.7 billion for state and local law enforcement agencies, including $8.8 billion to put 100,000 police officers on the streets in community policing programs, and $1 billion for drug enforcement; $8.3 billion to states for construction of new prisons and development of prison alternatives; $2.6 billion for federal enforcement agencies, including $1 billion for Immigration and Naturalization Service and U.S. Border Patrol; $1.8 billion in direct funding for local anticrime efforts such as drug treatment, education, and jobs; $1.3 billion for "drug court" programs providing at least 600,000 nonviolent offenders with substance abuse services over six years. In sum, over two-thirds of its $30 billion budget was earmarked for law enforcement.

Another example of the crime control model at work is the 1996 Anti-Terrorism and Effective Death Penalty Act. This bipartisan legislation authorizes, among other things, more than $1 billion over five years to strengthen antiterrorism activities, including the hiring of more than 1,000 new law enforcement officers. It also "toughens" the penalties for terrorist crimes and conspiracies involving explosives, and curtails the number of *habeas corpus* appeals under which state-imposed death sentences can be challenged in federal court on constitutional grounds.

State expenditures mirror the federal outlays on crime control. In California, for example, police budgets increased 126 percent between 1968 and 1974, compared with only a 50 percent increase for the courts, which also suffered a decrease in per capita personnel (Pontell 1984, 51–55). More recent data confirm this (Bureau of Justice Statistics 1997). Nearly every state spends over half of its criminal justice funds on policing (Bureau of Justice Statistics 1997). This funding policy gives rise to a "structural imbalance" in the criminal justice system, reducing the capacity of nonpolice agencies to handle violators and thereby undermining the crime control capacity of the system as a whole.

Public Policy and Criminal Stereotypes

Every president since Johnson has called for some form of "war on crime." The passing of the Omnibus Crime Control and Safe Streets Act in the late 1960s drew attention only to certain crimes and certain criminals. Despite using such broad expressions as "lawlessness in America," they considered the real crime problem to be the overt threats to public order and prevailing institutions represented in street crimes—muggings, forcible rapes, burglaries, assaults, and armed robberies—and the activities of junkies and dope pushers, militant activists, and other so-called radicals. Except for the last two groups, the bulk of those identified as the real threat to law and order are minorities and lower-class individuals living mostly in the poverty areas of the nation's cities (Chambliss 1999). Nineteenth-century officials dubbed such persons "the dangerous classes."

Because current crime policies show little evidence of changing focus, people have no incentive to alter their long-held stereotypes of the criminal. On the contrary, current policies merely reinforce these stereotypes. Americans are encouraged to view the streets as the unsafe turf of the criminal

class. They are encouraged to distrust less well-off neighbors and to demand speedy and harsh disposition of criminal offenses. The destruction of an entire city block in Philadelphia in 1985 when police dropped a bomb on political deviants (members of the group MOVE) is testimony to the link between stereotypical images of the dangerous class and crime-control policy.

A more recent example of criminal stereotyping at work is found in the practice of **racial profiling**. This term describes a practice in which a person's race or ethnicity strongly influences police decisions to stop, search, or make an arrest. It came to national attention in the mid-1990s following a highly publicized case in New Jersey. Over a short period of time, twenty-five African-Americans had been pulled over by the New Jersey State Police in one particular area of the state's turnpike, I-95. The defendants' cars were stopped and subsequently searched, and drugs were found. Defense attorneys suspected that their clients were pulled over only because they were African-American. A study was commissioned to see if a higher proportion of African-Americans were using that part of the highway or if African-Americans were simply being pulled over more frequently (Lamberth 1998). The study found that blacks did not use the road more frequently nor did they violate traffic laws more frequently than other racial groups. It appeared that race was the key to the traffic stops. Armed with corroborating testimony from state troopers, a New Jersey state court found Lamberth's study compelling, and ruled that the police had been engaging in racial stereotyping. "Driving While Black" (DWB) is the expression commonly used to refer to this type of racial profiling.

The American Civil Liberties Union has been at the forefront of attempts to outlaw racial profiling, and its latest report on the subject shows that while the problem is widespread, a number of states have passed legislation designed to curb the practice (Harris 1999). On June 9, 1999, President Clinton issued an executive order directing the Justice Department and three other federal agencies to improve data collection at all levels of law enforcement to address the problem of racial profiling. Even so, recent U.S. Supreme Court decisions—particularly *Whren v. The U.S.* (1996) and *Wyoming v. Houghton* (1999)—have given police almost unlimited authority to stop and search any vehicle they want, including its passengers. This trend serves crime control far more than it does due process.

Stereotyping can also result in the view that criminals are categorically "bad" people and victims of crime are categorically "good" people. This has been called *moral polarization*—the "tendency to locate participants in criminal events on opposite and extreme sides of a moral continuum" (Claster 1992, 196). In reality, as we have seen, criminality and victimization are interwoven, and sometimes cannot be easily distinguished from each other.

The targets of crime policy (and also many victims of crime) feel oppressed by the authorities (Allen 1974, 75–76). Crime control policy further alienates and aggravates the disadvantaged segments of society when they realize that middle-class criminality escapes the serious attention of the state. With all of the money spent on projects and programs dealing with drugs, burglary, robbery, and street crimes generally, the government has little left over to spend on policing the middle class, even if it wanted to.

This does not mean that street crimes should receive no attention or even that they should receive less attention than they do. The issue is how much and what kind of attention they receive *relative* to other forms of criminality. The relative lack of attention authorities give to white-collar, state, and corporate crime is hard to justify because its negative impact on society is greater than that resulting from street crimes. Chapter 6 looks at this issue in detail.

Jeffrey Reiman (2001) provides an interesting interpretation of this problem. He believes that the criminal justice system has failed to reduce crime and to protect society precisely because that failure "serves the interests of the rich and powerful in America." How can that be? Reiman asserts that this failure performs an ideological service by funneling discontent toward those depicted as responsible for crime—the poor, minorities, the lower classes—and away from the rich and powerful. At the same time, the system focuses on individual wrongdoing rather than on the organizations and institutions that make up social order, thus "implicitly conveying the message that the social conditions in which crime occurred are not responsible for the crime." If social conditions

are not responsible for crime, then cries for fundamental change in the social order are without substance; the "radical" threat can be resisted by a united middle class urging continuation of prevailing policies. As William Chambliss (1999) demonstrates in a recent book, criminal stereotyping gives us an inaccurate picture of both victimization and victimizers.

CHAPTER SUMMARY

This chapter began with the observation that the media image of the crime scene is highly distorted. The emphasis on crimes that are especially violent or sensational helps fuel widespread fear of crime, which leads many people to retreat behind locked doors, making the streets even more dangerous for those who venture out.

Criminologists try to uncover the "truth" about crime and criminals. The chapter discussed various concepts, definitions, and perspectives that criminologists have developed. The legalistic definition of crime is behavior that violates the criminal law; criminals are people who engage in that behavior. Others have argued that the definition of crime need not be based on law. Another definition proposed is that *crime* and *criminal* are labels attached to behavior, events, and individuals by people in positions of authority or power. This text favors a definition that sees crime as both a behavior and a status.

Criminal law formally creates crime by defining it into existence. It is the application of law, however, that criminalizes actual behavior, people, and events. This process is influenced by interests, the things that people value. When interests are in conflict, as they often are, law usually reflects the interests of the more powerful groups in society. As later chapters will show, even laws supported by broad public consensus—rape statutes, for example—may actually serve the interests of the more powerful (males) at the expense of the less powerful (females).

Public policy on crime is shaped by historical forces as well as by the attitudes and beliefs of people in power. The crime control model emphasizes order with justice and pays most attention to the capacity of society to catch, prosecute, and dispose of a high proportion of guilty defendants. The due process model emphasizes justice with order and sees the crime control function as secondary to the protection of individual liberties and the right to equal treatment under law.

American public policy on criminal matters is dominated by the crime control model. Government spending is used largely to improve apprehension and conviction of criminals rather than to prevent crime in the first place or to ensure that the rights of offenders and victims are protected. Criminal stereotypes abound, and this clouds our understanding of other threats to life and property, such as white-collar and corporate crime.

KEY TERMS

conflict perspective (p. 12)

crime (p. 9)

crime control model (p. 17)

criminal (p. 9)

criminalization (p. 9)

criminology (p. 5)

decriminalization (p. 9)

due process model (p. 17)

functionalist theory (p. 12)

labeling perspective (p. 9)

mala in se (p. 12)

mala prohibita (p. 12)

procedural rules (p. 14)

racial profiling (p. 19)

social control (p. 10)

substantive law (p. 14)

RECOMMENDED READINGS

Barak, Gregg. 1994. *Media, Process, and the Social Construction of Crime: Studies in Newsmaking Criminology*. New York: Garland.

Best, Joel. 1999. *Random Violence: How We Talk about New Crimes and New Victims*. Berkeley and Los Angeles: University of California Press.

Chambliss, William J. 1999. *Power, Politics, and Crime*. Boulder, CO: Westview.

Criminal Justice Collective of Northern Arizona University. 2000. *Investigating Difference: Human and Cultural Relations in Criminal Justice*. Boston, MA: Allyn and Bacon.

Currie, Elliott. 1998. *Crime and Punishment in America*. New York: Henry Holt and Company.

Friedrichs, David O. 2001. *Law in Our Lives: An Introduction*. Los Angeles, CA: Roxbury.

Henry, Stuart, and Mark Lanier. 2001. *What Is Crime? Controversies over the Nature of Crime and What to Do about It*. Lanham, MD: Rowman & Littlefield.

Roberts, Julian V., and Loretta J. Stalans. 1997. *Public Opinion, Crime, and Criminal Justice*. New York: Westview.

RECOMMENDED WEB SITES

American Society of Criminology

A professional association for criminologists and all other students of crime.

http://www.asc41.com

Criminal Justice Links

An enormous site intended to facilitate access to several hundred Web sites related to crime and criminal justice. Hosted by Cecil Greek, School of Criminology, Florida State University.

http://www.criminology.fsu.edu/cj.html

APB News

A site devoted entirely to breaking news and current happenings in criminal justice.

http://APBnews.com

CRIME DATA
AND THE METHODS
OF CRIMINOLOGY

The newspaper headlines read "Crime is Down," "Murder on the Decline," or "Hate Crime on the Rise." What does this mean and on what information are these claims based? Indeed, how do we even know how much crime there is in the United States? Fortunately, both the government and criminologists have devised various ways to measure the volume of crime. In addition, researchers have developed ways of identifying where crimes occur, the relationship between offenders and victims, and the age, gender, and race of those involved in crime. In the first section of this chapter, we will describe how crime data are constructed and gathered; the second part of the chapter provides a review of the basic research methods used by criminologists to study crime and punishment.

Science requires that valid and reliable data be used to build knowledge. If a data source or research strategy is poor or inappropriate for studying the problem at hand, then the results are questionable. Just as it is important to consider the source when hearing a story, it is also important to consider the source when using information on crime and criminality.

TYPES OF CRIME MEASUREMENT

There are three major sources of crime data in the United States: (1) information on crimes submitted by police agencies to the Federal Bureau of Investigation (FBI); (2) information on crime victimization gathered through interviews with citizens; and (3) information on crime and delinquency supplied through interviews with citizens who admit their own criminality. Each of these sources is discussed in turn.

Uniform Crime Reports (UCR)

The most widely used national data source on official crimes and criminals is the FBI's **Uniform Crime Reports (UCR)**. These reports were the brainchild of J. Edgar Hoover, late director of the FBI. Over sixty years ago Hoover recognized the need to compile nationwide data on crime as an aid to law enforcement and research on crime and criminals.

When you read or hear about crimes rates, UCR statistics are often the primary source of the information. The UCR is compiled by the FBI based on police department reports of crime. Crimes generally come to the attention of the police when a victim or observer reports a possible crime or if the police happen to discover one through routine patrol, detective work, or informants. Police departments report their crime statistics to the FBI on a monthly basis. The specific offenses reported under the UCR are divided into two categories: Part I and Part II. According to the FBI (1997, 1), Part I offenses—also called **index offenses**—are "crimes most likely to be reported and most likely to occur with sufficient frequency to provide an adequate basis for comparison." The following are Index Offenses with brief definitions (Appendix I contains the full UCR definitions of offenses):

Criminal Homicide: The willful killing of one human being by another.

Forcible Rape: The carnal knowledge of a female forcibly and against her will.

Robbery: The taking or attempting to take anything of value from the care, custody, and control of a person by force or the threat of force.

Aggravated Assault: An attack by one person upon another for the purpose of inflicting severe or aggravated bodily harm.

Burglary: The unlawful entry of a structure to commit a felony or a theft.

Larceny-Theft: The unlawful taking away of property from another.

Motor Vehicle Theft: The theft or attempted theft of a motor vehicle.

Arson: Willful or malicious burning down or attempt to burn a dwelling house, public building, motor vehicle or aircraft, or the personal property of another.

Notice that four of these eight crimes involve violence or the threat of violence against a person, while four are crimes against property. Also notice in these definitions: Male victims of rape are excluded; attempted murder is not formally considered criminal homicide; and robbery involves elements of both theft and the use or threat of violence.

The Federal Bureau of Investigation assembles and disseminates crime data from police reports. While criminologists often look to the UCR for information on crime trends and patterns as well as some offense-specific information, the extent to which the data accurately reflect the real threat of crime is debatable.

Part II offenses contain a range of crimes that vary significantly in their frequency and seriousness. There are twenty-one crimes defined as Part II offenses ranging from simple assault, forgery, and vandalism to gambling, prostitution, vagrancy, drunk driving, and drug abuse (again, see Appendix I).

The FBI's annual UCR report, titled *Crime in the United States* (available at <www.fbi.gov/ucr/ucr.htm>), contains a wealth of data, including the following:

- Aggregate statistics on the overall crime rate, and trends over the past few years
- The relative frequency of Index Offenses (see Figure 2.1), trends over the past few years, and for some, the relationship between the offender and victim
- Statistics on the race, gender, and age of some offenders and victims
- Data on the amount and type of crime in various cities, counties, and states
- Data on the police **clearance rate**: The percentage of reported crimes that result in an arrest
- Data on law enforcement personnel, including those on college campuses.

UCR CRIME RATES   The FBI presents much of its data in the form of rates. A **crime rate** is a very important concept, as we shall see. It is conventionally computed by dividing the number of crimes known to police in a jurisdiction by the population of the jurisdiction. The result is multiplied by 100,000 to avoid fractions. To illustrate, suppose we look at the states of Arizona, California, and Florida. The relevant figures for 1998 are shown in the table below:

STATE	POPULATION (1)	INDEX CRIMES (2)	CRIME RATE (3)
Arizona	4,669,000	306,985	6,575
California	32,667,000	1,418,674	4,342
Florida	14,916,000	1,027,123	6,886

The Index crime rate for Arizona, shown in column 3, was computed as follows:

$$\frac{306,985}{4,669,000} \times 100,000 = 6,575$$

Rates are more useful for comparative purposes than absolute numbers. This can be illustrated

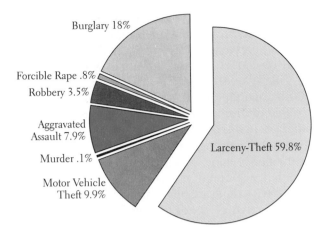

Burglary 18%

Forcible Rape .8%
Robbery 3.5%

Aggravated
Assault 7.9%

Murder .1%

Motor Vehicle
Theft 9.9%

Larceny-Theft 59.8%

▲ FIGURE 2.1

Distribution of Index Offenses, 1999

Source: Federal Bureau of Investigation, *Crime in the United States* (Washington, D.C.: U.S. Department of Justice, 2000), 8.

by using the above information. If you heard that California had around five times as many crimes as Arizona and half again as many as Florida you might think California a less safe place to live than either of the other states, and especially Arizona. But the overall chances of being victimized by crime were actually *higher* in Arizona and Florida than in California. Column 3 shows that California had the lowest crime rate of the three states even though column 2 shows that it had the most official crime. Rates take population size into account, making them a better basis for comparisons than absolute numbers. Based on the rates in this example, California *seems* safer than the other two states.

MODIFICATION TO THE UCR: THE NATIONAL INCIDENT-BASED REPORTING SYSTEM   In 1991, the FBI initiated a more comprehensive and detailed reporting system known as the **National Incident-Based Reporting System**, or **NIBRS**. All 17,000 state and local enforcement agencies now report their crime data to NIBRS. The plan is to replace the UCR with this incident-based system (Bureau of Justice Statistics 1994, vii).

The difference between the traditional UCR and NIBRS is basically this: Under NIBRS, individual police records on each official criminal incident and related arrest—rather than monthly summaries—will make up a data base that can be used

by criminal justice practitioners, policymakers, and researchers to answer a wide variety of questions. Information on crime incidents will be taken directly off the reports officers make at the scene, as well as from reports maintained by prosecutors and the courts. An immediate advantage of NIBRS is that all offenses within a given crime incident can now be recorded, as opposed to only the most serious offense, which is the case with the UCR. Another advantage concerns the breadth of information that will be available. Under NIBRS, information will be available on a wide range of details, from demographic information, time of day, weapon use, victim resistance, location of offense and residence of victims and suspects, to police response times, whether or not the crime was completed, and what eventually happened to the suspect, if there was one. In addition, NIBRS will contain incident-based data on the entire list of Part 1 and Part 2 offenses.

The promise of NIBRS is substantial but as yet unfulfilled. The U.S. Department of Justice has reported that NIBRS was not moving along as quickly as hoped. Implementing the NIBRS has proven to be difficult, but even when fully operational, NIBRS will still capture only official police-generated data. Nevertheless, the FBI reports that, as of July 1999, eighteen states have been NIBRS certified, eighteen states are in the process of testing NIBRS, and an additional six states are developing NIBRS with plans to test in the future (available at <www.fbi.gov/ucr/faqs.htm>).

DRAWBACKS OF THE UCR   The UCR has many limitations. For example, most white collar, corporate, and state crimes are excluded, as are federal crimes. In multiple offense situations, as when a robbery also involves an assault or a weapons offense, only the most serious offense is recorded. In addition to these limitations, there are three other problem areas: Many crimes are not reported to the police; there is routine underreporting of crime by the police; and some areas and populations are overpoliced. These will be discussed in turn.

Underreporting of Crimes to the Police   Perhaps the most significant problem with the UCR is that it only provides information on those crimes that come to the attention of the police. Indeed, we know that there is a massive amount of crime that never becomes known to the authorities. Those crimes that do not show up in the official UCR statistics are referred to as the **"dark figure in crime."**

National surveys indicate that only around 35 percent of all serious crimes are reported to the police, and the situation is not much different in other countries, such as Canada, Australia, and Britain (Bureau of Justice Statistics 1997; Bastion 1995; Mirrlees-Black, Mayhew, and Percy 1996). Although it is true that more serious crimes tend to be reported more often than less serious crimes, differences among serious crimes make some more likely to be reported than others (Gottfredson and Gottfredson 1988; Bureau of Justice Statistics 1987, 1994; Mirrlees-Black, Mayhew, and Percy 1996). For example, crimes resulting in high losses or injuries that require medical attention tend to be reported more often than other crimes. Murders are reported most often—it is hard to ignore a dead body. Among other serious offenses, motor vehicle theft heads the list at around 75 percent being reported, followed by aggravated assault (59 percent), and robbery (58 percent).

The reporting situation with violent crimes is complicated. On the whole, violent crimes are more likely to be reported if they involve female victims or weapons, or if they result in injuries (Gottfredson and Gottfredson 1988; Bureau of Justice Statistics 1994). Surprisingly, assaults involving strangers are no more likely to be reported than incidents involving people who know each other. This is a recent change and may be due to the fact that domestic violence has received a lot of negative publicity over the past few years. The major exception to this pattern is sexual assault: Assaults by strangers are more likely to be reported than assaults by acquaintances or family members.

Why do many violent crimes go unreported to the police? The most frequent reason given by victims is that the incident is "personal" or "private" (Maguire and Pastore 1998, 189). This reason is less likely to be given when the victim is attacked by a stranger (Harlow 1991a, 3); in these cases victims who don't report the crime usually say they felt nothing could be done. In fact, this is the most common reason for not reporting any type of serious crime. The second most common reason is that the victim felt the police would not want to be bothered. These responses may reflect unpleasant prior experiences with the police, or a belief that the police are uncaring or incompetent.

Sometimes a decision not to call the police is the result of fear of reprisal by the offender. This is most likely to arise with domestic violence or incidents involving friends. Victims feel that reporting the offender to police will result in more violence against them, if not immediately then later on. Yet national surveys have shown that calling the police may actually prevent future domestic violence (Bureau of Justice Statistics 1987, 32). Victims who reported being assaulted by their husbands were three times less likely to be assaulted again than victims who did not call the police. This crime-preventing aspect of the complainant role is recognized by some crime victims: Among those who reported a crime to police, one out of five did so because they believed it would prevent a similar incident from happening again (Bureau of Justice Statistics 1994, 100).

Underreporting by the Police   Although the public has a very important role in producing official data on crime, the police have the last word. This is true of both data on crime and data on criminals. A complainant may call the police to report a crime but the police decide whether or not the incident will be treated as a crime. This is called the **founding decision.** Since the police have considerable discretion in deciding whether or not to treat a complaint as a crime, the amount of crime officially recorded is directly shaped by how that discretion is exercised. This means that a rise (or decrease) in published crime rates may reflect changes in police founding decisions rather than changes in the amount of crime itself. One study of this issue has shown that a twenty-year upward trend in violent crime rates from 1973 to 1992 was largely due to greater police productivity in recording and reporting crime (O'Brien 1996).

The founding decision is sometimes inaccurate and may even be intentionally falsified. Internal audits of police founding practices in Chicago and in Portland, Oregon, found that 50 to 70 percent of "unfounded" felony crimes had been incorrectly labeled (Schneider 1977). Accusations of deliberate falsification are difficult to document, but not hard to imagine. In one study of founding behavior by English police, the authors discovered several reasons why the police would not record an incident as founded even though it was in fact a crime (Kinsey, Lea, and Young 1986):

- The police considered it too trivial.
- The victim was unlikely to prosecute the offender.
- The incident was "not police business."
- The crime was too difficult to investigate or prosecute.
- The incident was not "real" crime.

Underrecording of crime by police is related to the type of crime involved and the people victimized by it (Kinsey, Lea, and Young 1986; Elias 1993). Fights among lower-class and minority individuals, or domestic assaults involving female victims are examples of underrecorded crimes. In Canada, some police officers in one large city made a distinction between the public—whom they served—and "the dregs," or "scum" (Shearing 1979). The scum, drawn mainly from lower-class minority groups, were often not taken seriously when they complained of crime.

Overpolicing   Since poor and minority neighborhoods tend to experience an underrecording of crime, it may come as a surprise to learn that police also tend to concentrate law enforcement efforts in the same neighborhoods. These areas become overpoliced relative to other parts of the city (Hagan, Gillis, and Chan 1978; Smith 1986). To some extent this reflects the distribution of crime itself: Violent crimes such as robbery, aggravated assault, and murder tend to be concentrated in the inner city. But it also reflects stereotypes held by both police and the public about the origins, characteristics, and dangers of "real" crimes and "real" criminals. Police go where they expect to find real criminals committing real crime. Using computerized Geographic Information Systems (GIS) to map crime locations, many large urban police forces today keep track of crime "hot spots" and concentrate their personnel in those areas (Sherman, Gartin, and Buerger 1989). A hot spot may be a city block, a bar, an intersection, or even a residence.

Since overpolicing and underrecording of crime tend to occur in the same parts of the city, the impact on police clearance rates is substantial. Overpolicing inflates the numerator of the clearance rate

(the numbers of arrests) while underrecording of crime lowers the denominator (the number of crimes known to the police). The resulting clearance rate is thus artificially inflated, suggesting that there is greater police efficiency in a community than is really the case. It distorts the true picture of a community's experiences with crime: Underrecording downplays the suffering that occurs in inner-city areas and poorer neighborhoods, while overpolicing subjects residents to increased surveillance and risk of arrest. The result can be a sense of neglect on one hand and a sense of abuse on the other (Elias 1993; Kinsey, Lea, and Young 1986). In any case, the true clearance rate is typically lower than the published statistics indicate.

National Crime Victimization Survey (NCVS)

Every year since 1973 the U.S. Department of Justice has sponsored a nationwide survey of 49,000 households to find out more about crime in America. Called the National Crime Survey until 1991, and now called the **National Crime Victimization Survey**, or **NCVS**, the program has become an international model. The Bureau of Justice Statistics (BJS), which runs the survey, calls NCVS "the only national forum for victims to describe outcomes of crime and characteristics of violent offenders" (Bureau of Justice Statistics 1997, 21). Approximately 100,000 individuals aged twelve and over are interviewed each year by trained personnel from the U.S. Bureau of the Census.

The NCVS begins with a series of screening questions done by telephone or in face-to-face interviews with respondents. These questions identify whether the respondent recalls being personally involved in a crime during the previous year. For example, here is Question 42 from the NCVS Basic Screen Questionnaire used in the 2000 survey:

42a.   People often don't think of incidents committed by someone they know. Other than incidents already mentioned, did you have something stolen from you or were you attacked or threatened by:
   (a) someone at work or school?
   (b) a neighbor or friend?
   (c) a relative or family member?
   (d) any other person you've met or known?

42b. Did any incidents of this type happen to you?

42c. How many times?

These questions help jog the respondent's memory and the answers tell interviewers where to go next. When probing about some incidents, interviewers are able to identify elements that indicate the event involved other crimes as well. For example, here is the way interviewers can establish whether a case of vandalism might have been a hate crime:

46g. Hate crimes are motivated by dislike for members of specific groups.

Was any of the vandalism just discussed motivated by dislike for:

(a) people of your race?

(b) people of your religion?

(c) people of your ethnic background or national origin?

(d) people with disabilities?

(e) people of your gender?

(f) people because of their sexual orientation? (U.S. Bureau of the Census 2000, 8)

Sometimes an incident is revealed not to be a crime; other times it turns out to be a different crime than initially believed. For example, a broken window may at first suggest a case of attempted burglary but further questioning could reveal that it was more likely vandalism. In addition, detailed questioning provides information about such things as the actions of offenders and victims, the extent of injury or loss, the type of weapon used, and the reasons for reporting or not reporting the incident to police.

LIMITATIONS OF VICTIMIZATION SURVEYS Victimization surveys have their limitations. First, findings are based only on recall, and people's memories are often flawed. Second, respondents may intentionally deceive interviewers, though this is a risk that carefully constructed questionnaires and well-trained interviewers can reduce. Deception is more likely to be a problem for some crimes and some victims than for others. For example, it

is likely that victimization of women and children is underreported by victimization surveys because of embarrassment or fear. "Indeed, their assailant may be in the room at the time of the interview" (Hough and Mayhew 1983, 21). It has been found that the simple step of using female interviewers in a nonthreatening setting helps uncover more domestic violence (Mirrlees-Black 1995).

Another problem with victimization surveys is the possibility that they overestimate the proportion of crimes involving black suspects. This is less likely to result from victims intentionally lying about a suspect's race than from the fact that some victims hold stereotypical images of criminals. In one interesting study of this issue, white and black subjects were asked to describe a picture they had been shown of a white man holding a razor during an argument with a black man; a majority of the white subjects recalled that the black man had been holding the razor! Black subjects were more likely to recall the picture accurately (McNeely and Pope 1981). It is possible, too, that errors in racial identification could be made if some white offenders conceal their race by wearing masks and gloves, or by blackening their hands and face when committing crimes at night.

Victimization surveys nevertheless provide useful information on a broad range of issues. For example, researchers can learn about the protective measures victims take when they are assaulted, robbed, or raped; about relationships between victims and offenders; about the distribution of crimes in time and space; and about the nature and timeliness of the police response. NCVS data have also shown us that the risks and burdens of crime victimization are not born equally. This is particularly true of violent crime, as Box 2.1 illustrates. Except for sexual assaults, those more likely to be victimized by violent crime are males, teenagers, blacks and Hispanics, and people from low-income or urban households.

VIOLENCE IN THE WORKPLACE The NCVS has also provided the first national data on violence in the workplace. Survey respondents were asked if they had been a victim of a crime while working or on duty. From 1992 to 1996, an estimated 2 million violent victimizations occurred in the workplace each year (Warchol 1998). Occupations rank

BOX 2.1   WHO IS VICTIMIZED MOST BY VIOLENT CRIME?

The burden of crime victimization is not borne equally. This is particularly true of violent crime. NCVS reports show which Americans are more and which are less likely to be victimized by violent crimes.*

1 in 17 males
1 in 24 females

1 in 9 young people age 12–15
1 in 8 teenagers age 16–19
1 in 10 young adults age 20–24
1 in 16 adults age 25–34
1 in 25 adults age 35–49
1 in 66 adults age 50–64
1 in 196 persons age 65 and older

1 in 20 whites
1 in 17 Hispanics
1 in 16 blacks

1 in 12 households with incomes less than $7,500
1 in 25 households with incomes of $75,000 or more

46.3 victimizations per 1,000 urban households
35.5 victimizations per 1,000 suburban households
27.6 victimizations per 1,000 rural households

Women are 6 times more likely than men to experience violence committed by a spouse, an ex-spouse, or an intimate friend.

The risks of a woman being assaulted by a spouse or former spouse, or by a current or former boyfriend or girlfriend, are about equal across ethnic and racial lines.

In 1995, the rate of rape and sexual assault of women was almost ten times the rate for male victims.

Consistently over the history of NCVS, the least likely victims of any type of violent crime are people 65 years and older; the most likely victims are people 12–24 years of age.

---

*Violent crimes are rape, sexual assault, robbery with or without injury, aggravated assault with injury, and simple assault with minor injury. The data includes attempts to commit robbery or rape, and threats of assault involving weapons.

Sources: Bureau of Justice Statistics, *Changes in Criminal Victimization, 1994–1995* (Washington, D.C.: U.S. Department of Justice, 1997); Bureau of Justice Statistics, *Fiscal Year 1996 at a Glance* (Washington, D.C.: U.S. Department of Justice 1996); Bachman and Saltzman, "Violence against Women: Estimates from the Redesigned Survey," *BJS Special Report* (August, 1995), 1–8; Kathleen Maguire and Ann L. Pastore, eds., *Sourcebook of Criminal Justice Statistics* (Washington, D.C.: U.S. Department of Justice, 1999).

differently in terms of the number of nonfatal victimizations that occur for every 1,000 workers. Criminal justice occupations have the highest rates, followed by taxi drivers, people in retail sales, and people working in mental health. Most of the victimizations involved assaults, but over 80,000 robberies and over 50,000 sexual assaults were reported on average each year. A third of the time victims faced armed offenders. As with most crimes other than sexual assault and domestic violence, men were more often victimized than women.

Not surprisingly, commercial establishments and public locations were more dangerous than any other workplace locale. When attacked, most victims offered no resistance or took nonconfrontational actions, such as trying to persuade or bargain with the offender, or fleeing or hiding. Even so, nearly 10 percent of all workplace crimes resulted in the victim needing medical attention.

COMPARING THE UCR AND NCVS   The NCVS was designed to complement the UCR. The two programs are not directly comparable for as we have seen they use different methods, calculate crime rates differently, and provide different kinds of information. However, sometimes it is possible to manipulate the data from both programs to overcome some of the differences between them. Even though the NCVS still records more crimes, long-term trends in some offenses look remarkably similar in both UCR and NCVS data sets. For example, if robberies of commercial establishments such as gas stations, convenience stores, and banks are excluded from the UCR, the long-term rates closely correspond with those of the NCVS, which measure noncommercial robbery.

The Costs of Missing White-Collar Crime   Not surprisingly, the National Crime Victimization Survey provides virtually no information on crimes that victimize society rather than individuals—for example, drug offenses, treason and espionage, or environmental crimes. Nor does it collect information on crimes committed in connection with a person's job, such as embezzlement, price-fixing, or bribery. The UCR does hardly any better in this regard, reporting only on fraud and embezzlement. In fact, it would not be easy to collect information on white-collar crimes under either format. There is little systematic policing of the workplace, and

agencies that investigate such crimes do not generally report them to the FBI's UCR program—even if there was a category to put them in. In addition, people often have no idea what to call it or where to report it if they are victimized. Being the target of consumer fraud at an appliance store is different from having one's purse snatched or coming home to a ransacked house.

The absence of a regular national data collection effort designed to measure white-collar crime is unfortunate because the costs to individuals and society are far above those associated with street crimes and personal offenses against individuals. The most recent estimate of yearly financial costs associated with crimes such as burglary, robbery, homicide, rape, physical and sexual assault, drunk driving, and arson is $105 billion (Miller, Cohen, and Wiersema 1996).

Now consider the financial costs of white-collar crime. Although there has been no comprehensive study, here are some estimates of the yearly financial losses to victims and society (Friedrichs 1996; Maguire and Pastore 1996; Chambliss 1999): tax evasion, up to $300 billion; securities fraud, $5 billion; bank fraud, $20 billion; insurance fraud, $40 billion; employee theft, $25 billion; and computer-related crimes, $10 billion and rising every year. Together, these costs are more than four times greater than those associated with common personal crimes. And the figures do not include price-fixing and other restraint-of-trade practices, bribery, political corruption, industrial espionage, or violations of occupational health and safety regulations. Nor do the figures include environmental crimes. A major part of the dark figure of crime will remain hidden as long as there is no systematic national effort to collect victimization data on white-collar crime.

Self-Report Surveys

A well-known nationwide survey illustrates the **self-report** technique. In the mid-1970s, criminologists at the Behavioral Research Institute of the University of Colorado interviewed a representative sample of American youth born from 1959 through 1965 to find out about their delinquent activity (Dunford and Elliot 1984). A group of 1,725 adolescents were surveyed in 1977, making up the first "wave" or "panel" of the study, called the **National Youth Survey (NYS)**. The youths were interviewed again in 1978, 1979, 1980, and 1981. Now adults, they were again interviewed in 1984, 1987, 1990, and 1993. As you would expect, some of the original sample dropped out of the study because researchers could not find them or they refused to participate further. By 1993, only 78 percent of the original sample remained. This respondent loss is referred to as *attrition*, and it is a problem faced in all studies that follow the same group of people over time.

The subjects of the National Youth Survey were asked whether they had committed any of an extensive list of delinquent and criminal activities during the year preceding the survey. Box 2.2 (on page 32) lists the items, and, where appropriate, the year they were added to the original 1977 survey. The list shows a mixture of serious and less serious offenses, from joyriding and minor theft to assault, strong-arm robbery, and weapons offenses. The original survey also included some *status offenses*—for example, cheating on school tests, skipping classes, running away from home.

The NYS has produced a wealth of information about delinquency and crime, and criminologists are still learning new things from it. Because the study collected information on both the prevalence and incidence of delinquency and crime over a number of years, it is possible to identify the frequency of offending as well as its seriousness and duration (Barlow and Ferdinand 1992, 45–49). The NYS confirmed, for example, that although most delinquency is sporadic and minor in nature, a small group of "chronic delinquents" is responsible for a disproportionate amount of all types of self-reported delinquency (Dunford and Elliot 1984). Although some authors have criticized general youth surveys because they underrepresent truly serious chronic offenders who are incarcerated during the interview periods (Cernkovich, Giordano, and Pugh 1985), the NYS is generally recognized as one of the best self-report surveys.

SHORTCOMINGS OF SELF-REPORT SURVEYS   In the early days of self-report studies, especially those using adolescents, the surveys were full of questions about status offenses, with only one or two tapping participation in serious crimes. Not surprisingly, the prevalence of self-reported delinquency turned out to be similar across class, race, and gender lines (Hindelang, Hirschi, and Weis

1979). Critics argued that the surveys trivialized juvenile crime by underemphasizing serious offenses. More recent surveys have tried to correct this imbalance by including more questions addressing major crimes such as robbery and assaults involving injuries or weapons. Although overall rates of self-reported delinquency still do not vary much by class, race, or gender, serious offending involving violence is more commonly reported by males, lower-class individuals, and African-American youth (Barlow and Ferdinand 1992, 60–69).

Although self-report studies now tap more serious crimes, they have largely neglected white-collar crimes, especially corporate crimes. There are two major reasons for this. First, it is difficult to penetrate the "protective walls of secrecy behind which corporate executives conspire to commit crime" (Box 1983, 86). Second, even if corporate executives were willing to consider being questioned about illegal activity, the researcher has little to offer in the way of inducement. Adolescents in school no doubt enjoy the momentary distraction from regular studies, but the situation is surely different for executives, who may also feel that they are taking unnecessary risks by opening up to strangers. The few in-depth studies of corporate crime that have involved personal interviews were completed only after elaborate steps had been taken to ensure confidentiality and to gain the trust of respondents (Jackall 1988; Clinard 1989).

Trust is important in all interview situations but especially so with crime, a topic that is often embarrassing or humiliating, or involves behavior that would ordinarily get a person into serious trouble. An interview subject may well wonder whether cooperation is worth it, so interviewers must be adequately trained to overcome such negative reactions. Even then, problems may remain. For example, those people who agree to be interviewed may have had different experiences with crime from those who refuse; clearly, this would bias the results. Some respondents may conceal past criminal activities, and others may exaggerate them. Some youths think it "cool" to report doing things that in fact they have never done. Although all these problems create potential pitfalls in the use and interpretation of self-report studies, the knowledge gained still adds new pieces to the puzzle of crime in America and helps uncover the dark figure of crime.

BOX 2.2   SELF-REPORTED DELINQUENCY ITEMS FROM THE NATIONAL YOUTH SURVEY

The following items make up the self-report delinquency measure used in the 1976–1993 National Youth Survey. This list omits status offenses but includes some items added to the original 1977 questionnaire with dates shown in parentheses.

Question: How many times in the past year have you

1. purposely damaged or destroyed property belonging to your parents or other family members?
2. purposely damaged or destroyed property belonging to a school?
3. purposely damaged or destroyed other property that did not belong to you?
4. stolen (or tried to steal) a motor vehicle, such as a car or motorcycle?
5. stolen (or tried to steal) something worth more than $50?
6. knowingly bought, sold, or held stolen goods (or tried to do any of these things)?
7. carried a hidden weapon other than a plain pocket knife?
8. stolen (or tried to steal) an item worth $5 or less?
9. attacked someone with the idea of seriously hurting or killing them?
10. been involved in gang fights?
11. sold marijuana or hashish? ("grass," "pot," "hash")
12. stolen money or other things from your parents or from other members of your family?
13. hit (or threatened to hit) a teacher or adult at school?
14. hit (or threatened to hit) one of your parents?
15. hit (or threatened to hit) other students?
16. sold hard drugs such as heroin, cocaine, and LSD?
17. taken a vehicle for a ride (drive) without the owner's permission?
18. had (or tried to have) sexual relations with someone against their will?
19. used force (strong-arm methods) to get money or things from other students?
20. used force (strong-arm methods) to get money or things from a teacher or other adult at school?
21. used force (strong-arm methods) to get money or things from other people (not students or teachers)?
22. stolen (or tried to steal) things worth $5 to $50?
23. stolen (or tried to steal) something at school such as someone's coat from a classroom, locker, or cafeteria, or a book from the library?
24. broken into a building or vehicle (or tried to break in) to steal something or just to look around?
25. used or tried to use credit cards without the owner's permission? (1978)
26. used checks illegally or used phony money to pay for something (includes intentional overdrafts)? (1979)
27. tried to cheat someone by selling them something that was worthless or not what you said it was? (1979)
28. purposely set fire to a building, car, or other property or tried to do so? (1980)
29. hit or threatened to hit your supervisor or other employee? (1986)
30. forged or copied someone else's signature on a check or legal document without their permission? (1993)
31. made fraudulent insurance claims, that is, falsified or inflated medical bills or property or automobile repairs or replacement costs? (1993)
32. beaten up on someone so badly they probably needed a doctor? (1993)

Source: Kathleen Maguire and Ann L. Pastore, eds., *Sourcebook of Criminal Justice Statistics, 1995* (Washington D.C.: U.S. Department of Justice, 1996), Appendix 11.

METHODS OF CRIMINOLOGICAL RESEARCH

There are a variety of ways that criminologists carry out their research. The method and design of a study depends on what the researcher wishes to study, whether theory is to be tested or created, and the previous research on the subject under study. Selecting one method over another can also be based on the time and cost involved, as well as the researcher's particular skills. The major forms of criminological research include (a) surveys, (b) ethnographies, (c) case studies, (d) comparative and historical research, (e) experiments, and (f) content analyses. Before discussing each method, it is important to keep in mind some basic issues about social research.

Some Basic Issues in Research

DEPENDENT AND INDEPENDENT VARIABLES An important issue in most research is the specification of independent and dependent variables in a study. A variable is anything that can vary in quality or quantity, for example, age, gender, crime rates, or attitudes toward punishment. Much scientific research attempts to show that change in one variable is influenced or caused by change in another variable (or variables). The first variable—the one being influenced—is called the **dependent variable**; the second variable—the one doing the influencing—is called the **independent variable**. For example, suppose that a criminologist has hypothesized that concentrated poverty within a population is the cause of higher rates of violent crime and sets out to study this relationship by collecting relevant data from U.S. cities (Lee 2000). The primary independent variable in this analysis would be concentration of poverty; the dependent variable might be the homicide rate. The selection of independent and dependent variables for any study is influenced by many things, including the previous research conducted on the subject, the insights of theory, and, of course, the individual intellectual interests of the criminologist.

VALIDITY AND RELIABILITY Researchers try to insure that their measurements of variables are valid and reliable. Texts on research methods cover this topic in detail. Briefly, **validity** refers to the extent to which the method captures what it is designed to measure. Since the nature of social reality is very complex, attempts to measure key concepts and ideas may not work well. Measuring instruments tend to be "vulnerable to contamination from various sources outside (external) or inside (internal) the instrument itself" (Champion 2000, 377). So researchers struggle to find ways of reducing the contamination, a task made more difficult in many studies by the absence of standard measures in the social and behavioral sciences. Even if standard measures do exist—such as crime rates based on the Uniform Crime Reports—they may be a weak or misleading measure of this dependent variable. The Uniform Crime Reports may provide a better measure of police productivity than of crime rates.

Researchers also aim for **reliability** in their studies. Reliability refers to the extent to which particular methods or instruments yield consistent results when used repeatedly. For example, suppose a criminologist is interested in studying the attitudes of property offenders through the use of a questionnaire. If the subjects are interviewed in October, and then reinterviewed in November, the answers should be the same or similar if the instrument is reliable. If significant differences emerge between the two survey dates, then either the instrument is not reliable or something significant has happened to change responses. And this points to an enduring problem: Reliability—or lack of reliability—can only be established conclusively when other influences can be ruled out.

RESEARCH ETHICS Research should always be conducted ethically. Research ethics refers to basic principles that prescribe the appropriate ways to conduct research. One of the underlying concerns in most social research is protecting the rights of the people whose attitudes and behaviors are being studied. Generally, ethical research allows participants to drop out of the study at any time; protects the anonymity and/or confidentiality of participants; and secures the voluntary, informed consent of participants. This is particularly important when a study might result in physical or mental injury, or damage to a person's reputation or relationships with others. Ethical researchers always alert participants to possible dangers associated with their work.

The American Society of Criminology (1999) has recently proposed a draft Code of Ethics for its members. Here are a few items from that document:

- Criminologists should not misuse their positions as professionals for fraudulent purposes or as a pretext for gathering intelligence for any organization or government.
- Criminologists should not mislead respondents involved in a research project as to the purpose for which that research is being conducted.
- Subjects of research are entitled to rights of personal anonymity unless they are waived.
- The process of conducting criminological research must not expose respondents to substantial risk of personal harm. Investigators must make every effort to ensure the safety and security of respondents and project staff. Informed consent must be obtained when the risks of research are greater than the risks of everyday life. All research must meet the human subjects requirements imposed by educational institutions and funding sources.

Colleges and universities have created Institutional Review Boards (IRBs) to help guard against unethical research being carried out under their auspices. All university research involving human subjects must be reviewed by an IRB, although class-related projects may be exempt. It is always a good thing to check with your instructor before engaging in any research activity that involves human subjects.

Survey Research

The use of surveys is perhaps the most popular method of conducting criminological research. **Survey research** generally involves administering a questionnaire to a group of people in order to understand their attitudes, experiences, and behavior. The best surveys use *representative random samples* of relevant populations, meaning that people in the population have an equal chance of being picked. Randomness reduces bias and allows for generalizations beyond the people actually included in the study.

The quality of survey designs differs dramatically, sometimes because of simple things such as cost

The use of surveys, a popular method of conducting criminological research, usually involves administering a questionnaire to a group of people in order to understand their attitudes, experiences, and behavior.

and time. At one extreme, students often carry out "research" as a class project. But students generally have neither the time nor money to engage in serious survey research, so they will "sample" a few people on campus or some of their family and friends. These "convenience" samples may leave the student with impressions and suggest hypotheses for future study, but the results are of little scientific value. At the other extreme, the National Crime Victimization Survey collects data on a representative random sample of 49,000 households (in any given year) and is able to generalize to the entire U.S. population over age twelve, which is about 240 million people.

While some criminologists do conduct national surveys with random samples, this is unusual. Indeed, the NCVS and NYS are exceptions to the custom. Most of the time, criminologists will try to randomly sample a university, city neighborhood, school district, or some other regional population.

For example, one recently published article in *Criminology*, the official journal of the American Society of Criminology, used data collected from a questionnaire given to 2,425 public school students in Edmonton, Canada, in order to test a well-known criminological theory (LaGrange and Silverman 1999). Another study in the same edition of the journal surveyed around 34,000 students enrolled in Philadelphia middle schools in order to understand student misconduct in schools (Welsh, Greene, and Jenkins 1999).

Surveys are generally designed for *quantitative* analysis, a process that reduces information to numbers that can be manipulated mathematically. After the responses are collected, researchers generally store the data on computer disks and then use statistical software packages such as SPSS to identify relationships among the study's variables.

Ethnographic Research

One way of tapping meanings and common patterns in attitudes and behavior is through **ethnographic research**. In criminology, ethnographic research generally involves far-ranging interviews and discussions—sometimes over many hours or days—during which subjects give detailed accounts of their criminal activities and associated lifestyles. Ethnographers often spend considerable time in the natural environments of their subjects, either as *participant observers*—doing many of the same things group members do, though not necessarily committing crimes—or as *unobtrusive observers*—watching but not participating in the group. Criminologist Paul Cromwell (1999) has assembled a remarkable volume of ethnographic studies titled *In Their Own Words: Criminals on Crime*. It covers thieves of all sorts, gang members, rapists, murderers, drug dealers, and doctors who defraud the Medicaid system. Jeff Ferrell and Mark Hamm's (1998) book *Ethnography at the Edge* includes a collection of very interesting and sometimes shocking accounts of the experiences of criminological ethnographers.

A recent example of ethnography is a study of the street life of residential burglars in St. Louis (Wright and Decker 1994). Some of the problems mentioned earlier were also experienced in this study: convincing subjects to participate, gaining trust, assessing the truthfulness of what subjects said—and protecting the researchers' own safety.

Safety is often a problem in field research dealing with crime, all the more so if researchers spend hours and hours with their subjects on their own turf. A social researcher who was studying Chicago area gangs in the 1950s told how boys would constantly test him by frightening, "baiting" or "ranking" him, and subjecting him to minor acts of violence (Spergel 1964).

Even locating the interview subjects in the first place was a problem for the St. Louis researchers. The authors solved this by using the *snowball technique*: A former student of theirs was a retired criminal with hundreds of offenses—but very few arrests. The authors hired him to put the word on the street that active burglars were being sought for interviews. One person told another, and through these informal referrals the authors eventually built up a sample of 105 active burglars (Wright and Decker 1994). These burglars described their lives and crimes, and seventy of them agreed to visit sites of successful burglaries they had committed to reconstruct the crime. The researchers were able to place targets in their neighborhood context, and also to develop a clear picture of how these offenders typically went about their business of residential burglary.

Other outstanding examples of ethnographic research include Martin Sanchez Jankowski's (1991) study of several street gangs and Jeff Ferrell's (1993) field research on an urban graffiti subculture. Both of these works helped separate myth from fact in understanding gangs and people who engage in graffiti writing. Jankowski's (1991, 13) methodology is quite interesting and the following excerpt from his book *Islands in the Street* helps us better understand ethnography:

> … I participated in nearly all the things they (gang members) did. I ate where they ate, I slept where they slept, I stayed with their families, I traveled where they went, and in certain situations where I could not remain neutral, I fought with them. The only things that I did not participate in were those activities that were illegal.

The main advantage of ethnography is that it allows a researcher to gain in-depth information about experiences, beliefs, and behaviors that might otherwise go unnoticed through other research methods (Muzzatti 2000). As a general rule, surveys give the researcher more breadth, while ethnography gives more depth.

One type of ethnography is called the *life history*, often referred to as **biographical research**. This way of gaining knowledge about crime has been used throughout the twentieth century by some very famous criminologists, among them Clifford Shaw. Shaw (1930) wrote *Jack-Roller: A Delinquent Boy's Own Story* based on interviews and interaction with a boy named "Stanley." Only twelve when Shaw met him, Stanley had already run up an extensive arrest history and had spent almost half his life in institutions. By the time he was seventeen, Stanley had thirty-eight arrests, mostly for petty offenses but also for assault and "jackrolling." Jackrolling involved robbing drunks or homosexuals. In Stanley's own words: "We sometimes stunned drunks by 'giving them the club' in a dark place near a lonely alley. It was bloody work, but necessity demanded it—we had to live" (Shaw 1930, 85).

Through Stanley's story and those of other delinquent youths, Shaw shows how delinquent attitudes and practices develop and are transmitted from boy to boy, and also how individual delinquent careers develop. Friendships, neighborhood traditions, and relationships with parents played important roles in the development of delinquent careers, Shaw found. In addition, the work of Shaw and his colleagues helped in the construction of delinquency prevention programs, such as the Chicago Area Project. This program, which lasted many years, focused on changing a delinquent child's social environment through neighborhood reconstruction organized via community self-help projects. Since Shaw's day, biographical research has contributed a great deal to our understanding of criminality (e.g., Sutherland 1937a; Chambliss 1972; Klockars 1974; Steffensmeier 1986).

Case Studies

Case studies, while not as popular as surveys and ethnography, have been a mainstay of criminological research for some time. **Case studies** involve the detailed reconstruction of an event or process in order to develop or test theories or ways of understanding crime. This method is generally qualitative in design, but quantitative analyses can also be conducted.

Recent studies of state-corporate crime provide excellent illustrations of the case study method.

State-corporate crimes result from the cooperation or shared activities of both a governmental agency and a private corporation. Case studies have been conducted on the 1986 space shuttle *Challenger* explosion (Kramer 1992); on the deaths of two dozen workers in a fire at a chicken-food processing plant in North Carolina (Aulette and Michalowski 1993); on the environmental crimes committed through the production of nuclear weapons (Kauzlarich and Kramer 1993, 1998); and on the 1996 crash of ValuJet flight 592 in the Florida Everglades (Matthews and Kauzlarich 2000). In all of these examples the researchers collected as much information about the cases as possible, using both primary sources such as interviews and secondary sources such as governmental reports, investigations, and internal organizational memos. Using multiple sources of data in case studies increases the validity and reliability of a study (Yin 1994).

Good case study research produces a precise and multidimensional analysis of how and why a crime or event happened. They also aim to create or test new conceptual or theoretical ideas that shed light on why the crime occurred and perhaps how similar crimes might be explained. Diane Vaughan's (1996) monumental case study of the space shuttle *Challenger* explosion is one example of the rich insights that can be derived from the case study method.

Comparative and Historical Research

Long ago, French sociologist Emile Durkheim (1964b, 65) observed that there is no known society without crime. "Its form changes, but everywhere and always, there have been men [sic] who have behaved in such a way as to draw upon themselves penal repression." In order to find out whether and how crime varies from place to place, or from time to time, criminologists use **comparative or historical research** methods. Ideally, comparative research compares different societies at the same point in time; historical research examines the same society at different periods in its history. The methodologies can be combined, though this strategy also combines their difficulties and limitations.

These difficulties and limitations include the costs and time involved, language barriers, political

There are a number of barriers to comparative research in criminology, yet it is one of the most important endeavors in the field because there is much to learn about crime in one society by studying it in another.

obstacles, lack or poor quality of data, noncomparable definitions of crime and delinquency, and the ethnocentric tendency of researchers living in one society or time period to see their own as the "standard" against which to measure others. *Ethnocentrism* can be illustrated by the assumption held by some prominent criminologists that American views of crime and delinquency can be applied everywhere. At the very least, researchers must be sensitive to the fact that in other societies and time periods, the actions and meanings associated with crime are likely to differ from their own (Beirne 1983).

If these difficulties can be overcome, the benefits of comparative and historical research are considerable. One clear benefit of this method is in its ability to test criminological theories. Do theories developed in the Western world have any applicability to crime in Yugoslavia, Zimbabwe, or Iraq?

If criminology as a social science is truly interested in finding universal laws, we must test our theories in many areas around the globe (Barak 2000; Heiner 1996). Comparative and historical criminologies also have the benefit of allowing us to understand our own culture by examining its history or its similarities to and differences from other cultures. For example, in the United States, laws prohibiting child labor, domestic assault, and many drugs were not passed until the twentieth century. Likewise, there are a number of countries, particularly postindustrialized Western countries, that placed those laws on the books at roughly the same time. However, there is a significant difference in, for example, the nature of drug laws globally—in some countries like India and the Netherlands, marijuana possession and consumption is not criminally prohibited.

Louise Shelley's (1981) book *Crime and Modernization* is an excellent example of the benefits of historical and comparative research. Shelley analyzed crime data going back about 200 years in several countries. Her main finding is that the process of modernization significantly affects crime. First, modernization brings about gradual social change in the norms of a culture, so that the small, homogeneous community no longer has the ability to practice successful social control. The traditional norms of a community, Shelley continues, become less powerful in times of great change. Shelley also found that as societies advance, violent crime decreases and property crime increases. It was also found that those countries with lower overall crime rates in the modern period (such as Sweden and Japan) have managed to somehow insulate themselves from the full effects of modernization because of the extremely resilient nature of their cultures' traditional norms and values.

Experiments

When researchers wish to establish whether one variable causes another, they will think first of conducting an experiment. The **experimental method** is generally considered the ideal way to measure causation because the experimenter can control the research process. A "true" or "classic" experiment requires showing that independent variable X causes dependent variable Y. An experiment tries not just to show that variables are related, or "correlated," but that they operate in a linear and temporal (time-related) way. To satisfy the three criteria of causation—association, temporal order, and the exclusion of rival causes—the true experiment is usually conducted in a controlled laboratory setting, with the subjects randomly assigned to either experimental or control groups. Those subjects in the experimental group are exposed to manipulation of the independent variable, *X*, while those assigned to the control group are not. Then researchers examine whether the groups experience change. If there is a change in the experimental group and not in the control group, one has a stronger case for causation. However, the experiment ought to be repeated with other subjects for the sake of both reliability and validity.

In truth, criminologists rarely conduct the classic experiment. The ethical problems associated with experimenting on human social behavior are obvious, but it would also be very difficult to control the entire research process when studying crime and delinquency. The less a researcher has control over the research process, the less compelling and more questionable the findings will be. Some criminologists who wish to use the experimental method will attempt to conduct a *field experiment*: conducting research in a natural setting in which social behavior occurs. A classic example of this method is the Provo (Utah) experiment designed to study the effectiveness of a community treatment program for youths who had committed serious offenses and/or were repeat offenders (Empey and Erickson 1972). The 326 boys were randomly assigned to either probation or incarceration in one of four groups: probation experiment group, probation control group, incarceration experiment group, or incarceration control group. The boys assigned to the experimental probation group were placed in a special community treatment program, while their control counterparts were placed on regular probation. Those boys assigned to experimental incarceration were also placed into the social community treatment program, while their control counterparts were placed in a state training school. As you can see, this field experiment allowed the researchers to see which group of boys would re-offend less than the others. Ultimately, the results of the study were mixed (largely due to other methodological problems), but

it did show that community-based group-centered treatment was more beneficial as an alternative to incarceration than as an alternative to regular supervised probation.

Content Analysis

In Chapter 1 we discussed the images of crime portrayed by the media. We argued that the images are highly distorted, leading one to believe that crime rates have increased of late, that violent crime is at least as widespread as property crime, and that white-collar crimes are less injurious than traditional street crimes. One method criminologists have used to understand how newspapers, films, news shows, and other mediums create certain impressions of crime is through **content analysis**: A careful and scientific examination of the substance and spirit of representations of crime in print, audio, and/or video. Content analysis allows a researcher to understand how media agents "frame" the problem of crime. Two recent content analyses show how enlightening this method can be.

First, Jerin and Fields (1994) were interested in the type of subjects covered in the newspaper *USA Today*. Specifically, they were interested in the daily section of the newspaper called "News from Every State." The researchers analyzed and coded 26,301 news summaries for 1990 and found that, while crime-related and criminal-justice-related news stories were not as common as other topics (such as government and politics), crime-related stories were more frequently about murder than drug offenses or white-collar offenses. Then they compared the crime rates of each state with the type and quantity of crime stories in the newspaper and found that some states with low crime rates had a disproportionate number of crime-related stories. Jerin and Fields (1994, 200) concluded that major factors in whether a crime is reported by the media are "the circumstances surrounding the crime, the public nature of the offender or victims, or the humorous nature of the incident."

Melissa Hickman Barlow, David Barlow, and Theodore Chiricos (1995a; 1995b) published two articles based on their content analysis of *Time* magazine. These criminologists examined not only what types of crime were given attention, but also the overt and subtle messages conveyed by the articles. They found that *Time* presented very superficial analyses of crime-related issues by, for example, ignoring the employment status of the offender, providing racially biased representations, and generally supporting dominant political ideology.

CHAPTER SUMMARY

This review of data sources and research methods hardly does justice to a complicated topic. However, you should now have a much better understanding of the strengths, weaknesses, and utility of the information about crime and criminal justice presented in the chapters that follow. It is important to remember that no one research strategy or type of data stands above all the rest; each has its drawbacks and each has its benefits. In the last analysis, the appropriateness of a given method or body of data depends on the research questions being addressed.

Information on crime, criminals, and the justice system comes from a variety of sources: local police departments, who report to regional clearing houses and ultimately to the FBI; the National Crime Victimization Survey; and thousands of studies conducted by university researchers, governmental offices, and private corporations. The data collected are used to help test or form theories of crime, instruct social policy, and provide resources to criminal justice and social service agencies. It is crucial when using this data to understand that the "official" crime rate is an estimate of the real amount of crime based on reports to police or reports by victims or offenders. As such, the data must be carefully interpreted to avoid confusion and distortion.

Criminologists employ a variety of research methods. There are some near-universal issues a scholar must attend to: research ethics, validity, and reliability, among others. The major methods of criminological research are survey, ethnography, case study, comparative and historical research, experiments, and content analysis. Some of these methods are quantitative and others are qualitative, but all of them are used to gain a clearer understanding of the nature of crime. Most criminologists aspire to be objective and value-free in their research, although that goal is more difficult to reach than might be expected.

KEY TERMS

biographical research (p. 36)

case study (p. 36)

clearance rate (p. 24)

comparative research (p. 36)

content analysis (p. 38)

crime rate (p. 24)

dark figure in crime (p. 26)

dependent variable (p. 33)

ethnographic research (p. 35)

experimental method (p. 37)

founding decision (p. 26)

historical research (p. 36)

independent variable (p. 33)

index offenses (p. 23)

National Crime Victimization Survey (NCVS) (p. 27)

National Youth Survey (NYS) (p. 30)

National Incident-Based Reporting System (NIBRS) (p. 25)

reliability (p. 33)

self-report (p. 30)

survey research (p. 34)

Uniform Crime Reports (UCR) (p. 23)

validity (p. 33)

RECOMMENDED READINGS

Champion, Dean. 2000. *Research Methods for Criminal Justice and Criminology*. Upper Saddle River, NJ: Prentice Hall.

Ferrell, Jeff, and Mark S. Hamm. 1998. *Ethnography at the Edge*. Boston, MA: Northeastern University Press.

Renzetti, Claire M., and Raymond M. Lee. 1993. *Researching Sensitive Topics*. Newbury Park, CA: Sage Publications.

Sanchez Jankowski, Martin. 1991. *Islands in the Street: Gangs and American Urban Society*. Berkeley, CA: University of California Press.

Shelley, Louise I. 1981. *Crime and Modernization: The Impact of Industrialization and Urbanization on Crime*. Carbondale and Edwardsville, IL: Southern Illinois University Press.

Tontodonato, Pamela, and Frank E. Hagan, eds. 1998. *The Language of Research in Criminal Justice: A Reader*. Boston, MA: Allyn and Bacon.

Wright, Richard T., and Scott H. Decker. 1994. *Burglars on the Job: Streetlife and Residential Break-Ins*. Boston, MA: Northeastern University Press.

RECOMMENDED WEB SITES

Federal Bureau of Investigation

Reports and data on crime and criminal justice. Access to the UCR.

http://www.fbi.gov

Bureau of Justice Statistics

Access to victimization data and other criminological and criminal justice reports.

http://www.ojp.usdoj.gov/bjs

National Criminal Justice Reference Service

Access to all federal government criminal justice data and research, and links to other government publications.

http://www.ncjrs.org

VIOLENT CRIME

On April 20, 1999, Eric Harris and Dylan Klebold walked into their small-town high school in Littleton, Colorado, and killed twelve fellow students and a teacher. Harris and Klebold reportedly spewed racist phrases and voiced their hatred of athletes. Immediately afterward they committed suicide. Videotapes they had made and evidence at the scene indicated that they had planned an even more destructive rampage than actually occurred. The news media flocked to the scene and reporters—and police—spent the next days and weeks digging up all sorts of information about the killers, their victims, the families involved, and the community. A lot was made of the killers' apparent hatred of student athletes, their interest in Nazism, Goth music, and guns. Yet two years later, despite an extensive investigation and commentary from all sorts of experts, no adequate explanation of this terrible crime has been forthcoming.

Thankfully, mass murders such as that in Littleton are rare. The violence discussed in most of this chapter may seem less interesting and less heinous, but there is much, much more of it. It includes homicide, aggravated assault, simple assault, and robbery. Definitions are given in Box 3.1. This chapter does not address violence committed by or on behalf of states or corporations; that topic is discussed in Chapter 6.

VIOLENCE IN U.S. HISTORY

The Puritans came to America largely to escape repression. Perhaps because of this, violence by New Englanders was generally a rare occurrence. Violence in the name of justice, however, was not. Consider what happened during the celebrated Salem witch hunts. In one year alone, a score of executions were carried out in the name of justice—and more were to die before the witch scare died down (Erickson 1966, 149).

Some people believe that violence is never right, that it is immoral and without justification no matter what the circumstances. Others think violence can be justified, though only under exceptional circumstances, such as for self-defense. Others contend that violence can be justified by its accomplishments: a greater good or the prevention of a greater evil (Runkle 1976). Much of the violence that has marked America's history has been justified on the grounds that it brought about important, constructive changes in American society. The Revolutionary War, the Civil War, the Indian wars, frontier vigilante justice, and labor violence have been called examples of "positive" violence (Brown 1969). The fact that thousands of people were killed, maimed, orphaned, and left homeless has been played down. The end apparently justified the means.

During the nineteenth century, riots plagued the major cities; feuds erupted in Kentucky, Virginia, West Virginia, and Texas; guerrilla bands roamed the Midwest in search of glory and fortune; outlaws plundered the frontier regions of the country, often chased by bloodthirsty posses; citizens formed groups of vigilantes; workers seeking the right to unionize took to the streets and were met by police and hired thugs; lynch mobs plagued the

Box 3.1   Definitions of Criminal Violence

The following offenses make up the bulk of the crimes discussed in this chapter. Here are the relevant Model Penal Code definitions:

Criminal Homicide: A person is guilty of criminal homicide if he [sic] purposely, knowingly, or negligently causes the death of another human being. Criminal homicide is murder, manslaughter, or negligent homicide.

Murder: Criminal homicide constitutes murder when (a) it is committed purposely or knowingly; or (b) it is committed recklessly under circumstances manifesting extreme indifference to the value of human life.

Manslaughter: Criminal homicide constitutes manslaughter when (a) it is committed recklessly, or (b) it is a homicide which otherwise would be murder except that it is committed under the influence of extreme mental or emotional disturbance for which there is reasonable explanation or excuse.

Negligent Homicide: Criminal homicide constitutes negligent homicide when it is committed negligently.

Aggravated Assault: A person (a) attempts to cause serious bodily injury to another, or causes such injury purposely, knowingly, or recklessly under circumstances manifesting extreme indifference to the value of human life; or (b) attempts to cause or purposely or knowingly causes bodily injury to another with a deadly weapon.

Simple Assault: A person (a) attempts to cause or purposely, knowingly, or recklessly causes bodily injury to another, or (b) negligently causes bodily injury to another with a deadly weapon, or (c) attempts by physical menace to put another in fear of imminent serious bodily injury.

Robbery: A person in the course of committing a theft (a) inflicts serious bodily injury upon another, or (b) threatens another with or purposely puts him in fear of immediate serious bodily injury....

Source: Excerpted from the *Model Penal Code*, copyright 1962 by the American Law Institute. Reprinted with the permission of the American Law Institute.

South and dealt their own brand of justice; and the mass destruction of Native Americans continued. Wherever it surfaced, conflict seemed destined to be violent.

Resorting to violence as a means of resolving disputes continued into the twentieth century. The labor movement was marked by violence as it confronted stubborn bosses and politicians. Especially violent were the clashes in the country's mining areas. In a mining strike against the Colorado Fuel and Iron Company, from 1913 to 1914, over thirty men, women, and children lost their lives (Brown 1969, 55). The first half of the twentieth century also witnessed other forms of group violence: During and after Prohibition, gangland killings became routine events in some cities, Chicago in particular; the Ku Klux Klan became a national organization and brought its hatred and prejudice to bear on blacks, Catholics, Jews, and "radical" whites in brutal beatings and killings.

Throughout the 1960s and 1970s overall levels of violent crime rose steeply in the United States. The National Commission found about a 47 percent increase in the official rates for murder and nonnegligent manslaughter between 1958 and 1968. Rates for aggravated assault showed even higher increases, around 100 percent. FBI data confirm that aggravated assault rates continued to rise during the 1970s, although more slowly. From 1987 to 1991 serious assaults and homicides were on the rise after a leveling-off period during the mid-1980s (Federal Bureau of Investigation 1991, 9, 24). However, National Crime Survey figures in the 1980s suggested that the police picture overstated the increase in assault rates. In fact, fewer assaults were reported in those surveys than at any time since the NCVS program began in 1973 (Bureau of Justice Statistics 1988b).

THE CURRENT PICTURE

Official rates of murder and nonnegligent manslaughter vary around the country. New England states typically have the lowest rates, while Southern and Western states lead the country. Rates also vary by size of city. The highest rates are found in cities with over 250,000 population, and the rates tend to decline along with city size. Homicide is primarily a large-city phenomenon. However, for many years rural rates have been slightly higher than the rates for many small- and medium-sized cities. One reason may be that the distance from and quality of medical services in rural areas make assaults more likely to turn into homicides (Barlow 1985a; Giacopassi, Sparger, and Stein 1992; Long-Onnen and Cheatwood 1992).

More detailed information about official homicides is found in arrest data. Fortunately, official statistics on homicides are among the best available. Homicides rarely go unreported and suspects are usually apprehended and charged with the crime. Police departments generally take great pride in their ability to solve homicides, which is made possible by the existence of a corpse and the crime's typical circumstances. Although they have declined since 1970, probably due to increases in the proportion of stranger murders, clearance rates for homicide are markedly better than those for any other index crime. Figure 3.1 shows the clearance rates for seven offenses.

As Figure 3.2 shows, after rising continuously during the 1960s and then remaining steady throughout the 1980s, homicide rates in the United States have declined dramatically in recent years. In fact, people are now less likely to be victims of

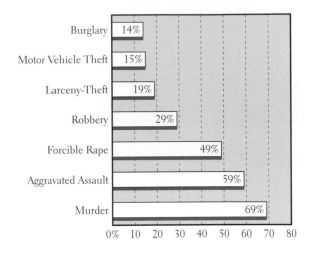

▲ FIGURE 3.1

Police Clearance Rates for Select Offenses, 1999

Clearance rates refer to the percentage of crimes reported that result in arrest. Here are rates for seven FBI Index Offenses. Note that clearance rates for property crimes are substantially lower than those for violent crimes. Since robbery involves elements of both, it is not surprising that it lies in between violent and property crimes.

Source: Federal Bureau of Investigation, *Crime in the United States, 1999* (Washington, D.C.: U.S. Department of Justice, 2000), 202.

homicide than in any other year going back to 1967. Whether this decrease is due to demographic changes, particularly the decrease in the proportion of people in the crime-prone age range of 15–24, the strong economy, other social and cultural changes, or criminal justice policies is a matter of great debate. However, the police in some cities have been claiming much of the credit, perhaps not without some justification, as Chapter 9 explains (see also Barlow 2000, 274).

About half of the arrests for homicide occur in cities over 250,000; of all those arrested in 1999, 90 percent were males and 51 percent of the arrestees were under the age of twenty-five. African-Americans accounted for 52 percent of the arrests, while 46 percent of arrestees were white. According to FBI data, 30 percent of murders arose from arguments and 17 percent occurred in conjunction with other crimes such as robbery and rape (Federal Bureau of Investigation 2000, 17).

The victims of homicides, national data show, are preponderantly male and usually between twenty and thirty years old. Most victims are of the same race and socioeconomic status as the offender,

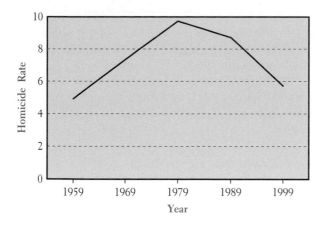

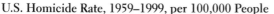

▲ FIGURE 3.2

U.S. Homicide Rate, 1959–1999, per 100,000 People

Source: Federal Bureau of Investigation, *Uniform Crime Reports 1950–2000* (Washington D.C.: U.S. Department of Justice).

Homicide in Large Cities

Although official statistics on homicide are valuable for assessing gross patterns and trends, those who wish a more complete picture will find a number of in-depth urban studies to which they can turn. The pioneering study of homicide was conducted by Marvin Wolfgang (1958) in the mid-1950s. Wolfgang looked at homicides that had come to the attention of Philadelphia police from 1948 to 1952. He investigated a host of variables, including race, sex, age, temporal patterns, spatial patterns, motives, and offender-victim relationships.

Since the publication of Wolfgang's study, there have been other urban investigations of homicide. These studies tend to confirm the following observations about homicide:

1. Young black adult males are most likely to be identified as offenders and victims.
2. Offenders and victims tend to be of low socioeconomic status and to reside in inner-city neighborhoods.
3. Homicides usually occur during the late evening and early morning hours of the weekend.
4. Around half of the known homicides occur in either the offender's or the victim's home.
5. Homicides do not follow consistent seasonal patterns. They do not, as prevalent myth has it, occur significantly more often during the hot months of the year.
6. Offenders and victims are usually acquainted and often live in the same immediate neighborhood.

which often means poor and half the time means black. For example, in 1999, 83 percent of white murder victims were killed by a white, and 93 percent of African-American murder victims were killed by an African-American (Federal Bureau of Investigation 2000, 17). FBI data also show that a young black male living in one of the nation's larger cities has a better chance than anyone else of being arrested for homicide or of being the victim of one. Table 3.1 provides further information on the risks of victimization for different groups of people. Clearly, the risk is not shared equally, nor has it been for as long as national data have been collected (Roth 1994a).

TABLE 3.1   **Lifetime Probability of Being Murdered, by Age, Sex, and Race, 1997**

AGE	MALE	FEMALE	WHITE MALE	WHITE FEMALE	BLACK MALE	BLACK FEMALE
10	137	519	249	741	35	186
15	138	529	251	753	35	189
20	160	581	284	825	41	206
25	216	680	356	953	57	243
30	283	794	442	1,088	76	290
35	364	976	544	1,309	101	368
40	462	1,221	663	1,588	133	481
45	589	1,509	820	1,876	174	638
50	766	1,875	1,032	2,280	231	826

Note: Numbers indicate the reciprocal odds ratio for victimization likelihood. Each number (*x*) should be interpreted as a 1 in *x* victimization probability.

Source: Federal Bureau of Investigation, *Crime in the United States* (Washington, D.C.: U.S. Department of Justice, 2000).

7. Strangers are killed most often during the commission of another felony, such as robbery, rape, or burglary.

Recent homicide trends indicate that (1) the homicide offender is getting younger—the proportion of offenses committed by persons under age twenty-five has been rising, (2) interracial homicides seem to be on the rise, though the increases are small, and (3) the proportion of homicides involving strangers has been increasing over the past few years, though it still remains lower than the proportion involving people who know each other (Federal Bureau of Investigation 1999, 17; Fox and Zawitz 1999).

Disaggregating Homicide

Even though most killings occur in the context of an argument or dispute of some sort, homicide is not a unitary phenomenon:

> Homicide is not one type of event, but many.... Homicides that begin as different types of confrontation have different characteristics, occur in different areas of the city, affect different segments of the population, and have different strategies for prevention. (Block and Block 1991, 6)

When homicide rates are compared across space or time, **disaggregation** uncovers important variations that would not otherwise be seen. Disaggregating is a technique that breaks down the total into its constituent parts. Various criteria have been used to identify the different parts—the weapon used, the relationship between offender and victim, the time and place of occurrence, and the context or circumstances of the killing.

Studies of Chicago homicides demonstrate the value of disaggregation in studying homicide trends (Block 1991; Block and Block 1991). The Blocks broke down the aggregate Chicago homicide figures for a 25-year period into two underlying categories: "instrumental," in which violence emerges out of a goal-oriented predatory attack (such as robbery) where the purpose is not primarily to kill or injure; and "expressive," where violence erupts spontaneously as part of a confrontation and as an end in itself. These two categories are considered opposite ends of a continuum, and they "seldom occur in their pure form. Thus, the acquisition of

money or property may occur as an afterthought in expressive violence, or it may be an additional way of hurting the victim" (Block and Block 1991, 7; see also Katz 1988).

The Chicago researchers found five contexts (called "syndromes") in which violent crimes like homicide and aggravated assault occur (Block 1995):

1. *Interpersonal disputes:* Disagreements between people regardless of their relationship;
2. *Instrumental felony offenses:* Violent crimes committed during the commission of another felony;
3. *Group-based violence:* Examples include gang-related violence;
4. *Chronic offenders:* Individuals with a very long history of violent offenses;
5. *Politically motivated violence:* Violence intended to further a political or ideological cause.

Other researchers have broken homicide down by the relationship of the victim and offender and have shed new light on topics that have interested criminologists for years. The relationship between income inequality, unemployment, poverty, and homicide is one such topic. A recent study of 190 U.S. cities found that while socioeconomic variables are linked to homicide regardless of victim-offender relationship, "poverty and unemployment are more important factors in acquaintance homicide than in other categories" (Kovandzic, Vieraitis, and Yeisley 1998, 592). Since this study also found that the racial composition of cities was a crucial factor relating to variations in homicide rates, the authors recommend further research involving disaggregation by race.

RACE AND HOMICIDE   It is generally recognized that the complexities of homicide in America will not be unraveled until homicide data are disaggregated by race. It is well known that African-Americans are disproportionately victimized and arrested for homicide, yet a more complicated picture emerges when one examines this relationship by county, state, and region (Hawkins 1999). It turns out that urban, rural, and suburban areas have different homicide rates by race. One study found that rates of both black and white homicide are related to changes in the local economy: The decrease in the availability of entry-level jobs results in greater economic deprivation, which in turn raises levels of violence (Shihadeh and Ousey 1998). Here is another fact to consider: African-Americans in the North are predominantly living in cities, while in the South there are sizable proportions of African-Americans who live in suburbs and rural areas. Black-white homicide arrest and imprisonment ratios are closer in the South, which suggests that the place of residence might be a significant variable in understanding racial differences in homicide (Hawkins 1999; Stark 1987).

There is good ethnographic research that bolsters the argument that homicide is not a unitary phenomenon, and therefore that disaggregation is important, particularly by race. Consider Elijah Anderson's study of violence in poor inner-city black neighborhoods in Philadelphia. Here's how Anderson accounts for the higher rates of violent crime in these neighborhoods:

> The lack of jobs that pay a living wage, limited basic public services (police response in emergencies, building maintenance, trash pickup, lighting, and other services middle class neighborhoods take for granted), the stigma of race, the fallout from rampant drug use and drug trafficking, and the resulting alienation and absence of hope for the future. (Anderson 1999, 32)

Anderson (1999) also found that these conditions foster a **code of the streets** within the inner city. This code, which entails a need for respect, not being "dissed," and being treated "right," is "normative for only a segment of the community" (1999, 32–33) but other blacks are drawn under its influence. Thus, black families that are regarded as "decent" (the subjects' own words) and not into the "street" culture oftentimes feel compelled to act in accordance with the code for their social, and even physical, survival. For many inner-city youth, violence is everyday fare. In one review of the literature, it was found that 20 to 40 percent of schoolchildren in inner-city neighborhoods have seen someone shot, stabbed, or killed in street violence (Green 1993; see also Berton and Stabb 1996).

GENDER AND HOMICIDE   The people most often victimized by and arrested for homicide are male. But what about female victims and offenders? Most studies suggest that the reasons women kill and the circumstances surrounding female violence are different from those attributed to males. Female homicides are often precipitated by the violence of the men they kill (Browne, Williams, and Dutton 1999). Most spousal homicides follow this pattern, and the wives who eventually become murderers have often been physically abused by their husbands over a long period of time. Ironically, the men are usually killed with their own weapons (Browne 1987).

Comparing abusive intimate relationships that end in homicide and those that involve lesser violence, it has been found that women who kill

- were assaulted more frequently
- sustained more serious injuries
- were more frequently raped and sexually assaulted
- were in relationships where the male had higher levels of alcohol and drug use
- experienced more death threats from their intimate

Unlike their male counterparts, women who kill generally have less extensive criminal histories, and they are rarely the first to use potentially lethal violence in an altercation. Also unlike males, women are most likely to kill their domestic partners than others. However, "women are two times more likely to be killed by their male partners as men are by their female partners" (Browne, Williams, and Dutton 1999, 150). We discuss some of the reasons for this in Chapter 4.

Mann (1996) studied a sample of all the women arrested for homicide in six major U.S. cities in the years 1979 and 1983. She found that women who kill do so in the home they share with the victim. Indeed 70 percent of the murders were domestic. One respect in which female homicides mirrors male homicides concerns the presence of alcohol: Mann found that more than 33 percent of the women and 50 percent of their victims had been drinking at the time of the murder. We will return to this issue later in the chapter.

Aggravated Assault

Aggravated assault is not as thoroughly researched as homicide. What is known about it, however, suggests a striking resemblance to homicide. This should not surprise anyone, because the essential difference between the two is the existence of a corpse. One study of 1,200 homicides and 32,000 serious assaults in Dallas over a period of five years found the following:

> Except for their fatality, homicides share socio-economic, temporal, racial, age, and gender characteristics.... Differences between homicides are due primarily to (1) variations in the lethality of weapons, and (2) the analytical mixing of primary (i.e., personal injury is the immediate objective of the assailant) and secondary (i.e., injury is incidental to some other immediate objective, for example, rape or robbery) homicides. (Harries 1989, 37; see also Miethe and McCorkle 1998)

Those arrested for aggravated assault are disproportionately young black males who come from low socioeconomic backgrounds and reside in large cities. The victims also fit this characterization; however, Native Americans experience the highest rates of aggravated assault victimization of all racial and ethnic groups (see Box 3.2). Most studies have focused on who is victimized by whom, and they show that whites and blacks are generally victimized by members of their own races. But in one study, the author turned the question around and asked, "Who do members of each race choose as victims?" (Wilbanks 1985). This analysis of nationwide victimization data showed that whereas 81.9 percent of black victims were assaulted by black offenders (the usual way of looking at things), 55 percent of black offenders had assaulted *white* victims. This is probably a result of opportunity rather than any sort of race-related motivation on the part of offenders. Whether this pattern holds for different regions and cities, different time periods, or other racial and ethnic groups was not explored.

BOX 3.2   NATIVE AMERICANS AND VIOLENT CRIME VICTIMIZATION

There are about 2.5 million Native Americans living in the United States (about .9 percent of the total U.S. population). Victimization data shows that they are more likely to be violently victimized (excluding homicide) than whites, Asians, and African-Americans:

Rates of Victimization per 1,000, Averaged from 1992 to 1996

	NATIVE AMERICANS	WHITES	AFRICAN-AMERICANS	ASIANS
Aggravated Assault	35	10	16	6
Rape/Sexual Assaults	7	2	3	1
Simple Assault	70	32	30	15

Interestingly, arrest data shows that Native Americans do not commit a seriously disproportionate amount of these offenses. For example, they accounted for only 1 percent of all arrests for aggravated assault, 1 percent for sexual assault, and 1 percent for other assaults. There is evidence to suggest, however, that Native Americans may be sentenced more harshly and serve a greater proportion of their sentences than other groups (Nielsen 2000, 51–52; also see Nielsen and Silverman 1996).

Sources: U.S. Department of Justice, *American Indians and Crime* (Washington, D.C.: author, 1999); and Federal Bureau of Investigation, *Crime in the United States* (Washington, D.C.: U.S. Department of Justice, 1998).

Box 3.3   MYTHS ABOUT SERIAL MURDER

Myth 1: Serial murder has reached epidemic proportions. In fact, it is extremely difficult to obtain data on this crime. No scientific evidence has shown that serial murder is on the rise (Fox and Levin 1999).

Myth 2: Serial killers are unusual in appearance and lifestyle. Many serial killers, on the contrary, look "normal" and oftentimes are not obviously alienated from the workforce or community (Egger 1998; Fox and Levin 1999).

Myth 3: Serial killers are insane, sex-starved, and/or totally sociopathic. Some serial killers divide the world into "good" and "bad" people, and would not consider killing their parents or children, the "good" people (Fox and Levin 1999).

Myth 4: Serial killers had terrible childhoods and were beaten and sexually abused; they are also likely to have been adopted. The evidence simply does not support these claims. While some serial murderers have come from abusive families, more have not (Egger 1998; Fox and Levin 1999).

Myth 5: Serial killers prey on anyone who crosses their path. Most of the time, serial killers are looking to victimize someone who fits their definition of "expendable," "bad," or "scum." A disproportionate amount of prostitutes, skid-row alcoholics, and drug addicts are victimized by serial killers (Egger 1998).

As with homicides, aggravated assaults often occur inside the home or around bars and street corners. Not surprisingly, knives, blunt objects, and fists are the weapons most often used (were guns more often used, assaults would more often be homicides). As with homicide, victim actions often contribute to the initiation of violence. Verbal confrontations between males, especially, are prone to result in physical attacks, not just in American cities but universally (Polk 1991).

Serial Murder

Serial murder is an extremely rare but much publicized phenomenon. The best estimates of the numbers of serial killers and their victims indicate that serial murder represents "an extreme fringe of the American homicide problem" (Egger 1998; Jenkins 1994, 29), certainly no more than 1 percent of all homicide victims each year, and probably a lot less. The myth that serial murder has become an epidemic has perhaps subsided a bit in the 1990s, but several other myths continue to survive. Box 3.3 identifies some of these.

As one type of multiple murder, **serial murder** generally refers to killings that take place over weeks, months, or years, often with an inactive period in between. In contrast, **mass murder** is a multiple murder that occurs within minutes or hours generally in one place, while **spree-killings** are multiple murders that occur over a day or two (Fox and Levin 1999). A stereotypical image of the serial killer emerged during the 1980s: that of a lone white male in his thirties or forties whose killings are motivated by sex or thrill-seeking. Dahmer, Bundy, and Gacy all fit this image. However, this stereotype has been challenged by some who note that serial killers do not always act alone nor from sexual motives (Egger 1998; Fox and Levin 1999; Jenkins 1994). Further, while most American serial killers have been male and white, there have been serial killings by women and nonwhites as well, and some authors suggest (but do not document) that serial killing by women is increasing (Hickey 1991; Holmes and Holmes 1994).

Still, the paucity of women and blacks among officially documented serial killers begs the question "Why?" Regarding black offenders, Jenkins (1993) has suggested that the low level of black involvement might result from the way in which law enforcement agencies identify and investigate murder: When victims are black, he suggests, police may be "less likely to seek or find evidence of serial murder activity." Using the case of Calvin Jackson, an African-American serial killer who murdered a number of poor, isolated, and elderly residents of a New York apartment building, Jenkins shows that the police did not establish any link among the killings until Jackson confessed. The oversight is explained as follows:

> [T]he police approach a suspicious death with certain preconceptions that depend on both the nature of the victim and the social environment in which the incident occurs. In some contexts, a sudden death can be explained in many ways without the need to assume the existence of a random or repeat killer; serial killer activity is thus less likely to be noted. This is particularly true of urban environments characterized by poverty, isolation, transience and frequent violence. (Jenkins 1993, 47)

Jenkins' argument might explain some of the disparity in black/white involvement in serial murder, but how much is unclear, and in any case it remains an untested proposition. It is important to remember that among the population as a whole, African-Americans make up only around 14 percent. This means that for every 100 white serial killers we should expect to find 20 black serial killers. Consider how few serial killers are identified in any given year. Hickey (1997) estimates that there have been between 2,526 and 3,860 victims and 399 serial killers in the entire period from 1800 to 1995. We would need to find very few black serial killers to bring their proportion in line with the black/white ratio in the U.S. population as a whole. On the other hand, we would need a lot more to bring the black/white ratio in line with that of homicide arrests generally.

The issue for women is clearly different since they constitute 51 percent of the population but only 17 percent of Hickey's count of serial killers. Quite a few women serial killers would have to be discovered to bring male/female proportions in line. On the other hand, what we know about homicide in general would not lead us to expect more female involvement. In fact, the ratio of known female to male serial killers is actually *higher* than that expected, based on the proportion of all arrested homicide offenders who are female (around 10 percent). Simply put, in the absence of further research specifically addressing the issue of minority and female involvement in serial murder, the disparities by race and gender will remain something of a mystery.

Perhaps the most interesting aspect of serial murder from a sociological point of view is the way in which the phenomenon has been elevated in social consciousness from a rare, aberrant occurrence into a pressing social problem. Philip Jenkins (1994) believes that the American public "discovered" serial murder during the 1970s, thanks largely to aggressive media coverage of a few sensational cases (Juan Corona; David Berkowitz, the "Son of Sam" killer; Kenneth Bianchi and Angelo Buono, the "Hillside Stranglers"; John Wayne Gacy; Ted Bundy; Wayne Williams, the Atlanta Child Murders; and the California Freeway Killings, actually two serial killers operating independently). The considerable attention given to this infrequent form of killing, Jenkins argues, helped support conservative crime control policies and agendas during the 1980s and early 1990s.

School Violence

It is impossible to discuss criminal violence these days without saying something about the problem of violence in the schools. Fifty years ago, school teachers worried about students talking out of turn, gum chewing, dress code infractions, cutting in line, and littering. By 1980, a survey found that they worried about far more serious concerns: drug abuse, pregnancy, suicide, rape, robbery, and assault (*CQ Researcher*, September 11, 1992, 797). From 1986 to 1990, an estimated 48 people died and 156 were wounded from gunshots in public and private schools in just ten states. From 1992 to 1999, 211 children died as a result of violence in U.S. schools (Hinkle and Henry 2000). Not surprisingly, high schools account for the greatest proportion of gun-related incidents on school property (about 60 percent), but this still leaves 40 percent occurring in junior high and elementary schools.

Several high profile murders were committed by high school students in the 1990s, leading many Americans to believe that school violence was on

BOX 3.4   RECENT SHOOTINGS AT U.S. SCHOOLS

March 7, 2001: An eighth-grade girl shot a female classmate once in the upper body at a small school in Williamsport, Pennsylvania.

March 6, 2001: A 15-year-old, Charles Andrew Williams, was arrested for the fatal shooting of two students at Santana High School in California, near San Diego. Thirteen others were wounded.

January 10, 2001: A 17-year-old gunman fired shots at Hueneme High School, about 60 miles north of Los Angeles, before taking a student hostage.

May 26, 2000: A 13-year-old honor student allegedly killed his teacher, Barry Grunow, on the last day of classes in Lake Worth, Florida.

February 29, 2000: A 6-year-old boy shot and killed his 6-year-old classmate at Buell Elementary School in Mount Morris Township, Michigan.

December 6, 1999: A 13-year-old student fired at least 15 rounds at Fort Gibson Middle School in Fort Gibson, Oklahoma, wounding four classmates.

November 19, 1999: A 13-year-old girl was shot in the head in school at Deming, New Mexico, and died the next day. A 12-year-old boy later pleaded guilty and was sentenced to at least two years in juvenile prison.

May 20, 1999: A 15-year-old boy opened fire at Heritage High School in Conyers, Georgia, wounding six students.

April 20, 1999: Two students at Columbine High School in Littleton, Colorado, killed 12 students and a teacher and wounded 23 before killing themselves.

May 21, 1998: Two teenagers were killed and more than 20 people hurt when a teenage boy opened fire at a high school in Springfield, Oregon, after killing his parents.

May 19, 1998: An 18-year-old honor student opened fire at a high school in Fayetteville, Tennessee, killing a classmate who was dating his ex-girlfriend.

April 24, 1998: A 15-year-old opened fire at an eighth-grade dance in Edinboro, Pennsylvania, killing a science teacher.

March 24, 1998: Two boys, 11 and 13, killed four girls and a teacher in Jonesboro, Arkansas.

December 1, 1997: A 14-year-old boy killed three students and injured five at Heath High School in West Paducah, Kentucky.

October 1, 1997: A 16-year-old in Pearl, Mississippi shot two students to death and wounded seven others after stabbing his mother to death.

February 19, 1997: A 16-year-old boy killed his principal and a student. He injured two others.

Source: "Other Recent School Shootings," *St. Louis Post-Dispatch*, 6 March 2001, A-10. On-line at <http://www.post-net.com/eaf.nsf/ByID/86256739007E113186256A060067ECA8>.

the rise and out of control (see Boxes 3.4 and 3.5). Understandably, the Colombine High School massacre, mentioned earlier, drew most attention because it was the worst instance of school killings in U.S. history. Yet available data show that school violence has either declined or held constant over the past several years (Hinkle and Henry 2000; U.S. Department of Education 2000). The most recent statistics show the following:

- From 1992 to 1998, violent victimization rates at schools went from 48 to 43 crimes per 1,000 students.
- From 1995 to 1999, students who reported

Box 3.5   COMMON CHARACTERISTICS OF RECENT SCHOOL SHOOTINGS

It is quite natural that we seek to understand the causes of school shootings, for they represent one of the greatest fears of parents—the fear of outliving their children. After the Columbine massacre, several law enforcement agencies, including the U.S. Secret Service and the Federal Bureau of Investigation, conducted case studies of school shootings. Based on a study of 37 such incidents from 1994–2000, the Secret Service concluded the following:

The incidents are seldom impulsive. Over 75 percent of the offenders planned the attack several days if not weeks in advance. Three-quarters were known to hold a grievance at the time of the shooting.

The offender often notifies someone of his intentions well before executing the attack. In most cases, the offender notified at least one friend of his intentions.

It is difficult to provide a single "profile" of the school shooter. Offenders ranged in age from eleven to twenty-one, came from a variety of socio-economic classes, and represented many different racial and ethnic backgrounds. They also differed markedly in their academic performances.

Most offenders have access to guns and have previously fired such a weapon. Two-thirds of the offenders procured the weapons from their home.

Most offenders feel that they have been bullied or threatened. Over two-thirds of the offenders reported having felt bullied, threatened, or injured by others prior to the incident. Some scholars believe that the inability to cope with such exclusion and ostracism serves as a motivational force for violence (U.S. Secret Service National Threat Assessment Center 2000).

One of the goals of criminology is to search for the causes of crime so that it can be controlled or prevented. Clearly, more studies of school shootings and school violence more generally are warranted, yet some criminological theories are already helpful in understanding these events, as we discuss in later chapters of this text.

that they were victims of both property and violent crimes fell from 10 percent to 8 percent.

- From 1993 to 1997, students in grades 9 through 12 who reported carrying a gun, knife, or other weapon on school property during the previous 30 days dropped from 12 percent to 9 percent (U.S. Department of Education 2000, 1).

During the 1990s, the problem of school crime and violence gained enough attention for the U.S. Congress to pass the Safe and Drug-Free Schools and Communities Act of 1994. This legislation required the National Center for Education Statistics (NCES) to collect data on the amount and

seriousness of crime and violence in elementary and secondary schools. The following are some findings from the study of the 1996–1997 school year:

- 57 percent of public elementary and secondary school principals reported one or more incidents of crime/violence.
- 10 percent of all public schools experienced one or more serious violent crimes. Overall there were around 4,000 incidents of rape or other type of sexual battery, 7,000 robberies, and 11,000 physical attacks or fights in which weapons were used.
- Physical attacks or fights without a weapon led the list of reported crimes in public schools, with about 190,000 such incidents.

Columbine High School shooters Eric Harris, left, and Dylan Klebold, right, shocked the nation with their murderous rampage in Littleton, Colorado. Although school shootings are extremely rare, they have received growing attention in the popular media and in academic quarters.

- Large schools had a ratio of 90 violent incidents per 100,000 public school students, compared with the medium-size schools with 38 serious violent crimes per 100,000. (National Center for Education Statistics 1999, 3)

The problem of school violence is understood by most criminologists as a reflection of trends in the larger society (Elliott, Hamburg, and Williams 1998; Kramer 2000). If, for example, youths become more alienated from conventional norms and values, one is likely to see a rise in violence both in and outside of the schools (Yogan 2000). In this sense, school is "a microcosm of society" (Lawrence 1997, 4).

Children are three times more likely to be victimized outside of school than in school (U.S. Department of Education 1999, 1), yet school crime is a community problem that requires a "team" approach for solutions. This means that parents, the police, organizations, and educational programs should be synchronized so that youths are receiving consistent definitions unfavorable to violence from as many agents of socialization as possible. It also means that schools should consider offering violence prevention programs (including those focused on coping skills) and counseling, and should adopt a more proactive approach to identifying and helping children who might be prone to violence (Elliott, Hamburg, and Williams 1998). This latter approach has gained increased popularity in the wake of the Colombine murders.

Mass Murder

Some recent school killings are also properly characterized as mass murders. Aside from the Columbine killings, several other school killings involved multiple victims murdered over a short period of time: In 1998, Michael Johnson and Andrew Golden killed four students and a teacher in Jonesboro, Arkansas; in 1996, mass murders occurred on school grounds in Pearl, Mississippi, and in West

Peducah, Kentucky. Sometimes mass murders on school property have involved outsiders and adults, as was the case in 1989 in Stockton, California, when Patrick Purdy shot and killed five Southeast Asian children while they played during recess.

Of course, mass murders can take place almost anywhere. During the period 1965–2000, they occurred in fast food restaurants, in post offices, in an on-line brokerage firm, on a commuter train, outside the CIA, in an insurance company office, in a university lecture hall, and, most famously, from a university tower. A determined killer needs only the opportunity to become a mass murderer.

What do we know of mass murder and mass murderers? Two of the best-known criminologists to have studied mass murder are James Alan Fox and Jack Levin (2000). In their latest book, *The Will to Kill*, Fox and Levin describe the typical mass murderer as follows:

> Most mass killers do not just snap and start shooting anything that moves. Typically, these murderers generally act with calm deliberation, often planning their assault days, if not months, in advance … mass murderers tend to be quite selective in targeting their victims. They aim to kill those individuals they are convinced are responsible for their miseries, frequently ignoring anyone not implicated in the plot against them. (Fox and Levin 2000, 117)

The offenders are most often middle-aged males, but the sex and age of the victims of mass murderers vary considerably. Furthermore, victims come from all social strata. However, it appears that victims are more often white than members of minority groups. This matches the race of the most common offender. Victims of the mass killer may be classmates, coworkers, relatives and family members (including young children), or complete strangers. Most often, the underlying motivation for mass murder is the resolution of intense anger brought about by frustration and feelings of injustice. Interestingly, most mass murderers think of themselves as law-abiding citizens, not criminals (Fox and Levin 2000, 125). In this respect, mass murderers are similar to terrorists and hatemongers; they all see their actions as justifiable and rational responses to circumstances they find distasteful, offensive, or threatening.

Robbery

Robbery, unlike the typical murder and aggravated assault, is almost always an instrumental crime designed to gain property or money. It is considered a violent crime because it involves the threat or use of force. The Model Penal Code definition is given in Box 3.1 (on page 43); the FBI's definition is found in Appendix A.

According to the FBI statistics, there were 409,670 reports of robberies in the United States in 1999. Each year robberies account for about 4 percent of all Index Offenses and result in approximately $500 million in losses (Federal Bureau of Investigation 2000, 28). The National Crime Victimization Survey, however, has consistently found evidence that there are perhaps twice as many robberies as are reported in the FBI's Uniform Crime Reports. Recall from Chapter 2 that the NCVS interviews victims of crime, so it generally finds more crime than that reported to police. Like most crimes, the robbery rate has decreased considerably in the past decade. In fact, since 1993 it has decreased about 40 percent according to NCVS data (Bureau of Justice Statistics 2000, 10).

Official data and studies by criminologists (e.g., Conklin 1972; Gabor et al. 1988) have consistently shown the following regarding robbery:

- Robbery occurs most frequently in the more highly populated cites of the country. Larger cities experience higher rates than smaller cities, and the lowest rates are found in rural areas (Bureau of Justice Statistics 2000).
- Robbery usually involves offenders and victims who are strangers. Although the percentages vary from study to study, estimates of the proportion of incidents involving strangers reach as high as 80 percent, though the more probable figure for the United States as a whole is around 60 to 70 percent (Bureau of Justice Statistics 2000).
- Offenders tend to be younger males. Males between the ages of fifteen and thirty predominate in arrest statistics for robbery. Black males are more likely than white males to be identified as the offenders in robbery incidents. Fifty-four percent of those arrested in 1999 were African-American; 45 percent were white (Federal Bureau of Investigation 2000).
- Victims are usually white males over age twenty-one. Males are much more likely than

females to be the victims of robbery. Whereas offenders are more likely to be black, the most likely victims are white males. Robbery is also more likely to be an interracial offense than any other violent crime (Bureau of Justice Statistics 2000).

- Robbery tends to take place "on the street." Although the percentages vary from city to city and from one part of a city to another, nationally, around 59 percent of recorded robbery incidents occur in the open—in alleys, outside of bars, in streets, in parking lots, or in playgrounds (Federal Bureau of Investigation 2000).

- Offenders usually have a weapon of some sort. The most typical robbery is an armed robbery with knives and handguns the preferred weapons. Robbery by a stranger is more likely to involve a firearm than robbery by an acquaintance. Not surprisingly, therefore, guns are used most frequently in commercial robberies. Black victims are more likely than white victims to face an armed robber, especially one armed with a gun. However, weapons are rarely used to inflict injury.

- Victims tend not to be injured or to be only slightly injured during the commission of a robbery. Victimization data show that seven out of ten victims are not injured. One in twelve robbery victims, however, is seriously injured, from broken bones to gunshot wounds or rape. The most likely situation in which a robbery victim is physically attacked is when the incident involves two or more armed offenders who rob a female late at night. However, white robbery victims are more likely than black victims to be physically attacked. No matter who the victim is, resistance significantly increases the chance that the victim will be injured, but it also increases the likelihood that the robbery will be unsuccessful.

This last point deserves further explanation. In a study of armed robbers in St. Louis, Missouri, it was found that most armed robbers attempt to create an "*illusion of impending death*" when they confront a victim (Wright and Decker 1997). The robber threatens the victim with death to increase the probability of victim compliance. The robber implies that if the victim does comply, only property will be taken, not life. Two statements from Wright and Decker's (1997, 132) interviews with active armed robbers illustrate this point.

One offender stated the following:

Robbery itself is an illusion. That's what it's about.... Here is a person that you stick a gun in his face, they've never died, they don't know how it feels, but the illusion of death causes them to do what you want them to do.

Several offenders use language like this in confronting their victims:

This is a robbery. Don't make it a murder!

Injury is more likely to occur in cases in which the offenders are unarmed than when they are armed. Robbery infrequently involves shooting or stabbing. It is far more likely to involve kicking, shoving, beating, or knocking down. On the other hand, fatal injury is far more likely to occur in armed robbery than when robbers are unarmed (Cook 1987, 366). The greater likelihood of violence erupting in unarmed robbery incidents is not hard to explain. First, the absence of a gun, knife, or club means that offenders have no obviously deadly weapon with which to intimidate the victim. "Lacking a credible threat," Riedel (1993, 155) writes, "the offenders will be unable to convince the victims to surrender the goods." This is consistent with Wright and Decker's St. Louis research. With a gun or knife present, actual violence may be unnecessary—the victim is sufficiently intimidated and offers no resistance. Second, much unarmed robbery involves a sudden attack. A successful sudden attack robbery depends as much on the element of surprise and the speedy commission of the theft as it does on intimidation. The robber, bent on taking as much as possible as quickly as possible, uses violence in an instrumental way: It helps ensure that the victim is in no position to resist even if he or she wanted to do so, and it makes escape more likely. It may also lessen the chances that the victim will be clearheaded enough to identify the robber for the police.

For obvious reasons, robberies of street drug dealers are seldom reported to the police. In this case, the offender usually takes precautions against being fingered, assaulted, and possibly killed on the street by the victim or the victim's associates. Such precautions are the use of extreme intimidation, using a disguise, selecting a stranger to rob, and becoming hyper-vigilant on the street after the offense (Jacobs, Topalli, and Wright 2000).

"DOING STICKUP"   Jack Katz (1988) argues that the violence in "doing stickup" is more than simply a means of securing compliance from the victim. "The more closely we examine violent interactions in robbery, the more we will appreciate that situational rationality will not do for the final analysis" (181). Katz believes that violence, especially killing, in robberies reflects "a commitment to be a hard-man—a person whose will, once manifested, must prevail, regardless of practical calculations of physical self-interest" (187). The use of violence among "career" or "heavy" stickup men, Katz argues, is a way of demonstrating to victims and to themselves that they really mean it. However, "[t]he ultimate challenge for the would-be stickup man is to convince himself not to give up" (194).

The stickup man anticipates violence at any time, anywhere. This is part of the "chaos" that career criminals live with, according to Katz. It is bound up with the constant threat posed by police, victims, other hardmen, and even the "action" lifestyle typical of hardmen: heavy drinking and partying, sexual exploits, drugs, gambling, being "on the run," fast and heavy spending, and (consequently) persistent episodes of criminal activity week after week.

Katz constructs his picture of stickup men from the vantage point of offenders themselves. What are they trying to do? His analysis is based on detailed police reports of Chicago robberies, ethnographies of street criminals, and autobiographical life stories such as that by John Allen (1977), whose criminal life began in his early teens and extended well into adulthood. The use of violence in these men's lives originates in the adolescent claims of the "badass" and becomes increasingly a persistent aspect of an existence framed by chaos and the never-ending challenge of demonstrating control.

Viewed in this light, the apparently "senseless"—that is, unprovoked, unnecessary, irrational—violence described in accounts of some robberies takes on new meaning. In his Boston study, Conklin (1972) found that one in six robbers with guns and one in three with knives used force even though victims offered no resistance. A bank robber interviewed by Letkemann (1973, 110) tells of seemingly gratuitous violence during a bank robbery:

> So they froze there—their reaction is one of extreme fear and they drop to the floor and sometimes we select the strongest person—the manager especially or another teller which is very big—a six-footer, or something like that, you know. And we won't say a word, we just walk up to him and smack him right across the face, you know, and we get him down.

Katz (1988, 189) argues that for "both the offender and the victim, the perception of whether the victim is resisting or not, is not as clear-cut as researchers often assume...." Katz illustrates with the following example:

> A 33-year-old male is sitting in his car when he is approached by a male of about 25, who opens the car door, displays a handgun, and demands money. The victim gives all his money. The offender then begins hitting the victim, requesting more money. The victim gives his wallet to the offender, who then runs off. (Katz 1988, 189)

Violence is a way to manage the uncertainties and suspense inherent in the robbery confrontation; however, the robber's understanding that he is able and willing to use violence (and that he is comfortable with it) transcends the specific event and is part of the "spiritual commitment" that transforms occasional and adolescent muggers into persistent offenders. The barrier to going on with robbery is the robber's inability to manage fear and uncertainty.

PROFESSIONAL AND AMATEUR ROBBERS   According to Conklin (1972), two main types of professional criminals are involved in robbery: those who do it almost exclusively and those who have other "lines" (such as burglary) but may occasionally commit a robbery. The professional robber is one who engages in robbery almost exclusively and for whom it is the main source of income. Relatively few robbers are properly called professionals; nevertheless, they are responsible for a disproportionate number of armed robberies and for most of the big jobs.

Professionalism means more than quasi-membership in a criminal subculture. It means developing skills, talents, know-how, competence, viewpoints, a way of life. It means weighing risks, choosing among alternatives, planning, using caution, and subscribing to a code of conduct. Professionalism in robbery means that robbery is a part of one's way of life. Einstadter (1969) found that many professional robberies had been fully planned and calculated and were not incidental to some other form of crime. His subjects also considered themselves robbers and had spent considerable time in that line of work. When professional robbers work together, proceeds are shared equally, and if arrested, team members are on their own—they are under no obligation to keep quiet, nor are their colleagues under any obligation to help them. If they do "rat," however, they will lose their share. The group has little cohesion. Members come in and leave the team as occasion necessitates, and leadership roles are filled more or less at will. Members of the team and other professional robbers are expected to deal honestly with one another, at least as it bears on the work itself. Members have a fatalistic attitude toward events that might transpire during a robbery. Other aspects of the professional robber's code and social organization concern cooperation, partnership consensus, planning the "hit," assigning roles (usually done on the basis of skill and knowledge), and decision making.

Many of the forms of robbery that in the past were the primary activity of professionals are now committed as often, if not more often, by amateurs—those who are unfamiliar with the skills, techniques, and other professional aspects of career robbery. Bank robbery is an example. The amateur status of many contemporary bank robbers is confirmed by newspaper accounts of robbers who hold up tellers while cameras take clear pictures of their undisguised faces. Other accounts describe robbers who try to rob drive-up facilities in which tellers are protected by bullet-proof glass and are sufficiently hidden from view so that they can summon the police via silent alarm systems.

Indications of amateurism in bank robbery are also found in estimates of the amounts of money lost in such robberies and in the arrest rates of the past few years. Not only are arrest rates higher now for bank robbery than for any other felony property crime, but, considering inflation, the average amount lost has apparently decreased during the past seven decades. In 1932, the average loss was $5,583, compared with $3,177 in 1991, and $4,802 in 1998. Of course, some of the long-term decline is due to changes in banking procedures in the handling of cash. A professional will know this, however, and will not waste time on petty "scores" unless hard-pressed. Considering the impact of inflation, bank robbery is certainly less lucrative than it used to be.

Research on amateur robbers suggests that quite a few take a "highly casual approach to their crimes" (Feeney 1999, 122). Unlike professional robbers, over half of Feeney's (1999) sample had done no planning at all and a third did only minor planning. The motivations for the robberies were found to be tremendously variable: Some needed money for drugs, housing, food, and clothes, while others, interestingly enough, were simply bored or "angry at the world."

Hate Crime

Hate or **bias crimes** do not necessarily involve violence, but physical assaults, even murders, are their hallmark. In 1990, under the Hate Crime Statistics Act, the FBI began a program of systematic data collection on hate crime. The FBI's definition of hate crime has recently been revised to include acts targeting people with disabilities. It now reads as follows:

> Hate crime, also known as a bias offense, is a criminal offense committed against a person, property, or society which is motivated, in whole or in part, by the offender's bias against a race, religion, disability, sexual orientation, or ethnicity/national origin. (Federal Bureau of Investigation 2000, 58)

The official FBI record on hate crime in the United States in 1999 is represented in Table 3.2. It is important to note that groups such as the Southern Poverty Law Center and the Anti-Defamation League find that FBI figures consistently undercount the amount of hate or bias crime in the United States. For example, in 1997, 1,571 anti-Semitic incidents were reported by the Anti-Defamation League, but the FBI reported 1,087. In 1994, the FBI reported 209 hate crimes against Asians and Pacific Islanders, but the National Asian Pacific American Legal Consortium reported 452 such crimes.

TABLE 3.2   **Hate Crime Offense Distribution and Most Victimized Groups**

OFFENSE DISTRIBUTION, 1999

CRIME TYPE	NUMBER OF OFFENSES
Murder	17
Rape	6
Aggravated Assault	1,120
Simple Assault	1,766
Intimidation	3,268
Robbery	129
Burglary	112
Larceny-Theft	103
Motor Vehicle Theft	14
Arson	48
Destruction/Damage to Property	2,654
Other	64
Total	**9,301**

MOST FREQUENTLY VICTIMIZED GROUPS BY HATE CRIME INCIDENTS, 1999

RACE	NUMBER OF INCIDENTS
African-Americans	3,542
Caucasians	970
Asians	363
Multi-Racial Groups	316
Native Americans	49
RELIGION	
Jews	1,198
Protestants	49
Catholics	41
Muslims	34
SEXUAL ORIENTATION	
Homosexual Males	1,025
Homosexual Females	216

Source: Federal Bureau of Investigation, *Uniform Crime Reports* (Washington, D.C.: U.S. Department of Justice, 2000), 58–60.

Most hate crimes involve simple assault, intimidation, or damage to property. Contrary to the overall crime distribution, however, the majority of hate crimes are crimes against the person, not property offenses. While very few people are murdered because of hate or bias, several recent incidents have drawn attention to the gravity of hatred-inspired violence.

In the mid-1990s, at least a dozen Southern black churches were set on fire, vandalized, and damaged. It is suspected that the offenders were racist white youths venting their rage and hatred at an extremely vulnerable target—small Christian churches with congregations composed largely of impoverished African-Americans. Another case that drew world-wide attention because of its brutality, was the 1998 murder of a young black man named James Byrd, Jr., in Jasper, Texas. Byrd was chained to a pickup truck by three young white males who then drove off, dragging Byrd behind. His body was found in pieces when the police arrived at the scene (State of Texas 1998).

Hundreds of Jewish synagogues and community centers were destroyed, damaged, or defaced by fire and graffiti during the 1990s. Jews have encountered significant violence, discrimination, and prejudice for centuries, not only in the United States and Germany, but in many areas of Eastern and Western Europe. Jews have been one of the most victimized groups in history. The Nazi Holocaust alone resulted in the loss of six million Jews. Unfortunately, anti-Semitism is still strong today in the United States, in part because of deeply

Students in a California school walk past a door painted with a swastika. African-Americans are most victimized by hate crime; Jews are the most victimized religious group.

imbedded stereotypes, myths, and conspiracy theories about Jews.

Finally, the age-old hate crime of violence against homosexuals has recently received more attention in the wake of the 1998 murder of a University of Wyoming freshman. Matthew Shepard was lured from a bar into a truck, robbed, beaten severely, and tied to a fence outside of town where he was left to die. His attackers, two young white males, were characterized as extremely homophobic (State of Wyoming 1998). They were convicted, but escaped the death penalty largely because Shepard's father agreed to a sentencing bargain before that phase of the trial took place. Here is part of a statement Mr. Shepard made to the court following the sentencing agreement:

It has been stated that Matt was against the death penalty. Both of these statements are wrong. We have held family discussions and talked about the death penalty. Matt believed that there were incidents and crimes that justified the death penalty. For example, he and I discussed the horrible death of James Byrd, Jr. in Jasper, Texas. It was his opinion that the death penalty should be sought and that no expense should be spared to bring those responsible for this murder to justice. Little did we know that the same response would come about involving Matt. I, too, believe in the death penalty. I would like nothing better than to see you die, Mr. McKinney. However, this is the time to begin the healing process. To show mercy to someone who refused to show any mercy. To use this as the first step in my own closure about losing Matt. Mr. McKinney I am going to grant you life, as hard as that is for me to do, because of Matthew. Every time you celebrate Christmas, a birthday, or the Fourth of July, remember that Matt isn't. Every time that you wake up in that prison cell, remember that you had the opportunity and the ability to stop your actions that night. Every time that you see your cell mate, remember that you had a choice, and now you are living that choice. You robbed me of something very precious, and I will never forgive you for that. Mr. McKinney, I give you life in the memory of one who no longer lives. May you have a long life, and may you thank Matthew every day for it. (http://www.wiredstrategies.com/shepardx.html)

The national ledger on hate crime is murky, but few experts doubt its extensiveness. One of the biggest problems in gathering data is that many victims of hate crimes do not report the attacks, often out of fear or simply because they consider it a private matter—as many victims of violence do anyway. Another problem is that law enforcement officers and prosecutors may have differing interpretations of the definitions of crimes motivated by hate or bias (Federal Bureau of Investigation 1997). Nevertheless, some believe that hate crime is on the increase in the United States, particularly crimes against gays and lesbians (see Levin and McDevitt 1993).

Some perpetrators of hate and bias crime have links to white supremacist groups such as the Skinheads, the White Brotherhood, the Invisible Empire (part of the Ku Klux Klan), the Christian Patriot Defense League, or the confederacy known as the Aryan Nations. But whites certainly have no monopoly on hate crime. Homophobia and racism are only two of the many underlying motivations for hate. Besides, hate does not have to be organized to result in violence.

Nor is hate crime a distinctly American problem. The Australian National Committee on Violence published a report on racist violence, suggesting that racist attacks were on the increase in that country, and that much of it was organized (National Committee on Violence 1989). The Skinheads originated in England, where for many years they operated as a loosely knit national group of young racist thugs. Skinheads are now found in the United States, as well as in Germany, Canada, the Netherlands, and other parts of Europe (see Hamm 1993, 1994). They tend to be associated with the conservative far-right, although their beginnings in England grew out of an attempt among working class youths to set themselves apart from society by showing pride in their blue-collar roots and sharing a common interest in Reggae music (Aronowitz 1994).

Hamm's (1993, 1998) studies of American Skinheads appears to be consistent with research done on this group in other areas of the globe. For the most part, Skinheads are likely to be white youths in the working class who became radicalized through music, the Internet, and hard-to-find racist books, films, and journals. Interestingly, many of those in his sample were from nonabusive families, had high school diplomas, and some were enrolled in colleges and universities.

Gang Violence

What is a gang? While there are many definitions of *gang* currently in use, Moore (1998) offers a useful perspective based on criminological research. **Gangs** (as opposed to youth groups), can be distinguished in the following ways:

1. The group in question must define itself as a gang. An indicator of this is that the group has adopted a name, such as "Crips" or "Bloods."
2. There exists significant socialization and the transmission of norms and values amongst the group members. This means that the primary agents of socialization are found in the "street," not in the family, school, or other conventional groups and institutions.
3. A group is more likely to be a gang if it recruits members and becomes institutionalized in the community.
4. A group is more likely to be a gang if it has been involved in a sufficient number of illegal incidents that have prompted negative responses from formal social control agencies and the larger community.

The juvenile gang provides the setting in which many young inner-city males explore violence. The ideals of masculinity, toughness, excitement, and reputation are stressed in gang activities (see Sanchez-Jankowski 1991; Moore 1998). Members must show that they can take care of themselves when threatened or provoked, and much emphasis is placed on the conquest and dominance of women (an issue of great relevance to discussions of sexual violence).

Gang members often carry weapons, and are more likely to use violence or the threat of violence to solve problems and gain respect. When approved by the group, violence can be used as a means to achieve prestige, honor, and recognition. Some criminologists believe that the meanings associated with violence for some groups of Americans reflect the existence of a **subculture of violence** (e.g.,

Wolfgang 1958; Wolfgang and Ferracuti 1967). Within this subculture, aggression is expected and legitimized in situations where it is not supported by the dominant culture. "Quick resort to physical combat as a measure of daring, courage, or defense of status appears to be a cultural expectation...." (Wolfgang 1958, 189).

Viewed in this way, violence has positive consequences for male gang members. It deters rivals and improves a youth's competitive edge at the same time that it enhances a member's reputation and social status (see also Horowitz 1987; Daly and Wilson 1988, 129). Not only does violence help gang members gain a tough reputation for themselves and their gang, but it helps protect that reputation. Ruth Horowitz (1987, 44) reports how members of a gang "gathered in an alley to discuss how they could regain the reputation they had lost when [two of their] members were beaten." All favored some sort of violent response. Sanders (1994), in the best ethnographic study of juvenile gang violence to date, shows how drive-by shootings are understood and justified by gang members in terms of rivalry, honor, protection, rationality, and defense.

Two additional points about youth gangs need emphasis. First, drug trafficking and other criminal enterprises are commonplace activities of many big-city gangs. As a result, a certain amount of instrumental violence surfaces as gangs compete with rivals and try to protect themselves from police. But again, the well-publicized gang-drugs-violence connection may be overstated: A three-year study of four of the largest street gangs in Chicago (Black Gangster Disciples Nation, Latin Disciples, Latin Kings, and Vice Lords) found that of 288 gang-motivated homicides, only 8 were related to drugs. The most prevalent context in which murder and assault occurred among the gangs was turf-related (Block and Block 1993). Of course, the findings of this study may not generalize to other locations (see Goldstein [1993] for a study of East Harlem in New York City).

Second, there is little evidence to suggest that youth gangs in general have adopted murder and mayhem as a way of life, or even that they are predisposed to violence. Youth gangs provide comradeship and a way to have a good time. While the adventures of adolescence often bring gang members into conflict with middle-class ideals and the law, most youths mature out of crime and go straight.

Whether they are male or female, inner-city youths who suffer from impoverishment and are aware that their lives are unlikely to improve find that violence bolsters feelings of self-worth and helps them achieve status among their peers.

Based on interviews with members of nineteen African-American gangs in Milwaukee, Hagedorn (1991) concludes that black gangs are part of an urban minority underclass—members tend to stay involved in gangs into adulthood, and the persistence of neighborhood gangs is supported not only because there is a lack of work but because neighborhoods in poverty lack effective social institutions. There are no chain grocery stores, no banks or check-cashing facilities, no alcohol or drug treatment facilities, and no community agencies. Neighborhood segmentation, drug dealing, and periodic shootouts contribute to tensions and reinforce gang violence.

The plight of African-Americans living in the inner-city is summed up in this quote from Elijah Anderson, which also contains a warning:

A vicious cycle has thus been formed. The hopelessness and alienation many young inner-city black men and women feel, largely as a result of endemic joblessness and persistent racism, fuels the violence they engage in. This violence serves to confirm the negative feelings many whites and some middle-class blacks harbor toward the ghetto poor, further legitimating the oppositional culture and the code of the streets in the eyes of many poor young blacks. Unless this cycle is broken, attitudes on both sides will become increasingly entrenched, and the violence, which claims victims black and white, poor and affluent, will only escalate. (Anderson 1994, 94)

SITUATIONAL FACTORS AND VIOLENCE

It is important to recognize that whether or not people are predisposed to violence when they enter a situation, the likelihood of violence can be influenced by factors that are present in, or develop out of, the situation itself. Examples of situational elements that promote violent outcomes are guns, alcohol, victim precipitation, and the encouragement of witnesses. While such situational factors raise the risk of homicide and serious injury in any encounter, they are most likely to be implicated in expressive homicides, where violence is an end in itself (Block 1993, 302).

Guns and Violence

Guns are used in large numbers of violent crimes, but mostly by men. The most recent National Crime Victimization Survey reports that guns were used in the commission in 25 percent of all violent crimes, including 24 percent of robberies, and 6 percent of assaults (Rennison 2000, 9). As Figure 3.3 shows, the most common murder weapon in the United States is a firearm. Among firearms, handguns were used in 80 percent of gun homicides in 1998 (Fox and Zawitz 1999). A classic study of 9,054 handgun murder victims in 1986 found that half were blacks, a victimization rate nearly eight times that for whites (Rand 1990). Blacks aged 20–34 were victimized at a rate nine times greater than the population as a whole, regardless of age. In contrast, white rates of victimization were only slightly higher than average. Male rates of handgun murder victimization were five times those for women. A majority of all victims were shot and killed during arguments, but nearly 30 percent were killed during a robbery or other crime. Recent data shows that 90 percent of gang-related killings involved guns (of all types), compared with around 60 percent of argument-related homicides, and 70 percent of homicides occurring during the commission of another crime (Fox and Zawitz 1999).

Estimates of the number of firearms in private hands in the United States vary, and it is important to recognize their source. One should be wary of estimates made by people with financial or political interests in guns. Probably no one claims to know the exact number, and so any figure must be treated as a more or less educated guess. Having said this, academic estimates from the late 1970s placed the figure at 120 million, plus or minus 20 million, with handguns making up about 30 percent of the total (Wright and Rossi 1981). In 1985 it was estimated that the number of handguns in private hands was 65 million, roughly two per household (*Newsweek*, October 14, 1985). Recent studies estimate that 200 million firearms are privately owned in the United States (Bureau of Alcohol, Tobacco, and Firearms 2000). National opinion surveys show that about 36 percent of those interviewed report having at least one gun in their home (The Gallup Organization 1999). Among teenagers, handgun ownership appears to be on the rise, and in one survey of incarcerated juveniles, 86 percent claimed to have owned a gun at some point in their lives, while 83 percent owned a gun at the time of their arrest (Wright, Sheley, and Smith 1992). A survey of high school students in Seattle found a much smaller percentage admitted owning a handgun (6.4 percent), yet 34 percent reported they had easy access to handguns (Callahan and Rivara 1992).

About 25 percent of private guns are kept for protection and self-defense, also the primary reasons voiced by children who carry guns (Wright and Rossi 1981; Wright, Sheley, and Smith 1992, 70). Clearly, many Americans are fearful for their lives or property. By comparison, relatively few people actually die from a firearm—around 30,000 annually.

In response to growing concern about the problem of assault-style weapons, on May 5, 1994, Congress voted to ban nineteen assault weapons despite vigorous opposition from the gun lobby. President Clinton quickly signed the bill, and gun shops were immediately inundated with orders for the guns from thousands of potential customers (and needless to say, prices skyrocketed). This step certainly has considerable symbolic value for the peace and

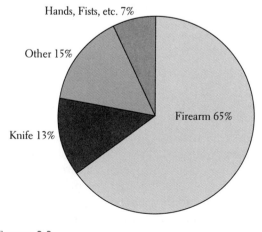

▲ FIGURE 3.3
Distribution of Murder Weapons, 1999

Source: Federal Bureau of Investigation, *Uniform Crime Reports* (Washington, D.C.: U.S. Department of Justice, 2000), 18.

antigun lobbies, but its impact on the practices of criminals may actually be small: A survey of state prison inmates estimated that fewer than 1 percent of all inmates used an assault weapon in committing their crime (Bureau of Justice Statistics 1993a, 18). Furthermore, the federal Bureau of Alcohol, Tobacco, and Firearms traced 56,509 firearms for law enforcement agencies during the 1990–1991 period, and found that two of the top three most frequently traced guns were cheap semiautomatic handguns: the Raven Arms MP-25 (about $60), and the Davis Industries P-32 ($85–$100).

In 1993 the Brady Law was passed by Congress; it requires a five-day waiting period before the sale of a handgun. During that time, local authorities are required to make a "reasonable effort" to find out if the buyer has a felony record, a history of mental illness or drug use, or some other problem that would make the sale illegal. Solid studies on the effects of the Brady Law are hard to find, but the public generally supports waiting periods for handgun purchases.

Some claim that if people could not readily acquire guns, there would be less killing. Others argue that the availability of guns has no bearing on homicide rates—that people kill, not guns. The debate on the issue is fierce and seems unlikely to be resolved in the near future. Since guns are a fact of life in the United States and have been widely owned for at least two centuries, talk of civilian disarmament generally falls on deaf ears. Powerful interest groups such as the National Rifle Association (NRA) and the highly profitable gun industry, which earns over $2 billion a year, strenuously resist any stringent controls. Actor Charlton Heston became president of the NRA in 1998, and was reappointed for an unprecedented third term in 2000. The pro-gun lobby claims widespread support, and indeed, opinion surveys consistently report that most Americans believe they have a right to own a firearm, though opinions are divided on whether handguns should be banned in the respondents' own communities (Bureau of Justice Statistics 1998). In view of the demographics of homicide, discussed earlier, it is perhaps no surprise that blacks are much more likely to favor stricter gun control laws than are whites. Thus, in 1997, a Gallup Poll found 94 percent of black respondents favoring stricter gun laws, versus only 62 percent of whites (Maguire and Pastore 1998, 143).

The presence of a gun does not mean a murder will occur. Millions of Americans have access to guns, but relatively few kill or are killed by them. Nor does the widespread availability of firearms in the United States account for all the disparity between U.S. homicide rates and those of other countries. As Messner and Rosenfeld (1994, 25) put it, "even if none of these weapons were ever used in another killing, the United States would still have the highest homicide rate of any advanced industrial nation." Yet the presence of a gun increases the probability that someone will die if a dispute erupts and neither party can successfully defuse the situation. The gun is a situational factor providing an easily accessible opportunity for murder.

The situational importance of guns to homicide is revealed in studies in Chicago (Zimring 1972) and St. Louis (Barlow 1983; Barlow and Schmidt Barlow 1988). Both studies found not only that guns were more lethal than knives but also that some guns were more lethal than others. In Chicago, .38 caliber handguns were twice as deadly as .22s; .32 caliber handguns were more lethal than .25s; and .25s were more lethal than .22s. The St. Louis study found that 47.7 percent of those victims shot by "large-caliber" weapons (i.e., .38, .357, .44, or .45) died, compared to 33.3 percent of those shot with .32 or smaller caliber handguns. In further contrast, only 18.5 percent of stabbing victims died.

It should be pointed out that the relative lethality of different firearms is affected by the location of the wound. In general, wounds to the head are more likely to be fatal than wounds to other parts of the body. However, Barlow's study also found that the difference in lethality between large-caliber and small-caliber handguns virtually disappeared in head-wound cases. Shoot someone in the head and it matters little whether the gun is a .357 magnum or a .25 caliber derringer (Barlow and Schmidt Barlow 1988).

According to interviews with prison inmates, when used in the commission of crime, guns (and knives) are carried primarily for purposes of scaring the victim or for self-protection (Bureau of Justice Statistics 1993a, 18). Typically, when killings occur in which guns are used, there has been a predictable chain of events: One person acquires a firearm; two or more people come within reach of the firearm; a dispute escalates into an attack; the weapon is fired; it causes an injury; and the injury is serious enough to cause death (Roth 1994, 2).

Roth (1994) suggests that when viewed as a chain of events, the problem of guns and violence can be analyzed as a series of measurable risks. For example, greater gun availability increases the overall risks of firearm deaths as well as the likelihood that a gun will be selected as weapon of choice in the first place; greater availability increases the ease and lowers the cost of acquiring a gun; selection of a gun as a weapon of choice actually reduces the risk of death in some crimes (in robberies and rapes, for example, guns generally intimidate victims into surrendering) but significantly raises it in others (assaults, for example, where the intent is to injure, though not necessarily to kill).

Alcohol and Violence

Just as guns turn up as the weapon used in most homicides, so alcohol emerges as a situational element in many homicides and assaults. Wolfgang found that alcohol was present in 63.6 percent of 588 homicide cases in Philadelphia. Other studies have found alcohol to be present in similar or greater proportions (Wolfgang 1958, 136; Bureau of Justice Statistics 1998). More often than not, both offender and victim had been drinking immediately before or during a homicide or assault.

Does this mean that alcohol in some way caused the violence? Most authors acknowledge the statistical association between alcohol and homicide but do not speak of the relationship in causal terms. True, alcohol is a psychoactive drug, meaning that it produces mental changes in people who consume it. Some scholars believe that alcohol directly increases aggressive tendencies through its pharmacological effects (see Roth 1994). The kind of changes and how extensive they are depend on numerous factors, including the quantity consumed, the consumer's physiological state, the consumer's tolerance for the drug, and whether or not he or she has just eaten. There are also social factors to keep in mind: Alcohol is often consumed in settings where expectations of violence may exist (e.g., at some sporting events, in notorious bars, and during binge drinking sessions among males).

In short, alcohol is best viewed as a precipitating factor in violence. To the extent that alcohol lowers social inhibitions and reduces anxiety and guilt,

people who have been drinking may act more aggressively than would otherwise have been the case. The underlying dispute may have erupted anyway, and the individuals concerned may have been predisposed to seek a violent solution. Without the situational influence of alcohol, however, fear, anxiety, guilt, and social inhibitions are there to serve as constraints. On the other hand, being drunk may be a factor in violence for an entirely different reason. People who anticipate getting into a dispute may prepare themselves by getting drunk. Being intoxicated may provide a convenient rationalization, besides the courage, for violence (Kantor and Straus 1987).

Victim Precipitation

It is often argued that many homicide victims precipitate their own deaths. Many years ago Hans von Hentig (1948) said that killers are often driven to murder as much by their victims' actions as by their own inclinations. This is most likely to occur when those involved know each other well. Tensions and mutual aggravations reach the point at which people see reconciliation only through violence. This can occur suddenly or develop over a long period of time. The violence is an outcome of interaction and not merely the result of a killer's actions.

A standard definition of **victim precipitation** is given by Wolfgang (1958, 252):

> The term victim-precipitated is applied to those criminal homicides in which the victim is a direct, positive precipitator in the crime. The role of the victim is characterized by his having been the first in the homicide drama to use physical force directed against his subsequent slayer. The victim-precipitated cases are those in which the victim was the first to show and use a deadly weapon, to strike a blow in an altercation—in short, the first to commence the interplay of resort to physical violence.

Examples given by Wolfgang (1958, 253), taken from Philadelphia police files, illustrate typical situations of victim-precipitated homicide:

> During a lover's quarrel, the male (victim) hit his mistress and threw a can of kerosene at her. She retaliated by throwing the liquid on him, and then tossed a lighted match in his direction. He died from the burns.

A victim became incensed when his eventual slayer asked for money which the victim owed him. The victim grabbed a hatchet and started in the direction of his creditor, who pulled out a knife and stabbed him.

Identifying the number of victim-precipitated homicides is virtually impossible because doing so requires knowledge of the interaction between victim and offender. Because one party is dead, recreation of the incident must rely on accounts by the killer or witnesses. Estimates have nevertheless been made, and these range from around 25 percent of homicides to upwards of 50 percent. The picture for nonlethal assaults is even more uncertain, especially since so many incidents are hidden. In all probability, a high proportion of assaults are precipitated by the victim's actions, but even pinpointing who the victim is may be moot since both parties may be injured and each is likely to blame the other for "starting it."

VIOLENCE AS A SITUATED TRANSACTION

All social situations possess unique characteristics, yet so many violent incidents look alike that the similarities lead one to ask whether there is some typical dynamic characterizing the events. David Luckenbill (1977) looked at homicide incidents with just this question in mind. He found evidence of six stages in the interaction between actors in the typical homicide drama. We may call this phenomenon a **situated transaction**.

In the first stage, one person insults or offends another. To onlookers the action may not seem particularly offensive, but the person to whom it is directed is angered by it. In stage two, the offended individual sees that the insult is directed at him or her personally. Sometimes this clarification results from meanings assigned by onlookers or friends; sometimes it derives from the history of interactions between the parties involved, as when, for example, a husband has previously fought with his wife and now interprets the present situation as similar.

Stage three involves decisions about reactions to the insult or affront. The offended individual may excuse the other's behavior, rationalizing that the person is just drunk, joking, or acting "crazy." If such face-saving techniques do not work or are inappropriate, the individual must retaliate or back down. Retaliation is usually the route taken in homicide situations and those in which someone is severely injured.

In a search for the situational, proximate, or close-in causes of murder, Katz (1988, 13) asks "What is the killer trying to do in a typical homicide?" He believes that many murders represent an impassioned attack, or "righteous slaughter," in which the killer makes a last-ditch effort to defend his basic worth. Insults about sexual prowess (for men) or continued sexual violation (of women) are felt to be deeply humiliating. When humiliation turns to rage, the would-be killer tries to settle things once and for all. In rage, the killer "confirms his humiliation through transcending it. In rage, he acknowledges that his subjectivity has been overcome by implicitly acknowledging that he could not take it anymore. But now the acknowledgment is triumphal because it comes just as rage promises to take him to dominance over the situation" (Katz 1988, 26).

Sometimes death or injury occurs in stage three. If not, a fourth stage may be entered, in which counterretaliation takes place. In stage four the original offender continues or escalates the insulting behavior, perhaps using violence. In this stage, onlookers may take sides in the dispute, escalating and even directing the conflict.

In stage five both parties are unable to back down without losing face, and weapons will be produced if they have not already appeared. In Luckenbill's study, many disputants already carried guns or knives with them. Others used bottles, pool cues, and other handy implements, or temporarily left the situation to get a gun or knife. With weapons at hand, one party either kills the other quickly or a battle ensues.

Throughout these five stages, no one has given much thought to the police. In stage six the police enter the picture. Some killers flee, some are restrained by onlookers, some are aided by friends, and some call police themselves. The interactions themselves have thus created a new situation in which outsiders are involved and must be reckoned with.

This view of violent situations is not intended to describe all murderous encounters. However, as a depiction of the most "normal" homicide and serious assault, it describes the dynamics well. Conflict,

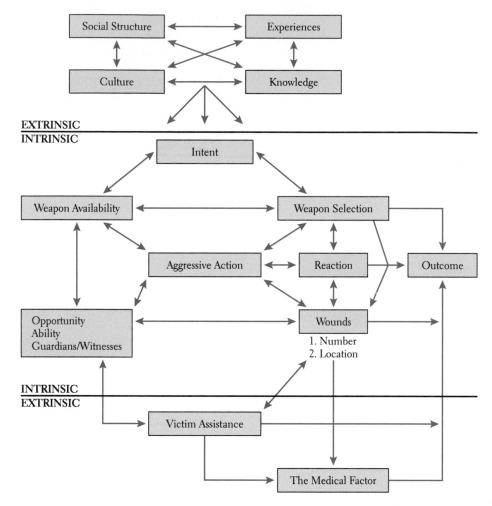

▲ FIGURE 3.4
The Violent Event: Elements and Linkages

victim precipitation, face-saving, retaliation and escalation, and the presence of weapons conspire to
produce deadly violence. That many situations also
involve alcohol, drugs, or partying makes defusing
the process a difficult, if not impossible, task. One
often hears about people who have tried to break
up a fight only to be injured or killed themselves.

Looking at violence as an event draws attention
from background factors and toward the situational
elements that are intrinsic to violent encounters—
victim precipitation, weapon availability and selection, witness behavior, offender-victim interaction,
number and location of wounds, action and reaction, and the impact of opportunity and ability.
There is also the medical factor. When victims do
not immediately die, there is a chance that emergency medical care can be delivered in a timely
fashion and a life saved. Figure 3.4 illustrates how
the intrinsic factors in violent events are linked with
one another, and also with extrinsic factors that are
in the background (e.g., culture, social structure,
experience, and knowledge) or introduced into a
situation after an attack occurs (e.g., victim assistance and the medical factor).

CHAPTER SUMMARY

This chapter has explored the character and extent of murder, assault, robbery, and other violent crimes. The United States ranks first in homicide among industrialized countries, and has for many years. Homicide offenders and victims are most likely to be young males of relatively low socioeconomic status who know each other. The same is true of nonlethal assaults, which are like homicides in most respects. The essential difference between a homicide and an assault is the existence of a corpse.

Robbery is a crime that involves an attempt to gain possession of material belongings through the use or threat of force. Robbers may be professional or amateurs, but oftentimes they attempt to create "the illusion of impending death" when confronting a victim during a street robbery. This raises the likelihood that the offender and the victim will leave the transaction without physical harm.

Serial murder is an infrequent but strangely attractive area of interest for people around the globe. A far more frequent type of violence is hate crime, which stems from racial, homophobic, religious, antidisability, and ethnic biases. Schools are in some ways a microcosm of the broader society, and violence in grade schools and high schools is still infrequent but an emerging concern for criminologists and the general public. Gang violence, studied by criminologists since the 1950s, has also received much attention. An understanding of gang behavior requires attention to the social and structural pushes and pulls youths become subject to as they pass through adolescence and the teenage years.

Certain situations are prone to turning violent: The presence of a weapon, the consumption of alcohol, and victim precipitation are examples of situational elements that contribute to violent outcomes. Many violent events follow similar stages in which someone is offended by an insult and the offended person retaliates in a face-saving ritual that in turn provokes a counterreaction.

KEY TERMS

code of the streets (p. 47)
disaggregation (p. 46)
gangs (p. 60)
hate (or bias) crime (p. 57)
mass murder (p. 49)
serial murder (p. 49)
situated transaction (p. 65)
spree killings (p. 49)
subculture of violence (p. 60)
victim precipitation (p. 64)

RECOMMENDED READINGS

Anderson, Elijah. 1999. *Code of the Streets*. New York: W. W. Norton and Company.

Egger, Steven A. 1998. *The Killers among Us: An Examination of Serial Murder and Its Investigation*. Upper Saddle River, NJ: Prentice Hall.

Jenkins, Philip. 1994. *Using Murder: The Social Construction of Serial Homicide*. New York: Aldine De Gruyter.

Miller, Jody. 2001. *One of the Guys: Girls, Gangs, and Gender*. New York: Oxford University Press.

Miller, Jody, Cheryl L. Maxson, and Malcolm Klein. 2000. *The Modern Gang Reader*. 2d ed. Los Angeles, CA: Roxbury Publishing.

Short, James F. 1997. *Poverty, Ethnicity, and Violent Crime*. Boulder, CO: Westview Press.

Wright, Richard, and Scott Decker. 1997. *Armed Robbers in Action*. Boston, MA: Northeastern University Press.

RECOMMENDED WEB SITES

Anti-Defamation League
A good source for information on anti-Semitism.
http://www.adl.org

Southern Poverty Law Center
Copious amounts of information on all varieties of hate crime and racial discrimination.
http://www.splcenter.org

Safe and Drug Free Schools Program
Information and reports on school safety.
http://www.ed.gov/offices/OESE/SDFS

CHAPTER

4

VIOLENCE AGAINST WOMEN AND CHILDREN

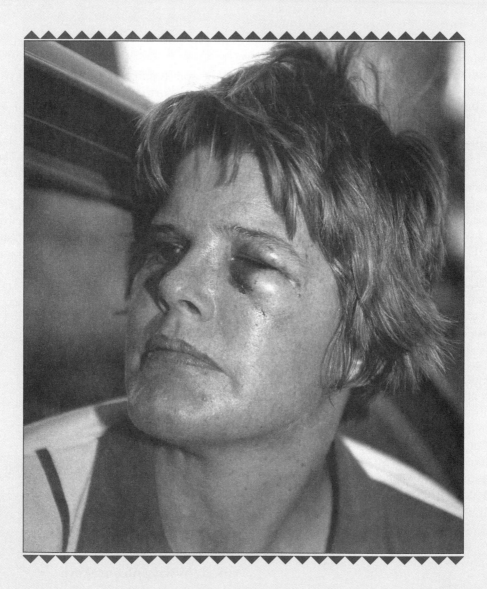

Not long ago, domestic violence, rape, and other sexual assaults were only mentioned in sensational news stories and discussed in secretive whispers. Even the scientific community kept the subject at arm's length. The sensitive nature of the subject may account for some of this, but the historical failure to address these acts seriously may have a deeper meaning: It is women and not men who are the usual victims of sexual assault and domestic violence, and female problems are not viewed with urgency in patriarchal societies. In addition, it was long believed that sexual assault was a rare thing that cropped up from time to time, but not often enough to merit real concern, even among women.

In recent years, sexual assault and domestic violence have become major areas of writing and research. This development is largely due to the efforts of women who have sought to dispel the myths and mystique surrounding rape and the sexual abuse of children, and who have fought to help the victims.

DOMESTIC VIOLENCE

Much violence, including homicide and serious assault, occurs in the home. **Domestic violence** can be defined as crimes committed by and against one or more family members, cohabitants, or intimates.

If anyone doubts that violence is widespread in the American family, consider the following facts:

- A recent Gallup poll indicates that 53 percent of people in the United States personally knew of a situation where a women had been physically abused by her boyfriend or husband (Maguire and Pastore 1998, 193).
- In the same survey, 15 percent of the respondents reported physical abuse by their spouse.
- In cases in which the victim-offender relationship is known, about a third of all female victims of homicide were killed by their husbands or boyfriends. Three percent of males were killed by their wives or girlfriends (Federal Bureau of Investigation 2000, 17).
- Nationally, as many as 4 million children are physically abused by family members, and over 2 million wives are beaten by their husbands (Crowell and Burgess 1996; Smolowe 1994, 21).
- One in five girls and one in ten boys experience at least one incident of incestuous abuse by the time they are eighteen years old (Fraad 1997, 17). (It should be noted that in some cultures, genital contact between a child and mother or father is not considered deviant [DeMause 1998].)

Characteristics of Domestic Violence

Women are much more likely than men to be victims of domestic violence, therefore, much of what is called "family violence" and "domestic violence" is in fact *violence against women* (Kennedy Bergen 1998).

The typical assailant is a husband, the next most common an ex-husband. Yet there is much evidence that the problem of intimate violence is not limited to heterosexual relationships. Although estimates vary, partner violence in lesbian relationships has been found to be frequent and serious enough to warrant the concern of social scientists, public officials, and domestic violence workers (Renzetti 1998; Tuel and Russell 1998). However, studies of lesbian battering have been conducted with very small samples and therefore are not very good measures of prevalence. The same is true of studies of intimate violence among men in homosexual relationships (Merrill 1998). One cannot say with confidence that there is more or less violence in gay and lesbian relationships than in heterosexual relationships.

Uncovering family violence directed at women and children is not easy, partly because there is uncertainty and disagreement about what constitutes criminal violence in family settings (Mihalic and Elliott 1997). When does a spanking of a child or other disciplinary action become abuse or crime? Consequently, even the most nonthreatening interviews often fail to uncover cases of family violence that respondents have not defined as such. This may explain why in victimization surveys parental abuse of children is less often reported than spousal violence.

In addition, many people believe that what happens within the family is a private matter, and this view is shared by men and women. NCVS surveys have consistently shown that around 60 percent of women who did not report being attacked said they considered the matter a private or personal one or they felt the offense was minor. When victims do make a decision to call officials for help, however, some find that they are physically restrained from making the call to police, or threatened with more violence (Fleury, Sullivan, Bybee, and Davidson 1998). In the end, the most common reaction among victims who seek assistance is to approach relatives, friends, or neighbors; however, it often takes more than one episode of abuse before a battered woman seeks any assistance.

There is no typical female victim of spousal abuse, nor is it easy to predict when an assault will occur or its level of violence, although the majority of known incidents do not result in serious physical injury (Crowell and Burgess 1996; Kennedy Bergen

Whether they report their victimization to the police or not, most female victims of domestic assault and rape turn to their friends or family members for guidance and support.

1998). Where there is spousal abuse there are also likely to be abusive relationships among other family members, including abuse of children (Kennedy Bergen 1998). This provides an intergenerational link for domestic violence among family members, and helps explain why violent adults often recount experiencing abuse as children (Heis 1998). In one study investigating this "cycle of violence," being physically abused as a child or as an adolescent significantly increased the odds of future delinquency and adult criminality, and such children had the highest probability of future arrests for violent crime (Brezina 1998; Office of Justice Programs 1996; Widom 1992). Indeed, a man who commits domestic assault is very likely to come from a violent home in which his parents hit him as well as each other (Hanson, Cadsky, Harris, and Lalonde 1997).

Although most incidents of family violence do not result in severe physical injury, there is a tendency for incidents within a family to escalate in frequency and severity with the passage of time (Crowell and Burgess 1996; Bureau of Justice Statistics 1994). People often wonder why most battered women do not end their abusive relationships by leaving their husbands or boyfriends. The answer is complex, but revolves around vulnerability and values. Battered women who leave are often subject to criticism from family and society because they leave, or if they stay they may be labeled emotionally dependent, unmotivated, or dysfunctional. It is not unusual for battered women to feel some responsibility for the battering behavior of the offender: The violence reflects their failings or shortcomings as a wife or mother. Financial vulnerability may also play a role in the decision to stay, especially if there are children (Crowell and Burgess 1996; Homer, Leonard and Taylor 1985). A low-income or unemployed mother often faces a frightening "Catch-22": If she leaves with her children her weak financial situation may threaten her children's welfare (they might even become homeless); if she stays, their physical safety may be in jeopardy, and she may be prevented from seeing them. Women in rural areas are more likely to face major obstacles in seeking help or leaving a violent intimate relationship:

> Isolation, inadequate transportation and communication, the prevalence of guns in the home, social norms and values in rural communities, the nature of policing in rural areas, the lack of social and health care services, and inadequate housing all make it more difficult for rural battered women to deal effectively with the abuse. (Orchowsky 1998, 1)

Some women stay in the hope that by changing their own behavior the battering will end. It rarely, if ever, does.

When young children are victims of family violence, the potential for serious injury is always present, even though fatality rates are relatively low. Typical child injuries from severe beatings include brain damage, skull and extremity fractures, internal bleeding, and other traumas. While this type of violence can be found in all social classes, evidence indicates that it is more commonly found in poor families. In this respect, family violence reproduces the uneven class representation found for homicide and aggravated assault in general.

Significant social and psychological harms are caused by acts of violence in the family. However, women abuse also takes place in dating relationships. A recent study has "challenged the idea that

Sexual, physical, and emotional abuse in dating relationships is much more common than most people think. The abuse crosses class and race lines, but the offenders are most often younger men.

violence is mainly found in marital relationships" by conducting research on women abuse on both U.S. and Canadian college campuses (DeKeseredy and Schwartz 1998, 65). Surveys of college men and women show that around 75 percent of men admit having been psychologically abusive and nearly 15 percent admit physical abuse. Sexist and patriarchal beliefs on college campuses not only encourage abuse of women, they legitimize it as well. The same study found that men who abuse their partners or girlfriends in college share a number of characteristics. They tend to have patriarchal views on the family, friends who perpetrate and legitimize abuse of women, experience with pornography, and they drink and/or use drugs often and frequently with their dating partners (DeKeseredy and Schwartz (1998, 123). We shall return to these features and their relationship to crime later in this chapter.

RAPE

Around the early 1970s, this argument surfaced in the emergent feminist literature (Brownmiller 1975; Russell 1983): There is a popular image of rape that has been fostered by males and that sustains certain myths about rape and the rapist. This image emphasizes the violence of male attackers who appear from nowhere to vent their repressed sexual desires by raping unsuspecting females who do everything possible to prevent the rapist from succeeding. This popular view reflects and perpetuates the following ideas:

- Males dominate females.
- A woman's body, especially her vagina, is man's property, and, like any other property, can be stolen by those to whom it does not belong. (Historically, when a married woman took the name of her husband it signified a property relationship.)
- "Good" women will defend that property at almost any cost.
- Normal males will not need to resort to force in order to acquire the sexual property represented by a woman—they learn to do it in other ways.

Armed with these images, society is encouraged to believe that true rape is infrequent, extreme behavior, whereas "normal" male sexual—and political, economic, legal, and cultural—domination of women by males is considered appropriate and acceptable.

Rape and the Criminal Law

Not surprisingly, then, the popular image of rape has been mirrored in legal definitions of the offense. Common law tradition long emphasized lack of victim consent, physical resistance, the use of force, actual penetration of the vagina, and no prior offender-victim sexual intimacy. Physical injuries, torn clothing, and disarray at the scene of the alleged rape were just some of the things courts looked for in establishing that force occurred and was met by active resistance. Under common law, the victim was expected to resist vigorously and repeatedly. Modern courts, though recognizing that resistance is not a clear-cut issue, are inclined nevertheless to treat active physical resistance as an important factor in establishing that rape actually occurred. Historically, prosecutors screened out cases where evidence of force and active resistance was weak, and that practice still continues.

Offender-victim relationships are also important. Rape accusations are looked upon with suspicion in cases where there is anything more than passing acquaintance. However, jurisdictions now acknowledge that it is possible for a husband to rape his wife, although there are often legal loopholes (Kennedy Bergen 1996). Traditionally, a rape defendant who could show that he has had prior sexual intimacies with his accuser has a strong point in his favor if the case reaches court.

With the advent of so-called **rape shield laws**, states are sometimes allowed to bar evidence of previous consensual sex between victim and suspect. U.S. Supreme Court Judge Sandra Day O'Connor once said: "Rape victims deserve heightened protection against surprise, harassment and unnecessary invasions of privacy." By the mid-1980s most states as well as the federal government had introduced some version of rape shield laws.

Even in states with rape shield laws, testimony about the prior sexual activity of the victim may be permissible in cases that do the following:

1. Raise the issues of consent by showing prior sexual conduct between the victim and the defendant
2. Show that the defendant was not the source of semen nor the contributor to pregnancy nor the cause of venereal disease
3. Attack the victim's credibility by contradicting her earlier testimony on her past sexual conduct (Allison and Wrightsman 1993, 179)

From the time of the earliest legal codes, the true rape victim has been pictured as a sexually naive woman, usually a virgin. Indeed, the Code of Hammurabi and the ancient Jewish laws specifically distinguished between virgins and nonvirgins in their treatment of rape. According to these early codes, a married woman could not be raped, but if she were sexually assaulted by someone other than her husband, both parties could be charged with adultery, a capital offense. However, ancient Jewish laws did not rely solely on the distinction between virgins and nonvirgins, for they ignored the virginity of those women raped within the city walls.

In such cases, complicity was assumed, "for the elders reasoned that if the girl had screamed she would have been rescued" (Brownmiller 1975, 20).

The traditional view of rape has focused on penile-vaginal intercourse, but feminists have been successful in getting states to change rape laws to include oral and anal sex and the use of any object to effect even the slightest degree of penetration. Russell (1983, 43) makes the following comment about the traditional definition:

> The focus on [penile] penetration of the vagina has often been seen as a vestige of an outdated patriarchal notion that female purity and virtue requires a vagina that has not been penetrated. According to this perspective, a female who has experienced all manner of "foreplay," including oral or anal sex, whether voluntary or involuntary, may still be regarded as a virgin.

The Official Record on Rape

According to the FBI, 33 out of every 100,000 women are victims of rape each year in the United States. This rate is based on 89,107 reported rapes in 1999. The FBI considers not only completed rapes under its definition, but assaults and attempts to commit rape as well. As you might expect, however, the true rate of victimization is far, far greater. Some estimates put the figure at ten times the official rate, but many of these are based on definitions of rape that include almost any unwelcome sexual contact. The National Crime Victimization Survey (NCVS), which has recently revised its questions on rape and sexual assault, shows 141,000 completed rapes in 1999, a victimization rate of approximately 60 per 100,000. The NCVS also shows that there were 60,000 attempted but not completed rapes that year, a rate of 30 per 100,000.

There is one point of agreement between these two official counts of rape: Both the UCR and the NCVS report that the rate of *completed* rapes has declined or has remained stable over the past seven years. However, Figure 4.1, based on victimization data, shows a small increase in the number of rapes and sexual assaults in 1998 and 1999.

As far as *intra*gender rape is concerned—men assaulting other men, women other women—the picture is even more murky. Estimates of the extent of intragender sexual assault vary considerably, but there seems to be no question that the true rate is

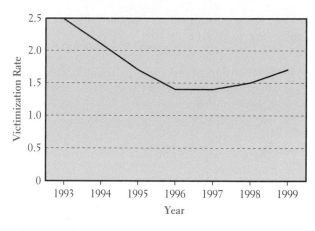

▲ FIGURE 4.1

Rape/Sexual Assault Victimization Rate per 1,000 Households, 1993–1999

While the rape and sexual assault victimization rate declined in the early to mid-1990s, recent data show that victimizations are on the rise.

Source: Bureau of Justice Statistics, *Criminal Victimization, 1999* (Washington, D.C.: U.S. Department of Justice, 2000), 10.

far greater than official records indicate (Allison and Wrightsman 1993, 48). Data collected under the National Incident-Based Reporting System show that just under 10 percent of reported sexual assaults are intragender, almost all of them males assaulting other males (Reaves 1993, 8). According to NCVS data for the years 1987–1991 and 1998, the rape victimization rate for males is 20 per 100,000 males, and presumably almost all of this is committed by other males (Bachman 1994, 2).

REPORTING AND NONREPORTING OF SEXUAL ASSAULT   The difference between police and other rates can be explained in large part by two things: victim reluctance to report offenses, and police labeling practices. For example, NCVS data show that during the period 1973 to 1987, almost half the 2,230,000 rapes cited by victims went unreported to police (Harlow 1991a, 13). NCVS statistics for 1998 suggest that the reporting of rape is even less, at 32 percent (Office of Justice Programs 1999, 6). A recent study of female college student victims of rape found that only 5 percent reported the rape to police (Fisher, Cullen, and Turner 2000). The likelihood that a victim will not report the offense increases if she knows her attacker, if no weapon is used, and if she is not physically injured.

The most common reasons given for not reporting a sexual assault are the following:

- It is considered private or personal, or the victim takes care of it herself.
- The victim fears reprisal.
- Police may be inefficient, ineffective, or insensitive.
- There is lack of proof, and/or no way to find the attacker.
- The victim reports it to someone else.

When victims do report the rape to police, the most common reasons are as follows:

- To keep the incident from happening again
- To punish the offender
- To stop the incident from happening
- To fulfill a victim's duty
- To get help (Office of Justice Programs 1998; also Bachman 1994, 12)

The reasons for reporting or not reporting a rape vary according to whether the victim was attacked by a stranger or an acquaintance. Victims of rapes by strangers are much less likely to consider the matter private or personal and are less likely to fear reprisal. Victims who did report rapes were more likely to cite punishing the offender or fulfilling one's duty when the rapist was a stranger (Harlow 1991a, 13). Other studies generally confirm these findings (e.g., McDermott 1979).

Using victimization data, Lizotte (1985) concluded that factors likely to make the legal case strong—offender is a stranger, he did not belong where the rape occurred, and the victim sustained injury—weigh more heavily in the victim's reporting decision in rape incidents than in other assaults. However, Lizotte also found that white women raped by black men were less likely to report the assault to police. He speculates this may be due to humiliation and embarrassment, or to failure to appreciate that the chances of prosecution and conviction are increased in this situation.

Victimization surveys unlock the door to the dark figure of crime, but how wide the door is opened is a matter of debate, especially with regard to crimes such as rape and sexual molestation.

Stanko (1990, 11) found that much violence against women is hidden, in that incidents are not easily called to mind even by victims who want to do so:

> One woman, a 63-year-old widow, assured me that she would not have very much to contribute to my study. When the interview was complete, she recalled being fondled by a shop owner when she was 8, feeling physically threatened by her brother as an adult, being attacked as a nurse while working at night in a hospital, and being hassled by men for sexual favors after the death of her husband.

As women began to talk more freely about rape, the manner in which rape complaints were received by police officials surfaced time and again as a factor in nonreporting. Rape victims are often subjected to intense and sometimes hostile questioning quite unlike that experienced by victims of burglaries, robberies, and other crimes. One victim gave this account of her experience:

> They rushed me down to the housing cops who asked me questions like "Was he your boyfriend?" "Did you know him?" Here I am, hysterical, I'm 12 years old, and I don't know these things even happen to people. Anyway, they took me to the precinct after that, and there, about four detectives got me in the room and asked how long was his penis—like I was supposed to measure it. Actually, they said, "How long was the instrument?" I thought they were referring to the knife—how was I supposed to know? That I could have told them 'cause I was sure enough lookin' at the knife. (Brownmiller 1975, 365)

In court, rape victims are subject to the rigors of a cross-examination in which they are required to recall, in explicit detail, the humiliating and frightening encounter with the alleged rapist. Of course, rape is a serious offense in all jurisdictions, and defense attorneys quite naturally seek to discredit the testimony of victims and demonstrate that a real rape did not occur. From the standpoint of the victim who wonders whether to report her rape to the authorities, however, the problem is a very real one and may only be resolved by a decision to keep silent.

People and Circumstances

Studies of rape during the 1960s and early 1970s suggested that the popular image of rape accurately depicts only a small portion of all rape incidents (see Amir 1971; Brown 1974). The publication of more recent research has left some of the earlier findings in doubt (e.g., Bachman 1994). Before turning to the conflicting evidence, however, points of agreement will be reviewed.

First, rape offenders and victims tend to be young, usually under twenty-five. In absolute terms, more white women are raped than black women, and more white men rape than black men. However, the probabilities of being a victim or an offender are significantly higher for African-Americans than for whites (Harlow 1991a). The most likely victims and offenders in rape incidents, regardless of race, come from relatively low socioeconomic neighborhoods in the nation's larger cities, again mirroring other interpersonal violence (Office of Justice Programs 1999; Bureau of Justice Statistics 2000, 7).

Second, rape is mainly an intraracial offense when seen from the victim's viewpoint—black women are most often raped by black men, and white women by white men. However, when viewed from the offender's standpoint, about half the black assailants in victimization surveys raped white women and white assailants almost never raped black women. The percentage of rapes that are interracial—black on white or white on black—increases considerably when there is more than one assailant.

Various reasons may be suggested to account for the white/black disparities in rape victimization. Opportunity may be a factor in that the greater mobility of white women relative to black women makes them more vulnerable to sudden-attack predatory crimes by strangers. However, it could also be that cultural and historical images of race and gender, reinforced by structured inequities, make sexual assault of white women appealing to some black males as a means of demonstrating power and control while demeaning whites in the process. On the other hand, for many black offenders this sort of politicization of rape may be far from their minds; they may choose white women as targets because mainstream white society bombards them with cultural stereotypes of the desirability and attractiveness of white women. The impact of such cultural stereotypes is surely heightened by the aura of forbidden fruit: Sexual intimacy between black men and white women is still frowned on in many quarters.

A third point of agreement in the research on rape is that most rapes are likely to occur in private or semiprivate locations such as homes, apartments, automobiles, or parking garages. This is especially true when the rapist is known by the victim. When strangers are involved, initial contact between the rapist and victim often occurs outdoors or in public places such as bars and theaters, but the single most common location for the actual assault is inside a home, usually the victim's (Office of Justice Programs 1997). Women living alone are most vulnerable to rape.

Fourth, rapists are usually unarmed. 1999 NCVS data show that 90 percent of rapes are committed without a weapon, 1 percent with a gun, and 1 percent with a knife (Bureau of Justice Statistics 2000, 9). When they are armed, rapists who know their victim tend to carry knives, while strangers are as likely to carry a gun as a knife (Bachman 1994, 12). Even though rare, the presence of a weapon significantly increases the probability that the rape attack will be completed.

Finally, the vast majority of women who are raped (72 percent in 1999) are victimized by someone they know; most of the offenders are identified as friends or acquaintances (Bureau of Justice Statistics 2000, 8). A study of college women victimized by rape found that 90 percent knew the offenders (Fisher, Cullen, and Turner 2000). Rapes by strangers account for about 28 percent of victimizations. About 22 percent of female rape victims are assaulted by an intimate, such as a boyfriend or husband. This picture is partly explained by convenience and opportunity, and partly by the fact that potential offenders more easily rationalize and justify sexual attacks against women they already have a relationship with or know well.

One point of debate is the extent of injury associated with rape. There is no question that the psychological trauma associated with rape victimization is severe and potentially devastating—"Rape Trauma Syndrome" is the medically accepted term for it—but what about physical injuries? An early national victimization survey looked in detail at the injury question, and McDermott (1979, 36–38) concludes the following:

> Briefly, most rape and most attempted rape victims who were attacked were injured. Injuries included rape and attempted rape injuries, as well as additional injuries.... [M]ost often the additional injury was in the form of bruises, cuts, scratches, and black eyes. These survey data on injury suggest that the element of violence in rape is the physical force used to attempt and/or achieve sexual intercourse with a woman against her will. Generally, it does not appear to be violence in the form of additional, capricious beatings, stabbings, and so forth.

Both popular and legal images of rape place considerable emphasis on the violence of rape and the physical resistance of the victim. The impression gained from Amir's Philadelphia study is that rape victims put up token verbal resistance. The national victimization surveys, using a different categorization of resistance, established a rather different picture. Most victims took measures to protect themselves by screaming, by trying to use some form of physical force against the attacker, or by attempting to flee. A study of rapes in London also found that most victims took protective measures (Smith 1989).

When potential victims resist a rape attack they increase the chances that the rape will not be completed, but at the same time they may increase the risk of more serious injury. A review of the available research "suggests that resistance does not result in an increase in *severe* injury ... and that it is the attacker's level of aggression and not the victim's level of resistance which is more directly correlated with injury" (Grace 1993, 23). While most of the research focuses on the victim, it is the offender's *perception* of the effectiveness of resistance that is surely an important element in his behavior.

One study using NCVS data found that when victims resist *with a weapon* the chances of further injury are significantly reduced. The authors conclude that since victims cannot predict what an attacker will do, "the best course of action for most rape victims is to resist, preferably with a weapon" (Kleck and Sayles 1990, 161). The authors also list attracting attention, running away, and hiding as appropriate types of resistance if victims do not

have a weapon at hand. However, any blanket recommendation about resistance as a strategy for women (or men) should acknowledge research showing that resistance is least likely to be successful when the attack occurs indoors, and when the offender is someone the victim knows (see Grace 1993, 21).

Marital Rape

Legal developments in recent years have led to a significant change in the scope of rape laws: A husband may be held liable for rape if he forces sexual intercourse on his resisting wife. This possibility has existed for many years in Norway, Sweden, and Denmark and in many formerly communist countries, but only since the late 1970s has Anglo-American law encompassed the idea. By the early 1990s, a number of Australian states, Canada, New Zealand, and Great Britain had abolished the marital rape exemption. Earlier, in 1980, the Israeli Supreme Court had dismissed a husband's appeal of his conviction for marital rape, arguing that the Talmud prohibits forced sexual intercourse between a man and his wife (Russell 1983, 336).

In America today the possibility of rape in marriage is recognized in all states and by the federal criminal code (Kennedy Bergen 1996; Allison and Wrightsman 1993, 89). One landmark decision that helped pave the way for the burgeoning of laws against marital rape was a 1985 Georgia Supreme Court ruling that upheld the conviction of a man who raped and sodomized his wife. The court argued that the marriage vow does not mean that a wife must always submit to a husband's sexual demands (Reid 1989, 152).

This represents a significant departure from legal tradition going back hundreds, even thousands, of years. These traditions were born of patriarchy, with the wife always the loser. Matthew Hale, the seventeenth-century English jurist, whose caution on rape (that it is easy to charge and difficult to defend) has long guided judges and legislators, was unquestionably a misogynist (Geis 1978b; Kennedy Bergen 1996). Recent changes in wife rape laws also reflect the influence of the feminist movement, showing yet again how important the pressure of organized interest groups is in the realm of law.

There have been few studies of marital rape. One of the earliest and well-known studies was conducted by Diana Russell (1983). She conducted interviews with 930 women aged 18 and over living in San Francisco, and of these women, 644 were or had been married and were the major focus of her study. Russell defined rape as forced sexual activity that involves intercourse, oral sex, anal sex, or forced digital penetration. One in seven of these women had been the victims of at least one completed or attempted rape by a husband or ex-husband; 10 percent had been the victims of both rape and other forms of physical abuse; and 15 percent had been victims of either rape or other abuse, but not both. Most of the completed incidents involved penile penetration; 9 percent involved anal or oral sex. Thirty-one percent were isolated cases; but another 31 percent involved more than 20 different attacks, sometimes over a period of weeks or even over a period of more than five years. Alcohol was frequently present before or during the incidents, though Russell (1983, 156–166) points out that no simple connection could be identified: Sometimes it appeared to be a factor and sometimes it did not.

The demographics of Russell's marital rape cases are particularly striking in light of other research on rape. White rapists were slightly overrepresented, and husbands were equally likely to hold lower-class, middle-class, or upper-middle-class jobs. Most of the husbands had at least some college education, and fewer than 20 percent were living at or below the poverty line at the time of the first incident. The majority of rapists were between the ages of 21 and 35. These findings depart from those commonly reported for rape in general. Russell warns against generalizations, however, as her study was plagued by refusals from many of the subjects initially contacted for interviews. On the other hand, it is probable that if cases such as those described by Russell were fully represented in victimization surveys, the demographics of sexual assault would look less young, less black, and less lower class.

Angela Browne's (1987) interviews with battered wives disclosed that many had also been raped. But the interviews also disclosed that women who eventually killed their husbands were more likely to report that they had been raped often and violently. Many of these women felt that the only way out of their fearful and humiliating marital life was by the death of their tormentor; yet most were also sorry that their husbands had died (Browne 1987, 140–141).

Finkelhor and Yllo (1985) conducted in-depth interviews with fifty women who had been sexually abused by their spouses. They constructed a typology of rapes based on their findings:

- Battering rapes: The sexual violence is part of a generally abusive relationship.
- Nonbattering rapes: The sexual violence grows out of other sexual conflicts; for example, a long-standing disagreement over the timing or setting of sex, or even the act itself.
- Obsessive rapes: These reflect bizarre sexual obsessions on the part of the male, perhaps related to pornography, sometimes a result of the need for force or ritual in order to get aroused.

Battering rapes were the most common, obsessive rapes the least common.

One of the most recent studies on marital rape was conducted by Raquel Kennedy Bergen (1996). She interviewed forty survivors of wife rape and found that they had very different experiences. Some were physically forced into the act, others were physically battered as a means to rape, and still others were sadistically raped. Many of the women had difficulty defining their rape as indeed "rape":

> They may see sex in marriage as their obligation, or laws and stereotypes about "real rape" in this society may hinder their ability to name their experience wife rape … having redefined their experiences as rape, many women decide to end the violence. (Kennedy Bergen 1996, 94)

Ultimately, many of the victims traced the source of their rape to the husbands' desire to take control or to levy punishment, or to their view that sexual assault of a wife was a matter of "entitlement."

Date Rape

Historically, dating has been an important social institution for both males and females. For the female it marked the conventional road to courtship and marriage and provided the opportunity to practice her "proper" role as the deferential, acquiescent, admiring, and passive partner. For the male, dating provided the conventional road to marriage but in addition gave him the chance to demonstrate independence, masculinity, and action. As the expected initiator of sexual play, the male has been encouraged to view his female companion as a sexual object to be won. His success is measured by how far he gets.

The goal of success in this particular demonstration of masculinity may not be shared by the man's female friend. When this happens, the interaction may become a physical confrontation. Influenced perhaps by the effects of a few drinks or by what he has wrongly interpreted as sexual acquiescence by his female companion, the rejected male refuses to back off. He reaches a point at which, in his own mind (and, he presumes, in the minds of other males), his masculinity is put to the test (see Schwartz and DeKeseredy 1997; Weis and Borges 1973). Indeed, "For many young women, negotiating adolescent heterosexuality is also negotiating sexual safety. How to say no or yes, without losing companionship, intimacy and the status involved in coupledom, is learned from experience. Young women juggle sexuality and safety and, at the same time, keep their eye on their social respectability." (Stanko 1990, 94)

Certainly, not all males subscribe to the masculine ideal of sexual conquest, nor do most dates end in physical confrontations and sexual assault. However, studies indicate that rape and attempted rape during a date are by no means rare, and when they occur, offenders come from all walks of life. Studies on college campuses show that both male and female students—in some cases as many as 27 percent of those interviewed—could recall instances in which they had committed or been the victims of sexual assault during a date and as many as 60 percent recall being petted, fondled, or kissed against their will (Schwartz and DeKeseredy 1997; Murphy 1984; Warshaw 1989; Feltey 1991; Allison and Wrightsman 1993, 6).

A recent study based on nearly 4,000 interviews with a nationally representative sample of college women found that 1.7 percent reported being raped and 1.1 percent reported being victimized by attempted rape (Fisher, Cullen, and Turner 2000). Including the possibility of multiple victimization, relative parity in victimization in the summer months as in the academic year, and assuming enrollment in college for five years, a disturbing statistic surfaces: Up to one-quarter of college women may be victimized by completed or attempted rape

in their years at college. This statistic needs to be viewed with caution, as it may represent the high end of rape victimization for college women. While further studies are needed to clarify the exact percentage, women are clearly vulnerable to sexual victimization in all sorts of contexts, including institutions of higher education.

Many, perhaps most, date rapes go unreported, but one thing is clear: It is unlikely that date rape will fade from the cultural landscape anytime soon. And this is partly because of enduring myths and misconceptions about rape.

Myths and Misconceptions about Rape

Some, perhaps many, males are quick to point out that rape can be justified. Such a view is characteristic of a patriarchal society in which social interaction is gender-based and males are structurally and culturally dominant:

> Rape and sexual violence against women are reproduced and legitimated through culturally mediated interpretative devices which justify, excuse, and glorify male violence against females. Rape myths, techniques of neutralization, or, more generally, patriarchal ideologies provide the linguistic rationalizations and interpretive frameworks for assessing the rape incident, for making sense of what happened, and for legitimating the sexual scripts governing male-female interactions. (Matoesian 1993, 13)

A number of myths and falsehoods mark the female as a legitimate target of male sexual aggression (see Box 4.1). Some women, it is said, need to be raped: They have stepped out of line; they are not passive or submissive and thus must be reminded of their place. Some women, it is said, deserve to be raped: They have been too submissive, and thus any man can have them, or they have (heaven forbid) rejected the male as a sex partner altogether. Then again, some men say, "When a woman says no, she really means yes," or "in their hearts all women want to be raped."

A survey of Minnesota men provides evidence of the prevalence of such views. Seventy-one percent of the respondents believed that women have an unconscious desire to be raped, and 48 percent felt that going braless and wearing short skirts was an invitation to rape (Hotchkiss 1978).

Box 4.1   Some Myths about Sexual Assault

Despite dramatic cultural changes over the past few decades in the United States, myths about rape and sexual assault endure:

- Women are sexually assaulted because they "ask for it" in some way.
- Sexual assault cannot happen to a respectable woman.
- Only the young or beautiful are sexually assaulted.
- Most women fantasize about rape and actually enjoy it.
- Sexual assaults are usually a spontaneous result of an urgent need for sex.
- Most sexual assaults are interracial.
- Most sexual assault victims react hysterically.
- Men cannot be sexually assaulted.
- Sexual assault only occurs in dark alleys and isolated areas.
- Most victims are assaulted by strangers.
- Rape is no big deal; it's only sex and most women aren't really hurt anyway.

If you think rape myths are a thing of the past, recent research has shown that they still exist (Johnson, Kuck, and Schander 1997; Schwartz and DeKeseredy 1997). One study found that of the 143 college students surveyed, about 33 percent of the respondents said that men "have sexual urges they cannot control" and 43.9 percent thought that "all men are capable of rape, given the right situation" (Johnson, Kuck, and Schander (1997, 696). This study also found that "males and those upholding traditional gender role beliefs were more likely to accept certain myths that blame the woman, excuse the male, and justify acquaintance rape compared to females and those who supported less traditional gender role beliefs" (p. 697).

One of the best ways to look at the absurdity of rape myths and justifications is by applying them to bank robbery. Among possible justifications would be the following:

1. The bank says "yes" to a loan and then changes its mind.
2. The bank has led the applicant to believe he/she will receive a loan.

3. Through advertisement, the bank has got the loan applicant "excited."
4. The bank has given the person a loan before.
5. The applicant "really needs" the money.
6. The bank has loaned other people money.
7. The loan officer goes to a party with the applicant where he knows drinking and drug use will be going on (Sanders 1983, 266).

It is not surprising that progressive people, feminist groups, and some politicians are calling for urgent and continued efforts to educate people of all ages and backgrounds on the realities of sexual violence. This is one step toward removing the myths and confusion surrounding rape and other sexual abuse. In spite of this, many people, women included, persist in blaming the victim.

Blaming the Victim

It is not unusual for victims to be blamed for their suffering, and this practice diverts attention from the real causes of victimizing behavior (see LaFree 1989). Implied **victim blaming** phrases might be:

"Don't hitchhike"; "Don't accept when a new acquaintance invites you to his apartment for drinks"; "Don't go out at night on your own"; "Don't wear sexy clothes"; "Don't initiate sexual play"; and, above all, "Don't promise what you won't deliver!" If you are a woman, be what you are supposed to be: vulnerable, demure, passive, dependent, and proper.

Although victim blaming seems to be a generalized response to rape in our culture, it is most likely to surface in the following situations:

- When there has been a prior association between the assailant and victim
- When the victim has behaved in a nontraditional way
- When the rape occurred close to the victim's home
- When the community as a whole espouses patriarchal values and has rigid sex-role traditions
- When observers see themselves as vulnerable to rape but have followed "rules" to avoid it

A study of events following the infamous "pool table" gang rape of a woman who stopped into a bar for a drink in New Bedford, Massachusetts, shows also that victim blaming may be linked to a community's efforts to defend itself in the glare of publicity (Chancer 1987).

Some victim blaming is really a denial that women are "rapable." Consider this comment from a male juror:

> I don't think a woman can be raped.… I ask why are they out at that time of the night? What did they do to provoke it?… A judge over in Ohio told me that a woman can run faster with her pants down than a man, and I believe that.… If you want to say rape, then she must be unconscious. She can scream and kick if she's awake and doesn't want it. (LaFree 1989, 225)

Myths about rape impede the search for understanding and reinforce the stereotypes and bigotry that often surround them. This is no less true in the case of intragender rape:

> Myths about the nature of rape impede awareness and recognition; many people assume that male-to-male rape occurs only among homosexual or

heterosexual men who are incarcerated and have no other sexual outlet. In actuality, like female victims, most male victims are assaulted by an acquaintance. Furthermore, neither the perpetrator nor the victim is necessarily homosexual. (Allison and Wrightsman 1993, 48–49)

Pornography and Rape

Pornography mostly involves the objectification of women so that their body parts are defined as sex instruments. Furthermore, in some pornography, rape is represented as a part of sexual relations, and the victim is usually depicted as being aroused by the experience, if not actively enjoying it (Ashley and Ashley 1984). Several studies of convicted rapists have discovered that many of the victimizers justified their violent infliction of pain on the grounds that the victim had experienced an orgasm (Scully and Marolla 1985, 253).

If there is a causal relationship between pornography and sexual violence, it remains unclear despite (or perhaps because of) the 1986 report of the Commission on Pornography headed by former Attorney General Edwin Meese. This commission did no research of its own nor did it even conduct a comprehensive literature review, relying instead on testimony at six public hearings around the country. Much of the testimony was composed of horror stories from people claiming to have been victimized by pornography and from representatives of antipornography groups (see also Baron and Straus 1990, 189). Testimony from social scientists was inconsistent and often cautionary, but a majority of the commission's members chose to ignore this fact.

There seems to be growing consensus that the portrayal of women in pornography, especially pornography depicting force or violence, provides cultural approval of the sexual objectification of women and their subordination to the desires and commands of men. To that extent, pornography provides part of the culturally acquired vocabulary that can be used to justify and excuse male sexual violence directed against women. In their study of state variations in rape rates, Baron and Straus (1990) found a positive correlation between the circulation of sex magazines and rape rates among states, and their interpretation of the finding is consistent with this argument.

However, these authors also caution against censorship of pornography on the following grounds:

1. It "paves the way for prohibition of controversial or unpopular political ideas, including feminist ideas, and helps to establish a social climate in which censorship is morally acceptable."
2. There is no scientific evidence that pornography without violent content increases aggression toward women.
3. "Violence, not sex, is the real problem."
4. "Pornography is less violent than other media."
5. "Pornography is no more sexist than other media."
6. There are more important ways that society can combat violence and sexism (Baron and Straus 1990, 190–191).

Many rapists see women "as sexual commodities to be used or conquered rather than as human beings with rights and feelings. Rape is not an idiosyncratic act committed by a few 'sick' men. Rather, rape can be viewed as the end point on a continuum of sexually aggressive behaviors that reward men and victimize women" (Scully and Marolla 1985, 261–262). According to a study of 132 rapists, these rewards are numerous, including revenge and the ability to exact punishment, to express anger, and to exercise power and control (Hale 1997). The study found that some women were raped because they had had an affair, some because they filed for divorce, and yet others merely because the offender was having a "bad day."

Sexual Aggression, Psychological Profiles, and Evolutionary Theory

Most males do not commit sexual assaults, certainly not violent rapes. It is a short step from this observation to the commonly held idea that those who do must be suffering from some sort of psychological pathology or disorder. This notion certainly fits well with the popular image of rape.

Research on the subject is inconclusive but generally does not support explanations of rape and sexual assault based on mental pathologies, brain damage, or personality disorder. Most studies show convicted rapists to be psychologically normal or, at most, suffering from some sort of neurosis. On balance, there is little impressive evidence that rapists are in general psychologically abnormal (Hagan and Gust-Brey 1999; Scully and Marolla 1985, 253). Some probably are—the particularly brutal, perhaps, or serial rapists who choose many different victims—but as a general explanation of sexual assault, psychic pathology or disorder theories are of limited use. The most promising approach is one that links structural and cultural factors with situational inducements, as was the case with explanations of violence in general.

If there is a common mental attitude among rapists, then Russell (1983, 123) probably captures it best in her description of the "patriarch." When she speaks of husbands who rape, she makes it clear that the description would fit many males:

> [Patriarchs] see themselves as superior to their wives because they are men; they believe their wives are their property and that it is the duty of their wives to accommodate them sexually whenever they want; they believe they should be the boss in the marriage, and that wives who behave in an insubordinate fashion deserve punishment … they subscribe to a sexual double standard in which it is acceptable for husbands to have other sexual attractions or affairs, but it is totally unacceptable for their wives to do the same.

Even as culture and gender stratification influence sexual attitudes and related behaviors could it also be that sexual aggression has biological roots? A theory advanced by Lee Ellis (1990) explains male sexual aggression as an evolutionary trait spawned by the interplay of genetics and the environment. Briefly put, Ellis's theory is that males need expend little time and energy copulating, whereas women must invest more than nine months and considerable energy to produce offspring and keep them alive. Driven by the biological imperative to procreate, males emphasize quantity rather than quality and are pitted against each other as well as against the potentially resistant female. The appearance of sex-aggressive genes drives up the prevalence and frequency of rape, especially if female counterstrategies also evolve.

If procreation lies at the heart of sexual aggressiveness, which this theory argues, then rape should be ubiquitous among human and nonhuman animals. Ellis argues that it is. Furthermore, he contends that sex is the primary motivation in most rapes, despite what many authors and most, if not all, feminists claim (1990, 65). He supports this argument with the observation that the most likely victims of rape are women in their child-bearing years.

In a more recent version of the evolutionary perspective, Wilson and Daly (1998) suggest that violence is related to the sexual rivalry and possessive motives of males. They assert that "… men's preoccupations with sexual exclusivity and sexual rivalry are dominant motives in homicides everywhere." The sexual assault of women by men, then, may also be related to these evolutionarily grounded emotions and mechanisms, as jealousy and anger often spike when men feel threatened by the loss of sexual possession/ownership. Assaults, homicides, and rape may result (Wilson and Daly 1998; also see Polk 1998; Thornhill and Palmer 2000).

Evolutionary theories are very controversial, but should be given consideration if the behavior in question is universal or cross-species. A basic conflict of interest exists between males and females when it comes to controlling their own bodies. Since men generally have greater physical strength than women and are the penetrators, they can force copulation on a woman. But since males are also in competition with each other over access to females, strategies evolve to moderate and control that competition without turning the tables in favor of the female, who might then be able to deny any male access to her body. From this perspective, rules about family relations, about incest and child sexual abuse, and about "appropriate" male and female behavior are social constructions with biological roots.

SEXUAL ABUSE OF CHILDREN

Although the most likely victims of rape are older teenagers and young adults, children, including the very young, are sometimes the victims of sexual assaults. The U.S. Department of Health and Human Services (1997, 4) identifies four basic types of **child maltreatment**: (1) physical abuse, (2) neglect, (3) emotional abuse, and (4) sexual abuse. We will focus on the latter, which is defined as the "exploitation of a child for the sexual gratification of an adult, as in rape, incest, fondling of the genitals,

exhibitionism, or pornography." Estimates of the extent of child sexual abuse range from one in every two girls and one in every five to six boys, to one in every six to eight girls and one in every ten to twenty boys (Stanko 1990, 56). As Figure 4.2 shows, more than half of all females who have been raped were victimized before their eighteenth birthday.

As with the rapist, there is a popular image of the child molester. He is the stranger who lurks around playgrounds, parks, and other places where children wander and who lures or drags his victims into his car or home where he then sexually assaults them. This image is no more accurate than the one of rape and the rapist. For example, the child molester is not usually a stranger. Several studies show that this type of context is rare, accounting for only 3–4 percent of all sexual assaults on children (Schneider 1997). In studies both here and abroad, researchers are finding that in most cases of child molestation the offender and victim are acquainted with each other (Schneider 1997; Stanko 1990). Over 70 percent of the perpetrators of sexual abuse against children are males, while most charged with neglect are female (U.S. Department of Health and Human Services 1997, 13).

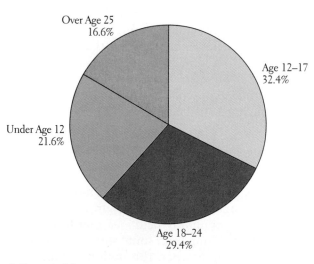

▲ FIGURE 4.2

Distribution of Rape by Age Groups

Victimization surveys show that younger women are more likely to be raped than older women. More than half of rape victims in 1998 were under age 18.

Source: Office of Justice Programs, *Prevalence, Incidence, and Consequences of Violence against Women* (Washington, D.C.: USGPO, 1998), 6.

It is estimated that one in five sexually abused boys go on to molest children sexually (Watkins and Bentovim 1992). Female incest victims are more likely than nonsexually abused females to die at a young age, commit suicide, become addicted to hard drugs and alcohol, prostitute themselves, and suffer a host of psychological and developmental problems (Fraad 1997). One study found that 38 percent of women and girls who were incestuously victimized by their fathers attempted suicide (Fraad 1997).

Most experts believe that molesters rarely resort to physical violence, and when a child does offer resistance it is most likely overcome by threats of deprivation (loss of love, affection, privileges) or by rewards (candy, money) (Schneider 1997). Victim resistance and use of physical coercion by offenders most often occur in sexual incidents involving strangers, which is what one would expect. Victim compliance is problematic when love and affection or familial ties are absent.

Some important points of agreement among researchers are that child molesters come from all walks of life, are of varied ages, engage in different sorts of sexual acts, and choose different types of child victims. About the only common characteristic is that they are most often males who target young females—the most likely victim is eleven to fourteen years old (Vander-May and Neff 1984).

There are four basic types of child sexual abusers:

1. The regressive offender who turns to children after rejection by those in his own age group
2. The fixed offender who is fixated and fanatically obsessed with children as sexual objects
3. The exploiting offender who generally desires power over children and obtains this power through sexual means
4. The sadistic offender who gains sexual pleasure by inflicting physical pain or killing children (Bartol 1995)

Sadistic offenders are the least common and the exploiting offender is probably the most common. According to a recent study of 140 child molesters, Fisher, Beech, and Browne (1999) found that they have lower levels of self-esteem and higher levels of loneliness and personal distress, and have little empathy for victims. This may underscore the motivations for the regressive offender and the exploiting offender.

Most sexually abused children are victimized by someone they know. The most frequent group of offenders are family members, including fathers, grandfathers, uncles, and males in step-families. The next most frequent group of offenders are those nonfamilial acquaintances such as neighbors, babysitters, teachers, and members of the clergy (Schneider 1997). In cases in which family members or relatives of the molester are victimized, the offense has usually been committed over a period of weeks, months, or years. Given the ongoing intimate but nonsexual interaction between relatives and family members, this is not surprising. In addition, the sexual encounters themselves may have developed in an atmosphere that encouraged physical demonstrations of affection and love. Incestuous desire on the part of both adult and child may be a natural—though not condoned—consequence of close, personal, and satisfying relations between family members. Thus, what begins as a loving nonsexual relationship between an adult and a child may, with the passage of time, expand to include repetitive sexual interactions (White 1972, 160–171).

As noted, most societies do not condone incest or other sex acts between family members or between adults and children in general. It is hard to imagine that molesters are, as a group, unaware that they have moved beyond acceptable boundaries of sexual conduct. Like other sex offenders, a few may be mentally deficient or suffering from severe psychiatric disorders, but most are clearly aware of their transgressions, and like many other criminals they disavow their actions or try to justify them (Schneider 1997).

When asked to account for their actions, child molesters explain away their conduct in various ways: by blaming it on a temporary loss of sense or rationality ("I was drunk"; "I didn't know what I was doing"; "everything went blank"); by blaming it on the behavior of the victim ("she wanted me to do it"; "he started it"); or by blaming it on conditions of family life or on other personal troubles. A classic study found that the most common single response to the question "Why?" was to blame the offense on a temporary loss of rationality (McCaghy 1967). The offenders most likely to deny their deviance in this way were those who had used force to obtain compliance and those who had molested female children.

Finding Out about Sexual Molestation

Learning the details surrounding cases of child molestation is not easy, especially when very young children are victimized. Except when brutal physical abuses are involved (a small minority of known cases), even the nature of the sexual encounter itself may be difficult to determine. From the standpoint of criminal law, the nature and gravity of the offense hinge on the details of the encounter. Especially important when the victim is an older child, fourteen or fifteen years old, are the issues of resistance and consent. Did the child resist? Did the child consent to the sexual act or even encourage it? Was compliance secured by the use or threat of physical force? In dealing with those questions, investigators are often confronted with conflicting pictures of an incident.

Studies of child testimony and related issues have been reviewed in a special issue of *Prosecutors' Perspective* (Vol. II, January 1988). The studies were performed by psychologists, social workers, lawyers, physicians, and sociologists and appeared in various scholarly journals. One of the major conclusions of these studies is that even young children remember details and testify more accurately than is generally believed. This has been supported by recent research, which, for example, estimates that less than 10 percent of children's portrayals of the events could be reasonably judged as false (Schneider 1997). However, one potential problem for the prosecutor in sexual abuse cases is that child victims remember much more about the actions that took place than about when and where they took place or the identity of the offender. The view that there is a pressing need for better methods of interviewing children is widely shared and government-funded research is now addressing the problem.

Not surprisingly, many children who are sexually abused find it difficult to report their experience to the authorities, especially so if they were victimized by a family member or acquaintance. Even after reporting, children face other problems. One study found the following:

> Participants (sexually abused children) reported little support from parents when disclosing sexual abuse. Participants who disclosed sexual abuse described being discouraged from initiating protective action against a boyfriend, father, friend, or relative. A female participant who had been sexually abused by a stranger stated that after disclosure, her father threatened to file charges against the abuser, yet called the participant who was raped a "whore." (Champion 1999, 712)

Significant numbers of legitimate complaints of child sexual abuse are designated as "unfounded" by authorities. One study looked at 576 reports of sexual abuse received by the Denver Department of Social Services and found that 47 percent had been designated unfounded. However, after review, the authors concluded that only 8 percent of these cases were probably fictitious reports. The remainder had been classified as unfounded primarily because of insufficient information or because appropriate suspicion could not be substantiated through investigation (Jones and McGraw 1987).

Various strategies have been advanced to reveal the facts behind reports of child sexual abuse. These range from the use of anatomically correct dolls to videotaping testimony and the use of closed circuit television so that victims can testify in court from another room (see Freeman and Estrada-Mullaney 1988; Whitcomb 1985). The U.S. Supreme Court ruled in *Maryland v. Craig* (1990) that alternatives to courtroom confrontation of the witness can be made available only to children expected to suffer severe emotional trauma if made to testify in the traditional manner. In addition, innovative methods may not be necessary in most cases of abuse.

The primary reason for concern over courtroom testimony of child victims is the trauma associated with it. Available research indicates that most children deal with the experience reasonably well, but long-term effects are less predictable. Three studies of the problem found that while children score high on anxiety and stress prior to their involvement in the court process, most improved with the passage of time, regardless of their experience in court. Further, the improvements in these children's mental health were directly associated with the strong support of their mothers (Whitcomb, et al. 1994). However, an important difference in findings also emerged: In one study, children who testified showed more improvement in their mental health than those who did not, while in the other two studies the reverse was found. The report concludes (p. 5): "Based on these studies it cannot be stated conclusively that testifying is either harmful or beneficial to sexually abused children." The authors advocate long-term follow-up research, including direct interviews with the children, as the next step in addressing the issue.

Any complete and accurate picture of child molesting and the child molester is far away. Much research still is needed, and the greater willingness of people to talk about sensitive sexual issues will aid in that endeavor. Even so, most incidents of child molestation will remain hidden, particularly those offenses in which physical force and abuse are not employed and those that involve offenders and victims who are familiar with each other and are associated in continuing relationships of a nonsexual kind. Many states now have child abuse hot lines and mandatory reporting laws. These will undoubtedly result in many more cases coming to light, but there is a downside: Some parents will not take their child to a counselor or seek other help precisely because they do not want the incident hotlined.

REACTIONS TO DOMESTIC VIOLENCE, RAPE, AND SEXUAL ABUSE OF CHILDREN

Although a problem for centuries, domestic violence has only recently become the subject of a formalized criminal justice response. Rape and sexual acts with minors, on the other hand, have long been regarded as heinous crimes. Even when legal codes were in their formative stages, little sympathy was extended to rapists, child molesters, and those committing incest with children. The usual penalties were death, banishment, and, in recent years, long prison sentences. Notwithstanding this tradition, public and official reactions to offenders have not been clear-cut. Though generally punitive, reactions have depended on who the offender is, who the victim is, and what kind of interactions the two had.

Reactions to Domestic Violence

The conventional response to domestic violence has been a restrained one at best, and more typically one of disinterest. This reflects a reluctance to get involved in family disputes: When men were asked by researchers what they would do if a friend was hitting his partner in front of them, this reply was typical: "Nothing … it's none of my business is it?…

it's between those two. I'd tell him he was out of order afterwards and that he should go back and make sure she's alright but I wouldn't interfere" (Bush and Hood-Williams 1995, 13). Even many victims feel that domestic violence is a private matter.

Some police officers believe that responding to domestic disturbances is not real police work. It is often seen as "uninteresting and unexciting, ranking alongside lost dogs, rowdy youth and bothersome drunks" (Grace 1995, 1). Even when serious violence is involved, a recent study of police actions in Chester, Pennsylvania, found support for a leniency hypothesis: Police there treated men who beat their wives more leniently than men who engaged in similar violence in other contexts (Fyfe, Klinger, and Flavin 1997). A study of the police response in London during the 1980s found that it was often slow, and that when police did arrive it was not uncommon for them to side with the assailant, who was rarely arrested (Edwards 1986; cited in Grace 1995). This picture also fits the situation in Australia, Canada, and the United States.

Besides being reluctant, the conventional police response to domestic violence is a *reactive* one (Sherman 1992, 208). This is largely because domestic disturbances are considered unpredictable events—and this includes the type and degree of violence involved. This unpredictability discourages the development of proactive policing strategies. Furthermore, although few people would question police who invaded a home because they thought someone was about to be stabbed, raped, or murdered, they would probably be alarmed if police routinely monitored and inspected homes or planted informants so as to prevent domestic disputes from occurring. More details about the traditional police response to "domestics" are found in Barlow (2000, 300–303).

CHANGING RESPONSES TO DOMESTIC VIOLENCE
The women's movement can claim much of the credit for bringing domestic violence into the open. By the 1980s, police departments around the country found themselves being sued for denying women victims of domestic violence equal protection of the law. A now-famous experiment conducted in Minneapolis in the early 1980s—but not confirmed by subsequent replications in other

cities—also gave impetus to change by showing that domestic assailants who were arrested were less likely to commit repeat offenses during a six-month period following the experiment (Sherman and Berk 1984). From 1984 to 1986, the proportion of urban police departments encouraging officers to make arrests grew fourfold and several states made arrests mandatory (Sherman 1992, 203). Special prosecution units were also established in some states to ensure vigorous prosecution (Fagan 1996).

Would more aggressive "proactive" criminal justice strategies reduce the incidence of domestic violence and perhaps also the homicides that sometimes result from it? For example, by keeping track of calls to specific addresses, police can identify "hot spots" of domestic violence. In Milwaukee, for example, the police found that couples with seven or more prior reports over a three-year period will have another one during that time period. If police acted on that prediction, they would be wrong in only one out of four cases. In addition, there are various other ways proactive policing might be conducted. For example, high-risk couples or families with repetitive police visits might receive letters (sent via mail or delivered by officers) that threaten more severe penalties the next time an incident occurs. This sort of approach could be tested experimentally. Another idea is repeat random visits by patrolling police to households with a specified number of prior domestic violence calls (Goldstein 1990, 104–114). Families would be notified that police would be calling periodically to see how things were going.

Even if successful policing strategies could be developed for dealing with domestic violence, there will probably be little change in the people most likely to be targeted by the criminal justice system. The policing of domestic conflicts will continue to focus on the lower classes. Not only are lower-class people stereotypically linked with violence, as we have seen, but their lack of resources and their self-help traditions mean that personal problems are rarely addressed through counseling, mediation, education, or restitution—forms of social control that are available to the middle and upper classes (Manning 1994, 89). In other words, the policing of domestic violence will likely remain concentrated in neighborhoods where there is already a disproportionate police presence.

Reactions to Rape

Most state codes have at one time or another identified rape as a capital crime, and those offenders most likely to receive the death penalty have been blacks. Since 1930, there have been 455 executions for rape; of those executed, nearly 90 percent were blacks. To these legal executions one must add the hundreds of blacks who were lynched for alleged sexual offenses against white women. The feeling among some whites, particularly in the South, seems to have been that only the most severe penalty matches the outrage committed when a black man violates the social taboos surrounding white-black relations and has sex with a white woman. Whether rape was actually committed—and in numerous cases this certainly was not established—seems to have been largely beside the point. A black simply did not become "intimate" with a white, especially a white woman. The charge of rape justified the imposition of death, which matched the legal punishment for rape. Also important, it exonerated the white female, who, whites could argue, would never have consented to sexual intimacies with a black. The charge and the punishment thus reinforced racist practices.

The general sense of what "true" rape and molestation are affects trial and sentencing. Important to this image are the characteristics of the victim and how she behaved before and during the rape. If she is a virgin, a minor, or very old, and if there is circumstantial evidence that she put up resistance and was overcome by force, the offender is likely to be convicted and receive a severe sentence.

The moral categorization of women as "rapable/virtuous" and "nonrapable/unvirtuous" (MacKinnon 1989, 175) is a manifestation of patriarchy that is reproduced in courtroom behavior. In rape trials, patriarchy, law, and the dynamics of courtroom behavior blend together and reproduce the relations of domination that structure interaction between men and women in everyday life (Matoesian 1993). Acquittals are often a matter of transforming a woman's rape into an act of consensual sex (Sanday 1996). Years ago, judges in a Philadelphia court, for example, admitted placing considerable weight on the victim and her behavior. They acquitted defendants when they perceived that

Thousands of blacks were lynched in the South during the late nineteenth and early twentieth centuries. Many were accused (usually falsely) of raping a white female, and judicial proceedings, if any, were swift and always under the control of whites.

"[w]ho gets to say what, when they get to say it, and how much they get to say is contingent upon the social organization of the courtroom system, the distribution of power among its participants, and the larger system of patriarchy within which these actions are embedded." Matoesian demonstrates that the moral categorization of the victim is not determined by virtue of her standards, but "according to male definitions through which rape is organized, interpreted, and legitimated." Through analyzing trial talk as it occurred, he shows how defense attorneys succeed and fail in convincing the court that the victim was no victim at all. The strategy is to impugn the victim's sexual/moral character, even though rape shield laws ostensibly forbid this. One illustration: In pretrial motions in one case, the judge ruled that the marital status of an unmarried pregnant victim could not be introduced; the defense attorney "consistently referred to her as 'Miss' during the trial."

Post-trial interviews with jurors show how blame can be attributed to some victims of rape (LaFree, Reskin, and Visher 1991). Defendants were more likely to be acquitted when there was evidence of the victim's drinking, drug use, or extramarital sex. However, these characterizations were cited most often in cases where the defense attorney had argued for consensuality or diminished responsibility. If the defense attorney does not impugn the victim's character as the story is reconstructed in court, it appears jurors accept the implication that she is rapable (see also LaFree 1989, 200–233). Furthermore, as Sanday (1996) and others have noted, jurors were actually told by judges in the United States that accusing someone of rape is easy but much harder to be defended, even if one is innocent.

There is no better way to sum up the tragedy of rape and sexual assault generally than from a woman's perspective. Elizabeth Stanko (1990, 85–86) writes the following:

> Wherever women are, their peripheral vision monitors the landscape and those around them for potential danger.... For the most part, women find they must constantly negotiate their safety with men—those with whom they live, work and socialize, as well as those they have never met. Because women are likely to be physically smaller

the sex had been consensual (described by some judges as "friendly rape," "felonious gallantry," "assault with failure to please," and "breach of contract") or that the charge was the result of "female vindictiveness" (Bohm 1974).

But how did they arrive at this judgment? How do defense attorneys transform a woman's rape into a consensual act? Matoesian (1993) explores these very questions through an analysis of trial talk—the verbal exchanges between prosecution, defense attorney, defendant, victim, witnesses, and judge. Talk is "socially structured" in that

Elizabeth Stanko believes that women must constantly be on guard against physical violence. Although women are certainly vulnerable when alone in places that attract predatory criminals, most violent and sexual assaults actually occur in the home.

than men, as well as emotionally and economically dependent on them, they must bargain safety from a disadvantaged position.... The very people women turn to for protection are the ones who pose the greatest danger.

If the criminal justice "management" of sexual assault of women is to do more than merely mirror the sexism of a patriarchal society, it must be recognized "that all women are entitled to be protected from rape and whatever a woman's behavior, there is no justification for rape" (Box-Grainger 1986, 32). An excerpt from Marge Piercy's famous poem about rape is stark in its portrayal of victim blaming:

> ... There is no difference between being raped and being run over by a truck except that afterwards men ask if you enjoyed it.
> There is no difference between being raped and being bit on the ankle by a rattlesnake except that people ask if your skirt was short and why you were out alone anyhow.... (Marge Piercey, "Rape Poem," in Odem and Clay-Warner, 1998, 3)

Reactions to Sexual Abuse of Children

Sexual assault of children commonly provokes severe reactions. Just the attempt to sexually molest a minor is generally near the top of public polls on the seriousness of crimes. Judicial attitudes toward sexual assault of young children are generally severe. When pubescent children are involved, marked variations in official reactions have been observed. Again, much is made of the victims themselves and of their apparent role in triggering the offense. Two examples from England illustrate. In one case, a young man had numerous episodes of sexual intercourse with a fourteen-year-old girl he had met at a dancing school. "It was accepted that the girl was a very willing participant." In another case, a married father of four children had repeated acts of sexual intercourse with his fifteen-year-old sister-in-law. Circumstantial evidence was entered to support the view that the girl "had been the real instigator." In both of these cases an appeals court reduced the sentences imposed by the trial judge on the grounds that the victims wanted sex and willingly participated in the act (Thomas 1967).

A retrospective study of 350 cases of child sexual abuse occurring in a Texas county from 1975 to 1987 found that prosecution and conviction was more likely when: (1) there was medical evidence to substantiate the charge; (2) the suspect made a statement of implication; (3) the time between the incident and the reporting of it was relatively short; and (4) the seriousness of the offense was greater (Bradshaw and Marks 1990). Another Texas study found that a victim/witness program designed to help children in the difficult process of prosecution affected cases in a variety of ways: It (1) increased the percentage of convictions at trial from 38 to 72 percent; (2) resulted in fewer plea bargains; (3) increased the percentage of offenders receiving prison terms from 25 to 48 percent; (4) increased the average length of sentence for all child sex abuse cases, whether pled or not (Dible and Teske 1993).

If there is some ambivalence in the societal response to sexual victimization of older children, even the sentences handed down to molesters of young children are sometimes light—for example, probation with counseling. This usually occurs as a result of plea bargains in which defendants plead guilty to misdemeanor sex offenses. When convicted of felony sexual assault, mandatory sentencing laws in many states make imprisonment inevitable, and most states now force the offenders to register with authorities after they have served time and (where appropriate) completed parole. This information is then made public, under the so-called Megan's Law.

In 1995, New Jersey passed Megan's Law, named after seven-year-old Megan Kanka who was raped and murdered by a known child molester who had moved in across the street. Megan's Law requires authorities to notify communities of convicted sex offenders in their neighborhoods. By 1998, thirty-six other states had enacted similar laws (*Washington Post*, 24 February 1998, 3). Megan's Law has been upheld by the U.S. Supreme Court despite objections that it violates the constitutional rights of people who have already been punished for their crimes. Some states have also passed new laws allowing certain repeat sex offenders to be committed to secure mental facilities indefinitely after they have completed their prison sentences. A civil proceeding is held, and the burden of proving why commitment should not occur rests with the defendant.

CHAPTER SUMMARY

This chapter has discussed domestic violence and sexual assault and abuse of women and children. Both legal and scientific perspectives have been shaped by historical conflicts of interest between men and women, and by the societal dominance of males and adults.

Domestic violence is kept largely under wraps but affects a large number of women and children. Victims often remain silent, and offenders often don't see themselves as criminals. Violence among intimates is regarded as a private affair. There has even been a tendency among police officers here and abroad to treat domestic violence as not worthy of serious police activity. Considering that women and children are the most common victims of domestic violence, this sends a strong message that it's okay for adults, men in particular, to use physical force against other family members. Men who persist in using violence generally escalate the seriousness of the attacks, sometimes to the level of homicide; at the same time, some victims turn the tables and murder their assailant.

In recent years feminists have led the way to more open and enlightened exploration of domestic violence and sexual assault. Research findings show that sexual assault is widespread; that it often involves people who know each other or are related; that victims are often humiliated and frustrated in their search for justice; and that reactions to rape are influenced by myths, stereotypes, and prejudices that generally serve the interests of men.

Current explanations of sexual assault focus on domination rather than on sex. The sex act itself is less important than what it represents—the humiliation of another person through intimate violation of that person's body and mind. Some people argue that high rates of sexual assault reflect the existence of subcultures of violence, while others suggest that aggressive male dominance of females is also valued in middle-class culture and encouraged through the institution of dating, through pornographic imagery, and by prevailing stereotypes of "proper" womanhood as weak, passive, and submissive to the male.

Sexual assault of children is also widespread, and most of it remains hidden from authorities. Child molesters come from all walks of life, but the offenders are most often male, and the victims are more often girls than boys. When questioned by authorities or researchers, many heterosexual child molesters either disavow their actions or blame them on the victim or on forces beyond their control.

KEY TERMS

child maltreatment (p. 82)

domestic violence (p. 69)

rape shield laws (p. 72)

victim blaming (p. 79)

RECOMMENDED READINGS

Brownmiller, Susan. 1975. *Against Our Will.* New York: Simon & Schuster.

Fisher, Bonnie S., Francis T. Cullen, and Michael G. Turner. 2000. *The Sexual Victimization of College Women.* Research Report. National Institute of Justice. Available at <www.ncjrs.com>.

Kennedy Bergen, Raquel. 1998. *Issues in Intimate Violence.* Thousand Oaks, CA: Sage.

Odem, Mary E., and Jody Clay-Warner. 1998. *Confronting Rape and Sexual Assault.* Wilmington, DE: SR Books.

Renzetti, Claire M. 1992. *Violent Betrayal: Partner Abuse in Lesbian Relationships.* Thousand Oaks, CA: Sage.

Renzetti, Claire M., Jeffrey L. Edleson, and Raquel Kennedy Bergen. 2001. *Sourcebook on Violence against Women.* Thousand Oaks, CA: Sage.

Sanday, Peggy Reeves. 1996. *A Woman Scorned: Acquaintance Rape on Trial.* New York: Doubleday.

Searles, Patricia, and Ronald J. Berger. 1995. *Rape and Society: Readings in the Problem of Sexual Assault.* Boulder, CO: Westview.

RECOMMENDED WEB SITES

Violence against Women Program, U.S. Department of Justice

Information, links, and reports on crimes against women.

http://www.ojp.usdoj.gov./vawo

National Organization for Women, Violence against Women Page

A wide range of studies, positions, and data on crimes against women.

http://209.207.163.32/issues/violence/index.html

National Clearinghouse on Child Abuse and Neglect

Volumes of information on all forms of child maltreatment.

http://www.calib.com/nccanch

VARIETIES OF NONVIOLENT THEFT

Consider how many opportunities there are for theft around your college or university. There are books and book-bags left lying around, cars to be broken into, and office, computer, and classroom equipment in plain view of perhaps thousands of people each day. All American universities are now required to publish crime statistics under a 1990 federal law known as the Jeanne Clery Act in honor of a woman murdered on a college campus. These statistics suggest that while most college and university campuses have lower than average overall crime rates, they are certainly not immune to crime, including theft (Fisher, Sloan, Cullen, and Lu 1998).

Theft is the most common class of crime in most societies. It is also the crime least likely to result in arrest when reported. If people do not themselves steal, then they are victims of theft, or they hear about thefts involving someone else. Many people may be the victims of theft without even knowing it. Only three conditions are necessary to make theft possible: (1) goods or services capable of being stolen, (2) someone from whom they can be stolen, and (3) someone to do the stealing. Box 5.1 provides Model Penal Code definitions of some of the offenses covered in this chapter; FBI definitions are found in Appendix A.

As one might expect, the legal notion of theft is not uniform across different societies. If property or material possessions do not exist, people are unlikely to have any notion of stealing. The types of possessions that can be stolen, the methods used, and the kinds of people who are victims all are influenced by culture, by the way people live, and by their attitudes and values.

In a society that places a premium on the acquisition of personal property, theft is likely to be a serious offense. However, those same values may encourage the very behavior that is condemned. If possession of material wealth is highly valued, then people may stop at nothing to accumulate it. If people could acquire whatever they wanted through culturally acceptable channels, then theft might not exist. But when some people are systematically excluded from access to acceptable channels of acquisition or cannot acquire what they want even with such access, then stealing may be an alternative way to achieve material wealth. Though it is popular to think that thieves are primarily the poor and disadvantaged, people from all walks of life, even those with all kinds of advantages, steal from others. This will be discussed in Chapter 6. This chapter concentrates primarily on forms of common theft committed outside the context of legitimate work.

THEFT IN HISTORY

Theft has a long and interesting history. In early legal codes theft was a rather vague term, though most known codes maintained laws identifying theft as punishable behavior. More interesting, perhaps, is that many of these early codes tried to distinguish among different methods of stealing and different classes of victims. For example, the

Box 5.1 MODEL PENAL CODE DEFINITIONS OF SELECTED FORMS OF THEFT

THEFT BY UNLAWFUL TAKING OR DISPOSITION

1. *Movable Property*: A person is guilty of theft if he unlawfully takes, or exercises control over, movable property of another with purpose to deprive him thereof.
2. *Immovable Property*: A person is guilty of theft if he unlawfully transfers immovable property of another or any interest therein with purpose to benefit himself or another not entitled thereto.

THEFT BY DECEPTION

A person is guilty of theft if he purposely obtains property of another by deception. [Deception includes creating a false impression of value, law, or intent; prevention of another from acquiring information that would affect his or her judgment of a transaction; failure to disclose lien or other legal impediment to enjoyment of transferred property; failure to correct a false impression previously created or reinforced by the deceiver.]

FORGERY

A person is guilty of forgery if, with purpose to defraud or injure anyone, or with knowledge that one is facilitating a fraud or injury to be perpetrated by anyone, the actor:

1. alters any writing of another without authority; or
2. makes ... executes, ... or transfers any writing so that it purports to be the act of another who did not authorize that act, or to have been executed at a time or place or in a numbered sequence other than was in fact the case, or to be a copy of an original when no such copy originally existed; or
3. utters any writing which he knows to be forged in a manner specified in paragraphs (1) or (2).

BURGLARY

A person is guilty of burglary if he enters a building or occupied structure or separately secured or occupied portion thereof with purpose to commit a crime therein, unless the premises are at the time open to the public or the actor is licensed or privileged to enter.

RECEIVING STOLEN PROPERTY

A person is guilty of theft if he purposely receives, retains, or disposes of movable property of another knowing that it has been stolen, or believing that it has probably been stolen, unless the property is received, retained, or disposed with purpose to restore it to the owner. "Receiving" means acquiring possession, control, or title, or lending on the security of the property.

BOX 5.1, CONTINUED

BAD CHECKS

A person who issues or passes a check or similar sight order for the payment of money, knowing that it will not be honored by the drawee, commits a misdemeanor. For the purposes of this section … an issuer is presumed to know that the check or order (other than a postdated check or order) would not be paid, if:

1. the issuer had no account with the drawee at the time the check or order was issued; or
2. payment was refused by the drawee for lack of funds, upon presentation within thirty days after issue, and the issuer failed to make good within ten days after receiving notice of that refusal.

CREDIT CARDS

A person commits an offense if he uses a credit card for the purpose of obtaining property or services with knowledge that:

1. the card is stolen or forged; or
2. the card has been revoked or cancelled; or
3. for any other reason his use of the card is unauthorized.

Source: "Varieties of Nonviolent Theft as Defined by the Model Penal Code," excerpted from the *Model Penal Code.* Copyright 1962 by the American Law Institute. Reprinted with permission.

Roman law of the Twelve Tables designated theft by night as a more serious offense than daylight theft. The Code of Hammurabi placed the interests of church and state above those of the citizenry as a whole: Those who stole from temples or royal palaces were punished by death, whereas those who stole from private citizens merely had to pay compensation.

It is mainly in English law that the roots of modern criminal law conceptions of theft are found. Even before the Norman conquest of 1066, theft was an offense. Many people are familiar with the adage "Possession is nine points of the law," but in early English law, possession was everything. It was in terms of possession that theft was identified and the thief so labeled. Ownership was a notion quite alien to early English society. One did not own something; it was in one's possession. To identify theft it was necessary to show, first, that the thief

did not have lawful possession of the object in question and, second, that the person who claimed lawful possession could rightly do so. In practical terms this meant that to establish theft it was important to produce the thief, and the best way to do this was to catch the person red-handed.

Similar to the American "posse," the English chase was thus an integral part of the theft scene. If the suspect was caught while transporting stolen goods from the crime scene, then the theft was "manifest" and justice could be meted out swiftly and severely (and often was). If the chase was unsuccessful or the lawful possessor had failed to pursue the thief, then the theft was "secret" and justice was often slow and tortuous. All things considered, it was certainly in the interest of the victim to catch the thief in the act of fleeing with the loot.

Another important aspect of common law conceptions of theft was a civil law violation: trespass.

The common legal term for theft was (and still is) *larceny*. Larceny was an extension of trespass. Under Roman law, larceny (*latrocinium*) was defined as almost any type of deceit and trickery, but this was not the case in England. Larceny meant laying hands on another's possessions without permission. "Simply to lay a hand on a man's thing without his permission would be trespass; therefore it was argued that there could be no larceny without trespass" (Turner 1966, 267). Larceny went beyond trespass in the notion of *animus furandi* (intent to steal); trespass turned into larceny when the trespasser intended to steal from the victim. The notion of trespass is still retained in many state laws dealing with theft.

Regarding what could be stolen, the idea of "movable" possessions remained central in emerging criminal law. The old charge that the thief "stole, took, and carried away" emphasizes this idea. In medieval times the most prized movables were agricultural chattels—farm animals such as oxen, cows, horses, and pigs, which often also served as money. Not surprisingly, these were the movable possessions to which early theft laws most often applied. But the creators of law have never been bound by tradition. One Anglo-Saxon king declared: "Men shall respect everything the king wishes to be respected, and refrain from theft on pain of death and loss of all they possess" (Attenborough 1963, 137). Though the king put the matter bluntly, the point is obvious: Those who shape legal conceptions of what can be stolen are in a position to impose their own ideas about what is valuable and to determine what will and will not be deemed stealable (Hall 1952).

The actual value of goods has traditionally been irrelevant to the identification of theft. It matters little whether you steal a coat worth $5,000 or one worth only five cents—a theft has still been committed. But value clearly does matter in what happens to the thief. From at least Anglo-Saxon times, distinctions in theft have been based on the value of the property taken. Just as today many states treat theft under $150 (or some other figure) as petty theft and anything more than that as grand theft, similar distinctions have been made throughout the history of theft laws. The penalties for grand theft, a felony, are more severe. If value is an indication of seriousness, which such rules imply, then such distinctions may be justified on the grounds that they provide a workable solution to the problem of "making the punishment fit the crime." Some authors have argued, however, that distinctions of value merely reflect the operation of class interests, ignoring the fact that what to one person may be a great loss to another may be trivial. More wealthy theft victims realize more in the way of "justice" than do poorer ones, whose losses may actually be more significant (Mannheim 1946).

Interests and Theft Laws

Criminal law is constantly changing. For one thing, legal formulations prove inadequate when confronted by changing social conditions and interests. Theft laws have continually been revised and extended, and one result is that new forms of theft keep emerging. One particularly significant development in criminal theft occurred during the late 1400s, and it shows the impact on criminal law of emergent social conditions and interests (see Hall 1952).

The **Carrier's Case** involved a man who was hired to carry some bales of merchandise to Southampton, an English port city. Instead of doing this, he broke open the bales and took their contents. He was subsequently caught and charged with felony theft. As the larceny law then stood, however, his actions did not legally constitute theft: He had entered an agreement in good faith, and he thus had lawful possession of the bales. Under the possession rules he could not steal from himself or from the merchant who hired him. After much debate a majority of the judges in the case finally found him guilty of felony theft and in doing so extended the law of larceny to cover cases of "breaking bulk," as it was called.

Most people would probably argue that this verdict and the legal precedent it established are reasonable enough. After all, if you hire a truck driver to deliver goods, you would surely be angry if the driver stole them. But if no laws could be applied in your particular case, then what satisfaction could you hope to receive? To judge from the Carrier's Case, successful resolution of the problem would depend on how much pressure you could bring to bear on authorities to protect your interests. It so happens that at the time of the Carrier's Case, the judges were faced with a number of outside pressures:

The most powerful forces at the time were interrelated very intimately and at many points: the

New Monarchy and the nouveau riche—the mercantile class; the business interests of both and the consequent need for a secure carrying trade; the wool and textile industry, the most valuable by far in all the realm; wool and cloth, the most important exports; these exports and foreign trade; this trade and Southampton, chief trading city with the Latin countries for centuries; the numerous and very influential Italian merchants who brought English wool and cloth inland and shipped them from Southampton. The great forces of an emerging modern world, represented in the above phenomenon, necessitated the elimination of a formula which had outgrown its usefulness. A new set of major institutions required a new rule. (Hall 1952, 33)

So, as William Chambliss (1975, 7) states: "The judges deciding the Carrier Case had, then, to choose between creating a new law to protect merchants who entrusted their goods to a carrier or permitting the lack of such legal protection to undermine trade and the merchant class economic interests. The court decided to act in the interests of the merchants despite the lack of a law."

The revision and expansion of theft laws continued to the present day. Many of the changes were designed to plug gaps and crevices in prevailing common law. Embezzlement, for example, emerged in its modern form in 1799 when Parliament passed a statute to cover cases of servants misappropriating goods placed in their possession in the course of employment. It was later extended to cover brokers, bankers, attorneys, and others in positions of trust as agents for third parties.

Embezzlement statutes covered only the illegal transfer of possession. For cases of ownership fraudulently acquired—as when one signs over property to another after being tricked into doing so—the law remained inadequate until a statutory decree in 1861 created the offense of obtaining goods by false pretenses. This new offense was basically an extension of the earlier common law crime "larceny by trick and device."

THEFT: THE CURRENT PICTURE

Much theft, like all crime, remains beyond the reach of bureaucratic data collection. Accordingly, national data on theft are extremely difficult to assess and interpret. When one considers the fact that

only a relatively minute number of thefts are ever solved, the difficulties become obvious.

Published national data provide an idea of the dimensions of the theft problem from the standpoint of the criminal justice system. In 1999, burglary, larceny-theft, and motor vehicle theft accounted for 10,128,411 of the index offenses reported by the FBI (2000). This represents about 90 percent of all index offenses. Incidences of all three offenses steadily increased during the 1960s, with burglary and larceny continuing to climb, though more slowly, during the 1970s. During the 1980s all three offenses increased again, according to police figures. As Figure 5.1 shows, property crime rates, like the rates for most crimes, consistently declined in the 1990s.

The published national data indicate other characteristics of these three index offenses:

- Rural rates are substantially below those found in both cities and suburbs.
- The young tend to be most victimized.
- The higher one's income, the *higher* the rate of victimization for *personal theft*. The higher one's income, the *lower* the rate for *burglary* victimization.
- African-Americans are more likely to be victimized than whites and Hispanics.

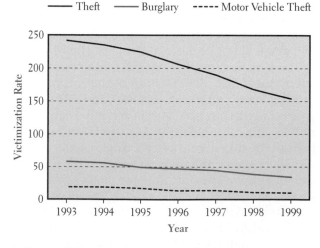

▲ FIGURE 5.1

Property Crime Victimization Rates, 1993–1999, per 1,000 Households

Source: Bureau of Justice Statistics, *Criminal Victimization, 1999* (Washington, D.C.: U.S. Department of Justice, 2000), 10.

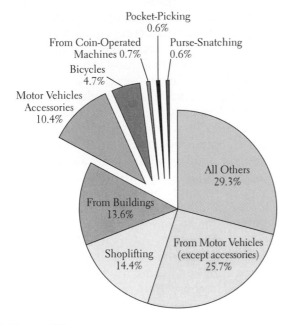

▲ FIGURE 5.2
Distribution of Larceny-Theft Offenses, 1999
Source: Federal Bureau of Investigation (Washington, D.C.: U.S. Department of Justice, 2000), 48.

- Most thefts are not reported to the police. If reported, less than 20 percent are cleared by arrest.
- The most common form of larceny-theft involves thefts related to motor vehicle parts, accessories, and other contents (see Figure 5.2).

Specialization and Varieties of Theft

Thieves rarely spend all or even most of their time in one particular line of theft (Cromwell 1999). Explaining why most thieves diversify, one professional thief had this to say:

Stealing for a living isn't just being a burglar or stick-up man. You've got to be able to look around and recognize opportunities and be able to take advantage of them regardless of what the conditions are. A lot of people think once a stick-up man, always a stick-up man. Well, you can't run around stickin' up people every day of the week like a workin' man. Maybe something worth-while sticking up only shows up every two or three months. In the meantime you're doing this and that, changing around, doing practically anything to make a dollar. (Martin 1952, 117)

Some thieves develop interests and talents so that they can concentrate on specific crimes. They "have a line." Some express interest in the theft of only certain types of merchandise—for example, credit cards, jewelry, or furs—and others see their talents put to the most productive (and secure) use in one line of work—picking pockets, sneak theft, forgery, or con games. On the whole, however, thieves are generalists rather than specialists. Some may even be adamantly opposed to specialization: It reduces the chances of remaining anonymous and increases the risks of being "fingered" for a caper known to be their style. Professionals give recognition to those who can say they "have a line," but this denotes their preference and skill rather than day-to-day activity.

Varieties of theft involving high levels of skill, organization, and planning and those requiring substantial resources (some big cons) are usually outside the reach of the typical amateur. Many types of theft attract both professionals and amateurs, however. Within these types, some of the major characteristics distinguishing amateurs from professionals are arrest and conviction history, size of the heist, level of technical skill involved, and type of fencing arrangement employed. Amateurs tend to be arrested and convicted more often, to leave with smaller payoffs (or none), to employ little in the way of manipulative and technical skills, and to steal for themselves or for their friends. Both professionals and amateurs are involved in burglary, sneak theft, forgery, and auto theft. Amateurs rarely perform confidence swindling, counterfeiting, or extortion.

SHOPLIFTING: THE FIVE-FINGER DISCOUNT

When people steal from under the nose of their victims, it is commonly called **sneak theft**. Examples include shoplifting, pocket picking, and "till tapping" (stealing from cash registers).

Of the many varieties of sneak theft *not* committed by employees, shoplifting has no equal. The number of shoplifting incidents and the total dollars lost from this crime are unknown and impossible to determine, but the estimates are staggering. While over 1.1 million shoplifting incidents were reported to the police in 1998, estimates as early as 1984 put the real figure closer to 200 million incidents per year (Federal Bureau of Investigation

1999; Baumer and Rosenbaum 1984). What about the cost of it all? Authors of the respected *National Retail Security Survey* (1999) estimate that the U.S. retail industry alone loses about $33.4 billion each year from theft, and that $11.5 billion of that is from shoplifters. The remaining amount is lost by, in order of frequency, employee theft, administrative errors, and vendor fraud. The average shoplift results in a loss of $142–$212 (Federal Bureau of Investigation 1999; National Retail Security Survey 1999). The dollar amount of the theft is important because in many jurisdictions, a theft over $350 dollars is considered a felony and therefore could result in more serious punishment.

Shoplifting is not new, nor have the methods changed much in a hundred years. To be sure, there have been changes in the architecture of stores and in the overall character of the shopping experience, but shoplifters still employ time-honored methods: concealing items under their clothes, hiding them in false-bottomed cases, "bad bagging" them (putting them in well-worn shopping bags), and using "booster boxes" (cartons and packages that appear sealed but in fact have an opening through which to put lifted items) (see Edwards 1958, 4–15; Klemke 1992).

Shoplifting is dominated by amateurs and opportunists, and it cuts across age, sex, race, economic status, and educational distinctions. It used to be thought that females stole from stores more frequently than males did—a reasonable belief, perhaps, in light of traditional sex roles and what official data tell us about gender and crime. However, more recent evidence suggests that males steal just as often as females and tend to steal more items per visit (Buckle and Farrington 1984; also see Klemke 1992). Few shoplifters are kleptomaniacs and most say they steal simply because they didn't *want* to pay for the item, not because they *couldn't* possibly pay for the item (Cromwell, Parker, and Mobley 1999). One shoplifter explained it this way: "I did it because I didn't want to pay for anything. I've got better things to do with my money"(Cromwell, Parker, and Mobley 1999, 62). Box 5.2 provides similar insights about college students who shoplift.

Reactions to Shoplifting

Reactions to shoplifting and shoplifters reveal an intriguing facet of this crime. Time and again, studies indicate that although most shoplifters are never apprehended, those who are sometimes face little

Most large department stores take shoplifting seriously and devote considerable resources (such as security camera surveillance) toward the protection of their property. Smaller stores often cannot afford to be as vigilant.

BOX 5.2   THE THRILL OF SHOPLIFTING

Jack Katz (1988) has argued that shoplifting, like vandalism and joyriding, is a sneaky crime that often provides the offenders with a "thrill." This thrill (part of the seduction of crime) is more powerful than criminologists have realized in the past. The "sneaky thrill" of shoplifting is evident, according to Katz (1988, 52), because of the seduction of the objects in time and place, the possibility of getting caught, and the sense of euphoria one experiences when doing and recounting the act. Here are some quotes from Katz's criminology students who recounted their thoughts on shoplifting.

ON THE ATTRACTION

"I felt an overwhelming urge ..." (55).

"I'm not quite sure why I must have it, but I must" (55).

KEEPING UP NORMAL APPEARANCES

"I proceeded to make myself look busy as I tried on several pairs of earrings. My philosophy was that the more busy you look the less conspicuous" (60).

"The whole time as we approached the exit I remember looking at it as a dark tunnel and just wanting to run down and disappear ..." (62).

AFTER THE EXIT

"Once outside the door I thought Wow! I pulled it off, I faced danger and I pulled it off. I was smiling so much and I felt at that moment like there was nothing I couldn't do" (64).

"... the thrill of getting something for nothing, knowing I got away with something I never thought I could, was wonderful" (64).

These quotes suggest that there is a lot more going on in the decision to shoplift than the interest in having "more things" or "saving a few bucks," at least according to Katz's sample.

more than a scolding, and are sent on their way after returning or paying for the merchandise. The shoplifter's chances of a lenient reaction depend on age, sex, ability to pay, attitude, apparent social class, and whether or not he or she is a known or suspected professional. Overall, it appears that the value of the stolen items is the best predictor of whether the shoplifter will get by with a verbal scolding or whether police will be notified and prosecution pursued (Hindelang 1974; see also Cromwell 1999).

Because detection and arrest of shoplifters are commonly the responsibility of store personnel, arrest and prosecution are largely influenced by the policies of store management. The typical store policy is usually one of caution and leniency. The primary objective is to deter shoplifting while avoiding anything that might hurt store business. Store management usually wants to avoid embarrassing situations on the shop floor that might adversely affect the attitudes and behavior of customers. Equally, it wants to minimize the time and expense involved in carrying through official prosecution of suspects. Finally, it wants to avoid unnecessary publicity that might mark the store as unfriendly, harsh, or as a place frequented by shoplifters (Cromwell, Parker, and Mobley 1999; Klemke 1992; Waltz 1953). If the store can recover the items or obtain payment through informal and discreet means, then its interests are partially met.

Other aspects of the informal approach should be kept in mind. Store management knows that most pilferers are amateurs and that when confronted with their attempted theft, most are shaken up so badly that they will do almost anything to avoid official attention. Further, they will probably refrain from stealing in that store again, at least for a time. Studies have shown that typical pilferers are what the criminal subculture labels as "square johns," those who neither systematically involve themselves in criminal pursuits nor identify themselves as criminals. They are typically people who adhere to the dominant cultural values and spend most of their time in legitimate pursuits. When caught, amateurs (particularly adults) display their commitment to dominant values and strenuously deny that they have done anything wrong or that they are criminals. Here is a typical verbal response from the amateur on being apprehended:

> I didn't intend to take the dress. I just wanted to see it in the daylight. Oh! what will my husband do! I did intend to pay for it. It's all a mistake. Oh! my God! what will mother say! I'll be glad to pay for it. See, I've got the money with me. Oh! my children! They can't find out I've been arrested! I'd never be able to face them again (Cameron 1964, 164).

To arrest a misdemeanor suspect (the usual case in shoplifting incidents) is to do so at peril because lawsuits charging false imprisonment or false arrest may result (Cromwell, Parker, and Mobley 1999). Not surprisingly, retailers in recent years have pressured legislatures to amend regulations dealing with the apprehension of suspected shoplifters. Most states now permit store personnel to detain suspects under certain broad conditions and without fear of civil suits charging false arrest or imprisonment. This may mean an increase in police arrests (and thus, an increase in official rates of shoplifting), though the considerations reviewed in this section will continue to play an important part in management decisions. In addition, since shoplifting is usually a misdemeanor committed by amateurs, authorities may decline to arrest or prosecute whenever jail space is tight, as happened in St. Louis several years ago (*St. Louis Post-Dispatch*, 28 January 1993, 4A).

The informal handling of shoplifters may have important ramifications for the way shoplifting is viewed by those arrested as well as by the general public. The fact that many shoplifters are generally law-abiding suggests that in order to engage in shoplifting in the first place—which they recognize is wrong and illegal—they may have convinced themselves that in their case it is not really theft, certainly not crime. As already seen, many apprehended amateurs think of their actions this way. How do they arrive at this conception? How is it that what they do is not crime but what someone else does—for example, robbery and burglary—is crime?

What society views as crime is influenced partly by prevailing cultural conceptions of crime and partly by the consequences of criminal behavior. If people do things they expect will result in being labeled criminal, then to be so labeled comes as no surprise and reinforces the belief that the act is criminal. But if people are not sure that the actions are criminal or if they have adopted the view that they are not, there will be no reason to alter their view when reactions do not match what they think happens to "real" criminals committing "real" crimes. So, upright citizens who occasionally shoplift and who are treated informally and discreetly by store personnel will be under little pressure to alter their conception of themselves or their behavior: They believe that what they do is not criminal and the criminal is quite another sort of person.

Interestingly enough, American business practices may encourage amateur shoplifting in other ways. Businesses spend billions of dollars every year on campaigns designed to convince Americans that they need and want items offered for sale. Already attuned to the values of an acquisitive society, Americans are reminded constantly to spend as much money as they can. They are continually exhorted to buy now, buy more, buy better, and pay later. During the Christmas shopping season, when shoplifting is at its yearly peak, the glitter and the temptation are at their height. Even if people cannot afford an item, they are discouraged from forgetting about it and instead are exhorted to find a way to buy it. When continually pushed to conceive of the meaning of life in material terms, people are measured by what they possess, what they can afford, and what they consume, rather than by who they are and what they are (Berlin 1996).

BURGLARY

Burglary is the illegal entry of a structure (usually a house or store) with the intent to commit theft. According to victimization surveys, burglary is the most common and, to many Americans, one of the most frightening among felony crimes. Victims often report that they felt as if their very person had been violated. People cherish the privacy and security of their homes and feel anger and resentment when these are breached. Women have a very special and justified fear: that an intruder will rape as well as steal. There is some research to support this concern, as violence is likely to erupt in about 30 percent of incidents in which someone is at home during a break-in.

British researchers using data from the British Crime Survey have compiled a list of the most significant risk factors associated with household burglary (Mayhew, Maung, and Mirrlees-Black 1993, 136–138). Among those risk factors were the following:

- Inner city location
- No security devices
- Only one adult living in a household (this risk was heightened for people living alone in an apartment)
- Being away from the residence during the evening

However, when researchers checked to see whether the different variables might "interact," that is, influence each other, it was discovered that houses without security devices are more vulnerable to burglary regardless of whether they are left unoccupied in the evenings. By the same token, security devices were more important for people living alone than for households with two or more adults.

During the past few years, the fears of middle-class homeowners have heightened as suburban burglary rates have increased faster than central city rates. Communities have organized "crime watch" groups to patrol their neighborhoods in an attempt to protect themselves from the burglar and other criminals.

Whether committed in the suburbs, in rural areas, or in cities, most burglaries are the work of relatively unskilled individuals who commit occasional burglaries among a variety of other offenses, and who live in or near the places they burglarize (Shover 1991). They look for cash and for items that can be readily disposed of via fences and pawnshops. Their methods are scorned by professionals, often known as "good burglars." Professionals take pride in their ability to gain entrance without force and noise and to pull a job speedily and profitably. The unskilled, often youthful burglars are called "door shakers," "kick-it-in men," "loidmen," and "creepers," names that reflect their amateur techniques (Pileggi 1968).

Good burglars choose targets they have selected in advance, sometimes after carefully casing them (Wright and Decker 1994, 62–102); sometimes they work in well-oiled teams with each member assigned a specific role based on experience and expertise; and they always work with quiet speed. In search of a lucrative target, the professional must deal effectively with security systems. The ability to disarm alarms separates the good burglar from both the amateur and the aspiring professional (Letkemann 1973; Wright and Decker 1994).

A number of research efforts during the past decade have aimed at identifying the major contours of burglary offenses and offenders. There is considerable agreement about the main characteristics. Losses are moderate, usually under $1,400 (Federal Bureau of Investigation 2000); most involve cash and cash-convertible items such as televisions, radios, and stereos; residential burglaries usually take place during the daytime, those of commercial establishments at night, often on weekends; and most involve forced entry. It is perhaps significant that the clearance rate (proportion of incidents resulting in arrest) tends to be higher for burglaries in which there is no loss at all or only a small loss. Presumably these are uncompleted burglaries, whose numbers are higher than might be expected—up to 33 percent of all incidents in some studies (e.g., Conklin and Bittner 1973). They are often the work of amateurs who cannot find what they want or who are discovered or frightened away before they have started work.

According to the British Crime Survey, burglaries are more likely to occur in the evening or late at night than at any other time, and daytime burglaries most often occur during the afternoon (Mayhew, Maung, and Mirrlees-Black 1993, 50). Forty percent of victims reported they were at home at the time of the burglary, most of them sleeping. This figure is rather surprising in light of the consistent findings from American studies showing the reluctance of burglars to enter occupied dwellings. In Wright and Decker's (1994, 110) study of St. Louis burglars, nine out of ten burglars interviewed said they "*always* avoided breaking into a residence when they knew or suspected that someone was at home." The British data are not based on interviews with offenders, but it could be that British burglars are more confident of their ability to avoid detection, or are simply less concerned about risks than their American counterparts.

Those arrested for burglary in the United States are disproportionately young and male. In 1999, 69 percent of those arrested were white and 29 percent were African-American (Federal Bureau of Investigation 2000, 43). Approximately 87 percent of arrested burglary suspects are male, a gender gap that is greater than for any index crime but rape. When women are involved, they are more likely than men to work in partnerships or in groups, although men also work in teams at least some of the time (Wright and Decker 1994). Most adult burglars have prior arrest records, often for burglary.

Once inside a building, burglars must find the cash or goods. If burglars are interested in cash, as many are, finding it is not always simple. Skilled burglars try to anticipate the behavior of their victims:

> In commercial establishments, [the burglar] may find it in the expected places, such as safes, cash registers, or in deliberately unexpected places, such as one shoe box among several hundred others. In residential dwellings, the burglar's task may be even more difficult, since the places where cash may be found are less predictable. A home does not have a cash register, nor, necessarily, a safe. Therefore, the burglar must make quick interpretations as to the most probable location of cash.

> The mental activity here is really a game of wits— or operating on the basis of reciprocal expectations. He proceeds on the assumptions he has regarding routine family behavior, and he anticipates uniformities in architecture as well as in styles of placing valuables. (Letkemann 1973, 55)

Among residential burglars in St. Louis, two main kinds of searches were identified: the *brief search* and the *leisurely search* (Wright and Decker 1994). In the brief search speed is the essence, and most burglars would head straight for the master bedroom where cash, jewelry, and guns are most likely to be found. Sometimes the kitchen would also be searched, but only if time permitted and doing so did not divert the burglar from his usual "script." The leisurely search was mentioned by a small number of burglars who liked to make an exhaustive search of a residence if they felt reasonably certain of not being interrupted.

In professional burglary, safecrackers are at the top of the status hierarchy, and their work makes some of the greatest demands on a thief's skill. Safecracking has been explored in detail by Letkemann (1973). Among the basic tools and equipment are "grease" (nitroglycerine), made from a combination of sulphuric acid, nitric acid, and glycerine; soap, which must be pliable and is used for funneling grease into the door; and "knockers and string" (detonators and fuses). The most common technique of safeblowing is the so-called jam shot, a procedure consisting of ten coordinated steps that, if done correctly, force the door of the safe to swing open on its hinges. When done incorrectly, the door is blown off the safe, or worse, the door and the safe buckle.

Professional safecrackers must remain knowledgeable about technological advances if they are to stay in business, and those who have been in the field long recognize the importance of information sharing. Safecrackers share information on jobs, on techniques, on new developments, and on any related aspects of their line. Letkemann suggests that the already fairly strong social bonds linking safecrackers have been strengthened as a result of greatly restricted access to dynamite (a ready source of grease), and the resulting need to make their own nitroglycerine: "It enabled leaders to screen new 'recruits' and necessitated the development of a stronger subculture based on mutual aid and group loyalty" (1973, 88).

Sophisticated professional burglary has been swallowed up by the growing numbers of amateur burglaries committed by those in search of immediate economic rewards. It may be that increased activity and decreased use of cash as a medium of exchange will help drive all but the most organized and skilled burglars into other "professions." On the other hand, the low risks of arrest coupled with initial successes may encourage many inexperienced burglars to continue in this line. They build their skills, their pride, and their fencing contacts. As they develop friendships with other crooks and lose contact with "straight" friends, their commitment to burglary increases and they become new experts, replacing retiring or imprisoned professionals (Cornish and Clarke 1986, 13). This does not mean they drop other criminal activities; rather, they add burglary to a list of offenses they feel competent to commit successfully when the opportunity and incentive arise.

Why Burglary?

The question "Why?" can be asked of offenders in any crime and the answers are bound to vary across offenses and offenders. But similar answers are also bound to appear and if these cluster around a particular offense then criminologists can rightly claim to be a little closer to identifying the motivations behind particular crimes and to establishing differences in motivations among crimes. Unfortunately, the time, energy, and resources required for an in-depth comparative analysis of offender motivation across crimes would probably be prohibitive, and so research designed to uncover the whys and wherefores of crime tends to be more limited in focus. This research is nevertheless crucial to building an understanding of specific crimes from the offender's perspective, and ultimately it helps us with the larger jig-saw puzzle.

Such is a recent study of burglary by Wright and Decker (1994). This is a ground-breaking work that does not rely on information from imprisoned offenders (as many studies have) but is based on interviews with *currently active* burglars located by the researchers themselves through a "snowball" sampling strategy. This method involves recruiting an initial subject "who then is asked to refer further participants. This process continues until a

suitable sample has been built." See Wright and Decker (1994, 16–25) for a complete account of their method and its pitfalls.

Wright and Decker's study sought answers to the whys and wherefores of burglary, and the authors wondered, like Katz (1988), what it feels like to do the crime. The immediate motivation for burglary appears no different than that for robbery: "a pressing need for cash" (p. 36). One burglar put it this way:

> Well, it's like, the way it clicks into your head is like, you'll be thinking about something and, you know, it's a problem. Then it all relates. "Hey, I need some money! Then how am I going to get money? Well, how do you know how to get money quick and easy?" Then there it is. Next thing you know, you are watching [a house] or calling to see if [the occupants] are home. (Wright and Decker 1994, 36)

The frequency of committing burglary is determined largely by how much money the offender has in his pocket at any one time. The money from burglary is then spent to maintain "high-living," or what Katz (1988) calls a life of "action." Much of this life involves getting and using drugs. It also includes wearing good clothes and gold jewelry and being able to flash money around, especially in the pursuit of women, whose conquest is the *sine qua non* of masculinity (see Messerschmidt 1994).

But why burglary over legitimate work or some other crime? Many burglars speak of needing cash on the spur of the moment, and not being able to get it legitimately, whether through work or from friends and relatives (Wright and Decker 1994; Tunnell 2000). As for why burglary over some other crime, the answer is varied: Some burglars said this was their "main line," others had moral objections to alternatives such as robbery, and some had simply gone along with the suggestions of others. One subject reported, "I got a friend that do burglaries with me. He usually the one that sets them up. If he ain't got one set up, then I might go off into somethin' else" (Wright and Decker 1994, 53). A few respondents mentioned the excitement of burglary, or its challenges. Excitement is also one of the things that drives auto thieves, as we see in the next section.

AUTO THEFT

The movie *Gone in Sixty Seconds* glorified auto theft and emphasized the skills and risks involved. However, scholarly studies of auto theft are scarce, despite the fact that this crime is better reported and more costly per incident than any other street crime. Estimates of the direct losses to victims alone are put at over $7 billion. Auto theft is also a major contributor to the nation's felony crime figures, representing around 1.1 million offenses in 1999 (Federal Bureau of Investigation 2000, 50). The rate of completed and attempted auto theft rose steadily during the 1980s, though it now shows signs of declining. (Some of this decline may be a result of new technologies such as satellite tracking systems and engine kill switches; however, research has yet to produce definitive answers). Unlike most other major crimes, auto theft is almost always reported to the police—insurance claims are the primary reason for this. The cars that are most likely to be stolen in any given year remain popular targets even as they age. Box 5.3 provides a list of the most stolen cars in the United States.

NCVS data also show that the risk of being victimized by car thieves is not born equally (what else is new?): households headed by blacks are twice as likely to be victimized as those headed by whites, and nearly three times as likely when the rate is calculated on the basis of vehicles owned by each racial group. Also, like most other street crimes, rates of victimization are higher in central cities and lowest in rural areas, and higher for renters than for homeowners (Bureau of Justice Statistics 1999, 8; 2000).

A comparison of international rates of auto theft shows that this crime is even more prevalent in other developed countries (Clarke and Harris 1992). Using Interpol data for 1987–1988, Clarke and Harris show that the United States is ranked below England and Wales, Denmark, Australia, Sweden, and Norway regardless of whether the auto theft rate is computed in terms of 1,000 people or 1,000 cars, and it also ranks lower than Scotland, Northern Ireland, France, and Spain when the rate per 1,000 cars is used. The high rates of vehicle ownership in the United States suggest that "more people, perhaps especially the young, have

BOX 5.3   TOP TEN MOST STOLEN CARS IN THE UNITED STATES

Car thieves select their targets with a number of things in mind: availability, market for parts, and larger consumer trends. Thus, it should not be surprising that the recent explosion in popularity of Sport Utility Vehicles and Pickup Trucks has extended to thieves as well.

1. Honda Accord
2. Toyota Camry
3. Oldsmobile Cutlass
4. Chevrolet Full Size Pickup
5. Honda Civic
6. Toyota Corolla
7. Jeep Cherokee
8. Chevrolet Caprice
9. Ford Taurus
10. Chevrolet Cavalier

Source: National Insurance Crime Bureau. Press Release, November 14, 2000, "SUVs, Pickups, Mini-Vans at Top of Thieves' Shopping List."

legitimate access to a car" and therefore are less motivated by the opportunity to steal one, especially for recreational (joy-riding) use (Clarke and Harris 1992a, 8).

Types of Auto Theft

These aggregate figures on auto theft obscure the different types of auto theft and their motivations. There are four basic contexts for auto theft: (1) joyriding: vehicles are stolen simply to be ridden around in for fun and recreation; (2) transportation: a vehicle is stolen for personal use so that the thief can get from one place to another; (3) to commit other crimes: a car is stolen to be used as transportation to and from a crime scene; and (4) profit: a car is stolen so that it can be sold or dismantled for parts that can be sold separately or combined ("chopped up") with other stolen parts to make "new" vehicles that are nearly impossible to trace (Fleming 1999).

A significant amount of auto theft appears to be for profit, and while most are relatively simple operations, some thieves are involved in quite complex schemes. There are four complex insurance frauds involving auto theft:

- *Duplicate Title Frauds*, in which a person sells a car, obtains a duplicate title, then reports the car stolen, then surrenders the duplicate title to the insurance company for payment.
- *Counterfeit Title Frauds*, where a heavily financed car is reported stolen and the insured provides a duplicate title listing himself as sole owner.
- *Paper Vehicle Frauds*, a fictitious vehicle is registered and then insured, then "stolen" so the insurance can be claimed.
- *Salvage Vehicle Frauds*, similar to the preceding except that they involve actual vehicles sold as salvage, which are then registered, titled as operational, insured, then reported stolen (The Illinois Motor Vehicle Theft Prevention Council 1993, 5–7).

Available research only allows inferences about the dynamic qualities of auto theft, including the perceptions, decisions, and reactions of car thieves themselves. A small sample of 100 car thieves provided information on these issues in a British study (Light, Nee, and Ingham 1993). Obviously, their views and experiences may not be typical even of British car thieves, let alone thieves operating in the United States or elsewhere. The main findings of the study, to some extent supported by the work of Fleming (1999), are summarized as follows:

- Most offenders began to steal cars in their early- to mid-teens, with the help of more experienced offenders.
- The influence of friends, the excitement of stealing cars, and boredom were the reasons given for first getting involved in car theft.
- Over time the opportunity to make money from car theft seems to have become more important, and over a third progressed to "professional" car theft for financial gain.
- Over half described themselves as "specialists," stealing cars more or less to the exclusion of other crimes. Specialists were more likely to have had a youthful obsession with cars.
- Car alarms appeared to be of some deterrent value. A third said all alarms deterred them and another quarter said some makes and models did.
- While accepting that car theft was morally wrong, most offenders did not consider it a serious crime.
- The excitement of car theft seemed to overcome any appreciation of the threat of punishment. Nine out of ten said they were not deterred by the prospect of being caught.
- Most of those who said they had stopped stealing cars put this down to increased responsibilities and maturity. The threat of penal sanctions seemed relatively unimportant in stopping offending.

Perhaps more than some other crimes, auto theft is complicated by its mixing of instrumental and expressive motives. When thieves steal cars to make money, the motive is clearly financial and the crime often has the hallmarks of the specialist; when cars are stolen for joyriding or as a gag, the crime is usually opportunistic and often ends with the vehicle being dumped somewhere in much worse condition. In both cases, however, the crime usually involves more than one person, which is also the case with confidence games, to which we now turn.

CONFIDENCE GAMES

Swindlers have been around for centuries. Swindlers and con artists rely on people wanting something for nothing, and they often say, "you can't cheat an honest man." There are no national data on **con games**, thefts committed through apparently legitimate but fraudulent means. Neither the FBI's Uniform Crime Reports nor the NCVS list them as an individual item. Partly because of this, most of the research has been impressionistic and anecdotal (Friedman 1992, 21).

Variations on the con game are numerous: Lists of different swindles compiled through the years show as many as 250 variations (Inciardi 1975). For at least 200 years, two of the most common con games have been "ring dropping" and "purse dropping." Both involve simple techniques of manipulation, and both take advantage of the victim's gullibility and desire to make easy money. In ring dropping, a worthless piece of jewelry is dropped by one member of the con team (the "roper" or "steerer") near a stranger (the victim or "mark"). A second member of the team (the "insideman") rushes forward to pick up the jewelry and, after showing it to the mark, agrees to share the proceeds if the stranger will sell it. The mark is persuaded to leave something of value with the insideman as security—a token of good faith. The climax of the game is obvious—the insideman absconds with the security, leaving the mark to discover that the jewelry is worthless.

The game just described is one variety of swindles commonly referred to as "short con" or "bunco." The aim in short con is to fleece marks of whatever they have with them at the time or can obtain in a matter of minutes. In a short con, the amount of preparation needed and the size of the take are generally small. It can be put into motion at a moment's notice and the score is usually a matter of dollars and cents (Roebuck and Johnson 1964). Another common version of the short con is the "pigeon drop," which operates along lines similar to ring dropping but requires more manipulative abilities by the bunco artist. In the typical pigeon drop, the victim is invited to share money that has supposedly been found by one member of the confidence team, but in order to qualify for a share the mark must first demonstrate good faith by putting up some of his or her own money. This money is then mixed with money supposedly put up by the con artist, but in fact the money is switched and the victim ends up with a bag full of worthless paper.

The successful con artist must accomplish at least three things: (1) Make the mark trust the con operator; (2) make the mark believe that his or her part in the enterprise will be rewarding; and, most important, (3) convince the mark to part ("temporarily," of course) with some of his or her own money. Clearly, a good deal of smooth talking and friendly persuasion is usually necessary. This is where good con artists excel (Roebuck and Johnson 1964, 236).

Big-con operators often adhere to a sequence of steps, each of which must be successfully accomplished if the con is to work. As each step is completed, it becomes more difficult for the con artists to abandon the enterprise and more likely that the swindle will succeed. Seven major steps in the sequence have been identified (Gasser 1963, 48–51):

Step 1: Tying into the mark—finding a victim, gaining his confidence, getting him ready for step two.

Step 2: Telling the mark the tale—showing the victim what is at stake for him, and how he can get hold of it.

Step 3: Initial money gaff—letting the mark make some money to show how easy it is.

Step 4: Putting the mark on the send—sending the victim for money.

Step 5: Playing the mark against the store—fleecing him of his money.

Step 6: Cooling out the mark—see explanation below.

Step 7: Putting the mark in the door—getting rid of the victim.

One of the most important steps in the sequence of events is "cooling out" the victim. Con artists recognize that victims will be angry when they discover they have been duped. Accordingly, they take a special step, the purpose of which is to reduce the chances that the mark will cause trouble. They hope the mark will be convinced to forget the whole incident.

Generally, con artists avoid using violence, even if it means losing the score (Roebuck and Johnson 1964). How, then, do they cool out the mark? One method is to create a twist whereby victims become apparent accessories to a felony (sometimes murder) and hence think they have committed a crime. From being a victim, the mark is now a criminal, facing a prison sentence if caught. Of course, the whole situation is contrived; the con artists stage a fake murder. For example, the mark in the excellent film *The Sting*, assuming himself to be an accessory to murder, was only too glad to forget the whole incident.

Erving Goffman (1952) has discussed a second method of cooling out the mark. This method relies on "the art of consolation." Instead of generating fear in victims, the con artists help them redefine the situation and themselves so that they feel more comfortable with the outcome. By emphasizing that it was extremely hard to con the mark or that the mark presented a real challenge, the con operators help the victim regain a positive self-image. Although the stakes are higher, this method is rather like the situation in which a chess opponent who has just beaten you proceeds to commend you on your play and the challenge you offered. You have still lost the game, but you feel much better. Redefining the situation for the mark provides "a new set of apologies ... [and] a new framework in which to see himself and judge himself" (Goffman 1952, 456).

It is in the nature of confidence games and swindles that the best targets are people with money but without the means to adequately protect themselves from the swindler's clever deceit. Elderly people are particularly vulnerable and it should come as no surprise that they are more often targeted than any other group. A 1990 national survey of bunco investigators representing 331 police departments in 39 states focused on the elderly as victims in three types of swindles: the pigeon drop, the "bank examiner" swindle, and home improvement and repair frauds (Friedman 1992). Since the first has already been described and the last is taken up in Chapter 6, we will describe the bank examiner scheme. In this fraud, the mark is asked to help check out the honesty of a local bank teller suspected of stealing. The prospective victim is asked to help with this investigation by withdrawing a large sum of money from the bank in cash, often several thousand dollars, and making sure the withdrawal is handled by the suspected teller. When the victim returns home he or she is met by a "bank examiner" who takes the withdrawn money for "laboratory analysis" after giving the victim an official-looking receipt (Friedman 1992, 27–28).

Friedman's survey found that the victims of these three types of swindle were very similar: Most were white, unmarried women between sixty-five and seventy-nine years old, living alone, and not working outside the home. When investigators were asked what characteristics would make an elderly person attractive to swindlers, the most common responses were being friendly to strangers and showing visible signs of financial assets such as expensive clothes and jewelry. Some differences among the three types of fraud emerged when investigators were asked to describe the typical characteristics of the bunco artists: Pigeon drop swindlers are most likely to work in teams of two, home improvement swindlers in teams of three or more; home repair swindlers are most likely to be white males, while pigeon drop teams are mixed race or black and mixed gender; on all dimensions, bank examiner swindlers tend to fall in between, according to police investigators.

FENCING STOLEN PROPERTY

Fencing overlaps the worlds of criminal enterprise and legitimate work. It binds theft to the larger social system. Without someone to dispose of stolen property (a **fence**), thieves would have to rely on their own connections, and the costs and risks of crime would increase substantially. For the rest of society, the fence provides an opportunity for people to buy something at less than market price.

The legal requirements for demonstrating that fencing has occurred are complex and help explain why police and prosecutors rely on highly specialized enforcement strategies in combating the crime. In America, as in England, there are four elements to the crime: (1) The property must have been stolen; (2) the property must have been received or concealed (though a fence may not have actually seen or touched it); (3) the receiver must have accepted it with the knowledge (in some states, merely the belief) that it was stolen; and (4) the property must have been received with criminal intent.

One must remember also that most fencing is carried on by "lay" or amateur fences, people who periodically deal in stolen property in networks involving family, friends, neighbors, and coworkers (see Klockars 1974; Henry 1978). Lay receivers may be essentially law-abiding ("square johns") or may dabble in other forms of crime (Shover 1973). The thieves they connect with are often young, usually amateurs, and many will not know professional fences. They have no alternative but to unload their booty on friends and acquaintances.

Ethnographic research on burglary shows that a majority of burglars sell directly to the public (Cromwell, Olson, and Avary 1991; Wright and Decker 1994). There are four main ways of doing this (Sutton 1993, 5): (1) selling directly to friends or neighbors; (2) selling at auctions, markets, car-boot (trunk) sales or through classified ads; (3) selling to strangers in bars, clubs, amusement arcades, or laundromats; and (4) selling to unsuspecting or unquestioning pawnbrokers and second-hand dealers.

Selling to strangers is probably more risky than the other methods, and this undoubtedly accounts in some measure for the fact that it is mentioned less often by active thieves. Even so, Wright and Decker (1994, 188–192) found this method used by twelve of the ninety burglars who spoke to them about disposing of hot property. A carefree attitude is expressed by some burglars:

> Man, just like if I see you on the street I walk up and say, "hey, you want a brand new nineteen-inch color TV?... You say, "Yeah," and give me seventy-five dollars. I'll plug it in for you. (Wright and Decker 1994, 189)

Professional "businessman" fences and thieves are better organized and better connected than amateur thieves and lay fences. They buy from thieves with the intention of reselling, and they often keep a stock of goods on hand. The relationship between professional thieves and fences is one of mutual support. Though many professional fences remain on the periphery of professional theft, they are often a useful source of tips and information for thieves. By acting as a source of information, fences retain better control of their own business because they know what is "coming down," and which goods will be available. This works to the advantage of both fence and thief.

Networking

Connections are vital to the fence, whose business is essentially word-of-mouth. The importance of networking was first established by Marilyn Walsh (1977). She identified three types of networks: (1) kinship networks, dominated by family ties, often with young members stealing and older members selling; (2) work-a-day networks, often based on employer-employee relations, as when a fence with a legitimate business receives stolen merchandise from an employee; and (3) play networks, groups of "good" burglars and fences who meet socially and exchange information. Other research has documented the extensive contacts of successful fences. Carl Klockars (1974) and Darrell Steffensmeier (1986) found that fencing requires resourcefulness, charisma, ingenuity, and a good grasp of market practices and the rules of economic competition. Pricing norms and prevailing market conditions are used to determine what is "fair," and a sense of justice is developed based on the risks borne by the thief. The motivation for being fair with thieves is rarely altruism. It stems from the need to maintain a good reputation and good relations with valued customers. In this respect the fence is no different from anyone whose knowledge and power provide temptations to exploit others that must be overcome if the goal is long-term prosperity.

To give the impression that fencing is primarily an entrepreneurial activity carried out by astute business people who make a good living at it ignores the extensive hidden trading among "ordinary people." A word, then, about Stuart Henry's (1978) important work. Henry studied amateur fencing, or "on-the-side" trading, as he calls it. He used information provided by friends, fellow workers, neighbors, relatives, university colleagues, and even the local hairdresser.

Most of the amateur trading took place within loose networks of collusion, and a participant's job usually provided the opportunity and incentive to get involved. But Henry points out that the incentive was rarely need or greed. He believes that on-the-side trading is largely inconsequential, if not actually unprofitable, from a material standpoint: Things are sold for no more, and often less, than they cost. A beer or a promise of favors returned is often sufficient payment. As one participant put it: "No one really makes any money. Not real money.... The bloke who sells it is not actually making anything either" (Henry 1978, 89). The real profits are of a social nature—forging and maintaining good relations with acquaintances, neighbors, and workmates, and the fostering of "community spirit." To be sure, these social benefits may have a material side, but Henry's informants rarely mentioned it.

All this may help explain why amateur trading is so extensive and why participants do not think of themselves as criminals. They see themselves as ordinary people who are not doing anything really dishonest. Since they do not "need" to steal, the stereotype of the "real" criminal doesn't apply: "People in ordinary, honest jobs know that they do not have to fiddle, pilfer, or deal in order to earn a living" (Henry 1978, 76). Thievery is certainly more justifiable if its criminality can be defined away.

CRIMES VIA THE COMPUTER

The increasing availability of personal computers has provided many new opportunities for criminal activity. In 1999, the FBI investigated 115 percent more cases of computer-related crime and arrested 950 percent more suspects than in 1996 (National Infrastructure Protection Center 2000). While many thefts and frauds by computer are committed by employees against their employers (discussed in Chapter 6), our focus here is on nonoccupation-related computer crimes. We begin with hackers.

Hackers are people who break the security of an organization's computer network. Emmanuel Goldstein, editor of *2600: The Hacker's Quarterly* once said: "While it's certainly possible to use hacking ability to commit a crime, once you do this you cease being a hacker and commence being a criminal. It's really not a hard distinction to make" (CNN 2000).

Many hackers are simply motivated by the challenge of figuring out how to beat a security system. Both a science and an art, hacking involves a high level of skill, knowledge, commitment, and creativity. It also takes higher than average intelligence to be a successful hacker.

The motivations for hacking vary. Sometimes hackers are simply interested in understanding how systems work and how they can be compromised. Some hackers have compared the challenge and high they receive with cracking a code (*ZNET*,

Most computer hackers are young and intelligent males. They put in long hours, often in isolation, breaking into computer networks. Some hacking is criminal, some is not, but all hackers are often motivated by the intellectual challenges hacking poses.

2000). Some hackers vandalize, deface, or otherwise disrupt networks and Web sites, but do not actually steal information, commodities, or cash. They can nevertheless cause considerable harm. In February of 2000 such hackers deployed a program known as "Stacheldraht" that disabled at least eight corporate Web sites (including CNN, Amazon.com, and E*trade). These are called "denial of service attacks." They send commands to other hackable "zombie" supercomputers (in this case computers at Stanford University) that flood a targeted Web site with thousands of simultaneous requests. This disrupts the site's normal operation and may cause it to crash.

Similar attacks may come in the form of e-mail bugs and viruses that compromise (and sometimes destroy) e-mail networks and servers. The computer programmer who created the 1999 Melissa computer virus recently pleaded guilty to causing $80 million in damages as a result of system damages to computer networks. In any case of sabotage, the affected Web sites and networks can be rendered useless for a period of time, and companies can lose serious money in sales, repairs, and additional security and software expenses (National Infrastructure Protection Center 2000). Equally serious consequences may result when hackers vandalize government Web sites. This happened when several hackers recently cracked into the U.S. Senate and FBI Web sites and posted offensive comments about members of these organizations. Presidential candidate George W. Bush Jr.'s Web site was defaced in similar fashion in 1999.

One of the most common forms of hacker computer crime is breaking into the network system of a credit card company or credit service bureau, stealing confidential information, and then using that information to obtain loans, cash advances, and of course, merchandise.

In some cases, the stolen information is "kidnapped" and held for ransom. "Maxim," the nickname of a criminal hacker, recently hacked into an on-line compact disc store, stole 300,000 credit card numbers, and threaten to published them on the Internet unless he was paid $100,000 in ransom. The company, Euniverse, refused to pay the ransom and Maxim did indeed post some of the data on a Web site. The FBI has yet to learn the real identity of Maxim. In another twist on an old crime, two men reportedly made about $370,000 in illicit stock gains as a result of posting phony stories about NEI Webworld, a Dallas-based printing services company. The bogus postings pushed the price of NEI's stock up from 13 cents to more than $15 per share. Both have been charged with a single count of conspiracy to commit securities fraud.

The range of crimes that can be committed via the computer is staggering: fraud, theft, extortion, piracy, intimidation, and even espionage. It is impossible to predict the future of computer crime, just as it was impossible for people ten years ago to understand how dramatically their lives would be transformed with the advent of e-mail, the Internet, and on-line commerce.

Entire subcultures have developed around computer hacking. So-called cyberpunk or phreak groups, like other subcultures, often have unique norms and customs, such as specialized vocabularies and nicknames. The well-publicized release of legendary hacker Kevin David Mitnick from prison illustrates this subcultural element. Mitnick was found guilty a few years ago of hacking into corporate Web sites and stealing software. Many fellow hackers protested the treatment of Mitnick and argued that while he did commit computer crimes, a five-year prison sentence was not justifiable. He is regarded as a martyr in the hacker community. A Web site devoted to his cause reads as follows:

> The greatest injustice in the prosecution of Kevin Mitnick is revealed when one examines the actual harm to society (or lack thereof) which resulted from Kevin's actions. To the extent that Kevin is a "hacker" he must be considered a purist. The simple truth is that Kevin never sought monetary gain from his hacking, though it could have proven extremely profitable. Nor did he hack with the malicious intent to damage or destroy other people's property. Rather, Kevin pursued his hacking as a means of satisfying his intellectual curiosity and applying Yankee ingenuity. These attributes are more frequently promoted rather than punished by society. (http://www.kevinmitnick.com/home.html)

Fair enough, but these same apologists would probably laugh at the idea of people attempting to justify other forms of theft on the grounds that the offender didn't mean to steal, it was only out of curiosity. That defense is usually reserved for young children.

PROFESSIONAL THEFT

Professional theft has a history going back at least to Elizabethan times, when "conny-catching" (a type of swindling) was a full-time profession. Through the years other varieties of theft became the focus of professionalization, with shoplifting and pocket picking two of the more common ones. Much of what is known about professional theft and the professional thief has come from firsthand accounts by thieves (both practicing and reformed), many of which are of the "as told to" variety. Among the best known are *The Professional Thief*, edited by Edwin Sutherland; Ernest Booth's *Stealing Through Life; My Life in Crime*, reported by John Bartlow Martin, and *Box Man: A Professional Thief's Journey*, as told to William Chambliss. To those must be added an assortment of books and articles focusing on professionalism in specific types of theft—for example, confidence games, burglary, forgery, and pocket picking.

By far the most influential work on professional theft has been Sutherland's *The Professional Thief* (1937b). Sutherland used the written accounts of one professional thief ("Chic Conwell") to illustrate the complex assortment of behavior characteristics, attitudes, organizational features, subcultural patterns, and views of the world that together make up a way of life shared by professional thieves.

In describing the world to which he belonged, Chic Conwell tells us that professional thieves (1) "make a regular business of stealing"; (2) acquire their skills and professional know-how through tutelage by and association with already established professionals; (3) develop highly skilled work techniques, the most important of which is the "ability to manipulate people"; (4) carefully plan everything they do in connection with their business; (5) look upon themselves as different from amateurs and superior to them, particularly those who indulge in sex crimes; (6) have a code of ethics that "is much more binding among thieves than that among legitimate commercial firms"; (7) are "sympathetic" and "congenial" with each other; (8) view successes and failures as "largely a matter of luck"; (9) have an established vocabulary of criminal slang, the main purpose of which is to enhance "we-feeling" and promote ease of intraprofession communication; (10) rarely engage in only one specialized form of theft (the notable exception being pickpockets, or "cannons"); and (11) usually operate in gangs, "mobs," or partnerships whose life span is generally short unless they are consistently successful (Sutherland 1937b, 2–42).

Summarizing Conwell's account of professional theft, Sutherland (1937b, ix–x) offers this conception of the profession:

> The profession of theft is more than isolated acts of theft frequently and skillfully performed. It is a group way of life and a social institution. It has techniques, codes, status, traditions, consensus, and organization. It has an existence as real as that of the English language. It can be studied with relatively little attention to any particular thief. The profession can be understood by a description of the functions and relationships involved in this way of life. In fact, an understanding of this culture is a prerequisite to the understanding of the behavior of a particular professional thief.

A key feature of professionalism is the maintenance of a system that confers status and prestige. Status distinctions are based on a variety of things: type of theft engaged in, skill and technical competence, success, connections, and commitment. As in any other profession, participants confer prestige and recognition upon one another and distinguish the entire fraternity from outsiders, those who do not belong.

Within the ranks of professional thieves, certain specialties stand out. Confidence men and safecrackers have traditionally been considered at the top of the pecking order. Their work involves considerable skill and ability, and the payoffs can be substantial for those who succeed. At the other end of the status hierarchy are those whose jobs usually have a small payoff, involve more modest levels of skill and risk, and whose victims are typically individuals or small businesses. Cannons (pickpockets), "boosters" (professional shoplifters), and small-time burglars are examples of low-status thieves. Here is how two thieves view shoplifting (King 1972, 81):

> A booster is just about the lowest thief there is. Nobody has much to do with them. I mean, I seen one yesterday as a matter of fact. I saw this one, then talked to this other guy who was a meter-robber; you know, a guy who robs parking meters. They make a lot of money. I was talking to this friend and he said he saw Charlie boosting the other day. I told him: "Gee, Charlie Jay? Man, I can remember when he was a real high-classed thief." "Oh," he said, "he's down at the bottom now." In our estimation he's down dragging bottom because he's boosting. And he used to be a real high-classed thief at one time.

It appears that "good" thieves also do not think much of women who venture into crime. In a rare investigation of the issue, Steffensmeier and Terry (1986) interviewed forty-nine male thieves, most of them experienced, some of them probably ranking as professionals. These thieves identified various traits that they felt were particularly important to their trade, but that women were perceived to lack. In their view, successful thieves are physically strong; they have "heart" ("guts" or courage); they are aggressive when they need to be; they have endurance; they can be trusted when the chips are down; they are emotionally stable; they stay calm and cool under pressure; and they command respect. Most thieves claimed to have committed crimes with women at one time or another, but in no cases were the women full partners in the crimes, being relegated instead to peripheral sex/service roles, for which they received a less-than-equal share of the "score." Even in crime, it seems, women are treated as second-class citizens.

In contrast to professional thieves, a considerable amount of property offenders are not skilled in the finer techniques of theft. These offenders have been called **persistent thieves**, who continue their involvement in property offenses even after an arrest. These thieves often use the proceeds of their crimes to "party" (i.e., to consume heavy amounts of drugs and alcohol in a group setting) (Shover and Henderson 1995; Shover and Honaker 1992; 1999). The phrase **life as party** refers to: "… the enjoyment of 'good times' with minimal concern for obligations and commitments that are external to the person's immediate social setting." This may include unconventional sleeping hours, just "hanging out" at home for days listening to music or watching television, and frequenting bars, taverns, lounges, and parks. Contrary to the professional thief, those stealing for party pursuits often do so spontaneously and unprofessionally. Several studies (e.g., Shover and Honaker 1999) have shown that these offenders commit their crimes when they are high and drunk, hardly a very professional way to go about their thievery.

CONVERGENCE OF PROFESSIONAL CRIME AND OCCUPATIONAL CRIME

Some criminologists believe that professional crime has been converging with the more avocational activity of people who commit crimes in connection with their work, that which is often called "occupational crime" (discussed in the next chapter). Hagan and Benekos (1992) see a number of parallels in the attitudes and behaviors of professional thieves and avocational offenders, and they find professional thieves, corporate offenders, and small businesses working together in a variety of scams and frauds. Consider the use of argot. In the 1980s, stock market, banking, and other occupational

thieves developed a whole new jargon, "S&L-ese." Hagan and Benekos (1992, 4) illustrate:

> Using RAP accounting and beards and straw borrowers, go-go thrifts busted out many S&L's as well as Fizzlic itself. With "cash-for-trade" and "dead horses and dead cows" land flips and paper parking they managed to Ponzi the American public— "the weak, the meek, and the ignorant" as well as the feds. With daisy chains and inflated appraisals, paper was kissed, loans scraped and walking money was produced from brokered deposits and invested in junk bonds. If revolving doors or fees could not buy off the professionalism of accountants, lawyers and members of Congress, white knights could be used to rescue Zombie thrifts.

The convergence of professional theft and occupational crime is seen most clearly in the realm of financial frauds and investment scams, according to Hagan and Benekos. Examples are phony accident claims, where professional thieves team up with lawyers and physicians to milk insurance companies; "mile busting," the practice of rolling back automobile odometers, prevalent among used car dealers in some areas of the country, and estimated to cost the American public $4 billion a year; "Boiler Room" frauds, where high pressure salespeople use rented offices and telemarketing to sell bogus products, often disguised as charities; oil, gas, and precious metal investment frauds; business opportunity and franchise frauds, where con artists with slick catalogues and phony testimonials sell the American dream to would-be entrepreneurs; Pyramid schemes, where those who get in on the ground floor can make a killing, but later investors rarely get rich and usually lose money as people drop out and the pyramid collapses; and "dead horses for dead cows," involving collusion among failing S&Ls (see Chapter 6) in which bad assets (dead horses) are swapped, and payment on delinquent loans postponed.

Hagan and Benekos (1992, 13) suggest that an "enterprise model" of crime such as that proposed by Smith (1980) best describes what is happening in professional crime. In this model, the economic activity of individuals and organizations ranges from totally legitimate at one end to totally illegitimate at the other. Most enterprises range somewhere in between, but all are driven by one underlying motive: profit. In Smith's (1980) view, the legality of the legitimate pharmacist (the "paragon") and the illegality of the drug dealer (the "pariah") put them at different ends of the continuum even though both kinds of entrepreneur are doing essentially the same thing. Hagan and Benekos (1992, 13) argue that in the S&L debacle, "the paragons (legitimate thrift operators) adopted the principles of con artists."

AGING PROPERTY OFFENDERS

There comes a time in most criminals' lives when they think seriously about "retiring" from crime. For some it comes relatively early, perhaps in their twenties or thirties; for others the decision may not come until they are in their fifties or sixties. Little is known about the later stages of criminal careers, a fact that Neal Shover (1983; 1985) has sought to rectify in a study of "ordinary property offenders." These are people who primarily commit nonviolent crimes of theft, though they sometimes venture into robbery or drug sales.

Shover interviewed fifty subjects, thirty-six of whom he classified as "unsuccessful" because their many crimes rarely paid off and they experienced multiple contacts with the criminal justice system. Shover classified five offenders as "successful"— they saw crime as a means of livelihood and were successful at it, though all had been incarcerated at least once. The remaining seven were "uncommitted"; that is, they were infrequent offenders who rarely planned their crimes, rarely made much money from them, and did not think of crime as their occupation (Shover 1985, 24–26, 97). For uncommitted offenders, the experience of being arrested and jailed had a strong impact that usually jolted them into reaffirming their noncriminal identity.

Though based on a small sample, Shover's unsuccessful group probably mirrors the experience of many high-frequency offenders who begin their criminal careers at a relatively young age and persist well into adulthood when not confined in the penitentiary. In Shover's group, the youngest was thirty-nine and the oldest seventy-two. Four men were still involved in crime at the time of the interviews, though their current crimes paled in comparison to the burglaries and robberies of their youth.

Shover (1983) identified five experiential contingencies that influenced the criminal behavior of the "unsuccessful" property offenders as they aged:

1. An *identity shift*: Some subjects realized that crime was a dead end and they began to dissociate themselves from the "foolish," "dumb," even dangerous behavior of their youth.

2. *Incommodious time*: Many became aware that time was a diminishing resource and thus worried about how to make the best of their limited futures. Many feared dying in prison.

3. *Aspirations and goals*: Some developed new priorities and goals, such as family, "contentment," or a pension. One said:

   > "I don't want to live that kind of life any more. I want peace. I want joy and harmony. I want to be with my children and my grandchildren…. I want to be with my mother. And when she passes on—I was in prison when my daddy died, I got to come home for five hours in handcuffs to see him—and when my mother passes on, I want to be there with her." (Shover 1983, 212)

4. *Tiredness*: Many grew tired of the problems and deprivations of crime and failure; they had simply had enough. If it was not age itself that weakened them, it was the criminal justice system that wore them down.

5. *Interpersonal contingency*: Ties to another person, such as the development of a satisfying relationship with a woman, and ties to a job, for legitimate employment provides both immediate rewards and prospects of a secure future. Besides, the routine activities of work rarely leave time (or energy) for the criminal pursuits of the ordinary property offender.

Not all the men experienced all these contingencies, but for those who did, the change from a criminal lifestyle was likely to be abrupt and permanent. Even so, Shover (1983, 216) concludes that "even offenders who committed serious crimes while young are capable of, and do, change as they get older." Shover believes that in essence the decision to refrain from crime is due to a perception of increasing costs and decreasing benefits (see also Cusson and Pinsonneault 1986). As one subject put it: "I'd rather be a bum in the street, than a millionaire in the penitentiary" (Shover 1985, 124).

The five experiential contingencies listed influence the decision-making calculus by making crime more of a risk.

CHAPTER SUMMARY

This chapter has examined shoplifting, burglary, computer crimes, and confidence games, as well as fencing, which helps support them. The social organization of professional theft was also examined, as well as the convergence of professional theft and occupational crime, the subject of Chapter 6.

Stealing has a long history and is found in some form in many societies. Without private property, however, the concept of theft is moot. Theft laws have been shaped by conflicting interests and by the power of property owners to protect that property. A society that values the acquisition of material wealth but also has gross inequalities in the distribution of material resources finds itself encouraging theft, as appears to have happened in the United States. Many thefts are not reported to the police, but even those that are usually remain unsolved. In this respect, most forms of theft are low-risk crimes, a fact that also contributes to high offense rates.

Most thieves are opportunists who sporadically shoplift, forge checks, or burglarize a business or residence with minimal planning or skill. Many do not think of themselves as criminals, either denying their crimes altogether or blaming their actions on situational pressures. Professional thieves, on the other hand, maintain a complicated system of roles and norms in terms of which participants gain status, prestige, and professional identity. In between the rank amateurs and the professionals are "ordinary property offenders," people who spend many years at crimes of all sorts, usually beginning at an early age, often spending considerable time in prison, and rarely making much money at crime. As they grow older they commit fewer crimes, and many eventually quit the largely unsuccessful criminal lifestyle to "go straight."

Fencing provides an important link between legitimate society and the world of theft. Without it, neither theft nor thieves would prosper, and with it, it is possible for ostensibly "straight" society to cash in on the criminality of others.

KEY TERMS

burglary (p. 101)
Carrier's Case (p. 95)
con games (p. 106)
fence (p. 107)
hackers (p. 109)
life as party (p. 112)
persistent thieves (p. 112)
sneak theft (p. 97)

RECOMMENDED READINGS

Cromwell, Paul. 1999. *In Their Own Words: Criminals on Crime*. Los Angeles, CA: Roxbury.

Hobbs, Dick. 1995. *Professional Criminals*. Aldershot, UK: Dartmouth Publishing Co.

Hollinger, Richard C. 1997. *Crime, Deviance, and the Computer*. Aldershot, UK: Dartmouth Publishing Co.

Shover, Neal. 1985. *Aging Criminals*. Beverly Hills, CA: Sage Publications.

Tunnell, Kenneth D. 1992. *Choosing Crime: The Criminal Calculus of Property Offenders*. Chicago, IL: Nelson-Hall.

Tunnell, Kenneth D. 2000. *Living Off Crime*. Chicago, IL: Burnham Inc. Publishers.

RECOMMENDED WEB SITES

The International Association of Auto Theft Investigators

Reports, statistics, and links on all kinds of thefts.
http://www.iaati.org

Illinois State Police

Information on dozens of frauds and con games.
http://www.state.il.us/isp

ZDTV

Reports, information, and links on various facets of computer crime.
http://www.cybercrime.com

CHAPTER

6

VARIETIES OF WHITE-COLLAR CRIME

So far the text has focused on what are "traditional" or "street" crimes. Robbery, rape, murder, assault, burglary and other thefts are traditional crimes in a number of senses. First, they are among the activities that most readily come to mind when people think of crime. Second, they are the conventional targets of criminalization. Third, they have long been the prime focus of law-enforcement efforts. And fourth, it is primarily around these kinds of crime that criminologists have framed their theories.

Robbery, burglary, assault, and rape may be called traditional crimes but this does not mean they are the most common forms of crime or that they create the most victims, the highest economic costs, or the greatest damage to social institutions. The crimes discussed in this chapter have a far greater impact on society, and often on individual victims as well. A closer look at occupational and organizational crimes will show that "crimes in the suites" deserve far more attention than they commonly receive in the press, and in criminology.

Types of White-Collar Crime

The term **white-collar crime** was coined in 1939 by Edwin H. Sutherland. He defined it as crimes committed by people of respectability and high social status in the course of their occupations. Sutherland also observed that criminologists had virtually ignored the illegal activities of those in business, politics, and the professions, concentrating instead on the world of lower-class criminality emphasized in crime statistics and in the criminal justice system. Lawbreaking, he argued, goes on in all social strata. Restraint of trade, misrepresentation in advertising, violations of labor laws, violations of copyright and patent laws, and financial manipulations were a part of what Sutherland called white-collar crime.

Over the years since Sutherland's groundbreaking work, other criminologists have refined the definition of white-collar crime. One of the earliest of these was Clinard and Quinney's (1973) effort to define white-collar crime in more operational terms. They split the concept of white-collar crime into **corporate crime**—crimes organizationally based and directed toward reaching corporate goals—and **occupational crime**, crimes committed by individuals in the course of their occupation for their own personal gain.

Another advance in white-collar crime research came when scholars argued that organizations are social actors in their own right and can be studied criminologically because they persist over time, develop and maintain procedures, and pursue goals

(Hall 1987). Furthermore, "[p]reoccupation with individuals can lead us to underestimate the pressures within society and organizational structure, which impel those individuals to commit illegal acts"(Schrager and Short 1978, 410). Thus, "the principal rationale for distinguishing organizational crime is the assumption that organizational dynamics, conditions, and constraints ... play a major part in their onset and course"(Shover and Wright 2001, 3). **Organizational crime** can be defined as

> illegal acts of omission or commission of an individual or group of individuals in a legitimate formal organization in accordance with the operative goals of the organization, which have a serious impact on employees, consumers, or the general public. (Schrager and Short 1978, 411)

Organizational crimes may be committed by private or public organizations. Thus, corporate crime is a type of organizational crime.

Another type of white-collar crime is **governmental crime** (sometimes called political crime), which may be committed by organizations or by individuals. There are several forms of governmental crime:

1. State Crime: Illegal or socially injurious acts of omission or commission by an individual or group of individuals in an institution of legitimate governance which is executed for the consummation of the operative goals of that institution of governance (Kauzlarich 1995, 39).
2. State-Corporate Crime: Illegal or socially injurious actions that result from mutually reinforcing interaction between institutions of political governance and institutions of economic production and distribution (Kramer and Michalowski 1991, 5; also see Matthews and Kauzlarich 2000).
3. Political White-Collar Crime: Illegal activities carried out by political officials for direct personal benefit (Friedrichs 1995, 94; 1996).

Clearly, there are many different offenses that fall within the realm of white-collar crime. Apart from the illegal activities already mentioned (restraint of trade, unfair labor practices, and so on),

there are embezzlement, a variety of consumer frauds, thefts by computer, music and record pirating, prescription law violations, employee pilfering, food and drug law violations, bribery and other forms of corruption by public officials, kickbacks, illegal wars, and violations of human rights—the list could go on and on. As might be anticipated from this list, white-collar crime is by no means a new problem; it dates from the first time people regularly put time, energy, and ability into a sustenance activity for which they received some form of reward.

As suggested by this discussion, white-collar crime varies by its organizational complexity and in its consequences for victims. One study looked at eight different offenses—antitrust violations, securities fraud, mail fraud, false claims, credit fraud, bribery, tax fraud, and bank embezzlement—in terms of these two dimensions. Securities and antitrust violations were at the high end of both dimensions, and tax fraud, credit fraud, and bank embezzlement at the other end (Weisburd, et al. 1991). The other offenses fell in between. When compared with "common crimes," in this case postal theft and forgery, the authors found that their white-collar crimes differed noticeably from the common crimes on these same two dimensions. Postal theft and forgery were less likely to victimize organizations, had mostly local impact, involved little potential gain, victimized far fewer people, were much less likely to involve five or more co-conspirators, and seldom involved a pattern of offending. The largest difference pertained to duration of the crime: Very few common crimes lasted more than a year, while half the white-collar crimes did. We shall return to a comparison of occupational and street crimes in a moment.

WORK AND THE HISTORICAL DEVELOPMENT OF LEGAL CONTROLS

The regulation of economic behavior has a long history. Long before the modern era there was widespread appreciation of the dangers and injustices of unregulated marketplace behavior. It requires little imagination to see how important orderly and fair economic relations must have been during a time when most people lived in small villages and knew each other.

However, the Industrial Revolution eventually pushed market exploitation "into the shadows, camouflaged by its remoteness, the diffuse nature of the harm it inflicted, and the obscurity of the source of the harm" (Geis 1988, 15). As a result, the public sense of injustice and indignation waned. As a fledgling capitalist society applied itself to the practical problems of making capitalism work, industrial power and wealth reached heights never before imagined. During the late nineteenth century, there emerged a drive to check corporate power and the economic abuses spreading from it. First the railroads and later corporations in general became the target of regulatory reforms. However, rather than a systematic response to problems, the regulatory movement consisted of sporadic responses "to a series of disasters" (Geis 1988, 21), from coal mine explosions to deformed babies born to mothers who had taken thalidomide (Hills 1971, 151).

The Role of Interests

The full flavor of laws relating to occupations is lost unless the role of special interests is considered. Besides the fact that many past laws were weighted in favor of elites so that the penalties for violation were less the higher one's social status, few laws formalized the obligations of masters and employers toward their servants, slaves, and employees. In addition, some laws were clearly designed to consolidate ruling-class control over economic and political activities and thus over the production and distribution of wealth and material advantages. Consider, for example, laws against criminal fraud.

FRAUDS   When people induce someone to part with money or valuables through the use of deceit, lies, or misrepresentation, they commit fraud, or what was called a "cheat" in earlier times. Under English common law, criminal liability extended only to situations in which (1) some false token or tangible device of trickery was involved and (2) the activity was such that reasonable prudence could not guard against it and any member of the general public was a potential victim (Turner 1966). Under common law, a personal fraud directed against a private individual was no crime, because it was customary to assume that individuals would exercise due caution in their financial dealings with

others and because when an individual was deceived, civil remedies were available.

With the rise of capitalism, entrepreneurs throughout the business community urged Parliament to broaden the range of criminal liability associated with fraudulent practices. In 1757 a statute was passed establishing the crime of "obtaining property by false pretenses." Subsequently adopted in the American colonies, this law has remained one of the few specifically criminal statutes dealing with fraud.

Despite the extensive victimization associated with consumer fraud, the courts until recently had operated on the principle of *caveat emptor*—buyer beware. The idea was simply that in making purchases, consumers have only themselves to blame if they are "taken." Reasonable as this may sound, it actually encourages victimization in the modern marketplace, where the complex nature of many products, services, and organizations are such that even knowledgeable purchasers find it almost impossible to protect themselves against fraud. For example, given modern supermarket packaging practices, shoppers can rarely inspect the products they want to buy in more than a superficial way.

PURE FOOD AND DRUG LAWS   Interest in the regulation of the food and drug businesses first gained prominence during the nineteenth century, as cities grew and consumers became increasingly removed from agricultural producers, and the possibilities for adulteration, spoilage, exploitation, and fraud increased. Public awareness of the problem was stirred partly through the changing experience of buying itself, but mostly by newspaper editorials, and by articles and books that stressed the dangers of existing business practices, sometimes in lurid and frightening detail.

The first major federal legislation aimed at regulating the food and drug businesses was introduced in 1880 and soundly defeated, as were many subsequent bills: "It and other efforts like it were defeated by a durable alliance of quacks, ruthless crooks, pious frauds, scoundrels, high-priced lawyer-lobbyists, vested interests, liars, corrupt members of Congress, venal publishers, cowards in high office, the stupid, the apathetic, and the duped" (Mintz 1970, 78–79). When Congress finally passed the Federal Food and Drug Act of 1906, it was only the first step in what has turned out to be a long and hard battle between public interests and the food and drug industries.

The 1906 law made it illegal to manufacture or introduce into the United States any adulterated or misbranded food or drug. Offenders could have their products seized, and those convicted of violating the law would be subject to criminal penalties. Thus a new area of occupational crime was born. But it has been argued that the new law contained inadequate regulation of advertising, and provided no provisions applying to cosmetics or the use of health devices (Quinney 1970). Indeed, "nearly 100 years after public interest was first mobilized, Americans could count on one hand the number of truly significant bills designed to regulate the powerful industries supplying their food, pharmaceutical products, and cosmetics" (Quinney 1970, 79).

If it were not for the efforts of Ralph Nader, the American public might still be buying meat products largely unregulated by legal controls. In 1906 Upton Sinclair had described the disgusting conditions of meat slaughterhouses in his highly popular novel, *The Jungle*. In 1967 Nader found that we were still "in the jungle." His investigation found meat that was contaminated with disease and spoiled carcasses—even manure and pus—and often sold in a deceptive and fraudulent manner. While cases of this magnitude are rare now, deliberate selling of unsafe food still happens. For example, in January of 2000, a Grand Rapids, Michigan, food distribution firm pled guilty to selling adulterated and contaminated meat and poultry to a Detroit retail grocer (Food Safety and Inspection Service 2000).

Like many problems related to consumer protection and safety, these appalling conditions in the meat and food industry are partly the result of the inadequacy of existing federal and state laws and partly of the pitiful efforts to enforce them. Both problems are blamed on the cozy relationship among the U.S. Department of Agriculture (USDA), state agriculture agencies, and the meat production and processing interests. When Congress passed the Wholesale Meat Act of 1968—bringing intrastate meat processing under federal jurisdiction and establishing stricter controls—another small victory for public welfare was achieved and the range of legal penalties extended. However, the Reagan administration systematically undermined the law by cutting back on expenditures for enforcement, and

states have generally done no better. The Clinton administration, however, has increased efforts to control the quality of food with its support of the Food Quality Protection Act of 1996. It remains to be seen whether the Bush administration will respond to the matter.

THE COSTS OF WHITE-COLLAR CRIME

It is now appropriate to return to a matter raised in the opening paragraphs of this chapter: the costs of white-collar crime to individuals and society. A brief look at some of these costs should support a more balanced view of the impact of crime and be a reminder that societal reactions to a particular form of crime are not necessarily an accurate reflection of its impact on people's lives, their communities, and their institutions.

Financial Costs

The financial costs of white-collar crime far exceed those resulting from traditional crimes. This reflects the greater frequency with which white-collar crimes are committed and also the fact that a single offense can result in losses running into millions of dollars. Estimates place tangible financial losses resulting from traditional street crimes such as burglary, murder, and robbery at $105 billion per year (National Institute of Justice 1996; Miller, Cohen, and Wiersema 1996). By contrast, losses attributed to fraud alone have been estimated at $400 billion per year (Association of Certified Fraud Examiners 1999). Other white-collar crimes cost the public billions more: The savings and loan disaster of the late 1980s may end up costing more than $500 billion (Chambliss 1999, 152); the extent of losses from employee theft are hinted at by an executive who observes, "We've got 24,000 employees; if half of them make $5 in forbidden personal calls a month, that's three-quarters of a million right there" (Baker and Westin 1987, 12); price-fixing costs at least $60 billion a year (Simon 1999, 106). Although the overall financial costs of white-collar crime cannot be estimated with confidence—there are simply too many types and no systematic data collection for most of them—they are huge relative to street crimes. A recent conservative estimate puts the costs of street crime at only 6 percent of the costs of white-collar crime (Rosoff, Pontell, and Tillman 1998, 16).

Damage to Institutions and Moral Climate

Deception, fraud, price-fixing, bribery, kickbacks, and violations of trust undermine principles of honesty and fair play. They also foster a moral climate in which lawlessness provokes little indignation—especially when its victims are vague entities such as "the public," "the consumer," "the corporation," and "the government"—and occurs largely free from any sense of guilt on the part of offenders. This results in the erosion of economic and political institutions. Looking out for number one, beating the system, getting something for nothing, or doing a favor for a price become accepted and expected practices for all social strata. When there is pervasive and unpunished thievery and corruption among leaders in business, the professions, and government, street criminals can easily rationalize their own illegal conduct as no different from that of their "betters" (Kauzlarich, Matthews, and Miller 2000; Simon 1999).

Personal Health and Safety

Arguably the greatest losses from white-collar crime involve personal health and safety. Occupational and organizational crimes pose health and safety hazards in numerous ways:

- Companies violating safety standards for their products (cars, tires, electrical appliances, toys, nightclothes, Christmas tree lights, and many others) expose their customers to possible injury or death.
- Physicians who do unnecessary surgery expose their patients to the risk of surgical complications.
- Pharmaceutical companies conspiring to fix high prices threaten the well-being of those who need but cannot afford their products.
- Mine and factory bosses who violate health and safety regulations expose their workers to injury, disease, and death.
- Companies manufacturing or selling contaminated food products or mislabeled drugs expose their customers to unnecessary health hazards.

Now consider how state crime may produce physical injury and death:

- Illegal wars and invasions have easily cost the lives of millions of people in the twentieth century.

- U.S. governmental projects such as the manufacture and production of nuclear weapons have resulted in hundreds of thousands of deaths and perhaps millions of health problems.
- Illegal radiation experiments and nuclear weapons testing have claimed the lives of thousands of U.S. veterans and civilians. Thousands more have had their health compromised by such state actions.
- State regulatory agencies that ignore their mandate to protect workers, consumers, and the environment have directly and indirectly led to death and injury (Kauzlarich and Kramer 1998; Matthews and Kauzlarich 2000).

There can be little doubt that when the health and safety of the population as a whole are considered, the threat posed by occupational, organizational, and political crime far exceeds that posed by traditional crimes. This is not to minimize the dangers associated with rape and robbery but, rather, to place the two broad categories of crime in perspective. It is easy to overlook the dangers posed by white-collar crime because these are often less visible, less direct, and appear less concrete than those of street crimes. They are also commonly committed by people or groups in positions of considerable power. Yet these crimes are extensive. Take, for instance, the physical dangers associated with environmental pollution in the air, water, soil, workplace, and home. Millions of Americans are exposed every day to known carcinogens and other potentially lethal substances, often because corporations and businesses fail to meet environmental standards or find legal ways to circumvent them (Clifford 1998).

In Missouri, the entire population of Times Beach was forced to evacuate because dioxin-tainted waste oil was sprayed on the roads to keep the dust down. Times Beach was a modern ghost town, with some former citizens suffering the delayed effects of dioxin (called "Agent Orange" during the Vietnam War). Many thousands of industrial workers will become ill or die because they work under conditions that needlessly expose them to carcinogens and that cause severe respiratory ailments. Those in the rubber, steel, asbestos, coal, and chemical industries are especially vulnerable to such diseases. One of the most costly industrial disasters of all time has been tied to "unlawful, willful, malicious, and wanton" disregard for human safety—the December 1984 gas leak at the Union Carbide pesticide plant in Bhopal, India, which claimed 2,000 lives and injured 150,000 to 200,000 more. The Indian government eventually charged Union Carbide with moral responsibility and legal liability for the leak. For its part, the company accepted some responsibility but denied any criminal negligence.

As with most forms of crime, the risks and costs of being victimized by occupational crimes are not borne equally. The young, poor, and elderly are especially vulnerable to environmental crimes and to frauds of all sorts. As the population ages, we can expect to see more and more victimization of the elderly—not only by fast-talking salespeople, but also by corporate marketers who capitalize on their fear of change, their susceptibility to illness, their fear of having inadequate insurance, and their loneliness.

OCCUPATIONAL CRIME: VIOLATING THE LAW FOR PERSONAL GAIN

The motivations for occupational crime are varied, and not simply economic. They include empire-building, protection of top management from hostile takeovers, and the defense of activities that carry great prestige or confer respect. This section explores crimes that are primarily committed by individuals for their own gain, and in violation of loyalty to their employer or client.

Embezzlement

There were only about 17,000 arrests for embezzlement in 1999 (Federal Bureau of Investigation 2000, 217). Embezzlement suspects are usually white, middle-class, middle-aged males, quite unlike the prevailing stereotype of the criminal. However, this police description of the typical offender may not be an accurate portrayal of the bulk of people embezzling from their employers or clients. In terms of age and gender, Gottfredson and Hirschi (1990) believe that the typical embezzler is no different from the typical street criminal, that is, a young male, although their evidence for this claim is far from compelling.

When the embezzler is a woman, she is usually a lower-level employee rather than an executive (Daly 1988). Indications are that male and female

rates of embezzlement are converging (Hirschi and Gottfredson 1987, 961). It is not clear why this is so, but some believe it reflects increased employment of women in positions of financial trust, while others attribute it to the economic marginalization of many women, who find themselves in financial straits with families to support. It is probably a combination of both.

The embezzler has been called "the respectable criminal" (Cressey 1965). Respectable or not, estimates of the frequency and costs of embezzlement are staggering. In 1967, the President's Commission on Law Enforcement and the Administration of Justice put the annual cost at more than $200 million; that figure is dwarfed by a 1974 estimate of $4 billion. Today's figure is certainly much higher.

The respectability of embezzlers mentioned by many authors acknowledges not only the relatively high occupational status of many offenders but also the fact that they rarely have a delinquent or criminal record prior to their embezzling activities and rarely think of themselves as real criminals. According to a study of 1,001 embezzlers conducted some years ago, the typical male embezzler is the epitome of the moderately successful family man. He is "… thirty-five, married, has one or two children. He lives in a respectable neighborhood and is probably buying his own home. He drives a low- or medium-priced car and his yearly income is in the top forty percent of the nation's personal income distribution" (Jaspan and Black 1960, 24–25). The female embezzler also fits the picture of a respectable American, though her income was found to be in the bottom third of the nation's income distribution—a reflection of sex discrimination in jobs and salaries more than anything else.

In a classic study, Donald Cressey (1953) describes interviews with 133 embezzlers in penitentiaries in Illinois, Indiana, and California. His findings regarding the "etiology" of embezzlement—the factors leading up to it—show that embezzlers typically committed offenses after (1) coming up against a "nonshareable" financial problem; (2) recognizing that they could secretly resolve the problem by taking advantage of their positions of financial trust; and (3) engaging in rationalizations and justifications to protect their self-image as a trustworthy employee or partner.

By a nonshareable problem, Cressey means almost any kind of financial difficulty the individual feels cannot be resolved by enlisting the help of another. It could be some unusual family expense or gambling debts, once thought to be the major cause of embezzlement. It could even be linked to attempts to keep up a particular standard of living. Rationalization occurs before or during the act of embezzling. Many of Cressey's subjects, and especially those who had been independent business-people, reasoned that they would be merely "borrowing" the money or that it really belonged to them anyway. The embezzlers-to-be often argued that they were merely adhering to a standard business practice, borrowing against future earnings. Looked at sequentially, then, a nonshareable problem leads to the search for a personal and secret solution; a position of financial trust provides the means to solve the problem; and rationalization provides the excuse.

One study could not substantiate Cressey's emphasis on the nonshareable financial problem as an impetus to embezzlement. Embezzlers were apparently driven to their crimes by temptation and avarice, and their jobs provided the opportunity and the means (Nettler 1974). A study of female embezzlers also challenges Cressey's explanation (Zeitz 1981). In this research, subjects were more likely to justify their crimes in terms of family needs than in terms of a nonshareable problem.

Another point being made by some criminologists is that embezzlement is more likely to be trivial and persistent than a carefully thought-out, last-ditch solution to a pressing financial problem (Gottfredson and Hirschi 1990; Croall 1989). This view receives some support from private security experts, who recommend that the best way to find embezzlers is to give employees a vacation that requires someone else to take over their duties: Embezzlers will resist the offer for fear their schemes will be uncovered in their absence. A recent case came to light at our university precisely because the clerk involved had not taken a vacation for over a year and thus drew the suspicions of her supervisor. She had been taking relatively small amounts of money over the course of three or four years, though in the aggregate her embezzlement reached hundreds of thousands of dollars. In any event, the explanation of embezzlement is not yet a matter of consensus.

Fiddling at Work: Part of the Hidden Economy

Operating within the legitimate world of work is a hidden economy in which goods and services are produced, stolen, or exchanged on the sly. There is no official record of this "fiddling," and the income obtained from it is rarely, if ever, taxed. Much of the activity is itself criminal, though rarely thought of as such by the participants or the general public. This quote illustrates the range of activities that make up the hidden economy:

> A number of specific fiddles make up hidden property crime. These include … taking company stock home to doing jobs "on the side."… Personal use of the firm's telephone, photocopying, or mailing service accounts for a certain amount of the kind of fiddling which may be claimed as perks, and over-estimates of petrol [gasoline], food and travel allowances that appear as inflated expense accounts might also be seen in this light. In addition, there are a number of other … fiddles … such as short-changing, overloading, overestimating, under-the-counter selling, buying off-the-back-of-a-lorry [truck] goods, fiddling time, dodging fares, and smuggling duty-free goods. Nor should we neglect the numerous tax and social security fiddles involving undeclared income, falsely claimed allowances and misrepresented welfare benefits and rebate claims: nor corporate fiddles, such as computer fraud and industrial bribery. (Henry 1978, 4–5)

Collectively, these fiddles cost billions of dollars. In the United States, theft by retail employees is estimated by employers to account for almost 43 percent of their inventory shrinkage (National Retail Security Survey 1999). Surveys of top management representing large and small firms across the United States show that no single generalization adequately describes the considerable differences in the nature and seriousness of employee crime across companies. However, executives are more likely to think that petty thefts, small frauds, and abuse of services are a more serious problem than large-scale thefts and frauds, violence, or sabotage (Baker and Westin 1987).

This section focuses on pilferage on the job. There are many forms: Sometimes it is casual, sometimes systematic and repetitive; sometimes workers pilfer alone, at other times in more or less organized groups; and sometimes the pilferage victimizes the employer, sometimes the customer or

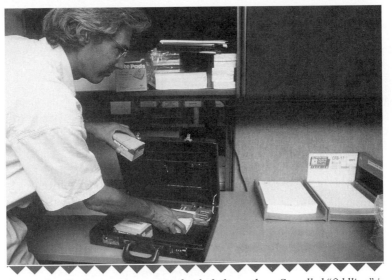

Some jobs offer better opportunities for theft than others. So-called "fiddling" is estimated to cost businesses billions of dollars each year.

client, and sometimes other workers. However, cash is rarely stolen directly, and the income obtained through fiddling at work is generally considered secondary to that obtained legitimately (Henry 1978).

Certain jobs are associated with certain kinds of pilfering and pilferers. Mars (1983) identifies four types of work situations depending on the extent to which jobs constrain and insulate workers or foster reciprocity and competition among them and the extent to which they give workers group support and control. Job pilferers are categorized as "hawks," "donkeys," "wolves," or "vultures."

1. *Hawks*: Hawks are found in jobs that stress individuality, competition, autonomy, and creativity. The jobs provide only weak group support because workers largely control their own activities. Independent salespersons, successful journalists, small-business people, academics, and other professionals are likely to be hawks, but so too are waiters and owner-operator cabdrivers. Hawk fiddles usually involve the manipulation of time and work performance, and the scale of the fiddle increases with the status of the fiddler. Mars shows how accountants, lawyers, physicians, management consultants, and even university instructors are able to capitalize on their status and freedom from

group control. Favorite fiddles of hawks are padding expense accounts and charging for work not actually performed. Professors have multiple opportunities to engage in hawkish fiddles, and as Box 6.1 (on page 124) shows, it appears as though quite a few criminologists do engage in minor forms of occupational fraud and fiddling.

2. *Donkeys*: Donkeys are in jobs characterized by isolation and relatively rigid constraints. Assembly line workers, supermarket cashiers, and retail sales people are good examples. "The donkey type of fiddle is an appropriate response to this minimal autonomy. Since the job isolates the worker, the worker fiddles in isolation" (Mars 1983, 71). New workers may learn of fiddling among their fellows, but there is no group support for it, nor is it practiced as a group activity. Bar stewards who give short-measured drinks and pocket the difference between what each bottle would have brought in and actually does bring in, and cashiers who fiddle change or pocket money after ringing "no sale" on the till are examples of donkey fiddlers. Mars observes that donkey fiddles are often not motivated by material gain but, rather, by the worker's greater measure of personal control. In addition, the absence of group controls may give rise to excessive fiddling, as when a short-order waiter skimmed

BOX 6.1   THEFT AND FRAUD BY CRIMINOLOGISTS

A recent study of a nationally representative sample of criminologists shows that fiddling and fraud exist among the ranks of those who study crime for a living. In *Criminologists: Are We What We Study?* Matthew Robinson and Barbara Zaitow (1999) present data based on a sample of 1,500 (N=522) criminologists. Results of the study show the following:

- 84 percent of the respondents reported that they had used departmental office supplies (pens, paper, copying, etc.) for personal rather than professional use; 11 percent admitted to using grant money for personal use.
- 20 percent falsified travel receipts for reimbursement for things like conference attendance and participation.
- 18 percent admitted they had misrepresented their income to obtain a reduced membership fee in a professional organization. (Membership fees are often graduated).

Respondents were also asked to report on their nonoccupationally related involvement in crime. A few of the findings: 22 percent admitted they had at least once engaged in burglary and 66 percent had at least once in their life driven a vehicle under the influence of alcohol.

Are criminologists, then, essentially "the pot calling the kettle black"? While the authors are cautious about concluding anything about the prevalence of fraud and theft by criminologists compared to other groups, they did indeed establish that some criminologists do engage in the very behaviors they study.

$150 a day for a year before being found out (Mars 1983, 87).

3. *Wolves*: Wolf fiddlers operate in packs and are found in jobs in which the work is organized into crews: longshoremen, miners, prison guards, and garbage collectors are found in "wolfpack" jobs. The group comes to exercise a lot of control over the individual, and pilferage is organized and controlled by the group. Individualists are not welcome, and membership in the wolfpack is not automatic, but comes through acceptance by other members. Members are held together by mutual dependence and trust, with much testing of the latter.

Dock pilferage by longshoremen in Newfoundland is typical of the wolfpack. Longshore work gangs are close-knit, with controlled membership and a ranking system based on skill and trust that effectively controls any particular member's access to cargo by allocating work responsibilities. Only through access to cargo can a dockworker pilfer, and so jobs with such access are essential. On the other hand, the nature of dockwork makes it important to have group support in order to pull off a fiddle. Since individual workers rarely have both access and support, dock pilferage remains group centered.

4. *Vultures*: Vultures hold jobs that offer autonomy and freedom but are subject to overarching bureaucratic control that encourages group influence. Vulture jobs are selling jobs, postal delivery, truck driving and other traveling jobs, taxi driving, and many service jobs. Fiddling tends to be exercised individually, but mutual self-interest keeps employees tied in a bond of sometimes uneasy cooperation. The relative instability of vulture occupations means that under the surface of cooperation there is competition, and when a particular fiddle threatens others' jobs, they close ranks against the offender.

One of us (Barlow) experienced a vulture fiddle. During a college vacation he was a delivery driver for Harrods department store in London, England. On the first day of work he learned from a co-driver that two breakfasts, a two-hour lunch period, and an hour-long afternoon tea break on top of seven hours of delivering always produced a healthy overtime check. He also learned that his co-driver expected him to conform to this schedule and that if he did not, it would not look good for the other drivers who were doing the same thing. The company supposedly knew about the time fiddle and so long as it did not become unreasonable, store management accepted it, he was told, in return for the drivers' staying nonunion. The other author of this text experienced vulture fiddles in a variety of jobs he took in college.

Obviously, employee theft is not a unitary phenomenon, occurring as it does in a great variety of contexts and involving different organizational characteristics, different levels of sophistication, and varying degrees of group support. On the other hand, some authors have argued that an underlying motive or drive behind much employee theft is worker perception of injustice in the workplace. Marginal, temporary, and socially isolated workers are at greatest risk of committing theft since stealing provides a means of obtaining justice for their grievances (Tucker 1989).

Tests of these hypotheses show inconsistent results. Interviews with retired garment workers found that employee theft was rarely selected because workers had grievances involving equity (Sieh 1987). Rather, theft was explained in terms of work group influence and institutional supports promoted by the Garment Workers Union. The idea that crime is driven by adversity (perceived or real) is an old one, and it has been the focus of considerable theory and research (see Chapter 11). Reasonable as the argument seems (most people would accept that angry and frustrated people often lash out at the perceived cause of their problems), as a general explanation of workplace theft, this view has a difficult time accounting for the fact that employee theft seems to be a universal phenomenon found in all types of organizations, including those where there is no evidence of low employee morale, job dissatisfaction, or perceived injustices.

POLITICAL WHITE-COLLAR CRIME

Political white-collar crimes are those violations of law by individuals in a position of governmental trust *for their own personal gain*. Political crimes committed for organizational gain are discussed later. Political white-collar crime manifests itself in two different, though often related, forms: (1) activities designed to bring about economic gain and (2) activities designed to perpetuate or increase political power (Friedrichs 1996). Government officials who accept or demand kickbacks in return for a vote for legislation favorable to some individual or special group are engaged in corrupt activities that promise economic gains. Politicians who arrange to have cronies stuff ballot boxes with the names of nonexistent voters are engaged in corrupt practices designed to keep them in office or to put them there. Needless to say, those who gain economically from corrupt activities may also gain political power, and those who gain political power may also gain financially. Thus it is sometimes difficult to separate the economic from the power dimension of political corruption.

Finding out about political corruption is not easy, and this is as true for the criminologist as it is for the general public. One reason is the insider-outsider barrier that politicians erect in their dealings with others who are not part of the political establishment. Another is the cronyism characterizing relations among politicians and their friends in business and government. This encourages a "politics is politics" attitude among insiders, who would rather look the other way than make public trouble for a colleague. During the entire history of the U.S. Congress, only seven senators and nineteen representatives have been censured by their colleagues, although others have resigned before they could be censured.

A third reason for the difficulty of learning about political corruption is that the agencies responsible for policing the politicians are themselves run by politicians. If an investigation of a particular official or agency is called for, it will usually be pursued without fanfare and rarely will result in the pressing of formal charges. Even when an investigation is reliably known to be underway, heads of the responsible agencies will often deny it. Fourth, there are no official statistics on the kinds of occupational crime committed by those in politics and government. One looks in vain for "official misconduct," "high crimes and misdemeanors," "bribery," "influence peddling," and so forth, in the annual Uniform Crime Reports. In fact, the only specifically occupational crime listed at all is embezzlement, which victimizes the establishment.

Political corruption is publicized primarily through the efforts of journalists and those who keep watch on the government in the public interest (e.g., Ralph Nader and Common Cause). Chicago has borne the brunt of media scrutiny for years, which has not blunted its reputation as the most politically corrupt city in America. From 1985 to 1988, federal grand juries indicted 265 public officials and government employees for corruption (*St. Louis Post-Dispatch*, 16 October 1988). Often, corruption comes to light because persons involved in it turn informer and approach the media or federal authorities. Someone who has been indicted may also "snitch" on others as part of a plea bargain.

Crimes for Money

Political crimes that come to light are usually notable because they have been committed by high officials, have involved substantial losses to the taxpayer, or have represented a systematic and extensive violation of public trust or civil rights. During the past few years, political corruption at the national and international levels has so dominated the headlines that local scandals seem mild by comparison. Actually, the victimization brought about by local corruption may have a more far-reaching and harmful effect on the lives of Americans. When, as happened recently in a mid-sized Illinois city, school board officials misappropriate thousands of dollars in school funds, it may take years to overcome the damage to local education, not to mention public trust.

In the course of their political careers, government officials sometimes find their past catching up with them after they have moved to national prominence. Such was the case with former Vice President Spiro Agnew, and former Labor Secretary Raymond Donovan. It was revealed in Agnew's case that while governor of Maryland, and earlier while a county official, he had received kickbacks from contractors doing business with the county and state governments. Upon these disclosures,

Agnew resigned the vice presidency and subsequently pleaded "no contest" to an income tax violation charge ("no contest" is not a plea of guilty but the defendant is still convicted). In Donovan's case, grand jury indictments charged him with fraud and grand larceny while he was in the construction business. Another case involved Judge Otto Kerner, formerly the governor of Illinois. Kerner was tied to an Illinois scandal involving offers of racetrack stock to politicians. Subsequently he was convicted of numerous criminal offenses, including perjury, and became the first federal judge ever to spend time in prison. Former Congressman from Illinois Dan Rostenkowski served prison time for illegally siphoning funds to support his personal lifestyle and political aspirations. These cases, in which bribery and kickbacks were prominent, clearly involve corruption for economic gain.

Another, more recent, example comes from Louisiana, where former Governor Edwin Edwards was convicted of seventeen counts of racketeering, extortion, and fraud in connection with riverboat gambling licenses (CNN.com, 9 May 2000). Edwards had been the target of federal investigations for decades, but this was his first conviction. His son and other prominent Louisiana politicians and businessmen were also convicted in this case. Government prosecutors claimed that Edwards and his fellow conspirators extorted more than $3 million from casino license applicants.

Political white-collar crime is encouraged by the tight links between politics and business. In addition to the fact that business provides financial support for political campaigns and governments disperse billions of dollars worth of contracts to industry, many government officials retain a financial interest in their business pursuits while in office. Members of Congress remain active in businesses ranging from real estate and insurance to construction, law, oil, and gas. Temptations to abuse their political connections abound, particularly when proposed laws or government contracts influence their personal finances and those of business colleagues.

ABSCAM   A major scandal involving several U.S. congressmen was uncovered in the 1980s. In the undercover FBI operation known as ABSCAM, one of its operatives posed as a wealthy Arab businessman seeking to obtain residency permits. Contacts were set up between the "Arab" and various congressmen to whom large sums of money were offered in exchange for help. The FBI video-taped the meetings, and when the prosecutions eventually took place, the public saw films of elected representatives gleefully filling their pockets and briefcases with money.

Although all the offenders were initially convicted, some later filed successful appeals, which were heralded by many in Washington as the fitting end to an affair in which the FBI, not members of Congress, was the culprit. Accusations of entrapment and violation of privacy flowed from all sides, and if anyone emerged tarnished by the episode it was the FBI and the Department of Justice. Indignation like that directed at ABSCAM is noticeably lacking when similar police practices are directed at drug traffickers.

Crimes for Power

Corruption for the purposes of acquiring, retaining, or increasing one's political power also occurs at all levels of government. Violations of fundraising laws, ballot box stuffing, nepotism, and exchanging favors for votes are some examples. As this is being written, Congress has called for an investigation of possible improprieties in former Vice President Al Gore's fundraising activities.

The most famous example of political crimes for power at the national level is the 1972 Watergate scandal. Brought to light after a bungled burglary attempt at the Democratic National Committee headquarters in the Watergate hotel and apartment complex in Washington, D.C., the affair resulted in the first resignation of a U.S. president and touched people in all areas of national politics. Due in part to vigorous investigative journalism by *Washington Post* reporters Carl Bernstein and Bob Woodward, the American public was given a two-year, in-depth look at political corruption at its worst. Not only had the White House been deeply involved in the scandals, but also included were a former secretary of the treasury, the attorney general of the United States, officials of the FBI, CIA, and Internal Revenue Service, persons connected with organized crime, international terrorists, and even some street criminals.

The central theme around which the Watergate affair revolved was clearly one of political power. The involvement of the Committee to Re-Elect the President, the activities of White House staffers, and the routine subversive manipulation of government agencies by Richard Nixon and his allies bear this out. Here was an incident, or rather a combination of incidents, in which maintaining and extending power stood as the central goal. Nixon's supporters and staffers committed various illegal actions: They used the U.S. Postal Service for fraudulent and libelous purposes, an aspect of the "dirty tricks" used to discredit Democratic opponents; the Watergate break-in itself was for the purpose of "bugging" the Democratic National Committee headquarters and scrutinizing its files; they pressured the IRS to harass political opponents and Nixon's alleged enemies; they encouraged the FBI and CIA to obstruct justice so that these and other criminal activities would not come to light and, if they were revealed, would not be linked with the White House; they paid "hush money" to the Watergate burglars; and they misused public funds and solicited campaign contributions in violation of federal laws.

In the summer of 1974 the House of Representatives' Judiciary Committee voted to impeach President Nixon. He was charged with obstruction of justice and failure to carry out his constitutional oath and duty to uphold the laws of the United States. He resigned on August 9, 1974. Much still remains unknown about political corruption in Richard Nixon's administration. Nixon is dead, making it unlikely that the true nature of his offenses will ever come to light. One is certainly left wondering whether anything would have come to light had it not been for the ill-fated break-in at the Watergate and the tenacity of two young reporters in search of news.

ORGANIZATIONAL CRIME I: CORPORATE CRIME

Organizational crimes arise in connection with business and governmental pursuits that are not the central purpose of the business or government. They are committed on behalf of business or state interests, sometimes by individuals, sometimes by groups; they surface among the self-employed and among executives of companies large and small. The discussion here will concentrate first on **corporate theft and fraud**, which are activities that violate laws governing commerce and trade. We will then address **corporate violence**, crimes that result in physical and social injury, pain, or death.

Corporate Theft and Fraud

This section explores a number of examples of corporate crimes involving theft or fraud. As noted earlier, this type of crime is arguably more extensive, and certainly more costly, than street crimes committed by individuals seeking personal gain.

RESTRAINT OF TRADE   The first relevant federal statute relating to trade was the Sherman Antitrust Act of 1890. Designed to curb the threat to a competitive, free enterprise economy posed by the nineteenth-century spread of trusts and monopolies, this act made it a criminal misdemeanor for individuals or organizations to engage in restraint of trade by combining or forming monopolies to that end. In 1974, Congress made restraint of trade a felony, thus making it possible for convicted offenders to receive prison terms of a year or more. Antitrust violations contribute to the persistence of a "closed enterprise system," the very antithesis of what American business is supposed to be.

There are three principal methods of restraint of trade: (1) consolidation so as to obtain a monopoly position, (2) price-fixing to achieve price uniformity, and (3) price discrimination, in which higher prices are charged to some customers and lower prices to others. From the standpoint of those engaging in these practices, they make sense: The less the competition and the greater the control over prices, the larger the profits. But small and independent businesses will lose business, and the public at large will face higher prices and lose its discretionary buying power.

The most common violations of restraint-of-trade laws are price-fixing and price discrimination. **Price-fixing** is an example of "horizontal" restraint of trade because it involves people or organizations at the same level in the chain of distribution (i.e., manufacturing, wholesaling, or retailing). Examples of price-fixing include any agreement or understanding among competitors to raise, lower, or stabilize prices. **Price discrimination** represents "vertical" restraint in that it involves conspiracies across different levels, for example, between manufacturers and retailers.

Sutherland (1949) describes a case involving Sears, Roebuck and Goodyear Tire Company: Goodyear charged Sears a lower price than its own independent Goodyear dealers for identical tires, allowing Sears to charge a lower retail price to the disadvantage of the Goodyear independents.

In his investigation of seventy of the largest American corporations over a fifty-year period, Sutherland found that many of the suits charging restraint of trade through price-fixing or price discrimination were brought by private interests rather than by the Federal Trade Commission or the Department of Justice, the two agencies given primary responsibility for enforcing restraint-of-trade provisions. When corporate officers break the law on behalf of their organizations, criminal justice officials do not seem particularly aggressive in ferreting out violations and bringing charges. But this should hardly come as a surprise, given the close relationship between business and politics. Indeed, in Europe and the Far East, governments have historically encouraged cartels, whose price-fixing activities are legendary.

PRICE-FIXING CONSPIRACIES   In 1961, twenty-one corporations and forty-five high-ranking executives in the heavy electrical equipment industry were successfully prosecuted for criminal violations of the Sherman Antitrust Act. They had been involved in a price-fixing and bid-rigging scheme that, over nearly a decade, had bilked local, state, and federal governments (and taxpayers) out of millions of dollars on purchases averaging nearly $2 billion a year.

In carrying out their scheme—called by the trial judge "the most serious violations of the antitrust laws since the time of their passage at the turn of the century"—executives of the conspiring companies would meet secretly under fictitious names in hotel rooms around the country. Referring to those in attendance as "the Christmas card list" and to the meetings as "choir practice," the conspirators arranged prices for equipment, allocated markets and territories, and agreed on which companies would supply the low bids on pending government contracts. The participants covered their tracks well and were discovered only because officials of the Tennessee Valley Authority had received identical sealed bids on highly technical equipment. The companies involved in the conspiracy ranged from such giants in the electrical equipment business as General Electric, Westinghouse, and Allis-Chalmers, to such smaller firms as the Carrier Corporation, the I.T.E. Circuit Breaker Company, and Federal Pacific (for more on this famous price-fixing conspiracy, see Ermann and Lundman 1982, 86–95).

This price-fixing conspiracy illustrates extensive collusion among corporations who have found a way to prosper without having to compete. Needless to say, cooperation is preferred when the benefits outweigh the risks of competition. Equally important, the cooperators usually gain over those who refuse to or simply cannot participate in the collusion. This advantage is precisely what restraint-of-trade laws are designed to curb, for its consequence is obvious: Fewer firms stay in business, and the prices of goods and services rise when the survivors exercise their monopoly power, keeping new competitors away and setting artificially high prices—in effect stealing from their customers. The cost of those higher prices can be staggering. In the heavy electrical equipment conspiracy, the cost approached $3 billion, "more money than was stolen in all the country's robberies, burglaries, and larcenies during the years in which the price fixing occurred" (Geis 1978c, 281). There are countless illustrations of price-fixing, although rarely will those accused of it admit the practice. Cullen, Maakestad, and Cavender (1987, 60) have argued that "conspiracy to set prices has become a way of life in some industries."

THE SAVINGS AND LOAN FAILURES   When savings and loan companies began to fail around the country in the late 1980s, alarm bells sounded in homes and businesses everywhere and in Washington, D.C. Long thought to be among America's most stable and trustworthy institutions, the local savings and loan suddenly looked weak and vulnerable. Since the government insures savings up to $100,000 in individual accounts, small investors were not hurt; however the private aggregate cost to taxpayers is estimated at over $500 billion. Mismanagement and mistakes in operating a business are not necessarily indications of criminal activity. Many believe that the S&L collapse was a product of systemic changes resulting from the deregulatory frenzy of the Reagan years (but see Ayres and Braithwaite 1992), and the rise of the junk bond

market. Deregulators took the position that "the free enterprise system works best if left alone" (Calavita and Pontell 1990, 312). The opportunities and incentives for S&Ls to embark on risky ventures were simply too compelling, given the freeing of controls and the prospects of huge short-run profits. A sort of "casino" economy emerged in which speculation and deregulation created expanded opportunities for fraud and embezzlement (Calavita and Pontell 1991). "Participants in this epidemic of fraud included both those who deliberately entered the thrift industry in order to loot it and legitimate thrift operators who found themselves on the 'slippery slope' of insolvency, unlawful risk taking, and cover-up" (Pontell and Calavita 1993, 240).

As details surrounding the collapse of Lincoln Savings and Loan—the largest thrift failure in U.S. history—emerged, it became clear that deceit, conspiracy, political corruption, and all manner of financial irregularities were involved. A sort of "collective embezzlement" occurred, in which S&L executives siphoned off funds for personal gain, at the expense of the institution, "but with implicit or explicit sanction of its management" (Calavita and Pontell 1990, 321). On December 4, 1991, a Los Angeles jury convicted S&L owner Charles H. Keating Jr. on seventeen counts of securities fraud. On April 10, 1992, he was sentenced to ten years in prison and fined $250,000; how does one measure this punishment against the estimated $2.6 billion the collapse of Lincoln is estimated to have cost American taxpayers?

FRAUDS IN ADVERTISING, SALES, AND REPAIRS   Consumers become the victims of corporate fraud in many different ways, including misrepresentation in advertising and sales. Misrepresentation in advertising means that what prospective buyers are told about a product is untrue, deceptive, or misleading. Sometimes the misrepresentation concerns the quantity of a product or the actual contents of a package or container; sometimes it concerns the effectiveness of a product; and sometimes it involves lack of or insufficient information about a product or service such that buyers are misled. An illustrative case involved Chrysler Corporation. In 1987 the company admitted selling cars that had been driven by executives as "new" cars. Another example is an ad campaign by Ralston Purina, the makers of

Puppy Chow, in which the company seemed to be claiming that its product cured cancer (*St. Louis Post-Dispatch*, 27 November 1991, B1).

The fact that a fine line divides fraudulent from legitimate sales promotion becomes evident as one considers a problem faced by nearly all businesses: creating a need for their products and services. Many of the things considered necessities today—canned foods, refrigerators, automobiles, insurance policies—either did not exist a few decades ago or were thought of as luxuries, certainly not necessities. They have come to be thought of as necessities largely because the companies selling them have convinced the public to do so. When things are necessities, people "need" to purchase them.

In their efforts to convince people of a need for goods and services, businesses use a variety of different ploys. *Fraudulent ploy* is to make false claims as to the effectiveness of a product in doing what it is supposed to do. Those who believe the claims will see a need for the product. An example is the advertising plan followed some time ago by the makers of Listerine. In their campaign, the makers sought to create a need for Listerine as a mouthwash, a fairly new idea at the time; to establish that need, they presented fake claims as to the germ-killing powers of the mixture.

It is only a short step from these strategies to those the common swindler uses. Consider the activities of the Holland Furnace Company. This company was in the business of selling home heating furnaces. With some 500 offices and a sales force in the thousands, the company put its resources to work on a fraudulent sales promotion involving misrepresentation, destruction of property, and, in some cases, what amounted to extortion:

> Salesmen, misrepresenting themselves as "furnace engineers" and "safety inspectors," gained entry into their victims' homes, dismantled their furnaces, and condemned them as hazardous. They then refused to reassemble them, on the ground that they did not want to be "accessories to murder." Using scare tactics, claiming that the furnaces they "inspected" were emitting carbon monoxide and other dangerous gases, they created, in the homeowners' minds, a need for a new furnace—and proceeded to sell their own product at a handsome profit. They were so ruthless that they sold one elderly woman nine new furnaces in six years for a total of $18,000. The FTC finally forced the company to close in 1965, but in the meantime, it had done some $30 million worth of business per year for many years. (Leiser 1973, 270)

Consumer fraud figures prominently in a list of the "Top 100 Corporate Criminals of the 1990s" (see Box 6.2). Twenty of the cases were instances of fraud in the electronics, medical, and financial service industries. Consider, for example, the recent legal problems experienced by State Farm Insurance Company.

A $238 million dollar lawsuit accused State Farm of several fraudulent practices involving the sale of whole life and universal life policies from January 1982 to December 1997. This lawsuit, which State Farm settled without admitting wrongdoing, claimed that policyholders were told to switch policies so they could receive greater benefits. In reality, these greater benefits were for the company, not the customer. Customers were also intentionally deceived about the rate of return on their policies and were given unreasonable predictions about the possible dividend (Associated Press 1999). At about the same time, State Farm was found guilty of fraud in the use of generic replacement parts in auto body repairs. Auto body shops generally need the permission of insurance companies when installing replacement parts. State Farm mostly approved the use of generic replacements parts, not the more reliable original-equipment parts from car manufacturers. While State Farm acknowledges that it did recommended and approve the use of aftermarket parts rather than the "true" replacements, it claimed the practice was not illegal. The judge did not agree and slapped a $1.2 billion fine on the insurance company. This is believed to be the largest cash settlement against an insurance company. The case is under appeal (*Kansas City Star* 1999).

THE BCCI CASE The Bank of Credit and Commerce International (BCCI) was established in 1972 by Pakistani financier Agha Hassan Abedi. BCCI became the first multinational bank originating out of the Third World. Headquartered until recently in London, regulated (in a very loose way) by Luxembourg, and backed by Middle East oil revenues, BCCI had by 1990 over $20 billion in assets in 75 countries with more than 400 branches and subsidiaries (*Newsweek*, 22 July 1991, 37; *Time*, 29 July 1991, 42). It gained a reputation for

Box 6.2   The Top Corporate Criminals of the 1990s

Russell Mokhiber (1999), editor of the journal the *Corporate Crime Reporter*, has recently published a list of the top 100 corporate criminals of the 1990s. Here are the top ten from that list:

1. F. Hoffmann-La Roche, Ltd., was fined $500 million in an antitrust case for conspiring to fix prices of several different types of vitamins. (*Corporate Crime Reporter* 21, no. 1 [May 24, 1999].)

2. Daiwa Bank, Ltd., was fined $340 million for fraud relating to the cover-up of massive securities trading losses and defrauding bank regulators. (*Corporate Crime Reporter* 9, no. 3 [March 4, 1996].)

3. BASF Aktiengesellschaft, a German company, was fined $225 million in an antitrust case in which the bank conspired to raise and fix the prices of several types of vitamins. (*Corporate Crime Reporter* 21, no. 1 [May 24, 1994].)

4. SGL Carbon Aktiengesellschaft was fined $135 million in an antitrust case stemming from attempts to fix the prices of graphite electrodes. (*Corporate Crime Reporter* 19, no. 4 [May 10, 1999].)

5. Exxon Corporation and Exxon Shipping companies were fined $125 million for the violation of environmental laws that resulted from the grounding of the *Exxon Valdez*. (*Corporate Crime Reporter* 11, no. 3 [March 18, 1991].)

6. UCAR International, Inc., was fined $110 million for antitrust activities associated with attempting to fix the prices of graphite electrodes.

7. Archer Daniels Midland was fined $100 million for antitrust conspiracies to fix prices in the lysine and citric acid markets. (*Corporate Crime Reporter* 40, no. 1 [October 21, 1996].)

8. Banker's Trust was fined $60 million for financial crimes committed by falsely recording several millions of dollars as income and reserves that were in truth unclaimed customer funds. (*Corporate Crime Reporter* 11, no. 1 [March 15, 1999].)

9. Sears Bankruptcy Recovery Management Services were fined $60 million for fraud relating to reaffirmation practices which led bankrupting Sears customers to believe they still owed the company money from previous credit card charges. (*Corporate Crime Reporter* 7, no. 1 [February 15, 1999].)

10. Haarman & Reimer Corp. was fined $50 million for antitrust activities relating to the fixing of prices in the citric acid market. (*Corporate Crime Reporter* 5, no. 4 [February 3, 1997].)

More information on these and other corporate crimes can be found in the above-cited editions of the *Corporate Crime Reporter* and on the Web page <http://www.corporatepredators.org/top100.html>.

Source: Used with the permission of Russell Mokhiber and the *Corporate Crime Reporter*.

offering first-rate service to its large depositors, and for asking no questions. BCCI also knew exactly where to go in the political hierarchy of Western nations to get counsel and representation for its expansion—for example, to Clark Clifford, who "sat atop three branches of the capital's permanent government—law, money, and politics" (*Wall Street Journal*, 14 June 1991, 4). Clifford, a man of formerly unquestioned respect and integrity, became chairman of First American Bankshares following its purchase by Saudi investors in 1981 with money loaned by BCCI. The investors eventually defaulted and BCCI (secretly, according to Clifford in Congressional testimony) became the owner of First American.

In sixteen years of expansion, BCCI was not the legitimate banking operation it appeared to be. And there is evidence that officials in many countries, including the United States, England, Peru, and Argentina, knew it. They knew that BCCI was heavily involved in shady activities, and far from doing anything about it, found their own illegal uses for the bank.

Drug trafficking was arguably BCCI's downfall. Indicted by a federal grand jury in 1988 for laundering millions of dollars in drug money, BCCI eventually pleaded guilty and was fined $14 billion in 1990 (*Time*, 22 July 1991, 46). Subsequent investigations produced an incredible array of charges: gunrunning, bribery and corruption, smuggling, terrorism, securities theft, property theft of all sorts, influence peddling, insurance fraud, covert operations for the CIA, bank fraud, espionage, extortion, kidnapping, and the violation of other domestic and international laws. The bank was closed down in July 1991, its assets frozen. In January 1992, BCCI pled guilty to racketeering; Clifford was indicted seven months later, along with his law partner, and many more indictments and convictions will surely follow.

Electronic technology has made international money transfers simple to commit and a nightmare for police:

> Bank-to-bank transfers of illegal funds can ... be accomplished easily with the complicity of bank officials. The bank transfers by wire between its own (rather than a customer's) account and accounts in correspondent banks, making the laundering of personal funds appear as legitimate bank business. Without other leads, bank-to-bank transfers of illegally obtained funds are almost impossible to distinguish from normal banking transactions. Furthermore, the sheer volume of all wire transfers made and the speed with which they are accomplished, make it extremely difficult to trace these funds or document their illegal nature. (Webster and McCampbell 1992, 5)

Corporate Violence

While many corporate crimes result in economic harms, a sizeable amount of corporate crimes are violent. It is clearly a myth that white-collar crimes can be correctly called "economic crimes." Here we review several instances of violent corporate crimes committed as a part of a company's pursuit of profit, a major cause of most forms of corporate crime.

VIOLENCE AGAINST CONSUMERS   Most of us rely on corporations to provide us with the commodities we use in our daily lives. We assume these products will not expose us to unreasonable threats to our life and safety. Unfortunately, this assumption can be in serious error, as we shall see in the following illustrations.

Ford Motor Company's *Pinto* was designed in the late 1960s to compete in the "small car for a small price market," which at the time was controlled by Volkswagen. Ford president Lee Iacocca and other executives directed the Pinto to be produced quickly, weigh under 2,000 pounds, and cost less than $2,000 dollars. While the Pinto was being tested prior to its release into the marketplace, a major problem in the fuel system was discovered. When rear-ended, the Pinto's gas tank often ruptured. The problem could be fixed by placing a rubber bladder or flak within and/or around the tank or by locating the tank in a safer area. Ford executives rejected these avenues because the assembly line was already tooled for production, and it would cost the company several millions of dollars to redesign and produce a safer car. As a direct result of the deadly design of the Pinto, dozens of drivers and passengers of the vehicle were killed or seriously burned in rear-end collisions over the next several years (Cullen, Maakestad, and Cavender 1987).

In the course of several successful civil suits against Ford and one unsuccessful criminal prosecution, it came to light that the company had made a conscious decision to risk the lives of consumers in order to make a profit. Ford calculated that a burn death would result in an average $200,000 loss and any injury less than death would cost them $67,000. Ford officials also calculated that the cost of fixing the problem with the Pinto's fuel tank placement would be a paltry $11 per vehicle. But with 11 million cars to fix, paying the estimated $49.5 million dollars it would cost in lawsuits for deaths and injuries would be a better business deal for the corporation. Ford was eventually forced to recall the Pinto after several successful product liability lawsuits (Mokhiber 1988). No one was ever sentenced to prison for the deaths.

Two widely publicized cases of corporate violence against consumers are also crimes against women and children (Fox and Szockyj 1996; Rynbrandt and Kramer 1995). First, the Dalkon Shield, an intrauterine birth control device, was marketed and sold by the A. H. Robins Company in the 1960s. The device was popular in part because it supposedly did not have negative side effects like the "pill." It was also marketed as an extremely effective way of blocking pregnancy (Mokhiber 1988). But because the shield was poorly designed (and poorly tested), it often caused severe pelvic infections, sterility, poor pregnancy protection, and the spontaneous abortions of fetuses. Twelve women also died from using this device. The Robins company, which knew of many of the problems with the Shield but did nothing to protect consumers, has escaped criminal charges but has paid nearly $1 billion in lawsuits (Mokhiber 1988).

Another corporate crime against women and children involved the sale and distribution of the drug *thalidomide*. Many women were given prescriptions for thalidomide as a tranquilizer and to combat morning sickness while pregnant. The producer of the drug, the German company Chemie Grunenthal, had information that the drug could cause major health problems, including severe disturbances to the nervous system. This information was ignored and then downplayed by Grunenthal for years, but the company was finally forced to come clean after overwhelming evidence of the drug's horrible side effects on fetuses. At least 8,000 children, the "thalidomide babies," were born with deformed genitals, eyes, and ears, brain damage, and shortened limbs. While Grunenthal escaped criminal fines, Distillers Ltd., a company later distributing thalidomide under the name of Distaval in Britain, was forced to pay millions of dollars to British and German victims of this drug (Mokhiber 1988).

VIOLENCE AGAINST WORKERS According to the Occupational Safety and Health Administration (OSHA 2000), there were 5.9 million work-related injuries and illnesses in 1999. OSHA also estimates that 6,026 workers died on the job that year. However, these statistics are conservative estimates of the risks involved in work. There is strong evidence to show that up to 100,000 workers in the United States lose their lives each year in the context of work (Friedrichs 1996). Many illnesses and injuries

are simply not reported to the authorities, whether that authority is the company, OSHA, or the U.S. Department of Labor. Some workers also know that whistle blowing to agencies like OSHA could cost them their jobs (OSHA 2000).

A study of mining disasters in five countries concluded that most of them were related to violations of workplace safety laws (Braithwaite 1985). Some of the violations were a cause of the disasters and others made the disasters worse than they should have been. Workers are not the only ones at risk in the mining industry. In 1972 in Buffalo Creek, West Virginia, an entire community was virtually destroyed by a dam break (Erikson 1976).

During the twentieth century, at least 100,000 U.S. miners were killed and 1.5 million injured. (Mokhiber 1988). Black lung disease, which took the life of one of this text's authors' (Kauzlarich) great-grandfathers, is still a major problem today. It is now called "coal workers' pneumoconiosis," and usually results from inhalation of and exposure to assorted coal dusts and silica (U.S. Department of Labor 2000). There is no doubt that many coal companies knew of the dangers of black lung but did nothing to prevent worker exposure to dangerous coal dust (Mokhiber 1988). Even today a few companies do not adequately protect their workers from contracting the disease (OSHA 2000).

Even if we use the conservative OSHA statistics, we get some sense of how routine violations of worker safety laws actually are in the United States. Federal and state OSHA agencies conducted 89,331 inspections in 1999. These inspections uncovered 280,158 violations of worker safety laws and resulted in over $159 million dollars worth of fines (OSHA 2000, 2). Here are some examples of these violations, most of which were classified as serious or willful:

- Four companies were fined a total of $410,900 for safety violations during the attempted repair of a tunnel beneath Boston Harbor. On July 21, 1999, two workers died attempting to remove underwater bulkheads on the tunnel (OSHA 2000b).
- Three companies were fined over $500,000 for safety violations that resulted in the deaths of three workers involved in the construction of Miller Park, home of the Milwaukee Brewers baseball team. The companies violated numerous regulations relating to maximum

crane loads, operations in poor weather conditions, and the physical placement of crews too close to a crane lift operation (OSHA 2000c).

- Dozens of companies have been fined for not providing protection to workers who perform duties while elevated. In one case, a worker fell to his death from a 600-foot-tall radio tower (OSHA 2000d, 2000e).

Other examples of corporate violence against workers could be detailed here. For example, the owners and managers of the Imperial Food Products company in Hamlet, North Carolina, routinely locked fire doors to prevent employees from stealing chickens. When a fire erupted in the plant on September 3, 1991, the workers were trapped—twenty-five were killed and another fifty-six were injured (Aulette and Michalowski 1993). Another case centers around the Johns Manville company's refusal to protect workers and others from exposure to asbestos. Even with the knowledge that the substance was harmful, Johns Manville allowed the product to be manufactured and distributed across the country. The company declared bankruptcy in the wake of a deluge of lawsuits (Friedrichs 1996; Mokhiber 1988).

VIOLENCE AGAINST THE NATURAL ENVIRONMENT   The natural environment can also be a victim of corporate violence. Like most corporate crimes, corporate degradation of the natural and physical environment is largely an outcome of the pursuit of profit. The costs of compliance with federal and state regulations are often greater than the costs of paying fines. The median fine for environmental crimes by organizations, for example, is $50,000 (Cohen 1998).

Perhaps the most devious environmental crime in U.S. history involves the actions of the Hooker Chemical Corporation who, in the 1940s, bought the Love Canal near Niagara Falls and filled it with dangerous toxic chemicals. The canal was eventually turned into a neighborhood playground and recreational area for nearby residents. Hooker had sold the land for $1 to the local school board and did not notify the board or the community of the hazardous material buried there (200 or so dangerous chemicals were dumped there over several years). As time passed, residents complained of

Harmful industrial pollution from factories like this constitutes a major form of corporate crime. Factories and other workplaces can pose another danger as well: In the United States, people are five times more likely to die from avoidable diseases and workplace injuries on the job than from homicide.

terrible odors emanating from the area, and high rates of emotional problems, miscarriages, and other illnesses were documented. It was also claimed that several died as a result of exposure to the chemicals (Mokhiber 1988). For years Hooker claimed it was not responsible for the problems, but eventually it was forced to pay millions of dollars to victims as well as to the federal government for the cleanup of the area (Mokhiber 1988).

When the *Exxon Valdez* ran aground in 1989, about 12 million gallons of oil fouled the ocean near Prince William Sound, Alaska. About 1,300 miles of beach were affected by the spill. At least 250,000 seabirds, 2,800 sea otters, 300 harbor seals, 250 bald eagles, and 22 killer whales were killed. Billions of salmon and herring eggs were eliminated as well (Exxon Valdez Oil Spill Trustee Council 2000). Thousands of people have been directly affected by the spill, and millions of dollars have been lost in tourism income and several commercial fishing enterprises have folded.

Hearings eventually determined that Exxon was responsible for the disaster: The company had allowed an incompetent crew to run the ship under a captain known to have a drinking problem. It had also made cuts in necessary staffing. Exxon entered into a criminal plea agreement in U.S. District Court that allowed them to pay only $25 million of a $150 million criminal fine. The company has also paid $100 million in restitution and $900 million toward the cleanup (Exxon Valdez Oil Spill Trustee Council 2000).

Small Business Crime

A variety of criminal activities are committed in the context of small business activity. Surprisingly, there are few studies of small business as a setting and context of crime. The following is a brief description of some of the factors that encourage criminal activity by companies, firms, or businesses that are owned by sole proprietors or business partners who directly supervise business activities and who personally authorize all transactions (Barlow 1993).

Mars's (1982) study of workplace fiddles, discussed earlier in this chapter, demonstrates that different occupational structures facilitate particular kinds of workplace crime that are then supported and routinized by the attitudes and inclinations of those working within them. "Hawks," for example, are found in jobs that stress initiative, autonomy, competition and control, the typical small business environment. "All share certain attitudes: The most common are a resistance to external constraint and a high value placed on independence. Our small businessman is, therefore, typically and almost by definition a hawk (Mars 1982, 42–43).

Tax fiddles are the archetypal offense, a version of which is described by one of Mars's informants, as follows:

> We fiddle part of our workers' wages. All the very small businesses that I know have to be in on this kind of fiddle. If you employ someone and he earns below the amount that allows him to get the maximum supplement as a low wage-earner—then you make sure he gets the supplement. You pay him just enough to qualify for the maximum and you make the rest of his wages up in cash. This is possible because we've got a lot coming through the till. (Mars 1982, 40)

Cash is the key here, as it is in other common tax fiddles such as avoidance of sales tax. Cash transactions bypass bookkeeping and therefore are difficult to monitor and trace.

In conjunction with bypassing the checks and controls of the official economy, some small businesses become involved in networks of collusion. Besides supporting the shadow economy, these networks bridge the worlds of compliance and crime and provide opportunities and incentives for a wide range of illegal activities. Collusion supports small business crime in various ways: through group norms and values that say it's OK; by offering protection; by disseminating information; and by forging connections between participants. Indeed, crime networks are largely indistinguishable from networks of legitimate exchange, and each appears to feed off the other. As noted earlier in this chapter, noncriminal and criminal opportunities work together to stimulate crime.

The structure of the legitimate economy is characterized by differences in the knowledge, control, and power held by some groups over others (Mars 1982, 138). This gives rise to various "fiddle factors" that facilitate small business crime as well as many forms of state and corporate crime more generally.

For example, consider retail and service businesses in high traffic areas that cater primarily to the tourist and convention trade. These contexts are fiddle-prone because they involve "passing trade": The parties to a transaction typically meet only once. Because business customers are usually strangers in the community, possibly also of different race, class, gender or ethnicity than "regulars," the conventional morality governing free exchange (i.e., don't cheat) is suspended or modified, thus increasing the chances of consumer fraud.

As noted with respect to fraud in maintenance and repair (which is dominated by small businesses), there is widespread ignorance among customers regarding what they need and don't need, how to satisfy a need, and what to pay. This ignorance constitutes another fiddle factor, and a clear parallel can be drawn between fraud in this context and fraud among physicians, lawyers, and other professionals (see Jesilow, Pontell, and Geis 1993).

Fidel Castro, president of Cuba, has survived numerous assassination attempts, some of which were supported by the United States. While political and state crime is an underdeveloped area of study in criminology, it may be one of the most important, for the harm caused by political elites and government organizations dwarfs that of traditional street crime.

ORGANIZATIONAL CRIME II: CRIMES BY STATES AND GOVERNMENTS

State crimes are socially injurious and/or illegal acts by states, state agencies, and state officials committed for the benefit of a state organization. These crimes cover a wide range of activities and, consequently, have a wide range of victims. These include: people targeted for genocide, individuals suffering from state-supported racism, sexism, classism; involuntary research subjects in government-sponsored projects; countries and nations oppressed by more powerful states; suspects in criminal cases; and even passengers on airplanes (Kauzlarich, Matthews, and Miller 2000; Mullins and Kauzlarich 2000). Here we discuss four major examples of state crime, beginning with the Iran-Contra affair during the Reagan administration.

The Iran-Contra Affair

The Iran-Contra affair, arguably the worst scandal during the administration of Ronald Reagan, was an international conspiracy designed to secure the release of American hostages in Lebanon through illegal sale of arms to Iran, and to shore up the Contra rebels in Nicaragua through illegal diversion of arms sales money to the rebels.

Investigations by congressional committees and by special prosecutors implicated members of the White House staff, the military, and the Central Intelligence Agency, and documented the involvement of businessmen and government officials from three continents. National Security Council aide Oliver North was at the center of the scandal, but other senior government officials were also implicated, though few have been charged and some convictions (including North's) were overturned on appeal.

It is interesting that the defense most often presented in state crimes is that "I did what I thought was in the best interests of the country." This appeal to national security diverts attention from the core issue (willful violation of the law by those entrusted to uphold it), protects the public image of the wrongdoers as people of honor who go out on a limb to protect the national interest, and conveys the idea that the accused have been wronged and are therefore the real victims. It also helps legitimize covert crimes by government officials and cloaks the secretive underside of national politics with an aura of decency and honor: The officials are doing their best to protect "Good" against "Evil." Appeals to higher loyalty are not confined to political criminals, it turns out, but are also invoked by common or garden-variety offenders and juvenile delinquents (see the discussion of "techniques of neutralization" in Chapter 12 for more on this).

U.S. Nuclear Crimes

The U.S. Department of Energy and a host of other federal agencies have funded or otherwise managed thousands of human radiation experiments. Several of these experiments have been conducted in violation of the Nuremberg Code, which outlaws nonconsensual, reckless, deceptive, and coercive experiments. Two sets of studies have been found to be particularly unethical and illegal (Kauzlarich and Kramer 1998).

From 1945 to 1947, a series of Manhattan Project and Atomic Energy Commission (AEC) supported plutonium injection studies were conducted on eighteen people. The subjects were expressly deceived into participating in the study. They were told that they were being *treated* for a life-threatening disease when in fact the studies were designed to help state officials understand the effects of plutonium on the human body in the case of nuclear war. The victims of these experiments, like many crime victims, were poor and uneducated. The second series of experiments in violation of the Nuremberg Code were prison radiation experiments conducted from 1963 to 1973. One hundred and thirty-one state prisoners in Oregon and Washington were subjects in a study to determine the effects of irradiation on the male reproductive system. Prisoners were given $25 per irradiation and informed of only some of the possible risks associated with the experiments. Prisoners are not in a position to exercise the type of free will envisioned by the Nuremberg Code. Clearly the victims of this state crime were poor, scientifically uneducated, and literally captive.

The production of atomic and nuclear weapons by the U.S. Department of Energy has resulted in massive environmental contamination. In violation of U.S. EPA laws, the Clean Water Act, and the Resource Conservation and Recovery Act, at least 17 areas in the country have been substantially damaged and polluted. In Hanford, Washington, 100 square miles of groundwater were contaminated with extremely high levels of tritium, iodine, and other toxic chemicals. Near the Savannah River Plant in the Carolinas, there have been massive releases of mercury into the air and tritium, strontium, and iodine into the soil (Kauzlarich and Kramer 1993, 1998).

There is evidence to show that there are higher rates of miscarriages, leukemia, and other health-related problems in the areas where nuclear weapons have been produced, stored, or tested. The human effects of environmental degradation as a result of the hundreds of nuclear weapons tests in the Western part of the United States are also examples of state crime. A recent study by the National Cancer Institute estimates that tens of thousands of people have developed thyroid cancer as a result of nuclear tests (Kauzlarich and Kramer 1998). The victims of these environmental crimes were not only the unknowing civilians who simply happened to be living near the test sites, but also military personnel who were forced to witness nuclear blasts and then tested for any negative side effects (Kauzlarich and Kramer 1998). In these cases, the victims were unfortunately easily exploitable because they were either unknowing, powerless, or in subordinate organizational positions (Kauzlarich, Matthews, and Miller 2000).

Finally, the development and use of weapons of mass destruction have been criminalized. On July 8, 1996, the International Court of Justice (ICJ) delivered an advisory opinion that the threat or use of nuclear weapons would generally be illegal. This historic ruling came in response to requests by the

The killing capacity of the nuclear weapon is unrivaled. The International Court of Justice recently declared the threat or use of weapons of mass destruction to be criminal, since their effects cannot be reconciled with the provisions of international law.

World Health Organization (WHO) and the United Nations General Assembly (UNGA) for advisory opinions on this important issue. In a complicated and controversial ruling, the ICJ stated that "... the threat or use of nuclear weapons would generally be contrary to the rules of international law applicable in armed conflict, and in particular the principles and rules of humanitarian law" (International Court of Justice 1996, paragraph 105 (2) E; Kauzlarich 1997; Kramer and Kauzlarich 1999). One of the relevant international laws the ICJ used to make their decision was the Nuremberg Principles (see Box 6.3).

Violations of Human Rights and Economic Terrorism

One of the most widely recognized forms of state suppression of political rights was the FBI's COINTELPRO program. Under this program, the political rights of dissident political groups like the Socialist Workers Party (SWP), the Southern Christian Leadership Conference (SCLC), the Black Panthers, American Indian Movement (AIM), and the Committee in Solidarity with the People of El Salvador (CISPES) were violated (Caulfield 1991; Churchill and Vander Wall 1990; Davis 1992). Covert attempts by the FBI to "neutralize" political dissent included such illegal tactics as wiretaps, bugging, mail-openings, and breaking and entering (Beirne and Messerschmidt 2000). Other activities included group infiltration and death threats (Churchill and Vander Wall 1990; Davis 1992).

Economic terrorism involves coercion through economic means that is directed toward the civilian population of the target country to bring about a desired political or economic change, or to simply "punish" the target country (Dowty 1994; Hass 1998; Hufbauer et al. 1990). The effects of economic sanctions range from moderate discomfort to more serious consequences, such as disease, malnutrition, and even death (Hufbauer et al. 1990). Consider the case of Cuba. The passage of the Cuban Democracy Act (CDA) in 1992, and the passage of the Helms-Burton Act in 1996 were major steps in tightening the economic sanctions

---

Box 6.3   THE NUREMBERG CHARTER

The Nuremburg Charter is an international law governing state behavior. The International Court of Justice referred to the following Nuremberg Principles when forming the opinion that the threat or use of nuclear weapons would generally be illegal.

a. Crimes against Peace: namely, planning, preparation, initiation, or waging of a war of aggression, or a war in violation of international treaties, agreements, or assurances, or participation in a common plan or conspiracy for the accomplishment of any of the foregoing.

b. War Crimes: namely, violations of the laws or customs of war. Such violations shall include, but not be limited to, murder, ill-treatment, or deportation to slave labor or for any other purpose of civilian population of or in occupied territory, murder, or ill-treatment of prisoners of war or persons on seas, killing of hostages, plunder of public or private property, wanton destruction of cities, towns or villages, or devastation not justified by military necessity.

c. Crimes against Humanity: namely, murder, extermination, enslavement, deportation, and other inhumane acts committed against any civilian population, before or during war, or prosecutions on political, racial or religious grounds in execution of or in connection with any crime within the jurisdiction of the Tribunal, whether or not in violation of the domestic law of the country where perpetrated (Kauzlarich and Kramer 1998, 32).

on Cuba. The tightening of the economic sanctions in 1992 created health problems for many Cuban citizens in the areas of malnutrition, water quality, and shortages of medicines and medical equipment (American Association for World Health 1997).

The outright ban on the sale of American foodstuffs has contributed to serious nutritional deficits, especially among pregnant women. This has led to an increase in low birth-weight babies. Food shortages have led to devastating outbreaks of neuropathy; the embargo has severely restricted access to water treatment chemicals and the parts needed for Cuba's water supply system (American Association for World Health 1997). This has led to rising incidences of morbidity and mortality rates from waterborne diseases. Finally,

> of the 1,297 medications available in Cuba in 1991, physicians now have access to only 889 of these same medicines—and many of these are available only intermittently. Because most major new drugs are developed by U.S. pharmaceuticals, Cuban physicians have access to less than 50 percent of the new medicines available on the world market. Due to the direct or indirect effects of the embargo, the most routine medical supplies are in short supply or entirely absent from some Cuban clinics. (American Association for World Health 1997, ii)

Historically, the use of economic sanctions has been viewed under both domestic law and international law as a "humanitarian" alternative to military force. Indeed, there have been instances where economic sanctions have been very successful in bringing about a desired change—the economic sanctions on Haiti and South Africa, for example. However, even when economic sanctions are "successful," sanctions and humanitarianism often collide:

> Although in theory sanctions are motivated by an implicitly humane rationale, their implementation often wreaks great havoc and civilian suffering. Inherent in sanctions policy are uncomfortable and, for the moment, still imprecise calculations about inflicting civilian pain to achieve political gain. Where tolerable civilian discomfort ends and full-fledged humanitarian crisis begins is an elusive boundary, particularly because pre-sanction conditions in many countries are often so marginal. (Weiss 1997, 30)

Each year since the passage of the CDA in 1992, the U.N. General Assembly has passed resolutions condemning the sanctions placed on Cuba. Cuba has maintained that the U.S. economic measures, which are intended to coerce changes in Cuba's political and economic institutions, violate principles of nonintervention and the sovereignty of states (Krinsky et al. 1993).

State-Corporate Crime

While the study of state crime is still in its infancy, a promising and important development has recently been made by Ronald C. Kramer and Raymond J. Michalowski (1990) through the introduction of the concept of **state-corporate crime**. State-corporate crimes are

> illegal or socially injurious actions that result from a mutually reinforcing interaction between (1) policies and/or practices in pursuit of goals of one or more institutions of political governance and (2) policies and/or practices in pursuit of the goals of one or more institutions of economic production and distribution. (Kramer and Michalowski 1991, 5; also see Aulette and Michalowski 1993, 175)

The concept of state-corporate crime has been used to examine the space shuttle *Challenger* explosion (Kramer 1992), the environmental devastation caused by U.S. nuclear weapons production (Kauzlarich and Kramer 1993, 1998), and the previously mentioned deadly fire at the Imperial Food Products chicken processing plant in Hamlet, North Carolina (Aulette and Michalowski 1993). Other examples of state-corporate crime include the I. G. Farben Company's involvement with Nazi atrocities, the Wedtech case involving defense contractor fraud (Friedrichs 1996a), and the violent and deadly crash of ValuJet flight 592 in May of 1996 (Matthews and Kauzlarich 2000).

Kramer and Michalowski (1990; 1991, 6) identify two forms of state-corporate crime. *State-initiated* crime occurs when corporations engage in organizational deviance at the direction of, or with the tacit approval of, the government. It includes cases such as the space shuttle *Challenger* explosion and the environmental and human injury caused by nuclear weapons production. In both of these instances, a government agency (NASA in the *Challenger* case and the Department of Energy in the nuclear weapons case) actively pursued a shared goal with a private corporation (Morton Thiokol and Rockwell International, respectively). The day-to-day manufacture of various parts for the space shuttle and nuclear weapons rests in the hands of private corporations. Both the state and the contracted corporation must produce a commodity in a timely and efficient way to achieve mutually held organizational goals.

The illegal corporate practices (environmental contamination and the manufacture of defective products) that resulted from such contractual relationships were strongly encouraged by the state agency involved (Kauzlarich and Kramer 1993, 1998; Kramer 1992; Matthews and Kauzlarich 2000). In the *Challenger* case, NASA pressured managers at Morton Thiokol into granting permission to launch the shuttle, even though scientists at Morton Thiokol expressed great concern that the O-rings would fail (Kramer 1992; Vaughan 1996). Here, a state agency initiated the socially injurious event. It was through this interaction that a private corporation and a public entity made a decision that ultimately led to the *Challenger* explosion.

The second form of state-corporate crime is *state-facilitated* crime. This occurs when "governmental regulatory institutions fail to restrain deviant business activities, because of direct collusion between business and government, or because they adhere to shared goals whose attainment would be hampered by aggressive regulation" (Kramer and Michalowski 1991, 6). For example, the Imperial Food Products fire in North Carolina did not simply result from the technical cause of injury (Imperial Food Products' decision to lock fire doors), but the twenty-five workers who died were the victims of "a series of social decisions made by a broad array of institutions." These institutions acted "like a noose … [that] … closed around Hamlet which brought about the death of 25 workers" (Aulette and Michalowski 1993, 203). Likewise, if it were not for very specific omissions by a number of institutional actors in both the private and public sector within a lax regulatory environment, ValuJet flight 592 would not have crashed in the Florida Everglades (Matthews and Kauzlarich 2000).

CHAPTER SUMMARY

This chapter has explored the many dimensions of occupational, political, and organizational crime. Such crime occurs in connection with a person's job, with work providing the opportunity and/or motivation for criminal activity. The financial, medical, and social costs of white-collar crime far exceed those of such conventional street crimes as robbery, burglary, drug sales, murder, and assault.

Occupational crimes are committed for personal gain. These include embezzlement, political white-collar crime, and a host of other offenses ranging from simple fiddles to high-tech manipulations costing thousands of dollars. Other white-collar crimes are committed on behalf of the organization, as in the case of corporate crime and state crime.

As we will discuss in later chapters, no one theory adequately explains white-collar crimes, partly because the term covers diverse situations. It seems safe to argue, however, that many people and organizations who commit work-related crimes regard their behavior as normal rather than deviant, or illegal but not criminal. Situational incentives are reinforced by norms and values that define the behavior as appropriate, even expected. Under such circumstances it is the people who refrain from offenses who are regarded as deviant.

On the whole, however, official reactions to most white-collar crimes are more lenient than reactions to most street crimes, and rarely will a convicted occupational criminal go to the penitentiary (Benson and Cullen 1998). Michael Blankenship (1993, xxi) wonders "What conclusions can we draw about a society that is willing to impose the death penalty on the poor and the powerless but permits members of the upper class literally to get away with murder?"

American culture strongly supports the drive for profits and power, and in doing so provides rationalizations for executives who bend the rules, for politicians who deal in favors, and for officials who look the other way. It should come as no surprise, therefore, that the factory worker, office clerk, and salesperson have little trouble justifying their relatively petty crimes. They are taking advantage of the opportunities before them in the same enterprising spirit. The irony is, however, that workers at all levels of responsibility and power actually have little choice in the matter: The structure and norms of work make occupational and organizational crime virtually inevitable.

KEY TERMS

corporate crime (p. 116)

corporate theft and fraud (p. 127)

corporate violence (p. 128)

governmental crime (p. 117)

occupational crime (p. 116)

organizational crime (p. 117)

political white-collar crime (p. 125)

price discrimination (p. 128)

price-fixing (p. 128)

state-corporate crime (p. 139)

state crime (p. 136)

white-collar crime (p. 116)

RECOMMENDED READINGS

Barak, Gregg. 1991. *Crimes by the Capitalist State*. Albany, NY: State University of New York Press.

Cullen, Francis, William J. Maakestad, and Gray Cavender. 1987. *Corporate Crime under Attack: The Ford Pinto Case*. Cincinnati, OH: Anderson.

Friedrichs, David O. 1996. *Trusted Criminals: White-Collar Crime in Contemporary America*. New York: Wadsworth.

Kauzlarich, David, and Ronald C. Kramer. 1998. *Crimes of the American Nuclear State: At Home and Abroad*. Boston, MA: Northeastern University Press.

Ross, Jeffrey Ian. 2000. *Varieties of State Crime and Its Control*. Monsey, NY: Criminal Justice Press.

Simon, David R. 2002. *Elite Deviance*. 7th ed. Boston, MA: Allyn and Bacon.

Tunnell, Kenneth D. 1993. *Political Crime in Contemporary America*. New York: Garland.

RECOMMENDED WEB SITES

Amnesty International

Abundant information on state and corporate crimes, especially violations of human rights.

http://www.amnesty.org

Association of Certified Fraud Examiners

Information and links on occupational and some organizational crimes, especially fraud and theft.

http://www.cfenet.com

Occupational Safety and Health Administration

This agency posts an enormous amount of information on matters related to worker health and safety.

http://www.osha.gov

Paul's Justice Page

A Web page with compelling examples of corporate and state crime.

http://www.paulsjusticepage.com/elite-deviance.htm

CHAPTER

7

ORGANIZED CRIME

organized crime activities. What most people have learned about organized crime, however, has come from the mass media. Apart from periodic news items, which are usually colorful and designed to demonstrate some special kind of inside knowledge, the entertainment industry has been a major window on organized crime. The success of films such as *Goodfellas* and *The Godfather* is evidence of the strong appeal of organized crime as entertainment. At best, the information available to the public via the mass media is fragmentary, superficial, and misleading; at worst, it is patently false and purely titillating. We also know that members and associates of the Italian organized syndicate **La Cosa Nostra** feel that there are widespread misperceptions about organized crime. Thomas Cupples (1997) interviewed 150 such persons and found that only 20 percent of the respondents believed that the mob is accurately depicted in movies (Cupples and Kauzlarich 1997).

THE EXISTENCE OF ORGANIZED CRIME

Over the years a belief has grown that thriving within the United States is a national alliance or cartel of organized groups of criminals, dominated by Italian-Americans and involved in an extensive range of illicit, often violent activities. As we shall see, this view is now strongly challenged. There is also controversy surrounding the definition of organized crime. Box 7.1 (on page 144) includes various definitions of the phenomenon. Note the vague wording.

The Case for a National Cartel of Crime Groups

In 1951 and then again in 1969, highly credible sources appeared to confirm that a national crime cartel does exist in the United States. First, the "Kefauver Committee" of the U.S. Senate reported the following:

1. There is a nation-wide crime syndicate known as the Mafia, whose tentacles are found in many large cities....
2. Its leaders are usually found in control of the most lucrative rackets in their cities.
3. There are indications of a centralized direction and control of these rackets, but leadership appears to be in a group rather than in a single individual.

Most Americans are familiar with the term *organized crime*, yet it is unlikely that many of them know much about it. They have probably heard of Al Capone, John Gotti, Joe Valachi, and Charlie "Lucky" Luciano. Most may also have heard of Eliot Ness, head of the "Untouchables," assigned to break up Capone's bootlegging operations during Prohibition. It is common knowledge that Chicago and the New York-Philadelphia-New Jersey area are major centers of

BOX 7.1   VARIOUS DEFINITIONS AND DESCRIPTIONS OF ORGANIZED CRIME

The vague wording in the following descriptions is indicative of the controversy surrounding the definition of organized crime:

Organized crime means the unlawful activities of the members of a highly organized, disciplined association engaged in supplying illegal goods and services, including but not limited to gambling, prostitution, loan sharking, narcotics, labor racketeering, and other unlawful activities of members of such organizations. (The 1968 Omnibus Crime Control Act, Section 3701)

Any enterprise or group of persons engaged in a continuing illegal activity which has as its primary purpose the generation of profits, irrespective of national boundaries. (1988 Interpol definition [in Bresler 1992])

Any group having a corporate structure whose primary objective is to obtain money through illegal activities, often surviving on fear and corruption. (Current Interpol definition [in Bresler 1992])

Organized crime groups are secret organizations that function outside the laws of the United States and operate for the purpose of making money at the expense of others. These groups have a distinctive organizational structure and are often motivated by greed. (2000 FBI "tour" description, <http://www.fbi.gov>)

4. The Mafia is the cement that helps bind the Costello-Adonis-Lansky syndicate of New York and the Accardo-Guzik-Fischetti syndicate of Chicago as well as smaller criminal gangs and individual criminals throughout the country....

5. The domination of the Mafia is based fundamentally on "muscle" and "murder." The Mafia is a secret conspiracy against law and order which will ruthlessly eliminate anyone who stands in the way of its success in any criminal enterprise in which it is interested. It will destroy anyone who betrays its secrets. It will use any means available—political influence, bribery, intimidation, etc., to defeat any attempt on the part of law enforcement to touch its top figures or to interfere with its operations (Tyler 1962, 343–344).

The findings of the Kefauver Committee were based on information supplied mainly by police officials and informants. Using basically the same kinds of information, Donald Cressey summarized his investigation on behalf of the President's Commission on Law Enforcement and the Administration of Justice as follows:

1. A nationwide alliance of at least twenty-four tightly knit "families" of criminals exists in the United States (because the "families" are fictive, in the sense that the members are not all relatives, it is necessary to refer to them in quotation marks).

2. The members of these "families" are all Italians and Sicilians, or of Italian or Sicilian descent, and those on the Eastern seaboard, especially, call the entire system "Cosa Nostra." Each member thinks of himself as a "member" of a specific "family" and of Cosa Nostra (or some equivalent term).

3. The names, criminal records, and principal criminal activities of about five thousand of the participants have been assembled.

4. The persons occupying key positions in the skeletal structure of each "family"—consisting of positions for boss, underboss, lieutenants (also called "captains"), counselor, and for low-ranking members called "soldiers" or "button men"—are well known to law-enforcement officials having access to informants. Names of persons who permanently or temporarily occupy other positions, such as "buffer," "money mover," "enforcer," and "executioner," also are well-known.

5. The "families" are linked to each other, and to non-Cosa Nostra syndicates, by understandings, agreements, and "treaties," and by mutual deference to a "Commission" made up of the leaders of the most powerful of the "families."

6. The boss of each "family" directs the activities, especially the illegal activities, of the members of his "family."

7. The members of this organization control all but a tiny part of the illegal gambling in the United States. They are the principal loan sharks. They are the principal importers and wholesalers of narcotics. They have infiltrated certain labor unions, where they extort money from employers and, at the same time, cheat the members of the union. The members have a virtual monopoly on some legitimate enterprises.... Until recently, they owned a large proportion of Las Vegas. They own several state legislators and federal congressmen and other officials in the legislative, executive, and judicial branches of government at the local, state, and federal levels. Some government officials (including judges) are considered, and consider themselves, members.

8. The information about the Commissions, the "families," and the activities of members has come from detailed reports made by a wide variety of police observers, informants, wire taps, and electronic bugs (1969, x–xi).

In Cressey's view, these crime families are organized along the lines of what sociologists call **formal organization**. In this structure, the labor is divided so that tasks and responsibilities are assigned primarily on the basis of special skills and abilities;

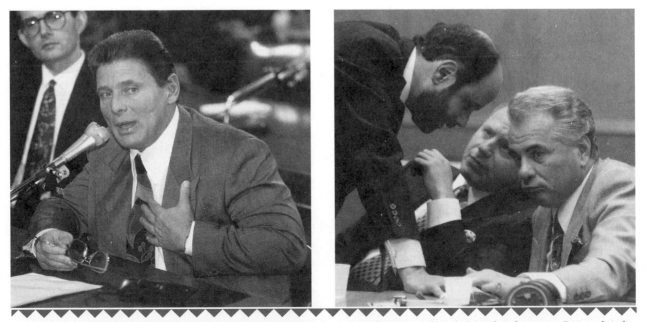

Information about organized crime activities is largely gathered through undercover work and through informants. One such informant, Salvatore "The Bull" Gravano (left), testified against his former associate John Gotti (right), once the head of the New York Gambino crime family. In April of 1992, following a highly sensational trial, Gotti was convicted of racketeering and murder. He is now serving a life sentence without parole in the federal penitentiary at Marion.

there is a strict hierarchy of authority; rules and regulations govern the activities of members and the relationships among them and with the outside world; and recruitment and entrance are carefully regulated. In short, the crime families are, like other formal organizations, rationally designed for the purposes of achieving specified objectives.

Many other law enforcement officials still favor this description of La Cosa Nostra (LCN). In testimony in federal court, Rudolph Giuliani documented the existence of specific LCN families in New York, Philadelphia, Cleveland, Chicago, Milwaukee, Kansas City, and Los Angeles; and he described nationwide coordinated LCN control of the nation's largest union, the International Brotherhood of Teamsters (see Block 1991).

Much-publicized recent successes by federal law enforcement officials in prosecuting reputed LCN members, primarily through the extensive use of wiretaps, lend credence to claims of LCN's existence and of considerable interaction among Italian-American crime families. However, Alan Block (1991, 13–14) believes they fall far short of proving the "big conspiracy," and he regards both the history of La Cosa Nostra and its sociology as clouded in mystery.

An Alternative View

Not all authorities on organized crime agree entirely with Cressey's depiction of a national network of crime families. The **revisionist view** emphasizes more or less organized local criminal gangs, some of whose activities inevitably bring them into working contact with groups operating elsewhere. Advocates of this view see no real evidence of any centralized direction or domination of these localized syndicates. "(T)erritory and organization are honored only in the breach" and there are "ceaseless disputes over rackets and territories" (Bell 1965; Block 1991, 8).

The notion of a formally organized, centrally directed, national alliance of Mafia families has been rejected by Reuter (1983). He does not dispute the existence of Mafia families—most have continued in the same recognizable form for at least fifty years. Rather, Reuter believes that the relations among them are the result of occasional venture partnerships, occasional exchange of services, and attempts to reduce the uncertainty that arises when business takes a family into unfamiliar territory. Reuter (1983, 158) also suggests that many of the connections among organized crime gangs resulted from Prohibition and from associations made while members served time in federal prisons.

Another point of contention concerns the degree and nature of organization. Some authors reject the idea that organized crime groups fit the formal organization model:

> Secret criminal organizations like the Italian-American or Sicilian Mafia families are not formal organizations like governments or business corporations. They are not rationally structured into statuses and functions in order to "maximize profits" and carry out tasks efficiently. Rather, they are traditional social systems, organized by action and by cultural values which have nothing to do with modern bureaucratic virtues. Like all social systems, they have no structure apart from their functioning; nor … do they have structure independent of their current "personnel."… Describing the various positions in Italian-American syndicates as "like" those in bureaucracies gives the impression that they are, in fact, formal organizations. But they are not. (Ianni 1974, 120–124)

A study of the South Philadelphia mob run by Angelo Bruno from 1959 until 1980, when he was assassinated, corroborates this view. Haller (1991) analyzed all files of the Pennsylvania Crime Commission dealing with Bruno and his successor, Nicodemo Scarfo. He found that two organizational structures appeared to operate simultaneously: (1) a family structure comprising a network designed to help the individual enterprises of members and constituting a "shadow government" of rules and expectations that facilitate members' legal and illegal activities; and (2) an enterprise structure comprising the legal and illegal businesses run by individual members of the Bruno family. This enterprise structure involved cost, risk, and profit sharing (sometimes with nonfamily members), and most of the business was carried on informally, through "deals, negotiations, [and] whispered conversations," and through decentralized operations involving minimal oversight. According to Haller, this system not only fit the life-style of the men but also provided to each participant wide discretion in doing "business."

Although some crime families or syndicates exhibit some of the elements found in highly rationalized bureaucratic structures, as Cressey showed, most do not. This distinction is important when one considers the growing organized crime involvement of blacks and Hispanics, and of street gangs, whom law enforcement officials have compared to the mobsters of Prohibition days. Some of these groups display only rudimentary organization, mostly operating in loosely connected networks, but others are highly organized.

Illegal Enterprise

Reuter's (1983) study of loan-sharking, gambling, and the numbers racket in New York City shows how illegality of products and services affects the organization of an economic market, keeping some enterprises localized and relatively small-scale. The illegal market differs from its legal counterpart in various ways: (1) Contracts cannot be enforced in a court of law; (2) assets associated with illegal operations may be seized at any time; and (3) participants risk arrest and imprisonment. These problems differ in significance from one illegal market to another, however; heroin trafficking carries more risk than operating a numbers game.

These problems call for control over the flow of information about the operation. Those who participate are at different risk and pose different levels of threat to others. The entrepreneurs who control operations are at greatest risk from their agents or employees, who know most about the business, but those risks are reduced by dividing up the tasks and responsibilities, by offering employees economic incentives, by ensuring that they are not employed elsewhere, by intimidating, and by recruiting based on family ties or the incorporation of employees into the family through rite or marriage. Risks to the employees come largely from other employees, thus encouraging entrepreneurs to keep operations small-scale and/or dispersed in time and space (Reuter 1983).

Another problem faced by illegal enterprise is financing. Reuter (1983, 120) found that credit works differently in illegal markets: (1) There are no accurately audited books; (2) the lender is unable to control any assets placed as collateral against a loan because the borrower is likely to demand secrecy, and, in any case, lacks court protection (as a

financer of criminal activities); and (3) the loan is to the individual entrepreneur and not to the enterprise, which has no legal existence apart from its owner. Therefore, the lender would have difficulty collecting from any successor.

These problems also constrain the growth of illegal enterprises, especially those in loan-sharking and gambling:

> Without smoothly working capital markets, the growth must be internally financed ... out of profits. In the heroin importing business, where each successful transaction may double the capital of the enterprise, this may be a minor restriction. For the numbers bank, with a relatively modest cash flow and a need for maintenance of a substantial cash reserve, this may be a very important constraint. (Reuter 1983, 121)

Mark Haller (1990), arguably America's foremost authority on the history of organized crime, reminds us that illegal enterprise existed long before La Cosa Nostra. Indeed, it shaped the underworld of American cities for over 100 years before the rise of Italian-American crime families. These enterprises included free-lance prostitution, street-corner drug dealing, and neighborhood bookmaking. Entrepreneurs sometimes got together in cooperative ventures giving rise to networks of collusion.

The cooperative ventures of illegal enterprise rested on three important factors, according to Haller: (1) police or politician oversight that involved regular payoffs (kickbacks), limited competition, and encouraged avoidance of scandals and participation in "honest" crime; (2) flexible partnership arrangements allowing several entrepreneurs to share risks, to pool resources, and to combine their capital, influence, and managerial skills; and (3) internal economics, that is, the need to develop cooperative relations between buyers and sellers in order to protect both from the vagaries of doing business in the illegal marketplace.

Distinguishing Characteristics of Organized Crime

It is unlikely that criminologists will soon reach a consensus on the issues under discussion here. Even if detailed and dependable information were forthcoming, how complete a picture could be drawn from it? When dealing with people who place a premium on secrecy and engage in criminal activities, one is rarely able to learn everything one needs to know. Even those in a position to know more than most (e.g., a participant who turns informant, such as Joe Valachi, whose testimony before the McClellan Committee was so influential; see Abadinsky 1990, 473–475) may know the facts about only some aspects of their own organization and thus cannot be considered authoritative sources of information on other aspects or other organizations (see Maas 1968). As Steffensmeier (1995, 269) notes: "No other area in the field is as difficult to define, describe ... and conduct research on...." Even so, criminologists generally agree on some important features of organized crime that, when taken together, distinguish this type of criminal activity from others.

First, organized crime is instrumental crime, the purpose of which is to make money. To accomplish this, participants organize in more or less complex networks. Second, most organized crime activities offer illegal goods and services. This does not mean, however, that those in organized crime have nothing to do with "traditional" crimes such as burglary or robbery. Stuart Hills (1971, 138–139) points out the following:

> It is the syndicate that has mostly controlled the importation and wholesale distribution of narcotics that, together with prohibitionist laws and police activity, compel most addicts to engage in burglary, robbery, and larceny to pay the exorbitant black-market prices. And it is the "fences," aligned with organized criminal groups, who allow thieves to convert their booty into cash. Organized crime has also been known to promote bank robbery, cargo hijacking, arson, and burglaries, sometimes in co-operation with individual professional thieves. This kind of crime has been called the "parasitic" activity of organized crime. (see Abadinsky 1990, 267–268)

A third important characteristic of organized crime is its connections with government and politics. Organized crime makes political and police corruption an integral part of its business. Indeed, political corruption is not merely a distinguishing feature of organized crime; it is critical to its survival (Beare 1998; Simon 1999). Take, for instance,

what a kingpin revealed to Cupples and Kauzlarich (1997: 20) about the need to protect illegal gambling activities:

> [P]olice corruption was a thriving business.... Bankers routinely paid protection money to ... the police department.... Basically you can't operate a numbers business without taking care of the cops.

The fourth feature of organized crime is its generational persistence. The syndicates or families involved in organized crime continue to operate despite the comings and goings of their members. Although the death or retirement of persons in leadership positions may result in significant changes, organized crime does not disappear, and individual organizations usually do not cease to exist. The persistence of organized crime can be explained in part by a fifth important feature: sanctioned rules of conduct (sometimes called "the code"). The survival of any group or organization is problematic if the behavior of members is neither predictable nor conforming to the evaluations of at least some other members of the group. Rules of conduct help establish conformity and predictability; sanctions for violations of the rules help ensure that conformity and predictability persist over time. Sanctions are related to a final characteristic: ability and willingness to use force and violence to accomplish the organization's goals. Reuter (1983) points out that reputation may be more important than actual behavior: A gang that has a reputation for violence can accomplish the same results with fewer bad consequences (see also Block 1991, 5).

When discussing what makes organized crime distinctive, some authors emphasize its organizational features, while others note that organized criminals are able to commit a greater variety of crimes, on a larger scale, than are other offenders (Steffensmeier 1995). Mark Moore (1986) believes that most recent research and policy has been guided by the first view rather than the second. For example, the Racketeer Influenced and Corrupt Organizations (RICO) Act of 1970 (see Box 7.2) focuses on the specific organization of criminal groups and their capacity to continue operations despite government opposition. "The policy goal ... is to weaken and frustrate the enterprise rather than control their criminal offending" (Moore 1986, 2). In addition, Moore argues, the organizational focus

BOX 7.2   THE RICO STATUTE

The provisions of the Racketeer Influenced and Corrupt Organization Act (1970) include the following:

- It shall be unlawful for any person through a pattern of racketeering activity or through collection of an unlawful debt to acquire or maintain, directly or indirectly, any interest or control of any enterprise which is engaged in, or the activities of which affect, interstate commerce.
- It shall be unlawful for any persons employed by or associated with any enterprise engaged in, or the activities of which effect, interstate or foreign commerce, to conduct or participate, directly or indirectly, in the conduct of such enterprise's affairs through a pattern of racketeering activity or collection of unlawful debts.
- It shall be unlawful for any person to conspire to violate any of (these) provisions.

Pattern of racketeering means at least two acts of racketeering activity within ten years of each other (excluding any period of imprisonment).

Racketeering activity includes the following: (a) murder, kidnapping, gambling, arson, robbery, bribery, extortion, or dealing in narcotic or other dangerous drugs ... and (b) any act indictable under the Organized Crime Act, including those related to bribery, embezzlement from pension or welfare funds, mail fraud, wire fraud, obstruction of justice, interference with commerce, robbery or extortion, (and) racketeering....

draws attention to the parallels between organized crime and legitimate enterprises. Indeed, these parallels are not lost on federal prosecutors, who routinely use RICO to crack down on corporate and other occupational crime, and who have recently used the statute to prosecute the recurring criminal activities of antiabortion groups—to which the U.S. Supreme Court gave unanimous approval in January 1993.

The Code

There is no conclusive evidence that one particular code, a set of sanctioned rules of conduct, is shared by the various criminal organizations. Investigators have found numerous obstacles to a definitive statement of what the code (or codes) might be, the most important being the veil of secrecy that surrounds organized crime and the difficulty of gaining access to its participants.

Cressey (1969, 175–178) combined snippets of information from informants with clues deduced from an analysis of the social structure of La Cosa Nostra and suggested the following as the **code of organized crime**:

1. *Be loyal to members of the organization. Do not interfere with each other's interests. Do not be an informer.* This directive, with its correlated admonitions, is basic to the internal operations of the Cosa Nostra confederation. It is a call for unity, for peace, for maintenance of the status quo....
2. *Be rational. Be a member of the team. Don't engage in battle if you can't win.* What is demanded here is a corporate rationality necessary to conducting illicit businesses in a quiet, safe, profitable manner....
3. *Be a man of honor. Always do right. Respect womanhood and your elders. Don't rock the boat.* This emphasis on "honor" and "respect"

helps determine who obeys whom, who attends what funerals and weddings, who opens the door for whom, ... and functions to enable despots to exploit their underlings....

4. *Be a stand-up guy. Keep your eyes and ears open and your mouth shut. Don't sell out.* A "family" member, like a prisoner, must be able to withstand frustrating and threatening situations without complaining or resorting to subservience. The "stand-up guy" shows courage and "heart."...

5. *Have class. Be independent. Know your way around the world....* A man who is committed to regular work and submission to duly constituted authority is a sucker.... Second, the world seen by organized criminals is a world of graft, fraud, and corruption, and they are concerned with their own honesty and manliness as compared with the hypocrisy of corrupt policemen and corrupt political figures.

In discussing the code, Cressey points out that it is similar to the codes adopted by professional thieves, prisoners, and other groups whose activities bring them into confrontation with official authority and generate the need for "private" government as a means of controlling the membership's conduct (see also Salerno and Tompkins 1969, 105–148).

Taking exception to Cressey's position, Ianni (1973, 150–155; 1998) argues that the presumption of a shared code is based on the questionable belief that there is a single national organization, and that each individual organized crime group has achieved similar levels of organizational sophistication and has shared similar experiences.

From his two-year participant observation of one Italian-American crime family operating in New York (the "Lupollo" family) and his later research on black and Hispanic groups in organized crime, Ianni found evidence of different codes for different groups. In the case of the Lupollo family, there were three basic rules for behavior:

> ... (1) primary loyalty is vested in "family" rather than in individual lineages or nuclear families, (2) each member of the family must "act like a man" and do nothing which brings disgrace on the family, and (3) family business is privileged matter and must not be reported or discussed outside the group. (Ianni and Reuss-Ianni 1973, 155; 1998)

Ianni found that black and Hispanic organized crime codes differed from the Lupollo rules, as well as from each other. For example, whereas the black and Hispanic groups emphasized loyalty and secrecy (as did the Lupollo family), some of these organized crime networks also stressed the rules "Don't be a coward" and "Don't be a creep" (in other words, "fit in" with the group). Some stressed the rule "Be smart" (know when to obey but also when to beat the system), and some stressed "Don't tell the police," "Don't cheat your partner or other people in the network," and "Don't be incompetent" (Ianni 1975, 301–305; 1998).

Which rules are stressed depends in large part on how the gangs came together in the first place. Gangs with shared family roots place a premium on rules supporting kinship ties. On the other hand, gangs with origins in youthful street associations and partnerships tend to stress rules underscoring personal qualities ("Don't be a coward"). Those originating in strictly business or entrepreneurial associations tend to stress rules emphasizing more impersonal, activity-oriented obligations ("Don't be incompetent"). The code adopted by a criminal organization reflects far more than the mere fact that it is a secret association engaged in regular criminal activities. How and why the participants came together in the first place, how long the organization has been operating, the cultural heritage of its major participants, and the nature and range of its activities all influence the code of a particular crime group.

While there may be different codes for different groups, a 1989 undercover FBI recording of an LCN induction ceremony obtained by Cupples and Kauzlarich (1997) suggests that Cressey's work is still relevant. The following is an excerpt of that ceremony, recorded in a home in Boston, with Joseph Russo (*consigliere* or counselor) and Biagio Di Giacomo (*capo* or captain) swearing in Carmen Tortora:

> RUSSO: In order to belong to us, to be a part of us, Carmen, you have to have truth and trust. Do you have that Carmen?
>
> TORTORA: Yes.
>
> RUSSO: This is what you want. Do you have any brothers, Carmen?
>
> TORTORA: One.
>
> RUSSO: If I told you your brother was wrong, he's a rat, he's gonna do one of us harm, you'd have to kill him. Would you do that for me?

TORTORA: Yes.

RUSSO: Would you do that favor?

TORTORA: Yes.

RUSSO: Anyone here asked for it?

TORTORA: Yes.

RUSSO: You know that. So you know the severity of this thing of ours?

TORTORA: Yes.

RUSSO: Do you want it badly and desperately? Your mother's dying in bed and you have to leave her because we called you. It's an emergency. You have to leave. Could you do that, Carmen?

TORTORA: Yes.

RUSSO: Alright. This what you want. We're the best people. I'm gonna make you part of this thing.

DI GIACOMO: We gonna baptize you ... Carmen ... you do not reveal any secrets of this organization ... to the rest of the world this does not exist ... they call it La Cosa Nostra, my organization. (Cupples and Kauzlarich 1997, 18)

Finally, Cupples and Kauzlarich's (1997) research on 150 members of La Cosa Nostra in Philadelphia lends some support to the claims of both Cressey and Ianni:

- Eighty-eight percent of the respondents claimed they were "honest."
- Ninety-five percent said that loyalty to the group was important to them.
- Only 30 percent considered themselves religious.
- Half considered themselves "aggressive."
- Seventy-three percent were employed outside of mob duties.
- Most (62 percent) had graduated from high school.

THE HISTORY OF ORGANIZED CRIME IN THE UNITED STATES

One of the most important factors likely to influence the activities, structure, and code of an organized crime syndicate is the length of time it has been in the business of crime. The crime syndicates one reads about most often—those identified as Italian-American and operating primarily in the Midwest and East—have been around for three-quarters of a century; others are relative newcomers, and some are just emerging. Understanding organized crime today requires understanding how it was in the past.

The origins of organized crime can be traced to the gangs of thugs that roamed the streets of New York and other cities and followed the frontier west during the nineteenth century. In New York City the earliest gangs were made up of the sons of immigrant Irish families. These immigrants constituted the core of poor people, who were deprived of political power and routinely discriminated against. In the eyes of many youths growing up during the period, survival and a path out of the ghetto lay in muscle and the willingness to use it. "The story of the early gangs—whether in New York, San Francisco, or the frontier—is told against a background of conflict; ethnic, economic, and political. It is the tale of men making their own law, legislating with their fists, striking out against real or imagined enemies" (Tyler 1962, 92).

From loafing and brawling, the New York gangs moved into extortion. They soon discovered that money was easily made through the intimidation of brothel owners, gambling proprietors, and others in the business of providing illicit services. More money came, and with it power, when it was discovered that politicians and businessmen would pay for their muscle. Gangs were hired to break up picket lines, to intimidate voters, to stuff ballot boxes, and to protect establishments from harassment by other gangs, not to mention the authorities. By the 1850s the gangs were the muscle behind Tammany Hall, the Democratic headquarters and the political heart of the city. With this new power, the gangs were able to open doors that formerly had been closed to the Irish. The docks were under their control, which meant work for Irishmen; now city hall felt their power, which meant city jobs for their fathers, brothers, and cousins.

Rags to Riches and the Quest for Respectability

The history of organized crime in America is to some extent the history of people seeking riches and respectability, and of social, legal, and political conditions providing both the incentive and means to attain them. Whether one looks at the nineteenth-century Irish gang, the Italian-American crime family, or the emergent African-American, Puerto Rican, and Cuban crime networks, the picture is essentially the same. It is a picture of migration and the herding of newcomers into ghettos, with few legitimate avenues of escape; of poverty, discrimination, and degradation; of corruption in politics and government; of laws rendering criminal many of the goods and services in public demand; and of material things held up as legitimate symbols of success and respectability but denied to the newcomers. Identifying the ghetto as the social setting in which organized crime is spawned, Ianni (1975, 89–90) wrote the following:

> The ghetto became a safe haven in which crime syndicates could grow and prosper. Two factors—immigrant slum dwellers' alienation from the political process and society's characteristic attitude that so long as "they" do it to each other crime in the ghetto is not an American problem—kept the police indifferent and absent and added to that prosperity. The immigrant and his children found organized crime a quick means of escaping the poverty and powerlessness of the slums. The successful gangster like the successful politician was seen as a model who demonstrated to the masses of lower-class co-ethnics that anyone could achieve success and power in the greater society. And if they did this while defying the police and other oppressors, so much the better. Then, when political power came to the group, partly as a result of these same illegal activities, access to legitimate opportunities became enlarged and assimilation was facilitated. The tradition became one of up and out.

Italian-Americans in Organized Crime

Over the years, virtually all ethnic groups have been involved in organized crime: the Irish, Eastern European Jews, Italian and Sicilian immigrants, Chinese and Cuban immigrants, Puerto Ricans, African-Americans, and WASPS, too, of course.

Of all these groups, the Italian-American immigrants made the most lasting impression on the organized crime scene and achieved, over the years, a dominating role in it. A study of the involvement of Italian-Americans in organized crime is thus particularly illuminating. It should be kept in mind, however, that it is an error to equate people of Italian descent with the mob (De Stefano 2000). In

some cases, this kind of stereotyping results in prejudicial and discriminatory actions against Italian-Americans seeking political office (Luconi 1999).

IMMIGRATION AND GHETTO RESIDENCY Between 1820 and 1930 an estimated 4.7 million Italians arrived in the United States. Many of the early immigrants traveled to the West and South and became farmers, fishermen, tradesmen, and craftsmen. Over 2 million Italians arrived between 1900 and 1910, 80 percent coming from southern Italy and Sicily. Poor, illiterate, and lacking occupational skills, many soon returned to Italy, but the majority remained in the East and congregated in "Little Italy" ghettos found in most urban centers, especially New York City. Like the Irish before them, they were desperate for a chance to improve their lot and achieve success and respectability in their new country. Also like the Irish, many found crime the easiest and quickest way up and out.

Unable to speak English, unfamiliar with American ways and big-city life, and dependent on one another for guidance and help, many Italian immigrants fell prey to exploitation. Apparently, crime among Little Italy residents was first of all crime against Italians: extortion, vendettas, and the kidnaping of brides. It was not, at first, organized crime, nor did Italian criminals often venture beyond the boundaries of the ghetto. A member of the "Lupollo" family related the following to Ianni:

> Can you imagine my father going uptown to commit a robbery or mugging? He would have had to take an interpreter with him to read the street signs and say "stick 'em up" for him. The only time he ever committed a crime outside Mulberry Street was when he went over to the Irish section to steal some milk so that my mother could heat it up and put in my kid brother's ear to stop an earache. (Ianni and Reuss-Ianni 1973, 55)

Yet this intra-ghetto crime was the beginning of Italian involvement in organized crime. By using muscle and by cashing in on ghetto conditions and police indifference to what went on in Little Italy, some immigrants became rich and powerful. They began to extend their illicit activities and hired other men to help them.

One key to wealth and power was extortion. Sometimes alone, sometimes with others, the extortionist would select victims from among newly arrived neighbors. Some extortionists associated themselves with the infamous "Black Hand," a loosely connected band that terrorized vulnerable immigrants. A favorite tactic was to send a letter demanding money, the letter being signed with a drawing of a black hand. Other letters would follow, each successively more blatant in its threats of physical violence. The fearful victim would search for help, which often came in the form of a man who was himself associated with the Black Hand. Sometimes the victim was able to secure a loan from a local source, thus helping enrich not only the extortionist but also the creditor. In this way, "respectable" members of the community grew wealthy from the activities of criminals. In either case, the victim went into debt, becoming more dependent and more vulnerable.

THE MAFIA CONNECTION   Sicilian-Italian immigrants brought their traditions with them. During the years of adjustment following their immigration, many naturally relied on their social and cultural heritage to help them, and the tendency to cling to old ways was heightened by the ethnic homogeneity of Little Italy. To understand Italian involvement in organized crime and the form it has taken, one must recognize the role played by the immigrant heritage itself.

Important to that heritage were the secret organizations that had flourished for years in southern Italy—among them the Mafia and the Camorra. The origins of the Mafia and the Camorra are generally traced to the early nineteenth century; the Camorra was centered in Naples, the Mafia in Sicily. Though their actual beginnings are unknown, they both flourished in large part because of the widespread political and social unrest characterizing the southern Italian and Sicilian societies during the nineteenth century (Block 1974; Ianni and Reuss-Ianni 1973, 30–40).

The concept of **mafia** was also important to the heritage. It refers not to the organization but rather to "a state of mind, a sense of pride, a philosophy of life, and a style of behavior which Sicilians recognize immediately" (Ianni and Reuss-Ianni 1973, 26). To describe someone as a mafioso does not necessarily mean that he is a member of the Mafia; it may simply mean that he is a man who is respected and held in awe. He is a man who seeks protection not through the law but by his own devices; he

is a man who commands fear; he is a man who has dignity and bearing; he is a man who gets things done; he is a man to whom people come when in need; he is man with "friends."

Though not all Italian immigrants were familiar with either the organization or the concept, those from southern Italy, especially western Sicily, undoubtedly were. Some of the immigrants themselves may have been mafiosi, in either meaning. In short, there is good reason to believe that Little Italy residents were familiar with Mafia ways and the spirit of mafia and that their behavior was affected by them. For example, Ianni noted that in the Italian ghettos, people went for protection or redress of grievances to informal "courts" held by mafiosi. In his testimony before the 1963 McClellan Committee of the Senate, Joe Valachi made much of the ties between the American Cosa Nostra and the secret organizations of southern Italy. One clear tie is the oath-taking ritual that changed little from that used in the early nineteenth century by both the Camorra and Mafia organizations:

> Flanked by the boss and his lieutenants, the initiate and his sponsor may stand in front of a table on which are placed a gun and, on occasion, a knife. The boss picks up the gun and intones in the Sicilian dialect: "Niatri representam La Cosa Nostra. Sta famigghia [age] La Cosa Nostra. (We represent La Cosa Nostra. This family is Our Thing.)" The sponsor then pricks his trigger finger and the trigger finger of the new member, holding both together to symbolize the mixing of blood. After swearing to hold the family above his religion, his country, and his wife and children, the inductee finished the ritual. A picture of a saint or a religious card is placed in his cupped hands and ignited. As the paper burns, the inductee, together with his sponsor, proclaims: "If I ever violate this oath, may I burn as this paper." (*Time*, 22 August 1969, 19)

This is not to say that Italian immigrants imported wholesale the Mafia or the Camorra. Rather, they imported a knowledge of the ways of secret societies and the spirit of mafia. This spirit seems to have been particularly important during early ghetto life, for those who grew rich—whether through crime or by essentially legal means such as loaning money in exchange for a part interest in a business—were able to cash in on the mafia idea. These men became the mafiosi and, like those back home, were feared while at the same time respected and upheld

The film Goodfellas *is a masterful account of a neighborhood Italian-American crime "family." Among other things, it demonstrates how organized crime attracts small-time thugs and fosters criminal careers, how members protect each other and counter threats to the family, and how the organization persists beyond the imprisonment and death of its key members. It also shows that even a criminal organization will not protect a psychopathic killer (played by Joe Pesci) or members who defy the rules.*

as models for emulation by the young. Ianni suggests that it was in the role of mafioso that Giuseppe Lupollo, grandfather of the crime family he studied, gained much of his strength. Abadinsky (1990, 32) describes the "boss" in a Mafia family as follows:

> The boss demands absolute respect and total obedience. His working day is spent in exchanges with numerous persons. With a word or two, a sentence, a shake of the head, a smile, or a gesture, he can set in motion a host of activities and operations involving dozens, if not hundreds, of persons. The boss is treated with a great deal of deference. People rise when he enters the room and never interrupt when he is speaking. If they are close to the boss, a kiss on the boss's cheek is considered an appropriate gesture of respect. If the boss rises and embraces an individual, this is considered a great honor, often reserved only for other bosses.

THE IMPACT OF PROHIBITION   Lupollo and other Little Italy residents grew rich and powerful through a combination of criminal and legal activities. Usually they worked alone or with other

members of their families. No secret organization tied them together, and the immigrants did not form a new Mafia or Camorra on American soil. Ianni and Reuss-Ianni (1973, 61) give three reasons why, until the 1920s at least, a Mafia-style organization did not emerge. First, they had not had enough time. The southern Italian immigrants were newcomers, and twenty years was hardly enough time to establish what had taken many decades at home. Second, the Italian immigrants had come mostly as individuals; hence they had to establish new patterns of organization and new sources of power and profit. Third, the traditional pattern of father-son respect and obedience was not reinforced in American schools and in church; especially in school, the lessons stressed individualism, not family loyalty.

The onset of Prohibition, however, added two of the missing ingredients. Prohibition provided the incentive and means to move outside the ghetto and offered substantial rewards to those who ventured into bootlegging and other liquor-related activities. The illegal market for alcohol provided the incentive for mafiosi to work together and establish contacts outside the ghetto. Prohibition also supplied new organizational models that replaced the traditional family model, which older immigrants stressed but their American-born sons tended to reject. The organizational model was that of the American crime gang of Irish and Jewish thugs, which offered lower-echelon positions to Italian youths who had gained criminal experience in ghetto street gangs. A working relationship with non-Italians, frowned on by the older generation of immigrants—called "Old Moustaches" or "Moustache Petes" by the youngsters—became an important feature of the new Italian-American involvement in organized crime.

What emerged was an Italian-American participation in organized crime that combined aspects of the old Mafia and the mafia spirit with strictly American contributions. Unlike the Italian Mafia, the new crime syndicates operated beyond the boundaries of the local community and employed non-Italians. Yet strong ethnic bonds persisted and became especially important as Italians began to secure positions within legitimate government as councilmen, judges, and police officers. Slowly, the domination of the older mafiosi was weakened as ambitious second-generation Italian-Americans sought leadership roles and lucrative fields of operation (drugs, for example) over the objections of their elders.

Toward the end of Prohibition, internal dissension threatened the power and profits of the Italian-American crime syndicates, as the Old Moustaches fought for authority with their younger Americanized counterparts. The Castellammarese War of 1930–1931 marked the height of the conflict. Originating in New York between the older Salvatore Maranzano faction and second-generation gangs under Giuseppe Masseria, the feud spread to Chicago and other cities. Although Maranzano was the victor, many of the Old Moustaches were killed, and it was Americanized gangsters such as Joe Adonis, Vito Genovese, Charlie Luciano, and Frank Costello who subsequently emerged as the powerful figures in the Italian-American syndicates.

After prohibition, Italian-American crime families continued to flourish and retain a dominant place in organized crime. This success was due to a number of events and conditions: the massive influx of Italian immigrants during the early decades of this century; the conditions of ghetto life to which they were subject; the indifference of authorities to what went on inside the ghettos; the immigrants' familiarity with, and fear of, the Mafia and mafiosi; the attempt by Mussolini to crush the Mafia and other secret societies, thus forcing mafiosi to seek shelter in America; the existence and successes of semiorganized American crime gangs; and widespread political corruption in urban areas. Most of all, it was due to Prohibition itself. Prohibition promised a quick and easy path to riches and provided the impetus for the mafiosi and other Italian-Americans to organize and venture outside the ghetto. Prohibition showed the criminal gangs in the ghetto how to increase their money and power. In short, Prohibition helped organized crime come of age.

THE MONEY-MAKING ENTERPRISES OF ORGANIZED CRIME

During Prohibition, crime syndicates made the manufacture, distribution, and sale of alcoholic beverages their major business. Although extortion, blackmail, robbery, prostitution, gambling, and the sale of protection had been lucrative enterprises, bootlegging outweighed them all. Suddenly the law had made illegal something much in demand by all segments of the population. Fortunes could be made by those who cared to break the law and could organize to do it.

When Prohibition came to an end in 1933 the black market quickly fell apart. This did not mean that no money was to be made by dealing in booze; only much less. Actually, organized crime continues to dabble in the liquor business. Some jurisdictions are still "dry," and others permit only beer or only certain labels to be sold. Even where liquor of any sort is legal, however, money can still be made. With the right connections, profitable liquor licenses can be bought on behalf of the syndicate; through control of bottling, warehousing, and distributing, syndicate liquor finds its way into legitimate outlets (Dorman 1972, 129).

Organized crime is not restricted to any one kind of activity, legal or otherwise, and, like any entrepreneur, must keep up with changing times or go out of business. To fill the void created by the repeal of Prohibition, organized crime turned its attention to new avenues of profit and has continued to branch out ever since.

Criminal Enterprises

The major enterprises providing illicit profits are gambling, usury (loan-sharking), drug trafficking, theft, and **racketeering** (criminal network schemes). In all these areas, the money to be made is enormous. Though one can only guess, it is generally held that profits from each one of these areas run into billions of dollars every year. Estimates of the annual gross from gambling enterprises go as high as $50 billion; drug trafficking is estimated to be a $75 billion business; and a conservative estimate of the gross from loan-sharking is $10 billion. Even the sale of sex, not one of the big money-makers, is estimated to gross over $2 billion a year. Recalling that organized crime avoids most, if not all, of the overhead and taxes legitimate businesses have to absorb, these gross figures indicate tremendous incomes for organized crime—a conservative estimate of the net profits would be 30 percent of the gross.

GAMBLING   Though some speculate that the money-making possibilities of illegal gambling may be on the decline following the spread of state lotteries, gambling remains one of the principal sources of income for organized crime (Pennsylvania Crime Commission 1989). LCN capo Thomas Del Giorno once said that many people got their start in the mob through gambling and that it was steady, "relatively easy money" (Cupples and Kauzlarich 1997, 20). Anastasia (1993, 49) has noted that mob-related sports betting in Philadelphia is as pervasive as "soft pretzels and, in most cases, is considered as harmless as bingo."

Most of the money from gambling is made from the policy, or numbers, racket. Legend has it that the term *policy* originated from the nineteenth-century practice among the poor of gambling with money set aside for insurance policy premiums; Cressey, however, suggests that the term came from the Italian word for lottery ticket, *polizza*. Whatever the truth, one fact is clear: Policy, or numbers, betting is predominantly a feature of urban slum life.

Numbers betting is a simple concept and easy to do. The gambler simply picks any three-digit number and bets that this number will correspond to the winning number, selected by some predetermined procedure. Over the years, winning numbers have been computed from the number of shares traded on a stock exchange, the daily cash balance in the U.S. Treasury, and the payoffs at local pari-mutuel racetracks. At one time, the number was simply drawn from a revolving drum. The odds are 1,000 to 1 against the bettor, whereas payoff never exceeds 600 to 1.

The numbers racket attracted organized crime not only because of the immense profits to be made from it but also because the game requires organization, money, and a good deal of corruption in the right places—things only organized crime had. Although small-scale games, involving small bets and a small betting clientele, have existed in the past, they were neither very profitable nor very secure for those who ran them. To work, the numbers racket needs organized crime. The boss of a New Jersey crime network explains why:

> Everybody needs the organization—the banker, the controllers, the runners, even the customers. Here's why. Only a big organization can pay up when the bank gets hit very hard. Suppose a lot of people play the same number one day. For example, when Willie Mays hit his 599th home run, a lot of black people played "600" the next day, figuring Willie was going to make it and so were they. If that number had come up, the banker would have been wiped out, and not only that, a lot of customers would have gone without their payoffs. The whole system would have collapsed.... There was another reason why they needed the organization. Only the organization had the money and the muscle to keep the cops and politicians from breaking up the game and shaking down the players and operators. (Ianni 1975, 59–60)

Reuter (1983) found that New York City numbers games were not highly coordinated, though some apparently independent banks may have been branches of a single owner (see also Haller 1991).

Though the specifics vary from place to place and from syndicate to syndicate, the numbers operation is organized along the following lines: The bets are picked up by "runners" from "numbers drops" in shops, factories, office buildings, and bars, or simply on the street. The runners pass the money and betting slips on to local "collectors," or "route men," in charge of their neighborhoods. The collectors pass the money and numbers tickets on to the "controller," who sends it on to the "district controller," who works for the "policy operator." The policy operator actually runs the enterprise and sometimes is known as the "banker" or "owner." He or she is usually one of a number of operators, all of whom pay a commission to the crime syndicate under whose overall supervision and control and in whose territory the racket operates. These policy operators may or may not be actual members of the crime family. At payoff time, the money simply follows the reverse route, usually starting at the "branch" or "district bank" run by the policy operator.

LOAN-SHARKING   Loan-sharking thrives because some people who need loans are unable or unwilling to secure them through legitimate lending institutions. Loan sharks will lend them the money, for a price. To make loans one needs money; organized crime has it. To ensure that the money is repaid, with interest, one needs organization and the ability to make collections; organized crime has them. Because usury is illegal, a lender must be able to collect without resorting to legal channels and without the interference of the law; organized crime accomplishes this through muscle and corruption.

Borrowers who come to a loan shark usually want quick loans with no questions asked. They may be gamblers in need of money to pay off debts or finance further play; they may be businesspeople faced with bankruptcy or wanting to invest in risky, perhaps illegal, ventures; they may simply be poor people in need of small loans but lacking the credit or collateral required by licensed lending institutions. The interest they will pay depends on how much they borrow, the intended use of the loan, their repayment potential, and what they are worth to the mob if they cannot make their payments. Generally interest runs anywhere from 1 to 150 percent per week, with most smaller loans at 20 percent per week—the "six for five" loan, in which each five dollars borrowed requires six to be paid back at the end of a week. Usually a set time is established for payments, and if the required payment is not made on or before that exact time, the borrower will owe another week's interest, computed from the principal plus the interest already accrued.

Various members of the South Philadelphia Bruno family operated loan-sharking businesses, and Haller (1991) uses two of them to illustrate contrasting operations within one crime family. On the one hand, there was Harry Riccobene, whose loans were mostly small (less than $1,000) and made to local hustlers and merchants. "Within their culture, borrowing informally from a loan shark was a normal and accepted business practice" (Haller 1991, 10). When customers fell behind in their payments, as most did, Harry used a combination of gentle chastisement and renegotiated (lower) payment schedules. Some of his agents did not approve of Harry's leniency, but Harry's revolving credit system prospered.

Also prospering was the loan-sharking operation of Frank Sindone, another Bruno family member. But Sindone's operation was different: He made much larger loans, up to $50,000 or higher, mostly to construction contractors and other legitimate businesses with credit and cash-flow problems. He also took his operation further afield, to South Jersey and the Pennsylvania suburbs. His agents operated relatively independently, sharing in the profits, and together Sindone and his agents "had mastered the orchestrated use of vicious, vulgar, and convincing threats of violence to the borrower and the borrower's family" when dealing with delinquent loans (Haller 1991, 12).

It is unusual for a borrower to be killed, for death means the money is lost forever. Though a killing may be committed occasionally to make the victim an example to others, the loan shark wants the money first and foremost, and if this cannot be obtained with threats, the loan shark will look for other ways to get it. Indeed, loans are sometimes made—at very high interest rates—not in the expectation that they will be repaid but for other purposes. The mob may be looking to garner a controlling interest in a borrower's business, and when loan payments falter, this provides the leverage necessary to bring this goal about. The borrower simply turns over all or a part of the business in exchange for a temporary delay of the payments. The Bruno family's Sindone liked to operate this way (Haller 1991, 12). This is one of the ways that organized crime secures a footing in legitimate business enterprises, though Reuter (1983, 101) thinks it is rare among the small-time loan sharks, most of whom would not know how to carry out profitable fraud schemes involving legitimate businesses.

DRUG TRAFFICKING Organized crime is involved in drug trafficking at all levels, but especially in importation and wholesale distribution. The need for organization, contacts, and large sums of money puts the business outside the reach of most individuals and small criminal groups (see Natarajan and Belanger 1998). This emphasis on importing and wholesaling does not mean, however, that organized crime is not interested in what goes on at the neighborhood and street levels of the drug scene. Since its own profits depend on a healthy drug traffic, it observes the street closely and helps keep open the channels through which the drugs flow. The syndicate also supplies loans to dealers—at least the bigger, more successful ones—and, through loan-sharking and fencing on the street, endeavors to ensure that money circulates so that buys can be made. Today much of the local heroin trade is controlled by black and Hispanic criminal groups, and this has been one of the avenues giving these groups access to the world of organized crime. The world of illicit drugs is discussed in greater detail in Chapter 8.

In 1984 the so-called Pizza Connection was uncovered when Italian and American police arrested over 200 suspected Mafia members, including 28 in America, after a high-ranking mafioso named Tommaso Buscetta turned informant. Buscetta had extensive operations in Italy and Brazil, and he detailed the existence of a Sicilian-based organized crime network operating outside the established American Mafia families. This network is reputed to have imported over 1,600 pounds of heroin since 1979, with a street value of $1.65 billion. Its American members were mostly pizza parlor operators—hence the name—located in rural parts of Wisconsin, Michigan, Oregon, and Illinois, and with connections in New York and Switzerland. In late 1988 another major drug ring was exposed, this one smuggling tons of marijuana into the United States from Colombia. Former race driver Randy Lanier and two associates were charged with engaging in a "continuing criminal enterprise," a federal charge carrying a mandatory life sentence. The three conspirators were said to have smuggled 646,000 pounds of marijuana over a seven-year period, and to have accumulated assets worth over $150 million (*St. Louis Post-Dispatch*, 6 October 1988).

THEFT Organized crime has been interested in theft since its earliest days. Today most organized crime efforts are directed at the kinds of thievery that promise high returns while avoiding high risk, such as truck hijacking, car-theft rings, thefts from warehouses and docks, securities theft, and fencing. Once again the organization, money, muscle, and contacts of organized crime are major factors in explaining syndicate activity in these areas.

Much has been made of syndicate involvement in securities theft and manipulation. Millions of dollars in securities disappear every year from the vaults of major brokerage houses; most of the lost bonds are stolen. Testimony before the Senate Committee on Banking, Housing, and Urban Affairs indicated that securities theft is a major problem these days and that behind much of the thievery lie organized crime syndicates (see also Abadinsky 1990, 291–294). While estimates of the actual amounts stolen are difficult to make, the yearly totals are generally thought to exceed $2 billion and may be much higher when thefts from the mails and manipulations during securities transfers are included (Conklin 1973, 121–127; Metz 1971).

To accomplish the theft and manipulation of stocks and bonds, organized crime needs insiders, persons employed by brokerage firms who have access to vaults or who routinely handle securities. Sometimes these important contacts are indebted to loan sharks and steal securities in exchange for a respite from their payments; sometimes extortion and intimidation are used to frighten employees into working with the underworld; and sometimes the mob manages to place one of its own into a position of trust within a brokerage firm. Once in syndicate hands, the stocks and bonds are often converted into cash. This can be accomplished by using the stolen securities as collateral for loans, as part of a company's portfolio of assets, or merely by reselling them through brokers here or abroad.

LABOR RACKETEERING During the nineteenth century, organized criminal groups learned that money could be made in the fields of industrial organization and employee relations. Faced with the prospects of strikes and unionization, companies called on criminal gangs to help them combat these threats to their power and profits. The companies paid well for the gangs' muscle, and the gangs, in turn, were happy to oblige. Infiltration of the union movement by organized crime soon followed, and with it came money and power for leaders of the fledgling unions. First the building trades and then service industries fell under the influence and domination of corrupt officials backed by gangsters. Money was collected from both employers and employees, organized crime playing off each side against the other (Hutchinson 1969).

Racketeering is explained not merely by the corruption of union and company officials nor by the fact that organized crime is in the business of making money any way it can. Rather, the spread of racketeering stems from a combination of conditions. Some are economic—for example, excessive entrepreneurial competition and an excess supply of labor. As Walter Lippmann (1931, 61) observed many years ago:

> Given an oversupply of labor and an industry in which no considerable amount of capital or skill is required to enter it, the conditions exist under which racketeering can flourish. The effort to unionize in the face of a surplus of labor invites the use of violence and terror to maintain a monopoly of labor and thus to preserve the workers' standard of living. Labor unionism in such trades tends to fall into the control of dictators who are often corrupt and not often finical about enlisting gangsters to enforce the closed shop. The employers, on the other hand, faced with the constant threat of cutthroat competition, are subject to the easy temptation to pay gangsters for protection against competitors. The protection consists in driving the competition from the field.

Additional conditions that support organized crime infiltration into unions include (1) the traditions of frontier violence, (2) cultural values stressing individualism, (3) an entrenched philosophy of acquisition, (4) an admiration for sharp practices, (5) a tolerance of the fix, and (6) a legacy stressing politics as a source of personal profit (Hutchinson 1969, 143). Companies and unions went along with the spread of racketeering because both saw benefits outweighing costs and because the conditions and temperament of the times presented no great obstacles. Actually, of course, both company officials and union leaders risk becoming pawns in the hands of organized crime syndicates. This is precisely what has happened over the years, with the costs borne not only by the union

membership but also by members of the general public who hold company stock or who are simply consumers of the companies' goods and services.

Nobody knows for sure how much organized crime syndicates make from labor racketeering. In 1958, the Senate Select Committee on Improper Activities in the Labor or Management Field found that $10 million in Teamsters Union funds had been siphoned off into the pockets of union officials and their gangster friends (Salerno and Tompkins 1969, 295). The Teamsters Central States Pension Fund is widely acknowledged to have been under the control of syndicate figures. It is known that the mob helped pick Teamster presidents Jackie Presser and Roy Williams. Police informants have tied both men to organized crime groups in Chicago, New York, Kansas City, and Cleveland (*Los Angeles Times*, 25 September 1985). The pension fund is worth billions of dollars, and millions have apparently been spent without the knowledge of the rank-and-file membership, whose money it really is (see also Block 1991; Abadinsky 1990).

Pseudo-Legitimate Enterprises

Apart from their patently illegal enterprises, organized crime groups have infiltrated the world of legitimate business. Though any complete list of the different businesses in which organized crime is involved would be impossible to compile, the following have been specifically identified: banking, hotels and motels, real estate, garbage collection, vending machines, construction, delivery and long-distance hauling, garment manufacture, insurance, stocks and bonds, vacation resorts, funeral parlors, bakeries, sausage manufacture and processing of other meat products, paving, tobacco, dairy products, demolition, warehousing, auto sales and leasing, meat packing, janitorial services, beauty and health salons, lumber, horse breeding, night-clubs, bars, restaurants, linen supply, laundries, and dry cleaning. There may well be no type of legitimate business enterprise in which organized crime does not have a financial interest.

Organized crime has sought involvement in legitimate businesses for a number of reasons. First is the obvious economic incentive: Legitimate businesses are additional sources of income. Second, legitimate businesses can provide a front for illegal activities; owning a trucking firm, for example, gives a crime syndicate the means of transporting stolen property or a cover for bootlegging. Third, legitimate businesses can serve as an important outlet for monies earned through criminal activities. Profits from the latter invested in businesses under syndicate control are made to appear "clean" (or "laundered") as are the wages and salaries received by syndicate members from the companies. These salaries constitute the members' visible sources of income, and they declare this income on tax returns in a continuing effort to avoid federal prosecution. (Needless to say, those receiving such salaries often contribute little or nothing to the actual day-to-day operations of the companies concerned). And fourth, legitimate business activity helps syndicate members avoid the costs and risks of continued exposure to law enforcement.

A final reason that organized crime has sought holdings in legitimate enterprises is respectability. Crime is not respectable work, and the profits from it are dirty money. A long-standing goal among higher-echelon mobsters, especially Italian-Americans with their traditions of family honor, has been the acquisition of respectability for their children and grandchildren, if not for themselves. Legitimate businesses provide a route to social acceptance. Instead of following in the footsteps of their elders, the younger generation is able to acquire the trappings of respectability by working in enterprises with no apparent connection to crime.

Peter Lupsha (1981) suggests that the pull of respectability may have been overstated. He sees organized crime as rational behavior selected not so much as a last economic resort but because it fits "one perverse aspect of our values, namely, that only 'suckers' work, and that in our society, one is at liberty to take 'suckers' and seek easy money, just as one is at liberty to be one" (p. 22). Organized crime families are not leaving the business in droves, nor are the children of members all leading exemplary lives: "A sufficient number of family members and relatives do stay in the business so that family control is maintained" (p. 20). Penetration of legitimate businesses is guided more by economic motives than any interest in respectability, in Lupsha's view.

Certainly, the legitimate enterprises are rarely, if ever, completely divorced from a syndicate's illegal enterprises, and for this reason it seems more

appropriate to call them "pseudo-legitimate" enterprises. A certain real estate company may appear quite legal and above-board; if organized crime has anything to do with it, however, all is not what it appears to be. Confounding the situation, companies in industries reputed to be racketeer-dominated often function in much the same way whether actually infiltrated or not, as found in the case of the vending machine industry (Reuter, Rubinstein, and Winn 1983).

Such is the case with state-sanctioned bingo games. A decade ago, the Pennsylvania Crime Commission completed a major investigation of organized crime's infiltration of bingo, the second-largest legal wagering game (after the lottery) in that state (Reilly 1992). Legal bingo is big business across the United States, with an estimated $4 billion wagered each year. The Commission found in Pennsylvania that fraud, racketeering, misrepresentation, and money laundering permeated the bingo industry, although casual observers would never know it. Many "charitable organizations" were created for the purpose of operating bingo games, with the organization acting merely as a front. Some legitimately run charitable bingo games have been run out of business by large-scale professionally run games under the control of organized crime groups. Studies of bingo in Kansas City and New York, and on various Indian reservations (where games may run 24 hours a day with jackpots as high as $50,000), suggest that organized crime's infiltration is widespread (Reilly 1992, 9–11). And why not? Profits are huge, and organized crime groups have little to fear from law enforcement partly because they keep a low profile, but also because there is little public concern over bingo.

Another example comes from the real estate industry. Real estate transactions provide excellent money-laundering opportunities: "For example, for a property worth $3 million, a money launderer offers to pay the seller $2 million in a visible transaction and $1 million under the table in cash. The launderer then sells the property for the fair market value of $3 million. The $1 million "profit" that the launderer makes is really only the drug [or gambling or prostitution] cash that has been cycled through the deal. He can now pay (or avoid) taxes on his profit and achieve an aura of legitimacy" (Webster and McCampbell 1992b, 6). Other illegal activities are typically involved as well (for example: obtaining false titles, credit, or loans; or bribing bank, title, or appraisal officials), showing the range of crimes that an apparently legitimate business transaction may conceal.

Organized crime moves into its pseudo-legitimate enterprises in various ways. Some use intimidation and force, and others use more normal avenues of business acquisition. When interested in a particular business, it is common for the syndicate to use the carrot-and-stick approach—in Don Corleone's words, "I'll make him an offer he can't refuse." Such a case was reported in the New York Court of Appeals in the late 1960s. An executive of several successful vending machine companies was simply told that he was to pass over to a certain family of interested persons a 25 percent share of his business interests. The request was backed up by assaults on his wife and various other forms of intimidation (Cressey 1969, 103). Another way to infiltrate businesses is to arrange, through extortion or bribes, to have syndicate associates placed in executive positions, so that eventually the company is controlled by the syndicate. Yet another way is to purchase large blocks of company stock through legitimate trading channels, though under the cover of fictitious names and companies. Finally, loan sharks may turn delinquent loans into a means of acquiring a controlling interest in a business.

Some criminologists argue that it is becoming increasingly difficult to distinguish organized crime activity from the broader realm of white-collar or occupational crime. Passas (1993), for example, suggests that the distinction should be abandoned in favor of an "enterprise" model that places the profit-making activities of organizations along a continuum from wholly legal to wholly illegal. This model accommodates the fact that there may be considerable mixing of legitimate and illegitimate activity within the same business or corporation. This mixing is often beneficial to both the professional criminal and the legitimate operator, neither being the reluctant partner (Passas 1993). This sort of argument parallels the points made in Chapter 6 about the convergence of professional crime and various forms of occupational crime.

The convergence of professional crime, occupational crime, and organized crime illustrates how difficult and perhaps pointless it is to attempt a demarcation of the worlds of compliance and of crime. The two are superimposed, one upon the other, and it would be difficult, indeed, for people to say with certainty that they live, play, or work among the truly law-abiding.

THE SURVIVAL OF ORGANIZED CRIME

Why does organized crime persist? The answer to this important question lies beyond the more obvious defenses that secret societies and groups erect against outsiders—secrecy, codes of conduct, mutual protection among members, and the like. Within the organization of crime syndicates are survival mechanisms that come into play whenever these more obvious defenses are inadequate. These include the roles played by public attitudes and behavior and the attitudes and behavior of those ostensibly responsible for combating organized crime. The nature of criminal law itself is a factor, especially as it focuses on moral choices and private behavior.

Role Imperatives

Two of the most important internal survival mechanisms appear to be the roles of "enforcer" and "buffer." These roles, assumed by select individuals in crime organizations, might well be called role imperatives, for without them (or something very similar) the survival of any crime organization would be threatened.

Donald Cressey (1969) goes so far as to argue that unless the division of labor provides for at least one enforcer, the organization in question is not a part of true organized crime. Ianni (1973), on the other hand, found only weak evidence of enforcer positions in the established division of labor and authority structure of the crime family he extensively studied. Methods of enforcement range all the way from verbal warnings to maiming or murder. A set of rules is not enough: From time to time threats must be enforced, and organized crime sees to it that they are. Organized crime has been likened to government in this sense: Not only do syndicates create their own rules, but also, like states, they have their own machinery for enforcing them and their own methods of doing it.

The **buffer** role identified by Cressey and others also enhances the organization's survival possibilities. The buffer is akin to the corporate "assistant to the president," whose tasks are primarily centered on internal communications and the flow of decisions in the hierarchy of authority. The buffer may also be likened to a spy, for he keeps tabs on what lower-level members do and say and reports back to his superiors. Without the buffer role, the smooth functioning of the organization would be impaired, and the decision-making process undermined. It is the buffer who keeps open lines of communication between leaders and followers, who passes down important messages from the top, who forewarns of internal dissensions and problems with operations at the street level, and who helps smooth out disagreements and conflicts.

Another role imperative is the **corrupter**. Since organized crime syndicates are in the business of crime, their survival greatly depends on the fix. To put the fix in and maintain important connections with those in government and law, organized crime groups typically have one or more members assigned to corrupt officials in order to preserve good relations with them. Corrupters may be found anywhere in the organizational hierarchy, and their job is to bribe, buy, intimidate, negotiate, persuade, and sweet-talk themselves "into a relationship with police, public officials, and anyone else who might help 'family' members maintain immunity from arrest, prosecution, and punishment" (Cressey 1969, 251–252). Moore (1986) suggests that corrupter roles emerge in response to the organization of law enforcement itself. If there is one enforcement agency that has jurisdiction over a particular illegal activity, then a centralized corrupter role will tend to develop. If many agencies have jurisdiction, however, corruption will have to occur on more "local" levels to be effective.

Cressey (1969, 248) calls the political objective of corruption the "nullification of government," and it is sought at two different levels:

> At the lower level are the agencies for law enforcement and the administration of justice. When a Cosa Nostra soldier bribes a policeman, a police chief, a prosecutor, a judge, or a license administrator, he does so in an attempt to nullify the law-enforcement process. At the upper level are legislative agencies, including federal and state legislatures as well as city councils and county boards of supervisors. When a "family" boss supports a candidate for political office, he does so in an attempt to deprive honest citizens of their democratic voice, thus nullifying the democratic process.

In his study of organized crime in Seattle during the 1960s, William Chambliss (1978) describes a crime network that extended from street hustlers, bookmakers, pimps, drug dealers, and gamblers to business people, politicians, and law-enforcement officials. Hotel, restaurant, club, and bingo-parlor operators were fronts for gambling and vice; police officers and prosecutors took bribes and offered protection, falsified reports, and covered up investigations; and politicians took campaign contributions of "dirty money" and exercised their licensing and legislative powers in support of the rackets, "one of the largest industries in the state" (Chambliss 1978, 54). This crime network depended for its survival on corruption at all levels of government, and for many years the corruption was there.

For nullification of government to work there must be officials willing or able to be corrupted. Some persons obviously are willing to be corrupted, but even if there were no willing corruptees, organized crime's muscle and its willingness to use it would probably ensure viable corrupter-corruptee relationships. The truth is, however, that organized crime rarely has to use muscle to nullify government, no matter what level. The nature of politics and government is such that those acting in violation of the law and those ostensibly responsible for its creation and enforcement readily enter into mutually beneficial relationships. Just how successful and important these connections are is evidenced by the fact that since its very beginning, organized crime has made one of its first tasks the establishment of working relationships with those in politics, government, and law enforcement. Because it pays off in security, organized crime will continue to pursue the nullification of government.

Legislation of Morality

Organized crime will continue to flourish if lawmakers continue to enact legislation rendering illegal any activities, products, and services demanded by significant numbers of the population. Organized crime makes the bulk of its profits in supplying illegal commodities and services. Drugs, gambling, sex, and other so-called vices are profitable precisely because criminal laws have the effect of driving the activities underground and into the hands of those willing and able to carry out illicit business. In this way, criminal laws create the very conditions conducive to the emergence and spread of organized criminal activities.

The legislation of morality is, then, yet another factor in the survival of organized crime. But apart from encouraging the emergence of black marketeering, laws designed to repress what some people think of as vices also help give "a kind of franchise to those who are willing to break the law" (Schelling 1967, 117). This is what Herbert Packer (1964) called "the crime tariff"; it serves to protect those among us who will break the law by supplying drugs or gambling opportunities to those who are unwilling to do so but who will take advantage of their availability. Journalist and social commentator Walter Lippmann (1931, 65ff) first drew attention to this unintended consequence of moral legislation when, seventy years ago, he noted the following:

> [W]e have a code of laws which prohibit all the weaknesses of the flesh. This code of laws is effective up to a point. That point is the unwillingness of respectable people to engage in the prohibited services as sellers of prohibited commodities.... The high level of lawlessness is maintained by the fact that Americans desire to do so many things which they also desire to prohibit.... [They] have made laws which act like a protective tariff—to encourage the business of the underworld. Their prohibitions have turned over to the underworld the services from which it profits. Their prejudice in favor of weak governments has deprived them of the power to cope with the vast lawbreaking industries which their laws have called into question.

Professionalization of Deviance: Outlaw Motorcycle Gangs

Another factor in the persistence of organized crime is what we might call the *professionalization of deviance*. From relatively unsophisticated, intemperate, and rebellious beginnings, many organized crime groups eventually distance themselves from overt criminal activity, especially the violent kind, that is likely to draw unwanted attention and result in arrests and prosecutions. Their ongoing criminal activity is overshadowed or hidden by the trappings of legitimacy and professionalism. As we saw earlier, involvement in pseudo-legitimate businesses is one way to accomplish this.

It has been suggested that Outlaw motorcycle gangs in the United States have gone through this kind of evolution since the 1950s. Loves (1992) sees a five-stage process: (1) the 1950s found social rebels, many ex-servicemen in search of danger and excitement, banding together in the style of Marlon Brando in the movie *The Wild One*; (2) during the 1960s a stereotypical biker image emerged, the "Potborskis," described as "hard riding, hard drinking, rough and tough." Tattoos, initiations that included assaults, rapes, and urinating on prospective members, indulgence in "perverse" sex, crazed parties, and drug trafficking are common; (3) drug trafficking gains a more prominent place and with it comes wealth and power, territorial battles with other biker clubs, and involvement in money laundering through bike repair shops and tattoo parlors; (4) the selective recruitment of members and rejection of Potborskis that began during the preceding stage becomes more and more important as the club starts developing its outside connections with both criminal and legitimate organizations, and hires accountants, lawyers, real estate experts, and other professionals; drug distribution becomes more sophisticated as does money laundering; the focus is more and more on making money and expanding the club's influence in politics and the economy; colors and other identification and overt criminal activity are rejected in favor of a more positive public image; (5) during the final stage the operation goes further underground and a pool of criminal associates becomes the source of criminal expertise when needed. However, so much money is being made from drug sales that clubs in this stage cannot launder it on their own and enlist the expertise and connections of high-powered accountants or lawyers. Loves (1992, 13) concludes the following:

> They take over whole industries and launder money through investments as diverse as overseas property development and share investment. The outward trappings of wealth are used to impress professionals and attract potential customers. They think more in terms of a corporate image and structure than of a "bike gang."

It must be born in mind that Loves's account represents the view of an investigator who spent four years gathering police intelligence on Australian, Canadian, and American bikers. It would be very interesting to see how Outlaw bikers themselves describe developments over the past thirty years. There is no question that the brotherhood of Outlaw bikers has been under intense and persistent police surveillance. The FBI is reputed to have set up clubs of its own in order that its agents might bypass the probationary ("Striker") period (Wolf 1991, 14). However, Wolf (1991) suggests that the international-biker-organized-crime-conspiracy theory favored by the police vastly overstates the situation, and ignores the considerable variation among biker clubs in their involvement in criminal activity of any sort. Wolf's participant observation of a Canadian Outlaw biker gang, The Rebels, brought him to this conclusion:

> The Rebels are outlaws but they are not professional criminals. When I rode with them, laws were sidestepped, bent, and broken, but rarely for profit. Criminal acts were usually confined to minor misdemeanors such as the possession of soft drugs, weapons offences, occasional assaults, mischief, and drunk-driving charges, along with a plethora of vehicle violations and traffic tickets.

The true picture of Outlaw biker gangs is probably one in which they are ranged on a continuum of professionalism, organization, wealth, and influence. Even so, the claim that professionalization of deviance contributes to the prosperity and long-term survival of criminal groups is not in dispute.

Attitudes and Behavior of the General Public

Organized crime depends for its profits and power on the widespread demand for its services. By demanding its products and services, the public helps organized crime survive and prosper. Convicted LCN killer Nicholas Ceramandi reported the following to Cupples and Kauzlarich (1997, 18):

> We serve needs. People come to us when they can't get justice, or to borrow money that they can't get from a bank … politicians, doctors, lawyers, entertainment people all come to us for favors … there's got to be a reason … we are the best … there are no favors we can't do … people need us and we give them what they want.

In more sociological terms, this is this way the LCN can be seen as functional. It performs a function that no other institution does, and since there is a demand, there will be a supplier, at least according to functionalist reasoning.

In addition to the actions of the public, their attitudes and perceptions also help organized crime survive. How Americans view crime and criminals helps shape the crime scene itself. In the case of organized crime, public perceptions and attitudes are probably more fuzzy and mixed than anything else, but there is no evidence that the public perceives organized crime as a real problem deserving stringent control.

The lack of a rigorous public opposition to organized crime reflects the fact that use of its services is widespread, and also that many people remain unconvinced that these services are particularly harmful. Moreover, many people probably have only a vague idea of what organized crime really is, and popular films like *The Godfather* and *Goodfellas* present a picture full of excitement and mystery. Indeed, the mystery surrounding organized crime gives it the appeal (tinged with fear) of the unknown. Even when people consume products and services supplied by organized crime, they rarely come in contact with persons who represent themselves as members of a crime family or syndicate, and those who are encountered have no distinguishing marks about them to suggest that they are part of organized crime. Stuart Hills (1971, 130) points out: "Many of the customers who place a friendly bet with that nice old man in the corner bar do not perceive, in fact, that this criminal bookmaker is a businessman—not an unorganized individual gambler."

Perhaps the most important reason that public perceptions and attitudes about organized crime are ambivalent at best is that those to whom society customarily looks for clues and guidance in thinking about crime have themselves presented a fragmented and warped picture. Politicians, government officials, and law-enforcement agencies have tended to stress the individual character of crime and criminality and to downplay its organizational features.

Beyond this, the stereotype of the dangerous criminal fostered by authorities fits the mugger, rapist, burglar, and dope pusher, not Vito Genovese, Carlo Gambino, or Sam Giancana. Whether government officials purposely play down organized crime and systematically keep information about it from the public is hard to say. Salerno and Tompkins (1969, 271) think this might be the case: "Too much effort spent exposing organized crime could be damaging in future elections." The healthy publicity given Rudolph Giuliani and other federal prosecutors may actually have diverted public attention from the mundane and parasitic activities of most organized criminals.

Future Trends

Organized crime is undoubtedly here to stay, at least for the foreseeable future. But changes are afoot, just as changes occurred in the past. Ethnic succession has brought Chicanos, Puerto Ricans, and Cuban-Americans into prominent positions in organized crime, especially in the highly populated Northeast and in Chicago and Miami (see Ianni 1998). African-Americans have also claimed a more prominent place in organized crime, moving beyond their traditional urban numbers rackets into drug trafficking and prostitution (see Venkatesh 1998). There is also evidence to suggest that Russian organized crime syndicates in the United States have grown considerably since the dissolution of the Soviet Union (Friedman 2000). However, the presence of the Russian mob in the United States is often exaggerated and sensationalized (Rawlinson 1998). William Kleinknecht (1996) has noted that Asian and Caribbean groups are also emerging in the United States. As yet they are neither as well-organized nor as far-reaching in their activities as are Italian-American crime syndicates. But the die seems to be cast: Italian-American domination of vice should decline in urban centers where large populations of African-Americans and Hispanics are concentrated.

According to Ianni (1998, 127), the same ghetto conditions that spawned early organized crime helped produce the contemporary ethnic succession:

It is important to note in this context of ethnic succession that none of these characteristics of or attitudes toward organized crime are culture bound:

The structures of poverty and powerlessness, rather than the structures of the black and Puerto Rican cultures, seem most responsible.

In addition, the Italian-American crime syndicates themselves may have helped bring about change. Established organized crime groups inevitably came to employ ghetto residents as soldiers, lower-echelon pushers, and numbers runners in their own neighborhoods. Streetwise blacks, Chicanos, Puerto Ricans, and Cubans became vital links between the organization and street-level buyers of commodities and services. With involvement came knowledge, contacts, and, for some, wealth. With involvement also came efforts to control the business in one's territory. An added incentive for Cuban involvement was the establishment of a cocaine and heroin connection from South America through Cuba and Miami.

Although mainly restricted to their own ethnic neighborhoods, the crime networks of blacks and Hispanics are emerging as the new forces in the organized delivery of drugs and sex and are gaining more control over the numbers racket and loan-sharking in the ghetto. In order to extend and expand, however, these newcomers will have to accomplish what the Italian-Americans did before them: "(1) greater control over sectors of organized crime outside as well as inside the ghetto; (2) some organizing principle which will serve as kinship did among the Italians to bring the disparate networks together into larger criminally monopolistic organizations; and (3) better access to political power and the ability to corrupt it" (Ianni 1974, 36; 1998). Although the first requirement may well be the easiest to meet because of their growing control over the drug traffic, much will depend on the willingness of established crime syndicates to allow a blossoming competition from these newcomers.

One can expect to continue hearing about organized crime. It should be apparent that organized crime is a consequence of numerous social, cultural, political, legal, and economic conditions, many of which seem destined to persist. The apparent international growth of organized crime, especially in Russia and areas in Southeast Asia, is interesting in this vein. Viewed from a rationality-opportunity perspective, as well as functionalist reasoning, organized crime will continue to flourish as long as illicit goods and services are demanded and capable people are willing to organize to supply them for a profit. As new opportunities for criminal enterprise appear, they will be grasped by criminally motivated individuals in a position to prosper from them.

One of the more interesting directions this line of reasoning takes us is reflected in the recent explosion of research on international organized crime (Geis 1997, 1998; Passas 1999). The FBI has also extended its international investigations of organized crime to an unprecedented level. It now has Russian and Chinese organized crime "squads." The United Nations has also recently taken notice of the threat of global organized crime networks by establishing a special committee to promote an international Convention against transnational organized crime. The committee is focusing on three areas not traditionally associated as main organized crime activities: the trafficking of women and children, migrants, and firearms. Clearly the range of activities available for organized crime groups can and will change as cultural and structural forces shape supply and demand.

conditions that provide both the incentives and means to attain them. Over the years virtually all ethnic groups have been involved in organized crime, though Prohibition is probably the most significant event in its history. Prohibition helped organized crime come of age and lent it a distinctly American character while promoting the fortunes of ambitious Italian-American crime families. In recent years, trafficking in drugs from Mexico and South America has likewise promoted the fortunes of ambitious black, Hispanic, and Vietnamese crime groups.

Organized crime survives mainly because there is widespread demand for the illegal goods and services that it provides, because public officials are willing to be corrupted, and because moral entrepreneurs are successful in getting the authorities to criminalize activities that many people find pleasurable. In short, organized crime is functional. In addition, however, the existence of marked ethnic and racial inequality in an acquisitive society helps explain both the appeal and suitability of black-market enterprise for population groups isolated from the economic, social, and political mainstream.

CHAPTER SUMMARY

This chapter has explored the nature and role of organized crime in the United States. Criminals are considered part of organized crime if they combine into groups for the purpose of providing illegal goods and services or to engage routinely in illegal activities that profit the group. Political corruption is an integral part of organized crime as is the ability and willingness of participants to use force in pursuit of the organization's goals and to ensure that members abide by its rules. Although there is disagreement on the extent to which organized crime is organized, it is generally agreed that even rudimentary organization means that participants are able to commit a wider variety of crimes on a larger scale than are other criminals.

The history of organized crime in America is to some extent the history of people seeking riches and respectability, and of the social, legal, and political

KEY TERMS

buffer (p. 161)

code of organized crime (p. 149)

corrupter (p. 162)

formal organization (p. 145)

La Cosa Nostra (p. 143)

mafia (p. 153)

racketeering (p. 156)

revisionist view (p. 146)

RECOMMENDED READINGS

Adler, Patricia A. 1993. *Wheeling and Dealing: An Ethnography of an Upper-Level Drug Dealing and Smuggling Community.* 2d ed. New York: Columbia University Press.

Chambliss, William J. 1988. *On the Take: From Petty Crooks to Presidents*. 2d ed. Bloomington, IN: Indiana University Press.

Haller, Mark H. 1991. *Life under Bruno: The Economics of an Organized Crime Family*. Philadelphia, PA: Pennsylvania Crime Commission.

Ianni, Francis A. J., and Elizabeth Reuss-Ianni. 1973. *A Family Business: Kinship and Control in Organized Crime*. New York: Russell Sage.

Kleinknecht, William. 1996. *The New Ethnic Mobs: The Changing Face of Organized Crime in America*. New York: The Free Press.

Passas, Nikos. 1994. *Organized Crime*. Aldershot, U.K.: Ashgate.

RECOMMENDED WEB SITES

The Nathanson Centre for the Study of Organized Crime and Corruption

A major reference service for academic and popular studies of organized crime.

http://www.yorku.ca/nathanson/default.htm

Organized Crime Registry

Articles and information on various facets of organized crime.

http://members.tripod.com/~orgcrime/index2.htm

CHAPTER 8

PUBLIC ORDER CRIME: PROSTITUTION AND DRUGS

Nothing inherent in an act makes it a crime, though some crimes carry the stigma of "sin" as well as illegality. Over the centuries, societies have grappled with the problem of what to do about activities that many regard as sinful and yet many enjoy. As long as these behaviors are kept from public view, it is easy to deny that they really exist. Prostitution, pornography, drunkenness, and drug addiction are rarely hidden from the public eye, however, and for that reason are often considered threats to public morality and order and so are made illegal.

This chapter deals primarily with the public order crimes of drug use and prostitution. In their criminal aspects, drugs and sex have some marked similarities:

- Participants in these crimes often do not view themselves as criminal, nor are they viewed as criminals by significant portions of the population.
- The criminal sides of sex and drugs have legal counterparts that are sometimes difficult to distinguish from them except for their legality.

For example, it is legal to buy and sell alcohol and caffeine but not heroin or marijuana. It is legal (in most places) to view pornography on the Internet but not to dance nude in a bar.

- Illegal sex and drugs are sources of pleasure and tremendous profits. The profits, more than the pleasures, are a direct consequence of criminalization. The black market drives up prices and profits, and entrepreneurs willing to take risks pay no taxes on their profits.
- Illegal sex and drugs are prime targets of organized crime, with all three feeding off one another. For example, many prostitutes are drug addicts, and vice versa. Organized crime controls large segments of drug trafficking and criminal sex, and through the profits it makes, extends its control, protects itself from enforcement, and increases the market for its products and services.
- The laws that apply to sex and drugs reflect both consensus and conflict, with special interests prominent in both their substance and enforcement.
- Enforcement of laws dealing with drugs and sex requires a special type of policing: the use of informants and undercover police. It is also a major area of graft and corruption in the criminal justice system.
- Much of the behavior that is criminalized in both areas is said to be "victimless," in that participants consider themselves willingly involved rather than being offended against.
- Both areas of crime are prime targets of moral entrepreneurs, who see the behavior involved as evidence of declining morals and unreasonable permissiveness and who continually organize campaigns to broaden the laws and increase the penalties.

These, then, are some of the similarities. A more detailed, individual examination of these public order crimes follows.

SEX, CRIME, AND LAW

Historically, criminal labels have been applied to sex on the basis of four considerations: (1) the nature of the act, (2) the nature of the sex object, (3) the social setting in which sex occurs, and (4) the existence of consent.

Some sexual behaviors are considered criminal regardless of the people and circumstances involved. In most states it is illegal to engage in anal intercourse or analingus (oral stimulation of the anus), and in some states oral sex of any sort is prohibited. However, the nature of the sex act itself is often coupled with other considerations in designating the behavior as criminal.

Most criminal codes limit legal sex to partners who are human, adults, and not members of the same family except as marital partners. Many states outlaw sex when the partners are not married (fornication) or are married but not to each other (adultery). Even when the act itself and the partners are legal, a crime may still be committed if the act is performed in public: Sex in parks, restaurants, theaters, automobiles, trains, or anywhere else where it could reasonably be witnessed is usually an offense.

Last is the important question of consent. No matter what is done, with whom or where, a crime may be committed if a partner withholds consent or is legally considered incapable of giving it (he or she is mentally ill, for example, or drugged, or a child). However, as seen in Chapter 4, not all women are truly protected by laws against the rape of a wife by a husband.

The Shaping of Modern Sex Laws

In the earliest legal codes, relatively few sexual activities were illegal. Incest, adultery, fornication, and defilement of virgins were commonly prohibited.

With the spread of Christianity, an ever-increasing collection of sexual prohibitions emerged in law. As the church spread its gospel and increased its power in law and public policy, the foundations of modern sex laws were set in place. In England, for example, the church was quick to impose severe restrictions on sexual freedoms. At the heart of the church's stand was "a definite and detailed code of behavior regarded as obligatory [for] all Christian believers. At the center of the code was the fixed principle that pleasure in sex was evil and damnable. It was not the sex act itself which was condemned, but the pleasure which was connected with it" (Wright 1968, 20–21).

The church viewed sex in extremely narrow terms. Heterosexual copulation for the strict purposes of procreation was the rule, and then only within the framework of marriage. Any sexual activity or relationship not meeting these criteria was viewed as inherently wrong and evil. If the sex act

was not "straight" intercourse, furthermore, it was considered "unnatural," "perverted" behavior.

These views and restrictions did not make the church successful in suppressing sexual expression. On the contrary, by all accounts it failed dismally. Even priests found it hard to abide by church rulings on sexual matters, and there are accounts of monks murdering their superiors when the latter sought to deprive them of heterosexual or homosexual outlets (Taylor 1965). Even as late as the sixteenth century, the papal heads of the Roman Catholic church were notorious for their debauchery, incestuous conduct, and sexual adventures.

The failure of the church and its ecclesiastical courts to control sexual expression, even among its own ranks, left religious leaders searching for alternative ways to control sex. They turned to the state for help, reasoning, perhaps, that the criminal justice system would succeed where they had failed. In addition, state authorities were growing less content to give the church sanctioning power over any area of human conduct, including sex. They saw punishment as the proper domain of the state, and besides, why allow the church to levy fines when these could be paid into the royal treasury?

Henry VIII was one of the first English kings to enact specific sexual legislation. His buggery statute of 1533 made it a felony for a male to have anal intercourse with another male or for a female to have intercourse with an animal. Urged on by Protestant and later by Puritan leaders—and quite in keeping with their statutory expansion of the criminal law—Henry's successors continued to enact sex laws. Thus by the eighteenth century almost every conceivable sexual activity and relationship could be made to fit common law or statutory provisions.

Vagueness in Sex Laws

Henry VIII's buggery statute was vague, leaving unclear whether anal intercourse with a female was included or whether male sex with an animal was a crime. Unfortunately, many of our sex laws today are unclear regarding what exactly constitutes a crime.

Part of the problem unquestionably derives from the reluctance of legal authorities to describe in plain language what have always been sensitive matters. Writing in the late sixteenth century, Sir Edward Coke found it hard to break with that tradition and may himself have contributed to its perpetuation. His attitude is summed up in his now famous reference to buggery as that "detestable and abominable sin, among Christians not to be named." In regard to a description of the penetration of the vagina during intercourse—an essential element in legal definitions of carnal knowledge—he could only bring himself to say, in Latin, "the thing in the thing" (Gigeroff 1968, 11).

The U.S. Supreme Court has not improved matters much. Consider on the one hand its ruling in *Wainwright v. Stone* (1973). In this case the Court supported the continued enforcement of a Florida statute outlawing sodomy, defined only as "an abominable and detestable crime against nature." On the other hand, there is the matter of obscenity. Here, in *Miller v. California* (1973), the Court appeared to have abandoned jurisdiction, leaving judgment largely up to "the average person," applying "contemporary community standards." From one perspective this might be hailed as progressive, since it allows for variations in community standards. From another it places considerable enforcement discretion in the hands of local authorities, does not reduce the likelihood of breaches of First Amendment freedoms, and encourages the activities of moral entrepreneurs, those who work for enactment and enforcement of moral prohibitions (see Becker 1963).

Just what violates community standards depends, of course, on the standards themselves. Yet few attempts are made to poll the moral views of the electorate, especially those pertaining to sex. In *Pope v. Illinois* (1987) the Supreme Court ruled that a work is obscene if a reasonable person applying objective social standards would find the work lacking in social value. Far from clarifying the question of standards, the case leaves undetermined what "reasonable" means, as well as "social value" and "objective." Justice Stevens, who dissented in this ruling, suggested that a work is protected if anyone finds merit in it.

More recently, attempts to define obscenity and pornography on the Internet have met with much resistance. The 1996 federal Communications Decency Act attempted to criminalize indecent or obscene materials on the Internet. However, the Supreme Court ruled that the Act violated the First Amendment's guarantee of free speech. Federal attempts to regulate "decency" or the distribution of "offensive material" will generally fail, since the Supreme Court has historically found such terms extremely vague and therefore devoid of meaning.

Prostitution

Some sex offenses are **victimless crimes**, meaning that they are between consenting adults who voluntarily engage in an activity that happens to be illegal. Adultery, fornication, the sale and purchase of pornographic literature, and prostitution are possible examples. This section focuses on prostitution, which some consider a victimless crime, but as we shall see, can and does result in social and physical harms.

As many as one million male and female prostitutes are working at any given time in the United States (San Francisco Task Force on Prostitution 2000). Yet prostitution is in violation of criminal codes in all states except Nevada, in which county governments decide on legality. Prostitution has not always been illegal in the United States (Daly 1988, 174), and in some Western societies it is tolerated today. In Germany, Holland, and Denmark, for instance, female prostitutes are pretty much left alone as long as they ply their trade in designated areas and fulfill other requirements such as licensing and payment of taxes.

SELLING SEX: THE PROSTITUTE AT WORK Prostitutes work in various ways (Romenesko and Miller 1989; McCaghy and Capron 1994). At one end of the spectrum and most numerous are the streetwalkers, or street hookers. These women may be readily encountered on the street, particularly where cheap hotels, bars, and mass transportation terminals are to be found.

The streetwalker is at the bottom of the pecking order among prostitutes. She works where the risks are greatest; she has little or no control over what clients she takes; she must put up with all kinds of weather; she must generally give a good portion of her earnings away for "protection"; and she must usually work long hours to make enough from her "tricks" (paying customers, sometimes called "johns") to meet her financial obligations.

There are three kinds of female streetwalkers in big cities:

1. *Daytimers*, the "classiest" group who usually work office buildings, mostly comprises white, out-of-work models and actresses, and housewives supplementing their family income.
2. *Early evening girls*, who finish by 11 P.M., are full-time, independent professionals working in and around hotels.
3. *All the rest* are those who do not fit into the first two categories, including the old, the very young, the unattractive, and the desperate, who work far into the night and turn as many tricks as they can (Sheehy 1973, 30–32). The latter category would include women with drug addictions, who commonly render their "services" in a car, an abandoned building, a cheap hotel, or a crack house (French 1994).

Even the "classiest" streetwalkers—those working office buildings or conventions—rarely gross more than $300 a day. The streetwalker does well to stay in business for more than a few years, and her earning capacity declines rapidly after she passes her twenty-second or twenty-third birthday. Male prostitutes also work the streets; most are older teenagers and young adults. They rarely regard themselves as homosexuals, and prefer to be called *hustlers* (McCaghy and Capron 1994, 442). Various roles are possible, and as with female streetwalkers, young men and boys can be seen selling and negotiating on streetcorners, sometimes standing close together displaying their wares in what is known as the "meat rack."

Next up the social ladder are prostitutes who work in brothels (also called bordellos, cathouses, or whorehouses). Until World War II, brothels were the major outlet for prostitution in the United States. In major cities, brothels numbered in the hundreds, and they were usually located close together in areas that came to be known as "red light districts." Run by madams, who were often working prostitutes at one time, these brothels sometimes had a "stable" of twenty or thirty women working in shifts. Typically, half the woman's earnings went to the madam to pay for room and board (see Wiltz 1999).

In Amsterdam's "red light district" prostitutes display themselves at windows and invite passersby to join them. Hardly less flagrant than the behavior of some prostitutes in the United States, this practice is thought to be safer for the women.

Over the second half of the twentieth century, the number of brothels declined, mostly as a result of cleanup operations by city councils pressured by local citizen groups. Brothels still operate as the major context of prostitution in Nevada (the state frowns upon the streetwalker), and most large cities in the United States have brothels that maintain themselves solely through a system of informal referrals. Gone are the days, though, when a visitor could simply appear on the doorstep of a common brothel and buy himself sexual pleasure (Wiltz 1999). The closing of brothels made the business of prostitution more unpleasant and dangerous for both clients and prostitutes (Daly 1988, 199).

A recent study of male sex workers (MSWs) in Australia found that clients were primarily contacted through advertisement and escort services (Minichiello, Marino, Browne, and Jamieson 1999). The study also found that half the surveyed

MSWs considered themselves as "gay," 31 percent as bisexual, and 5.5 percent as "straight." The MSWs reported that their clients were mostly middle-aged and middle-class.

Toward the top of the prostitution pecking order are call girls. Though the operating methods differ, the established call girl usually secures her clients through individual referrals by customers or trusted friends (Bryan 1965). She conducts the sexual transaction in her own apartment or in the office, home, or hotel room of her client. Many call girls work independently and exercise considerable discretion in their choice of clients. Most topflight call girls are in their early twenties; they are generally from middle-class backgrounds, and some have a college education. The successful call girl is physically attractive, well-groomed, and articulate, and she makes a pleasant date for those men who can afford the $300 or $400 it takes to purchase her company for an evening. By using the telephone rather than the street, call girls can be highly selective regarding customers. The 1994 conviction of the "madam to the stars," Heidi Fleiss, drew massive public attention to the organized call-girl business.

BARS AND MASSAGE PARLORS AS PLACES OF PROSTITUTION   Public bars and nightclubs have long been frequented by prostitutes (Weinberg, Shaver, and Williams 1999). These women often operate with the support of bar management. Prostitutes find bars good places for hustling. For one thing, they can work indoors; in addition, they have a constant flow of prospective clients, they can mingle with the crowd and thus not be too obvious, there are people around who can come to their rescue if trouble should arise, and they can choose their clients.

Massage parlors are a lucrative setting for prostitution. Though some establishments provide only therapeutic massages by trained personnel, many of the thousands of parlors from coast to coast basically offer one service: sex. The range of sexual activities purchased extends from simple "handjobs"—which are permissible in some jurisdictions—to "blow-jobs," "straight" sexual intercourse, and anything else the customer may desire and the "masseuse" is willing to do. The profits can be enormous for owners of these parlors: Between 1985 and 1989, four massage parlors located just across the Mississippi river from St. Louis generated $3,349,047 from prostitution, and paid their owner $4,000 a week (*St. Louis Post-Dispatch*, 19 July 1994, B1).

Massage parlors are good fronts for prostitution because they provide a legal setting for customer contacts. "Employees" need not solicit business; it comes to them. A typical customer is looking for more than a massage. Furthermore, the masseuses are not dependent on the customers' purchase of sex because they receive a commission (usually 30 to 35 percent) on any legal massage they give—and these can cost customers $100 an hour if they want frills such as nude masseuses, champagne, and special baths. Other advantages to prostitution in this setting include a comfortable work environment, a potentially speedy turnover in customers, and some protection against arrest and criminal conviction for prostitution. Massage parlor prostitutes are protected from arrest and conviction partly by the semi-private character of the parlor and partly because by leaving it up to the customers to do the soliciting, they can minimize chances of a legal arrest. An undercover cop who first solicits sex and then arrests the masseuse may well be acting illegally under the rules of entrapment. These rules usually are interpreted as follows: Police may not entice a person into committing a crime and then use the offense and evidence of it to bring about a criminal conviction if the person would not normally have voluntarily committed the offense in question.

THE PIMP   A key position in the world of prostitution is held by the **pimp** (Miller 1986; Romenesko and Miller 1989). Though there is no way of knowing exactly what proportion of prostitutes work under the control of pimps, it is certainly the majority, and may be as high as 90 percent in some places (Farley, Baral, Kiremire, and Sezgin 1998). For a pimp, prostitution is the road to financial success; he reaps the real profits from the billion-dollar business, not his women. Despite this arrangement, many prostitutes would quickly fail in business without their pimp. Ironically, though, the fact that the pimp controls their earnings means that the typical female street hustler "cannot save or plan for the future *independently* of men" (Romenesko and Miller 1989, 132).

The pimp's importance comes partly from the nature of prostitution itself and partly from his own business acumen and ability to manipulate people. Because prostitution is illegal, those involved are constantly threatened by arrest. Pimps can help protect prostitutes from legal troubles as well as provide financial and other assistance such as posting bail. Pimps help defend their prostitutes against competition by establishing and maintaining control over a particular territory. Independent prostitutes do not have that kind of security. Pimps also offer protection against physical or financial threat posed by drunks, toughs, and customers who want something for nothing. Most prostitutes have little control over male access to them—indeed, they must make that access as free as possible—and when confronted by a troublemaker it is nice to have someone in the wings who can deal with the problem.

The dangers of prostitution open up a role for the pimp. Even so, his success also hinges on his adeptness in establishing and maintaining the prostitute's dependence on him and his control over her. Control and dependence are the central features of what is, at its heart, a relationship of exploitation. To establish that relationship, the pimp demonstrates that the practicing or would-be prostitute needs him for both material and emotional reasons. He shows his material importance by taking care of room and board, clothing, and medical expenses and by running the business profitably. On the emotional level, the pimp is there when the woman needs affection, advice, and love, but he also disciplines her when she falters.

In Miller's classic (1986) study of street hustling, the pimp is called the "man," the prostitutes are his "wives-in-law," with the "bottom woman" running the "household" and accorded the greatest respect. This pseudo-family structure is explored in depth by Romenesko and Miller (1989), who write: "The establishment of an emotional tie between the 'man' and the woman is an extremely important element of the 'turning out' process. Even though a woman discovers relatively early that a 'man's' affection is conditional (depending upon her payment, respect, and obedience to him), she believes being 'taken care of' financially, socially, and emotionally 'to be worth it" (p. 126).

Once caught up in his grip, the prostitute quickly learns the extent of her dependence on him and the risks of attempting to leave the fold. If she does decide to leave she risks not only her

financial security but also her physical safety, for beatings, assaults, and even murders are not uncommon. He may have no further use for her, but the violence sends a message to other pimps and to his remaining women: He "owns" his women and all decisions are his to make. A traditional patriarchal structure thus creates and feeds off the vulnerability, emotional and financial, of those women caught up in the sexual marketplace of the street.

This phenomenon is similar to the **Stockholm syndrome**, normally associated with terrorist kidnappings that last days, weeks, or months. This syndrome is

> a psychological strategy for survival in captivity ... useful in explaining the traumatic bonding which occurs between women in prostitution and their pimps/captors. When a person holds life-or-death power over another, small kindnesses are perceived with immense gratitude. In order to survive on a day-to-day basis, it is necessary to deny the extent of harm which pimps and customers are capable of inflicting. Survival of the person in prostitution depends on her ability to predict others' behavior. So she develops a vigilant attention to the pimp's needs and may ultimately identify with his view of the world. This increases her chances for survival.... (Graham, Rawlings, and Rigsby 1994 as cited in Farley, Baral, Kiremire, and Sezgin 1997; 1997, 407)

ENTERING INTO PROSTITUTION   Prostitutes risk not only police arrest and criminal punishment but also such work-related hazards as disease, injury, theft, and exploitation. Why, then, do some women become prostitutes? One long-standing explanation is that they are forced into prostitution by unsavory characters who use devices of compulsion ranging from kidnaping, blackmail, to forced crack or heroin addiction. Doubtless some women are forcibly introduced to prostitution. But current thinking on the subject places less emphasis on the role of force and more on a voluntary, though often reluctant, decision to enter prostitution and the circumstances surrounding that decision. It seems likely that when considered as a whole, only a small minority of prostitutes are explicitly forced into the profession.

Nevertheless, a woman may feel that she has no real choice in the matter, and some look upon their entrance into prostitution as something forced upon them by circumstances beyond their control. One circumstance often mentioned is financial insecurity. Simply stated, some women enter prostitution because they need the money, as William Sanger observed in New York over a hundred years ago (see Daly 1988, 177). They may have a child to support; they may be out of work and unable to find a full-time job; or they may have pressing financial obligations, such as paying medical bills or financing a drug addiction, which they cannot hope to meet through conventional, legal kinds of work.

Several recent ethnographic studies have shown that prostitution is a significant source of income for crack-cocaine-addicted females (Ratner 1994). While the levels of crack use have declined of late, many lower-class, crack-addicted women sell or exchange sex for crack. The women are often so desperate for money that they will perform sexual "tricks" for next to nothing, just to get a little closer to a hit on the crack pipe. Others give sexual favors to crack dealers or crack house operators in exchange for drugs. One crack-addicted woman put it this way:

> The rock is the pimp.... We go out there, we get all this money, first person we run to is to the dope man. The rock is the pimp.... So that's why they call us strawberries, 'cause we get the rocks and we will have oral sex, have you, have your brother too, all at the same time to get this cocaine. (Feucht 1997, 135)

Another put it this way:

> I really didn't want to be with them, but I wanted to get high, so I just went ahead and had sex with them to get the money and go on and buy my [rock]. (Feucht 1997, 136)

In any case, these women have very little control over their lives (Ratner 1994). They also hold the lowest status on the street—the crack whore is disdained not only by the so-called "professional" street prostitutes, but also by her clients (Boyle and Anglin 1994).

Despite the well-documented relationship between drug addiction and prostitution, Ronald

Akers (1973, 166) warns that one should not misinterpret the nature of the financial incentives in prostitution:

> This may sound trite or overly simplistic, but the nature of the monetary incentive in prostitution is often misunderstood. The woman need not be in dire or desperate economic straits; escape from poverty is only one way (and probably not the most frequent way) in which prostitution is economically inspired.

The choice, Akers argues, is often not between starving or becoming a prostitute but, more commonly, between a low-paying, low-status, but respectable job and a relatively high-paying job that happens to be illegal and not respectable. Most of the women interviewed by Romenesko and Miller (1989) had held "straight" jobs, but these were usually low-paying and often part-time: for example, fast food attendant or cook, box checker at a department store, bakery shop clerk, hot dog stand attendant, go-go dancer, waitress, beautician, and cashier.

The loss of respectability and the risks of arrest and criminal punishment are thought to be offset by the economic rewards anticipated from prostitution. Unfortunately, many prostitutes find that financial stability is as difficult to achieve in this world as it is in "straight" society. For one thing, if there is a pimp around, he receives and controls all the money. As in straight society, men run the underworld (Romenesko and Miller 1989; Miller 2001).

Most people to whom prostitution would offer financial attractions do not become prostitutes. For the few who do, it seems that additional considerations facilitate their entry into the prostitute role. One factor appears to be experience in sex at a relatively early age, and another is a set of verbalized opinions favorable to prostitution (McCaghy and Capron 1994, 444–446). Women who have had early sexual experiences have less difficulty accepting the idea of sex as normal, even among strangers.

REACTIONS TO PROSTITUTION   Prostitutes are generally looked upon with mild intolerance by society and its legal officials. Unless community pressure to do something about prostitution builds up, police and courts rarely go out of their way to make life difficult for prostitutes. It seems that when police do take the trouble to arrest streetwalkers or to raid local brothels and illegal massage parlors, they do so more to harass them and get some "action" than to enforce the law. When prostitutes go before a judge, they typically pay a small fine and are back on the street within hours. FBI figures from 1998 show that 63,000 persons were arrested for "prostitution and commercialized vice" (Federal Bureau of Investigation 1999). Only 1.4 percent of the arrested were under the age of eighteen. To put these total arrest figures in perspective, this represents less than 1 percent of all arrests, and about 2 percent of the arrests for sex and alcohol/drug offenses combined (Federal Bureau of Investigation 1999).

Opinions favorable to prostitution are bound to vary, but some notable ones are "prostitution is no worse than any other kind of job"; "people don't really look down on the prostitute"; "the prostitute is necessary, for without her marriages would fail, some men would have to commit rape to get laid"; and "the prostitute gives men what their wives and lovers won't" (Jackman et al. 1963; Bryan 1966). This reasoning gels with the recent social and intellectual movements of scholars, activists, and prostitutes who refer to prostitution as simply "sex work" and prostitutes as "sex workers."

This view clashes with those of the religious right and some progressives, although some members of the latter group have argued that prostitution is not a crime against women, but a sign of a new era of women's liberation. In this vein, the past few decades have witnessed the proliferation of sex worker unions, voluntary organizations, and political action groups. Such groups lobby for the legalization of prostitution, the protection of sex workers under state and federal labor laws, and enhanced medical services.

Some feel, however, that prostitution, like pornography, is essentially a crime against women. Many studies show that a disproportionate number of women and girls entering prostitution are sexually abused, drug addicted, poor, and of color:

[P]rostitution itself is violence against women.... [We] understand prostitution to be a sequel to childhood sexual abuse; [we] understand that racism is inextricably connected to sexism in prostitution; [we] understand that prostitution is domestic violence, and in many instances—slavery or debt bondage.... (Farley, Baral, Kiremire, and Sezgin 1997, 405)

Whichever view is correct, there is little doubt that debates about the morality, legality, and harmfulness of prostitution will continue. For example, some local jurisdictions take prostitution so seriously that they publicize the name of arrested clients in newspapers and on Web sites. Other jurisdictions form police stings that pose a female police officer as a prostitute and then arrest a "client" when payment is arranged. In most cases, however, the criminal punishment for solicitation is about as harsh as a speeding ticket.

Pornography

Pornography, like prostitution, has been around for centuries, and also like prostitution, pornography generally arouses feelings of mild intolerance in the general population. Yet as one might expect, attitudes toward pornography vary considerably from one segment of the population to another. Women and the elderly, married individuals, less-educated people, political conservatives, and religious traditionalists are more condemning of pornography than their counterparts (Woodrum 1992). Even so, people holding strong negative views about pornography, including its effects on relations between men and women, do not necessarily feel that it should be criminalized. Some are caught on the horns of a dilemma: "Are the potential solutions worse than the perceived problems?" (Thompson, Chaffee, and Oshagan 1990).

The explosion in sales and rentals of pornographic videotapes, the success of Internet porn sites, and the growth of sex-oriented cable and satellite channels indicate that many Americans want to view sexually explicit material, at least in the privacy of their homes. Middle-class people can now do in private what before necessitated a trip to the seamier parts of town. In this way they maintain a public front of decency while avoiding the dangers of predatory criminals in sleazy neighborhoods. One major exception to this tolerance should be noted, and that is child pornography, the depiction of children engaging in sexual activities with each other or with adults. Severe penalties have now been introduced by most states for offenses of this sort, whether it is accomplished by print or electronic media.

The fight against pornography is continuing in some circles, and it has brought together strange bedfellows: On the one hand are such moral entrepreneurs as Citizens for Decency Through Law and the Christian Coalition, who see pornography as a reflection of a larger moral decay, and on the other are progressives who see pornography as a manifestation (and perpetuation) of sexual stereotyping, in which women are seen as "vile whores" who deserve, and probably want, to be sexually abused by men (Baird and Rosenbaum 1998; Lederer 1980). Both groups argue that at its best, contemporary pornography, with its "sexualization of violence" (Ashley and Ashley 1984), trivializes male sexual aggression and at its worst actually encourages crimes of sexual assault. A feminist version of this argument is summed up this way:

> In keying male arousal to the objective presentation of female biological sexedness (i.e., pussy), pornography creates and maintains a practice of the sexual within which rape is not a *conceptually* deviant practice, even if it is considered to be a morally deviant practice. Pornography creates and maintains the objectified female sexuality that makes male sexual satisfaction through rape possible (and also empirically inevitable). Thus pornography both creates and maintains women's rapability. (Vadas 1992, 97)

There are at least two reasons why it is unlikely that the war against pornography waged by these groups will succeed: First, commercial sex is big business and growing bigger; second, America still remains a largely patriarchal society.

DRUGS AND ALCOHOL

This chapter began with the assertion that nothing inherent in any activity makes it a crime. Rather, activities and those who engage in them become criminal when they are so labeled by persons with the authority to do so. Sometimes acts similar in substance are labeled differently—some are called crimes; others are not. This is especially true of drug-related acts. Most Americans are consumers of drugs, but some do nothing illegal, whereas others do. The world of drugs, then, has two sides, the legal and the criminal. Although this is a criminology text and as such focuses on crime, one cannot hope to grasp the realities of the criminal side of drugs and their use without at the same time considering the legal side. Indeed, understanding the legal use of legal drugs gives insights into the illegal use of drugs and drug-related crime.

Here the word **drug** will refer to any **psychoactive substance**. A psychoactive substance is one having the capacity to alter mental states. Identifying an "altered mental state" requires a subjective assessment by the drug user, which sometimes complicates the identification of a substance as a drug. However, there is widespread agreement on the following examples of currently abused drugs: alcohol, nicotine, caffeine, opiates, hallucinogens (LSD, DMT), cocaine, heroin, barbiturates ("downers"), amphetamines ("speed"), ecstasy ("X") marijuana, tranquilizers, and analgesics (pain killers).

Marijuana and the Drugging of America

There have been two trends, beginning nearly forty years ago, that together explain much of the current drug problem, in particular its criminological aspects. First was the growing recreational use of drugs, especially among the young; second, there was a marked growth in the production and marketing of legal drugs. In the opinion of many experts, the first trend was helped along by the second.

IN SEARCH OF SELF: MARIJUANA   The preeminent illegal drug is marijuana. According to recent national surveys of use among high school students, 47 percent claimed to have used the drug during the year before being interviewed (Maguire and Pastore 2000, 230). Around 26 percent of the students said they had used marijuana at least once in the past thirty days before the interview. College students generally report a greater level of drug use than high school students. And while inner-city neighborhoods have received considerable publicity as drug-ridden, recent studies suggest that inner-city youth are no more at risk of becoming drug users than are other youths; however, they are more at risk of becoming sellers of drugs, including marijuana (Greenwood 1992, 446).

Figure 8.1 shows a steep decline in the use of illicit drugs among Americans during the 1980s to early 1990s, although in recent years their use appears to be increasing. Figure 8.2 shows a gradual decrease in the late 1980s among high school seniors in the use of marijuana and cocaine, and relatively little change in use of alcohol and cigarettes. Since then, however, there has been an increase in cigarettes and marijuana use among high school seniors, and a slight increase in illicit drug use among the general population.

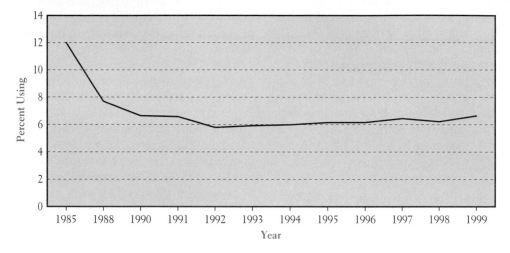

▲ FIGURE 8.1

Americans Reporting Current Use of an Illegal Drug, 1985–1999

The percent of Americans reporting that they used an illicit drug "during the past month" declined from 1985 to 1992, but shows signs of increasing again.

Source: Kathleen Maguire and Anne L. Pastore, eds., *Sourcebook of Criminal Justice Statistics, 1999* (Washington, D.C.: U.S. Department of Justice, 2000); and <www.health.org/newsroom/releases/aug00/9.htm>.

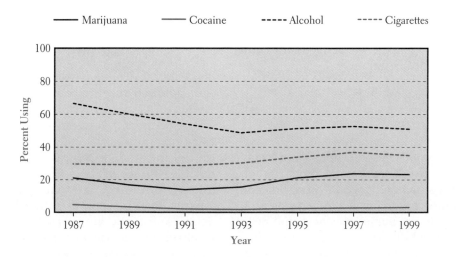

▲ FIGURE 8.2

Drug Use Trends among High School Seniors, 1987–1999

The numbers shown here represent the percent using the drug in question "during the past 30 days."

Source: Kathleen Maguire and Anne L. Pastore, eds., *Sourcebook of Criminal Justice Statistics, 1999* (Washington, D.C.: U.S. Department of Justice, 2000), 237.

Marijuana is readily available: The majority of studies have found that around 85 percent of high school seniors surveyed think it would be easy to buy marijuana where they live (Maguire and Pastore 2000). Furthermore, the availability of marijuana appears to have been increasing in recent years, with expanded domestic cultivation.

Marijuana (cannabis) comes from the Indian hemp plant *Cannabis sativa* and has been used for centuries. The resin, called *charas* by Hindus and known as *hashish* today, was used for spiritual purposes by Native Americans and as a medicine by the ancient Chinese. When the buds and top leaves of the hemp plant are cut and dried, they can be eaten or smoked. The mixture is less potent than hashish, and the Indians called it *bhang*; it is now called marijuana, weed, or pot, among other terms. Over half of the marijuana supply in the United States comes from Mexico, although imports from Colombia, Venezuela, and Jamaica have increased (National Narcotics Intelligence Consumers Committee 1993).

According to the U.S. Drug Enforcement Agency (2001), almost all of the marijuana smuggled into the United States is

> concealed in false compartments, fuel tanks, seats, and tires of private and commercial vehicles, pickup trucks, vans, mobile homes, and horse trailers. Larger shipments, up to multi-thousand kilogram amounts, usually are smuggled in tractor-trailer trucks in false compartments and among legitimate bulk shipments, such as agricultural products.

Domestic cultivation of marijuana is at an all-time high, with indoor operations found in all fifty states. Kentucky, Illinois, Hawaii, Tennessee, and Indiana are the nation's top five cannabis-producing states. Indoor cultivation is highest in Washington, California, Colorado, Florida, and Oregon (Drug Enforcement Agency 2001).

Marijuana's legal status in the early 1990s (and that of some other well-known recreational drugs) is summarized by Schlosser (1994, 52):

> Marijuana is currently classified as a Schedule I controlled substance, implying that it has a high potential for abuse, no officially accepted medicinal uses, and no safe level of use under medical supervision. Heroin, LSD, and peyote are other

Schedule I drugs; cocaine and phencyclidine (PCP) are listed in Schedule II, allowing doctors to prescribe them. Under federal law it is illegal to buy, sell, grow, or possess any amount of marijuana anywhere in the United States. Penalties for a first offense range from probation to life imprisonment, with fines up to $4 million, depending on the quantity of marijuana involved.

Box 8.1 (on page 180) shows recent criminal penalties for the possession of cannabis in Illinois.

How did marijuana emerge as America's most popular illicit drug? The answer lies partly with the growth of countercultures during the late 1950s and subsequent confrontations with "the Establishment" on college campuses during the 1960s. The "beat" generation that emerged in New York and San Francisco in the 1950s emphasized an alternative lifestyle of autonomy, drugs (especially pot), music, free sexual expression, aversion to routine employment and politics, and disregard for the law (Polsky 1967). Hippies succeeded the beats and made famous the Haight-Ashbury district of San Francisco. They claimed a similar lifestyle, though jazz was replaced with acid- or folk-rock, and marijuana was joined by LSD. Hippies also enjoyed "putting on straights" and "blowing their minds" by rejecting all that was valued by the dominant, middle-class culture. By the end of the 1960s the hippie culture, if not its ideology, had spread to all parts of the country, and rock music was one of its major vehicles.

Another factor in marijuana's increasing popularity was the growing disenchantment among young people, especially college students, with the policies and practices of American government. Use of illegal drugs became a way of underscoring their opposition to the Establishment. In addition, marijuana and psychedelics were touted as a way to "expand the mind," to "trip," to "get your head right." They were perfect for the "now" generation, those who searched for meaning and heightened self-awareness (Carey 1968).

DRUGS AS A WAY OF LIFE   Another trend that encouraged illicit drug use was the growth of drug use in general. In America, drugs have become a way of life for the healthy as well as for the sick. Beer, wine, liquor, tea, nicotine, coffee, and myriad pills and potions are daily fare for many respectable

BOX 8.1   YEAR 2000 CRIMINAL PENALTIES FOR THE POSSESSION OF CANNABIS IN ILLINOIS

One part of the recent "War on Drugs" is the increased severity of criminal sentences. Here one can see signs of this practice in the criminal penalties for possession of cannabis in the state of Illinois.

Amount of Cannabis	Criminal Penalty
Less than 2.5 grams	Up to $1,500 fine and/or up to 30 days in jail.
2.5 to 10 grams	Up to $1,500 fine and/or up to 6 months in jail
10 to 30 grams	1st Offense: Up to $2,500 fine and/or up to 1 year in jail
	2nd Offense: Felony up to $25,000 fine and/or 1–3 years of prison.
30 to 500 grams	1st Offense: Felony up to $25,000 fine and/or 1–3 years of prison.
	2nd Offense: Felony up to $25,000 fine and/or 2–5 years of prison.
500 to 2000 grams	Felony up to $25,000 fine and/or 2–5 years of prison.
2000 to 5000 grams	Felony up to $25,000 fine and/or 3–7 years of prison.
over 5000 grams	Felony up to $25,000 fine and/or 4–15 years of prison.

Criminal penalties for the sale, manufacture, and possession with intent to sell cannabis are more severe. For example, selling 10 grams of cannabis could land one in prison for 1–3 years. Selling 30 grams could land a person in prison from 2–5 years, the same length of time a person convicted of involuntary manslaughter or reckless homicide would serve.

Source: National Crime and Justice Learning Center 2000.

Americans. Even children are targets: Aspirins are named after saints, vitamins are made to look like cartoon characters, and beer that is not really beer is marketed as if it were beer.

With the exception of caffeine, and perhaps aspirin or ibuprofen, alcohol and tobacco are the drugs used most often (Barton 2000). Caffeine is a stimulant found in coffee, tea, hot chocolate, cola beverages, and in some over-the-counter pills for dieting and preventing sleep. Half of all Americans drink at least one cup of coffee per day, and coffee drinkers consume an average of 3.3 cups per day (National Coffee Association 2000). Studies also suggest that children and teenagers are consuming more caffeine than ever before (Cordes 2000), as

the overall consumption rate of carbonated soft drinks, many of which contain caffeine, has risen 111 percent since 1970 (U.S. Department of Agriculture 2000).

Drugs are big business. The message conveyed by advertisers is that drugs are normal, natural, and good for you. Often they are shown making problems and difficulties go away. Drugs bring "the good things in life" and even confer respectability, the ads proclaim, subtly or otherwise. People will feel better and look younger and fit in with others if they use drugs, though the word drug is rarely used, of course. In 1994, the tobacco industry responded to growing congressional interest in banning smoking in all public places, and to the

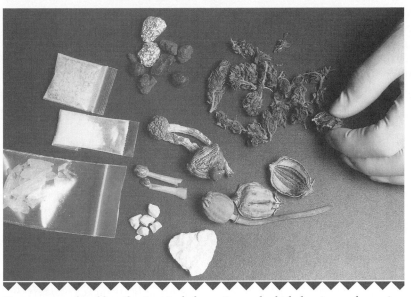

Drugs commonly sold on the street include marijuana, hashish, heroin, crack, cocaine, speed, mushrooms, and opium.

possibility of regulating tobacco under Food and Drug Administration rules, with a vigorous ad campaign impugning the scholarship and integrity of their opponents. Today, there are stricter rules on tobacco advertising, fewer places where smoking is allowed, and billions of dollars in civil settlements against the tobacco industry. Given the social and legal setbacks the tobacco industry has sustained in the 1990s, it is not unreasonable to wonder if the possession and distribution of tobacco itself will be criminalized in the years to come. On the other hand, with an estimated 66.8 million Americans (30 percent of the U.S. population) reporting some use of tobacco in 1999, it seems unlikely that tobacco products will be criminalized in the near future (U.S. Department of Health and Human Services 2000, 3).

With so many drugs around and with so many respectable people selling and using them, it is small wonder that America has a drug problem. People grow up anticipating a place for drugs in their lives. That first cigarette, puffed courageously in some secluded spot, that first can of beer, downed with much bravado in a friend's car, are milestones along the road to adulthood. Most youthful experimenters know they are breaking the law, but that

merely adds to the adventure. What is "cool" about doing something that children are supposed to do? Anyway, there must be something to smoking, drinking, popping pills, or else why would parents and other adults spend so much time and money doing it, and why would all those advertisements encourage it? In this vein, Erich Goode (1972, 126–128) noted that, "The legitimate drug industry is, both directly and indirectly, responsible for much of the illegal drug use taking place today. The 'pusher' should be sought not only on the street but in the physician's office, the pharmacy, the tavern—and the home."

Those likely to use illegal drugs are precisely those who have grown up in a social environment in which legal drugs are commonly used (Abdelrahman, Rodriguez, Ryan, French, and Weinbaum 1998). No matter whether it is cocaine, heroin, marijuana, or the psychedelics, studies consistently show generational continuity in drug use and in the progression from legal to illegal drugs (Vega and Gil 1999). Of course, thousands of those who use legal drugs do not "progress" to illegal ones, and many who do usually discontinue their use after one or two episodes; they do tend to remain consumers of legal drugs such as alcohol—in fact 105 million Americans (47.3 percent of the U.S. population over the age of twelve) consumed alcohol in 1999 (U.S. Department of Health and Human Services 2000, 3). The important lesson is that illegal drug use is most likely to be found in a climate favorable to drug use in general. In fact, the most significant correlate of illegal drug use is the consumption of legal drugs.

Cocaine

Cocaine is extracted from the leaves of the plant Erythroxylon coca, which is found in South America. Coca leaves have been chewed for at least 3,000 years by South American Indians. Cocaine use in America is not well-documented but does not seem to have been particularly extensive until recently. It was first used medicinally as an anesthetic in eye surgery in the early 1900s. It was also "used by many people in the form of tonic, wines, and teas" (Chaiken 1993, 3). It was once a popular "yuppie" drug, and its street use grew in the 1980s, especially in the form of crack. As Figure 8.2 shows, cocaine use declined from 1987 to 1993, although it has been slowly rising since then.

The major site of coca cultivation continues to be Peru, but trafficking is dominated by Colombia, where the raw paste or cocaine base is converted into cocaine hydrochloride (HCl) for distribution to the United States. Generally, cocaine HCl is 90 percent pure when imported. The usual route of importation is through Mexico, followed by the Caribbean. Cocaine confiscations by the Drug Enforcement Administration (DEA) peaked in the early 1990s, from 399 pounds in 1977 to 81,823 pounds in 1987 to 173,391 pounds in 1992. DEA confiscations have tailed off in recent years, and are now closer to the levels of the late 1970s (Maguire and Pastore 2000). Part of this is explained by more multi-federal agency involvement in drug investigation. For example, the combined DEA, FBI, U.S. Customs, and U.S. Border Patrol cocaine seizures have increased from 218,697 pounds in 1989 to 264,630 in 1998 (Maguire and Pastore 2000).

Cocaine use has been controlled since the Harrison Narcotics Act of 1914 restricted its manufacture, distribution, and sale. It is illegal in all states. Cocaine is not, in fact, a narcotic; it is a stimulant that acts directly on the "pleasure" or "reward" centers of the brain. It is so powerful that it undermines the brain's ability to regulate such functional necessities as sleeping, eating, and handling stress. Users describe the "high" as elation, warmth, vigor, friendliness, and arousal (Farrington 2000; Grabowski 1984). Because the subjective effects are so pleasant, cocaine is considered a prime target for abuse.

CRACK If anything accounts for the explosive growth in cocaine use in America during the 1980s it is **crack**—a cheap, smokable form of cocaine. Crack, unlike other forms of cocaine, is inexpensive: In New York City in 1985, a pea-sized rock of crack cost $40 (*Newsweek*, 28 November 1988); it now costs less than $15. Like most commodities, the price does vary considerably from location to location. For example, in St. Louis, Missouri, an "eightball" of crack (1/8th of an ounce) sells for about $200, while the same quantity costs half that in Chicago (personal interview, March 2000). Crack is easy to make and extremely fast-acting. It is produced by processing street cocaine with ammonia or baking soda to remove hydrochlorides. The resulting crystalline mixture gets its name from the crackling sound that the residues of baking soda make when the mixture is smoked (Inciardi 1987).

Drug dealing structures are not well studied, but some similarities appear to exist across drug types and may help explain the popularity of crack in the 1980s and early 1990s.

First, the structure of distribution is better characterized as groups of dealers and individual entrepreneurs, rather than as a single, highly organized and centralized criminal operation; and second, entrance and acceptance into dealing groups are based on familiarity, friendship ties, situational factors ("the right place at the right time"), and available capital (Hunt 1990, 181; Jacobs 1999a, 1999b).

Crack can be manufactured in anyone's kitchen, and the "step from crack manufacturer to crack user is a short one" (Hunt 1990, 179). Thus the entire crack business can be a local, neighborhood affair (Bourgois 1995). Many crack dealers, however, try to be careful about their own use of crack because of its tendency to get in the way of good business decision making. Many do, however, smoke marijuana or consume other drugs (personal interview, March 2000; Jacobs 1999b).

The presence of neighborhood gangs and cliques facilitates the production and distribution of illegal drugs. True, illicit drugs have been a feature of street-corner society for decades (see Merry 1981; Schwendinger and Schwendinger 1985), but the intensity of trafficking grew after crack appeared on the scene. Traditions of street drug use, black market enterprise networks, protection of "turf," anonymity, and high rates of truancy and unemployment combine with ease of manufacture to promote trafficking in crack (Barr, Farrell, Barnes, and Welte 1993). Nevertheless, street gangs vary widely in the extent of their involvement in drug-related crime in general and with cocaine. For example, in Chicago, whereas cocaine dominates the illegal activity of the Vice Lords and Black Gangster Disciples Nation, it is much less prominent among members of the Latin Kings and Latin Disciples (Block and Block 1993, 3–4).

One ex-drug dealer explains the lure of trafficking from the standpoint of underclass black youths:

> See, where I come from, young people don't dream of becoming doctors, lawyers, teachers, or even professional athletes. They dream of becoming big-time drug dealers. Kingpins. I'll stand witness.... When I show people the pictures of my previous lifestyle and the material things I had, it's not to brag. It's just you can't tell them the whole truth without letting them see the traps—money, cars, fine women, bad rep and the feeling you're a big man. In some neighborhoods, if you aren't a drug dealer, you'll never get a girlfriend. Talk about pressure, especially for a teenager. (Alexander 1994, 33)

The decrease in crack use of late has placed considerable strain on dealers who now compete in a high risk-low return environment. Bruce Jacobs (1999a, 1999b) has studied both heroin and crack dealers in St. Louis and finds plenty of evidence to show that heroin has replaced crack as the drug of choice in the inner city. Many former crack dealers now prefer to sell heroin, while those who still sell crack often supplement their inventory with heroin. There are many interrelated reasons for this change in drug use and dealing: Demand for crack is down; heroin is in some ways more powerful and profitable than crack; some crack users have died or gone to prison and have not been replaced; and there is increasing social stigma surrounding crack

use even among those on the "street." Some criminologists believe that heroin has assumed the role crack once occupied (Inciardi and Harrison 1998; Jacobs 1999a, 1999b). One reason for this is the different pharmacological and psychological effects of the drugs. One user put it this way:

> You get a better high out of it [heroin]. A crack high only last like maybe one, two, three, maybe five minutes man and then it's gone ... [with heroin] you spend [the same amount of money] ... and get high all day, get high for two or three days.... (Jacobs 1999a, 564)

While crack use and dealing is declining across the country, the drug problem is far from over. Cheap and potent forms of heroin, as we will see shortly, are becoming the major concerns of communities and law enforcement agencies across the United States.

Designer Drugs

During the 1980s a new breed of drugs appeared on the streets of some cities—the "designer drugs." Underground chemists, who seemed to work mainly in California, manufactured "analogs" of compounds available in existing pharmaceutical products. The motivation for producing designer drugs is not new discoveries for medicinal science, but profit. The pharmacology professor who invented the term "designer drugs" believes that a single "world-class medicinal chemist" was responsible for the fentanyl analogs that appeared on California streets in the early 1980s (Baum 1985, 10). The compound fentanyl is a powerful narcotic manufactured under the tradename Sublimaze by Janssen Pharmaceutica of Belgium. Fentanyl is about 100 times as potent as morphine. It is very short-acting and is used as an anesthetic in up to 70 percent of all surgical procedures in the United States. Fentanyl is also just as addictive as heroin or morphine, and the "high" associated with it, though short-lived, appears to be very similar to that associated with heroin (Baum 1985, 7–8).

A more recent example of a designer drug that has received considerable law enforcement and popular attention is "Crystal Meth" (street methamphetamine). Easily produced in "meth labs," the drug has the effects of concentrated speed and is very addictive. Stepped-up law enforcement efforts in response to several deaths and thefts related to the drug have netted thousands of arrests of meth "cooks" and users, especially in areas of the Midwest, and in Utah and California. In fact, the U.S. Drug Enforcement Agency (2001) seized 2,155 meth labs in 1999, compared to only 852 ten years earlier.

Heroin

The millions of Americans who routinely consume psychoactive substances with little thought that they are addicts, or even drug users, stand in stark contrast with the estimated 600,000–800,000 hardcore heroin addicts (Jacobs 1999a; National Institute on Drug Abuse 2000). Heroin has historically born the brunt of public and legal intolerance, and the world of most heroin addicts is quite different from that of other, "respectable" drug users. It is a world in which getting the "shit" (or "horse," "smack," "skag," "junk," "tragic magic") and staying alive and out of jail consume much of every waking day.

The heroin that an addict craves has often traveled thousands of miles and passed across numerous links in a complex underground chain of importation and distribution. Over the past decades, the primary foreign sources of heroin have been the Middle East, Afghanistan, Pakistan, India, the Far East, Mexico, and Colombia. During the 1970s, Mexico emerged as the major foreign source, with an estimated 80 percent (10 tons) of the 1975 domestic supply originating there. Today, Pakistan and Afghanistan compete with Mexico, Colombia, and the "Golden Triangle" (Burma, Laos, and Thailand) as the major U.S. sources.

The mechanics of importation vary according to the location and availability of raw opium—Mexico became an important source only after America withdrew from Vietnam and the Turkish government cracked down on opium production. Local dealers and vendors always remain the important final links in the chain and effectively control dealing at the street level. It is the pusher, the small-time vendor, who provides the addict and user with heroin. Pushers are usually addicts themselves; today, as they have for decades, pushers finance their own drug purchases through sales to others (Dunlap, Johnson, and Manwar 1997; Preble and Casey 1969).

Recall that heroin has replaced crack cocaine as the drug of choice in the inner city. According to Jacobs (1999a), heroin is usually dealt on the street in one of two forms: (1) buttons, which can be purchased for about $10 each, are pills that contain black tar heroin and crushed sleeping pills, and (2) the more recent pure tar heroin, which is of better quality and sold for about $20 a tenth gram. Neither require that the user "shoot up"—both can be snorted. This might make the drug more desirable to casual or recreational drug users, as illustrated in Plano, Texas, a few years ago when nineteen young "middle-class white cheerleaders, football players, and preppies" died as a result of taking $10 "chiva" heroin capsules (Gegax and Van Boven 2000).

FINANCING ADDICTION   Heroin can cost an addict hundreds of dollars a day. Where do addicts get their money? Most addicts finance their addiction through a combination of legitimate work and various sorts of hustle: begging, borrowing, stealing, drug pushing, and prostitution. In a classic study in Florida, selling drugs ranked first, followed by (for men) burglary, shoplifting, and robbery and (for women) prostitution, shoplifting, and prostitute theft from johns (Inciardi 1979). It was estimated that in one year alone, the sample of 356 Florida addicts committed a total of 118,134 offenses. Another classic study examined the lifestyles of 124 black, male, inner-city heroin addicts in Chicago, New York, Washington, D.C., and Philadelphia and presents a good picture of the economics of heroin addiction. (Hanson et al. 1985; for another view, see Faupel 1991). Most of the addicts interviewed were unskilled opportunists who rarely began the day with any money. Their "overwhelming preference" was to get money in the quickest, least violent, and least risky way (Beschner and Brower 1985, 36). As with the Florida addicts, legitimate work was an important, but usually insufficient, source of income. To supplement it, most addicts engaged in a variety of hustles, some legal, some not. For half the addicts the main hustle consisted of thefts, robberies, or con games; most would also try to borrow money from family and friends.

The Hanson et al. study distinguished four types of addict hustlers:

1. *Opportunistic hustlers* will take any opportunity, legal or not, that comes along. They start early in the morning so as not to miss any

opportunity, but beyond that they do little planning. Versatility is their hallmark, and the target is open.

2. *Legitimate hustlers* seldom engage in crimes, raising money by offering goods and services in the neighborhood to people they know. No job is rejected, no matter how menial, and their day is dictated by the routine activities of the neighborhood. They are also versatile and prepared to take drugs in exchange for services. They do not generally deal with strangers.

3. *Skilled hustlers* engage in crimes and hustles that require more skill and risk but are also more lucrative: picking pockets, specialized shoplifting, burglary. Targets are selected for vulnerability, the addicts usually work with a partner, and hustles are planned.

4. *Dope hustlers* raise money through drug trafficking. They are usually lower-echelon participants, getting drugs on consignment and selling them to fellow addicts in their own neighborhood. They may also offer services to others in exchange for dope (Hanson et al. 1985).

A Fields and Walters interviewee (1985, 64) explicates the services a dope hustler might offer:

Like sometimes there are people that don't know where to cop. We get their money and cop for them and get a taste. My biggest advantage is that I know, uh, I am real tight with most of the people that get in big quantity. I always know when the [good] stuff is comin' through. I always have people who want me to get it for 'em. I'm like the middleman. I got a credit line with most guys.

Besides "copping," dope hustlers may also "steer" customers to sources or "route" them to a particular dealer in exchange for drugs or cash (Johnson et al. 1985).

ADDICTION AS A CAREER   Many heavy drug users appear to have a career of use during which they are initiated into a drug's use, become regular users, and then "mature" out of using it. Trevor Bennett (1985) analyzed heroin addiction according to these career stages and the decisions that users and addicts make. His approach is predicated on the assumption that people are self-determining,

deliberate, and responsible and that their behavior is goal-directed, episodic, self-limiting, and mundane.

1. *Initiation:* Initial use occurs among friends and under the influence of a normative structure providing justification and support for its use. Bennett correctly points out that some of the normative supports may exist before the drug is ever taken. Bennett's own study of six groups of addicts from 1982 to 1984 found that 90 percent were introduced to the drug by friends or acquaintances, and many had made a conscious decision to try heroin some time before they actually did so. This is consistent with current research on many types of drugs (Abdelrahman, Rodriguez, Ryan, French, and Weinbaum 1998).

2. *Continuation:* Heroin users generally progress slowly toward addiction, some taking many months to reach that point. The majority of Bennett's subjects took over a year from first use to the point where they were using heroin daily, and many reported long gaps without use in between. "One addict reported that he usually gave up opioids during the summer months so that he could pursue his favorite sports. During the winter months he injected heroin on a daily basis" (1985, 25). Bennett also found considerable variation in the amount consumed from day to day, suggesting purposive decision making.

3. *Cessation:* Addicts can mature out of addiction, quitting heroin for a variety of reasons: because of a new job, family responsibilities, or an effort to change lifestyles. In Bennett's Cambridge study, all the subjects were current users, and half said they had no interest in quitting permanently. The others were confident they would quit within ten years, but only if certain other things occurred; for example, if they moved away from their associates and contacts or if their lives changed dramatically in some other way.

Bennett's study indicates that the behavior of heroin users can be self-regulated and manageable. Furthermore, they are not slaves to their addiction in the sense of having lost all self-determination. A similar position was taken by Fields and Walters (1985, 71–72) in a study of African-American heroin addicts in the United States. Other, more rewarding, things may temporarily supplant an addict's use of drugs, may lead to reduced levels of use, or may lead the addict to quit altogether (see also Shaffer and Jones 1989). Unfortunately, studies of ghetto use indicate that many of the conditions most likely to result in cessation—a good job, a stable family life, involvement in "straight" society—are out of reach of many inner-city addicts (Anderson 1999; Hanson et al. 1985). The problem is exacerbated by, and is partly the result of, the criminal involvements of many ghetto addicts. Submerged in crime, an addict's horizons rarely extend beyond the neighborhood and a small group of drug-using friends.

These observations are in line with a study of 32 hard-core heroin addicts (including fourteen women and twenty-three blacks) by Faupel and Klockars (1987) (see also Faupel 1991, 1999). Copping, dealing, and shooting heroin take place at the intersection of conventional and criminal roles and are structured by the availability of the drug. Faupel and Klockars describe a pattern in which "stabilized junkies" (addicts whose routine activities have incorporated regular and controlled heroin use and who have relatively easy and predictable access to the drug) may become destabilized—often after a binge of "free-wheeling" heroin use—and find themselves caught up in a ceaseless round of hustles, opportunistic crimes, and (consequently) arrests, and able to score only "street dope," heroin that is diluted ("stepped on") many times. This is the archetypal street junkie, whose life is "a continuous but typically unsuccessful effort to stabilize life structure and increase heroin availability" (Faupel and Klockars 1987, 64). For the inner-city street junkie, respite from this struggle often comes only with jail (temporary) or death.

The Link between Drugs and Crime

Where there is illicit drug use, there is often other crime. Much of the associated crime relates to financing drug use, abuse, and addiction (see Cromwell 1999; Wright and Decker 1994, 1997). This instrumental crime is most likely to be found among people who are poor, unemployed, or unemployable and among those who are heavy users. Many inner-city crack and heroin addicts belong to both groups (Hunt 1990).

Studies in Baltimore and Harlem confirm that heroin addicts who are frequent users commit crimes at a much greater rate than lower-level users. In Harlem, addicts participated heavily in drug distribution, with daily users averaging 316 drug sales per year plus 564 episodes of copping, steering, or routing. In all, daily users generated an average of $11,000 in cash per year from crimes of all sorts (Johnson et al., 1985). In Baltimore, a sample of 354 known users drawn from 7,510 users arrested or identified by police between 1952 and 1976 committed four to six times the amount of crime when frequently using than when not using or using occasionally (Ball, Shaffer, and Nurco 1983). The Baltimore addicts admitted to nearly 750,000 offenses, mostly thefts, drug sales, and various cons, over the course of nine and a half years.

The relationship between level of drug involvement and crime is confirmed in a study by Anglin and Speckart (1988). These authors found not only that as the level of use increased, so did the amount of criminal activity, but also that a shift seemed to occur in the criminal activities of high-level users to more profitable types of crime. Daily use of a narcotic drug was the best predictor of stepped-up criminal involvement among the 671 male addicts studied. However, even after addiction was terminated, a "subsistence" level of crime continued (see also Nurco et al. 1988).

More recently, Wright and Decker (1994, 39) found that 59 of 68 burglary offenders who used proceeds for pleasure-seeking pursuits specifically mentioned how the money would be used to buy drugs: "For many of these respondents, the decision to break into a dwelling arose as a result of a heavy session of drug use. The objective was to get the money to keep the party going."

There is little argument that drug use and crime are related (see Faupel 1999; Harrison and Gfroerer 1992; Harrison 1992). The nature and direction of that relationship remains a matter of dispute. In fact, drug use and crime may be connected in various ways:

- Drug use may give rise to crime.
- Crime may give rise to drug use.
- Drug use and crime may be reciprocal—each giving rise to the other.

All three views find support in criminological research, as does another:

- Commitment to a life of "action" produces both drug use and crime.

Most studies of chronic criminal offenders find heavy drug use and drug sales in their backgrounds, often beginning in their early teens (Harrison 1992). What is not clear is how much of that crime is explained by their drug use. The financial pinch that forces many drug users—especially the young and poor—into instrumental crime is clearly a factor; but it is difficult nevertheless to disentangle the offenses that are driven by drug abuse from those that are not and would have occurred anyway. As far as violence is concerned, it appears that drug (and alcohol) users who commit violent acts were likely to have been aggressive before they started using drugs (Fagan 1990). So, too, one should recognize that there is a kind of systematic violence associated with the world of illicit drug use—violence that derives from the milieu rather than the drug-using behavior of individuals within it. Territorial fights, robberies of dealers and subsequent retaliation, the elimination of informers and punishment for selling adulterated (or fake) drugs, are examples (Hunt 1990).

The Drug Use Forecasting (DUF) program established in 1987 by the National Institute of Justice measures drug use among men and women arrested for crimes in twenty-four cities around the United States. Voluntary and anonymous urine samples are tested. The results vary from city to city, but the overall picture shows that a majority of arrestees test positive for an illegal drug, in some cities as high as 75 to 80 percent of the men and women who are tested (see National Institute of Justice 1993). Although the DUF program does not tell us anything about the causal relationship between drug use and crime, and certainly tells us nothing about offenders who escape arrest, the program does confirm that where there is crime there is a strong probability that illicit drug use also will be found.

Although it is popular to think of drug use driving crime, criminal activity itself may lead to drug use among offenders. There are various ways this can happen:

(1) People who "earn" money like to spend some of it on pleasurable things; (2) a risky but successful venture should be celebrated; (3) a risky venture may need some special courage or other mental preparation; (4) the peer networks that facilitate delinquency and crime also facilitate drug use; and (5) drugs may substitute for cash or other profits. (Barlow and Ferdinand 1992, 109)

Studies have shown that serious drug use is more likely to be an aspect of the lifestyles of chronic delinquents and criminals than chronic criminality is of the lifestyles of serious drug users. In part, this reflects the better economic backgrounds of chronic drug users compared to those of chronic delinquents. On the other hand, as illegal income increases, so does discretionary buying power, which means more money is available for drugs (Cromwell 1999; Collins, Hubbard, and Rachel 1985; also see Faupel 1991, 1999).

For various reasons people cling to the idea of a causal connection between drug use and antisocial behavior, even though association does not mean that one causes the other. The idea helps one account for criminal behavior without imputing criminal intent. If a person were not "under the influence," a crime would not have happened. The drug becomes an excuse, a rationalization. Another reason pertains to enforcement: It is because people believe that illegal drugs cause terrible crimes that they accept and support severe penalties and secretive police tactics used against drug offenders. Ordinarily, people abhor "snitches" and distrust those who go about in disguise pretending to be what they are not.

Reactions to Drug and Alcohol Use

Reactions to drug and alcohol use are ambivalent at best, despite what the press and politicians might lead people to believe. For one thing, the possession, sale, and use of illegal drugs are often viewed as victimless crimes because they usually involve willing participants. Second, an individual can easily violate a drug law without being detected. Who is to know that a person is carrying two or three joints, some illegal pills, or a day's supply of heroin? The police can expect little help from the public, partly because of concerns about privacy, but also because of fear of reprisals. Third, some Americans remain unconvinced that the best strategy for dealing with the drug problem lies with the criminal law (see Box 8.2 for the debate around this issue). And the more proactive the police become, the more people begin to worry about their constitutional rights.

The law enforcement response to drugs emphasizes the supply side of the problem: Make illegal drugs more difficult to obtain by eradicating crops, disrupting smuggling, seizing drugs at the border, arresting dealers and pushers, and shutting down crack houses and clandestine laboratories. This is the core of the war on drugs, and some experts believe it is destined to fail (Blumstein 1993; Gaines and Kraska 1997). This is largely because a strong market for drugs persists even after the supply is

Box 8.2   CRIMINALIZE OR DECRIMINALIZE DRUGS? TWO OPPOSING VIEWS

The following summary of the two sides in the drug decriminalization debate is based on the work of two prominent scholars who have conducted considerable research on drug use and abuse in America: Arnold Trebach and James Inciardi.

For Decriminalization: Trebach

1. There is no scientific basis for distinguishing between legal and illegal drugs. All can be harmful yet all can be used without material harm.
2. Drug prohibition is linked to crime and violence.
3. Justice has turned to profit-making (e.g., asset forfeiture).
4. The huge costs of the drug war have few beneficial returns.
5. The drug war diverts attention from real social problems, such as racial hatred, criminal violence, and AIDS.
6. "The seductive powers of drugs are overrated." There is no evidence that legalization would produce huge numbers of new addicts.
7. Criminalization causes more harm than the drugs themselves. For one thing, criminalization spawns crime.

Trebach's Major Reform Proposal: "Deal with virtually all illegal drugs as we now deal with alcohol."

Against Decriminalization: Inciardi

1. Drug prohibition seems to be working since most Americans do not use illegal drugs.
2. Drug legalization would produce health and behavioral problems that would "far outweigh the current consequences of prohibition."
3. Cocaine, especially in crack form, is especially dangerous, and legalization would only make it more available, more attractive, and more troublesome.
4. Any reduction in the violence currently associated with drug trafficking and distribution will be offset by increases in violence associated with the psychopharmacological properties of drugs.
5. The American public wants the war on drugs to continue, and voluntary treatment in the absence of criminal justice controls doesn't work.

Inciardi's Major Reform Proposal: More humane use of the criminal justice system, plus compulsory treatment for those arrested.

Source: Based on Arnold S. Trebach and James A. Inciardi, *Legalize It? Debating American Drug Policy* (Washington, D.C.: American University Library, 1993).

interrupted. This rather pessimistic view is all the more disturbing when one considers how much is spent on the war on drugs: over $28 billion by federal, state, and local governments in 1996. Around half of all the money is spent on the enforcement activities of federal, state, and local police.

Because illicit drug offenses are mostly consensual crimes and because they are not readily observed, police enforcement strategies emphasize undercover work and the use of police informants. By infiltrating the ranks of users, undercover narcotics officers—or **narcs**—are able to develop trusting relationships with users and pushers and thus keep tabs on the people and places associated with the illegal drug industry.

To maintain their cover, narcs must often live among the "enemy" and to all appearances become one of them. This is a difficult role that carries various risks and costs beyond the obvious one of personal danger. A first-hand investigation of the junkie's world in New York, Houston, Austin, and Los Angeles found that narcs often had difficulty separating themselves from that world, even though they despised it and their goal was to destroy it (Jackson 1969b). Some officers succumbed to temptation, others ended up with severe stress disorders. Keeping their lives separated, remembering "who I really am, and what I am really doing here" sometimes

took tremendous willpower and self-confidence. This picture hasn't changed, as we see from a narc's observation in a more recent study of undercover police work:

> I identified very strongly with the bad guys.... Even though these people were breaking the law ... I realized everything wasn't black and white.... It didn't take me long to get into the way of thinking like the crooks I was running with. I started identifying with these people very quickly. (cited in Pogrebin and Poole 1993, 388)

Helping law enforcement are **police informants**, known pejoratively as "snitches." Usually drug abusers or sellers themselves, informants are cultivated by police, who use the information they receive to develop cases. The informants' own crimes are often used as a means to induce them to work for the police. Under threat of arrest and a jail sentence, would-be informants find they have little choice. If they don't cooperate, police can spread word on the street that they are snitches.

STOPPING DRUG SMUGGLING: THE FEDERAL INTERDICTION EFFORT   A major federal enforcement effort is directed at the interdiction of drug trafficking at the border, on the high seas, or in countries involved in production or trafficking. The U.S. Customs

Drug smuggling from Mexico to the United States is big business, and the profit margin is enormous. Small wonder that people from all walks of life are involved, and that an equally wide range of techniques are employed. Drugs are mostly smuggled in by truck, but also via automobile, mule, and even stomach.

Service deals with land border smuggling with the cooperation of other federal agencies, while the U.S. Coast Guard employs more than 135 seagoing vessels and 180 aircraft in their marine interdiction efforts. Smuggling by air is handled by the Department of Defense, although the military is prohibited from making arrests (Bureau of Justice Statistics 1993, 146). The DEA is also involved, primarily as an investigative and intelligence gathering agency, which includes posting agents in foreign countries.

Combining the seizures of the major federal agencies involved in drug interdiction suggests the staggering magnitude of international drug trafficking. But seized drugs represent merely the tip of the iceberg. The drug pipeline is tough to breach, not only because the major importers, wholesalers, and distributors are well-organized and equipped, but also because the profitability of small quantities of these drugs make large shipments unnecessary. It is like looking for a needle in a haystack. The diversity of drugs also contributes to the difficulties facing police: "Crack, powder cocaine, heroin, PCP, 'pills'—each drug type has a different volume, different user demographics, and a different relationship to dealer and user crime" (Kleiman and Smith 1990, 73).

The major obstacle to effective control of drug trafficking at home and abroad is the simplest to identify and the hardest to overcome: Illicit drugs are in high demand, and people are willing to pay the price. The lure of high profits means there will always be plenty of people willing to pit themselves against authorities. Even as the authorities become more organized and sophisticated in their enforcement efforts, so do the traffickers.

DRUG AND ALCOHOL ARRESTS: A MAJOR POLICE ACTIVITY

As Figure 8.3 shows, the police make many drug arrests, but mostly for possession (79 percent). When combined with alcohol-related arrests in any given year, more arrests are made for drug-related offenses than for any other category of crime. Over the past twenty years, drug and alcohol-related arrests account for around 30 percent of all arrests. Despite the downward trend in self-reported drug use during the 1980s and early 1990s, police agencies did not slow down in making arrests. Leaving out alcohol offenses, drug arrests as a percent of all arrests grew from 5.7 percent in 1983 to nearly 10 percent in 1996.

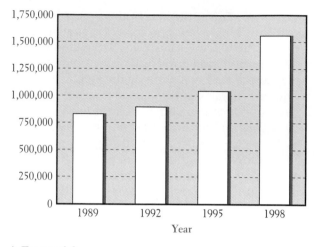

▲ FIGURE 8.3

Drug Abuse Arrests, 1989–1998

Source: Federal Bureau of Investigation, *Crime in the United States* (Washington, D.C.: U.S. Department of Justice, 1999).

Arrests on charges relating to alcohol far outnumber other drug arrests. Over 65 percent of more than 3 million drug/alcohol arrests in 1999 were alcohol-related. The offenses are usually public drunkenness, the violation of liquor laws governing sale and consumption, or driving while intoxicated—the most common alcohol offense. Alcohol-related offenses constitute this country's number-one law enforcement problem, representing almost a quarter of all police arrests.

Over the past few years, drug arrests of African-Americans have been rising faster than those of whites. The spread of crack in inner-city neighborhoods certainly accounts for some of the difference, but the complete story is not that simple. Many drug arrests are incidental to other police actions, and when police target minority neighborhoods with a reputation for crime and social disorder such actions are likely to uncover many drug violations that might have escaped detection in other neighborhoods (Klofas 1993). In fact, most drug arrests are not made by specialized narcotic units but by police on routine patrol, whose nondrug stops and searches reveal evidence of drug-related crimes.

Many police departments are discovering that increasing the number of drug arrests by itself is an ineffective way of dealing with the drug problem in their communities. Some departments have adopted what are called **problem-oriented policing** strategies that go beyond arrests. The four primary objectives of problem-oriented drug enforcement are as follows:

- To increase the effectiveness of police in battling local drug problems by addressing the underlying community problems that spawn them
- To increase reliance on the knowledge and creative approaches of patrolling officers to analyze problems and develop solutions
- To encourage police to tap diverse public and private resources in a cooperative effort to solve community problems
- To develop a closer involvement with citizens and let them see that police address the needs of the public (Bureau of Justice Assistance 1993, 6)

Under this model, patrolling police officers are trained in problem-solving methods and are encouraged to assess and analyze situations as they arise and to develop action plans for dealing with them that go beyond making arrests. Case studies in seven cities and evidence from "hot spot" experiments suggest that the approach has much promise, but long-term success will depend on the continuing support of police departments and the communities they serve (Uchida, Forst, and Annan 1992; Weisburd and Green 1995).

MADD AND DARE: ARE THEY WORKING? Drunk driving stands as a constant reminder of the dangers of complacency toward alcohol. The majority of all auto fatalities and accidents are attributed to drinking before or while driving. Private organizations such as MADD (Mothers against Drunk Drivers) and SADD (Students against Driving Drunk), and government-sponsored campaigns such as RID (Remove Intoxicated Drivers) have pressured lawmakers into revising drunk-driving laws. In the past few years all states have passed new laws or toughened existing statutes.

So far the results are not promising: DUI arrests have actually gone down from their peak in the mid-1980s. The risks of being arrested while driving intoxicated are less than 1 percent, and even when people are stopped by the police, violations continue (Lanza-Kaduce 1988; Linsky et al. 1986; but see Piquero and Paternoster 1998, for a study of the deterrent effects).

Declines in drug and alcohol use among young people during the 1980s made good press for groups such as Mothers against Drunk Driving. However, one study tells a different story (Lundman 1991). City police in the early 1970s were not much interested in drunk driving and made DUI arrests infrequently. With the founding of MADD in 1980, DUI arrests initially grew, but then actually declined from 1984 through 1989. Apparently, while MADD inspired initial increases in arrests, it turned out that the criminal justice system often could not handle the influx of new offenders, and the police soon discovered there was no point in making arrests since offenders were quickly released (Kinkade and Leone 1992). Experiences such as these leave the police and public understandably frustrated. In light of the massive increases in incarceration of drug offenders, they also reinforce the view that alcohol-related offenses such as drunk driving are not all that serious. A lesson to learn is that policy changes do not necessarily have the effects that are intended.

The school DARE (Drug Awareness and Resistance Education) program is popular with parents, teachers, police, and many students. Research on its effectiveness, however, shows mixed results.

Another area of controversy concerns the Drug Abuse Resistance Education, or DARE, programs that target fifth and sixth graders. The typical program includes seventeen weekly lessons taught by uniformed police officers trained by Los Angeles-based DARE America. The officers give lectures and assign homework on the dangers of drugs, alcohol, and gangs. Some schools offer DARE lessons to younger children as well, while others offer a supplemental curriculum for junior high and high schools. In 1997 the DARE program received $750 million in federal funding (Glass 1997).

Despite generally favorable responses from teachers, parents, and young children alike, there are two major problems with DARE: (1) The bulk of research indicates that it does not work in the long run (Dukes, Stein, and Ullman 1997; Rosenbaum and Hanson 1998), and some suggest that it may even have a "boomerang" effect: "DARE graduates are *more* likely to use marijuana" (Glass 1997, 20); and (2) a fierce lobby exists, coordinated by DARE officials and backed by the White House and the U.S. Justice Department, that is resisting the research evidence and any attempts by school districts to scale back or end DARE programming. Instead, DARE supporters are calling for *more* DARE (and therefore more DARE funding) on the grounds that its messages need repeating and reinforcement throughout a child's school years.

CHAPTER SUMMARY

This chapter has examined prostitution and offenses involving drugs and alcohol. To some extent, these activities are prohibited as violations of prevailing moral standards and because they threaten to interfere with the orderly functioning of society. The discussion in this chapter has shown, however, that special interests also play a major role in the creation and enforcement of these so-called public order crimes.

There are many similarities in the criminological aspects of drugs and sex, including the fact that participants usually do not think of themselves as either criminals or victims. Prostitution thrives because there is widespread male demand for sexual encounters and a more or less organized network of suppliers prepared to meet that demand for a price. If there is a victim in prostitution it is the prostitute herself. Among the various participants—prostitute, customer, pimp, or procurer—it is the prostitute who runs the greatest risk of arrest, jail time, assault, robbery, disease, and dependency.

Many authors believe that prostitution results from, and contributes to, a system of gender stratification in which women are subordinate to, and serve the interests of, men. Even though few women are forced into prostitution, the economic options open to many poorer women, especially single mothers, are such that prostitution is a rational choice from among a restricted number of unpromising alternatives.

Reactions to prostitution are generally lenient, as one might expect in a society where laws are created and enforced primarily by men. The same is largely true of reactions to other consensual sex crimes, although enforcement of laws prohibiting prostitution may well become more systematic and repressive.

Offenses involving alcohol generally enjoy lenient reactions on the part of both the public and legal officials. This is hardly surprising given widespread social drinking, the failure of Prohibition, and the fact that powerful liquor interests spend millions of dollars advertising the pleasures of drinking and lobbying state and federal officials on their behalf.

In contrast, offenses involving heroin, cocaine, hallucinogens, and to a lesser extent marijuana, are the focus of extensive enforcement efforts and can result in penalties that are more severe than those given to burglars, robbers, and rapists. Influenced by fears of a crumbling morality among youth and by the view that drug use causes other crime, the current furor over illicit drug use largely obscures the fact that much of the current drug problem in America is explained by three related historical processes: growth in recreational use of drugs; growth in the production and marketing of legal drugs; and the selective creation and enforcement of prohibitions dealing with essentially similar behaviors. This observation does not deny that the growing use of heroin is a serious problem that needs to be solved, but it serves as a reminder that crime is invariably shaped by social, political, and economic history rather than by the criminal motives of evil, or merely weak, individuals.

KEY TERMS

crack (p. 182)

drug (p. 177)

narc (p. 189)

pimp (p. 173)

police informant (p. 189)

pornography (p. 176)

problem-oriented policing (p. 190)

psychoactive substance (p. 177)

Stockholm syndrome (p. 174)

victimless crime (p. 171)

RECOMMENDED READINGS

Inciardi, James A. 1999. *The Drug Legalization Debate*. Thousand Oaks, CA: Sage.

Inciardi, James A., and L. D. Harrison. 1998. *Heroin in the Age of Crack Cocaine*. Thousand Oaks, CA: Sage.

Jacobs, Bruce A. 1999b. *Selling Crack: The Social World of Streetcorner Selling*. Boston, MA: Northeastern University Press.

Miller, Eleanor M. 1986. *Street Women*. Philadelphia, PA: Temple University Press.

Ratner, Mitchell S. 1994. *Crack Pipe as Pimp: An Ethnographic Investigation of Sex-for-Crack Exchanges*. New York: Lexington.

Wilson, Hugh T., ed. 1999. *Annual Editions: Drugs, Society, and Behavior*. Sluice Dock, CT: Dushkin/McGraw-Hill.

RECOMMENDED WEB SITES

National Institute on Drug Abuse

An outstanding source of information on drug types and addictions.

http://www.nida.nih.gov

U.S. Drug Enforcement Agency

Statistics, policies, programs, and interdiction effort information.

http://www.usdoj.gov/dea

Prostitutes' Education Network

A site maintained by a group attempting to repeal prostitution laws and increase sex workers' rights.

http://www.bayswan.org/penet.html

Prostitution Research and Education

A site maintained by activists, scholars, and organizations interested in drawing attention to the harmfulness and exploitative nature of prostitution.

http://www.prostitutionresearch.com

CHAPTER

9

CRIMINOLOGY, CRIMINAL JUSTICE, AND CRIME

If we use the legalistic definition of crime—that the state creates crime—then it must also be, in some measure, the state's responsibility to deal with it. For this reason alone, crime and criminal justice are intertwined. This means that a comprehensive understanding of crime and criminality depends on knowledge of how the criminal justice system works. While most people correctly see criminal justice as the state's reaction to crime and criminals, some others see it as a *cause* of crime as well. This is also correct, not only because the actions of authorities may encourage criminal activity, but also because some of those actions may be criminal in themselves. The study of the relationship between crime and criminal justice might be called a *criminology of criminal justice*.

Rather than provide a comprehensive description of the American criminal justice system—there are whole textbooks on this subject—this chapter looks instead at the criminology of criminal justice. After a brief introduction to the major actors and decision points in the system, the chapter discusses the nature and consequences of discretion, the crime-prevention function of the police, and the relationship between crime and punishment. The chapter also looks at crimes and other abuses committed by criminal justice authorities.

CRIMINAL JUSTICE: ACTORS AND DECISIONS

Criminal justice is a society's system of roles and activities for defining and dealing with crime. In the United States today, criminal justice involves the actions of the following:

- State and federal legislatures, where rules governing crime and justice are enacted into law
- Administrative agencies such as the Internal Revenue Service and the Food and Drug Administration, which create rules that carry criminal penalties if violated
- Local, state, and federal law enforcement agencies
- Prosecution and defense, made up of attorneys who practice criminal law and handle criminal cases in the courts
- Municipal, state, and federal trial courts where criminal cases are handled
- State and federal appellate courts, which rule on the constitutionality of actions taken by lower courts and by police and correctional agencies
- Probation and parole agencies that provide services to the courts and to correctional agencies
- Local, state, and federal correctional agencies, which carry out the punishment of convicted criminal offenders and oversee the operation of jails and prisons
- Justice professionals such as private detectives, medical examiners, expert witnesses, jury consultants, criminologists, and law professors
- Social service agencies providing treatment, counseling, and rehabilitation
- Private companies that provide goods or services to individuals and agencies involved in criminal justice or employ criminal justice personnel
- Special interest groups, such as the National Rifle Association (NRA), the American Civil Liberties Union (ACLU), the National Association for the Advancement of Colored People (NAACP), and the National Organization for the Repeal of Marijuana Laws (NORML)

- Private citizens who are crime victims, witnesses, or complainants, or who have ties with offenders or criminal justice personnel
- Criminal suspects, defendants, and offenders

The relationship between these different actors is shown in Figure 9.1, a "road map" of criminal justice in America (Barlow 2000, 35). Decisions made at one point in the road flow along it and influence decisions made at other points. The core agencies, or pillars, of the criminal justice system are the police, courts, and corrections. However, actions taken outside the core influence what happens inside, and vice versa. For example, in March 1997, the U.S. Supreme Court, the nation's highest appellate court, ruled unconstitutional a legislative decision by the State of Florida to take away from certain prison inmates the "good time" they had earned toward their release. Florida was forced to release hundreds of offenders who had served portions of lengthy sentences for murder, robbery, rape, and other serious crimes. The Court had upheld the rights of prisoners but many private citizens and justice officials were concerned by the prospect of a mass release of violent criminals. In response, special interest groups and the state legislature immediately sought ways to stop the release, and police organizations geared up for trouble.

The criminal justice system is a part of society's formal social control apparatus. Three overall goals unite the three core agencies of the system:

1. Track down and punish those found guilty of committing crimes.
2. Maintain order.
3. Promote justice.

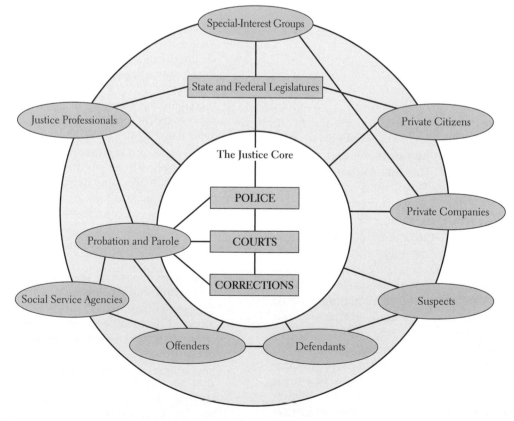

▲ FIGURE 9.1
Criminal Justice System Relationships

Table 9.1 lists the immediate goals and primary activities of the police, courts, and corrections. It is easy to see how one area relies on another. For example, a primary goal of the police is the detection and arrest of suspects. Unless that is accomplished, the courts have no one to process, and therefore cannot achieve their goals of determining guilt or innocence and promoting justice through fair punishments. Likewise, if no one is declared guilty by the courts, the goals of corrections cannot be achieved. Like any other system, the whole achieves its purpose only if the parts, or subsystems, accomplish theirs.

TABLE 9.1 **The Goals and Primary Activities of the Criminal Justice System**

OVERALL GOALS OF THE SYSTEM
Track down and punish those guilty of committing crime Maintain order Promote justice

THREE FUNCTIONAL AREAS OF THE SYSTEM	
POLICE	
PRIMARY GOALS	PRIMARY ACTIVITIES IN SUPPORT OF THE GOALS
Enforce the law Maintain order Prevent crime	Detection and investigation of crimes Identification and arrest of suspects Routine patrol, surveillance, and intelligence gathering Education and training of officers and citizens, including children (e.g., bicycle safety, DARE) Community and problem-oriented policing
COURTS	
PRIMARY GOALS	PRIMARY ACTIVITIES IN SUPPORT OF THE GOALS
Determine guilt or innocence of suspects Set the appropriate penalty upon conviction Uphold the cause of justice, including due process	Prosecution and defense of suspects Pre-trial hearings Impartial bench and jury trials Plea negotiations Sentencing Appeals of conviction or sentence Provide probation and parole services in conjunction with corrections
CORRECTIONS	
PRIMARY GOALS	PRIMARY ACTIVITIES IN SUPPORT OF THE GOALS
Apply court-ordered punishment Maintain safety and security of correctional personnel and the community Uphold due process and other constitutional rights of offenders	Design and implement correctional programs Design, construct, and run prison and jail facilities with appropriate levels of security Carry out the death penalty (in states where legal and prescribed) Provide probation and parole services in conjunction with courts

Decision Stages in the Criminal Justice System

The criminal justice system comes alive through the actions of the people who work in it and those who are "processed" by it. From the vantage point of criminal suspects, defendants, and victims, there are various key decision points that have markedly different outcomes depending on the actions taken. This section briefly describes where those points are in the system, the actions that may be taken, and their consequences. Figure 9.2 presents a flow chart summarizing the formal criminal justice process. The arrows show where the suspect or defendant goes after each decision is made. Some decisions involve considerable discretion, where criminal justice personnel act on the basis of their professional judgment; others are governed by strict rules allowing little leeway. Highly discretionary decisions are indicated by a ✓+.

KEY POLICE DECISIONS   The key decision points for police involve whether or not to do the following:

- Treat an event as a possible crime.
- Investigate the crime.
- Make an arrest.
- Turn the suspect over to the prosecution.

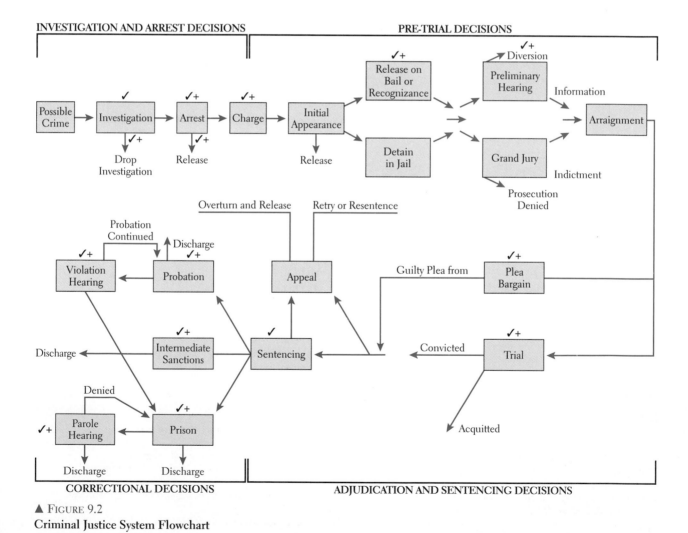

▲ FIGURE 9.2
Criminal Justice System Flowchart

Most police decisions are highly discretionary. Even though the police rely heavily on complaints from the public, they must decide that an event is a possible crime and then investigate it in order to set the wheels of criminal justice in motion. It may be minutes or many months before a suspect is found, but only then can the police contemplate making an arrest. Arrest decisions are influenced by many things, but the essential legal criterion is **probable cause**. This means that a person exercising reasonable judgment would believe that a crime is being or has been committed and that the suspect is responsible for it. Technically, suspects are arrested when they have been deprived of their freedom, or believe that they have been placed in custody.

A suspect may be released quickly if the police realize they have made a mistake or believe they do not have sufficient probable cause. The same suspect can be rearrested if circumstances change, however. Suspects have the right to remain silent once they are arrested, but many end up talking to the police. Innocent or not, some suspects implicate others, and the police are trained to listen carefully to anything said by a suspect. Normally, the suspect must be formally charged with a crime or released within 48 hours of being arrested. Suspects who are charged are turned over to the prosecution, and thus enter the court phase of the criminal justice process.

KEY DECISIONS OF THE COURTS   Suspects that are turned over for prosecution become *defendants*. During the court phase of the criminal justice process, the key decisions involve the following:

- Filing of a formal complaint or charge
- Granting or denying of bail
- Issuing of an "indictment" or "information"
- Entering of plea
- Plea negotiations
- Determination of guilt or innocence at trial
- Filing of an appeal
- Determination of sentence

One of the first decisions made in the court phase is bail. The U.S. Constitution does not guarantee a defendant's right to be released on bail pending trial, but it does prohibit "excessive" bail. Bail can be denied if the court has grounds to believe that a defendant will not return for trial, would pose a threat to the community if released, or will interfere with the police or prosecution in the preparation of the case. Bail turns out to be one of the most significant decisions for defendants because, among other things, freedom helps in the preparation of their defense while detention generally hinders it.

Other crucial decisions are made in the charging process. Many cases are screened out early in the process as prosecutors concentrate on pursuing cases they feel they can win or that they believe are important to the community, the criminal justice system, or themselves. When prosecutors take no further action, the case is called *nolle prosequi*; sometimes they may decide to pursue less serious charges than the crime itself might warrant. Prosecutors thus exercise considerable discretion in the charging phase.

Most felony cases go through one of two kinds of pretrial review designed to establish that there is sufficient evidence to proceed against the defendant. One is a **preliminary hearing**, held before a lower court judge who summarizes the charge(s) listed by the prosecutor in a document called an "information" and reviews the evidence. Prosecution and defense may each present testimony. Police procedures are sometimes challenged at this stage. If the judge or magistrate finds there is enough evidence to support the charges, the defendant is bound over for trial. The other review process, held in about half the states and in the federal system, is conducted in secret before a panel of citizens, usually twenty-three, called a **grand jury**. The grand jury dates back to the reign of Henry II in the twelfth century, when it was composed of a group of royal knights assembled by the sheriff to decide who should be brought before the traveling court. Over the years, the grand jury gained in popularity because it was not afraid to challenge the crown by refusing to indict political opponents of the king. This reputation helped make the grand jury popular in the American colonies.

Today, only the prosecutor presents testimony before the grand jury and there is no opportunity for cross-examination. To all intents and purposes the grand jury is an investigative arm of the prosecution. It sifts through the evidence presented and generates new evidence through the questioning of witnesses. If the grand jury accepts that there is probable cause to proceed with the case, it issues a *bill of indictment* listing the specific charges. In August 1998, President Clinton gave testimony before a federal grand jury investigating his relationship with Monica Lewinsky. The hearing was conducted via closed circuit TV and videotaped for the record. With congressional authorization, and over the objection of Clinton's lawyers, the videotape was released to the public a month later. Although these were unprecedented events, this grand jury hearing had the same purpose as any other: to determine if sufficient evidence of criminal wrongdoing existed to warrant prosecution.

Although the U.S. Constitution gives criminal defendants the right to a jury trial, approximately 90 percent of criminal convictions are the result of guilty pleas, and most of these are agreed upon by the prosecution and defense following some sort of negotiation. If the case goes to trial before a jury, the decision to convict must usually be a unanimous one. A guilty verdict sends the defendant on to sentencing; a not guilty verdict releases the defendant, who cannot normally be retried for the same offense. If the jury cannot make up its mind, it may be declared a "hung jury," and the defendant may be retried at the discretion of the prosecution.

Some convicted defendants may decide to appeal the conviction, which can take months or years to complete. The appellate court will be asked to consider whether the defendant's legal rights were violated in some way. If the court finds that they were, a new trial may be ordered or the defendant may be freed altogether. Defendants are usually sentenced even though an appeal is pending. In misdemeanor cases, convicted defendants are usually sentenced the same day; in felony cases, it may be three or four weeks before sentencing is carried out. Judges used to have considerable discretion in the sentences they handed down; today, many states have **mandatory sentencing**, which requires the court to impose a certain penalty for a given offense.

KEY DECISIONS IN CORRECTIONS   Even though the sentencing judge stipulates the penalties that will be imposed on a convicted offender, corrections officials have key decisions to make that impact offenders as well as the criminal justice system and the larger society. These decisions concern the following:

- Classification of offenders
- Prison and jail management
- Type and extent of services provided
- Inmate release and postrelease

Some corrections decisions are more discretionary than others. For example, federal and state laws as well as court rulings may require that certain types of facilities be made available and that offenders receive certain services or be treated in a certain way. Increasing numbers of law suits filed by inmates and other offenders under correctional supervision continually test the constitutionality of practices and procedures. In 1980 a total of 42,781 suits were filed in U.S. District Courts; by 1995 the figure had grown to 120,060 (Maguire and Pastore 1996, Table 6.77). Although most suits are rejected, corrections officials know that their actions are subject to a level of public scrutiny that was unheard of twenty years ago.

Felony offenders headed to prison are generally classified according to the security risk they pose, and their likely response to the available educational and treatment programs. In these times of mandatory sentencing, prison overcrowding, and reduced support for rehabilitation and other "liberal" programs, classification decisions focus on security rather than inmate needs. But overcrowding is also forcing release of some inmates long before their time is served. This is seen by many people as a distinct threat to the community and it fuels calls for more prison beds.

The new hope in correctional circles today lies with intermediate sanctions. The bulk of criminal offenders do not pose a serious safety risk to the community even though a majority of known felons are repeat offenders, and many commit new offenses while on probation or parole. Correctional officials around the country are challenging public fears and the skepticism of many politicians by advocating increased use of community-based corrections. The American Correctional Association lobbied Congress in 1996 to support legislation that provides alternatives to incarceration for the bulk of felony offenders.

An incarcerated offender's successful return into the community is never a foregone conclusion, and usually both offenders and correctional officials must work very hard at accomplishing it. More often than not the effort fails because offenders who leave prison have few marketable skills, few resources to fall back on, and few people willing and able to provide the emotional support and healthy companionship ex-inmates need to build a new life. Making matters worse is the stigma associated with street crime and prison time: Potential employers are reluctant to believe that ex-inmates are trustworthy, and the comment "once a criminal, always a criminal" sums up the view of many people. Notwithstanding the offense a person has committed—and ex-inmates have generally committed more serious ones—it is during the postrelease phase of the criminal justice system that some of the most crucial decisions are made. These decisions are made by members of the public, not criminal justice personnel.

The Criminal Justice System Is a Leaky Funnel

Pour engine oil in a funnel with holes in it, and not much oil will reach the engine. Figure 9.3 illustrates this phenomenon using the criminal justice system as the funnel and criminal suspects as the oil. One can easily see that few of the people who started the journey through the system ended up in prison.

Of course, it is unlikely that every one of the individuals arrested by the police for a felony crime actually committed it. But the picture is nonetheless sobering because it shows fairly convincingly that the system succeeds in weeding people out better than it does passing them through to the statutory punishment that defines a felony offense. This disturbs many people inside and outside criminal justice. However, other people are more disturbed by this fact: The people who get arrested in the first place are more likely to have committed conventional street crimes and are more likely to be from the lower classes and minority groups. These same people are the ones most likely to end up in prison. In this way, decisions made throughout the criminal justice system—including decisions about what constitutes serious crime in the first place—tend to have an accumulative, negative impact on minority individuals, especially African-Americans. It turns out this is true for juveniles as well as for adults (Pope and Feyerherm 1991). A combination of factors is responsible for this state of affairs: stereotypes of real crime and real criminals; bias and discrimination in the labeling practices of some criminal justice personnel; the nonrandom distribution of criminal opportunities and access to them; get-tough-on-crime policies that target street crimes, particularly drug sales; and the higher rates of violent crime among minorities and the poor who live in inner-city neighborhoods.

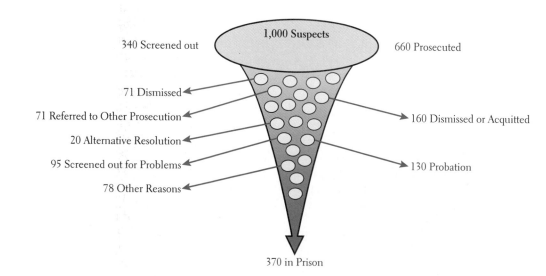

▲ FIGURE 9.3
The Criminal Justice System Is a Leaky Funnel

DISCRETION IN CRIMINAL JUSTICE

Discretion is exercised in situations where "criminal justice officials ... choose one action over another on the basis of their professional judgment" (Barlow 2000, 681). Examples of these situations include decisions to interrogate a suspect, to make an arrest, to prosecute a defendant, to negotiate a plea, to follow the recommendations in a presentence report, and to release an inmate onto parole. There are both positive and negative aspects to the exercise of discretion. On the positive side, discretion allows criminal justice personnel to take into account individual characteristics and circumstances of people they are dealing with. The exercise of discretion inevitably results in some individuals and groups being treated differently than others, and this points up a major problem: Discretion undermines the constitutional right of all Americans to be treated equally under the law (Barlow and Barlow 2000). Discretion means power and if it is abused, justice is compromised and respect for law—and for its enforcers—is diminished. This in itself may promote crime.

Police Discretion

In the daily routines of criminal justice, the police are typically the first officials to exercise discretion. Their decisions shape law in action, and "through the exercise of discretion [patrol officers] define and redefine the meaning of justice" (Brown 1988, 7). In similar circumstances one citizen may be arrested while someone else is let go; or perhaps one suspect's refusal to cooperate is handled in a different way than another's.

The scope of discretion, that is, the range of choices of action that can be made in a given situation, is enormous. Consider the case of traffic stops. There are at least 770 different combinations of actions that officers could appropriately take (Bayley and Bittner 1989, 98–99). This number is calculated by multiplying ten different actions officers could choose when making initial contact by seven strategies used during the stop and by eleven options for exiting the encounter (10 x 7 x 11 = 770). Here are some of the exit options that officers could select when dealing with the driver (Bayley and Bittner 1989, 98):

- Release the car and driver.
- Release the driver with a warning.
- Release the driver with a traffic citation.
- Arrest the driver for a prior offense.
- Arrest the driver for being drunk.
- Arrest the driver for actions during the stop.
- Insist the driver proceed on foot.
- Transport the driver somewhere without making an arrest.

Needless to say, dealing with traffic offenses is only one part of the police job; *all* routine police work involves choosing among alternative courses of action. Discretion is the core of policing.

Of necessity, the police engage in **selective enforcement** of the law. This means that "the police do not enforce all the laws all the time against every single violator" (Doerner 1998, 152). Some experts believe that the most important discretionary decisions are the *negative* ones, such as not to make an arrest, not to investigate a complaint, or not to make deals. These decisions establish the line between people "getting into trouble," and "getting away with it." They define the limits of the law.

There is a strong incentive for police officers to avoid taking official action and it is this: Once they decide to take such action, whether it is responding to a complaint, writing a report, or making an arrest, that decision is subject to review by others. A review can mean a rewarding pat on the back, perhaps even a promotion; but it may also bring criticism, suspension, even dismissal. Decisions to act unofficially or to do nothing, on the other hand, are rarely reviewed because they are usually of low visibility (Gottfredson and Gottfredson 1988, 50). By their very nature, "do nothing" decisions will not be scrutinized by third parties except in extraordinary circumstances. Negative decisions contribute an element of mystery to the routine actions of police officers while lessening both internal (departmental) and external (public and legal) controls.

DISCRETION AND THE FIELD INTERROGATION   Police officers may choose to question individuals in the field, either while on routine patrol or as part of an investigative assignment. This is called a **field interrogation**. It may be a simple question or two or it may be quite involved. The field interrogation is an integral part of the job, and another area in which discretion comes into play. Deciding whether to stop and question someone is an important decision for police as well as for the general public. It not only determines whether a citizen will be detained, if only for a short time, but it could also turn out to determine the outcome of a case. How the interrogation is handled may also determine whether citizens later complain about the police officer's behavior.

Studies of police field work show that officers are often very casual in their interviewing behavior, rarely taking detailed notes, sometimes none at all (Greenwood et al. 1977; Sanders 1977). Police carry information in their heads, often for many hours, sifting and sorting it until a picture forms that guides their subsequent decisions. Throughout the process, they are trying to establish "what really happened," and "who really did it." Interrogations are primarily designed to develop information, but they often help officers decide what actually happened and what to call it.

Verbal information secured during field interrogation may point to inconsistencies or inaccuracies in the accounts of victims or witnesses, and it may also be used to "trip up" suspects in subsequent interrogations. Minor inconsistencies may be ignored, even in homicide cases, but a major inconsistency will be taken seriously and investigated further, perhaps during future questioning or through the collection of new evidence. Throughout the process, police categorize and sort the verbal information they receive, combining it with impressions—the suspect is acting "guilty"—and with evidence from the scene or from witnesses.

It is often heard that police unfairly target women and members of minority groups when conducting field interviews. One recent study of ethnic differences in field interrogations found that more blacks than whites reported (1) being stopped while in a vehicle or on foot; (2) being questioned about an offense, having their house searched, or being arrested; and (3) being asked for documents or to provide a statement (Bucke 1997).

▲▼

A Denver police officer takes notes as he talks to residents about a murder that took place nearby. Police exercise much discretion when conducting field work, especially when interviewing potential witnesses and conducting field interrogations.

In response to charges of ethnic or racial bias, police often argue that they are responding to proven stereotypes of "suspicious" persons. For example, "A police officer's experience indicates that young black men engage in robbery at a higher rate than young white men. Data on participation in crime supports this perception" (Walker 1992, 235). Sometimes ethnic groups are believed responsible for periodic crime waves, and the police take these generalized racial stereotypes as a common-sense basis for targeting their field interrogations. One New York City police officer made the following comment:

> One of the worst days in the police department is Good Friday. An awful lot of Gypsies steal on Good Friday.... Christ on the cross is supposed to have said, 'From now on and forevermore, Gypsies can steal and it's not a sin.'
>
> Good Friday is a big day for them. When I was working the Gypsies, we worked them for ten years, we would never take Good Friday off because it was a day we'd have to get up early and be on the run with them because they would be everywhere. (Fletcher 1990, 222)

As for field interviews of women, a study in Miami uncovered evidence suggesting that some male police officers went out of their way to stop women drivers for traffic violations (Fyfe 1989). Opportunities for sexual harassment are clearly present in the practice of field interrogation. Sex with female suspects has been called one of the "seductions of police work" for some male officers (Crank 1998, 141–145). It is part of the excitement, the thrill that always lies around the corner. Although undercover cops who work the drugs and vice details may have more routine contact with women in settings that promote sexual opportunities, patrolling officers find such opportunities in a variety of situations: during traffic stops of lone women, when dealing with a female victim, when offering a runaway girl a ride or a meal, when making a field interrogation of a female suspect, when responding to calls from lonely women. Not only do police have tremendous power by virtue of their job, including the power to overlook crimes in exchange for favors, they spend much of their time dealing with highly vulnerable and marginal populations. It is easy to be seduced by the opportunities for pleasure. Here is the story of one officer:

> I really didn't have any offers or even really think about it until I was assigned to a 1-man car and one night I stopped a female subject for running a traffic light. She was really [the] first. The way she acted I just kind of hinted that maybe we could reach an understanding and she picked right up on it. Well, she had enough moving violations that another one could take her license and I guess she didn't want that to happen. Anyway, I met her later that night and [we] had a wild session. I called again a few days later and she wouldn't even talk to me. Yeah, I've had a few similar experiences since but I'm real careful. (Sapp 1994, 195; quoted in Crank 1998, 142)

Studies on the extent of police sexual activity on the job are few and far between, although one analysis of recent surveys of municipal and county police officers suggests that it may be widespread. For example, it has been estimated that as many as 1,520 incidents of sexual harassment, *witnessed by other officers*, occurred in Ohio and 3,175 in Illinois during a one-year period (Crank 1998, 143, citing research by Martin 1994, and Knowles 1996). Presumably far more occurred that were not witnessed or not reported in the surveys.

HOW POLICE JUSTIFY FIELD INTERROGATIONS In general, the police justify field interrogations on the grounds that someone or something is suspicious. However, the authors of one analysis of field interrogations point out that the police are faced with a dilemma in explaining adequately to others why they behave the way they do. "If an officer has developed an ability to see and attend to features of scenes that most other persons do not notice, how can he show that it is 'reasonable' to stop and question a citizen?" (Daudistel et al. 1979, 90). The authors continue as follows:

> The fact that officers often cannot explain the reasons for their actions does not mean that they are always covering up for one another or that they always capriciously stop citizens on the street. It appears that most of the time, those who stop and question persons do so only if they feel that an interrogation might lead to the discovery of a crime. The concern with clearing crimes and making many arrests, however, has led to stopping some

persons more frequently than others.... So, although the frequent stopping of blacks and Chicanos, for example, may be viewed by the police as legitimate and necessary, this practice has also generated conflict in our society.... Most often the police do not see the complaints as legitimate, frequently responding to them by commenting, "If you were in our shoes you'd understand why we, the police, did what we did." (Daudistel et al. 1979, 91)

When officers stop and question citizens under dubious circumstances they will sometimes attempt to "cool out" cooperative "suspects" before letting them go. One method of cooling out is to provide a justification for the interrogation that sounds reasonable under the circumstances. Cooling out helps prevent complaints from being filed, and it also confirms the authority of the officer to make the stop and warns subjects that they should expect it to happen again. Here is an illustration:

Driving down a residential street an officer noticed some people, Mexican-Americans, moving some belongings from a house to a truck parked adjacent to the curb. It was about 9 o'clock in the evening. The patrolmen asked what was going on and was told that the people were moving. The patrolman frisked several of them and then checked one of them for warrants. The man had no warrants and the officer decided to stop [the interrogation]. Before leaving he told the people that burglars often tell the police they are moving and this was why they were questioned. (Brown 1988, 173)

"ACTION" AND STEREOTYPES OF "BAD GUYS"
Police stops are sometimes contrived events to overcome boredom. Many hours during a typical patrol shift are spent doing unexciting, routine things. Getting a little "action" spices things up while reaffirming the active, masculine culture of policing. But police do not target just anyone for this activity; they tend to choose individuals who belong to marginal groups in society and pose less risk of complaints or other negative repercussions. The following account from Memphis, Tennessee, illustrates:

Occupants of a police car actively looked for "deviants" on their beat to break the monotony of a quiet evening. To these officers, deviants included anyone whose clothes, hair length, mannerisms, or race did not conform with an officer's standards of acceptability. Thus, youths with long hair or garish dress—"hippies," as defined by the policemen—transvestites, and blacks were stopped and questioned at the pleasure of the patrolmen.

A typical scenario in a two-man squad car during periods of prolonged inactivity went something like this: Patrolmen Harry and Jack have had an uneventful evening when a car driven by some teenagers goes by. One of the youths stares (or smiles, or grimaces, or sneers, etc.) at the police car. Patrolman Jack turns to his partner and says, "Harry, let's pull that car over. Those kids are guilty of 'contempt of cop'!" Or one of the officers spots a pedestrian who appears likely to provide some "activity" and turns to his partner saying, "Jack, let's stop the fag (or hippie, or whore, or nigger, etc.) and ask him a few questions. That ought to liven things up." (Bent 1974, 17–18)

This section has shown that the exercise of police discretion has profound effects on the quality of justice and may on occasion contribute directly to the crime problem through its victimization of women and minorities. This does not mean that police discretion is inevitably a bad thing, nor that all police officers take unreasonable liberties with it. Realistically, the police could not do their jobs without the ability to exercise discretion, nor would the public stand for it.

Prosecutorial Discretion

Prosecutors do not proceed against all felony suspects brought to them by the police. Instead, they exercise considerable discretion, not only in deciding whether to proceed, but also in the selection of the particular charges that will be presented to the grand jury or at the preliminary hearing in open court.

One important factor affecting the decision to proceed with prosecution is the prosecutor's evaluation of the probability that the defendant will be convicted. Prosecutors avoid investing time and resources in prosecuting defendants who are unlikely to be convicted. Prosecuting only those suspects who stand a good chance of being convicted helps serve the state's interest in convicting guilty people. It also confirms that the prosecutor's judgment is sound and that the taxpayer's money is not being wasted.

Important as these considerations are in making the decision to proceed with prosecution, this is by no means the whole story. The prosecutor's exercise of discretion is influenced by many considerations. Some are bound up with questions of justice, some with practical matters involving resources, evidence, and witnesses, some with politics and community interests, and yet others with the organization and culture of the criminal justice system itself. Let us review each of these in turn.

First, a prosecutor often worries about questions of justice. There may be times when a conviction is virtually guaranteed but the prosecutor has doubts about the suspect's actual guilt. Despite a prosecutor's obvious professional interest in obtaining guilty verdicts, conviction of an innocent person does not serve the interests of justice, which prosecutors are sworn to uphold. Concern that a defendant may actually be innocent would lead most prosecutors to delay prosecution pending further investigation. The defendant may have to be released, but this does not stop the prosecutor from coming back later with new charges.

Now consider the problem of resources: It is rarely feasible to prosecute all defendants that prosecutors believe can be convicted, and so a choice must be made among them. A prosecutor may therefore focus resources on the prosecution of people suspected of more serious crimes, or of people with extensive prior arrests, or of people suspected of specific types of crime, for instance, drug offenses or violent crimes.

The decision to prosecute is sometimes influenced by private individuals and groups who are able to put pressure on the district attorney. The fact that chief prosecutors are usually elected officials helps explain their responsiveness to public opinion. It would not be in their interest to spend time prosecuting crimes the public does not care about. In many cities, police and prosecutors have been under pressure to do something about gang violence and drug trafficking.

Prosecution decisions are also influenced by the need to maintain good working relations with police and other members of the courthouse work group, including those who work directly with the victims of crime. In some communities, for example, victim advocacy groups strongly favor the prosecution of certain types of offenders, who previously may have been screened out—for example, those

suspected of domestic violence, or people arrested for spraying graffiti or other vandalism. Many police departments have special units to handle sex crimes. These units often work closely with victim advocacy groups to develop "prosecutable" cases.

Evidence sometimes comes to light that the police made legal errors in their handling of a case, such as violations of search and seizure rules. This puts prosecutors in a difficult position, and can cause strained relations with the police. When cases have been compromised in this way, prosecutors may still proceed with prosecution, but their chances of winning in court are significantly reduced.

As noted earlier, the boundaries of the criminalization process in any society are largely determined by negative decisions, that is, decisions to do nothing. In effect, negative decisions establish what people can get away with. Many criminal cases that come before prosecutors are screened out at an early stage or end up being dismissed later on. The decision not to prosecute is often made at an initial screening before the case is forwarded to the felony court. In most larger cities, this initial decision is handled by assistant prosecutors who staff a warrant office. Besides determining whether initial charges will be filed or the case screened out, the warrant office is the major liaison between the district attorney and the public and will also routinely advise the police on legal matters.

Prosecution policies in many jurisdictions turned tougher during the past decade, largely in response to public concerns over rising rates of violent crime in the home and by juveniles.

One change has been the adoption of "no-drop" policies that forbid prosecutors to drop a case merely because a victim declines to cooperate. Milwaukee, Wisconsin, has adopted this policy in regard to domestic violence arrests (Davis and Smith 1995). Under the old system, Milwaukee prosecutors pursued cases only when victims showed up at a charging conference held the day after arrest. Few victims showed up, and as a result 80 percent of cases were screened out. The new policy, adopted January 1995, virtually ignores the behavior—and desires—of the victim, and the prosecution rate has jumped from 20 to 60 percent.

A second change around the country is that prosecutors are taking a "tougher" line with some juvenile suspects. The rates of juvenile offenses involving guns and violence have been increasing over the past few years, and new laws have made it easier for prosecutors to take a hard line with juvenile defendants charged with violent crimes. This is reflected in the rising numbers of juveniles who are being prosecuted as adults (Davis and Smith 1995). From 1985 to 1992 the number of such cases grew from 7,200 to 12,300 (Butts 1997, 1).

Discretion in Sentencing

Although the use of mandatory sentences and the spread of "3-strikes" laws have significantly curtailed the discretion allowed judges during sentencing, sentencing disparities still exist and reflect the exercise of discretion. When different sentences are imposed on offenders convicted of essentially the same offense, we have sentencing disparity. This could be the result of bias on the part of judges. For many years, criminologists have documented sentencing disparities by *race* (e.g., Sellin 1935; Wolfgang and Cohen 1970; Thornberry 1973) and *class* (e.g., Hood 1972), and the question of gender bias has been receiving increased attention in recent years (e.g., Datesman and Scarpitti 1980; Morris 1987; Chesney-Lind and Shelden 1992). This section reviews some of the evidence on the effects of discretion in sentencing.

RACE AND SENTENCING One study of juvenile court sentencing practices looked at a sample of 159 counties in 17 states (McGarrell 1993). Minority youths were more likely than whites to be referred to court, to be detained, and to be placed outside the home. This disparity increased over the five-year period studied, although the increase varied significantly among the counties. On the whole, nonwhite referrals to court rose 38.5 percent versus only 4.3 percent for whites. The bulk of this increase can be attributed to the growing emphasis on drug enforcement during the 1980s: Juvenile drug referrals showed a 147 percent increase over the period.

The so-called War on Drugs has had a greater impact on African-Americans than on any other group. The stiff penalties for crack cocaine offenses have resulted in a huge increase in the incarceration rate of blacks. This has been called a "hidden effect" of the criminal law, and "politicized sentencing" to reflect the political character of drug enforcement (Barnes and Kingsnorth 1996; Mauer

2000). Politicians and high-ranking government officials have been enthusiastic supporters of harsh measures against illicit drugs at least partly because it means votes at the ballot box and more resources for their home state or county, or the agency they head. When the War on Drugs is examined from the perspective of race, however, a startling picture emerges.

Data on illicit drug use compiled through nationwide household surveys shows slight differences between overall drug use patterns by race: Whites are somewhat more inclined than blacks to have ever used an illegal drug. But imprisonment rates bear little relationship to use rates. The rate at which African-Americans were sentenced to prison for drug offenses was over *six times higher* than that for white defendants. The trend over the past decade has been for black imprisonment rates for drug offenses to increase while those for whites have remained stable or decreased (Tonry 1994). Though some of this difference is probably explained by legal factors such as prior record and the severity of the current charge—for example, "selling" versus mere "possession"—much of it reflects the tough sentencing of crack cocaine offenders, who are mainly black.

When sentences for drug trafficking and drug possession are compared, African-Americans still receive harsher sentences than whites. For example, the average sentences imposed by state courts in 1994 on white and black felony drug offenders were as follows (Brown and Langan 1998, 21):

Whites: possession—20 months
trafficking—33 months
Blacks: possession—31 months
trafficking—54 months

It is not possible to tell whether some of this disparity is due to blacks having worse criminal records than white drug offenders. However, even if that were true, the records themselves could reflect the cumulative impact of bias that occurred in earlier criminal justice decisions, for example by legislators, the police, or prosecutors. During the charging and plea bargaining processes, for example, prosecutors may take essentially the same events and reconstruct them into different crimes—carrying different penalties—on the basis of race

(Crew 1991). A recent study has found that, all other things being equal, young black males are more likely than any other age-race-gender group to receive the harshest of criminal penalties (Steffensmeier, Ulmer, and Kramer 1998).

RACE, SOCIAL CLASS, AND SENTENCING   Race and social class are intertwined in American society, as are gender and class. African-Americans and women tend on the whole to have lower socioeconomic status and power than whites and males. This makes distinguishing their individual relationship to sentencing more difficult.

It has been shown, for example, that the sentences given to juvenile offenders are affected by both race and class. In one study, the records of 9,601 juvenile court dispositions in Philadelphia were analyzed. Even when legal variables such as severity of offense and prior record were taken into account, blacks were more likely than whites to be prosecuted and institutionalized, and offenders of low socioeconomic status were more severely penalized than others (Thornberry 1973). More recent studies of the sentencing of juveniles have also shown class and race disparities (Leonard, Pope, and Feyerherm 1995).

A study of early releases from prison in Ohio found race to be the most important factor in determining releases in certain situations (Leonard, Pope, and Feyerherm 1995). For example, when the probation department had recommended against early release, whites were twice as likely as blacks to be released, even after controlling for criminal record, current offense, and other variables.

Although much of the research on case dispositions appears to show that race and class influence sentencing, a review of numerous studies found ten showing no association between class and disposition and seventeen studies showing no association between race and disposition (Box 1981). Many of these studies used different methods, and so caution must be exercised in any search for generalizations. Nevertheless, the author of a recent review of the relevant research raises a thought-provoking question:

> Even a single verified case of unequal sentencing because of racial status serves to illuminate flaws in the criminal justice system, and indeed ample research demonstrates that there are thousands of

such cases—can we dismiss the real world issue of judicial injustice toward minorities because of a lack of the precise methodological rigor demanded by some quantitative researchers?" (Mann 1993, 196)

Reanalysis of the evidence in some of the earlier studies has shown that the race and class effects on sentencing diminish when other factors such as prior record and circumstances of the offense are taken into account (Hagan 1974, 379). One study focused on racial bias in both capital (death penalty) and noncapital cases and reviewed more than fifty-five studies, mostly from the 1960s and 1970s (Kleck 1981). It concluded that there was little evidence of any general, overt racial discrimination in noncapital cases, but strong evidence of discrimination in capital cases in the South when the offense was rape. However, black defendants sometimes were treated more leniently than whites, especially when their victims were also black. Various explanations for the more lenient treatment of black-on-black offenders were suggested: (1) Blacks are devalued crime victims, hence offenses against them are considered less serious; (2) there exists a sort of white paternalism that promotes an "understanding" and forgiving attitude in dealing with conflicts within the black community; and (3) some judges may feel guilty about past discrimination or may be compensating for institutionalized racism or for any prejudice they might have.

Table 9.2 compares death penalty requests for various racial combinations of offenders and victims (Paternoster 1983). It clearly shows that when blacks killed blacks their offenses were least likely to be classified as capital murders, and when they were, the prosecutor was least likely to request the death penalty.

Other research on sentencing in capital cases confirms that the killing of white victims results in harsher sentences than the killing of blacks. One study found that defendants convicted of killing whites were over four times as likely to receive a death sentence as defendants who killed blacks (Baldus, Woodworth, and Pulaski 1985). This finding could not be explained by conventional legal factors such as the circumstances of the crime or offenders' past records. A later study of death penalty sentences in eight states—Florida, Georgia, Illinois, Oklahoma, North Carolina, Mississippi, Virginia, and Arkansas—found a "clear

TABLE 9.2   **Death Penalty Requests by Prosecutors in South Carolina, 1977–1981**

Over the years many experts have claimed that minorities, especially African-Americans, have been discriminated against in the imposition of the death penalty. A key player in any decision relating to the death penalty is the prosecutor, who decides in the first place whether to charge a defendant with capital murder, in effect requesting the death penalty. The figures below show that during a four-year period in South Carolina, death penalty requests were most likely when a black person killed a white person, and least likely when a black person killed another black person.

CATEGORY OF OFFENSE	NUMBER OF HOMICIDE ACTS	NUMBER OF HOMICIDES ELIGIBLE FOR THE DEATH PENALTY*	NUMBER OF ACTUAL DEATH PENALTY REQUESTS	PERCENTAGE OF ELIGIBLE HOMICIDES IN WHICH PROSECUTORS REQUESTED DEATH
Black killed white	148	111	54	48.6
White killed white	580	113	44	38.9
Black killed black	894	76	8	10.5
White killed black	54	16	7	43.8

*Capital murder cases are the only homicide cases for which the death penalty may be sought. They involve the commission of the willful homicide in conjunction with at least one other aggravating circumstance as defined by South Carolina's death penalty statute.

Source: Raymond Paternoster, "The Decision to Seek the Death Penalty in South Carolina," *Journal of Criminal Law and Criminology* 74 (1983): 754–787. Reprinted by special permission of Northwestern University School of Law, *Journal of Criminal Law and Criminology*.

pattern" of victim-based discrimination "unexplained on grounds other than race" (Gross and Mauro 1989, 110).

In one study, disparities in sentencing based on the race of offender and victims were most dramatic when the offenses were more serious. An analysis of 2,858 felony cases ranging from assaults to robberies and murder found that only in the case of murders and sexual assaults were marked racial disparities present in the sentences received (Spohn 1994). Why this should be so is unclear. Two possibilities are (1) that judges see black-on-white sexual assaults and murders as a serious threat to the power structure, of which they are a part, and (2) that the violent intimacy of the crimes themselves gives rise to racial bias. Yet a recent Florida study of decisions to increase penalties by use of habitual offender laws shows that racial disparities were more common for *less* serious offenses (Crawford, Chiricos, and Kleck 1998). The authors surmise that less serious offenses allow judges more room for flexibility in sentencing, including allowing nonlegal factors such as race to enter the picture. Only continued research will clarify the complex relationship between race and sentencing.

GENDER AND SENTENCING   A review of research on juvenile court dispositions concludes that girls receive harsher treatment than boys for lesser crimes but not for more serious offenses (Barlow and Ferdinand 1992, 130–134). To some extent this reflects the impact of gender on referrals to juvenile court. A national study of juvenile court data found that girls were three times as likely as boys to be referred to juvenile court for status offenses—that is, acts that would not be crimes if committed by adults—(Snyder and Finnegan 1987). Once in juvenile court, however, girls charged with status offenses were also more likely than boys to be incarcerated. This difference is an historical one (Chesney-Lind 1987a, 1987b, 1988).

What explains this difference in the treatment of boys and girls? One study looked at gender bias in 36,680 juvenile court dispositions in Nebraska over a nine-year period (Johnson and Scheuble 1991). Hypotheses were derived from two competing theories: sex role traditionalism and chivalry (or paternalism). The sex role traditionalism perspective predicts harsher punishment for females based on the argument that girls and women who commit crimes violate the traditional female role—being gentle, passive, and dependent. The chivalry model predicts an opposite gender bias: Female offenders will be given more lenient sentences because males—who dominate the criminal justice system—try to protect the "fairer sex."

The findings of this study support both models of gender bias. Overall, girls received more lenient dispositions than boys, suggesting a chivalry effect. Yet, harsher penalties for girls were found in the case of repeat offenders who committed more serious offenses, suggesting a sex role effect. Over the nine years, however, the trend was toward greater leniency for females—"higher odds for girls being dismissed and higher odds for probation and lock-up for boys" (Johnson and Scheuble 1991, 695).

One interesting study looked at sentencing practices as they take place in the courtroom (Daly 1989). Courts in New York City and Seattle placed considerable weight on the family ties of defendants. Thus, black women with spouses, dependent parents, or children benefited most from sentencing leniency, and single and married men with children or dependent parents also did better than other men. Likewise, a study of 61,294 criminal cases in Pennsylvania in the late 1980s found that gender had only a small impact on prison sentences; interviews with judges and courtroom observation showed that sentencing was influenced most by perceptions of a defendant's blameworthiness and by the practical consequences of incarceration (Steffensmeier, Kramer, and Streifel 1993). When defendants had families to support and good jobs to lose, judges tended to be more lenient. This conclusion has also been reached in a study of the sentencing of women in England (Hedderman and Gelsthorpe 1997).

To conclude this section on discretion in criminal justice, suffice it to say that most crimes do not end with an arrest, and most arrests do not result in jail or prison for the offender. This result is due in large part—though certainly not entirely—to the exercise of discretion. Unfortunately, discretion also results in some individuals and groups being more likely to be arrested and prosecuted, and to receive harsh punishments than others. These disparities tend to increase as the severity of the offense declines.

CRIMINAL JUSTICE AND CRIME PREVENTION

This section of the chapter considers whether and how the actions of the criminal justice system affect the amount of crime experienced in society. More particularly, can the criminal justice system prevent crime? This issue will come up again when we discuss opportunity-rationality theories of crime in Chapter 13. Here, let us start with the police.

Crime Prevention and the Police

When police teach youngsters how to avoid being kidnapped or resist pressures to use drugs, when they help business owners burglar-proof their premises or conduct neighborhood-watch seminars, when they place clearly visible surveillance cameras in subway stations, they are engaged in *crime prevention*. Even the mere visibility of patrolling officers provides the police patrol with a potential crime prevention aspect—people contemplating a crime may refrain from going through with it for fear of being caught and punished. When police enforce laws, they may also prevent crimes: Arresting a suspect may prevent a future crime, if not by that suspect, then by others who saw the arrest or know about it.

The law enforcement-crime prevention function of policing is the role that many police officers and many members of the public believe should be at the core of police operations. It certainly fits with the media image of policing, and the great success of crime-fighting fiction on film and in books suggests that the public appetite for it is vast. Yet most of the time the police—or more precisely, patrolling police officers—are neither actively enforcing the law nor actively preventing crime (Felson 1998).

PROACTIVE POLICING AND CRIME PREVENTION The traditional police response to crime is largely reactive: Crimes occur and the police respond. Reactive policing is unlikely to be a very effective crime prevention technique, although of course the police can prevent some crimes from being completed. Reactive policing is also not very effective for dealing with consensual crimes such as drug use and prostitution, nor for crimes occurring in neighborhoods where confidence in the police is low or the police are regarded as enemies.

To address these problems, police departments across the nation have adopted a strategy of policing known as **proactive policing**: taking an active role in uncovering crime and trying to prevent it. Various methods have been employed:

- Use of Decoys: Sometimes police pretend to be participants in crime, thereby inviting the real offenders to commit crimes in their presence. This strategy has been used for consensual crimes involving prostitution, homosexual activity in semipublic places such as highway rest areas and park restrooms, and in sting operations against the money-laundering activities of drug traffickers and the transactions of fences and thieves. In some situations, as when a rash of assaults has been taking place in a certain neighborhood, undercover police act as inviting victims, hoping to lure potential rapists and muggers into committing a crime.

- Directed Patrols: When crimes reach epidemic proportions, or when citizen complaints become politically embarrassing, police may turn to the "directed patrol." This involves concentrating patrol officers in particular locations or in surveillance of particular individuals or groups. This sort of saturation policing has been used successfully against youth gangs, as discussed below. Yet departments that adopt the strategy run the risk of merely moving crime to another neighborhood, outside the area of saturation. "Displacement" effects such as this are an age-old problem in crime prevention and they undermine proactive policing. The strategy of directed patrols has also been criticized for targeting black inner-city communities (Fishman 1998, 116).

- Crime-Focused Community-Relations Programs: One form of proactive policing is represented by the "gun buyback" programs that have sprung up around the country in recent years. Police departments ask citizens owning firearms, particularly handguns, to sell them to police with "no questions asked." The idea is to get guns off the street, thereby cutting down on the number of gun crimes. Thousands of guns have been turned in, often quickly exhausting the available buyback funds. But the success of buyback programs in actually reducing violent crimes committed with firearms is not proven (Rosenfeld 1996).

Aggressive policing such as that advocated in some proactive strategies is believed to contribute to crime reduction through its **deterrent effect**. The idea is that proactive policing raises the risks and costs of doing crime relative to its benefits, and this reduces the appeal of offending: "By stopping, questioning, and otherwise closely observing citizens, especially suspicious ones, the police are more likely to find fugitives, detect contraband (such as

stolen property or concealed weapons), and apprehend persons fleeing from the scene of a crime" (Wilson and Boland 1978, 373). Deterrence is working if potential offenders see these outcomes as too costly, and therefore refrain from committing crimes.

Aggressive policing may also lower crime rates by influencing the perceptions people hold of the likelihood of being arrested. As a rule, people have only a vague notion about the actual probabilities of arrest, which are low even for serious crimes. This means that potential offenders will rarely witness an arrest going down, and if they do, they won't necessarily know what the person is being arrested for. But if the police engage in a rigorous proactive program of arrests, even if this is mostly for relatively minor offenses such as drunkenness or traffic violations, "this is a very visible indicator of police activity … [and it may] send a signal to potential offenders that one's chances of getting caught are higher than they actually are" (Sampson and Cohen 1988, 165). Thus proactive policing may have a direct deterrent effect on crime by causing potential criminals to reconsider even when the actual risks of being arrested for a particular offense may not have changed.

This idea was tested in a study relating police arrest rates for disorderly conduct and driving under the influence (DUI) to the armed robbery rates for 171 American cities (Sampson and Cohen 1988). The study found that aggressive policing of the public order offenses directly reduced robbery rates in general, but most significantly in the case of robberies committed by adults and by blacks. Why? The authors suggest that proactive policing of public order offenses may be more visible to blacks than to whites because blacks see it not only in their own neighborhoods, but also in downtown and commercial areas where most whites are arrested. This may explain why proactive policing of whites influenced black robbery rates more than did proactive policing of blacks themselves. Overall, the authors concluded that aggressive police patrolling of public order crimes did have a deterrent effect on adult robbery.

In response to concerns about rising gun crimes among youth, the National Institute of Justice funded an experiment in directed police patrolling aimed at confiscating firearms that are illegal or illegally carried. When concentrated around gun crime hot spots, directed police patrols appear to reduce both the presence and use of guns at relatively modest cost. And it appears that the patrols did not result in a displacement of gun crime to other areas, where risks of police intervention are lower (Sherman and Rogan 1995). However, repeated tests of the strategy are needed, and there are still some possible hazards that need to be addressed. One of these is the possibility that intensified gun patrols provoke more violence "by making youths subjected to traffic stops more defiant of conventional society" (Sherman, Shaw, and Rogan 1995, 9).

This problem does not seem to have occurred in New York City, whose police claim that directed patrols have significantly reduced gun crimes (*New York Times*, 30 July 1995, 15). New York police first flooded a zone consisting of nine streets in northwest Harlem with plainclothes officers and detectives. Then the precinct moved many beat and uniformed narcotics officers from less violent streets to the "hot zone" to arrest low-level drug lookouts and dealers, often initially for minor violations. Meanwhile, patrolling officers in cars looked for legal excuses like lane changes without signaling to stop and question drivers of cars with out-of-state licenses. When approaching suspects in the target zone, officers first looked for a bulge that may be a gun. If they thought the suspect was carrying a gun or responding to their questioning in a suspicious or nervous way, they frisked for a weapon. In June 1995, 30th Precinct officers frisked 450 people, a 150 percent increase from June 1994. The frisks produced only a handful of gun arrests, but shootings began to decline. The police believe potential offenders were leaving their guns at home in anticipation of encounters with police.

Aggressive police patrolling may be part of the answer to gang-related crimes, as well as to street violence associated with drug trafficking. However, there may be a cost in civil liberties that some Americans will find objectionable. The strategy also tends to target minority and poor neighborhoods, which raises the problem of overpolicing discussed earlier. In cities with large minority populations there may be a political cost that elected authorities are reluctant to bear. This may explain why some police departments across the country have been reluctant to copy New York City's program.

Punishment and Crime Prevention

Punishment is any action designed to deprive someone of things of value because of something the person is believed to have done. Valued things include freedom, civil rights, money, health, identity, personal relationships, and life itself. Throughout the ages, rulers have devised all manner of punishments for people guilty of wrongdoing. The more serious an offense was considered to be, the harsher the penalties attached to it. Many people consider the harshest penalties to be those that cut offenders off from their families. Today, when a judge formally announces a sentence in a felony case, the penalty could be as little as twelve months on probation, or as severe as life in prison; in thirty-eight states and the federal system, the penalty may be death.

An ideal punishment, according to eighteenth-century philosophers Jeremy Bentham (1948) and Cesare Beccaria (1963), is both proportionate to the offense and sufficient to outweigh the pleasure derived from it. The second part is important for it helps explain how punishment prevents crime. Crime is prevented when people refrain from offending so as to avoid the pain of punishment. This prediction is the central idea behind deterrence theory, discussed in more detail in the next section and in Chapters 10 and 13. But deterrence is only one way that punishment might prevent crime. In fact, as Box 9.1 shows, there are least *ten* different ways that punishment may prevent crime. Only the first four on the list have received much attention in criminal justice circles; these are reformation, incapacitation, rehabilitation, and deterrence. Let's look more closely at these four possibilities.

REFORMATION   The idea behind **reformation** is that punishment conveys a sense of shame and remorse to some offenders, building their consciences and thus promoting conformity to the law. The original penitentiary was an early application of the idea that reformation occurs through punishment. Offenders were placed in solitary confinement so that they could reflect on the evil of their ways and be reformed through penitence. Even an arrest may have a reformative impact with some criminal offenders. Some amateur shoplifters and many people charged with white-collar crimes

BOX 9.1   PUNISHMENT AND ITS POTENTIAL TO PREVENT CRIME

Punishment has the *potential* to prevent crime in the following ways:

1. Deterrence: People are scared away from criminal activity by fear of the consequences if they are caught.

2. Incapacitation: Offenders cannot commit crimes because the opportunity or ability to do so has been removed or reduced. Imprisonment is considered an incapacitating penalty, and so are some forms of mutilation.

3. Reform: Punishment conveys a sense of shame and remorse to some offenders, and this promotes subsequent conformity. In the original penitentiary, offenders were placed in solitary confinement so they could reflect on the evil of their ways and through penitence be reformed.

4. Rehabilitation: The alteration of behavior by nonpunitive means so that the individual no longer commits crimes. While not punishment in itself, rehabilitation is often attempted within the context of punishment. Work release and prison education programs are examples.

5. Surveillance: When people are watched closely or monitored by electronic means, their behavior is made visible to others. This may prevent some crimes from occurring. Obviously, deterrence may be involved here, too.

6. Normative Validation: Punishment confirms and reinforces the view that an act is wrong. When a teacher or a judge says; "I'm going to make an example out of you" it reminds the offender and others how they ought to behave and what will happen if they do not.

7. Retribution: Punishing offenders in a just manner may prevent other crimes such as private vengeance or armed vigilantism. The "subway vigilante" Bernard Goetz is a real-life example. He shot three young men whom he claimed were about to rob him. He blamed his behavior on the inability of society to protect him from criminals.

8. Stigmatization: Punishment marks people as offenders, and the label "criminal" may stick to them long after the punishment is over. An individual may refrain from crime not because of the punishment itself, but because of the anticipated stigmatization that is associated with it. Laws requiring that neighbors be informed of convicted sex offenders in their midst are designed partly for their stigmatizing effect and partly to encourage surveillance.

9. Normative Insulation: People tend to be influenced by the people they associate with. If people could somehow escape the influence of criminals there would be less crime. Parents who keep tight reins on their children may contribute to normative insulation— which children undoubtedly see as a punishment! Electronic monitoring of offenders on probation may contribute to normative insulation as well.

10. Habituation: Punishment can lead to the development of habitual behavior that conforms to the law. For example, driving tends to be slower in places where police routinely use speeding traps to catch violators. Habituation differs from deterrence because conforming behavior may persist long after enforcement has ended.

Source: Jack P. Gibbs, *Crime, Punishment, and Deterrence* (New York: Elsevier, 1975). Used with the permission of Jack P. Gibbs, Ph.D.

Due to severe overcrowding, an auditorium at the Deuel Vocational Institution Correctional facility has been converted into prisoners' quarters. The prospects for reformation, rehabilitation, and deterrence are compromised by such makeshift arrangements.

experience a sort of moral jolt when arrested. The arrest demonstrates that they have slipped from law-abiding citizen to thief and prompts a return to lawful behavior—at least for a time. While true reformation implies a permanent change in behavior, even a temporary return to law-abiding behavior will have prevented some crime.

INCAPACITATION   Some forms of punishment render offenders no longer able to commit crimes. This consequence of punishment is called **incapacitation**. Potential offenders are incapacitated because punishment removes or diminishes their opportunities to commit crimes. Incapacitation is absolute when an offender is executed but it is relative for other forms of punishment. Consider imprisonment: Although putting someone behind bars reduces the opportunity to commit crimes, it does not rule out all offenses and may actually encourage some that the offender never before committed, such as homosexual rape.

Capital punishment is the surest way to prevent future crime through incapacitation. But it is not foolproof, because offenders might still commit crimes while awaiting execution. Indeed,

an infamous murderer awaiting execution in Illinois has found a way to delay his execution more than once—he has killed fellow prisoners, forcing new criminal investigations and trials, thereby postponing his own scheduled execution. It is surely preposterous to suggest execution as an incapacitation remedy for all types of offenses.

A study of persistent thieves found that imprisonment encourages a "rationalization of crime" (Shover and Henderson 1995). Inmates learn from others how and why they were "busted," and this encourages a more calculating approach to their own criminal activity. In addition, many inmates leave prison reassured by the fact that they survived the ordeal, claiming in retrospect that prison was no big deal: "For too many of those who pass through it once, the prison experience will leave them less fearful and better prepared for a second trip if that should happen" (Shover 1995, 241; Shover and Henderson 1995).

REHABILITATION   It is traditional to think of the terms *reformation* and *rehabilitation* as interchangeable, but this is incorrect. Reform is a direct consequence of punishment, whereas **rehabilitation** is the alteration of an offender's behavior by non-punitive means so that he or she no longer violates laws. While it is not in itself punishment, rehabilitation is usually attempted side-by-side with punishment. For almost a century the nation's correctional system has included some efforts at rehabilitation while offenders are confined. Work release, prison educational and vocational programs, and halfway houses for offenders about to return to the community are examples. How much effort is put into rehabilitation generally depends on the security level of the prison; the higher the security level, the less the emphasis on rehabilitation.

DETERRENCE   The **deterrence doctrine** argues that people refrain from crime because they fear the punishment that might follow. This idea has probably received more attention from the scientific community than any other perspective on punishment, *and many important people believe in it*. For this reason we will spend a little more time discussing it here as well as in Chapter 10.

It is conventional to distinguish between two classes of potential offenders who may refrain from crime because they fear punishment:

1. People who have directly experienced punishment for something they did in the past. If these people refrain from future criminal activity because they fear being punished again, this is **specific deterrence**.
2. People who have not experienced punishment themselves but are deterred from crime by the fear that they might get the same punishment experienced by others. This is **general deterrence**.

The distinction is important because the deterrent effect of experienced punishments may be quite different from that of threatened punishments. When a judge hands down a sentence and tells the offender, "This ought to make you think twice next time," the judge is thinking of the penalty as a specific deterrent; if the judge says, "I intend to make an example of you," the penalty's general deterrent value is being emphasized.

A second important distinction in deterrence research concerns three properties of punishment—severity, certainty, and speed. Beccaria and

Bentham believed that the deterrent impact of punishment is greater when it is applied with greater certainty, greater severity, and more swiftly. However, they considered severity to be less important as a deterrent than the others.

Over two hundred years have passed since Bentham and Beccaria lay the foundation of the deterrence theory of punishment. During that time a conventional wisdom emerged that punishment deters if it is certain, swift, and reasonably severe. But science has not confirmed that wisdom, and many experts would agree that "probably not" is the best answer to the question "Does punishment deter?" (Nagin and Paternoster 1991).

The inability of the scientific community to substantiate—or reject—the conventional wisdom (and political belief) that punishment deters crime must be difficult for many people to understand. Most of us can think of anecdotal illustrations of deterrence, from our own personal experience perhaps, or from hearing about other people who refrained from committing a crime because they were fearful of the consequences. But serious researchers find that the complexities of the subject present formidable obstacles to developing conclusive answers (Gibbs 1975; Gibbs and Firebaugh 1990; Stafford and Warr 1993). This is not to say that there has been *absolutely* no support in the literature of deterrence theory. Limited support of deterrence has been found in the areas of drunk driving (Piquero and Paternoster 1998; Walker 1998), luggage theft (Trivizas and Smith 1997), and crime more generally (D'Alessio and Stolzenberg 1999).

Most surprising, perhaps, is the fact that more than fifty years of research has yet to uncover a deterrent effect for capital punishment (Archer and Gartner 1984; Baile 1998; Cochran, Chamlin, and Seth 1994; Peterson and Bailey 1991). There is no good research that supports the oft-heard claim that there would be fewer murders if more killers were executed rather than sent to prison. Murders are often unplanned, spur-of-the-moment attacks, and alcohol is usually a factor in them. But even among hardened criminals who may think about risks in planning their crimes (Horney and Marshall 1992), fear of punishment does not seem to be a major factor in their decisions (Cromwell 1999; Shover 1995; Wright and Decker 1994, 1997).

People who kill are rarely executed these days, and never in public. There are those who believe that a return to public executions would reduce the homicide rate; however, there is no evidence to support this claim.

between crime rates and punishment (Sherman 1993). Sherman suggests that if punishment is seen as unfair or excessive, an attitude of "defiance" emerges. This defiance undermines any deterrent effect the threat of punishment might have had. It can also undermine any lingering respect for the law—a consideration in the sentencing of youthful and first-time offenders. Such a reaction has also been noted by Gilligan (1996) in his research on incarcerated murderers, and to some extent by Tittle (1995).

To summarize, deterrence clearly does not score high marks as the basis for a sentencing policy. Yet the lack of strong evidence does not mean that deterrence theory is disproved. The prospect of swift, certain, and relatively severe punishment may deter some individuals from committing crimes under some circumstances. The difficulty is figuring out who those individuals are, and which circumstances count. Thus, rather than reject the deterrence doctrine, more research on these complex issues would seem the more prudent course. It would also seem appropriate for politicians, judges, and other court officials to refrain from claiming that harsher punishments will deter crime. One might go as far to say that it is irresponsible for politicians to present such unproven claims as truisms. In this way, we were disappointed when both of the major candidates (Al Gore and George W. Bush) in the presidential election of 2000 flatly proclaimed in a nationally televised debate their belief in the deterrent value of capital punishment. They made no further comments, caveats, or qualifications on the subject, even though there was ample time to do so.

CRIMES OF THE CRIMINAL JUSTICE SYSTEM

Some actions taken by some criminal justice personnel result in the victimization of suspects, offenders, witnesses, victims, and even the general public. Some of these actions are also illegal, either because they violate procedural laws such as the constitutional protections against illegal search and seizure or cruel and unusual punishment, or because they violate the criminal law. This section looks at some of the ways in which citizens are victimized by the very people society employs to deal with crime and criminals.

On balance, the threat of formal punishments is much less worrisome to potential offenders than the threat of informal punishments imposed by relatives, friends, co-workers, or other close acquaintances (Cullen 1994; Tittle 1980; Paternoster, Saltzman, Waldo, and Chiricos 1983, 1985; Braithwaite 1989). The average law-abiding citizen "is afraid of losing his job, of being ostracized by his business associates and friends, of the possible alienation of members of his family, of having to leave his neighborhood or even his town" (Shoham 1970, 9).

One criminologist has argued that punishment may backfire under certain circumstances, and this may explain the lack of a deterrent relationship

Contexts and Varieties of Offenses

There are many ways that criminal justice officials may create victims in carrying out their work. Indeed, they run the gamut of occupational and organizational crimes discussed in Chapter 6. Some of these crimes are for personal gain, as when police officers take drugs or money from criminal suspects, and some are committed on behalf of organizational goals, as when correctional officers use excessive force when handling resistant inmates or when prosecutors ignore or hide evidence that might hurt their case in court.

While all criminal justice operations provide opportunities for crime, the enforcement of public-order crimes such as consensual drug and sex offenses is especially prone to lawbreaking. As noted earlier, police take a proactive approach in dealing with these offenses, and much of this work is undercover or involves informants. Armed with a strong public mandate but largely free from outside scrutiny, drug and vice officers have plenty of opportunities and incentives to break the law (Abadinsky 1990; Luttwack 1995). Sex and drugs are also big business, and money flows freely. By all accounts, it takes great self-control and immunity to the influence of corrupt peers for officers to resist the many opportunities and temptations in this line of policing (Jackson 1969; Progrebin and Poole 1993). Another context in which the opportunities and temptations for crime are strong is also largely hidden from public scrutiny: the prison. Furthermore, the public expects prisons to be harsh environments, so there is little interest in what goes on inside unless it seems extreme: deadly riots on the one hand, or a country club atmosphere on the other.

Indeed, for many years there existed a "hands-off doctrine" in correctional circles, allowing wardens to run their prisons pretty much as they liked. Although court rulings during the 1970s and 1980s severely curtailed authoritarian control strategies (Johnson 1987), the history of prisons has been a brutal one. Consider torture and segregation. Torture has been outlawed in America and Europe for over 150 years, yet cruel and vicious abuse of inmates has been documented. For example, in the late 1960s, physical torture was commonplace in the Arkansas prison system (Murton and Hyams 1969). In the Tucker prison farm, officers used the infamous "Tucker telephone" to punish inmates.

Electrical wires from the "telephone" were attached to the feet and genitals of inmates, who were then "rung up" with an extremely painful electrical charge.

Segregation is also associated with brutality and abuse of inmates. Often referred to as "the hole," segregation units are used to discipline inmates or to keep them isolated from other inmates—sometimes at their own request. In some prisons, the hole is also used as a way of punishing inmates who are considered "difficult" or "subversive" by correctional staff (Scraton, Sim, and Skidmore 1991, 85). Segregation units in older prisons were usually small, solid-walled cells, often without windows. Some sound terrifying: "When you step into the cell you see a box. That's the silent cell. Around this is all their strip-lights and big heaters. Also metal straps to keep the heat in. The inside is about three square yards. There are two spyholes, and two small air vents. It's a human furnace...." (Scraton, Sim, and Skidmore 1991, 84–85). In Pennsylvania during the 1960s, state courts ruled that inmates in segregation must have some light, so officials at one prison built a cell of Plexiglas known as the "glass cage"; bright lights were shone 24 hours a day (Hassine 1996, 100).

Understanding Police Corruption

Most of the research on crimes of the criminal justice system has focused on the police, society's first line of enforcement. Every few years, it seems, a tale of police crimes comes to light and receives national attention. This happened in New York City during the early 1970s, and the 1972 Knapp Commission found a widespread and "strikingly standardized" pattern of corruption involving patrol officers assigned to districts frequented by pimps, gamblers, and drug dealers. During the 1990s, in both New York and Chicago, commissions were appointed to investigate charges of racketeering, extortion, stealing, and conspiracy among police officers. All three commissions reported the existence of a **blue code of silence** (or "wall of silence"), a curtain of secrecy (Crank 1998, 56) that unites police against outside scrutiny and protects them against informants from within. Police don't "rat" on their own kind, and anyone who does risks injury or death, as New York City narcotics officer Frank Serpico found out in 1970. The most recent case of police corruption that has attracted national attention occurred in Los Angeles; it is described in Box 9.2.

Explaining police corruption is a difficult task. Some evidence shows that serious police crime is mostly the product of so-called "bad apples" in a department. These people are portrayed as "rogue" cops who shouldn't have been placed in a police uniform in the first place. Other research has found that corruption is fairly widespread, and that the very organizational structure and culture of policing itself contributes to corruption. For example, the police culture includes qualities and values such as solidarity, bravery, independence, the code of silence,

and an "us versus them" mentality (Kappeler, Sluder, and Alpert 1994). These features, along with significant opportunities to engage in crime, can be combined to help explain police crime. Police crime, as all crime, often has multiple causes.

A TYPOLOGY OF POLICE CORRUPTION An important step in understanding police crimes is to identify their similarities and differences. One of the few systematic studies of police corruption has identified eight types of police corruption (Roebuck and Barker 1974):

1. Corruption of authority means receiving unauthorized, unearned material gains by

BOX 9.2 CORRUPTION IN THE LOS ANGELES POLICE DEPARTMENT

More than 30 Los Angeles police officers have been suspended, fired, or imprisoned and more than 70 criminal convictions have been recently overturned because of corrupt and illegal police practices the past few years. Word about the LAPD "scandal" began to spread in 1999, when officer Rafael Perez admitted to stealing drugs, planting evidence on suspects, lying, and falsely testifying in court. Perez then fingered a number of police officers engaged in corrupt practices. He charged that such corrupt behavior was relatively common in the anti-gang unit for which he worked. Examples include the following:

- The unreasonable use of force against suspects, including brutal beatings and unwarranted uses of deadly force
- Theft of cocaine and other drugs from evidence lockers
- The planting of weapons and drugs on suspects
- Widespread perjury ("testilying") in courts of law
- The staging of fictitious crime scenes

Both the LAPD Administration, including the police chief, and the U.S. Department of Justice have admitted that while most LA cops are not corrupt, poor recruitment and the lack of supervision and training contributed to the corruption. Indeed, at least four of the officers involved in these crimes had criminal records or financial difficulties which should have eliminated them from the applicant pool. LAPD Chief of Police Bernard Parks has also admitted that some senior officers and administrators were woefully apathetic about monitoring and evaluating special units such as the anti-gang force.

Other organizational problems and ineptitude have been blamed for the corruption, and both federal and state investigations of the LAPD have recommended that major structural and personnel changes be made in the department.

Sources: <http://apbnews.com>; <http://www.cnn.com>; <http://latimes.com>.

virtue of police officer status. This includes free liquor, meals, discounts, and payments by merchants for more police protection. The corrupters are respectable citizens, there is considerable peer group support, there is little adverse departmental reaction, little organization is required, and the violation involved is primarily that of departmental regulations. This form of corruption is widespread, and most police officers know about it even if they have not participated themselves.

2. Kickbacks involve receipt of goods and services in return for referring business to a variety of patrons—doctors, lawyers, bondsmen, garages, taxicab companies, service stations, and so on. Corrupters are usually respectable persons who stand to gain from the scheme. Departments tend to ignore it, or actually condone it, depending on the respectability of the corrupter; however, this practice usually violates formal departmental rules. Peer group support is often substantial, though its degree may depend on the reputation and trustworthiness of the patron. The organization involved is relatively simple, consisting basically of the ongoing relationship between the business and the police officer.

3. Opportunist theft consists of stealing goods or money from arrestees, victims, crime scenes, or unprotected property. It involves no corrupter and is clearly in violation of criminal laws as well as departmental rules. Reaction from departments is usually negative, and the reaction is likely to be more severe if the value of goods or cash taken is high, if the public knows about the theft, and if the victim wants or is willing to prosecute. Peer group support depends on informal norms governing distinctions between "clean" and "dirty" money. Dirty money is money that comes from crime, especially drug trafficking; some police officers treat this as fair game. Little organization is involved in opportunistic theft; as the term implies, it is a spontaneous act that occurs when an appropriate situation arises.

4. Shakedowns are also opportunistic behaviors. They occur when the police know about a crime but accept money or services from suspects in exchange for doing nothing. The corrupter may be either respectable or habitually involved in criminal activities.

Shakedowns violate legal and departmental norms, and though peer group support is necessary for shakedowns to become routine, that support is often contingent on the suspect's criminal activity—bribes from drug dealers and armed robbers are frowned upon. Secrecy among participants is a key element of shakedowns.

5. Protection of illegal activities arises when corrupters want to continue illegal activities without risk of being arrested. Since they are doing something illegal, they purchase "protection" from police officers willing to be corrupted. Protection violates criminal and departmental rules and involves considerable collusion, peer group support, and organization. Though departmental reaction usually results in suspension, dismissal, or criminal charges, the severity and consistency of negative reactions may depend on the degree of community support of the illegal activities being protected.

6. The fix refers to quashing legal proceedings and "taking up" traffic tickets. Corrupters are suspects attempting to avoid arrest. Of course, the fix can occur anywhere in the criminal justice system—even in prison, where guards are paid not to "write up" an incident that could result in an inmate losing credit toward time served. Within policing, patrol officers, detectives, and even dispatchers may accept bribes to look the other way. The fix violates legal and departmental rules, and reaction is usually severe when cases are brought to light. In departments where the fix occurs frequently and with considerable regularity, it is a highly organized activity.

7. Direct criminal activities involve no corrupter, as the police alone are involved in the activity. Direct criminal activities include crimes of robbery, extortion, and other violence by police officers against suspects, victims, and citizens generally. Lack of peer group support and severe departmental reactions generally underscore the blatant criminal character of these practices. Even so, when officers engage in criminal activities in groups—whether stealing drugs or beating up suspects—the blue code of silence helps protect them from their law-abiding peers and effective control by their department or outside agencies.

8. Internal payoffs involve bribes within the police department for such things as hours,

assignments, promotions, control of evidence, and credit for arrests. By virtue of their job assignments, some officers are in a particularly good position to take payoffs. An example is the dispatcher, who can give, or deny, patrolling officers all sorts of favors that ease the burdens of a shift. The internal payoff system is usually highly organized and there is extensive peer group support. Departmental reaction is tolerant if it means a more satisfied work force and does not involve breaking high-priority rules.

Needless to say, these categories are not mutually exclusive in the life of any given police officer: He or she could be found engaging in more than one type at the same time. Furthermore, it is not uncommon to find progression from corruption of authority to more serious violations. This is why some police departments have outlawed perks and have made it a suspendable offense—what begins as "just being friendly" may end up as bribery, kickbacks, payoffs, and direct criminal activities. Such was the case with ex-New York City police officer Michael Dowd. On July 12, 1994, Dowd was sentenced to fourteen years in prison on racketeering and drug charges. According to his own testimony, what began as petty perks taken on the job ended in ongoing criminal activities, shakedowns, and regular use of the fix.

Recognizing that improper police actions include various dysfunctional behaviors not clearly encompassed by the above typology—for example, sexual harassment, discrimination, violation of civil rights, and verbal mistreatment—there is an alternative way of looking at police deviance (Barker and Carter 1994, 3–11). It rests on the distinction between two types of police conduct: occupational deviance and abuse of authority. *Occupational deviance* concerns activities made possible by the nature and organization of normal work activity. Some are occupation-specific:

> [M]any forms of deviance may be committed only by those who are in a given occupation. For example, only physicians can write fraudulent drug prescriptions and college professors may publish "research results" from false data in order to gain promotion, merit, and tenure. Similarly, only police officers can threaten to arrest in exchange for sexual favors or accept money in lieu of issuing a traffic ticket. The common elements in all of these

> acts is that they are committed by "normal" persons during the course of their occupational activity and the behavior is a product of the "powers" inherent in their occupation. (Barker and Carter 1994, 7)

Occupational deviance thus includes many corrupt practices as well as misconduct such as sleeping on the job. The key element is that occupational deviance has an internal locus: "It is concerned with how an officer performs as an organizational member, rather than the method by which the officer discharges his/her police duties" (Barker and Carter 1994, 9).

The second element in their model, *abuse of authority*, encompasses physical abuse such as brutality and misuse of force, psychological abuse, and legal abuse such as the violation of a person's constitutional rights. Unlike occupational deviance, abuse of authority has an external locus because it addresses the authority relation linking the police to the public—who make up the police "clientele"—and concerns the manner in which the police carry out their lawful function.

In addition to the distinction of locus, three other distinctions are noted by the authors. One concerns motivation, a second concerns police department liability, and the third involves peer tolerance. Abuse of authority is less likely to be motivated by personal gain or gratification, and largely because of this, is more likely to be tolerated by police peers. But it is also more likely to result in lawsuits claiming civil rights violations. This occurs because the police have exceeded their lawful exercise of authority and may have violated constitutional protections.

CHAPTER SUMMARY

Criminal justice and criminology are highly related areas of study. The core components of the U.S. criminal justice system are the police, courts, and corrections, but the system also includes public interests groups, lawmakers, and assorted private industries. The criminal justice system can be thought of metaphorically as a leaky funnel. Very few people who are arrested end up in prison. The discretionary decisions by the police, prosecutors, and courts account for most of the leaks in the funnel. There is an abundance of evidence to show that gender, race, and class are related to the exercise of discretion. For example, the data on capital punishment clearly supports the notion that due process varies by social status.

Many popular, political, and scholarly views on crime hold that the nature and form of the U.S. criminal justice system have something to do with the causes of crime. The relationship between criminal justice and criminal behavior is complex. The police can deter some crime through proactive policing and patrol. The courts may be able to prevent some crime by incarcerating criminals and providing opportunities for reformation and rehabilitation. The most politically popular justification for punishment, however, is deterrence, but the evidence on the effectiveness of the deterrence doctrine is mixed, and no study has clearly shown that the death penalty is a deterrent to crime.

Crimes by the criminal justice system, like crime generally, consist of many different activities. Some of these are blatant violations of the criminal law, while others are violations of administrative rules and regulations or constitutional protections. Nevertheless, they result in someone's victimization and may even target society as a whole by undermining respect for the law and encouraging lawbreaking generally. Although no criminal justice agency is immune from crimes among its members, the police have received most of the attention, perhaps because there are more of them and they have more opportunities for crime. Crimes of the police range from taking perks on the job—which can result in some people getting more police protection and others less—to theft, violence, and dealing drugs.

KEY TERMS

blue code of silence (p. 217)

criminal justice (p. 195)

deterrence doctrine (p. 215)

deterrent effect (p. 211)

discretion (p. 202)

field interrogation (p. 202)

general deterrence (p. 215)

grand jury (p. 199)

incapacitation (p. 214)

mandatory sentencing (p. 200)

preliminary hearing (p. 199)

proactive policing (p. 210)

probable cause (p. 199)

reformation (p. 212)

rehabilitation (p. 214)

selective enforcement (p. 202)

specific deterrence (p. 215)

RECOMMENDED READINGS

Barlow, David E., and Melissa Hickman Barlow. 2000. *Police in a Multicultural Society*. Prospect Heights, IL: Waveland Press.

Barlow, Hugh D. 2000. *Criminal Justice in America*. Upper Saddle River, NJ: Prentice Hall.

Henderson, Joel H., and David R. Simon. 1994. *Crimes of the Criminal Justice System*. Cincinnati, OH: Anderson.

Victor, Joseph L., and Joanne Naughton. 2001. *Annual Editions: Criminal Justice 01/02*. New York: McGraw-Hill.

Walker, Samuel. 2001. *Sense and Nonsense about Crime and Drugs: A Policy Guide*. 5th ed. Belmont, CA: Wadsworth.

Walker, Samuel, Cassia Spohn, and Miriam DeLone. 2000. *The Color of Justice: Race, Ethnicity, and Crime in America*. 2d ed. New York: Wadsworth.

RECOMMENDED WEB SITES

Sourcebook of Criminal Justice Statistics

A voluminous collection of criminal justice data in easy-to-read tables.

http://www.albany.edu/sourcebook

Mega-Links in Criminal Justice

Links to hundreds of criminal justice-related Web sites.

http://faculty.ncwc.edu/TOConnor

CRIMINOLOGICAL THEORY: ROOTS AND BRANCHES

What we now call criminology dates back to the middle of the eighteenth century. It has many roots and branches. The pioneers in the field were trained in a variety of disciplines. Cesare Beccaria (1738–1794) and Jeremy Bentham (1748–1833) were philosophers and students of law; Cesare Lombroso (1835–1909, regarded as the founder of criminology, was a physician and surgeon; Raffaele Garofalo (1852–1934) was a professor of law and a magistrate; Enrico Ferri (1856–1929) was a criminal lawyer and member of the Italian Parliament; Gustav Aschaffenburg (1866–1944) and William Healy (1869–1965) were psychiatrists. Although people from many disciplines continued to make important contributions to the field over the years, criminology found its primary academic home in departments of sociology, where it remains today.

CRIMINOLOGICAL THEORY

The most basic function of **theory** is *explanation*. Explanations are important because they help us figure out why things are the way they are, and they suggest what might be done to change things. Every academic discipline has theory, for it drives basic questions about the subject matter. In criminology, many of the theories attempt to explain why people or groups of people commit crime. Other theories attempt to explain why some places have higher crime rates than others, or under what social conditions the crime rate might rise and fall. A group of theories in criminology also explains lawmaking, the process by which certain behaviors and individuals are singled out for criminalization. Still other criminological theories attempt to explain such varied phenomena as the purpose of the criminal justice process, victimology, and the politics of crime and justice. In sum, the purposes of theory are as follows:

- To shed light on the topic under study
- To shed a *different* sort of light on the topic under study
- To frame a story about how and why crime occurs
- To point out the relationships between variables
- To inform and evaluate social and criminal justice policy
- To guide research and other forms of scholarly investigation
- To point out things that may not be readily apparent
- To critique existing sets of knowledge and assumptions

Many criminological theories are *oppositional*. Such theories develop from an explicit critique of existing modes of explanation. In the late eighteenth century, for example, Classical theory introduced the notion of rational choice to combat and defeat supernatural and demonological explanations of crime. In like manner, Edwin Sutherland introduced his theory of differential association by critiquing theories that held that poverty was a major correlate of crime. More recent theories reviewed in this chapter and the next, such as postmodernism and feminism, are also oppositional, for they include fundamental critiques of other explanations of crime when advancing their own theoretical statements.

The orientation of this text is sociological, which means that crime and criminality are discussed in terms of social structures and social processes. Individuals are part of the analysis, but only to the extent that they are connected with other individuals in social relationships.

For example, a sociologist might study the amount and kinds of crime committed by a class of people, or the relationship between the criminal behavior of people and the sorts of friends they have. Alternatively, a sociologist might ask how the characteristics of situations affect people's chances of being victimized by crime, or why the rate of a certain crime varies in space and time or from one group or class of people to another. A sociologist might also study the social origins of criminal definitions, as well as how their enforcement affects group life, including crime itself. Some sociologists are interested in why certain events and people are labeled criminal and others not; other sociologists look into the process of constructing criminal definitions itself—among scientists, perhaps, or on the street or in the courtroom.

Characteristics of Theory

Before reviewing particular theories of crime and criminality, it is helpful to consider characteristics of theories and ways in which they are similar and different. There are four main classifications of theory: (1) level of analysis, (2) paradigmatic structure, (3) range of explanation, and (4) causal locus. Let us review each of these classifications in turn.

LEVELS OF ANALYSIS   Some theories deal mainly with large-scale social patterns such as social change or the social, economic, and political organization of society. Crime is viewed as a property of whole groups of people rather than as a property of individuals. Because they focus on how societies are organized, these theories usually relate crime to social structure. They are called **macrosociological** theories, but this does not mean they lack relevance for the everyday lives of individuals. Rather, such theories attempt to make sense of the everyday behavior of people in relation to conditions and trends that transcend the individual as well as the individual's neighborhood and community.

Some other theories focus on the ways individuals interact with others and with the groups to which they belong. These are called **microsociological** theories, and most share an interest in the way social interaction creates and transmits meanings. They emphasize the social processes by which people and events become criminal. For example, as people move from situation to situation, they are confronted with all sorts of messages, rules, and expectations, some of which are not obvious. Through a process of sending, receiving, and interpreting messages, individuals help construct the social reality of which they are a part. Prominent examples of microsociological theory in criminology are Agnew's strain theory, Hirschi's control theory, and Sutherland's differential association theory, discussed in the next few chapters. Figure 10.1 shows some common independent variables associated with both microsociological and macrosociological theories. Table 10.1 further illustrates the differences between microsocial and macrosocial approaches to explaining violence.

Some theories seem to bridge the two levels. Laub and Sampson (1988), for example, predict that structural factors such as household crowding, economic dependence, residential mobility, and parental crime, through their effects on the way parents relate to their children day by day, influence the delinquent behavior of children. More recently, Barak (1998) has attempted to integrate

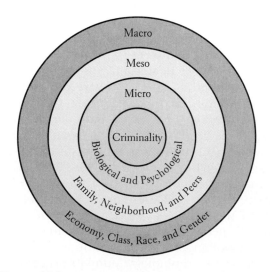

▲ FIGURE 10.1
Levels of Analysis and Common Independent Variables

TABLE 10.1 **Macrosocial and Microsocial Risk Factors for Violence**

	PREDISPOSING	SITUATIONAL	ACTIVATING
MACROSOCIAL	Concentration of poverty Opportunity Structures Decline of social capital Oppositional cultures Sex role socialization	Physical structure Routine activities Access to weapons Emergency medical services	Catalytic social event
MICROSOCIAL	Community Organization Illegal markets Gangs Family disorganization Pre-existing structures	Proximity of responsible monitors Participants' social relationships Bystanders' activities Temporary communication impairments Weapons: carrying, displaying	Participants' communication exchange

Source: Excerpted from Albert J. Reiss Jr. and Jeffrey A. Roth, eds., *Understanding and Preventing Violence* (Washington, D.C.: National Academy Press, 1994).

biological, psychological, and postmodernist approaches with sociological theories to provide an integrated criminology capable of explaining crime and criminal justice in a more multidimensional way. Scholars of organizational crime are also moving toward combining micro and macro perspectives (Kauzlarich and Kramer 1998; Vaughan 1992).

PARADIGMS AND CRIMINOLOGICAL THEORY Paradigms are broad assumptions and presuppositions about the nature of social life (*ontology*) and how knowledge is to be gained about social life (*epistemology*). Paradigms are far more fundamental than theories or perspectives (Ritzer 1999). There are two basic paradigms in criminology: the social facts or **positivist paradigm**, and the **social constructionist paradigm**. While some have argued that there are also Marxist, postmodernist, and feminist paradigms, we see these approaches as multidimensional—they combine elements of both the positivist and constructionist paradigms.

The positivist paradigm involves the assumption that knowledge can be gained about crime and criminal justice through the methods of science. Crime is considered an objective condition, or social fact, that can be analyzed and understood as an independent phenomenon, unrelated to differing definitions, claims, and conceptions of its development and constitution (Michalowski 1985;

Thomas 1982). The positivist paradigm would ask questions such as the following:

1. What is the nature, extent, and distribution of crime?
2. What is the etiology (cause[s]) of crime?
3. How can crime be controlled or reduced?

The social constructionist paradigm is antithetical to the positivist paradigm because it does not assume the objective existence of crime. It emphasizes instead how crime, law, and criminal justice have been and continue to be conceptualized by social actors—thus, the term *social constructionist*. Crime is not an inherent condition, nor is the law, the criminal, or the criminal justice system.

Criminologists operating from the social constructionist paradigm might ask the following questions:

1. Who defines crime and for what purpose?
2. How and why are labels attached to certain people and to certain acts at particular moments in time?
3. What are the consequences of the application of labels to people and groups over time?

Box 10.1 (on page 226) further illustrates these opposing paradigms.

Box 10.1   APPLICATIONS OF POSITIVIST AND SOCIAL CONSTRUCTIONIST PARADIGMS

What is this?

Social Constructionist: A Smiley Face

Positivist: A circle, two dots, and an arch

Here are examples of how criminologists from each of the paradigms might approach the subject of marijuana:

POSITIVIST PARADIGM:

Why do people use marijuana?

How can marijuana use be prevented?

How can the police more effectively suppress marijuana use and distribution?

Are DARE programs successful in decreasing marijuana use?

SOCIAL CONSTRUCTIONIST:

Why is marijuana use criminalized?

Who benefits from the criminalization of marijuana?

Who are the victims of the war on drugs?

What civil liberties are lost by the war on drugs?

Whose interests are served by the war on drugs?

GENERAL AND RESTRICTED THEORIES   Another important way in which theories differ is in the range of phenomena they try to explain. **General theories** are meant to explain a broad range of facts. They are not restricted to any one place or time. A general theory of crime, for example, is one that explains many (if not all) types of crime and can be applied to a variety of social and historical settings. Two of the most influential theories written in this vein are Braithwaite's (1989) theory of reintegrative shaming and Gottfredson and Hirschi's *General Theory of Crime* (1990). These theories will be discussed in Chapter 14.

A general theory subsumes more **restricted theories**; that is, theories designed to apply to a narrower range of facts. A restricted theory of crime might apply to one type of crime, or to various types under a limited set of circumstances. Most modern theories in criminology are regarded as restricted, but the development of general theory remains an important goal, and recent efforts are promising (see Chapter 14).

DISTANT AND PROXIMATE CAUSES Causation is not a simple concept, especially in the social and behavioral sciences. Think about your own behavior for a moment. Right now you are reading this book. How and why you are reading could probably be explained in many different ways; in other words, various causes might be at work. Some of the causes are closer or more immediate—called *proximate causes*—while others are more *distant*, or *background, causes*. A proximate cause might be that your professor just assigned this chapter to be read before your next class, which is tomorrow. An even more proximate (and perhaps more powerful!) cause might be that your parents just told you that they would buy you a new car if you got an "A" in your criminology class. A more distant cause is the expectation that you will follow your mother's footsteps and become a lawyer. An even more distant cause may lie in the fact that a university education is a requirement for many professional careers and increasingly for other jobs as well.

You look out the window and notice that a friend is not cracking the books like you. No surprise, since she's not a college student. But then you wonder why not. Because you know her you comfortably reject personal explanations based on her intelligence, her drive, and her commitment to getting ahead, and start thinking about background factors. You remember that neither of her parents has a university education; you recall that she has four brothers and sisters and that only her father works outside the home, as a house painter. You remember that one of her brothers is disabled and that a few years ago the father had an accident and was out of work for two years. You start thinking about other university students you know and about high school friends who never went to college or dropped out.

Even though it is only a small sample of people, you begin to see patterns. You realize that a university education is explained by a combination of proximate and distant causes, some of which relate to the individual, some to the community and larger society, and some to the social situations people move in and out of in the course of their lives. You recognize, as well, that some causes seem to have a direct impact while the effect of others is more indirect, working through their impact on something else. Some causes are both direct and indirect. For example, the impact of poverty on behavior may be indirect through its effects on family relationships, and direct through its impact on opportunities and access to them.

IDEOLOGY AND CRIMINOLOGICAL THEORY

The way criminologists visualize their field and its subject matter reflects their particular set of beliefs and values. These beliefs and values—called ideology—affect decisions about what to investigate, what questions to ask, and what to do with the knowledge gained. The intrusion of ideology is a normal aspect of the scientific enterprise, and the study of crime is no exception. There are three competing ideological perspectives in criminology: conservative, liberal, and radical/critical. The latter position includes feminist, Marxist, postmodernist, and peacemaking perspectives.

Conservative Criminology

Conservative criminology is identified with the view that criminal law is a codification of moral precepts and that people who break the law are morally defective. Crimes are seen as threats to law-abiding members of society and to the social order on which their safety and security depend. The "right" questions to ask about crime include the following: How are morally defective persons produced? How can society protect itself against them? The causes of crime are located in the characteristics of individuals. The solution to the crime problem is couched in terms of a return to basic values wherein good wins over evil. Until well into the twentieth century, most criminological thinking was conservative. In lay circles, the conservative view enjoyed a considerable boost during the Reagan and Bush years, and continued to enjoy some popularity throughout the Clinton administration.

Liberal Criminology

Liberal criminology began to emerge as a force during the late 1930s and early 1940s, and it has remained dominant ever since. The most influential versions of liberal criminology explain criminal behavior either in terms of the way society is organized (social structure), or in terms of the way people acquire social attributes (social process). Social structure is discussed in detail in Chapter 11 and social process is covered in Chapter 12. Here, a brief introduction to major theories within the liberal perspective will suffice.

Social structure theories include strain theory, cultural transmission theory, and conflict theory. *Strain* theory argues that when people find they cannot achieve valued goals through socially approved means, they experience stress and frustration, which in turn may lead to crime. *Cultural transmission* theory draws attention to the impact on individuals of the values, norms, and lifestyles to which they are exposed day to day. Delinquency and crime are learned through exposure to a criminogenic culture, a culture that encourages crime. According to *conflict* theory, society is characterized by conflict, and criminality is a product of differences in power exercised when people compete for scarce resources or clash over conflicting interests.

Social process theories include associational theory, control theory, and labeling theory. *Associational* theories assert that people become criminal through close association with others (family members, friends, coworkers) who are criminal. *Control* theory asserts that crime and delinquency result "when an individual's bond to society is weak or broken" (Hirschi 1971, 16). More room is allowed for individual deviance when social controls are weak. *Labeling* theory suggests that some people become criminals because they are influenced by the way other people react to them. People who are repeatedly punished for "bad" behavior may eventually accept the idea that they are bad, and their subsequent behavior is consistent with that identity.

Radical/Critical Criminology

Liberal criminologists locate criminogenic forces in the organization and routine social processes of society, yet they do not call for any change in its basic economic, cultural, or political structure. Radical/critical criminologists generally do. From a Marxist point of view, crime and criminal justice have reinforced and strengthened the power of the state and the wealthy over the "poor, Third World communities, and youth" (Platt 1974, 3). To some Marxists, crime and criminality are manifestations

of the exploitive character of monopoly capitalism, and current efforts to control crime are poorly disguised attempts to reduce freedoms and to divert attention from the real culprits—those who control capital. While Marxists are but one school of thought within radical/critical criminologists, the approach has largely been shaped by Marx's ideas, such as his call to work for social justice, encapsulated in the dictum: "The philosophers have only interpreted the world in various ways; the point, however, is to change it" (quoted in Tucker 1978, 143).

Feminist theories in criminology focus on how gender relations and patriarchy form the nature, extent, and distribution of crime, responses to crime, and victimization. Criminology, like most academic disciplines, has historically been male-centered, sexist, and unsympathetic to issues related to gender inequality and discrimination. Since the 1970s, however, advances have been made in the understanding of the gendered nature of crime and criminal justice. We discuss feminist criminological perspectives at length in the next chapter.

Another radical/critical criminological approach is postmodernism, which employs notions of chaos and unpredictability in the understanding of crime, and questions conventional ideas about the value of science in explaining crime (Milovanovic 1997). Postmodernism is clearly an oppositional theory, and is really "a loose collection of *themes* and *tendencies*" that include the rejection of scientific methods, the notion of Truth, and the legitimacy of the state (Friedrichs 1998, 83; Schwartz and Friedrichs 1994). Criminological postmodernism sensitizes us to the power of words, especially the so-called "crime speak," and how the use of language and articulation is linked to how we think about and define the supposed "being" of crime and justice (see Arrigo 1998; Henry and Milovanovic 1996, 1999). For example, a recent postmodern *constitutive* theory of crime holds the following:

- Language is never neutral. It is encoded with multiple desires and multiple ways of knowing.
- Certain conversations about crime are valued and esteemed over others. Crime talk provides one accented or anchored representation of reality.

- There is an inherent problem when crime talk signs are reduced to perpetuate conventional criminological meanings … this semiotic cleansing of being … denies … the possibility for emerging alternative or replacement narratives on crime, on criminal behavior, and on the criminal law.

- Theories of crime [are the] product of coterminous forces, the subject in process and economic conditions that give rise to notions of crime … (Arrigo 1998, 56).

There is a similar focus on the language of crime in the work of Henry and Milovanovic (1991, 1996, 1999). Indeed, everything around us and the words we use, including "prisons," "criminals," "police" etc., are products of human invention, which is imperfect, unpredictable, and often ruled by chaos and disorder. While postmodern and constitutive criminologies have yet to make a significant impact on the discipline of criminology as a whole, they clearly raise important questions (e.g., "How do we know what we know?").

Finally, radical/critical criminology has given rise to what is known as *peacemaking criminology*. This perspective holds that problems such as crime, injustice, and domination should be addressed through peaceful, healing, honest, and respectful avenues. Much of criminology and criminal justice is geared toward "warmaking," according to this perspective. Peacemaking criminologists argue this is the least effective way to bring about healing and therefore promote measures that aim to bring the victim and offender toward a harmonious and nonviolent relationship, provide support for the peaceful resolution of offender deviation from community standards, and create a system of justice that focuses on truth, not simply "winning" or vengeance (Pepinsky 1999; Quinney and Pepinsky 1991). As Hal Pepinsky (2000, 1), one of the founders of the perspective, recently penned: "The primary question I face as a U.S. criminologist is: Why are we so punitive in our wars on crime, and how can we transform that punitiveness into peacemaking?" Peacemaking criminology is not simply theoretical, but can be applied to a number of real-life situations, one of which is family group conferencing, discussed in Chapter 14.

All of these ideological positions—conservative, liberal, and radical/critical—can be found in the various theories reviewed in this and the next four chapters. Sociological criminology has been dominated by liberal perspectives, but the field has also benefited from important insights from the conservative and radical/critical camps. Box 10.2 (on page 230) illustrates the findings of an interesting study of criminologists' political ideology.

PHILOSOPHICAL FOUNDATIONS OF CRIMINOLOGY: THE CLASSICAL SCHOOL

The end of the eighteenth century in Europe was a time of great transformation. The beginning of the Industrial Revolution started to change how people lived and worked. People began moving to urban areas and working for wages from others, and capitalist economic organization was growing. The traditional authority of monarchies was increasingly tenuous as philosophers and scholars involved in the Enlightenment intellectual movement promoted the ideas of democracy, rationality, and free will. Intellectuals began to view people's behavior as a response to their rational choice, not as a result of supernatural forces. Demonological explanations of behavior, including criminal and deviant behavior, gradually lost their popularity (Pfohl 1985).

Cesare Becarria and Jeremy Bentham, both products of this new intellectual movement, were among the first European scholars to write on issues pertaining to crime and criminal justice. Their writings were not so much focused on explaining the causes of crime, but on how a rational, fair, and democratic criminal justice system should be designed. It is fair to say that the Classical School had two main foci: (1) a program for changes in the administration of justice, and (2) a limited theory of crime causation.

Regarding the relationship between the state and the control of its citizens, Becarria (1993, 9) wrote that "… every act of authority of one man [sic] over another, for which there is not an absolute necessity, is tyrannical. It is upon this then that the sovereign's right to punish crimes is founded." Essentially, Becarria and Bentham subscribed to the philosophy of **utilitarianism**, which holds that policies and deeds, particularly those associated with the government, should provide the greatest good for the greatest number of people.

Both Becarria and Bentham promoted the now commonly accepted procedural practices such as the presumption of innocence, judicial neutrality,

BOX 10.2   POLITICAL IDEOLOGY AND CRIMINOLOGISTS' THEORETICAL PREFERENCES

A recent survey of criminologists lends considerable support to the notion that political ideology is related to preferences toward certain kinds of criminological theories (Walsh and Ellis 1999). Of the 138 respondents to the survey, 70 identified themselves as liberal, 35 as moderates, 23 as conservative, and 10 as radical.

The study found that criminologists who regarded themselves as more politically conservative or moderate were more likely to favor theories that focus on low self-control and poor disciplinary practices as important causes of crime. Liberals were more likely to favor theories that focus on environmental factors that lead to crime, such as economic and educational inequality. Radicals, or critical criminologists, were even stronger in their belief that these factors are important in the understanding of crime. Moreover, those claiming to be radicals supported mostly Marxist and conflict theories; conservatives supported theories such as social control and self-control, which do not implicate larger social factors in the causes of crime; and those claiming to be liberal or moderate "fall in between" radicals and conservatives (Walsh and Ellis 1999, 14).

The authors of the study point out that it is unclear whether political ideology causes theoretical preference or whether the objective merits of theory cause a change in a person's ideology. This is an interesting question, for if ideology alone causes theoretical preference, what are the chances of establishing criminology as a real "science"? If, however, certain theories are found to be supported in the research and this causes a change in ideology, does this mean that the discipline is "objective" and committed only to the search for "truth"? The answers to these questions are not forthcoming, but what this study points out is that, indeed, criminology is (and perhaps has always been) "highly fragmented" by political ideology (Walsh and Ellis 1999, 14).

Source: Reprinted with the permission of the American Society of Criminology.

and proportionality in sentencing. They were opposed to the torture of prisoners and capital punishment, mostly because of the physical abuse suspects and prisoners suffered for centuries. Classical school scholars believed that punishment was a "necessary evil" and only justifiable if based on reasonable, humane, and rational processes. More specifically, Bentham (1948) believed that punishment should not be given when it is groundless, inefficacious, too expensive, or needless. Bentham also devoted many of his years to producing what is known as the **hedonistic calculus**: the listing of appropriate punishments for crimes based on the harm or injury they caused.

Classical school scholars also provided a rough theory of crime causation. They believed that criminal behavior resulted from the rational calculation of costs and benefits. The idea that people are **hedonistic** guided their work: People would be more likely to commit a crime if the pleasure (perceived benefits) from the behavior would outweigh the pain (perceived costs). As noted in Chapter 9, the threatened punishment for criminal behavior was thought to work best as a deterrent if it was (a) certain, (b) proportionate to the harm caused by the crime, and (c) swiftly imposed. This means that people would be less likely to commit a crime if they knew they would be caught and punished (certainty) soon after committing the crime (swiftness), and if the punishment mirrored the seriousness of the crime.

Becarria and Bentham's ideas have greatly influenced criminal justice policy. Their views on the causes of crime have in a sense "stood the test of time" since many people today appear to support deterrence policies. "Three strikes and you're out" policies and increased punishments for many offenses are consistent with the severity aspects of the theory. Ironically, the emphasis on due process that Classical school thinkers proposed is not as popularly supported now because some view it as counterproductive to deterrence and punishment. Witness the calls for eliminating appeals, quicker executions, and less "intrusive" procedural laws for police. Even though the Classical school thinkers published their work about 200 years ago, their ideas are relevant today as we shall see again in Chapter 13.

SCIENTIFIC FOUNDATIONS OF CRIMINOLOGY: POSITIVISM

The birth of criminology as *science* is usually traced to nineteenth-century Europe. By the latter half of that century the scientific revolution was well under way. The armchair philosophizing of the Classical theorists was grudgingly giving way to the logic and methodology of science. Observation, measurement, and experimentation were the basic tools of the scientific method, and their use in the study of human behavior heralded the development of disciplines now taken for granted—biology, anthropology, psychology, sociology, political science, and statistics. Thus was born the Age of Positivism, and crime was placed under the microscope of science. Theories now had to be spelled out, quantified, and falsifiable.

Positivism and Early Criminology

The notion that crime could be studied through the methods of science was established early in the nineteenth century by two authors whose work earned them an honored place in the annals of criminology. Working independently, Adolphe Quetelet (1796–1874) and André Michel Guerry (1802–1866) compiled the first criminal statistics and used them to make predictions and comparisons about crime. Others soon followed suit, and these early ventures into social statistics became a model for the later work of Emile Durkheim. "For the first time in history," Leon Radzinowicz (1966, 35) has observed, "crime became thought of as a social fact molded by the very environment of

Charles Darwin's work on animal evolution was a major impetus to the rise of positivism. Many intellectuals during that time were strongly influenced by Darwin's theory of evolution.

which it was an integral part." This was an important break with the classical theorists, who viewed criminal behavior as stemming from the exercise of free will in the pursuit of pleasure.

A major impetus to the rise of positivism was Charles Darwin's work on animal evolution. Darwin's followers argued that human behavior is largely determined by Homo sapiens' position on the evolutionary scale and by the ongoing battle for survival. However, the specific impact of these forces on an individual was considered a matter for empirical investigation.

Positivism is not without its critics. The objections are varied, but primarily they consist of the argument that the so-called "objective" depiction of "concrete facts" in the world obscures a reality that is socially constructed by the participants in it. The facts are "constructed meanings produced within specific cultural, political, and economic contexts" (Michalowski 1988, 18). Even the nature of crime itself cannot be taken for granted, as we saw in Chapter 1.

The debate about positivism versus social constructionism is unlikely to be resolved in the near future, and it is certainly possible for both to live side by side, and for criminology to profit from their contributions to our knowledge and thinking about crime. Gibbs (1988, 4) makes an important point, however: How else are scientific theories about crime to be assessed, if not by testing their predictions against a body of empirical data? This was the great insight of the early positivists, although there was actually very little research going on during this period (Garland 1985b, 128).

Biology and the Search for the Criminal Type

Influenced by positivism, early criminologists were convinced that they could uncover the causes of criminal behavior if they could apply the methods of science to the study of human beings. Deviance, they believed, was caused rather than chosen (Pfohl 1985). The major figure was Italian physician Cesare Lombroso (1911). Like many of his contemporaries, Lombroso believed that criminals must be

Cesare Lombroso helped establish criminology as a field of scientific study. He spent decades searching for the criminal type.

different from law-abiding people in some important way. The problem was to find out how they differed, and the search for the criminal type consumed much of his career.

As a physician attached to the army and later to prisons and asylums, Lombroso examined thousands of individuals. Profoundly influenced by the evolutionary doctrine, he searched for physiological evidence of the link between deviant behavior and biological forces. In 1870 he claimed a triumphant discovery: In his view, many of the criminals he had studied were *atavistic*—biological throwbacks to a more primitive evolutionary state. Such "born criminals" could be identified by five or more physical stigmata, or anomalies: an asymmetrical cranium, a receding chin, a low forehead, large ears, too many fingers, a sparse beard, protruding lips, low sensitivity to pain, and deformities of the eye.

But the born criminal was not the only type Lombroso identified, nor did he argue that criminal behavior was solely the result of biological forces. He distinguished other categories of criminals, including insane criminals (idiots, imbeciles, alcoholics, degenerates), criminaloids (those with less-pronounced physical stigmata and degeneracy, but pulled into crime by situation or environment), and criminals by passion (those who were neither atavistic nor degenerate, but drawn into crime by love, politics, offended honor, or other intense emotions).

Though the core of his theory was biological, Lombroso recognized the importance of precipitating situational and environmental factors. He mentioned poverty, emigration, high food prices, police corruption, and changes in the law as nonbiological determinants of criminal behavior (Wolfgang 1961, 207). However, it remained for one of his followers, Enrico Ferri, to undertake serious investigation of the impact of environmental factors (see Sellin 1937).

Lombroso and his followers had a tremendous impact on the emerging field of criminology. Especially important was the impetus their work gave to research on the individual criminal offender. For more than fifty years, scholars concentrated their efforts on describing and classifying criminals and on distinguishing them from noncriminals. (For a critical analysis of this movement, see Garland 1985b.) More recent work, however, has taken a different direction.

Some biologists believe that people are instinctively aggressive, basing their claim on studies of animal behavior. According to Konrad Lorenz (1971), nature gave animals an instinct for aggression for three reasons: (1) to ensure that the strongest males succeed in mating with the most desirable females, thus ensuring a kind of genetic quality control; (2) to protect the physical space, or territory, necessary for raising the young, securing food, and the like; and (3) to maintain hierarchies of dominance and through them a stable, well-policed society.

Following Lorenz and Desmond Morris—the author of *The Naked Ape*—Pierre van den Berghe (1974, 777) believes that human behavior is not "radically discontinuous from that of other species," and he advocates a biosocial approach to understanding human violence. Essentially, the argument is that humans, like animals, have predispositions to violence that are innate—that is, biologically grounded. Though conclusive proof of this is still unavailable, one promising indication is that aggression is a universal behavior pattern for a species: In humans, aggression has been observed everywhere, despite widely differing habitats, cultures, and technologies. The viewpoint receives additional support from the documented relationship between aggression and the male hormone testosterone and the discovery of "aggression centers" in the brain (van den Berghe 1974; Bailey 1976; Wilson and Herrnstein 1985).

Robert L. Burgess (1979; Burgess and Draper 1989) has drawn on evolutionary theory to explain variations in child abuse and family violence. Burgess argues that mature humans have two related problems. The first is to pass on their genes through successive generations, and the second is to protect their offspring despite limited resources. The solution is for parents to invest most in those genetic offspring who show the best prospects for surviving and reproducing and least in nongenetic relatives and/or those genetic offspring who show the worst prospects of surviving and reproducing.

The problems and their solutions will produce greater risks of abuse and neglect in families with stepchildren, in poorer families, in those with less education, in families with many children, in single-parent families, and in families whose children have mental or physical impairments. Burgess cites studies both in the United States and abroad that confirm these predictions (see also Daly and Wilson 1988b). However, it should be emphasized that child abuse is not inevitable in families with these characteristics and it is found in many families without them (see Ellis and Walsh 1997).

Daly and Wilson (1988a, 520) make the following observation about step-relationships and violence:

> In view of the costs of prolonged "parental" investment in nonrelatives, it may seem remarkable that step-relationships are ever peaceful, let alone genuinely affectionate. However, violent hostility is rarer than friendly relations even among nonrelatives; people thrive by the maintenance of networks of social reciprocity that will make them attractive exchange partners.... The fact remains, however, that step-relationships lack the deep commonality of interest of the natural parent-offspring relationships, and feelings of affection and commitment are correspondingly shallower. Differential rates of violence are one result.

As briefly discussed in Chapter 4, Daly and Wilson's evolutionary psychological perspective (1988a, see also 1998) explains the male propensity for violence as the result of the ubiquitous struggle over control and propagation. Green (1993, 32) explains it as follows:

> Wife-murder and wife-abuse represent the striving for control over the reproductive capacities of women. Killings arising out of trivial altercations aim to deter rivals from threatening one's interests; they give tangible proof that any such attempt will be met with severe punishment. The predominance of males is due to the greater need of men for additional resources with which to check rivals and attract women.

Finally, we should note that genetic and neurological explanations of crime continue to play some role in the modern day search for the causes of crime. Most theorists working in these areas agree that crime is best explained by studying how the social environment and internal physiological systems interact with one another to produce behavior (Ellis and Walsh 1997; Jeffery 1994). For example, it is quite true that the brain develops in concert with environment. Any changes in the functioning of the brain, then, may be related to behavior, including criminal behavior. This means that the nutritional content of food, adverse chemical interactions caused by drug use, and brain trauma or disease may be involved in criminal decision making (Jeffery 1994).

More recent genetic studies of twins and adoptees have found some evidence of a hereditary-based criminality, although the correlations are small and many of the studies have critical methodological limitations, such as the use of small samples and lack of controls for environmental influences (Gottfredson and Hirschi 1990; although see Ellis and Walsh 1997).

SOCIOLOGICAL FOUNDATIONS OF CRIMINOLOGICAL THEORY

Sociology has influenced criminology more than any other academic discipline. The broadest of all social sciences, sociology involves the study of social structure, culture, and interaction. Crime and criminal justice are part of the social structure, which includes social institutions, organizations, statuses, and roles. From a functionalist perspective, the criminal justice system is an institutional arrangement created and maintained to serve some social need (e.g., the protection of society from dangerous, violent, and/or undesirable individuals and groups of individuals). The law is also part of the social structure because it represents the highest form of legitimate authority and social control a society can create. A functionalist sociologist would also point out that in order to maintain social solidarity and equilibrium, criminal justice policy and law should reflect the *collective will of the people*.

From a conflict perspective, the criminal justice system and the law represent bureaucratic organizations that protect other elements of the social structure from major change. *Conflict criminologists* would examine how law and criminal justice policies represent the interests of economic and cultural elites, men, and other privileged groups. Whether one adopts a conflict or functionalist perspective on crime, criminal justice, or law, various roles and statuses arise from the creation of formal social control. People become police officers, judges, prosecutors, correctional officers, probation and parole officers, lawyers, and of course, criminals, as a result of the organization of criminal justice and law. Each of these statuses require

roles, the behavior within a status. Of course, how these roles are played varies from person to person and from context to context, especially since the criminal law allows criminal justice agents to exercise considerable discretion.

Crime, law, and criminal justice are cultural phenomena as well. This means that the study of norms, values, beliefs, ideology, consciousness, and other cultural social facts is indispensable for understanding what is considered crime, how societies attempt to control crime, and how larger belief systems shape elements of social control. For instance, the United States is one of the few Western industrialized nations that still practices capital punishment (Barlow 2000). This represents a unique cultural practice guided by distinct norms and beliefs. Furthermore, states are given the option of whether or not to have capital punishment, which underscores the cultural differences that may exist in various regions of the United States. The United States also has more laws than any other country. Sometimes these laws are hailed by the majority—*Three Strikes* laws are a good example; sometimes they are received with mixed support—for example, anti-domestic violence laws; and still others are much less popularly received, such as holding parents responsible for the misdeeds of their children.

The substance of law, crime, and criminal justice is inextricably tied to elements of social structure, which interact with a society's culture. In reality, norms and ideology influence social structure, and institutional practices help create norms and ideology. While it is important to understand the distinction between the cultural and structural worlds, criminological theories often employ elements of both of these phenomena in the explanation of crime. These theories are sometimes called "integrated" theories because they include elements of both social structure and social process. For example, Colvin and Pauly (1983) created an influential "Integrated Structural-Marxist" theory to explain delinquency on the basis of how parental positions in the workplace effect the process of parenting. Inevitably, one must consider the cultural sphere when framing a problem structurally. In other words, institutional arrangements, in this case a capitalist economy, have implications for how people develop norms and practices.

More recently, Heimer (1997) has called for the synthesis of social structural and cultural theories of violence. She explains that while criminologists recognize the interaction of structure and culture in the production of crime, few have actually built synthesized theories. Heimer (1997, 807) holds that "socioeconomic status is consequential for violent offending primarily because it affects the cultural contexts encountered by youths (e.g., family and peer contexts) and thus indirectly shapes the learning of cultural definitions about violent delinquency."

Several theorists have suggested that our interactions and subsequent behavior are *shaped*, not caused, by larger social forces. Like Colvin and Pauly (1983), such theorists as Braithwaite (1989a), Thornberry (1987), and Sampson and Laub (1993b) place interaction and subsequent behavior within larger structural and cultural contexts. The importance placed on social structure as a correlate or cause of crime varies from theory to theory. This point is illustrated well in this comment: "Structural factors will strongly affect family and school social control mechanisms, but ... their influence will be largely indirect (but not unimportant) in the explanation of delinquency" (Laub, Sampson, Corbett, and Smith 1995, 94).

Some theories of crime rest on the idea that social structure and culture are continually being constructed through the day-to-day interactions of individuals as they live their lives. This microsocial **interactionist perspective** (sometimes called symbolic interactionism) sees human beings as *active agents* in the construction of the social world they experience. The idea is that during interaction, people construct meanings, expectations, and implications that shape everyone's behavior and thus create a certain social reality for participants. This experience influences what happens in later interactions, although each interaction creates its own social reality. Social order is therefore fluid and ever-changing.

One of the most important elements of the interactionist perspective is the idea that actions arise out of situations (Blumer 1969, 85). Whether people are at home with their families, in school, at work, or at play, each situation presents opportunities, demands, tasks, obstacles, pleasures—and sometimes dangers—that must be taken into account and evaluated by the actor. That assessment provides people with the basis for understanding the situation and forming their actions.

Essentially, *the meaning of a situation for each participant* derives from the actions and reactions of the other participants.

For example, how do you decide that you are in control of a situation? By how others respond to you. Or consider how you know that a situation is safe or dangerous. You can "read" the situation through the actions of others, or you can put yourself in the shoes of another and imagine how they would act and what the likely results would be. Obviously, this becomes possible only when you have prior knowledge or experience of "situations and people like these." Social order is constructed as people agree on the meanings and implications of the situations they are in, and act accordingly.

With the interactionist view, the general assumption is that *both* consensus and conflict are factors framing any given social situation. However, some of the more prominent theories of crime drawing on the interactionist perspective have tended to emphasize conflict, as we shall see in Chapters 12 and 14.

Robert Merton (1975) once said that paradigms are "opposed to one another in about the same sense that ham is opposed to eggs: They are perceptively different but mutually enriching" (quoted in Ritzer 2000, 633). The same might be said about the relationship between social structure and culture in the understanding of crime.

Classical Sociological Theory and Criminology

The "Holy Trinity" of sociology includes Emile Durkheim, Max Weber, and Karl Marx. These scholars are considered the major founders of sociology, and their work has significantly influenced how sociologists think about the social world. We will briefly review the contributions each has made to the sociological study of law, crime, and social control.

MARX While Karl Marx said little about crime, some criminologists, especially radical/critical criminologists, recognize a substantial debt to this nineteenth-century scholar. Marx believed that a society's mode of economic production—the manner in which relations of production are organized—determines in large part the organization of social relations, the structure of individual and group interaction.

Under a capitalist mode of production, there are those who own the means of production and those who do not. The former group is known as the *bourgeoisie* and the latter as the *proletariat*. The bourgeoisie, or ruling class, controls the formulation and implementation of moral and legal norms, and even *ideas*. Both classes are bound in relationship to one another, but this relationship is asymmetrical and exploitive.

This relationship affects law, and by extension, crime. Laws are created by the elite to protect their interests at the expense of the proletariat. However, the image of law promoted to the masses is one that implies democracy and consensus. For example, nearly everyone would agree that killing another without legitimate reason should be criminal. However, what *are* those legitimate reasons? War? Air, water, and soil pollution by corporations for capital accumulation? Violations of worker safety laws that result in worker deaths? Marxists might point out that even presumably simple and well-supported laws may not work in the interests of the have-nots, though they may be perceived to be a representation of the collective will of a society. In this spirit, some Marxist-influenced scholars have noted the following:

> The fact is that the label 'crime' is not used in America to name all or the worst of the actions that cause misery and suffering to Americans. It is primarily reserved for the dangerous action of the poor. (Reiman 2001, 58)

> [I]t is not the social harms punishable by law which cause the greatest misery in the world. It is the lawful harms, those unpunishable crimes justified and protected by law, the state, the ruling elites that fill the earth with misery, want, strife, conflict, slaughter, and destruction. (Tifft and Sullivan 1980, 9)

Marxist criminology probably hit its high point in the 1970s after some of Marx's early writing were translated to English and made available in the United States. Marxist theories of crime are explored in more detail in Chapter 11.

DURKHEIM   Durkheim is regarded by some as the most important classical sociologist to influence the study of crime and law. The breadth of Durkheim's work is impressive, and in many of his

French sociologist Emile Durkheim argued that deviance serves important social functions. He also noted that deviance is normal and universal, as it is found in all societies.

writings one can see the intellectual debt criminologists owe to this macrosociologist.

Durkheim was a functionalist, and so it should not be surprising to find that he was concerned with how societies attempt to regulate behavior for the purposes of stability, control, and solidarity. Law, Durkheim believed, should ideally represent the collective will of the people. What should be considered criminal, then, are behaviors that compromise and jeopardize the social order. Durkheim (1893) used the term **collective conscience** to describe widely held social values and beliefs. He reasoned that something should be made (or considered) criminal if it offends the collective conscience, the normative standards of the society. Punishment, he argued, was necessary to reaffirm the collective conscience so that all members of society would understand the wrongfulness and immorality of criminal behavior. This, he explained, increases social solidarity.

Durkheim also pointed out that crime is not abnormal because it is found in every society. Crime and deviance are universal because every society must have norms and every society will have someone break those norms at one time or another:

> There is no society that is not confronted with the problem of criminality. Its form changes; the acts thus characterized are not the same everywhere; but everywhere and always, there have been men who have behaved in such a way as to draw upon themselves penal repression.... No doubt it is possible that crime will have abnormal forms, as, for example, when its rate is unusually high.... What is normal, simply, is the existence of criminality, provided that it attains and does not exceed, for each social type, a certain level, which it is perhaps not impossible to fix in conformity with the preceding rules. (Durkheim 1950, 64–66)

Crime and deviance are also functional because they provide avenues for social change. Here Durkheim meant that norm or law violation may make people become aware of required changes in society. Using the example of Socrates, Durkheim noted that challenges to established rules may enlighten others so that laws and norms may change along with other concurrent social changes:

> Nothing is good indefinitely and to an unlimited extent.... To make progress, individual originality must be able to express itself. In order that the originality of the idealist whose dreams transcend his century may find expression, it is necessary that the originality of the criminal, who is below the level of his time, shall also be possible. One does not occur without the other. (Durkheim 1950, 71)

The actions of people such as Martin Luther King Jr., Rosa Parks, and even Jack Kevorkian illustrate that lawbreaking or deviance can produce social change.

Durkheim made numerous contributions to criminology. Perhaps the most lasting was the introduction of the concept of **anomie**. In both *The Division of Labor* (1893) and *Suicide* (1897), anomie was explained as a social condition in which "normlessness" prevails. More specifically, anomie exists when systems of regulation and restraint in a society have diminished so much that individuals suffer a loss of external guidance and control in the goal-seeking endeavors. The structure regulating social relationships is disrupted and social cohesion and solidarity are undermined. Durkheim argued that anomie is more likely during periods of rapid social change, when traditional norms prove ineffective in regulating human conduct. This structural, macrosociological approach helped explain why some areas have a higher suicide rate than others. Suicide is often considered a very individualistic act more appropriately explained by psychological theories. However, Durkheim showed that suicide, as a social fact, is a phenomenon explainable by the study of large scale social currents and forces. Sociologist Robert Merton was heavily influenced by the concept of anomie and used it to build a theory of crime, reviewed in Chapter 11.

WEBER   German sociologist Max Weber is generally not considered an important contributor to criminology. However, a few criminologists (Turk 1969; Chambliss and Siedman 1982) have employed Weber's ideas to make sense out of the relationship between law, authority, and social structure. In our view, Weber's contribution to criminology rests in his work on the social impact of authority and bureaucracy.

Weber thought that authority is gained and sustained in three ways: by tradition or custom, through the charisma of individual leaders, or through rules and regulations in rational systems. The rational-legal basis of authority, Weber (1954, 215) writes, "rests on a belief in the legality of enacted rules and the right of those elevated to authority under such rules to issue commands." Legitimacy derived from the law gives criminal justice decision makers, especially the legislature, wide discretionary powers, a measure of protection from critics, and the right not to "give reasons for their actions" (O'Conner 1998, 13).

This last point is worth stressing. Indeed, it is politicians, not criminologists, who make law, despite the fact that many legislators have no formal education or training in fields such as criminal justice and criminology. At worst, this can be detrimental to community safety, and at best, a waste of resources. For example, publicly supported criminal justice programs (such as DARE) are developed more or less at whim rather than on the basis of scientific understanding. When programs are found through scientific tests to be worthless, rationality would dictate that they be changed or dropped, but this often does not happen.

But the legitimacy of criminal justice is not just blindly accepted by the masses—there are protests over police brutality; feminist groups and others have forced changes in sexist laws; people of color have fought and even died for the equality of justice; victims-rights groups have successfully lobbied to bring the victim "back in" to the criminal justice process; and most recently, people have questioned the state's procedures dealing with capital punishment cases. Clearly, there is some resistance, opposition, and critique of the way criminal justice is carried out, but Weber's point still remains valid: Few have called for the dissolution of the government or of the very positions that are held in governance. Despite all the criticism, the fundamental legitimacy of the criminal justice system has remained intact. Except in truly unusual cases, the authority of the state rarely loses legitimacy, as Friedrichs (1980, 541; 1982) notes: "Legitimacy is at the least a wholly desirable, and at the most an absolutely necessary, element of a stable and effective legal order."

Another important concept derived from the work of Weber (1954, 956) is *bureaucracy*, an organizational form that is characterized by written rules, hierarchy, specialization, and instrumental rationality. While criminal justice organizations possess many bureaucratic characteristics, one aspect is particularly pronounced: *rationalization*, defined as the tendency for people and organizations to pursue their goals by selecting *only* the most effective means. The argument goes like this: As societies advance, people are less inclined to "go with the flow" and instead follow established rules and regulations to meet their needs. In a rationalized world, decisions are made quickly according to principles of efficiency. While rationality can help a society run smoothly and efficiently, it can also be dehumanizing in that the self—who individuals really are—becomes controlled and the spirit subdued. Law is clearly an attempt at rationalization, and so are the policing, prosecutorial, and correctional institutions within criminal justice.

Modern organizations are largely bureaucratic and rationalized. A major problem with bureaucratic organizations is that they have difficulty dealing with the unique needs and abilities of people—including office holders—and with abnormal or unexpected events. There is a tendency to apply rules universally, and deviations from prescribed practices are frowned upon even if they meet the goals of the organization. Probation and parole officers, for example, often argue that they cannot be creative with their clients because of bureaucratic constraints. Those who commit crime are not a homogeneous group, and some offenders and groups of offenders may require special treatment. Imagine, for example, a group of sexual offenders and a group of genocidal governmental officials. Should these groups be treated in the same way? Are sex offenders themselves so alike that universal treatment and counseling programs will be successful? And how rational is it to treat people with different needs in the same way? Weber pointed out that sometimes rationalized actions spawn irrationalities, and therefore may lead to negative and counterproductive consequences.

Weber's sociology alerts us to the problems that authority, bureaucracy, and rationalization may cause in the successful control of crime in our society. The major lesson is that complex societies contain the very elements that may undermine the quality of life, including being safe from violence.

CHAPTER SUMMARY

This chapter began with a discussion of the nature and types of criminological theory. Theories reflect the values, beliefs, and academic disciplines of those who propose them. Conservative criminological theories explain crime in terms of the moral defectiveness of individuals. Liberal theories explain crime in terms of normal social conditions and processes that characterize group life. Radical/critical theories explain crime in terms of the exploitive character of capitalist society, patriarchy, or modernism.

Theories differ in other ways. Macrotheories deal with large-scale social patterns; microtheories focus on the interaction of individuals and on the manner in which meanings are created and transmitted in social situations. General theories explain a broad range of facts; restricted theories apply to a narrower range of facts. A general theory thus subsumes more restricted theories. However, the development of general theory is extremely difficult, and most modern theories in criminology are regarded as restricted. Paradigms structure how theorists go about viewing the world in a fundamental way. The social fact paradigm assumes the objective existence of social phenomena, while the social constructionist perspective guides the investigation of subjective, interactive, and definitional processes.

Classical theorists created a theory of justice and a simplified theory of the causes of criminal behavior. Many of both Beccaria and Bentham's ideas have remained relatively popular today. The scientific foundations of criminology are traced to nineteenth-century Europe and the rise of positivism. The development of new techniques of data collection and analysis and Charles Darwin's work on evolution spurred the application of science to problems of human behavior.

Employing a sociological approach to the study of crime allows the examination of social structure, culture, and interaction. Classical sociological theorists such as Marx, Durkheim, and Weber all influenced the development of criminology, though in significantly different ways.

KEY TERMS

anomie (p. 237)

collective conscience (p. 236)

general theories (p. 226)

hedonistic (p. 230)

hedonistic calculus (p. 230)

interactionist perspective (p. 235)

macrosociological theories (p. 224)

microsociological theories (p. 224)

paradigms (p. 225)

positivist paradigm (p. 225)

restricted theories (p. 226)

social constructionist paradigm (p. 225)

theory (p. 223)

utilitarianism (p. 229)

RECOMMENDED READINGS

Arrigo, Bruce. 1999. *Social Justice/Criminal Justice: The Maturation of Critical Theory in Law, Crime, and Deviance.* Belmont, CA: West/Wadsworth.

Bierne, Piers. 1993. *Inventing Criminology: Essays on the Rise of "Homo Criminalis."* Albany, NY: SUNY Press.

Gibbons, Don C. 1994. *Talking about Crime and Criminals: Problems and Issues in Theory Development in Criminology.* Englewood Cliffs, NJ: Prentice Hall.

Lynch, Michael J., Raymond Michalowski, and W. Byron Groves. 2000. *The New Primer in Radical Criminology: Critical Perspectives on Crime, Power, and Identity.* Monsey, NY: Criminal Justice Press.

Pepinsky, Harold E., and Richard Quinney. 1991. *Criminology as Peacemaking.* Bloomington, IN: Indiana University Press.

Ritzer, George. 1990. *Frontiers of Social Theory: The New Syntheses.* New York: Columbia University Press.

Williams, Frank P., and Marilyn D. McShane. 1998. *Criminology Theory: Selected Classic Readings.* Cincinnati, OH: Anderson.

RECOMMENDED WEB SITES

SocioSite Theory Page

A comprehensive page on sociological theory.

http://www.pscw.uva.nl/sociosite/TOPICS/ Theory.html

National Institute of Justice, Criminal Justice Publications, Criminal Justice 2000 Series

Four volumes of expert commentary on criminality, crime, and criminal justice.

http://www.ojp.usdoj.gov/nij/pubs-sum/ cj2000.htm

CRIME AND SOCIAL STRUCTURE

Sociological theories emphasize the social aspects of human behavior, including the organization, structure, and culture of group life as well as the interactions that occur among individuals and groups. Theories of crime that focus on social structure are generally macrosociological. They emphasize social conditions and patterns that transcend the immediate social situation. Theories of crime that focus on social interaction explain crime in terms of social process and are generally microsociological. They emphasize how the immediate social situation shapes the behavior of participants, and is in turn shaped by it. This chapter focuses on social structure, the next on social process.

There are two strains of liberal thinking in criminology. The earliest, and most influential, emphasizes the behavior of criminal offenders and explains that behavior in terms of social structure, or in terms of social process. The second strain of liberal thinking deals more with the causes and consequences of the application of criminal labels to people and events. It should be emphasized at the outset that some theories of crime defy easy classification because they bridge the conventional distinction between structure and process. This is true of the social disorganization theories advanced by the Chicago School and it is also true of conflict theory. In the end, all criminological theories are saying something about the behavior of individuals, for it is individuals who make and enforce the criminal law or who behave in ways that violate it. The theories are grouped in different categories to emphasize their similarities and differences, and to show how they build upon each other, and how they compete. Chapters 12 and 14 will also examine some theories of crime that purport to be general theories and/or to integrate structure and process.

CRIME AND SOCIAL DISORGANIZATION

Sociological investigations of crime and delinquency have given considerable attention to the so-called "sins of cities" (Moore 1964, 905). The basic argument is that decaying urban environments generate high rates of crime and delinquency. Two monumental nineteenth-century studies of life in London helped draw attention to the relationship between the behavior of individuals and the physical and social space they occupy. Henry Mayhew's *London Labour and the London Poor* and Charles Booth's *Life and Labour of the People of London* were early contributions to what is now called the field of human ecology.

Beginning in the early 1900s, sociologists at the University of Chicago published a series of studies of life in Chicago. Under the guidance of Robert Park and E. W. Burgess, these studies were designed to document the belief that problems such as crime and delinquency resulted from **social disorganization**. Simply put, the idea is that the amount of crime in a community depends on the ability of the community to regulate itself (Bursik and Grasmick 1995). Social organization is maintained by a group's commitment to social rules; when this commitment breaks down, social control breaks down. Members of the Chicago School believed that this breakdown in social control could occur through ecological changes, as when communities experience rapid population change through social mobility and migration.

By examining voluminous data on the city of Chicago, Clifford Shaw and Henry McKay (1942) were able to confirm that certain areas of Chicago experienced relatively high rates of crime and delinquency and that these areas also showed the telltale signs of social disorganization. They were close to the central business district and, consequently, areas of population transition. These areas of high crime were also characterized by overcrowding, physical deterioration, concentrations of minority and foreign-born residents, concentrated poverty, lack of home ownership, lack of locally supported community organizations, and concentrations of unskilled and unemployed workers. Further analysis showed that these areas also had other problems: high rates of infant mortality, tuberculosis, mental disorder, and juvenile delinquency (Shaw and McKay 1942; Morris 1958).

Shaw (1931a, 387) summarized the links between ecological change, social disorganization, and the development of "delinquency areas" as follows:

> In the process of city growth, the neighborhood organizations, cultural institutions, and social standards

in practically all areas adjacent to the central business district and the major industrial centers are subject to rapid change and disorganization. The gradual invasion of these areas by industry and commerce, the continuous movement of the older residents out of the area and the influx of newer groups, the confusion of many divergent cultural standards, the economic insecurity of the families, all combine to render difficult the development of a stable and efficient neighborhood for the education and control of the child and the suppression of lawlessness.

One of Shaw and McKay's most important observations was that the relative levels of delinquency and crime in local communities tended to remain stable over many years, despite changing ethnic and racial composition (Bursik 1988, 524; Bursik and Grasmick 1993, 1995). Thus, a city area with high rates of delinquency compared to other areas would tend to remain that way, as would an area with low rates relative to another. They

Chicago in the late 1920s, shortly before Shaw and McKay published their major works on social disorganization and crime.

showed this to be true of Chicago over a period spanning several decades. Shaw and McKay argued that delinquent values and traditions were being passed from one generation of residents to another; in other words a form of cultural transmission was taking place. In Shaw and McKay's view, the only way to combat the tendency for areas to become permanently crime-prone was to develop neighborhood organizations that could help promote informal social controls, and encourage residents to look out for each other's welfare (Sampson 1986, 1987; Stark 1987).

Shaw and McKay and their colleagues at Chicago had a major influence on the development of sociological criminology. They not only showed how social organization and culture unite to influence social behavior, but they drew attention to the processes by which youthful residents adopt the criminal lifestyles of an area and thus reinforce them. Even though their theory is essentially a macrolevel explanation of variations in group rates of crime, they clearly believed that interactions between parents and children, and between neighborhood youths themselves, helped mediate the influences of structure and culture (Bursik 1988, 521). Indeed, Shaw spent many years helping youths find alternative solutions to their problems, and he persuaded former delinquents and crooks to help him reverse the spread of delinquent values and lifestyles. The resulting Chicago Area Project became a model for delinquency prevention efforts.

Social disorganization theory fell out of favor in the 1960s—few criminologists identified themselves with the perspective. Various reasons can be advanced for this decline in popularity. For some it was sufficient to point out that many youngsters do not become delinquent despite living in high crime areas. Others wondered whether crime and delinquency are not a part of social disorganization rather than a result of it. Furthermore, how could one explain the emergence of highly organized, cohesive youth gangs in neighborhoods that are supposedly so disorganized? Finally, there was concern that the social disorganization model diverts attention away from the delinquency and crime of middle-class neighborhoods and from nonstreet crimes such as price-fixing and the sale of unsafe products.

On the other hand, there are signs of a rebirth of interest in social disorganization theory (Bursik 1988,

2000). One of the more recent theories developed in the tradition of the Chicago School is Rodney Stark's "Theory of Deviant Places" (1987). Using human ecology theory and other classic Chicago School concepts, Stark's theory focuses on the following variables: density, poverty, mixed use, transience, and dilapidation. He argues that poor and densely populated neighborhoods are likely to be mixed-use, and people tend to move in and out of these neighborhoods regularly. This can result in less community surveillance, more opportunities to engage in crime, and people who are disenchanted, cynical, or apathetic about their neighborhood.

Neighborhoods that are dilapidated are also often stigmatized, for they signify disorder and sometimes seem attractive to those who may be seeking deviant opportunities. Furthermore, Stark (1987, 901–902) proposes the following:

- More successful and conventional people will resist moving into a stigmatized neighborhood.
- Stigmatized neighborhoods will tend to be overpopulated by the most demoralized kinds of people and suffer from lenient law enforcement, which may increase the incidence of crime and deviance.

Many of the basic propositions of social disorganization theory have been supported by recent scholarly research. For example, one study found that "busy places" in neighborhoods in Seattle have higher rates of violent crime (Rountree, Land, and Miethe 1994). A study of Chicago neighborhoods found that the higher the level of informal community social control, cohesion, and trust, the lower the rate of violence in that area (Sampson, Raudenbush, and Earls 1997, 922). This study also found that the more willingness on the part of people to help others in a community, the lower the level of violence in that area. There is also evidence to show that even nonintimates, or those removed from a person's daily or weekly routines, can also exercise considerable control over people's involvement in crime (Bursik 2000).

Finally, we should consider how the dramatic increase in U.S. imprisonment rates over the past few decades may be negatively affecting neighborhood and community social organization. In this vein, a very interesting theoretical argument has been proposed:

> High incarceration rates may contribute to rates of criminal violence by the way they contribute to such social problems as inequality, family life deterioration, economic and political alienation, and social disorganization ... [and] undermine social, political, and economic systems already weakened by the low levels of human and social capital produced under conditions such as high rates of poverty, unemployment, and crime.... The result is a reduction in social cohesion and a lessening of those communities' capacity for self-regulation. (Rose and Clear 1998, 441)

In sum, this argument proposes that imprisonment takes away fathers, mothers, neighbors, and workers from the very social relationships that are needed to keep community crime rates low. For example, children are less likely to be well-supervised if one parent, or even an older brother or sister is incarcerated; family members devastated by the imprisonment of one parent may move in and out of areas to be nearer to the prison; and the growth of collective-political action movements that need young, energetic members is inhibited due to overincarceration.

It has been observed that the imprisonment boom has taken its largest toll on poor African-American communities (Mauer 2000; Whitehead 2000). Figure 11.1 suggests that this is indeed the case. In the Washington, D.C. area, nearly half of all young African-American men are under some form of criminal justice control (Whitehead 2000), and a recent study by the National Council on Crime and Delinquency (2000) clearly shows that the juvenile justice system still treats minority juvenile offenders more harshly than whites. In addition to all the other social organization problems resulting from imprisonment, further problems may develop once the offender is released from prison. Offenders may come back to the community more jaded, aggressive, and with an internalization of the stigma of being an "ex-con" or "criminal" (as we discuss in Chapter 12). While this hypothesis awaits further empirical test, it is important to recognize that while some communities may benefit from the removal of certain people from their neighborhood (i.e., "weeding out bad apples"), those same communities may also pay a great price (including furthered social disorganization) because of harsh incarceration policies (Currie 1997; May 2000).

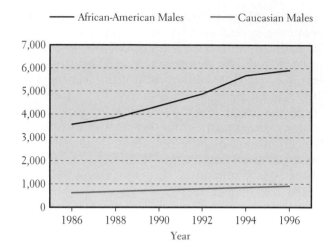

▲ FIGURE 11.1

Rate of African-American Males and Caucasian Males in Prison or Jail (per 100,000), 1986–1996

Compared to Caucasian males, African-American males have a much higher rate of imprisonment. From the social disorganization perspective, this further weakens community and familial solidarity, and leads to even further levels of social disorganization and crime.

Source: Kathleen Maguire and Anne L. Pastore, eds., *Sourcebook of Criminal Justice Statistics* (Washington, D.C.: U.S. Department of Justice, 1998), Table 6.24.

MERTON'S ANOMIE THEORY

Emile Durkheim's notion of *anomie* was extended and elaborated on by Robert K. Merton (1938, 1957), who made it a central feature of a *strain* theory of crime. According to Merton, a state of anomie exerts pressure on people to commit crime. While all societies establish institutionalized means, or rules, for the attainment of culturally supported goals, these means and goals are not always in a state of harmony or integration. The way the society or group is organized interferes with the attainment of valued goals by acceptable means for some of its members. A condition of anomie or strain therefore exists.

Looking at the United States in the 1930s, Merton saw an inordinate emphasis on material success, which was held up as achievable by all Americans. Not all segments of society, however, could realistically expect to have material success if they followed the rules of the game. Blacks and the lower classes were routinely excluded from access to legitimate means of achievement. The acceptable routes to success—a good education, a good job, the "right" background, promotions, special skills—typically were not routes open to them. Unfortunately, things are only marginally better today (see Farley 1998).

Strain is essentially the disjunction or lack of fit between socially desirable goals and the socially acceptable means to achieve those goals. Merton believes that various "modes of adaptation" are possible in response to the strain resulting from unrealized expectations: conformity, innovation, ritualism, retreatism, and rebellion (see Table 11.1). We will briefly discuss each of these adaptations to strain.

Many people will *conform*, simply accepting that they will never "make it big"—unless they win the lottery! Perhaps the "bite of conscience" (Wilson and Herrnstein 1985) holds them back from crime; perhaps they fear punishment; perhaps they have too much to lose, if not materially, then in terms of relationships with family and friends; perhaps they cannot recognize—or take advantage of—illegitimate opportunities. Merton prefers the idea that conformity reflects social acceptance of the rule of law.

Other people may engage in *ritualism*. They give up on the goals but continue to support the socially approved means. They cling "all the more closely to the safe routines and institutional norms" (Merton 1957, 151). Imagine the platoon leader who gives up on the apparently impossible task of taking the enemy position but berates his men for having dirty belt buckles, or the loyal corporate manager who gives up on being promoted himself but punishes his subordinates for not "playing the game."

Still others reject both means and goals. Such *retreatism* is an adaptation to anomic conditions in which people may even withdraw from society altogether. The inner-city heroin or crack addict is most often mentioned in this context. The drug-using, antiestablishment "hippies" of the 1960s and the short-lived commune movement also come to mind. On the other hand, some people substitute new sets of norms and goals, and Merton calls this adaptation *rebellion*. Unfortunately, the logical separation between these two modes of adaptation is unclear. For example, are the antiestablishment hippies retreatists or rebels? Can rebellion occur without retreatism?

The adaptation that Merton identifies most closely with crime is *innovation*. Innovators accept the goals, but they reject the institutional means and substitute illegal alternatives. Merton uses innovation to explain the relatively high rates of property crime among lower-class and minority segments of society. Their disadvantaged status coupled with the high cultural priority given to material success as a goal for all makes high rates of crime a "normal outcome" for those segments of society.

Merton's theory of anomic strain and crime had a profound influence on subsequent structural theories, despite some serious criticisms. In many ways his "theory" is merely a catalog of potential reactions to anomie: It does not tell us when to expect one mode of adaptation rather than another, or whether different segments of the population are

TABLE 11.1   Merton's Modes of Adaptation to Anomie

When confronted by a disjunction between legitimate means and socially approved goals—a condition of anomie, which produces strain—people may adapt in various ways. This table summarizes Merton's modes of adaptation.

ADAPTATION	SOCIALLY APPROVED GOALS	LEGITIMATE MEANS
Conformity	accept (+)	accept (+)
Innovation	accept (+)	reject (-)
Ritualism	reject (-)	accept (+)
Retreatism	reject (-)	reject (-)
Rebellion	reject and replace (±)	reject and replace (±)

Source: Adapted from Robert K. Merton, "Social Structure and Anomie," *American Sociological Review* 3 (1938): 672–682.

likely to select different adaptations. Katz (1988, 358, note 9) objects that Merton's theory is unconvincing as an explanation for "vandalism, the use of dope, intergroup fighting, and the character of initial experiences in property theft as sneaky thrills."

Another line of criticism repeats that directed at the social disorganization theory of Shaw and McKay: Too much is made of the high rates of crime officially observed among the lower classes. Even if the data are credible, the preoccupation with criminal behavior among the lower classes diverts theory and research from the behavior of other classes and from the power relations that exist between classes. More recent extensions of Mertonian strain theory, however, have been used to explain organizational crimes. Kauzlarich and Kramer (1998), for example, have specifically studied how state strain brings about innovation. They argue that state agencies use illegal means in order to achieve their operational goals, which may be legitimacy, national security, or political hegemony. For example, illegal human radiation experiments conducted by the U.S. government from 1940–1980 can be understood as the use of illegitimate means (violating international law and human rights) for the larger goal of winning the Cold War.

Another limitation of Merton's theory according to Messner and Rosenfeld (1996, 2000) is that there is no explanation of why the "success ethos" is so important in the United States. They argue that the larger U.S. *culture*, not simply its structure, prizes economic success over other forms of achievement. So, for example, good parenting and good grades in school are less valued because they produce no capital. Institutions such as the family, school, and community become visualized in economic terms, and potential informal social control mechanisms within the culture become sterile. Crime is then not so much a product of those who are unable to achieve the American Dream, but of those who are "locked in" to those values.

GENERAL STRAIN THEORY

Robert Agnew (1992) has redirected Merton's strain theory to the social-psychological (micro) level of analysis. Agnew's General Strain Theory (GST) starts with the assumption that negative relationships with others cause strain or stress in people's lives. Negative relationships are those "in which others are not treating the individual as he or she would like to be treated" (Agnew 1992, 50). According to Agnew, Mertonian strain theory relies too heavily on the relationships that prevent the individual from reaching positively valued goals. GST, however, considers this and two other sources of strain that may lead to crime and delinquency: (1) when other individuals remove or threaten to remove positively valued stimuli that one possesses, and (2) when others present or threaten to present a person with negatively valued stimuli (Agnew 1992, 50). Some examples might help clarify these sources of strain.

The first type of strain, the failure to achieve positively valued goals, suggests that people have in some way not met their goals and expectations, or have received unfair or inequitable outcomes in social relationships. Examples include not meeting one's expectation to earn good grades in school, wealth from working, and fair treatment by their parents, teachers, and peers. When others remove or threaten to remove things that a person positively values, that person is also likely to experience strain. Think of the kinds of stressful life events we encounter: Many people lose boyfriends, girlfriends, husbands, wives, and friends. How about when a child loses a parent? All of these negative events can place considerable stress on individuals, and may trigger involvement in crime. Finally, strain is also likely to develop when others present or threaten to present an individual with negative outcomes. Examples of this type of strain include a child who is abused, neglected, or otherwise criminally victimized (Agnew 1992). The child may deal with these negative relationships by attempting to escape the environment (e.g., running or staying away from home) or by exacting revenge upon the victimizers, who are usually family members. These different types of strain can overlap:

> [F]or example, the insults of a teacher may be experienced as adverse because they (1) interfere with the adolescent's aspirations for academic success, (2) result in the violation of a distributive justice rule such as equity, and (3) are conditioned negative stimuli and so are experienced as noxious in and of themselves. (Agnew 1992, 59)

Since most people probably experience these forms of strain, who is more likely to commit crime

Agnew's strain theory suggests that the removal of positive stimuli or the dissolution of close relationships causes strain. How kids deal with adversity and loss greatly impacts their future behavior, including their involvement in delinquency.

or delinquent acts because of the strain? Agnew suggests that it is those who do not *cope well* with the situations. Coping abilities, or adaptations, that moderate the effects of strain are things like the ability to "blow off," neutralize, or downplay the seriousness and/or significance of a stressful life event. For example, lowering one's standards for the accumulation of wealth or grade point average helps neutralize strain. Personality traits, temperament, and social learning and bonding variables ultimately, according to Agnew, help determine whether a person's adaptation to strain is criminal or not. The theory, therefore, complements leading criminological theories such as social control theory and social learning theory, discussed in Chapter 12 (Agnew 1992, 76). GST can also be melded with social disorganization theory, as Agnew (1999) has recently attempted to do in order to better understand community differences in crime rates.

Empirical tests of GST have generally confirmed the theory's value (Mazerolle 1998; Paternoster and Mazerolle 1994; White and Agnew 1992). Two recent studies have examined the theory's ability to predict gender differences in offending (Broidy and Agnew 1997; Mazerolle 1998). Both found that GST did not predict the differences in overall offending very well, but that it did account for some differences in violent offending by gender. Specifically, one study found that losing a parent or family member and having negative relationships with adults are more likely to be criminogenic for males but not females (Mazerolle 1998). This provides partial support to the notion that males tend to manifest anger and strain externally, while women more often direct these emotions internally. In this way and others, GST has been found to complement some varieties of feminist theory, discussed later in this chapter. Agnew's (1999) recent extension of GST to the community level of analysis is yet to be tested.

CULTURAL TRANSMISSION OF CRIME AND DELINQUENCY

As noted previously, ecological studies of crime and Merton's theory of anomie emphasized the high rates of crime officially observed among the poor. From 1940 to 1960, sociologists seemed preoccupied with explanations of criminal activity among the lower classes. Most of the theories produced in the period emphasized social structure, especially the ways in which the behavior of adolescents and young adults is shaped by the lifestyles and values to which they are exposed.

A number of theories focus on what is called the *delinquent subculture*. Any heterogeneous society is likely to have a parent, or dominant, culture and a variety of different subcultures. The dominant culture consists of the beliefs, attitudes, symbols, ways of behaving, meanings, ideas, values, and norms shared by those who regularly make up the membership of a society. Subcultures differ from the dominant culture and consist of the beliefs, values, and lifestyles shared by those members of society who belong to identifiable subgroups. For example, "Goth" kids, residents of a retirement community, homosexuals who have "come out," the hippies of the 1960s, and Polish-Americans who belong to clubs and organizations that emphasize their common heritage are *identifiable subgroups* whose members share a common subculture.

Some subcultures are merely different from the dominant culture, while others are in active opposition to it. Delinquent subcultures fit neither characterization exactly. According to Cloward and Ohlin (1960, 7), a delinquent subculture "is one in which certain forms of delinquent activity are essential for the performance of the dominant roles supported by the subculture. It is the central position accorded to specifically delinquent activity that distinguishes the delinquent subculture from other deviant subcultures [such as homosexual activists]." However, even in its support of delinquent activities, a delinquent subculture may nevertheless also share aspects of the dominant culture; for example, an emphasis on material possessions, or an acceptance of gender differences in social roles.

Subcultural theories of crime and delinquency begin with the assumption that people are socialized into the norms and values of the immediate groups to which they belong. In a sense, all people are conformists, but the values and norms with which they conform may be different from, or at odds with, those of the dominant culture, and the behaviors that result are sometimes illegal. In other words, some kinds of conformity turn out to be delinquent or criminal. So it is with the activities central to delinquent subcultures.

Cohen's Theory

One of the first sociologists to propose a subcultural explanation of crime—or, rather, delinquency—was Albert Cohen (1955). In *Delinquent Boys*, Cohen suggests that high rates of lower-class delinquency reflect a basic conflict between lower-class youth subculture and the dominant middle-class culture. The delinquent subculture arises as a reaction to the dominant culture, which is seen as discriminating against lower-class people. Told in school and elsewhere to strive for middle-class goals and to behave according to middle-class values (be orderly, clean, responsible, ambitious, and so forth), lower-class youth find that their socialization has not prepared them for the challenge. They become "status frustrated" as a result of their inability to meet middle-class standards, and in reaction turn to delinquent activities and form delinquency-centered groups.

Cohen describes the delinquency that results as nonutilitarian (e.g., stealing "for the hell of it"), malicious (enjoying the discomfort of others), and negativistic (taking pride in doing things because they are wrong by middle-class standards).

Cloward and Ohlin's Differential Opportunity Theory

Expanding on Merton and Cohen, sociologists Cloward and Ohlin (1960) developed a theory of delinquency and youth crime that incorporates the concept of opportunity structures. The authors point out that society provides both legitimate and illegitimate opportunities for behavior, and these opportunities (whether legitimate or not) meet different kinds of needs—some help a person achieve status (and with it, membership in the middle class), and others help a person achieve economic success. Not all youths aspire to the same things, and Cloward and Ohlin believe that those youth who aspire to economic success but are denied legitimate opportunities to achieve it are at greatest risk of becoming embroiled in gang subcultures.

Cloward and Ohlin's theory is more than a rehash of strain theory because the introduction of opportunity variables enables them to explain why a particular form or type of deviance arises in response to structural strain (see Cullen 1983b, 41–45). While anomie theory predicts that strain is a motivating force behind deviance and crime, it does not explain why one form of deviance (say, retreatism) occurs rather than another (such as innovation). Cloward and Ohlin (in Cullen 1983, 44) make the following argument:

> The pressures that lead to deviant patterns do not necessarily determine the particular pattern of deviance that results.... Several delinquent adaptations are conceivably available in any given situation; what, then, are the determinants of the process of selection? Among delinquents who participate in subcultures, for example, why do some become apprentice criminals rather than street fighters or drug addicts? These are distinctive subcultural adaptations; an explanation of one may not constitute an explanation of the other.

Applying opportunity theory to the world of business (conventionally thought to be a far cry from delinquency), Braithwaite (1989a, 33) shows how a criminal subculture of price-fixing might arise:

> Let us imagine, for example, that the government suddenly decides to double sales tax on beer in an effort to discourage consumption. The brewing companies might find as a consequence that legitimate opportunities are blocked for them to achieve their profit or growth targets. They might get together at trade association meetings to curse the government, to begin to suggest to each other that they have no choice but to conspire to fix prices, in other words to fashion a criminal subculture which rationalizes price fixing by blaming the government for it, appealing to the higher loyalty of saving the jobs of their workers, and which evolves new criminal conduct norms for the industry.

Cloward and Ohlin identify three delinquent subcultures to which lower-class youths may belong and that help structure a youngster's response to the absence of legitimate opportunities. These subcultures are criminal, conflict, or retreatist.

Criminal subcultures are characterized by illegal money-making activities and often provide a stepping-stone toward adult criminal careers. They tend to arise in slum areas where relatively well-organized age hierarchies of criminal involvement exist. This condition provides youth with adult criminal role models and encourages their recruitment into money-making crime. Also, the existence of adult roles such as "fixer" and "fence," which bridge the worlds of legitimate enterprise and crime, helps facilitate illegal money-making activities as an alternate route to economic success.

Conflict subcultures are dominated by gang fighting and other violence. They arise in disorganized slum areas with weak social controls, an absence of institutionalized channels (legal or otherwise) to material goals, and a predominance of personal failure. Violence is a route to status as well as a release for pent-up frustrations.

Finally, *retreatist* subcultures are marked by the prevalence of drug use and addiction. This subculture arises as an adaptation for some lower-class youth who have failed in both the criminal and conflict subcultures, or have not successfully accessed either the legitimate or illegitimate opportunity structures. Like Merton's retreatists, they disengage from the competitive struggle for success goals.

Miller's Lower-Class "Focal Concerns"

The works of Cohen and of Cloward and Ohlin focus mainly on youthful gangs, and to that extent they ignore a tremendous amount of delinquency and crime that is not gang-oriented. Their work also focuses on the organization and culture of the lower class, and to that extent it may not apply to lower-class behavior in other societies.

The same observations can be made of Walter Miller's (1958) well-known study of youth gangs, a study in which he delineates the special themes or issues prominent in lower-class youth culture. The material and social deprivations that are commonplace among the urban lower class contribute to the development of special themes, or **focal concerns**, as Miller calls them. Focal concerns command a high degree of emotional commitment. Among the focal concerns identified by Miller are "trouble" (a concern to avoid entanglements with the law), "toughness" (an ability to handle physical and emotional challenges), "smartness" (being able to con, hustle, or outwit others), "autonomy" (remaining free from domination or control by others), and "excitement" (getting kicks, avoiding the routine and the monotonous).

Some of the activities shaped by these focal concerns are delinquent or criminal, for the law reflects and supports the dominant standards of middle-class society. But even when given a choice not to engage in delinquency or crime, youngsters will often find the "deviant" activity more attractive because the norms of groups with whom they identify, as well as peer group pressures, point to it as a means of acquiring prestige, status, and respect.

The social structural theories reviewed thus far purport to explain the relationship between the organization or structure of society and the behavior of its people. The almost exclusive focus on lower-class delinquency obviously limits the scope of the theories, and none of them was initially advanced as a general theory.

Unfortunately, one of the undesirable (and probably unintended) consequences of the lower-class emphasis has been the respectability it has given the stereotypical view of crime and criminals. This view associates being criminal with being a member of the lower class. Interestingly, the considerable media publicity given to crimes by members of the middle and especially the upper classes sensationalizes their crimes, and by doing so seems only to confirm the idea that "real" crime is committed by the poor, the unemployed, and the disreputable. The misbehaviors of "real" criminals are, by definition, unsensational. We expect crime from the "criminal classes." The objection to the criminological emphasis on lower-class crime is essentially that it lends the weight of "expert opinion" to this popular stereotype. If this (i.e., the lower class) is where criminologists look to find crime, then it must be where crime really is!

CRIME AND INEQUALITY

A common thread runs through social structural theories of crime, a thread that explains to a large extent why they have been almost exclusively theories of lower-class crime. These theories see crime as a consequence of inequality in the distribution of material resources. Lack of economic opportunities, the social disorganization of inner-city neighborhoods, the subculture of youth gangs, and unrealized expectations of affluence are hallmarks of inequality. They are the products of a social organization that puts some people at a disadvantage in the competition for scarce resources. Crime is therefore an unexceptional consequence of economic, social, and political disadvantage.

This common thread reflects an assumption that is made about human nature: Human beings are basically good people. When they become "bad," it is because they are pushed or pulled into crime by adverse conditions. If the lot of the lower classes was improved, there would be less crime. Since food, clothing, and shelter are material resources, the bettering of conditions must begin with economic change that distributes material resources to segments of society where they are most needed. This is a major policy implication of social structural theories.

This implication poses a rather awkward dilemma: If criminological theory and research follow the traditional focus of social structural theories, criminologists will lend credence to stereotypical views of crime that emphasize its lower-class character. On the other hand, if theory and research do not address the lower-class connection, criminologists will be ignoring the real pains and problems of life at the bottom of a class society. In his classic book, Elliott Currie (1985, 160) reminds us that "harsh inequality is not only morally unjust but also enormously destructive of human personality and of social order. Brutal conditions breed brutal behavior. To believe otherwise [is] to [ignore] ... the genuine social disaster wrought by the extremes of economic inequality ... tolerated in the United States."

Structural theories take into account the relationship between economic inequality and crime.

Ethnographies of poverty and crime such as those by Hagedorn (1988) and Anderson (1990, 1999) illustrate with real life stories the profound impact that so-called *capital disinvestment processes* over the past few decades have had on the economic fortunes of inner-city youth, especially blacks and Hispanics (see also Petras and Davenport 1991). According to Hagan (1994, Chapter 3), residential segregation, concentrations of poverty, and recent increases in race-linked inequality have encouraged youths to view crime as a "short-term adaptive form of recapitalization." Illegal markets, especially drug dealing, have become a major part of the subsistence activities of many inner-city youths. Yet this does not mean that these youths and their adult counterparts have rejected conventional labor markets as a preferred means of subsistence. Quite the opposite, in fact. Hagedorn (1994, 216), for example, found in Milwaukee that most of the 236 underclass adult gang members he interviewed "are still struggling to hold onto a conventional orientation to life."

Let us, however, reconsider another view, one that takes strain theories to task, particularly the version developed by Merton. The argument is basically that inequality theories explain far less of the motivation for crime than sentimentality has dictated. Thus, Jack Katz (1988, 313–316) writes the following:

> The problem for Merton and materialistic theory is not simply with some youthful "gang" activity. There is now strong evidence that a high proportion of those who go on to especially "serious," "heavy," "career" involvements in criminality start in early adolescence, long before job opportunities could or, in a free social order, should become meaningful considerations.... So, a lot of juvenile forms of violent crime and an important segment of serious adult crime do not fit the sentimentality of materialism.... None of this argument denies the validity of the recurrent correlation between low socioeconomic status or relative lack of economic opportunity, on the one hand, and violent and personal property crime on the other. The issue is the causal significance of this background for deviance. A person's material background will not determine his intent to commit acquisitive crime, but a person, whether or not he is intent on acquisitive crime, is not likely to be unaware of his circumstances. Instead of reading into ghetto poverty an unusually strong motivation to become deviant, we may understand the concentration of robbery among ghetto residents as being due to the fact that for people in economically more promising circumstances, it would literally make no sense—it would virtually be crazy—to commit robbery....

Conflict, Crime, and Criminality

The social and economic inequities to which social structural theories draw attention are central to conflict theory. The conflict perspective sees a society shaped by conflicts among people who have competing self-interests.

Even though at any time a society may seem to agree on basic values and goals, the existence of scarce resources and the tendency for them to be allocated unequally means that someone (or some group) is benefiting at the expense of someone else. People on the "losing end" may not recognize or admit that their interests are in conflict with the interests of others, when in fact they are. As we pointed out in Chapter 10, during the nineteenth century Karl Marx and Friedrich Engels spent a great deal of energy trying to point out such unrecognized conflicts.

Even though the struggle over scarce resources may be unrecognized or unacknowledged, conflict theorists believe it is historic and ubiquitous. It usually consists of a struggle over three related things: money, power, and influence. Those who have more of them try to keep things the way they are; those who have less of them favor change so that they can obtain a bigger share. The groups with wealth, power, and influence are favored in the conflict precisely because those resources put them in a dominant position. It is the "haves" rather than the "have-nots" who make the rules, control the content and flow of ideas and information, and design (and impose) the penalties for nonconformity. Dominance means people are in a position to promote their self-interest, even at the expense of others.

Sometimes the struggle over scarce resources is blatant and bloody, but more often it is subtle and restrained. Conflict theorists point to various factors as part of the complex reasons for the restraint. For example, by controlling ideas and information, the dominant group is able to promote beliefs and values that support the existing order. In this way, the disadvantaged classes in society may develop what Marx and Engels (1947) called "false consciousness": a belief that prevailing social conditions are in their interest, when in fact they are not. Marx and Engels (1947, 39) illustrate how this happens in the case of law. As discussed in the last chapter, law is presented to the masses as "the will of the people," and this "juridical illusion" undermines the development of opposition and resistance among the disadvantaged. People are likely to feel uncomfortable challenging a law that they believe reflects public consensus. In reality, law reflects the interests of the ruling class, according to Marx and Engels.

A second way that the struggle over scarce resources is kept in check is through the *institutionalization* of conflict. Special mechanisms such as courts, tribunals, and (in modern times) arbitration and civil rights hearings are set up to settle disputes. Disputes between individuals and groups are often conflicts over the distribution of scarce resources. When institutionalized avenues of settling disputes exist, the underlying struggle tends to be moderated and obscured. Aggrieved parties in the immediate dispute are pacified if not by talk of "justice," then by the emphasis on procedures. Nowhere is this more evident than in the realm of crime, where victims often experience a complete loss of purpose as they face interminable delays and the intricacies of judicial procedure.

The *consensus view* (functionalist perspective) mentioned in previous chapters sees law and other political arrangements as useful for society as a whole, which justifies their existence. *Conflict theorists*, on the other hand, see them as useful for the dominant group(s), and perhaps even harmful to other groups or to the larger society. Law and politics protect the interests of the powerful, who in turn resist efforts to change them. It might be illustrative to consider how a conflict theorist might view the crime of rape.

RAPE LAWS: AN ILLUSTRATION OF CONFLICT   In the first place, far from meeting the needs of society as a whole, rape laws have historically served the interests of males, the dominant group, and have actually victimized the women they are ostensibly designed to protect. While there is clearly broad agreement that rape should be a crime (a consensus that has probably existed for centuries), we saw in Chapter 4 that rape laws have been written and enforced in such a way that males benefit.

For example, some criminal codes do not recognize rape in marriage, and in most jurisdictions, rape is a narrowly defined offense and successful prosecution depends as much on the victim's behavior as on the attacker's.

Second, conflict theorists are likely to view rape not merely as an unfortunate consequence of otherwise useful arrangements (such as dating), but as a manifestation of unequal power relations among males and females. Indeed, many scholars believe that most rape is an assertion of male control and domination. Other writers (e.g., Russell 1983), argue that rape extends patriarchy into the most intimate and private realm: Men not only control how women behave in general; they also control how their bodies will be used (see also Messerschmidt 1986, 130–156).

TURK'S CONFLICT THEORY   Austin Turk (1966, 1969) has developed a conflict theory of criminality, and his work illustrates many of the points made earlier. What makes Turk's work distinctive is his emphasis on authority and power relations rather than on economic inequality.

Turk begins by rejecting the conception of crime as behavior, arguing instead that crime is a status acquired when those with authority to create and enforce legal rules (lawmakers, police, prosecuting attorneys, judges) apply those rules to others (the "subjects" in authority relations). He then constructs a theory to explain this process of criminalization. Turk believes that criminology needs a theory "stating the conditions under which cultural and social differences between authorities and subjects will probably result in conflict, the conditions under which criminalization will probably occur in the course of conflict, and the conditions under which the degree of deprivation associated with becoming a criminal will probably be greater or lesser" (1969, 53).

Turk hypothesizes that conflict between groups is most likely when authorities and subjects disagree about a particular activity, but the actions of both groups (social norms) correspond with what they each think ought to happen (cultural norms). For example, if the authorities hold that marijuana use is wrong and refrain from using it themselves, but a group of subjects holds that marijuana use is okay and they use it, then conflict is likely because there is no room for compromise. In such a case, Turk argues, the authorities are likely to resort to coercion in order for their view to prevail. Conflict is least likely when neither authorities nor subjects act in accordance with their beliefs: Neither group is sufficiently committed to a value or belief to make an issue out of it. Other factors can affect the probability of conflict, including the degree to which subjects who resist are organized and the level of their sophistication. Conflict is more likely when norm resisters are poorly organized and unsophisticated.

Given the existence of conflict, the probability of criminalization depends on power differentials between authorities and subjects and on the realism of moves (i.e., tactical skills) employed by opposing parties. Criminalization is more likely when the power difference favors authorities and the moves adopted by resisters are unrealistic. Examples of unrealistic moves are those that (1) increase the visibility of an attribute or behavior perceived by authorities as offensive; (2) draw attention to additional offensive attributes or violate even more significant norms upheld by authorities; and (3) increase the level of consensus among authorities, for example, by turning opposition to a particular rule into an attack on the whole system; or (4) increase the power differences in favor of the enforcers (Turk 1969, 72).

Turk's theory has not been tested as much as other theories reviewed in this chapter, but one of the very few empirical studies found considerable support for the notion that poor organization and a lack of sophistication among norm resisters tend to produce conflict. However, the more specific claims of Turk regarding the relative importance of organization and sophistication were not supported (Greenleaf and Lanza-Kaduce 1995).

Further research is needed, but we should note that Turk's theory represents one of the finest examples of theory construction in criminology. Foremost among these issues is the nature of the relationship between those who create, interpret, and enforce legal rules and those who are subject to them. Crime has no objective reality apart from the meanings attached to it, and criminality is an expression of those meanings. As Turk makes clear, the structure of authority relations must be included in a comprehensive theory of criminalization (for a more recent statement along similar lines, see Chambliss and Zatz 1993).

Karl Marx wrote little about crime, but his critique of capitalism spurred others to apply his theories to crime. Radical criminology borrows from his theories on class struggle, the role of the capitalist state, and the impact of work and economic status on behavior and attitudes.

Marxist Criminological Theory

Turk's theory focuses on authority relations and explains how it is that some people are labeled as criminals. Marxist theorists go further, casting conflicts of authority and criminal labeling within a general theory of political economy having roots in the work of Karl Marx.

WILLEM BONGER ON CRIME AND ECONOMIC CONDITIONS As discussed in the previous chapter, Marx himself wrote little about crime. However, an intellectual follower of Marx, Willem Bonger, applied some of Marx's arguments to crime in capitalistic societies. In *Criminality and Economic Conditions* (published in English in 1916), Bonger observed that capitalistic societies appear to have considerably more crime than do other societies. Furthermore, as capitalism developed, crime rates increased steadily.

Under capitalism, Bonger argued, the characteristic trait of humans is self-interest (egoism). Given the emphasis on profit maximization and competition, and the fact that social relations are class-structured and geared to economic exchange, capitalistic societies spawn intraclass and interclass conflicts as individuals seek to survive and prosper. Interclass conflict is one-sided, however, since those who own and control the means of production are in a position to coerce and exploit their less fortunate neighbors. Criminal law, as one instrument of coercion, is used by the ruling class to protect its position and interests. Criminal law "is principally constituted according to the will of" the dominant class, and "hardly any act is punished if it does not injure the interests of the dominant class" (1969, 379–380). Behavior threatening the interests of the ruling class is designated as criminal.

Since social relations are geared to competition, profit seeking, and the exercise of power, altruism is subordinated to egoistic tendencies. These tendencies lead, in Bonger's view, to a weakening of internal restraint. Both the bourgeoisie and proletariat become prone to crime. The working class is subject to further demoralization, however, because of its inferior exchange position and its exploitation at the hands of the ruling class. "Long working hours and monotonous labor brutalize those who are forced into them; bad housing conditions contribute also to debase the moral sense, as do the uncertainty of existence, and, finally, absolute poverty, the frequent consequence of sickness and unemployment" (1969, 195).

In Bonger's view, economic conditions that induce egoism, coupled with a system of law creation and enforcement controlled by the capitalist class, account for (1) higher crime rates in capitalistic societies than in other societies, (2) crime rates increasing with industrialization, and (3) the working class character of official crime.

SAMPLES OF MARXIST CRIMINOLOGY: 1970S TO THE PRESENT   In the United States, the 1970s witnessed the first systematic statements on crime from a Marxist perspective. Many works by Marx (such as the *Economic and Philosophic Manuscripts* of 1844) became widely available to U.S. scholars at this time. We will now review several Marxist-inspired theories.

According to David Gordon (1971, 1973), most crime is a rational response to the structure of institutions found in capitalistic societies. Crime is "a means of survival in a society within which survival is never assured" (1971, 59). Gordon identifies three types of crime in the United States as the best examples of this rationality: ghetto crime; organized crime; and corporate, or white-collar, crime. These types offer a chance at survival, status, and respect in a society geared to competitive forms of social interaction and characterized by substantial inequalities in the distribution of social, economic, and political resources.

Involvement in different types of crime is explained by class position. Those in the upper socioeconomic classes have access to jobs in which paper transactions, large amounts of money, and unobtrusive communication are important features. Illegal opportunities are manifest in the many forms of white-collar crime. Those in the lower classes, especially those who are "raised in poverty," do not have easy access to money or nonviolent means to manipulate it. Accordingly, illegal activities tend to involve taking things by force or physical stealth.

Gordon sees duality in American justice in that the state tends to ignore certain kinds of crime—most notably corporate and white-collar crime—and concerns itself "incessantly" with crimes among the poor. According to Gordon, this duality is understandable only if one views the state through the radical perspective. First of all, government in a capitalistic society exists primarily to serve the interests of the capitalist class, and preservation of the system itself is the priority. So long as power and profits are not undermined, the offenses that tend in general to harm members of other classes receive little interest. Second, even though offenses of the poor tend to harm others who are poor, they are collectively viewed as a threat to the stability of the system and the interests of the ruling class. Furthermore, an aggressive lower class is a dangerous class, and the spread of ghetto crime (conveniently identified with African-Americans) to other parts of the nation's cities heightens the fears of the affluent classes who are in a position to influence policy. Gordon's critical approach provides a framework for explaining both the status of criminality and the behavior of the criminal (see also Spitzer 1975).

Richard Quinney is one of the most prolific and well-respected criminologists in the world. While Quinney has written on crime from a number of theoretical perspectives (e.g., social construction-ism, peacemaking), here we will consider his Marxist theory of crime first published as *Class, State, and Crime* in 1977. This work is really not a theory of crime causation, but a call for the use of Marxism in understanding law, justice, and crime.

Quinney starts with a number of presupposi-tions. First, understanding the meaning of crime in capitalist society must take into account how capitalist economics develop, how "systems of domination and repression" operate for the bene-fit of the capitalist class through the capitalist state, and an understanding of the forms of accommo-dation and resistance to capitalism. Additionally, Quinney (in classic Marxist form) writes that our ideas about crime and justice are largely created through our experiences in a capitalist society, and that justice is "an ideological and practical instru-ment in the class struggle" (1979, 6). Crime, ac-cording to Quinney, is a manifestation of class struggle as well:

> Much criminal behavior is of a parasitical nature, including burglary, robbery, drug dealing, and hus-tling of various sorts ... the behavior, although pursued out of the need to survive, is a reproduc-tion of the capitalist system. (p. 61)

Crimes such as murder, assault, and rape, he con-tinues, often stem from those who are already "brutalized by the conditions of capitalism" (p. 61). The solution to crime, according to Quinney and others working from this perspective, involves a fundamental restructuring of society on socialist principles (Quinney 1979).

Quinney viewed many criminologists as implicit agents of the capitalist state, for the discipline "seeks to control anything that threatens the capitalist sys-tem of production and its social relations" (p. 176). What Quinney meant is that by divorcing the study of crime from the study of domination, class, and capitalism, criminologists are involved in reproduc-ing the inequality caused by capitalism. Many mod-ern criminologists have taken issue with this claim, but from a Marxist view, it is defensible. Quinney's version of criminology at this time was clearly an extension of the work of Marx and Engels.

At about the same time, another Marxist-in-spired conceptualization of crime was offered by William Chambliss (1975). Chambliss argues the following:

- Acts are criminal because it is in the interests of the ruling class to so define them.
- The lower classes are labeled criminal and the bourgeoisie is not so labeled because the bour-geoisie's control of the means of production gives them control of the State and law en-forcement as well.
- Socialist and capitalist societies should have significantly different crimes rates since class conflict will be less in socialist societies.

In a similar vein, Steven Spitzer (1975, 352) ar-gued that people become candidates for formal so-cial control in a capitalist society when they "disturb, hinder, or call into question any of the following":

- Capitalist modes of appropriating the product of human labor (theft)
- The social conditions under which capitalist production takes place (those unable or un-willing to perform labor)
- Patterns of distribution and consumption in capitalist society (drug use)
- The process of socialization for productive and nonproductive roles (youths who refuse schooling or traditional family life)
- The ideology that supports the functioning of capitalist society (revolutionaries and other political deviants)

Many of these Marxist accounts have been crit-icized as overly instrumentalist. Instrumental Marxists, of which there are very few left, were economic determinists, believing that capitalism, capitalist interests, and the protection of capital causes crime and determines the content of crim-inal justice and law. Indeed, a major problem with the instrumentalist treatment of the structural sources of crime is its vision of the ruling class it-self. Sometimes the image conjured up is of a small band of powerful individuals in constant touch with one another who determine the destinies of all. At other times the image suggested a category broad enough to include almost anybody. Some early Marxists also portrayed those whose criminal actions were political as victimized prisoners of circumstance whose crimes were not their responsibility. Some radicals were against short-term reforms of the criminal justice system because such actions would undermine the militant opposition necessary for a socialist revolution.

As the years passed, Marxist criminology began to appreciate the insights of other theories of crime and more refined application of Marx's ideas.

David Greenberg (1977) developed an explanation of juvenile delinquency that focused on teenager's exclusion from the labor market. Perhaps the most compelling part of Greenberg's theory is that, since children and teenagers do not normally engage in "serious work," their ability to achieve status through money is problematic. Some parents, of course, have neither the means nor the desire to buy their children all the makeup, clothes, toys, concert tickets, and cars that youths might employ to raise their social status amongst peers. Youths, then, because they are often not capable of buying these items, might turn to delinquency to upgrade their lifestyle. While Greenberg's theory is far more complex than this, you can see how the lack of participation in a capitalist labor market might be connected to crime.

Another influential Marxist theory of juvenile delinquency was developed by Mark Colvin and John Pauly in 1983. Juvenile delinquency, they argued, begins with parenting. While this does not seem all that radical, they argued that parenting styles are influenced by people's relationships and experiences at work. They argue first that many delinquents come from working class families, where the breadwinners are employed in "dead end" jobs (so-called "Fraction I" jobs) and are subject to coercion, threats, and the possibility of dismissal at any time. Such jobs include nonunionized industrial, textile, and agricultural work. Workers in this category tend to be highly alienated from their jobs and this tends to carry over at home. Such parents are likelier to be punitive (sometimes physically), inconsistent, and generally more abusive than parents employed in other jobs. As a result of this type of parenting, children may become alienated from their parents, which leads to a greater likelihood of alienation at school and the association with other alienated peers. Along with the disadvantages of their class position, the table then becomes set for the formulation of delinquent attitudes and behavior.

Bohm (1998) has suggested that more workers today are employed in Fraction I jobs, and if Colvin and Pauly's theory is correct, higher rates of alienation and consequently criminal violence by juveniles might be expected.

Marxist criminology has matured immensely in the 1990s. Perhaps the best illustration of this change is found in Chambliss' **structural contradictions theory** (Chambliss and Zatz 1993). Rejecting theories that argue that the capitalist mode of production exclusively determines law, and by implication crime, the argument is made that every society attempts to resolve conflicts and dilemmas caused by fundamental contradictions. The creation of law, then, is more complicated than the ruling class plotting against the interests of the working class (see Figure 11.2). The basic contradiction within capitalism is between labor and capital. This contradiction

> produces conflicts between workers and capitalists, and for the state it creates a set of dilemmas. Should the state represent only the interests of capitalists, the conflicts will increase in intensity, with workers pitted against the state.... Were the state to side with the workers ... the system would likewise collapse and a new social order would have to be constructed. Faced with this dilemma, officials of the state attempt to resolve the conflict by passing laws, some which represent the interests of capitalists and some the interests of workers. (Chambliss and Zatz 1993, 10)

A major goal of the capitalist state has been to promote capital accumulation, and the state's regulatory function "must not be so severe as to diminish substantially the contribution of large corporations to growth in output and employment" (Barnett 1981, 7; Chambliss and Zatz 1993). For example, while state regulatory agencies have been created to help protect workers (Occupational Safety and Health Administration), the environment (Environmental Protection Agency), and consumers (Consumer Product Safety Commission), these agencies generally do not undermine an industry's fundamental contributions to the functional requirements of the economy (Matthews and Kauzlarich 2000). Sometimes regulatory laws are strictly enforced and sometimes they are not, but ultimately the laws will not be created or enforced if they seriously compromise capitalist accumulation.

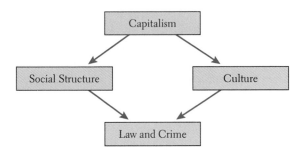

Instrumental Marxist Approach: Capitalism and capitalist interests determine the particular form of institutions, organizations, ideology, and social processes. Law is used to control the proletariat and to shield the crimes of the bourgeoisie.

Structural Marxist Approach: Capitalism and capitalist interests shape institutions, organizations, ideology, and social processes, which then further shape the political economy of capitalism. Law and crime are strongly influenced by the interests of the economy, not simply elites conspiring to control the proletariat.

▲ FIGURE 11.2
Instrumental versus Structural Marxist Criminological Theories

For in depth discussions of these perspectives, see Raymond J. Michalowski (1985) and William Chambliss and Marjorie Zatz (1993).

Marxist criminological research, not just theory, has also matured, although it has not grown at the rate many expected. Good research does exist, however. For example, Raymond Michalowski and Susan Carlson (1999) have shown that unemployment rates and new court admissions to prison can be linked to swings and qualitative changes in the U.S. capitalist economy. These changes include shifts in the productive dimension of the overall economy, the workforce, and various state interventions. Thus,

> periods with high unemployment, deteriorating job quality, low social-welfare benefits, and a growing surplus population of young, disaffected,

unemployed men … will generate a greater reliance on punitive strategies than periods that also may have relatively high levels of crime and unemployment but that also have improving job quality and/or relatively high levels of alternative income replacement or public-work provision for surplus population. (Michalowski and Carlson 1999, 227)

Left Realism

Several years ago British criminologists Jock Young and Roger Matthews started to systematically critique some radical Marxist criminological theories. Young and Matthews proposed that the "left idealism" of the radical perspective be replaced by "**left realism**." According to Young (1986, 1997), left idealism has tended to downplay the severity of crime and the fact that it is most often intraclass and intraracial. Rick Matthews (2001) explains it as follows:

> While not ignoring crimes of the powerful, new left realists have taken the position that the effects of street crime are both serious and real, that the criminal class is not revolutionary, and that critical (i.e., Marxian, conflict, feminist, and radical) criminologists must pay attention to it. What ties new left realism to Marxian criminology, however, is its emphasis on understanding crime within the larger political economy.

In addition, Young charges that left idealism has failed to build on past theories of criminal etiology and in consequence has failed in its theoretical mission to explain crime. For example, Young writes the following:

> There is no evidence that absolute deprivation (e.g., unemployment, lack of schooling, poor housing, and so forth) leads automatically to crime. Realist criminology points to relative deprivation in certain *conditions* as being the major causes of crime; i.e., when people experience a level of unfairness in their allocation of resources and utilize individualistic means to attempt to right this condition…. To say that poverty in the present period breeds crime is not to say that all poor people are criminals. Far from it: Most poor people are perfectly honest and many wealthy people commit crimes. Rather, it is to say that the rate of crime is higher in certain parts of society under certain conditions. (Young 1997, 30–31)

Young (1986, 25) believes that the central tasks of radical criminology still remain: "to create an adequate explanation of crime, victimization, and the reaction of the state."

The alternative—realist criminology—deals with that agenda while uncovering the reality of crime, "its origins, its nature, and its impact" (Young 1986, 21). Official data and research is not be rejected out of hand, nor will current definitions of crimes and their severity constrain the realist's search for this reality (Matthews 1986, 8). Left realism emphasizes going beyond appearances that pass as reality. A "central tension" in left realism is working both "in" and "against" the state. The question is this: How can the victimization and suffering of crime, especially among the lower classes, be reduced without extending the coercive and bureaucratic apparatus of the state? (Matthews 1986, 14; also see Schwartz and DeKeseredy 1997).

Like other social structural perspectives, one of the central ideas of realist criminology leads to the lower classes. But rather than looking there only for offenders, the realists see the lower class as a victim of crime "from all sides" (Young 1986, 23). The lower class generally, and racial minorities in particular, are doubly vulnerable to crime because they are victims of predatory street crimes as well as white-collar crimes: They are victims of the poor and the powerful (Young 1997, 2000).

In the tradition of both left realism and strain theory, Elliott Currie (1997) has recently made a number of theoretical observations about crime in *market societies*. These types of societies (e.g., the United States and Great Britain) are dominated by the pursuit of personal economic gain *in all facets of life*. This one-dimensional motivation comes at the expense of people's interest and ability to invest in powerful social, cultural, and human forces (so-called social capital) that are known to limit the amount of violence in any given society. Profound economic inequality and marginalization as well as the lack of stable and rewarding jobs are sure signs of market societies. Also, one finds that people have little or marginal interest in furthering the solidarity and integration of communities, neighborhoods, and families in market societies.

According to Currie (1997), market societies are *criminogenic*—they provide fertile grounds for crime to flourish—in a number of ways. First, while market economies like the United States can produce lots of jobs, many are low-paying and without benefits. So, even though the unemployment rate in the United States is currently quite low, many people are working very hard for very little. This continues to produce economic and social inequalities that, as we pointed out earlier, are positively related to the overall crime rate. Second, market societies tend to have limited formal and informal social supports. For example, the strains between family and work are profound for many working people. There is little formal support by employers or the government to provide paid parental leave, quality universal health care, or to do something about the disintegration of neighborhoods and communities. Third, market societies often place "competition and consumption over the values of community, contribution, and work" (Currie 1997, 161). We should therefore expect that in a "dog eat dog" world, people will care less about others' well-being, and not caring about other people will make it easier to victimize them. Fourth, Currie believes that it is possible that the amount of firearm violence in the United States could be reduced with more sensible gun regulation. The United States leads the advanced industrialized world in the rate of gun crime and violence—it also has the weakest national regulations on the sale and possession of guns. Finally, Currie notes that, at least in the United States, the lack of alternative political discussion leads people to believe that there is nothing that can be done about social problems like crime. Crime is thus easily divorced from its larger structural roots, which in turn lessens people's ability to envision a safer and less violent society.

Left realism is surely here to stay, for it provides a more holistic and richer approach to understanding the links between crime and the economy. In fact, the approach may soon be as recognizable as any other approach to criminological theory discussed in this chapter.

Varieties of Feminist Criminology

Feminism as a theory, perspective, and methodology has challenged many of the biases of traditional academic disciplines, including criminology. For years criminologists were mostly males who studied males, and therefore very *androcentric* (male-centered) (Flavin 1998). While there are many different forms of feminist criminology, at the most basic level **feminism** in criminology is about centering gender and its relationship to lawmaking, lawbreaking, and reactions to crime (Iadicola and Shupe 1998, 78; Daly and Chesney-Lind 1988). Several years ago Kathleen Daly and Meda Chesney-Lind (1988) published a landmark paper on feminism and criminology. In that paper, they identified five elements of feminist thought that distinguish it from other forms of social and political thought:

1. Gender is not a natural fact but a complex social, historical, and cultural product.

2. Gender and gender relations order social life and social institutions in fundamental ways.

3. Gender relations and constructs of masculinity and femininity are not symmetrical but are based on an organizing principle of men's superiority and social and political economic dominance over women.

4. Systems of knowledge reflect men's views of the natural and social world.

5. Women should be at the center of intellectual inquiry, not peripheral, invisible or appendages to men (Daly and Chesney-Lind 1988, 108).

These points suggest that a small physiological difference at birth between males and females (that is, our sex) becomes the basis for drastically different expectations and socialization throughout the life course. Open almost any introductory sociology textbook (e.g., Farley 1998) and read the chapter on gender. There you will find overwhelming evidence of the significance of (a) *gender role socialization*, the teaching of girls to be feminine and boys to be masculine, and (b) *gender inequality*, the differences in political, social, and economic power, authority, and status amongst men and women (also see van Wormer and Bartollas 2000).

Many criminologists who take gender seriously use these larger sociological realities to help understand things such as (a) different offending rates (b) differential involvement in types of crime, (c) police, prosecutorial, and judicial discretion in criminal justice, (d) institutional discrimination against women in criminal justice, and (e) differential victimization (Flavin 1998; Stanko 1995). This last area, which we discussed in some detail in

Chapter 4, has played a key role in the development of criminological research and theory on domestic assault, sexual assault, child maltreatment, pornography, and prostitution. While there is considerable debate amongst criminologists about the impact of feminism on criminology more generally (Rafter and Heidensohn 1997), there is little question that feminist criminology is a growing area of scholarship, and in our view, makes considerable contributions to the understanding of crime. Here we review some recent feminist contributions to criminological theory. For more comprehensive study of feminist criminological theory and scholarship, see Renzetti and Goodstein (2001), Maher and Daly (1998), and Miller (2001).

GENDER CLASS THEORY   As we have seen, social structural theories of crime that focus on class relations and economic inequality owe a heavy debt to Marx and Engels. However, some criminologists believe that an adequate theory of crime requires the incorporation of a second aspect of social structure, what Messerschmidt (1986) calls relations of reproduction. "[I]n all societies," Messerschmidt writes, "people need to reproduce, socialize, and maintain the species. Consequently, people organize into relations of reproduction to satisfy these needs" (1986, ix).

In capitalist societies such as the United States, "relations of reproduction take the form of patriarchal gender relations, in which the male gender appropriates the labor power and controls the sexuality of the female gender" (Messerschmidt 1986, ix–x). However, the domination of women as a group by men as a group is intertwined with class domination: "Women labor in both the market and the home, and suffer masculine dominance in each. But in addition, their experience in both realms is determined by their class" (1986, xi). In production and in reproduction, behavior is shaped by power relations that cut across both spheres. In the United States, "we do not simply live in a 'capitalist' society, but rather a 'patriarchal capitalist' society" (Messerschmidt 1986, 35). One can therefore distinguish two basic groups: "a powerless group, comprising women and the working class, and a powerful group, made up of men and the capitalist class" (1986, 41).

Messerschmidt endeavored to show how interlocking class and gender relations affect both criminal behavior and its control. For example, the well-documented gap between female rates of serious crime (which are low) and male rates (which are high)—the so-called "gender ratio problem" (Daly and Chesney-Lind 1988, 119; see also Chesney-Lind and Shelden 1992, 7–28)—is explained in terms of the lack of female opportunities for legitimate and illegitimate activities that results from the fact that women are subordinate, "and therefore less powerful in economic, religious, political, and military institutions" (Messerschmidt 1986, 43). On the other hand, males have power, which provides them with far more opportunities to commit crime. When class is brought into the picture, the argument is this: Lower-class males have less power, hence commit less crime, than capitalist and middle-class males, but in all social classes, males are more powerful than females. "Their powerful position allows some men to engage in crimes specifically as men to maintain their dominant position" (Messerschmidt 1986, 45). Rape and wife beating are examples.

While Messerschmidt combines existing research with left-liberal and radical commentary to substantiate his theory, John Hagan (1988) and his colleagues (Hagan, Gillis, and Simpson 1990) tested their version with data from interviews they conducted with 458 adolescents in Toronto, Canada. The results show promise: While the delinquency involvement of higher-class individuals was greater than that of lower-class adolescents, and while male rates were higher than those of females in all social classes, the gender differences were greatest in the highest ("employer") class and least in the lowest ("surplus") class. Many studies have since supported the notion of the significant effects of power differentials on delinquency and the intertwining of gender and class.

Hagan and his colleagues have also developed a *power-control theory* of crime that attempts to explain gender differences in offending. The theory focuses on the relations of girls and boys to their parents, and argues that in patriarchal (male-dominated) families, male delinquency will be greater because parents encourage, support, and socialize boys into masculine roles and behaviors. Girls in patriarchal families, however, commit less crime because they are more subject to regulation by their parents and are encouraged to adopt more feminine roles and behaviors. On the other hand,

girls in more egalitarian families, where each parent has equal power and status, are more likely to engage in delinquency because fewer controls are exercised over their behavior. In sum, the theory holds that "as women enter the paid labor market and assume more powerful positions in the workplace, mothers, and by extension their daughters, might become freer and less controlled. Thus, daughters could become more like sons in their willingness to take risks and in their involvement in delinquency" (McCarthy, Hagan, and Woodward 1999, 762).

What makes Messerschmidt's and Hagan's work important is its improvement over the traditional Marxist focus on only economic inequality, and particularly its specification of how class and gender together affect crime. Even so, the approach is not without its critics. Meda Chesney-Lind (1987), for example, objects that the work (Hagan's in particular) represents a "not-so-subtle variation" of the now discredited view that "liberated" females commit more crime (see Chapter 13). Hagan and his colleagues have indeed recognized the merit of such criticism, and have pointed out in a test of a revised power-control theory that there is a "further possibility that changes in women's work and family experiences might affect their relationships with their sons and their sons' fathers, thus altering, and perhaps diminishing delinquency among males" (McCarthy, Hagan, and Woodward 1999, 761). This richer, more dynamic power control theory has been empirically supported, and the revised power control theory now awaits further test.

TWO RECENT FEMINIST WORKS   Jody Miller (1998) has recently studied the differences between men and women robbers. Based on data from St. Louis (Wright and Decker 1997), Miller found that while the *motivations* for engaging in robbery for men and women were similar, the *accomplishment* of robbery was very different: (a) Women robbers targeted females victims more than men, and (b) some of the women robbers used men's perceptions of women as weak and sexually available to facilitate robbing males. In Miller's (1998a, 60) view, these differences suggest that women who commit violent crimes may do so quite differently from men because of the "gendered nature of their environment." Miller's (1998a, 61) research clearly supports much feminist criminological theory in that "... the differences that emerge reflect practical choices made in the context of a gender-stratified environment—one in which, on the whole, men are perceived as strong and women are perceived as weak." Research on girl gang members' victimization also suggests similar social processes and structures at work (Miller 1998b). In a different vein, Lisa Maher (1997) has found evidence that women who engage in violent crime often do so to protect or defend themselves. While Miller (1998) found that the motivations for men and women to commit robbery were similar, Maher found that women often "vicced" (robbed) male clients in part because of their increased economic marginalization and vulnerability to abuse and assault on the street. Women, then, according to Maher, can clearly have different motivations from men for engaging in violent crime. Many feminist theories also support this research finding.

The study of masculinities and crime has blossomed recently. Led by James Messerschmidt (1994; 2000, 6), **structured action theory** "emphasizes the construction of gender as a situated social and interactional accomplishment ... gender grows out of social practices in specific social structural settings and serves to inform such practices in reciprocal relation." The theory, then, is not purely structural, but contains aspects of social process and construction, discussed in Chapter 12. Essentially, the theory suggests that when men "do" crime or violence, they are often acting out a role within a specific social context that can be related to the presentation of masculinity. But this performance of masculinity is relative and intermittent. Obvious affronts to a boy or man's masculinity, such as insults and threats, are called *masculinity challenges*, and it is these challenges that can give rise to the motivation to violent behavior or masculine social action (Messerschmidt 2000). However, many threats to masculinity may not result in violent behavior.

Using structured action theory to help understand the identities of nine boys, Messerschmidt (2000, 139) notes that each of the boys, and all males presumably, construct or "do" gender differently. The difficult part is identifying who is most at risk and how to promote a "democratic manhood" in which men and boys separate violence, authority, and domination from being masculine. Closing this section with the words of Messerschmidt (1997,

185) seems appropriate. His take on the future directions of feminist criminology is consistent with ours: "[R]ather than conceptualizing gendered crime simplistically in terms of, for example, 'males commit violence and females commit theft,' new directions in feminist theory enable us to explore which males and which females commit which crimes, and in which social situations." Indeed, it seems quite fair to say that criminology can only benefit from this type of analysis.

CHAPTER SUMMARY

This chapter has focused on theories of crime that emphasize the relationship between criminality and social structure. Social disorganization theories argue that crime and delinquency result when there is a breakdown in social control. Members of the Chicago School believed that such a breakdown could result from ecological changes, as when communities experience rapid population change through social mobility and migration.

Strain theory, on the other hand, argues that when people find they cannot achieve valued goals through socially approved means, they experience stress and frustration, which in turn may lead to crime. Strain theory borrows heavily from the work of Emile Durkheim, who believed that crime rises when social relationships are disrupted and existing social norms are no longer effective in regulating goal-seeking behavior.

Advocates of both social disorganization and strain theories have made much of the relatively high rates of crime found among the lower classes according to police statistics. This preoccupation has diverted attention from the behavior of other classes and from the power relations that exist between classes. Some have argued that it has also perpetuated the popular stereotype that criminals come mainly from the lower classes.

Cultural transmission theories also seem preoccupied with lower-class life. These theories relate the criminal behavior of adolescents and young adults to the values, norms, and lifestyles to which they are exposed. Delinquency and crime are learned through exposure to a criminogenic culture. Delinquent subcultures sometimes form in response to the restricted opportunities that face economically disadvantaged youth. Delinquency and crime become a central activity within these subcultures, according to Cloward and Ohlin.

The almost exclusive emphasis on lower-class criminality reflects a common thread running through social structural theories: that crime is a consequence of inequality in the distribution of material resources. Conflict theory makes that inequality an explicit issue. Crime and criminality result because people in positions of wealth, power, and influence use their dominant status to create and apply criminal laws that protect their own self-interests. Radical/critical theory goes further, placing conflicts of authority and criminal labeling within a general theory of political economy rooted in the work of Karl Marx. This social structural view of crime focuses on class relations and on the consequences of economic and political exploitation.

Finally, new developments in criminological theory have been influenced by the conflict and radical camps. Realist criminologists believe that lower-class people generally, and racial minorities in particular, are the ones most vulnerable to crime, not only as offenders but also as victims who are preyed upon by the powerful as well as by each other. Feminist criminology has emerged as a relatively powerful force in criminology as of late. Rather than just treating gender as a "variable," feminist-inspired research has helped criminologists understand the meaning and significance of both masculinities and femininities and their relationship to crime and criminal justice.

KEY TERMS

feminism (p. 259)

focal concerns (p. 249)

left realism (p. 257)

social disorganization (p. 241)

strain (p. 245)

structural contradictions theory (p. 256)

structured action theory (p. 261)

subcultural theories (p. 248)

RECOMMENDED READINGS

Anderson, Kevin, and Richard Quinney. 2000. *Erich Fromm and Critical Criminology: Beyond the Punitive Society.* Champaign-Urbana, IL: University of Illinois Press.

Chambliss, William J., and Marjorie Zatz. 1993. *Making Law: The State, the Law, and Structural Contradictions.* Bloomington, IN: Indiana University Press.

Lynch, Michael J. 1997. *Radical Criminology.* Aldershot, UK: Dartmouth.

Maher, Lisa, and Kathleen Daly. 1998. *Criminology at the Crossroads: Feminist Readings in Crime and Justice.* New York: Oxford University Press.

Messner, Steven F., and Richard Rosenfeld. 2000. *Crime and the American Dream.* 2d ed. Belmont, CA: Wadsworth.

Passas, Nikos, and Robert Agnew. 1997. *The Future of Anomie Theory.* Boston, MA: Northeastern University Press.

Renzetti, Claire M., and Lynne Goodstein. 2001. *Women, Crime and Criminal Justice: Original Feminist Readings.* Los Angeles, CA: Roxbury Publishing.

Ross, Jeffrey I. 1998. *Cutting the Edge: Current Perspectives in Radical/Critical Criminology and Criminal Justice.* Westport, CT: Praeger.

RECOMMENDED WEB SITES

Critical Criminology Division of the American Society of Criminology

Many links and some research and theoretical statements on Marxist, feminist, and postmodern criminology.

http://www.critcrim.org

Crimetheory.com

A good site for information on a variety of criminological theories.

http://crimetheory.com

CHAPTER 12

CRIME AND SOCIAL PROCESS

Social process theories recognize that not all people exposed to the same social structure engage in the same behavior nor do people who come from dissimilar social environments necessarily behave differently. Social process theories are more microsociological theories concerned with how individuals acquire social attributes through interaction with others. A person's attributes identify a person in the eyes of others, distinguishing one person from another. When thinking about attributes it is important to keep in mind that their meaning is always contextual; how one person looks to another is always a matter of how other people in a similar situation look to that person.

Social attributes, such as being reliable or being "forward," convey messages about a person's behavior, status, and ideas. They are part of that person's social identity, and other people use them to determine how they should behave toward that

individual and to distinguish that person from others. A person is not born with these attributes, but acquires them through interaction with others. Criminality is a social attribute. People become criminals, and that status is confirmed when others treat them like criminals, and confirmed again when people so identified actually engage in criminal behavior.

THE PROCESS OF ASSOCIATION

In criminology, **social process theories** attempt to describe and explain the ways in which individuals become criminals. They deal with the links between an individual's interaction with others and that person's motivations, perceptions, self-conceptions, attitudes, behavior, and identity. Although many interactionist theories seem to place greater emphasis on the behavior of others than on the behavior of "self," the goal is the same: to explain the emergence and consequences of behavior. An underlying assumption is that criminal behavior can be explained within the same framework as any other behavior. A common theme in many social process theories is that criminal behavior is learned through interaction with others.

The Theory of Differential Association

In the 1939 edition of *Principles of Criminology*, Edwin H. Sutherland introduced **differential association theory**. According to this theory, criminal behavior patterns are acquired through processes of interaction and communication, just as are other behavior patterns. The principle of differential association accounts for the particular behavior pattern acquired through these processes: Individuals acquire criminal behavior patterns because they are exposed to situations in which the learning of crime outweighs the learning of alternative, noncriminal behaviors. Sutherland wanted it clearly understood that criminal behavior was not the result of biological or psychological *pathology*, but rather was one possible outcome of normal interactive processes. In their daily lives, people are participants in a variety of group situations in which they are exposed to the behavior and influence of others. What they "pick up" in these situations helps shape their own behavior. When a person is more involved with delinquent or criminal groups, he or she is more likely to become

Social process theories propose that criminal behavior is learned in a process of communication with others. For example, people are more likely to use drugs if their close friends do the same. This does not prove that differential association is correct, however; it is possible that kids who use illegal drugs simply seek out others who do the same.

delinquent or criminal as a result. The theory as a whole consists of the following nine propositions:

1. Criminal behavior is learned.
2. Criminal behavior is learned in interaction with other persons in a process of communication.
3. The principle part of the learning of criminal behavior occurs within intimate personal groups.
4. When criminal behavior is learned, the learning includes (a) techniques of committing the crime, which are sometimes very complicated, sometimes very simple, and (b) the specific direction of motives, drives, rationalizations, and attitudes.
5. The specific direction of motives and drives is learned from definitions of the legal codes as favorable or unfavorable.
6. A person becomes delinquent because of an excess of definitions favorable to violation of law (the principle of differential association).
7. Differential association may vary in frequency, duration, priority, and intensity.

8. The process of learning criminal behavior by association with criminal and anticriminal patterns involves all of the mechanisms that are involved in any other learning.
9. While criminal behavior is an expression of general needs and values, it is not explained by those general needs and values, since noncriminal behavior is an expression of the same needs and values (Sutherland and Cressey 1974, 75–77).

Figure 12.1 (on page 266) illustrates the process of differential association.

Three important observations should be made about this theory. First, the theory of differential association purports to explain noncriminal as well as criminal behavior. Noncriminal behavior emerges because of an excess of definitions unfavorable to law violation. Thus, if a child spends a great deal of time interacting intensely with people whose behavior and ideas stress conformity to the law, the child is likely to grow up a conformist (in terms of the law, at least).

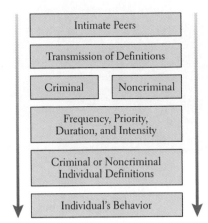

▲ FIGURE 12.1
The Process of Differential Association

Second, the theory can be used to explain variations in group rates of crime as well as individual criminality. Although the theory focuses on how individuals come to engage in criminal behavior, a compatible explanation of variations in rates of crime for whole populations is possible. Thus, relatively high crime rates are predicted for people and places having extensive exposure to definitions favorable to law violation, especially when there is a high probability that such definitions will be learned by a relatively large number of people. Shaw and McKay's delinquency areas, discussed in the previous chapter, would meet these criteria.

Third, the theory can be applied to white-collar crime as well as traditional street crime. Recall that Sutherland invented the term white-collar crime, and he soundly criticized other theorists (like Shaw, McKay, and Merton) for failing to consider those crimes situated within the context of work. A general theory of crime, then, according to Sutherland's view, could not rely on a class-specific model of criminal behavior. Variables like poverty or neighborhood disorganization are insufficient independent variables since one can learn criminal behavior and attitudes in any economic or neighborhood context.

It is fair to say that the theory of differential association has been very influential in criminology. It is, after all, hard to argue with the idea that people learn criminal ways from others. Yet few theories have been subject to more criticism: The language

is imprecise; the theory is untestable because major variables such as "definitions favorable or unfavorable to law violations" cannot be measured; the theory deals with the acquisition and performance of behavior and yet leaves out any mention of personality traits or other psychological variables; and the theory does not explain the fact that people often respond differently to the same situation. C. Ray Jeffery (1959) observes that since crime is learned, it must first exist. What accounts for the first criminal act? How does one explain crimes that are committed "out of the blue" or by people with no prior interaction with criminals?

Behavioral Learning Theories

According to *behavioral learning theories*, people tend to repeat activities for which they will be rewarded and to avoid those for which they will be punished. They also tend to copy others whom they see being rewarded. In this case the reward is experienced vicariously. The sanctioning effect of rewards and punishments may apply to any behavior.

One modification of Sutherland's original theory has been conducted by Robert Burgess and Ronald Akers (1966). They argue that Sutherland's formulation does not identify the mechanism by which individuals in fact learn. Taking a social learning approach, the authors restate Sutherland's theory in terms of **operant conditioning**—a view that argues a certain behavior is learned because past examples have been rewarded. Thus, people engage in crime because it has been more highly rewarded in the past than has other behavior. That some people become criminals and others do not is explained by noting that all people do not go through the same socialization process, nor are they exposed to the same nonsocial situations of reinforcement.

Another quasi-behavioral learning theory was proposed by Daniel Glaser (1956), who argued that all forms of interaction between an individual and his or her social environment be incorporated in a modified theory of "*differential identification*." "A person," writes Glaser (1956, 440) "pursues criminal behavior to the extent that he identifies himself with real or imaginary persons from whose perspective his criminal behavior seems acceptable." These people serve as behavior models, and they need not come into direct, personal contact with the individual. Hence Glaser acknowledges something that Sutherland did not: the possibility that portrayal of criminal roles in the mass media is linked with the adoption of criminal behavior patterns.

These modifications of Sutherland's theory have some parallels with a prominent theory that people learn violence by imitating or modeling the behavior of people they "look up to." Albert Bandura (1973) showed that the behavior of aggressive models is readily imitated by experimental subjects, whether observed in the flesh or via film. In one well-known experiment, Bandura played a film of a woman who beat, kicked, and hacked an inflatable doll. After witnessing the film, nursery school children, when placed in a room with a similar doll, duplicated the woman's behavior and also engaged in other aggressive acts.

Experiments such as these have established the existence of immediate imitation, but how enduring are the behaviors learned, and does each new situation have to be virtually identical with the one originally observed in order for similar behavior to occur? While the jury is still out on these questions, there is evidence that suggests imitated behaviors do survive over time and that people will generalize from the initial modeling situation to other, sometimes quite dissimilar, situations.

Violent behavior has its rewards. Many people learn about them quite early in life. They learn that conflicts can be won through violence, that violence can be effective as a rule-enforcing technique, and that violence helps people get their way in the face of resistance. They also discover that respectable people often reward violence used in their interest, especially against "outsiders" and people regarded as a threat. From history, they learn that violence helped make America a better place to live. Closer to everyday life, they see that successful use of violence often confers status, authority, and even riches.

This brief list by no means exhausts the rewards associated with violence. As people grow up they have many opportunities to learn that violence is rewarded. But they also learn that it has its costs. Violence is costly when used at the wrong time, in the wrong place, or against the wrong person. But since there are differences of opinion as to when the use of violence is wrong, the costs (and rewards) of violence in any given situation are perceived differently by members of different groups

(Stanko 1990). One cannot assume that because one person or group refrains from violence in a certain situation, others will too.

Peer Groups and Serious Delinquency

The observation that association with friends who are delinquent or criminal is associated with high rates of offending is not new, but continues to be reconfirmed in study after study (Gorman and White 1995; Knight and West 1975; Elliott, Ageton, and Huizinga 1985). Recall that the associational argument states when youths are involved with delinquent friends, the association encourages further delinquency. *How* it does it is a matter of debate, but various mechanisms are possible: the group's power to sanction behavior of members; the social rituals that confirm membership and confer status; the role models provided by the group's leader(s); the facilitation of activities that are not easily (or successfully) performed alone. The essential idea is that the delinquency of the group influences its members, and vice versa.

It all sounds simple enough, but the issue of peer influence remains controversial. In the first place, some studies have found that seriously delinquent youths are weakly attached to delinquent peers (e.g., Chapman 1986; also Gottfredson and Hirschi 1990, 154–157). They are loners. Other studies have found quite the opposite, at least for youths involved in illicit drug use (Kandel and Davies 1991). Youths in drug-using networks display extremely strong interactive ties with peers. Second, a study of incarcerated offenders found that group members who conformed to conventional standards were more popular than less conforming members (Osgood et al. 1986). Third, at least two observational studies, one in the United States (Schwendinger and Schwendinger 1985) and one in England (Parker 1974), have shown that occasional and serious delinquents participate side by side in the same streetcorner networks, and the occasionals remain sporadic offenders.

Another issue further complicates what appeared to be a simple matter. Rather than influencing a youth's propensity to commit crimes, it has been suggested that delinquent peer groups merely facilitate crime among individuals whose tendencies are already compatible with it (Linden and Hackler 1973; Gottfredson and Hirschi 1988). A network of delinquency-prone individuals creates and responds to criminal opportunities in its milieu. The type and frequency of criminal acts will be determined largely by that milieu. A chronic delinquent is most often a lower-class street-corner male who keeps company with other lower-class street-corner males. This suggests that, quite apart from the intimate interaction among peers, the social structure of lower-class street-corner society is conducive to high rates of street crime (Barlow and Ferdinand 1992, 60–79).

Testing Differential Association Theory

Testing the original formulation of differential association is not easy, and both the methods used and the results have been inconsistent. Usually researchers infer support (or nonsupport) of the theory and do not test it directly. This is largely Sutherland's fault because he did not specify how the theory might be tested, and he left major concepts undefined. We shall now review a few studies that have attempted to test differential association.

One study involved interviewing 1,544 students in nine high schools in the Southeast (Paternoster and Triplett 1988). The authors reported strong support for differential association. Friends' definitions of appropriate and inappropriate behavior and friends' actual behavior were significantly related to an individual's own use of marijuana, drinking behavior, petty theft, and vandalism. A study of over 1,000 Dutch children found great support for the idea that the frequency of contact with deviant friends significantly influences definitions favorable to deviant behavior (Bruinsma 1992). In another study, Warr and Stafford (1991) used National Youth Survey data (see Chapter 2) to evaluate associational theory. They found that peers' behavior—what they actually do—was a more important predictor of self-reported delinquency than peers' attitudes about behavior.

Two tests of differential association have been conducted from data obtained from the Richmond Youth Project, a self-report survey of over 4,000 high school students. The first study found that definitions favorable to law violation predicted delinquency more strongly than any other variable (Matsueda 1982; Matsueda and Heimer 1987).

However, in a recent reexamination of this data, it was found that the bonds to parents and friends more strongly explained delinquency (Costello and Vowell 1999). More specifically, the authors found that definitions favorable to law violation were shaped or mediated by other factors, especially measures of the social bond (discussed in some detail later in this chapter). A similar finding was made by Matsueda and Anderson (1998).

Indeed, tests of differential association theory are at the very least supportive of the *mediation hypothesis*—the notion that larger social and structural factors shape the content and form of definitions favorable or unfavorable to crime (Heimer 1997). This approach has been used to explain the gender differences in violent offending. A recent study by Heimer and DeCoster (1999) found the following:

- Learning violent definitions is an important predictor of violent delinquency.
- Aggressive peers and coercive discipline each has a larger effect on boys' than girls' learning of violent definitions.
- Emotional bonds to family influence girls' but not boys' learning of violent definitions (also see Alarid, Burton, and Cullen 2000).
- Accepting traditional gender definitions significantly reduces violence among girls, but does not influence violence among boys.
- Boys engage in more violent delinquency than girls in part because they learn more violent definitions and more traditional gender definitions than girls and have more previous experience with violent offending than girls.

How and with whom we associate varies in a number of ways (e.g., by age, location, gender, and time). In the case of gender, role socialization reflects larger social inequalities, which help shape definitions of socially acceptable and unacceptable behavior. These combined with many other socially learned customs, norms, and differential treatment help explain the massive differences in criminal offending by gender (Giordano and Rockwell 2000).

Differential association theory is also helpful in explaining the causes of occupational and organizational crime. Indeed, partial support of the theory has been found in a number of studies of white-collar crime (Kauzlarich and Kramer 1998). In some respects, white-collar crime

> may be better understood by reference to differential association than is true of conventional lower-class crime and delinquency, both because of the broader range of learning options generally available to the white-collar crime offender and the complex nature of the offenses themselves. (Friedrichs 1996, 229)

However, differential association theory is not equipped to explain the larger structural and organizational elements involved in facilitating many organizational crimes. This limitation has prompted many white-collar crime scholars to study how definitions of appropriate and inappropriate behavior are created and maintained in unique organizational climates.

For example, Vaughan's (1996) monumental study of the space shuttle *Challenger* explosion employs the notion of the **normalization of deviance**, a condition in which deviations from technical protocols gradually and routinely become defined as normative. Risky practices, which can be an outcome or a precursor to the normalization of deviance, are often caused by "environmental and organizational contingencies [which] create operational forces that shape world view, normalizing signals of potential danger, resulting in mistakes with harmful human consequences" (Vaughan 1996, 409). The 1996 crash of ValuJet flight 592 and many other organizational crimes are also partially explainable through the use of social learning theory (Matthews and Kauzlarich 2000).

SELF-CONCEPT

The discussion so far has drawn attention to the ways in which youths, in particular, come to adopt patterns of delinquent or criminal offending. Learning, communication, and interaction are the fundamental processes by which individuals acquire their social identities. These processes are also crucial to the development of an individual's personality—motivations, ideas and beliefs, perceptions, feelings, preferences, attitudes, values, self-control, inhibitions, and awareness or sense of self. Some authors have argued that a person's sense of self, or

self-concept, is a major element among the forces that control behavior.

Containment Theory and Self-Concept

One of the first to propose a link between self-concept and criminal behavior was Walter Reckless. Reckless (1973) believes that the individual confronted by choices of action feels a variety of "pulls" and "pushes." The pulls are environmental factors—such as adverse living conditions, poverty, lack of legitimate opportunities, abundance of illegitimate opportunities, or family problems—that serve to pull the individual away from the norms and values of the dominant society. The pushes take the form of internal pressures—hostility, biopsychological impairments, aggressiveness, drives, or wishes—that may also divert the individual away from actions supported by dominant values and norms.

But not all people faced with the same pulls and pushes become delinquent or criminal. To explain why some do not, Reckless advances **containment theory**. According to Reckless (1973, 55–56), there are two kinds of containment, inner and outer.

Inner containment consists mainly of self-components, such as self-control, good self-concept, ego strength, well-developed superego, high frustration tolerance, high resistance to diversions, high sense of responsibility, goal orientation, ability to find substitute satisfactions, tension-reducing rationalizations, and so on. These are the inner regulators.

Outer containment represents the structural buffer in the person's immediate social world that is able to hold him within bounds. It consists of such items as a presentation of a consistent moral front to the person; institutional reinforcement of his norms, goals, and expectations; the existence of a reasonable set of social expectations; effective supervision and discipline (social controls); provisions for reasonable scope of activity (including limits and responsibilities) as well as for alternatives and safety-valves; opportunity for acceptance, identity, and belongingness. Such structural ingredients help the family and other supportive groups contain the individual.

In Reckless's view, the inner control system, primarily self-concept, provides a person with the strongest defense against delinquency involvement.

Commenting on the results of a follow-up study of white schoolboys in high-delinquency areas in Columbus, Ohio, Reckless and Simon Dinitz (1967, 517) observe the following:

> In our quest to discover what insulates a boy against delinquency in a high delinquency area, we believe we have some tangible evidence that a good self-concept, undoubtedly a product of favorable socialization, veers slum boys away from delinquency, while a poor self-concept, a product of unfavorable socialization, gives the slum boy no resistance to deviancy, delinquent companions, or delinquent subculture. We feel that components of the self strength, such as a favorable concept of self, act as an inner buffer or inner containment against deviancy, distraction, lure, and pressures.

The work of Reckless and his associates has not gone without criticism, but interest in self-concept and its connection with criminality has remained very much alive in some circles. One study seems to confirm the importance of favorable family experiences in protecting a child against criminogenic influences, even in slum neighborhoods. Joan McCord (1991) used case records of visits to the homes of 232 boys as well as records of their juvenile and adult criminal activity covering a thirty-year period. She found that sons of mothers who were self-confident, offered leadership, and were affectionate and consistently nonpunitive in discipline tended to escape delinquency involvement. However, McCord also discovered that a different mechanism seemed to relate to whether a child subsequently became an adult criminal: a father's behavior toward wife and children. Apparently, fathers who undermine their wives, who fight with the family, and who are aggressive "teach their sons how to behave when they become adults" (McCord 1991, 412). Thus, juvenile crime may be more susceptible to control mechanisms, including self-concept, whereas adult crime may be more susceptible to the influence of role expectations. More recent extensions of this approach have focused on how different identities both between *and* within gender influence the process of constructing one's "self" and one's criminal offending and victimization (Giordano, Millhollin, Cernkovich, Pugh, and Rudolph 1999).

Techniques of Neutralization

One interesting theoretical contribution bearing on self-concept comes from David Matza and Gresham Sykes. Matza (1964) argues that individuals are rarely committed to or compelled to perform delinquent or criminal behavior. Rather, they drift into and out of it, retaining a commitment neither to convention nor to crime. This so-called **drift theory** is also applicable to some instances of organizational crime (Braithwaite 1989b).

In Matza's view, delinquents are never totally immune to the demands for conformity made by the dominant social order. At most they are merely flexible in their commitment to them. In a joint publication, Sykes and Matza (1957) argue that if delinquents do form subcultures in opposition to dominant society, they are surprisingly weak in their commitment to them. They show guilt and shame, though one would expect none; they frequently accord respect and admiration to the "really honest" person and to law-abiding people in their immediate social environment; and they often draw a sharp line between appropriate victims and those who are not fair game—all of which suggests that "the virtue of delinquency is far from unquestioned." In terms of the *dominant normative order*, the delinquent appears to be both conforming and nonconforming.

Sykes and Matza believe that in order to practice nonconformity, delinquents must somehow handle the demands for conformity to which they accord at least some recognition. In the view of these authors, delinquents handle those demands by learning to neutralize them in advance of violating them. That is, they redefine their contemplated action to make it "acceptable," if not "right." The authors identify five **techniques of neutralization** that facilitate the juvenile's drift into delinquency:

1. Denial of responsibility ("alcohol causes me to do it; I am helpless")
2. Denial of injury ("my action won't hurt anyone")
3. Denial of the victim ("he 'has it coming'")
4. Condemnation of the condemners ("those who condemn me are worse than I am")
5. Appeal to higher loyalties ("my friends, or family, come first, so I must do it")

Two other techniques of neutralization have been proposed and discussed in a classic study of occupational crime (Hollinger 1991; Klockars 1974; Minor 1981). They are *defense of necessity* and *metaphor of the ledger*. Defense of necessity relates to the fact that, among business offenders, illegal acts are seen as standard business practice and necessary in a competitive marketplace (Minor 1981, 298). Metaphor of the ledger relates to the idea that a person can build up "good" credit so that he or she can later do something "bad" without feeling guilty—a form of cashing in the credits.

More recently, scholars of state crime and elite deviance have found evidence of the operationality of techniques of neutralization (Cohen 1993; Kauzlarich, Matthews, and Miller 2000; Simon 1999). Indeed, one of the most important things separating state victimizers from their victims is the power to exert their will. Most often, victimizers do not acknowledge the degree to which their policies have caused harm while assessing the "effectiveness" of their policies to bring about desired change or to maintain their position of dominance. Unjust and injurious domestic and international policies can also be downplayed by neutralizing reasonable categorical imperatives (e.g., do no harm) by employing bankrupt utilitarianism, which may or may not be guided by ethnocentric paternalism. Harms are often neutralized by denying responsibility, dehumanizing the powerless for purposes of exploitation, and appealing to higher loyalties (i.e., the capitalist political economy and "national security") (Kauzlarich, Matthews, and Miller 2000; Simon 1999).

It has been argued that political policymakers attempt to "neutralize" the destructive and harmful effects of their policies, as in the long history of U.S. abuses in Latin and Central America:

U.S. policy makers have consciously decided (1) that the United States is entitled to control Central America and that the peoples of Central America are obligated to acquiesce in this power exercise; (2) that violence is permissible, and policy makers can live with themselves and conclude that they are ethical/moral persons and that these policies are ethical/moral even if they involve violence; (3) that the use of violence, intimidation, and threat of violence will produce the desired effect or minimize a more negative one; and (4) that the policy of violence and control will not unduly endanger

the United States, and the country will neither sustain physical harm nor suffer legal, economic, or political consequences that will outweigh the benefits achieved through this violence. (Tifft and Markham 1991, 125–126)

With respect to the historical treatment of Native Americans within the United States, "colonists quickly justified their violence by demonizing their enemies" (Takaki 1993, 43). However, the transference of one's own negative tendencies to another group is not something new. While Native Americans were seen as unruly, "God-less" savages, Takaki (1993) notes that the atrocities committed by the civilized whites against the Native Americans, were, in fact, savage. It is in this light, then, that Native Americans became an enemy worthy of indiscriminate killing. In much the same manner, the indiscriminate killing of the "Godless" communists of Central America were also justified:

[This] is a painful reality. Many of us face this reality with initial disbelief and denial, for it is difficult for us to see either the United States or ourselves as terrorists, as batterers. Terrorists and batterers are someone else. To emotionally experience, to actually witness the destruction, the horror, the reality of destabilization, starvation, torture and death by design, by public planning, is beyond our comprehension. (Tifft and Markham 1991, 131)

Empirical evaluations of the neutralization hypothesis are scarce, in part because of the difficulty of establishing what happens cognitively *before* a law violation occurs. Almost all research has looked at rationalizations after the fact, which provides at best only inferential evidence. The problem is one of establishing the causal order: neutralization before transgression.

In any case, with the exception of Agnew's (1994) study, the evidence is not very supportive in studies of most traditional street crimes. The absence of neutralizations, however, does not mean they might not have operated at some time in the mind of an offender. Neutralizations might arise after earlier transgressions and act as rationalizations for later ones, perhaps contributing to a "hardening" process that leads to a commitment to deviance (Hirschi 1971, 208). Hamlin (1988, 432) goes even further and calls the prior sequencing argument "a fallacy." He argues that the motives for doing things are created during the process of legitimizing actions that have been criticized or challenged.

Furthermore, neutralization may be necessary only for certain offenders. According to one scholar, "neutralization should only be necessary when a potential offender has both a strong desire to commit an offense and a strong belief that to do so would violate his personal morality.... If one's morality is not constraining, however, then neutralization or rationalization is simply unnecessary" (Minor 1980, 103–120).

There may be no adequate way to disentangle the causal order problem mentioned earlier even with longitudinal data, since definitional learning ("this is right to do, this is wrong," and "I'm OK, I'm not OK," etc.) occurs concurrently with rule breaking (Hollinger 1991). Even so, neutralization theory may have received a "bum rap" from critics, especially in light of the finding that neutralization may interact with age, younger people being less likely to neutralize than older ones (Hollinger 1991). Neutralization theory deserves continued attention, it appears (Agnew 1994).

CONTROL THEORY

Like Matza and others, control theorists emphasize the episodic character of much crime and delinquency, but unlike their colleagues they build in no assumptions about what motivates people to commit deviance. Indeed, "They assume that human beings are born free to break the law and will refrain from doing so only if special circumstances exist" (Box 1981, 122).

Travis Hirschi's Theory

The most prominent version of control theory is that of Travis Hirschi (1971). According to Hirschi, these special circumstances exist when the individual's bond to conventional, or moral, society is strong. As originally conceived, Hirschi's **social control theory** holds that this bond is based on four elements: *attachment, commitment, belief,* and *involvement. Attachment* refers to the individual's affective involvement with conventional others (e.g., parents, teachers, friends), including sensitivity to their thoughts, feelings, and desires. When that attachment is weakened, the individual is free to deviate.

Commitment is the "rational" component in conformity. It refers to the weighing of the costs and risks of deviance in light of that person's investment, or "stake," in conformity. "When or whenever he considers deviant behavior, he must consider the costs of this deviant behavior, the risks he runs of losing the investment he has made in conventional behavior" (Hirschi 1971, 20). The weaker the commitment to conformity, the lower the costs of deviance; hence the freer one is to deviate.

Hirschi defines *belief* as "a common value system within the society or group whose norms are being violated." But individuals differ in the strength of their belief in the moral validity of these social rules. If for some reason these beliefs are weakened, the individual will be freer to deviate. By including *involvement*, Hirschi suggests that deviance is in part a matter of opportunities to deviate. He argues that the more one is involved in conventional things, the less one has the opportunity to do deviant things. This is one of the weakest parts of the theory, as Hirschi himself discovered in his research with over 4,000 California junior high and high school students—as opportunities for criminal or delinquent activities increase along with opportunities for noncriminal activities (see Chapter 13).

Both the clarity of its exposition and the many research findings supporting it have given Hirschi's control theory a prominent place in criminology. A recent study by Robert Agnew (1985), however, questions its utility as an explanation of youth crime. Agnew studied a national sample of 1,886 male youths interviewed first in the tenth grade and again at the end of the eleventh grade. He

▲ FIGURE 12.2
Hirschi's Social Control Theory

Social control theory suggests that the closer the bond between children and parents, the lower the likelihood of juvenile delinquency. Hirschi's version of the theory is one of the more popular explanations of juvenile crime in the field of criminology.

found delinquency involvement to be remarkably stable over the two-year period, with the delinquency measured in the tenth grade accounting for 65 to 68 percent of the delinquency measured later.

In contrast, Agnew found that the social bond variables of parental attachment, school grades, and commitment explained only 1 to 2 percent of the variance in delinquency. Agnew speculates that as children grow older, the importance of the bonds discussed by Hirschi may diminish, but he does not rule out that they may be important among younger children.

Hirschi's social control theory has also been soundly criticized for overstating the importance of the social bond. A recent reanalysis of the Richmond Youth Project data by David Greenberg (1999) found that while social control theory has its merits, the strength of theory has been overstated by criminologists. For example, Greenberg (1999) found that (a) intimacy in communication between parent and child (a measure of attachment) is not highly correlated with delinquency, (b) there is a very modest negative relationship between involvement in school-related activities and delinquency, and (c) negative correlations between

aspirations to attain higher levels of education (e.g., college) and delinquency are also quite small. However, another recent study using the same data source found that measures of the social bond, especially belief, were the greatest predictors of delinquency (Costello and Vowell 1999).

One final comment on this prominent theory is in order. Some criminologists contend that control theory ignores the criminal activity of career offenders, as well as the crimes of people in positions of economic and political power (Box 1981; Hagan 1985). The "upperworld" individual is actually freed by conventional society to engage in "indiscretions" because these are not viewed as especially disreputable, much less criminal (Hagan 1985). Such a person may thus exhibit strong social bonds to conventional society and considerable involvement in illegal activities. Indeed, if we consider political and state crimes, many of the offenders would be considered very bonded to the social order because of their high levels of education, employment status, familial relationships, and belief systems. While there has been some support for social control theory in studies of occupational crime (Lasley 1988; Makkai and Braithwaite 1991), Hirschi's version is best suited to explain juvenile delinquency, not white-collar crime. At the very least, the theory must be broadened to include other forms of control and regulation, as found in the white-collar crime studies of Braithwaite (1989b), Kauzlarich and Kramer (1998), Simpson, Exum, and Smith (2000), and Vaughan (1996).

THE LABELING PROCESS AND ITS IMPACT

Up to this point, the focus has been on crime and delinquency as behavior, and on people who commit crimes and the distinctions between them and those who do not. The questions "What causes or influences criminal behavior?" and "What factors are associated with committing crime or becoming criminals?" are underlying concerns in the work reviewed. However, the conception of crime and the criminal that underlies such questions is not the only one recognized. Instead of viewing crime simply as illegal behavior and the criminal as one who engages in it, some criminologists draw attention to the behavior of other people with whom an individual interacts. Crime is a label attached to

behavior, and the criminal is one whose behavior has been labeled crime. Crime is thus problematic and a question of social definitions. Nothing intrinsic in behavior makes it a crime:

> Social groups create deviance by making the rules whose infraction constitutes deviance, and by applying those rules to particular people and labeling them as outsiders. From this point of view, deviance is not a quality of the act a person commits, but rather a consequence of the application by others of rules or sanctions to an "offender." *The deviant is one to whom that label has been successfully applied; deviant behavior is behavior that people so label.* (Becker 1963, 9)

Labeling theory, or the societal reactions approach, gained immense popularity in the fields of crime and deviance during the 1960s. This was also about the time that the social constructionist paradigm (Chapter 10) fully emerged in sociology. In its applications to the crime scene, labeling theory has been used to explain why individuals continue to engage in activities that others define as criminal, why individuals become career criminals, why the official data on crime and criminals look the way

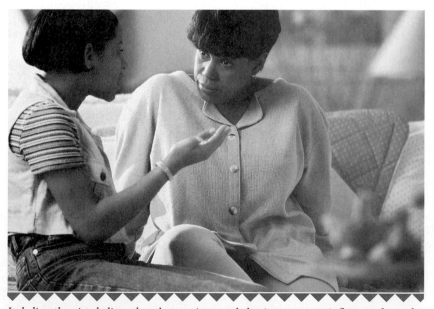

Labeling theorists believe that the reaction to a behavior or gesture influences future behavior. When children misbehave, parents often distinguish the act from the person, but in the criminalization process the label is often categorical, overshadowing other things the person might be.

Box 12.1   THE SAINTS AND THE ROUGHNECKS

William J. Chambliss (1973) followed the experiences of two small-town juvenile gangs whose members were students at "Hannibal High." The youths regularly broke the law. However, only the members of the Roughnecks were considered delinquent by officials and repeatedly arrested. The other gang, the Saints, largely escaped criminalization, and no members were ever arrested.

According to Chambliss, four factors played important roles in the differential response, and all related to the class position of the gang members. The Roughnecks came from the lower-class, while the Saints came from more "respectable" upper-middle-class families.

First, the Roughnecks were more visible. Unlike the Saints, whose members had access to cars and could escape the local community, the Roughnecks had little choice but to hang out under the surveillance of neighbors and local authorities.

Second, the outward demeanor of the Saints deceived parents and officials. Around authority figures, they wore masks of courtesy and obedience, and when accused of deviant behavior, they were apologetic. The Roughnecks, on the other hand, misbehaved openly and showed little regard for social customs or the feelings of others.

Third, when responding to the gangs' misbehavior, authorities displayed bias that favored the Saints. The Saints were characterized as typical adolescents who were merely sowing their wild oats as normal boys do.

Finally, in defining the Roughnecks as boys who get in trouble, the community reinforced the "deviance" of gang members and helped produce a self-fulfilling prophecy—deviant self-images promoted further deviance. The Saints, meanwhile, remained respectable in the eyes of the community, although in fact they continued to maintain a high level of delinquency.

Chambliss's study is one of the best examples of the application of labeling perspective to date. It clearly shows that "labeling, stigma, and negative self-images have a powerful impact in determining who we are and what we become" (Chambliss 1999, 120).

Source: William Chambliss, *Power, Politics, and Crime*. Copyright © 1999 by Westview Press, a member of Perseus Books Group. Reprinted by permission of Westview Press, a member of Perseus Books, LLC.

they do, why crime waves occur, why law enforcement is patterned the way it is, why criminal stereotypes emerge and persist, and why some groups in society are more likely to be punished, and punished more severely, than others. Box 12.1 describes a famous study by William Chambliss (1973) that illustrates some of these points vividly.

Though labeling theory gained popularity during the 1960s, it is based on the much earlier contributions of Frank Tannenbaum (1938) and Edwin Lemert (1951, 1972). Forty years ago, Tannenbaum pointed out that society's efforts at social control may actually help create precisely what those efforts are meant to suppress: crime. By labeling individuals as "delinquents" or "criminals" and by reacting to them in a punitive way, Tannenbaum argued, the community encourages those individuals to redefine themselves in accordance with the community's definition. A change in self-identification (or self-concept) may occur, so that individuals "become" what others say they are. Tannenbaum (pp. 17–18) described the process:

From the community's point of view, the individual who used to do bad and mischievous things has now become a bad and unredeemable human being. From the individual's point of view there has taken place a similar change. He has gone slowly from a sense of grievance and injustice, of being unduly mistreated and punished, to recognition that the definition of him as a human being is different from that of other boys in his neighborhood, his school, street, community. This recognition on his part becomes a process of self-identification and integration with the group which shares his activities. It becomes, in part, a process of rationalization; in part, a simple response to a specialized type of stimulus. The young delinquent becomes bad because he is defined as bad and because he is not believed if he is good. There is a persistent demand for consistency in character. The community cannot deal with people whom it cannot define. Reputation is this sort of public definition.

Even if people act in ways normally defined as good, their goodness will not be believed. Once stigmatized, they find it extremely difficult to be free of the label "delinquent" or "criminal." As Erikson (1966, 17) notes in *Wayward Puritans*, "The common feeling that deviant persons never really change … may derive from a faulty premise; but the feeling is expressed so frequently and with such conviction that it eventually creates the facts which later 'prove' it to be correct."

A bad reputation doesn't just affect individuals. Reuter, Rubinstein, and Winn (1983) describe the experience of corporations and even whole industries (for example, the vending machine business) whose bad reputations have led to an increase in crime. The reason, they argue, is that when labeled crooked, respectable people do not apply for jobs or work with such businesses, leaving them open and attractive to risk-takers and criminals; a kind of self-selection is going on, "bad" places attracting "bad" people.

Societal reaction to crime and delinquency helps turn offending individuals from seeing themselves as basically "straight" and "respectable" and toward an image of themselves as criminal. Thus, some people who are reacted to as criminals come to think of themselves as criminals, or at least they participate in what becomes a *self-fulfilling prophecy*. In a study of used car fraud, one of Braithwaite's (1978) informants said, "They think because you're a used car dealer you're a liar. So they treat you like one and lie to you. Can you blame the dealer for lying back?"

The term **secondary deviation** refers to the criminal acts associated with the individual's acquired status as a criminal and his or her ultimate acceptance of it (Lemert 1951, 1972). Secondary

deviation emerges from a process of reaction and adjustment to the punishing and stigmatizing actions of significant others, such as schoolteachers, parents, and law enforcement officials. Although initially the individuals engage for a short time in deviant acts that they regard as incompatible with their true selves (suggesting the need for the techniques of neutralization discussed earlier), they eventually come to accept their new identities as deviants and may well progress toward a career in deviance:

> The sequence of interaction leading to secondary deviation is roughly as follows: (1) primary deviation [initial acts of deviance prompted by any number of reasons]; (2) social penalties; (3) further primary deviation; (4) stronger penalties and rejections; (5) further deviation, perhaps with hostilities and resentments beginning to focus upon those doing the penalizing; (6) crisis reached in the tolerance quotient, expressed in formal action by the community stigmatizing of the deviant; (7) strengthening of the deviant conduct as a reaction to the stigmatizing and penalties; (8) ultimate acceptance of deviant social status and efforts at adjustment on the basis of the associated role. (Lemert 1951, 77)

Whether an individual moves from primary to secondary deviation depends greatly on the degree to which others' disapproval finds expression in concrete acts of punishment and stigmatization. In a later paper, Lemert notes: "While communication of invidious definitions of persons or groups and the public expression of disapproval were included [in earlier discussions] as part of the societal reaction, the important point was made that these had to be validated in order to be sociologically meaningful. Validation was conceived as isolation, segregation, penalties, supervision, or some kind of organized treatment" (Lemert 1974, 457). Support for the criminogenic impact of validation comes from Shannon's (1991) famous cohort study in Racine, Wisconsin, which found that boys who experienced repeated contacts with the police were at much greater risk of chronic delinquency.

Some critics have attacked labeling theory, arguing that many of its key assumptions are not supported by the bulk of available evidence (Wellford 1975). Indeed, Wellford (1975, 342) asserts that the supposed connection between punitive reactions, changes in self-concept, and secondary deviation is "a simplistic view of behavior causation, one that stresses the explanation of intellectual as opposed to behavioral characteristics of the subject." Critics argue that the claim that changes in self-concept produce changes in behavior has yet to be demonstrated. Some prefer to view behavior as situationally determined, and thus crime may well occur quite independently of the actor's self-concept.

Some criminologists seem to believe that labeling theory is essentially dead, or at the very least has fallen from grace in criminological circles (Wright 1994). Our view is different, as one of us indicated in this comment in response to Wright:

> To be sure, labeling theory has come in for its share of criticism—perhaps even a disproportionate share—but it is far from dishonored as a theoretical perspective on crime, nor is it about to be abandoned by the field. Consider Braithwaite's (1989) theory of reintegrative shaming [discussed in detail in Chapter 14]. Braithwaite clearly takes labeling theory seriously, giving it a prominent place in his own integrative theory of crime. Whenever shaming is stigmatizing, the predictions of labeling theory can be applied: Crime is likely to increase and criminal tendencies are hardened (see also Akers 1994, 135–137). Don Gibbons (1994, 37) has recently observed ... that "labeling themes can be identified in some of the 'new criminologies,' (feminist views, realist criminology, and critical approaches)." This is hardly an indication that labeling theory has fallen from grace or is anachronistic! (Barlow 1994, 2)

While differential association theory, social control theory, and varieties of strain/anomie theory are more frequently tested than labeling theory, several recent studies have found that labeling theory does explain some elements of crime and deviance. For example, because of the stigma surrounding being "mentally ill," people who may in fact be mentally ill might avoid treatment, keep their problems secret, or withdraw from the very audiences (friends, family) that might be able to help them improve the quality of their lives (Link and Cullen 1983; Triplett 2000). Criminal justice policies are also instructively viewed through labeling theory, as Triplett (2000) notes in the context of social reactions to juvenile delinquency in the 1990s. Furthermore, two studies found that the effects of labeling theory are not as direct as the initial authors of the theory suggest—it was found that the effects of labeling are mediated through differential association (Adams 1996; Downs, Robertson, and Harrison 1997). Another study found that the effects of labeling were far stronger—a child's perception of teacher disapproval was highly associated with delinquency, independent of prior delinquency. However, the effects of labeling were less direct when considering a child's delinquent peer associations (Adams and Evans 1996). Other research has found that the effects of labeling were highly significant in explaining adolescent drug use (Edwards 1993).

INTEGRATED THEORIES

Social process theories deal with the dynamic aspects of the relationship between individuals and their immediate social environments. They explain how it is that certain people learn criminal behavior patterns, and how they acquire criminal status. Where social structural theories focus on the relationship of organization and culture to values, norms, resources, and opportunities, social process theories consider how the actions of individuals and groups influence what people do and become.

Even though process has been separated from structure in this review of prominent theories, as we discussed in Chapter 10, the two are in reality intimately connected. One way to think of that connection is to visualize structure as setting the stage for process which in turn brings structure to life. When thinking about crime, structure promotes and restrains criminal activity among different segments of the population, while process determines which individuals within those segments will become criminally active (or be singled out for criminal labeling), and which will not.

Two questions are therefore relevant when considering why crime varies from place to place or from group to group: (1) How do social structures compare? and (2) How do the activities and experiences of individuals compare? Often it is not possible to answer both questions at the same time because the kinds of information or methodologies needed are not available or not used. Sometimes the criminologist who engages in research is simply not interested in process questions, for example, but wants to evaluate the relationship between structure and crime, perhaps at a class or societal level.

It is helpful, nevertheless, to illustrate how structure and process can be linked in research. While there are many integrated theories, one fairly recent study assesses the criminal behavior of individuals who live in different family and neighborhood environments (structure) and are exposed to different interactional experiences (process). The study is by John Laub and Robert Sampson (1988), and it reanalyses data compiled by Sheldon and Eleanor Glueck some forty years ago.

The Gluecks (1950) collected data on 500 officially defined delinquents and 500 nondelinquents. All subjects were white males growing up in poor, deteriorated neighborhoods close to the industrial and commercial zones of Boston. Their average age was just under fifteen. Data on all sorts of social, psychological, and biological variables were collected in a multifactor design. Despite a variety of criticisms leveled at the Gluecks' research design, the study remains a classic in the field (Laub and Sampson 1988, 357–361).

The reanalysis of the Gluecks' data by Laub and Sampson focused primarily on the relationship between family factors and delinquency. The family factors were divided into two categories that reflect the distinction between structure and process.

Structural factors included household crowding, economic dependence, residential mobility, and parental criminality. Process variables included parental discipline and supervision of a child, and emotional rejection.

Figure 12.3 shows the model developed by the authors. They hypothesize that parental child-rearing practices and other family management skills would be most directly related to the delinquent behavior of a child since they constitute the emotional atmosphere and control environment to which the child is exposed while growing up. Basing their argument on work by Hirschi (1983) and others, Laub and Sampson predict that good parenting skills and a supportive emotional climate help prevent the emergence of delinquency in a child because they enhance family social control.

The authors also predict, however, that parental discipline and family emotional climate are directly influenced by background factors such as economic dependency, irregular employment, and parental criminality. Thus, the structural variables influence delinquency through their impact on family process. "For instance, it is likely that residential mobility and irregular employment by mothers are related to difficulties in supervising and monitoring children. Similarly, family disruption not only affects supervisory capacity, but also attachment and disciplinary practices" (Laub and Sampson 1988, 367–368).

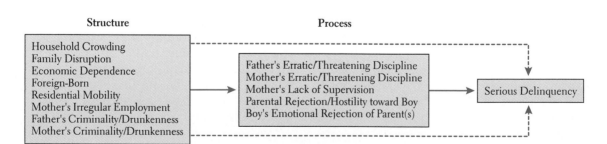

----- Broken line indicates hypothesized weak or insignificant relationship.
——— Solid line indicates hypothesized strong effect.

▲ FIGURE 12.3

Structure and Process United in a Model of Delinquency

Source: Taken from John H. Laub and Robert J. Sampson, "Unraveling Families and Delinquency: A Reanalysis of the Gluecks' Data," *Criminology* 26 (1988): 366. Reprinted with the permission of the American Society of Criminology.

In this manner, Laub and Sampson show how structure and process can be linked in the explanation of delinquency. When they reanalyzed the Gluecks' data to test this model, they found that the quality of family social control was indeed directly and strongly related to serious and persistent delinquency among boys. Equally important, however, was the finding that the social structural variables helped set the stage by directly influencing the ways in which parents supervise and discipline their children and the quality of the emotional relationship between parent and child.

The relationship between family life and delinquency, it must be said, is one of the most researched issues in criminology. Yet a review of nearly 300 studies came up with few clear-cut conclusions, except to reiterate that a relationship does exist—deviance begins at home (Wright and Wright 1994). The lack of definitive conclusions about the specifics of the link between family life and crime reflects in part the many inconsistencies plaguing the methods and findings of so much of the research. It also reflects problems in resolving the issue of causality:

> For example, when researchers observe an association between family conflict and delinquency, any one of three explanations may describe the actual relationship between the variables. Family conflict may, in fact, actually cause delinquency. Alternatively, having a delinquent child may create considerable conflict within the family. Or, perhaps family conflict and delinquency are unrelated, but increase or decrease in relation to one another because of their mutual relationship to yet a third variable, for instance, aggression proneness among family members. Researchers never prove causality but endeavor to eliminate alternative explanations by using more complex models and methods that allow them to rule out other possibilities. (Wright and Wright 1994, 2)

On the whole, one can safely say that family structure and family interaction *together with* external factors such as the economic condition, opportunity structure, quality of schools, and institutional stability of the neighborhood and surrounding community go a long way toward explaining the antisocial behavior of youth. How relevant these same factors are for explaining adult crime, especially occupational and public order crimes, is another matter. The fact that most youths "mature" out of crime by their late teens and early twenties indicates that something is operating to halt or perhaps even reverse the impact of these factors for a majority of children once they reach adulthood.

Some criminologists believe that key adult roles such as spouse, full-time worker, and parent make continued criminality too costly. Perhaps people become concerned about losing their family's respect (e.g., Rowe, Lindquist, and White 1989), or perhaps participation in family life bonds a person more closely to conventional society, including values and attitudes about marital, parental, and work responsibility (e.g., Thornberry 1987; Sampson and Laub 1990). On the other hand, Gottfredson and Hirschi (1990) argue that criminality reflects impulsivity, short-time perspective, and other characteristics of low self-control. Such individuals are unlikely to make successful marriage partners, parents, or workers as adults, just as they are unlikely to do well in school as children. Any relationship between marriage and family life and crime is therefore spurious, meaning that the three are related only through their association with low self-control.

Wright and Wright (1994) conclude that the research on this issue is inconclusive. But here is another thought: Some forms of crime—small-business crime and perhaps some occupational and professional crimes—may actually thrive on strong family and work relationships. Since the emphasis in most criminological research is on street crime, it is easy to forget that sneak theft, robbery, burglary, drug pushing, rape, assault, and murder actually represent just the tip of the crime iceberg. An adequate description and explanation of the relationship between family life and crime must surely move beyond these crimes into the world of business crime, money laundering, fraud, and bribery—offenses not usually committed by children, nor by people whose backgrounds automatically suggest a delinquent childhood.

The Life Course Perspective

A very promising integrated theory of crime has been proposed by Sampson and Laub (1992, 1993b), the same authors who reanalyzed the Gluecks' data. Their theory centers on the notion of the life course, through which all individuals travel from birth to death. The **life course** consists of *trajectories*, which are long-term sequences and patterns of behavior (for example, schooling, work-life, marriage, parenthood, or criminal career), and *transitions*, which are specific life events within a trajectory, such as first job, first marriage, going to college, or joining a gang.

Sampson and Laub review research showing that there are fairly stable attributes of individuals that are established early in life and that provide continuity and consistency as individuals age; aggression might be one, with adult manifestations in the form of spousal abuse and harsh punishment of children. But they also find evidence that a childhood trajectory may be modified or even halted by key life course events, such as getting married or getting a job or moving from one town to another. Sampson and Laub believe that in the transition to adulthood, it is not so much the timing of discrete life events such as marriage but, rather, "the quality or strength of the social ties" that result (Sampson and Laub 1992, 73).

Sampson and Laub argue that future theory and research should elaborate how continuity and change work together in an individual's life course to inhibit or promote antisocial behavior. In proposing a dual focus on continuity and change within the individual life course, they nevertheless recognize that structural conditions, including social opportunities and the actions of social control agencies, impact the life experiences of individuals and therefore the chances that an individual's criminal behavior will begin, end, continue, or undergo modification over time. Sampson and Laub (1993b) use natural histories compiled by the Gluecks in the manner of earlier work by Clifford Shaw (see Chapter 2) to illustrate their thesis.

Interactional Theory

Terrence Thornberry (1987) developed an **interactional theory of delinquency** that highlights the relationship between delinquency and the family, school, and peers. While attention to these factors is certainly not new, Thornberry argues that criminologists have only explored their recursive or unidirectional qualities. The theory unites more "process" than "structure" variables, but clearly is an integrated theory, as it combines the insights of

social control and differential association theory, among others.

Thornberry argues that instead of just studying how a person's commitment to school affects their belief in conventional or unconventional values, we should also consider how beliefs shape the commitment to school, which in turn may further influence beliefs which then may further affect commitment and so on. As Thornberry (1987, 876) explains "… bonding variables appear to be reciprocally linked to delinquency, exerting a causal impact on associations with delinquent peers and delinquent behavior; *they also are causally affected by these variables*" (our emphasis). Interactional theory, then, suggests that many of the variables in social control theory and differential association theory can affect one another in all sorts of ways. Again, most people would think that strong attachment to parents reduces the extent to which youths associate with delinquent peers. But is it not true that associations with delinquent peers could affect a child's bond with their parents? Is it not also the case that delinquent peers could affect delinquency, just as delinquency affects association with delinquent peers? (Matsueda and Anderson 1998). Figure 12.4 illustrates this line of reasoning for those in middle adolescence.

That the school, family, and peers have multiple and reciprocal effects is just part of the interactional theory. The second major part of the theory specifies how these variables affect people over the life course. This developmental approach, which is somewhat similar to that of Sampson and Laub, suggests that the importance of these factors *varies by age*. For the very young, the family is the most important agent of socialization; when youths enter into middle adolescence, friends and the school become more important than before; and as the person enters adulthood, work and families of procreation (second families) become salient. All of this suggests that at different points of our lives, certain groups and institutions have more or less significance to our attitudes, beliefs, and behavior. No doubt the journey from childhood to adulthood is marked with change. It only stands to reason, then, that criminal offending is shaped by these developmental changes, and a recent test of the theory has found some support for this line of reasoning (Jang 1999).

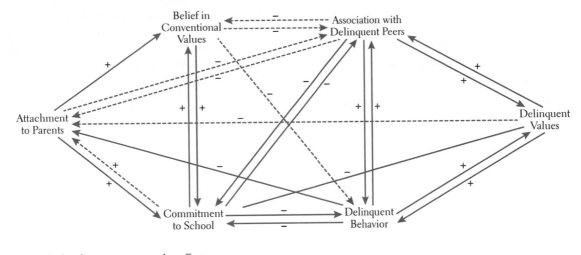

▲ FIGURE 12.4

An Interactional Theory of Delinquency

Source: Terrence Thornberry, "Toward an Instructional Theory of Delinquency," *Criminology* 25 (1987): 878. Reprinted with the permission of the American Society of Criminology.

CHAPTER SUMMARY

This chapter has considered the social processes by which people acquire the attributes of a criminal. A common theme running through many social process theories is that criminal behavior is learned through association with others who have criminal attributes. Associational theories focus on the ways in which relationships with others provide opportunities and incentives to learn criminal behavior patterns.

Self-concept theories of criminality suggest that a person's sense of self, which is grounded in the reactions of others, is an important element in the internal control of behavior. A strong self-concept is a defense against criminal influence. Neutralization theories suggest that self-respecting individuals will occasionally drift into crime or delinquency, provided they can rationalize their misdeeds so as to protect their self-image as essentially good and honest people.

Control theory, on the other hand, asserts that by nature people will tend to do whatever they want, including crime, so the important theoretical question is, "What stops them?" Hirschi believes that the more attached people are to the people, values, and activities of conventional (i.e.,

noncriminal) society, the less likely they are to become criminals.

Labeling theory revolves around the idea that crime is a label attached to behavior and to people; there is nothing intrinsic in behavior that makes it a crime. Labeling theory emphasizes how the stigmatizing reactions of others may turn an individual's infrequent or spontaneous criminal behavior into persistent involvement that matches a criminal identity.

The fact that Laub and Sampson discovered a more direct effect on behavior from family process rather than from structural background does not lessen the importance of social structure in the etiology of crime and delinquency. This is particularly true at the macrosociological level, where the structural characteristics and crime rates of whole communities are compared. Even at the level of individual behavior, the impact of social structure is felt through its effects on social process. Social structure sets the stage for the interactions and relationships that individuals experience and participate in. Social process theories deal with the interactions between individuals and their immediate social environment and the effect these interactions have on their behavior.

KEY TERMS

containment theory (p. 269)

differential association theory (p. 264)

drift theory (p. 270)

interactional theory of delinquency (p. 280)

life course (p. 280)

normalization of deviance (p. 269)

operant conditioning (p. 266)

secondary deviation (p. 276)

social control theory (p. 272)

social process theories (p. 264)

techniques of neutralization (p. 270)

RECOMMENDED READINGS

Barlow, Hugh D., and Theodore N. Ferdinand. 1992. *Understanding Delinquency*. New York: HarperCollins.

Gilligan, James. 1996. *Violence: Our Deadly Epidemic and Its Causes*. New York: Grosset/Putnam.

Hirschi, Travis. 1971. *Causes of Delinquency*. Berkeley, CA: University of California Press.

Lemert, Edwin M. 2000. *Crime and Deviance: Essays and Innovations of Edwin M. Lemert*. Edited by

Charles C. Lemert and Michael F. Winter. Lanham, MD: Rowman and Littlefield Publishers.

Sampson, Robert J., and John Laub. 1993. *Crime in the Making*. Cambridge, MA: Harvard University Press.

Shakur, Sanyika. 1993. *Monster: The Autobiography of an L.A. Gang Member*. New York: Atlantic Monthly Press.

Simpson, Sally S. 2000. *Of Crime and Criminality: The Use of Theory in Everyday Life*. Thousand Oaks, CA: Pine Forge Press.

RECOMMENDED WEB SITES

The Red Feather Institute

Criminologist T. R. Young summarizes and critiques many of the criminological theories discussed in this chapter.

http://www.tryoung.com/crime/002folk theories.html

Office of Juvenile Justice and Delinquency Prevention

A great resource for finding research and theory on juvenile delinquency.

http://www.ojjdp.ncjrs.org/index.html

RATIONALITY-OPPORTUNITY THEORIES OF CRIME

During the mid-1960s in the United States, rates of assault, rape, robbery, and other "street" crimes took an alarming upward turn and continued to rise dramatically throughout the 1970s. Crime quickly emerged as the number one problem facing the country, and President Lyndon Johnson created a commission to study the problem and offer solutions. Evaluations of existing theory and research as well as original research were undertaken by the commission. Two years later, the final report of the President's Commission on Law Enforcement and the Administration of Justice included more than twelve volumes.

Crime became a *cause célèbre* for the president and for Congress, which in 1968 enacted the Omnibus Crime Control and Safe Streets Act. Among other provisions, this act established the Law Enforcement Assistance Administration (LEAA), through which billions of dollars would eventually be funneled in the effort to combat crime. Scrambling to obtain pieces of this largesse were agencies ranging from universities wanting to fund research and to create academic programs, to police departments and correctional institutions wanting to professionalize, rationalize, and expand.

As the money flowed and the effort grew, so did crime. A sense of failure hung in the air. "Nothing works," was a popular lament. Efforts were redoubled and budgets grew. By 1976 the annual budget of LEAA stood at more than $1 billion. Still crime grew.

Mainstream positivistic theories and the crime-prevention strategies they informed, such as rehabilitation, came under attack from many quarters. Yochelson and Samenow's (1976, 1977) claim that criminals are calculating and hedonistic could not have appeared at a more receptive time. "It is not the environment that turns a man into a criminal," they wrote, "but a series of choices he makes …" (Yochelson and Samenow 1976, 247). This conclusion linked their research to an old idea, one found in the Classical school of criminology reviewed in Chapter 10: Criminals control their own actions and commit crimes when they believe the benefits of crime outweigh the risks. In other words, "crime pays." Not surprisingly, deterrence, the idea that authorities must make the choice to commit crime less attractive, became one of the hottest crime issues of the 1970s. As we noted in Chapter 9, it is perhaps one of the hottest issues here at the start of the twenty-first century as well.

Arguments in favor of deterrence have come from many quarters and have been promoted by some highly respected scholars. Taking a somewhat different tack, some scholars proposed an alternative strategy, but one also predicated on the assumption that criminals are rational actors. Why not reduce crime by manipulating the opportunities for its occurrence? Steering locks were introduced in automobiles, street lamps were made brighter, private security forces were beefed up, dead-bolt locks and home alarm systems were sold everywhere, new gun-control laws were proposed, and all varieties of environmental modifications were envisioned. Simply put, the idea was that many criminal events can be prevented if opportunities are reduced through "target hardening."

While overall crime has decreased in the 1990s, there is still much emphasis on how to make crime less attractive. This chapter traces these developments in both criminological theory and research.

RATIONALITY AND CRIMINAL DECISION MAKING

This section presents the criminological theory underlying deterrence and target hardening. First it briefly ventures back in time to classical criminology, which flourished in the late eighteenth century and is now undergoing a rebirth. The economic model of crime is a modern formulation of this classical view. The rationality model modifies the older approach in many aspects and introduces such interesting concepts as "crime displacement" and "able criminals."

Classical Criminology Revisited

As discussed in Chapter 10, Italian Cesare Beccaria and Englishman Jeremy Bentham are credited with forming many of the essential ideas of classical criminology. Writing in the late eighteenth century, these authors believed that criminals are free, rational, and hedonistic. Like other people, they choose among a variety of actions according to expected benefits. They avoid behavior that is likely to bring pain unless pain is expected to be outweighed by pleasure.

Although Bentham and Beccaria recognized that individuals are sometimes forced to engage in behavior they would not choose, the decision to act in a certain way is considered to be voluntary, and individuals are therefore responsible for their actions. "For classicism, it was an article of faith that each individual (except the mad and the infant) possessed the faculties of will, responsibility, and reason" (Garland 1985, 120).

The Economic Model of Crime

A more recent formulation of the classical view has been advanced by economists, among them Gary Becker (1968), whose work on crime was cited when he received the Nobel Prize for Economics in 1993. Many complicated models have been developed, but they all share certain key ideas. First, the approach "is predicated on the assumption that individuals choose to commit crimes" (Warren 1978, 439). Second, it is assumed that people choose the same course of action when confronted by the same alternatives. This is rationality as economists use the term. The choice itself is guided by maximization of satisfactions, or "utility."

Individuals evaluate possible activities according to utility. The utility of a crime is the expected gain weighed against the probability of being caught and convicted, and the monetary costs, real and foregone, if convicted. When the expected utility of a criminal act is greater than the utility of a noncriminal alternative, the economic model predicts that the crime will be selected.

The classical model of criminal behavior assumes that crime follows a calculation in which the perceived rewards, costs, and risks of alternative actions are compared. In itself this is a bold assumption because it not only implies that people are capable of making such calculations but also that they have the information necessary to do so.

Economists who develop models of criminal behavior often ignore noncriminal alternatives, concentrating instead on variations of estimated costs and benefits associated with crimes. The likelihood of a particular crime (robbery, for instance) is then calculated in terms of variations in the probabilities of arrest, conviction, and imprisonment, and in the economic losses (offenders' gains) for robbery, compared with other predatory property crimes. If the gains from robbery are small compared to the risks and costs, but the gains from burglary are greater, then a person acting rationally and voluntarily would choose to commit burglary.

VOLUNTARISM VERSUS DETERMINISM   The classical model is not accepted by those scientists who believe that people are "pushed" or "pulled" into crime by forces beyond their control. From this **deterministic** point of view, all assumptions of the classical model are questionable, especially the notion that choices are freely made. One cannot speak of free will, critics assert, when biological, cultural, or economic factors determine not only the choices but who can take advantage of them. In response, the advocates of **voluntarism** claim that it is reasonable to speak of free will, regardless of circumstances, whenever a person has a choice. If one can say yes or no to an action, the final choice is the exercise of free will.

These positions represent two poles between which more moderate views exist. One view is expressed in the observation that "offenders are not ineluctably propelled by social conditions. They have individual moral choice within the context of circumstances that beset them. After all, even though crime is distinctly related to poverty, only a tiny proportion of the poor at any given time commit crimes. Crime is a subjective choice in a given objective situation" (Kinsey, Lea, and Young 1986, 75).

The assumption that choice making is a fully rational exercise—a key assumption of the economic model and also implied in the writings of Beccaria and Bentham—is tempered by some authors who believe in a more limited rationality. It is argued, for example, that most people cannot know all the information necessary to evaluate all possible actions, but rather they reflexively react to opportunities that arise in ordinary situations (Trasler 1986, 20).

The limited rationality view holds that behavioral choices arise in peoples' lives routinely and some involve decisions to commit crime. These choices are structured by several factors, including the social distribution of opportunities and access to them; the knowledge, past experiences, and capabilities of individuals; the conditions that characterize and are created by the social situations in which individuals find themselves; and the measures taken by victims and authorities to prevent them. Behavioral decisions are made by individuals within the boundaries created by these factors. The chosen actions are rational to the extent that they are purposive (conscious and goal-oriented) and reasonable (efficient, economical) in light of goals and alternatives. It is not necessary to assume that criminals carefully plan and execute their crimes or use the most sophisticated techniques. Rational choice theories need only assume that some minimal level of planning or foresight occurs (Cornish and Clarke 1986a; Hirschi 1983; Newman, Clarke, and Shohan 1997).

Rationality and Crime

The **rational choice model** of decision making predicts that individuals think about the expected rewards, costs, and risks of alternative actions and choose actions best suited to their goals. If the model has merit, it should be revealed not only in the choice to commit crime, but also in the choice to commit one kind of crime rather than another, and in the decision to direct crime against one victim rather than another.

Research about these choices is still in its infancy, but some promising work has been done about the decision making of property offenders (Tunnell 1992, 2000; Wright and Decker 1994). This may reflect the prevalent view that property offenders are more likely to act rationally than, for example, drug addicts or rapists, whose crimes are popularly thought to be expressive rather than instrumental. (Despite its popularity, this view has been challenged throughout the text. Suffice it to say, many crimes involve rationality if only to the extent that they hardly ever occur in front of a police officer.)

Two examples of research on decisions by property offenders are Thomas Reppetto's (1974) study of residential burglary and robbery and Wright and Decker's (1994) study of burglars. Both studies show that offenders do have target preferences that were taken into account when they contemplated committing crimes. Burglars looked for unoccupied single-family homes (thus reducing the risk of being seen or heard), with easy access (thus reducing the amount of skill needed to gain entry), which appeared affluent (thus increasing the possible reward), and which were located in neighborhoods where offenders felt they "fit in" (another way to reduce the risk of being noticed) (Reppetto 1974). At the very least, most burglars want to know *something* about the people who live in the house and the types of things the house contains (Wright and Decker 1994).

The rationality model receives additional support from studies in England. Walsh's (1980) study of Exeter burglars found that although few burglars admitted doing much preplanning or "casing" of targets, most were very concerned about being seen, and avoided entering houses likely to be occupied. A second study of English burglars is more detailed and lends further support to the rationality model while pointing to the importance of situational cues in decision making. Using videotapes of thirty-six houses seen from a passing van, Bennett and Wright (1981, 1984) asked fifty-eight convicted burglars to evaluate the houses as potential burglary targets. Most of the burglars were very experienced so there is no indication whether the findings would apply to occasional thieves or beginners.

Although there was considerable variation in target choice, the burglars strongly agreed about certain blocks of houses or about one or two specific homes. When the authors grouped evaluations according to risk, reward, or skill factors, the authors found that the burglars most frequently mentioned risk of being seen or heard as the decisive consideration. Reward factors became more important than those connected with skill only when given as reasons to disregard a target. A house may not be worth burglarizing regardless of how easy it is to enter.

These studies did not investigate actual criminal behavior, only what offenders said about it. For that reason they give only inferential support for the rationality model. However, a study of actual robberies of convenience stores and the crime prevention effectiveness of various security measures found that only six of eighteen measures were significantly related to the frequency of being robbed, and only two of these in the expected direction: Stores with space around them and those with only one employee on duty were robbed more often (Calder and Bauer 1992). It is also true that criminals might not evaluate situational cues about ease of access and neighborhood surveillance all the time, especially when they are "desperate for money, feeling impulsive or bloody-minded, or simply too lazy" (Bennett and Wright 1981, 16; Shover and Honaker 1992).

It is important to remember that a full-fledged theory of criminal decision making needs to address not just the crime itself, but also the offender's initial involvement in crime. Such a theory must also account for decisions to continue and to terminate criminal activity (Cornish and Clarke 1986a, 1987). Traditionally, criminology has been more concerned with background influences such as social structure and prior experience and less with situational and transitory influences, which may influence certain types of criminal activity even more significantly.

Crime Displacement

Whenever criminally motivated persons decide not to commit a crime or to avoid certain victims in favor of others, the substitution is commonly referred to as **crime displacement**. Five types of displacement have been identified:

- Temporal Displacement: An offender substitutes one time of day, week, or even season for another.

- Spatial Displacement: An offender substitutes one street, neighborhood, area, or region for another.

- Target Displacement: An offender substitutes an easier, less risky, or more rewarding target in the same location.

- Tactical Displacement: An offender substitutes one modus operandi (method of operation) for another.

- Type of Crime Displacement: One type of crime is substituted for another, usually one that is less risky or more easily performed (Hakim and Rengert 1981).

Displacement is important for two reasons. First, its occurrence is predicted by the rationality model. The idea is that criminals generally take advantage of or seek the best criminal opportunities, those with the greatest rewards at the least risk and cost. Second, displacement is important because it is one of the potential costs of crime prevention efforts. For example, when criminal opportunities are reduced by police surveillance or other "target-hardening" measures, the net result may be an increase in crime in another place. Criminally motivated individuals simply move to the "safer" areas to commit crime. Therefore, one community may benefit from crime prevention efforts while another may suffer because of them. It should be kept in mind, however, that offenders often take big risks for very small gains (Wright 2000). This is partially explainable by the need to support a drug habit or a strong desire to continue "partying." As we discuss in Chapter 14, it can also be understood as an irrational, sensual, or thrill-seeking activity not readily understandable to the outside viewer (Katz 1988).

Research on crime displacement is sparse because it is extremely difficult to measure substitution behavior as it occurs. At the least, one would need to show that one criminal event occurred and some other did not because the offender changed his or her mind after evaluating the situation. Criminologists often infer displacement from studies of spatial or temporal changes in the volume of crime or by asking offenders if, when, and why they made substitutions. Most studies are further limited because they focus only on temporal or spatial displacement.

Spatial displacement is probably quite limited because "criminals prefer to operate in known territory." (McIver 1981, 32) This in itself is a sign of rationality, for familiarity reduces an offender's risk of being caught and may contribute to successful completion of the crime (Wright and Decker 1994). Nevertheless, some studies show that police crime prevention efforts resulted in "spillover" effects: Crime rates increased in neighborhoods adjacent to areas with more concentrated police enforcement. However, displacement is more likely to occur with property crimes, not with crimes of violence. The latter may be relatively impervious to displacement pressures because they are more likely to be spur-of-the-moment and tend to occur at the criminals' homes, near local bars, and so forth.

English studies lend tentative support to the displacement argument, at least for some crimes.

The Club is a type of target hardening that reduces the likelihood that the owner's car will be stolen. However, it takes many owners using this device for auto theft rates to be affected, and the principle of displacement predicts that many thieves will move on to easier targets or to different kinds of theft. The same holds true for car alarms.

When steering locks were introduced in new British cars as a target-hardening measure, the rates of auto crime did not drop significantly. Apparently many thieves turned their attention to the abundant older cars that did not have steering locks. In addition, determined thieves could quickly learn how to overcome the devices. This suggests that displacement brought about by changes in skill factors is probably limited to amateur and opportunistic thieves. However, a similar program in West Germany had the effect of dropping the overall rate of car theft because *all* cars had to be equipped with the device (Felson 1998; Mayhew, Clarke, and Hough 1992).

A third British study surveyed the impact of installing closed-circuit television in some London subway stations (Mayhew et al. 1979). Generally, stations with the greatest volume of traffic experienced more robberies and other property crimes. After authorities installed television cameras in high-traffic stations, the volume of robberies declined there but increased dramatically in stations without TV surveillance. On the other hand, other thefts declined throughout the subway system during the three-year test period. This finding suggests that an offense-specific spatial displacement took place rather than any general displacement. Apparently robbers took the new surveillance into consideration, merely changing location. Other, perhaps less committed or less experienced thieves were apparently more likely to view the TV cameras as evidence of a more concerted law-enforcement effort. Reacting to this perception, offenders reduced their activity, at least for a time.

Displacement is thus not an inevitable result of crime-prevention efforts such as target hardening (Felson 1998; Welsh and Farrington 1999). Prostitution is another case in point. A study showed that increased police enforcement in a North London suburb did not cause prostitutes to move elsewhere (Matthews 1986). Studies by Clarke and Mayhew (1988) of the effects of detoxification of the British gas supply on suicide rates showed marked decreases in suicides and no evidence that suicide-prone individuals were shifting to other means. Finally, the introduction of motorcycle helmets in various countries has apparently had the unintended consequence of reducing motorcycle thefts (presumably because thieves must carry a helmet with them), but there is no evidence that similar forms of crime, for

Signs warning criminals that neighborhood residents are on the lookout for crime seem quite sensible, but such signs stand little chance of deterring crime unless the criminals who read them feel that the risks of being caught are unacceptable.

example auto theft, have increased as a result (Mayhew, Clarke, and Elliott 1989).

It is unlikely that many offenders substitute new crimes for old when the calculus of risks, costs, and benefits changes. Income tax evaders, shoplifters, and employee thieves will not become burglars, con artists, and robbers. Some professional or habitual criminals may respond to such changes by increasing their skills and directing their energies only toward the most lucrative targets. They may become better criminals in the process, and they may also become more dangerous—willing to take greater risks, combining into more formidable groups, or increasing their willingness to use deadly force when confronted.

Those criminals most likely to shift from one crime to another, and least likely to continue a given line of crime in the face of increased risks and costs, are the less skilled but more experienced opportunistic offenders. They take advantage of easily accessible opportunities. They are unlikely to increase their efforts and risks in search of less hardened targets with which they may be unfamiliar or which may be too far from home. These are speculations, although a study of decision making among property offenders lends them credence (Tunnell 1992, 149). Considerably more work must be done in both theory and research to untangle the complexities of displacement (Felson 1998). The fact that there are many distinct techniques of situational prevention makes both tasks all the more difficult (see Box 13.1 on page 290).

Able Criminals

Some criminals reduce the risk and increase the likelihood of successfully completing a crime through planning, organization, and skill. This is the reasonable answer to overcoming risks when the anticipated rewards are compelling. It has the added benefit of increasing future rewards by improving the feasibility of undertaking more difficult but more lucrative crimes.

Though relatively few in number, a hard core of offenders is responsible for a large portion of the street crimes that come to police attention, as well as those that do not. For some of these offenders crime is a livelihood and they can make more money at crime than they ever could legally. These are the **able criminals**—experienced, and often

BOX 13.1   TECHNIQUES OF SITUATIONAL CRIME PREVENTION

There are several distinct techniques of situational crime prevention, including the following techniques:

1. Increasing Perceived Effort: Target hardening, access control, deflecting offenders, and controlling facilitators. Examples include steering locks, fenced yards, bus stop placement, and gun control.
2. Increasing Perceived Risks: Entry/exit screening, formal surveillance, surveillance by employees, and natural surveillance. Examples include border searches, police patrols, surveillance by bus conductors, and street lighting.
3. Reducing Anticipated Rewards: Target removal, identifying property, reducing temptation, and denying benefits. Examples include removable car radios and property marking.
4. Inducing Guilt or Shame: Rule setting, strengthening moral condemnation, controlling disinhibitors, and facilitating compliance. Examples include controlling access to alcohol and other drugs and the use of designated drivers.

Source: R. V. Clarke and R. Homel, "A Revised Classification of Situational Crime Prevention Techniques," in *Crime Prevention at a Crossroads*, ed. Steven P. Lab (Cincinnati, OH: Anderson, 1997), p. 24.

skilled, connected, and informed. They seek out opportunities even if that means charting new waters. In the United States, most predatory crimes seem to be committed by a core of relatively young but experienced offenders, many with a history of heavy drug use.

THE POSSIBILITY OF ARREST   Able criminals, and many others who violate the law, may actually spend little time contemplating the risks of crime. Several recent studies have found strong evidence of the apparent insignificance of arrest and punishment in criminal decision making (Shover and Honaker 1992; Tunnell 1992, 2000; Wright and Decker 1994, 1997). Interviews with forty-six persistent property offenders found that the majority gave little or no thought to the possibility of arrest and confinement. Here are some typical comments:

Q. Did you think about getting caught?

A. No.

Q. How did you manage to put that out of your mind?

A. [I]t never did come into it.... It didn't bother me.

Another subject said:

I wasn't worried about getting caught or anything, you know. I didn't have no negative thoughts about it whatever.

And another said:

When I went out to steal, I didn't think about negative things. 'Cause if you think negative, negative things are going to happen.... You just, you just put [the thought of arrest] out of your mind, you know. (Shover and Honaker 1992, 5)

Another study found evidence of a similar line of reasoning:

Q: As you did the burglaries, what came first—the crime or thinking about getting caught for the crime?

A: The crime comes first because it's enough to worry about doing the actual crime itself without worrying about what's going to happen to you if you get caught. (Tunnell 1990, 37)

Retrospective interviews are not without draw-backs, not least among which is the validity of re-constructions of events long past (Shover and Thompson 1992). It remains to be seen whether more proximal memories confirm the lack of a neg-ative relationship between perceptions of risk and criminal activity among able offenders.

Studying *active* offenders (those not imprisoned) has several obvious advantages over studies of in-carcerated persons. However, several recent studies of active burglars, robbers, drug dealers, and robbers of drug dealers generally support the findings of those studies conducted on prisoners, that most crimes are not well planned out. However, there is a tendency for incarcerated offenders to make it sound as though they are (Wright and Decker 1994).

As we discussed in Chapter 9, criminal justice policy is often misplaced in its assumption that ac-tive criminals seriously weigh the costs and benefits of committing a crime in a way envisioned by the average American. Just like any behavior, illegal be-havior manifests itself in a particular social context. This has been called the *socially bounded decision mak-ing process* by Shover and Honaker (1992). And as we mentioned in Chapter 5, living "life as party," being addicted to drugs like heroin and crack (in combination with economic marginalization) make all of this more understandable:

> The lesson here for theories of criminal decision making is that while utilities and risk assessment may be properties of individuals, they are also shaped by the social and personal contexts in which decisions are made. Whether their pursuit of life as party is interpreted theoretically as the product of structural strain, choice, or even happenstance is of limited importance.... If nothing else, this means that some situations more than others make it pos-sible to discount or ignore risk. (Shover and Honaker 1999, 20; see also Anderson 1999; Tunnell 2000)

All of this suggests, as we have discussed in previ-ous chapters, that popular notions of rational choice and deterrence are tenuous bases for building crim-inal justice policy.

OPPORTUNITY AND CRIME

Now it is appropriate to consider how the nature and distribution of opportunities for crime influ-ence criminal activity and shape the contours of crime for specific groups of people. It will be nec-essary to shift gears somewhat. So far, the exercise of will and the rationality of decision making in the face of choices have been discussed. Now it is important to think about the factors that shape those choices.

Crime as an Event

It will help to think of crime as an event. Crime is not an event until it has occurred, for an event is an occurrence or happening. A criminal event occurs when a situation fortuitously brings together factors that facilitate it. Advocates of a *situational* approach look at crimes that have occurred and ask what things came together to make them happen.

Crimes differ in so many ways that any attempt to identify basic elements shared by all criminal events would be doomed from the start (but see Gottfredson and Hirschi 1990; see also Chapter 14). A criminal event need not even have an offender present when it occurs. Some bombings and arson, forms of extortion, and many forms of consumer fraud take place when the criminal is elsewhere, even dead. The point is not as trivial as it may seem; detection, arrest, prosecution, conviction, and pun-ishment all rely on tying a suspect to the event. Strangely enough, some crimes occur only in the presence of police officers, as in resisting arrest and police brutality.

The **situational crime prevention** approach, sometimes referred to as crime opportunity theory, is based on ten principles:

1. Opportunities play a role in causing all crime.
2. Crime opportunities are highly specific.
3. Crime opportunities are concentrated in time and space.
4. Crime opportunities depend on everyday movements of activity.
5. One crime produces opportunities for another.
6. Some products offer more tempting crime opportunities.
7. Social and technological changes produce new crime opportunities.
8. Crime can be prevented by reducing oppor-tunities.

9. Reducing opportunities does not usually displace crime.
10. Focused opportunity can produce wider declines in crime (Felson and Clarke 1998, v–vi).

We shall discuss some of these principles in a few moments. First, however, it is important to note that the perspective holds that there are three minimal elements of a crime: (1) a motivated offender, (2) a suitable target, and (3) the absence of a capable guardian (Felson 1998). If any one of these elements is lacking, a criminal event will not occur. Notice that no mention is made of "capable" offenders, those able to "pull crimes off" (though they may later be caught). In fact, much crime is unsuccessful, making the distinction between completed and uncompleted crime an important one for theory and research. Indeed, the law has long recognized the distinction, treating attempted crimes less severely than completed ones. From the situational point of view the distinction is interesting because it prompts one to compare attempted and completed crimes in order to establish the differences, and to determine which elements account for the outcomes.

If there is a common element in all events, criminal or not, it is opportunity. An opportunity makes an event possible; a criminal opportunity makes a crime possible. One cannot rob a bank without the opportunity to do so—without the existence of banks. Notice, however, that banks provide not only criminal opportunities, but noncriminal ones as well. In fact, the purpose of most things is not crime, but their existence creates criminal opportunities. A functionalist would say that the above principle is a "latent dysfunction" of otherwise useful objects and institutions.

From a legalistic definition of crime, no event is criminal until those who create and administer the law say it is. While this is but one way to define crime (see Chapter 1), it means that two otherwise similar societies may have different criminal opportunities simply because the authorities in one society have labeled more (or different) activities as crimes. In one society, for example, people who take advantage of the opportunity to buy pornographic material may be committing a crime, while in another they would not be. Thus, the amount and kinds of crime committed among different jurisdictions depend on the existence of appropriate criminal labels. If the appropriate labels exist in all jurisdictions, then variations in the amount and kind of crime will reflect variations in criminal opportunities and access to them.

Social Change and Crime

As societies grow increasingly complex and as knowledge grows and technology advances, both noncriminal and criminal opportunities expand. The range of what is possible grows, and so does crime. This is probably what nineteenth-century Italian scholar Francesco Poletti meant when he observed that the more honest activity there is, the more dishonest activity there is. This would be true even if there were no changes in criminal law. But criminal law does change: Technological change makes new activities possible, and some will be labeled criminal if those in authority accept that they should be (see Michalowski and Pfuhl 1991). The U.S. government is obviously concerned: It has changed many of its currency bills now that advanced copying machines have made counterfeiting easier, and all bills now contain a metal strip embedded within the paper.

Consider what many people now take for granted: electronic fund transfers. Not long ago this computer-based service was known and used only by banks and large corporations. Now the automatic teller machine (ATM) is familiar to virtually everyone. Those with personal computers may also take advantage of home banking services. With the spread of electronic fund transfer has come growth in criminal abuse. Types of crimes resulting from this newer technology are the following:

- Unauthorized Use: This is when an access card is stolen and used without the permission of the authorized holder.
- Fraud by Legitimate Holder: For example, a person makes an authorized withdrawal and then denies any knowledge of it, demanding that the bank refund the money.
- Insider Manipulation: In this instance a bank employee steals directly from the machine, takes a card that should have been mailed to a customer, or creates a fictitious account by manipulating the computer.

The automatic teller machine (ATM) has made banking much easier but has also increased opportunities for crime, from fraud and theft to rape and robbery.

- Physical Attack: Automated teller machines often hold considerable amounts of cash and thus become targets of attempts to break them open. Customers who use machines can become robbery targets after they have withdrawn money (Bureau of Justice Statistics 1984a).

Of course, the growth of personal computers has opened up many opportunities for crime as well. As we discussed in Chapter 5, such crimes include theft, fraud, embezzlement, and blackmail. It is also true that contacts between people have become easier via chat rooms, instant messaging, and e-mail. Thousands of arrests, for example, are made each year of adults soliciting sex from minors and running or viewing child pornography Web sites.

Interestingly, Felson and Clarke (1998) note that the number of thefts of certain products are higher when they are growing in popularity or have just hit the mass market. Thefts are usually the lowest when a commodity is first introduced or when most people already have it. For example, levels of video cassette recorder (VCR) thefts have gone down since many people already have them and the potential rewards for the thief are negligible. The same may be said of hand-held calculators,

which are "mostly safe on your desk with the door open" (Felson and Clarke 1998, 22). However, when things are old enough to be in demand but new enough not to be easily purchased, thefts of those products are more likely.

Many criminologists believe that the global increase in crime throughout the past 150 years can be traced to an increase in criminal opportunities. In one classic American study, Leroy Gould (1969) showed that the significant rise in property crime rates from 1930 to 1967 directly reflected the growing abundance of property. Another classic study found that changes in English society not only increased the opportunities for property crime but also changed the nature of those opportunities (McIntosh 1971). A corresponding shift occurred from what is called "craft crime" to "project crime." Craft crime developed during Elizabethan times as cities grew and more people carried cash and valuables. The thief could steal small amounts from many victims and with practice could master a variety of skills. Pocket picking, shoplifting, gambling cheats, and con games were examples of craft crime. Project crime emerged as a by-product of industrialization. It is similar to the "planned operation"—a high-risk crime for high stakes (Einstadter 1969). It arises in response to the opportunity to steal large amounts from small numbers of commercial victims, such as banks and other businesses that go to greater lengths to protect their property by developing new methods that the criminal must then overcome. Innovations created by potential victims result in counterinnovations made by thieves. One does not hijack a Brinks armored truck alone, on the spur of the moment, or with a pocketknife.

Felson (1998) offers a more detailed description of the impact of social change on crime in his book *Crime and Everyday Life*. He shows why it is that the United States maintains high crime rates by focusing on crime as an event rather than on the number and motivations of criminals. He takes a **routine activities approach** and concludes that changes affecting where people live and work, where and when they interact, the type and storage of goods and services that are available, and the movement of goods and people have resulted in changing crime rates. For example, as cities became more dispersed, with more and more people living in single family homes and in the suburbs, and more and more property being spread over large and larger space, it also became more difficult for people to control their environment and prevent crime. Cities that had previously been "convergent," bringing people and property together, became "divergent," spreading them apart. Work organizations and schools also became bigger, drawing thousands, often from miles away. People can less readily monitor their own families under such circumstances, let alone the activities of strangers. Both informal and formal (i.e., police) social control is therefore hampered.

The Routine Activity Approach

Change sooner or later affects all social institutions, in addition to the environments in which people live, work, and play. The growth of cities, the smashing of the atom, the conquest of near space, the invention of the assembly line, the discovery of penicillin, the defeat of the Axis powers in World War II, the migration from southern states to northern states, the invention of the personal computer—all have affected our daily lives.

The relationship between change, opportunities, and criminal events has been explored in many studies. A routine activity is any recurring and prevalent goal-seeking activity. Work is a routine activity, but so are sex, child rearing, eating, going to the movies, and vacationing. Much crime is also routine activity.

Advocates of the approach argue that changes in noncriminal routine activities affect criminal opportunities by affecting the convergence in time and space of the elements necessary for a crime to occur. The basic proposition, as mentioned earlier, is as follows: "The probability that a violation will occur at any specific time and place ... is ... a function of the convergence of likely offenders and suitable targets in the absence of capable guardians" (Cohen and Felson 1979, 590).

This proposition is examined for both groups and individuals. At the group level, changing rates of predatory crime in America from 1947 to 1974 (and later to 1977) are largely the result of the dispersion of routine activities away from the household. Increased participation in work, play, and family activities outside the home increases the likelihood that suitable unguarded targets will be available to motivated offenders. To explain it another way, when fewer people stay at home, more household property is unguarded, and when more people leave home after dark or are alone, more people are unprotected. Looking at robbery from the standpoint of potential victims, for example, the chances of victimization are greater for people who are alone or away from home.

Another way of looking at routine activities is to think of the locations where crimes are likely to occur. Where would you expect handgun crimes to occur most often? Your answer will depend on the routine activities of typical offenders and victims, and on the relationship between the two. Thus, handgun crimes involving relatives are most likely to occur in the home; those involving strangers are most likely to occur on the street. Urban structure has an impact on violent crime and within that context the kinds of lifestyles (routines) people follow significantly affect their chances of being assaulted, robbed, or raped: People who go to bars, go to work, go to class, or go for a walk or drive at night are more likely to be victimized (Kennedy and Forde 1990; Wittebrood and Nieuwbeerta 2000). Similar findings have been discovered in studies of elderly theft-homicide victimization (Nelsen and Huff-Corzine 1998), homicide more generally (Caywood 1998), and gender differences in all forms of criminal victimization (Mustaine 1997).

Dangerous Places

Routine activities are carried out in a wide variety of places, and some are more dangerous than others. Crime risks differ in places that offer varying levels of guardianship to life and property (La Grange 1999). A place that offers few opportunities to observe what is going on, where anonymity is characteristic, and where strangers can come and go with ease lacks defensible space (Newman 1972).

Newman (1972) developed the idea of defensible space in a study of public housing projects in New York. He found that rates of serious crimes such as robbery increased along with the height of buildings, from 8.3 per 1,000 people in three-story buildings to 20.2 per 1,000 people in buildings sixteen stories or higher. He found also that more than half of the crime in high-rise buildings occurred in easily accessible corridors and other communal areas that were poorly monitored. He concluded that building design influences the opportunities for crime by affecting residents' surveillance and control of semipublic places.

Despite criticism of Newman's approach, the idea of defensible space has continued to draw attention. Other research shows that architectural features of the environment do influence the occurrence of crime, but that influence is mediated by such factors as age (the more young people, the more crime), household composition (the more single-parent families, the more crime), and size and density of both resident and surrounding populations (the more people in a given space, the more crime) (Pyle 1976). In fact, a growing consensus is that the value of defensible space in explaining crime rates is lessened by its almost exclusive emphasis on architectural features of buildings (Roncek 1981). What goes on in and around the buildings is the key. Anonymity and lowered guardianship are especially important in areas where people come together precisely for the purpose of having a good time—more bars and taverns mean more risk of crime (Roncek and Maier 1991). Good, recent research on matters pertaining to the notion of defensible space finds limited support for its overall significance in explaining crime (see Donnelly and Kimble 1997).

Access to Opportunities

The routine activity approach is a promising perspective on the relationship between criminal events and the organization of everyday activities. In the case of direct-contact, predatory property crimes, the perspective correctly predicts that younger people are more likely to be victims and offenders than older persons, as are the poor more than the rich, the unemployed more than the employed, the active more than the inactive, and urban residents more than rural residents. It also correctly predicts that small but *valuable* pieces of property left unguarded are the items most vulnerable to theft.

One factor that proponents of the routine activity approach have not researched is the manner in which the organization of routine activities influences the *range* of crime. This is not just a question of the nature of criminal opportunities, but of access to them.

Structural theories tell us that neither opportunities nor access are distributed evenly in time and space or throughout a population. Obviously, opportunities for auto theft are greater in areas where there are more cars, but getting to them, especially the more valuable ones, is not as easy for some thieves as it is for others. The opportunities for shoplifting are greater in areas where there are more stores, larger stores, and stores with open displays, but these stores may be clustered in certain areas only. The opportunities to pilfer at work increase as more people work and as work places grow larger and more impersonal, but only the employed can pilfer, and some employees can pilfer much more valuable things than others. The opportunities for executive crime—price-fixing, bribery and kickbacks, corporate fraud—increase as the economy expands, but relatively few people are able to take advantage of them. Of course, even though restrictions in access may effectively reduce the opportunities for a particular type of crime, they may actually increase the opportunities for other types. For example, higher rates of unemployment may result in lower rates of work-related crime and higher rates of loitering and public intoxication.

SPATIAL ASPECTS OF CRIME The spatial distribution of crime is affected by the constraints that govern behavioral decisions. Geographers have studied the locations where crimes occur and the movement of offenders to and from crime sites. Coupled with studies of target selection, this research offers insight into the links between criminal opportunities, routine activities, and criminal decision making.

"[O]ne of the striking things about criminals is that most of them behave as ordinary people most of the time" (Brantingham and Brantingham 1981, 35). In being "ordinary," people grow familiar with certain parts of the city—their neighborhoods, local shopping centers, entertainment districts, and areas where friends and relatives live. These areas constitute a person's "awareness" or "action" space. They are the familiar environment, the places a person knows well.

Choices are influenced by knowledge. Regardless of where the best criminal opportunities are located, criminals will tend to commit crimes within their action space. Studies of the distance between crime site and an offender's home show that this rarely exceeds two miles. There is also evidence that the number of crimes a person commits decreases as the distance increases from home base. (See Rengert, Piquero, and Jones 1999 for a discussion of the many complications involved in geographic analyses of crime.)

Motivated offenders living in places with few criminal opportunities have a problem. They must either forego some or all crime or move from their action space. Doing the latter increases the risks and costs of crime because (1) they are more likely to be unfamiliar with the territory, and therefore the targets and guardians; (2) they use more of their resources in travel, in getting their bearings, and in returning home; and (3) they are more likely to be recognized as strangers and therefore watched more closely by those who "belong" there.

These problems are exacerbated for people who lack the resources to find opportunities in unfamiliar places or who stand out because of some characteristic that cannot be easily hidden, such as race or sex. In a classic study of crime in Oklahoma City, it was found that African-American offenders had to forego areas they designated as having "easy marks" in favor of highly familiar areas (Carter and Hill 1979). For white offenders, easy marks and familiarity had equal weight in their selection of target areas. Further, it was discovered that black offenders had a much more restricted image of the city than whites, who moved from area to area more freely.

Offenders who commit crimes in areas beyond their action space may be "pulled" to those areas when the opportunities are especially abundant (such as in "red light" districts) or when the anticipated rewards are especially high. The rationality model predicts selection of those areas that maximize utility, and even high-risk areas may be selected when the expected returns significantly outweigh those from safer areas.

CRIMINAL RESOURCES   Access to criminal opportunities is governed by available resources. The greater the resources, the greater the range of accessible criminal activities. Some crimes require special skills (criminal computer hacking, counterfeiting, con games); some crimes require special equipment (computer software and hardware, record pirating, bombing, heroin production); some crimes require special planning (embezzlement, numbers running); some crimes require lots of money (cocaine and heroin importation, large-scale gambling, loan sharking); some crimes require prestige or social position (bribery, corporate crime, state crime, police corruption, welfare fraud); and some crimes require "connections" (drug dealing, fencing).

Despite (or perhaps because of) its obviousness, the resources aspect of criminal activity has not been carefully explored in relation to criminological theory (Agnew 1990). This is even more surprising given the long-standing interest in inequality noted in Chapter 11. Still, one can point to a few studies that address the issue of criminal resources. In an analysis of fraud in economic transactions, it was found that personal skills involving manipulation of people, use of status, management abilities, and technical expertise facilitated fraud and were important for the successful completion of the crime (Newman et al. 1981). Activities most likely to improve access to criminal opportunities are those related to work. Through work, people gain access to many resources and skills that can be channeled in either criminal or noncriminal directions.

Access to criminal opportunities influences not only which crimes are likely to occur but also the range of possible crimes. Criminal events occur more often if they involve relatively few resources. However, the range of criminal events is narrower when there are fewer available resources. Thus, those who are poor, unemployed, or otherwise disadvantaged in the competition for scarce resources are similarly restricted in access to criminal opportunities (Tunnell 2000). One would therefore predict that there would be less, not more, crime among such people and that the range of offenses they commit would be narrower. The first part of the proposition is predicated on the assumption that wealthier people have the same access to criminal opportunities as poorer people, with additional access because of their advantaged position. As demonstrated in Chapter 11, Messerschmidt (1986), Hagan (1988), and others have reached a similar conclusion about the distribution of criminal events in the class structure, though from an entirely different perspective.

Resources have been found to facilitate juvenile crime and delinquency. Agnew (1990), for example, discovered that youths with cars and other resources showed higher levels of delinquency involvement than other delinquency-prone youths. He concluded that resources confer power and autonomy and help to increase a person's ability to activate their predispositions, whether criminal or otherwise. This, in turn, increases their sense of self-efficacy as well as the potential profits from an activity.

Opportunities and Female Crime

Women and girls have been historically ignored by criminologists. Why? The answer is obvious: The field was founded by men and has been dominated by males ever since (Leonard 1982; Chesney-Lind and Shelden 1992, 2). If nothing else, this would tend to focus theory and research on the experiences and activities of men. Such an emphasis is, according to some, easily justified: Women commit fewer and largely petty crimes compared to men.

As we pointed out in Chapter 11, many criminologists believe this neglect has been detrimental to the study of crime and delinquency. Most prominent theories about crime are really theories about male crime and may not be valid when applied to women:

A theory is weak if it does not apply to half of the potential criminal population; women, after all, experience the same deprivations, family structures,

and so on that men do. To study only men or boys to assess whether or not delinquency springs from, for example, poverty makes little sense. Similarly, to refer to the "subcultural style" of working-class boys as a solution to the problems of redevelopment, housing, depopulation, and community solidarity begs an important question: How do working-class girls solve these problems? Theories of crime should be able to take account of both men's and women's behavior and to highlight those factors which operate differently on men and women. (Morris 1987, 2)

There is evidence to suggest that female rates of some crimes and delinquencies have been rising faster than those of males in recent years. It is certainly the case that the rate at which women and men are being sentenced to prison, jail, and probation for criminal conduct has risen. For example, Figure 13.1 shows that while the actual number of female murderers has declined dramatically in the past thirty years, more absolute numbers of women have been sentenced to death over that time span. Figure 13.2 (on page 298) shows that since 1928, the rate at which women are sentenced by U.S.

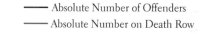

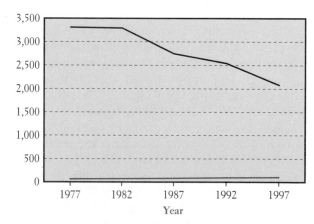

▲ FIGURE 13.1

Number of Sentenced Female Murderers in the United States and Actual Number of Women on Death Row, 1976–1997

Source: Kathleen Maguire and Anne L. Pastore, eds., *Sourcebook of Criminal Justice Statistics* (Washington, D.C.: U.S. Department of Justice, 2000).

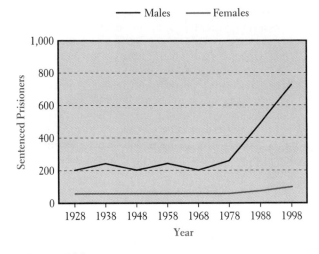

▲ FIGURE 13.2

Rate of Sentenced Prisoners by Gender, 1928–1998, per 100,000 Women and Men in the Population

Source: Kathleen Maguire and Anne L. Pastore, eds., *Sourcebook of Criminal Justice Statistics* (Washington, D.C.: U.S. Department of Justice, 2000).

state and federal courts has increased seven-fold, while the rate for men has risen four-fold. One explanation of the growth in female crime, and presumably sentencing, is couched in terms of opportunity theory and routine activities. The argument goes as follows.

The greater supervision and control of females, especially girls, restricts their routine participation in activities that are open to males, and hence the experience and opportunities that may lead to crime and delinquency (Hagan 1988; McCarthy, Hagan, and Woodward 1999). Historic to current practices encouraging females to remain "housebound" and schooled for mothering lessen the chances for equality, and to "make it" in what is essentially a man's world, except in the restricted contexts of marriage and "women's" work. Even when married women are employed in high status occupations, however, they are mostly responsible for housecleaning, cooking, and taking care of children (Farley 1998). In essence, women have been historically assigned the role of "auxiliary" in a man's world. This is true of criminal as well as noncriminal activities (Miller 1998a, 1998b, 2001). Through the years, researchers of delinquent gangs

have documented an auxiliary role for girls—as helpers, girlfriends, lookouts, but rarely as full participants (e.g., Thrasher 1929; Klein 1971; Campbell 1984). Apparently, men still run the underworld (Miller 1998a, 1998b; Romenesko and Miller 1989, 117). However, it appears that more females are involved in gangs:

> [F]ew would dispute that when it comes to serious delinquency, male gang members are involved more frequently than their female counterparts. However, this evidence does suggest that young women in gangs are more involved in serious criminal activities than was previously believed and also tend to be more involved than nongang youths—male or female. (Miller 1998a, 39)

Some authors believe the female criminal role is changing and that the shift reflects changes in the opportunities open to women. The expansion of Western economies has drawn many women into the labor force and out of the home. The women's liberation movement has pushed for equality between the sexes. The result, Adler (1975) and Simon (1975) suggested, has been a convergence of gender roles as many of the experiences and opportunities previously reserved for males (and a few "lucky" females) open to more and more females. In Adler's terms, a "virilization" of women has taken place, and the masculine female will become less distinguishable from her male counterpart in all areas of life, including crime. The changes, because they affect home life and the socialization process, presumably will filter down to young girls. This **liberation/opportunity theory** predicts that the crime rates of women and girls will increase and broaden.

The theory weakens under empirical scrutiny. Indeed, tests of the virilization hypothesis have found no support in studies of girls' delinquency nor has it been found that delinquent girls are less patriarchal or traditional in views (e.g., Cullen, Golden, and Cullen 1975; Giordano and Cernkovich 1979; Thornton and James 1980). One study, however, discovered that girls who expressed liberated views tended to be less delinquent than those who conformed to traditional gender roles. Figueira-McDonough (1986), on the other hand, suggests that the impact of liberated views may differ with the kind of school environment girls are exposed to: The more traditional and restrictive the

Here a two-year-old sits in a homeless shelter as her mother walks by. Homelessness among single women with children is part of the phenomenon sociologists call the feminization of poverty.

environment, the greater the pressures on liberated females to deviate. Steffensmeier and Allan (1988, 69) point out that "the emancipation hypothesis is at odds with the profile of the female offender, who is typically unemployed or has a poor employment history, espouses traditional sex role attitudes, manifests high emotional dependency on males, and has a high incidence of drug use or psychiatric history."

As for the new opportunities around which the theory revolves, most scholars have argued that there has been little real change. Females are still more likely to hold low-paying jobs that are often auxiliary to the "more important" and better-paying jobs of men. Some have suggested that many women are actually *less free* today than they were forty years ago. They are expected to contribute to family income, and yet child-care facilities are woefully inadequate. This is particularly burdensome on young single mothers, many of whom are teenagers (Morris 1987, 72). There is much merit to this approach, as it is clear the **feminization of poverty** continues into the twenty-first century. Quite simply, perhaps now more than ever, being a women, or living in a family with a female head

of house, is strongly associated with poverty (Farley 1998).

Another way that modern working women actually have less freedom, especially if they have children, is that such women inevitably work longer hours since they are subject to the "double burden" of wage labor plus housework and childcare (Messerschmidt 1986, 72–76). Messerschmidt finds no evidence that males (boyfriends, brothers, husbands) are taking up the slack in household chores and childcare created when women go to work. In many families that include working mothers, the daughters (but not the sons) take on added responsibilities. On the other hand, with more mothers working, children are less subject to parental supervision and some observers believe this will increase delinquency, especially among girls. Hagan's (1988) power-control theory of delinquency, reviewed in Chapter 11, takes this position.

Some authors believe that increases in separation and divorce and the rise of single-parent families during the 1980s and 1990s help explain the rising rates of female crime. The argument is that girls more than boys respond in delinquent ways to family discord and to the stresses of living in a single-parent family (Pornfeld and Kruttschnitt 1992). Figure 13.3 shows some possible aggregate level support for this line of reasoning.

Most recent theory argues that female crime has not really changed—it is still largely nonviolent, mostly petty, and linked to conventional female roles. If accessible opportunities have expanded for women, they have done so in relation to mundane activities that do not require special skills and resources. Women who are criminally motivated do what men do: They take advantage of the situations in which they routinely find themselves. What remains unclear is how much of the difference in male and female crime rates can be accounted for by opportunity/situation factors and how much by differences in inclination and motivation. It is also quite possible that sex interacts with other demographic variables (e.g., race) so that generalizations about female rates are misleading (see Hill and Crawford 1990). African-American female crime rates appear closest to white male rates, and it is important that future theory and research on female crime take this into account.

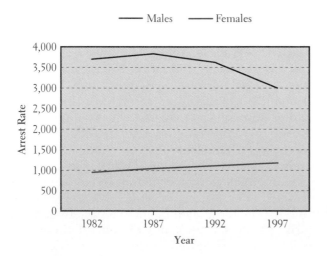

▲ FIGURE 13.3
Male and Female Juvenile Property Crime Arrest Rates, 1982–1997

Source: Eileen Poe-Yamagata, "Male and Female Juvenile Arrest Rates for Property Crime Index Offenses, 1981–1997," *OJJDP Statistical Briefing Book* (1998). On-line at <http://ojjdp.ncjrs.org/ojstatbb/qa072.html>.

CHAPTER SUMMARY

The central message of opportunity-rationality theories is, first, that crime cannot be understood apart from the nature and distribution of opportunities for both criminal and noncriminal behavior. Criminal opportunities are tied to the noncriminal activities that characterize a population. As these opportunities change, so does crime. Second, when criminals find themselves in situations in which they have opportunities to commit crime, the decision to do so or not to do so is a rational one.

Since neither the availability nor the accessibility of criminal opportunities is distributed evenly throughout society, modern theory generally asserts that behavioral choices are not exercised freely but within constraints resulting from conditions beyond control. Because of the uneven distribution of criminal opportunities, some criminals can participate in a wider range of crimes than others.

Geographers have demonstrated that criminal events cluster where opportunities exist, but sometimes the "best" opportunities must be foregone. Unfamiliar places tend to inhibit potential offenders, and this problem is compounded for criminals who are younger or less experienced or who have traits that would cause them to be noticed. Displacement, one of the potential costs of situational crime prevention, is predicated on the assumption that offenders alter their criminal behavior in response to changing risks and costs, but it has been seen that displacement is not an inevitable result of target hardening.

The routine activity approach brings rationality and opportunities together to explain the distribution of crime in time and space. Advocates of the approach argue that the everyday activities of people influence the convergence of criminally motivated individuals and suitable, unguarded, criminal targets.

The rational view of crime assumes that criminals think about their crimes before doing them, but does this apply to the apparently impulsive, spur-of-the-moment actions typical of many offenders? The best answer is a weak "yes." It is unreasonable to separate present behavior from past actions, and what may appear to be impulsive actions may be linked to previous actions that were preceded by rational thought. Furthermore, behavior that is routine and ordinary often takes place without much thought, but this does not make it any less rational. Finally, the narrow view that reason somehow does not belong in explanations for murder, rape, child molesting, drug abuse, and other so-called "expressive" offenses ignores the fact that the manner of execution and the choice of victim are rarely, if ever, mindless.

KEY TERMS

able criminals (p. 289)

crime displacement (p. 287)

deterministic (p. 285)

feminization of poverty (p. 299)

liberation/opportunity theory (p. 298)

rational choice model (p. 286)

routine activities approach (p. 294)

situational crime prevention (p. 291)

voluntarism (p. 285)

RECOMMENDED READINGS

Clarke, Ronald V. 1997. *Situational Crime Prevention: Successful Case Studies*. 2d ed. New York: Harrow and Heston.

Felson, Marcus. 1998. *Crime and Everyday Life*. 2d ed. Thousand Oaks, CA: Pine Forge.

Felson, Marcus, and Ronald V. Clarke. 1993. *Routine Activity and Rational Choice*. New Brunswick, NJ: Transaction Press.

Felson, Marcus, and Ronald V. Clarke. 1997. *Business and Crime Prevention*. Monsey, NY: Criminal Justice Press.

Newman, Graham, Ronald V. Clarke, and S. Shoham. 1997. *Rational Choice and Situational Crime Prevention: Theoretical Foundations*. Aldershot, UK: Ashgate.

von Hirsch, Andrew, David Garland, and Alison Wakefield. 2000. *Ethical and Social Perspectives on Situational Crime Prevention*. Oxford, UK: Hart Publishing.

RECOMMENDED WEB SITES

British Home Office

News, programs, and research on crime and crime prevention in England. Make sure to do a publications search, for many papers and reports on situational crime prevention are found here.

http://www.homeoffice.gov.uk/index.htm

National Criminal Justice Reference Service

This site provides an outstanding selection of reports on crime prevention, many through the lens of crime opportunity theory.

http://www.ncjrs.org

C H A P T E R

14

GENERAL THEORIES OF CRIME

The period of time from the mid-1980s to the mid-1990s may very well go down in history as the time criminology finally took stock of its achievements and rediscovered general theory. Six important theories of crime have appeared during this period of time, each purporting to explain a broad range of criminological facts that are not restricted to any one historical or social setting. The six theories are as follows:

- The sociobiological/learning theory by James Q. Wilson and Richard J. Herrnstein (1985)
- Jack Katz's (1988) theory of moral transcendence
- The theory of reintegrative shaming by John Braithwaite (1989a)
- The evolutionary ecological theory of expropriative crime by Lawrence Cohen and Richard Machalek (1988)
- The general theory of crime by Michael R. Gottfredson and Travis Hirschi (1990)
- The control balance theory by Charles Tittle (1995)

First, a word about general theory. As noted in Chapter 10, *general theories* explain a broad range of facts and are not restricted to any one time or place. This does not mean that a particular general theory has to explain all crime, but if exceptions keep turning up, its generality is obviously suspect. By the same token, successful tests of a general theory with a particular crime, say armed robbery, cannot be the basis for inferring that the theory applies equally well to, say, corporate crime or even to other forms of robbery. Only repeated tests of a theory with different people, places, or events will establish its degree of generality.

A General Theory of What?

As we have seen throughout this text, crime varies in many ways. There are variations from one population, place, and time to another, and from one individual to another; there are variations in the frequency with which people commit crimes (called the "incidence" of crime), and variations in the proportion of people who commit those crimes (the "prevalence" of crime); there are variations in the way crimes are committed, and in the consequences that follow for offenders as well as for victims; there are variations in criminalization, from the declaration that certain activities are crimes all the way to the imposition of penalties.

A general theory that explains all these variations would be impressive indeed. In the first place, it would need to explain variations at the individual level as well as variations at the societal level. The things that account for differences among individuals may not account for differences among societies, and vice versa. "There is some evidence, for example, that while unemployment is a strong predictor of individual criminality, societies with high unemployment rates do not necessarily have high crime rates …" (Braithwaite 1989a, 104). In the second place, a theory that accommodates all these variations would have to explain not only the behavior that constitutes crime, but also the propensity of people to engage in that behavior and the propensity of others to apply criminal labels to those people and acts.

A third reason such an all-encompassing theory would be impressive relates to the conceptualization of crime as an event. One way to think of crime as an event is illustrated by the routine activities approach, discussed in Chapter 13. In this conceptualization, crime occurs when opportunities and motivated offenders fortuitously come together in the absence of capable guardians. From this vantage point, a general theory of crime would have to explain variations in the situational matrix that gives rise to criminal events.

Another way to visualize crime as an event is in the form of a situated transaction that is constructed through the acts and reactions of participants as they occur *in situ*. In Chapter 3 we discussed murder from this perspective. Katz (1988) makes a distinction between "background" and "foreground" (or "proximate") factors in the explanation of crime, and this is relevant here. **Background factors** are the traditional focus of positivistic criminology: the biology underlying criminal behavior, the psychological determinants, the socioeconomic and cultural forces that push or pull people into criminal activity. **Foreground factors** have to do with the quality of the "lived experience" that is crime—in Katz's terms, the compulsions and seductions of crime felt by individuals as they live and breathe. Could a general theory of crime that accommodates background factors also explain the lived experience of crime?

The central concepts of a theory usually reflect the training of its author(s). It comes as no surprise when a sociologist includes social variables in a theory of crime, or when a psychologist includes personality variables, a biologist constitutional variables, or a geographer spatial variables. Yet some scholars see discipline boundaries as a hindrance to the development of a general theory of crime. Gottfredson and Hirschi (1990, 274) make this point, arguing that "much of the research generated by these disciplines is beyond the reach of their own explanations of crime." They "find no adequate positivistic theory that accounts for a range of well-documented facts about crime (e.g., the age curve [crime rates peak at age 20 to 24 and fall off rapidly thereafter], the gender gap, the disproportionate involvement of minorities, the high correlation between crime rates and rates of other 'deviancy'), and the characteristics of crime itself" (Barlow 1991, 231). And so Gottfredson and Hirschi claim to base their theory on a conception of human nature and of crime that escapes the fetters of disciplines.

If the disciplinary baggage theorists carry around restricts their ability to construct a general theory of crime, the competition among different theoretical perspectives within a discipline is surely more restrictive. This has led some criminologists to seek *integrated* theories that borrow from otherwise competing paradigms. In sociological criminology, for example, attempts have been made to unite control theory with rationality-opportunity theory, associational theory with strain theory, and cultural deviancy theory with control theory. These efforts expose some of the commonalities among ostensibly competing theories (Barlow and Ferdinand 1992, 201–222), though tests of integrated theories (usually with juveniles) have had mixed success. To the extent that an integrated theory explains a wider range of phenomena, it is more general than the individual theories of which it is constructed, and that makes theoretical integration a worthwhile challenge.

THE SIX THEORIES

These observations might well evoke pessimism about the possibility of constructing a general theory of crime. Yet the challenge has now been taken up, although it should be said that Katz (1988) makes no claim that his work constitutes a general theory. In truth, his is as much method as theory, but the two are so intertwined as to be indistinguishable, as we shall see. Here, then, are the six theories. There is space to do only a superficial job, and readers are strongly advised to read the original sources in their entirety. Always remember that the further removed one is from the original author, the more likely it is that arguments and ideas will be misrepresented. This is another good reason to read the original works.

We begin with two theories that share a common grounding in sociobiology, although one is an evolutionary theory and the other is a behaviorist learning theory.

Wilson and Herrnstein's General Theory

Wilson and Herrnstein (1985, 42) offer an integrative theory of criminal behavior that combines sociobiological, psychological (behaviorist), and rationality-opportunity perspectives on crime. Their theory is about "the forces that control individual behavior," and it incorporates behavioral, biological, and environmental factors to explain why some people commit "serious" street crimes and others do not.

An underlying assumption of the theory is that when individuals are faced with choices of action, they evaluate them according to their consequences and will prefer those with the highest anticipated ratio of rewards to costs. To the extent that individuals act on this basis, their behavior is rational. Therefore, both stealing and bestiality can be rational. Wilson and Herrnstein believe that individuals can choose to commit or not commit a crime, and for any given level of internal restraint (the "bite of conscience"), they will select crime over noncrime whenever the reward-cost ratio is greater for the crime than for the noncrime.

What any given individual considers rewarding (or costly) is part human nature (i.e., it satisfies such primary drives as hunger and sex) and part learned. These rewards may be material or nonmaterial, certain or uncertain, immediate or delayed. The evaluation of any particular action will be influenced by how well a person handles uncertainty and delay, which Wilson and Herrnstein believe is influenced by nature, temperament, and social environment. Aggressive individuals, for example, are inclined to be more impulsive and less able to delay gratification, a trait characteristic also of youth. The rewards of noncrime are often delayed, whereas the rewards of crime generally precede their costs and will therefore be preferred by less mature and more impulsive individuals. Finally, there is the important question of equity: Crime may be preferred to noncrime if it is perceived to correct an imbalance in distributive justice. Such an imbalance occurs when people feel that in comparison to them, others get more than they deserve on the basis of their contribution.

Wilson and Herrnstein's theory is controversial partly because of their claim that the theory is general enough to encompass most sociological theories of criminal behavior (1985, 63–66), partly because it is used to justify conservative crime control policies (pp. 528–529), and, perhaps most of all, because it links criminal behavior to constitutional factors. On the other hand, Wilson and Herrnstein have explored some new avenues and some old ones in a way that merits serious study.

A major criticism of their approach is its focus on "serious" street crime—murder, theft, rape—to the exclusion of other forms of criminality. A general theory of crime that explains only a small range of behaviors is not so general, and in any case it is certainly not established that embezzlers, con artists, organized criminals, genocidal state officers, and pilferers are constitutionally different from noncriminals, or for that matter, from other criminals. It is also curious that despite their declared focus on serious street crime, the voluminous research that Wilson and Herrnstein bring to bear on their theory often does not make that distinction. Finally, Wilson and Herrnstein's approach manifests the ideology of conservative criminology in its thinly veiled search for the criminal type (for additional criticisms, see Gibbs 1985).

Inferential support for Wilson and Herrnstein's theory (and also that of Gottfredson and Hirschi, discussed later) comes from a survey of college undergraduates by Nagin and Paternoster (1993). These authors asked students to describe their involvement in three distinctive offenses—drunk driving, sexual assault, and theft. Students were presented with various scenarios that were experimentally varied across the sample. They were asked to estimate the chances they would commit the act specified in the scenario, as well as the chances that they would be arrested; they were also questioned about their perceptions of the costs and benefits of committing the offense, and they were also given questions designed to measure their level of self-control.

Nagin and Paternoster found evidence of individual differences in the propensity to commit crime (individuals lacking self-control were more likely to say they would commit an offense), as well as evidence that students took vulnerability of the target and perceived benefits and costs of doing the crime into account. The authors thus concluded that individual differences and situational factors both influence the decision to commit crime—although in this case hypothetical crimes. The authors advocate more research along these lines, although less research has been conducted on Wilson and Herrnstein's theory as the years have passed since Nagin and Paternoster's study.

Cohen and Machalek's Evolutionary Theory

The evolutionary ecological theory proposed by Cohen and Machalek (1988) is also integrative, and what is remarkable is the simplicity of the result. The theory is heavily influenced by biological developments and is described as a general theory even though the authors apply it to a restricted range of crimes (although, see Vila 1994, for an attempt to extend the theory to all forms of criminal behavior). Even though the theory remains to be fully developed, it unites the perspectives of routine activity, structure, social psychology, and biology.

Cohen and Machalek (1988, 467) argue that variation in individual behavior is explained by the "alternative behavioral strategies" that are used as people try to meet their needs. Some of these strategies are *expropriative*, because they involve depriving others of valuable things. Many crimes are expropriative, and it is these crimes to which the theory is applied.

Behavioral strategies develop over time as people (like other organisms) strive to meet their needs. The successful strategies tend to become "major" ones. However, the more prevalent a strategy becomes within society, the more vulnerable the population is to "invasion" by alternative strategists, or to "nonconformists" who are willing to be creative. This is one way that new strategies evolve and behavior diversifies.

In addition, individuals differ in their physical and behavioral traits and resources. These differences may result in the selection (intentional or not) of different strategies, just as they may help or hinder a person's successful adoption of a preferred strategy. In this way, "conditional" strategies arise alongside major strategies, and again behavioral diversity grows.

Human beings possess intelligence, meaning they can think; however, people do not always act with conscious purpose. "It is thus unnecessary to assume that criminal acts are perpetrated by rational, calculating individuals who understand fully the strategic implications of their chosen actions" (Cohen and Machalek 1988, 479). Indeed, people may have resource advantages that they do not realize or intend, and yet these advantages explain why they have adopted a strategy. If a strategy works well it will probably be tried again, although the individual may never question or realize why it worked.

Cohen and Machalek argue that property crimes, as expropriative strategies, are promoted by various factors, some pertaining to individuals, others to the type and mix of noncriminal strategies that exist in a time and place. Deficiencies in social, cultural, and physical resources may promote criminal strategies (such as burglary) that are employed as alternatives to inaccessible noncriminal strategies. However, criminal alternatives may

also be promoted by resource advantages: "[An] individual who is rich in [resources] may be even more predisposed to commit a criminal act precisely because he or she commands the resources required to implement an expropriative strategy successfully" (Cohen and Machalek 1988, 483).

If both resource deficiencies and advantages promote crime, it is difficult to see how resource differences can explain individual or group differences in the selection of expropriative crime. Cohen and Machalek get around this problem by taking a conventional and conservative approach: People who are socially and economically disadvantaged are more likely to be exposed to values and experiences that encourage criminal behavior. They do not tell us why this should be so. On the other hand, resource variability can explain the type of crime selected, for as seen repeatedly in Chapter 13, access to criminal opportunities often requires the right combination of resources.

Because expropriative strategies arise as alternatives to legitimate production activities, they are promoted by the expansion and proliferation of noncriminal activities. For example, Cohen and Machalek (1988, 480) observe that "large-scale concentrations of producers offer rich and inviting opportunities" to both advantaged and conditional strategists. Once discovered, a particular theft strategy is likely to proliferate through conventional social-psychological processes such as imitation and social learning, and through independent discovery.

This brief sketch does not do justice to Cohen and Machalek's theory, which contains other elements and emphasizes the evolutionary dynamics that underlie the development and acquisition of behavioral strategies (see also Machalek and Cohen 1991; Vila and Cohen 1993; and Vila 1994). Nevertheless, it is important to note again that none of the elements described earlier is new. One can find them in the theories reviewed in the last several chapters. A new idea that does emerge is the notion that crime is shaped by "strategy evolution" in general, and that the characteristics, frequency, and mix of behavioral strategies explain the amount and types of crime that exist in any particular place, time, or group. An evaluation of their theory using real world data has not yet been accomplished; however, computer simulations have not disproved the theory (Vila and Cohen 1993, 907).

Gottfredson and Hirschi's General Theory of Crime*

Crime can be thought of as a form of cheating, where one person or group extracts resources from another without compensating the victim (Machalek and Cohen 1991, 223). What crimes have in common is the fact that they victimize. When crime is conceptualized this way, questions about the ubiquity and evolution of crime follow naturally enough, for how can societies survive in the face of such parasitic conduct? Gottfredson and Hirschi (1990) take a different approach in conceptualizing crime, although they acknowledge that suffering occurs. Much of the account that follows is taken from a critical review of their theory (Barlow 1991).

Taking classical (rational choice) theory as a starting point, Gottfredson and Hirschi argue that crime, as any other behavior, turns on the likelihood that it will bring pleasure. Its characteristics must, in general, be consistent with that result irrespective of the specific motives, interests, or talents of the people doing it. Gottfredson and Hirschi observe that most crimes are in fact attempts, and this implies something about the nature of crimes: They are unlikely to be carefully thought out, skillful acts involving special expertise, technology, or organization. Criminal acts are relatively easy and simple to commit, involve little skill or planning, and tend to be exciting, risky, or thrilling.

What makes crimes distinct from analogous acts is that they entail the use of force and fraud, and this helps make gratification immediate. On the other hand, force and fraud also threaten the self-interests of victims and are therefore universally resisted. Like Machalek and Cohen (1991) and Durkheim ([1893] 1964a) before them, Gottfredson and Hirschi see potential retaliation as the inseparable other side of crime. And so we have three other characteristics of crimes: They provide immediate gratification but also produce pain and suffering for victims and the risk of long-term costs for offenders.

Beyond the commonalities already noted, crimes will not occur unless an appropriate opportunity exists. That opportunity is defined by the logical structure of the crime itself, and therefore will vary from one specific offense (embezzlement) to another (rape). Gottfredson and Hirschi describe the "typical or standard" characteristics and the logical structures (necessary elements or conditions) of burglary, robbery, homicide, auto theft, rape, embezzlement, and drug use. The characteristics and elements of the offenses are strikingly similar. However, it is also apparent that the likelihood of any particular crime being committed is influenced by the availability of opportunities and a person's access to them, issues the authors do not explore. Presumably, the characteristics of situations and the personal properties of individuals jointly affect the use of force or fraud in pursuit of self-interest.

Gottfredson and Hirschi maintain that crimes are interchangeable not only among themselves but also with analogous acts that do not involve force or fraud. They call this the **versatility construct**. And so they end up rejecting traditional distinctions among crimes (e.g., petty and serious, personal and property, attempted and completed, street and suite) as "without import" and "a waste of time." They look for what crimes have in common as a basis for inferring what criminals have in common.

CRIMINALITY: LOW SELF-CONTROL   If crimes differ in opportunities for their commission, individuals differ in the extent to which they are vulnerable to the temptations provided by those opportunities. Gottfredson and Hirschi use the notion of *self-control* to represent that vulnerability, and criminality is synonymous with low self-control. **Criminality** refers to the propensity to use force and fraud in the pursuit of self-interest. Its characteristics are inferred from the characteristics of crime. In this way Gottfredson and Hirschi ensure that the conception of criminality is consistent with their conception of crime.

The traits associated with **low self-control** include short-time perspective; low diligence, persistence, and tenacity; a tendency to be "adventuresome, active, and physical"; a tendency to be "self-centered, indifferent, or insensitive to the suffering and needs of others"; and a tendency to have "unstable marriages, friendships, and job profiles." Since these traits are also implicated in many noncriminal acts (e.g., alcohol use,

---

*Parts of this section are reprinted with permission from Hugh D. Barlow, "Explaining Crimes and Analogous Acts, or the Unrestrained Will Grab at Pleasure Whenever They Can," *Journal of Criminal Law and Criminology* 82 (1991): 229–242.

accidents, smoking, running away, truancy) "crime is not an automatic or necessary consequence of low self-control" (Gottfredson and Hirschi 1990, 91). In other words, there is no theoretical basis for predicting which of many possible crimes and analogous acts will be committed by individuals with low self-control.

Gottfredson and Hirschi identify the major cause of low self-control as "ineffective parenting." However, individual differences among children (and parents) may affect the prospects for good parenting. Thus low intelligence tends to compromise the recognition of low self-control and the willingness or ability to do anything about it. Other factors affecting parental control and the prospects for effective socialization include parental criminality and anything that interferes with the monitoring and supervision of children. Gottfredson and Hirschi acknowledge that schools and other socializing institutions (marriage, work, Boy or Girl Scouts) may have a positive effect on self-control; but the further from early childhood one moves, the harder it is to make up for early deficiencies. Besides, the traits characteristic of low self-control are inconsistent with success at school, work, and interpersonal relationships. This fact explains, in their view, why delinquent youths end up in the company of each other ("birds of a feather") and why failure in school, marriage, and work correlates strongly with delinquency and crime (they all require diligence, hard work, and willingness to defer gratification).

THE STABILITY POSTULATE   Central to the theory is the proposition that levels of self-control are relatively stable throughout the life course. Put another way, "differences between people in the likelihood that they will commit criminal acts persist over time" (Gottfredson and Hirschi 1990, 107). This "stability postulate" is predicated on the belief that the early failure of control and socialization cannot readily be overcome later in life any more than effective control and socialization of a child can later be undone. Together with the notion that there are many noncriminal acts that are analogous to crimes, the stability postulate explains why the so-called age-curve of crime is invariant across space and across crimes, as well as why "[m]en are always and everywhere more likely than women to commit criminal acts" (p. 145).

To summarize, the central proposition of Gottfredson and Hirschi's general theory of crime is as follows: Crime rate differences among individuals are explained by the independent effects of variations in the characteristics of crime itself (i.e., the opportunity to pursue self-interest through the use of force or fraud) and variations in self-control (criminality, or the propensity to use force or fraud in the pursuit of self-interest). Criminal opportunities held constant, low self-control predicts relatively high rates of offending, low self-control earlier in life predicts criminality later in life, and criminality earlier in life predicts low self-control later in life.

SCOPE OF THE THEORY   Despite continued reference to "ordinary" or "common" crimes, Gottfredson and Hirschi call their theory general, going so far as to claim that the theory "is meant to explain all crime, at all times, and, for that matter, many forms of behavior that are not sanctioned by the state" (p. 117). In short, the independent effects of crime opportunities and criminality explain bait-and-switch scams in appliance stores, police brutality, bid-rigging, employee theft, fraudulent advertising, insider trading, tax evasion, smuggling, gang crimes, labor racketeering, prison rape, armed robbery, arson, burglary, murder, rape, and shoplifting; and they also explain drug use, accidents, smoking, and eating between meals. No specialized theories are needed because all crimes and analogous acts "provide relatively quick and relatively certain benefit with minimal effort" (Gottfredson and Hirschi 1990, 190).

Unfortunately, Gottfredson and Hirschi do not develop the opportunity (crime) side of their theory sufficiently well to predict which of all these varied acts individuals are likely to commit (at a high or low rate) at any given time, or when they might switch from one crime to another or from crime to a noncriminal but analogous act. Nor do they provide a basis for deducing what kind of social or cultural setting would experience a high (or low) rate of any particular crime or analogous act. Their treatment of these issues as theoretically irrelevant or inconsequential hardly lessens the theory's vulnerability to attack. In fact, it is quite clear that Gottfredson and Hirschi have a unique, and in our view, myopic understanding of crime, especially those committed in the context of an organization or institution.

CHAPTER 14 *General Theories of Crime*

The theory is most vulnerable in its application to white-collar crime, both organizational and occupational. Gottfredson and Hirschi present FBI arrest data on embezzlement and fraud to show that correlates of "white-collar" crime are similar to those of murder (and therefore other common crimes), and they also refer to "good research" that shows just how mundane, simple, and easy occupational crimes are and that the people who commit them also tend to commit analogous acts (drug and alcohol use, for example).

The evidence is at the very least inconclusive about these issues, and at most contrary to the claims of Gottfredson and Hirschi. Indeed, much research into organizational and occupational crime clearly challenges another assertion of their theory—that crime is more prevalent among those outside the occupational structure than among those in it (see Barlow 1991). The lack of consistent evidence of a relationship between unemployment and crime is one challenge, but another comes from abundant evidence that employee fraud and theft, though often mundane, are widespread in all sectors of the U.S. economy as well as in those of other countries. Furthermore, evidence of widespread crime in the fields of health, real estate, banking, insurance, defense contracting, and politics hardly supports the contention that high-end occupations are inconsistent with criminality (Reed and Yeager 1996; Yeager and Reed 1998).

Gottfredson and Hirschi do not assert that criminality is absent among corporate executives or other high-level employees, merely that it is less prevalent the higher one climbs the occupational ladder. Even if this is true, many of the crimes committed at the high end display characteristics opposite to those indicative of low self-control. Compared to low-end crime, high-end crime is much more likely to involve planning, special expertise, organization, delayed gratification, and persistence—as well as considerably larger potential gains with arguably less long-term cost. Such distinctions are also apparent when comparing the activities of fences with thieves, "good" burglars with "kick-it-in men," pickpockets with purse-snatchers. Gottfredson and Hirschi's theory can accommodate these observations in only one of two ways: Either temptations to commit force and fraud in the pursuit of self-interest overwhelm the resistance associated with self-control, or (many)

individuals with low self-control manage somehow to become managers, professionals, and entrepreneurs.

If their stability postulate is wrong, however, it is possible for people with low self-control early in life to develop it later and for individuals with self-control early in life to lose it later. Braithwaite's theory of reintegrative shaming (discussed later) presumes this to be true, while Gottfredson and Hirschi's theory requires that it not be. Recall that low self-control is inconsistent with effective control and socialization, and that includes socialization into as well as out of crime. Hence the groups and organizations to which offenders belong are regarded as facilitating crime among people who already lack self-control. Gottfredson and Hirschi thus dismiss as misguided (or poor) research suggesting that the social and cultural milieu of an organization generates criminality among its members. Besides, they argue, there is little social support of white-collar offenders because their offenses usually victimize the organizations in which they work and are detrimental to fellow employees.

Our reading of wide-ranging research is very different. Whether the subject is police corruption, employee pilfering, the ethics of corporate managers, antitrust violations, city politics, or state crime, one finds social support of criminality through subcultures of criminality—accommodating norms, goals, means, values, and networks of cooperation. Gottfredson and Hirschi's view that such support relates to the nature and context of crime itself rather than to the propensity of individuals to commit it would perhaps constitute a fatal counterattack if they could also show that self-control cannot be undermined by external (group) influence. This has not been established, however, and contrary to the general theory, rational choices are "far from being self evident and stable"; rather, they are "socially constructed in group interaction" (Yeager and Reed 1998, 894).

MINORITY CRIME Among the facts about crime in America are these: African-Americans constitute roughly 14 percent of the population; yet nearly 50 percent of those arrested for violent crime are black, as are 33 percent of those arrested for property crimes, 40 percent of those serving jail time, and 47 percent of those in state prisons (Maguire and Pastore, 2000). How would the general theory of Gottfredson and Hirschi explain these facts?

They reject traditional explanations of minority involvement in crime (e.g., inequality and subcultural theories) and resort to an emphasis on the self-control component of their theory. In their view, parental management of children is the key to understanding racial variations in crime; and within the realm of parenting, discipline is considered more important than supervision, which affects access to criminal opportunities. However, Gottfredson and Hirschi cite no evidence, saying only that "[p]artitioning race or ethnic differences into their crime and self-control components is not possible with currently available data" (p. 153).

On Gottfredson and Hirschi's side, the relationship between parenting and delinquency is one of the strongest in the literature, and evidence is piling up that the impact of structural factors (e.g., family composition, socioeconomic status) on delinquency is mediated by parental management. Nevertheless, if poverty, community disorganization, large family size, and family instability impact negatively on parental management, rates of crime and delinquency will be affected. Such structural conditions are prevalent in inner-city black communities (Anderson 1999; Wilson 1987), where rates of victimization by force and fraud are also high. Gottfredson and Hirschi do not explore the implications of this for their theory.

In rejecting inequality theories of race differences in crime, Gottfredson and Hirschi point out that "[offenders] tend to victimize people who share their unfortunate circumstances" (p. 152). True, but then this question arises: Are there race differences in the tendency for offenders to victimize people who are like themselves? According to their theory, crime is a matter of "proximity, ease, and convenience of rewards"; hence there is no a priori basis for predicting such differences. Nevertheless, studies of the urban distribution of crime indicate that black offenders have a more restricted image of the city than white offenders, who can move around more freely and need not concentrate their criminal activities in areas close to home, thereby foregoing "easy marks" (Carter and Hill 1979; Boggs 1964). This suggests that while most crime tends to be intraracial, crimes committed by whites are likely to be more dispersed and hence potentially more rewarding—but also more costly and risky—

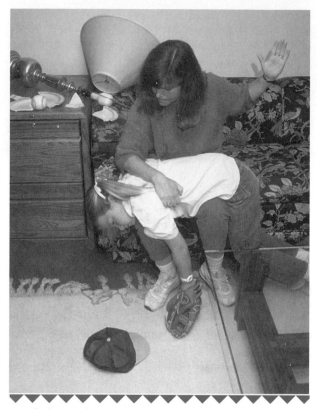

Gottfredson and Hirschi's general theory of crime and Braithwaite's theory of reintegrative shaming both identify parental discipline as an explanatory factor in crime. What would the authors have to say about this picture?

than crimes committed by blacks. If access to profitable criminal opportunities is skewed in favor of whites, Gottfredson and Hirschi are silent on the issue and its implications for their theory.

Gottfredson and Hirschi's general theory of crime has come under considerable empirical scrutiny since its publication (Pratt and Cullen 2000). An example of the most common approach to testing the theory is a study of drunk driving and self-control. Here a composite measure of low self-control was found to relate to DUIs for both men and women, and the authors found a strong risk-taking component to drunk driving—for example, not wearing seat belts. However, they also found that teenagers did not have higher blood-alcohol levels than others, and speculate that a minimum drinking age of nineteen might have been a factor. Furthermore, "it may be that teenagers express more of their criminality in other and more demanding (i.e., physical) ways" (Keane, Maxim, and Teevan 1993, 40). As seems fairly typical of tests of this general theory to date, self-control is found to relate to crime or analogous acts and therefore the theory cannot be rejected (Gibbs, Giever, and Martin 1998; Evans, Cullen, Burton, Dunaway, and Benson 1997; Paternoster and Brame 1998).

Braithwaite's Theory of Reintegrative Shaming

Like Gottfredson and Hirschi, Braithwaite (1989a, 1) believes that "there is sufficient in common between different types of crime to render a general explanation possible." However, Braithwaite explicitly rejects the idea that crimes are inherently similar, arguing instead that they are qualitatively similar by virtue of the stigma attached to them and by the fact that the offender makes a "defiant choice" in grasping the opportunity to perpetrate a crime:

> The homogeneity presumed between disparate behaviors such as rape and embezzlement in this theory is that they are choices made by the criminal

actor in the knowledge that he is defying a criminal proscription which is mutually intelligible to actors in the society as criminal. (Braithwaite 1989a, 3)

Braithwaite excludes acts that are formally crimes but whose criminalization is without support in the society at large, for example, "laws against marijuana use in liberal democracies or laws that create political crimes against the state in communist societies …" (p. 3). Braithwaite's theory applies to predatory crimes, acts that involve victimization of one person or group by another.

We encountered some of the ideas associated with Braithwaite's theory in previous chapters. But the theory is much more than this. Braithwaite offers yet another integrative theory, one that incorporates elements of major sociological theories of crime and delinquency: control theory, labeling theory, subcultural theory, associational theory, strain theory, and social learning theory.

Braithwaite's diagram of his theory is reproduced in Figure 14.1. The arrows indicate the direction or flow of influence between linked variables, and the

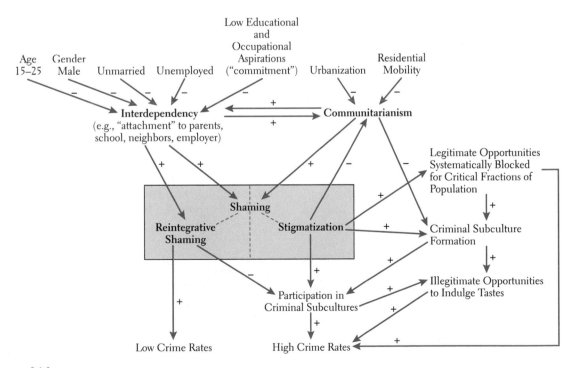

▲ FIGURE 14.1

A Summary of Braithwaite's Theory of Reintegrative Shaming

Source: John Braithwaite, *Crime, Shame, and Reintegration* (Cambridge, UK: Cambridge University Press, 1989). Reprinted with permission.

The village stocks were an example of punishment by discomfort and shame. Shaming without reintegration, however, creates crime rather than reduces it, according to Braithwaite.

signs indicate whether the relationship between them is positive (i.e., a plus sign indicates the more of one, the more of the other) or negative (i.e., a minus sign indicates the more of one, the less of the other).

On the integrative and original aspects of his theory, Braithwaite (1989a, 107) has this to say:

> The top left of [the figure] incorporates the key variables of control theory; the far right—opportunity [strain] theory; the middle and bottom right—subcultural theory; the right side of the middle box—labeling theory. With one crucial exception (reintegrative shaming), there is therefore no originality in the elements of this theory, simply originality of synthesis.

The central proposition of the theory is this: Crime rates of individuals and groups are influenced directly by processes of shaming. High crime rates result from shaming that stigmatizes, because rule-breakers who are shamed but not forgiven are more likely to become "outlaws" and to participate in subcultures of crime. This is referred to as **disintegrative shaming**, a stigmatizing approach that involves the following:

- Disrespectful disapproval and humiliation
- Ceremonies to certify deviance but no ceremonies to decertify deviance

- Labeling the person, not just the deed, as evil
- Allowing deviance to become a master status trait (Braithwaite 1995, 194)

On the other hand, when rule-breakers are shamed but then forgiven and welcomed back to the fold, the unpleasant, punitive experience of being shamed is offset by the pleasant relief of discovering that one is still accepted (loved, wanted, cared about) despite the transgression. This is what Braithwaite refers to as **reintegrative shaming**. The process of reintegrative shaming confirms the validity of the rules and reestablishes the transgressor's place as a member in good standing. This process involves the following:

- Disapproval while sustaining a relationship of respect
- Ceremonies to certify deviance terminated by ceremonies to decertify deviance
- Disapproval of the evil of the deed without labeling the persons as evil
- Deviance not being allowed to become a master status trait (Braithwaite 1995, 194)

Although Braithwaite hypothesizes that either kind of shaming is likely to be more successful at combating predatory crime than "punishment without associated moralizing and denunciation" (p. 86), systems of punishment that encourage reintegration should experience the lowest crime rates.

As a mechanism of social control, shaming works best among closely connected people whose fortunes, reputations, and futures are interdependent—as in families, for example, or among workmates, colleagues, and friends. Justice officials in Western industrialized societies are at a decided disadvantage: "Most of us will care less about what a judge (whom we meet only once in our lifetime) thinks of us than we will care about the esteem in which we are held by a neighbor we see regularly" (Braithwaite 1989a, 87). Interdependence among individuals has a societal correlate—*communitarianism*—which has three elements:

> (1) Densely enmeshed interdependency, where interdependencies are characterized by (2) mutual obligation and trust, and (3) are interpreted as a matter of group loyalty rather than individual convenience. Communitarianism is therefore the antithesis of individualism. (Braithwaite 1989, 86)

Western industrialized societies, with their high rates of urbanization and residential mobility, are more individualistic than less-developed agrarian societies. The model in Figure 14.1 shows that communitarianism has a positive effect on shaming, but is itself undermined by shaming that is merely stigmatizing. This is because shaming without reintegration makes criminal subcultures more attractive and encourages their formation "by creating populations of outcasts with no stake in conformity" (Braithwaite 1989a, 102). Criminal subcultures are also fostered by blocked legitimate opportunities, and once formed, they encourage crime directly by providing illegitimate opportunities and incentives to deviate from the norms of conventional society.

At the individual level, **interdependency** is associated with age, marital status, gender, employment status, and aspirations within societally approved opportunity systems. More so than other people, older teenagers and young adults—especially if they are male—are freed from the constraints and obligations of interdependency, as are single people, those without work, and those with a low commitment to legitimate ways of "getting ahead." Absent the close ties of interdependency, such people are less likely to be exposed to

or affected by shaming. They are more susceptible to crime because controls are weak.

EVALUATION OF THE THEORY   Braithwaite's work is an important contribution to criminological theory. Not only does he show how "old" competing theories can be integrated into one model, but his addition of the social-psychological variable, shaming, is a major innovation. Along with associational theories, his theory is one of the few that can be applied to occupational and organizational crimes. Other notable accomplishments are that the theory of reintegrative shaming can be applied at both individual and societal levels of analysis, and that it incorporates background and foreground variables, although discussion of the lived experience of shaming is largely limited to the mechanics of gossip (see Braithwaite 1989a, 75–77). The latter is certainly an area for future research and elaboration and will be considered when we discuss Katz.

Braithwaite suggests ways of testing his theory and even mentions modifications that could be made to accommodate additional variables. Few specific tests of the theory have been conducted to date, but at least a dozen or so studies have found some empirical support for its basic thesis (Chaplin and Cochran 1997; Hay 2001; Makkai and Braithwaite 1994; Vagg 1998). Despite the absence of focused tests, Braithwaite confidently asserts the merits of his theory by claiming that it accounts for the thirteen best-established findings in criminology, which no other existing theory can do. (Some of these were listed in Chapter 1 as "Facts about Street Crime.") Among these findings are the high rates of crime among males, people living in large cities, certain categories of young people (e.g., those with low aspirations, poor school performance, weak attachments to school or parents, or strong attachments to delinquent peers), and among disadvantaged people. The theory also accounts for the low rate of crime in Japan—an industrialized nation—when compared with other industrialized nations such as the United States (see Braithwaite 1989a, especially pages 61–66).

One of the theory's most interesting aspects is its implications for criminal justice policy in highly individualized societies such as our own. Given that reintegrative shaming works best in the informal contexts of family, friends, and neighborhood, a justice policy aimed at preventing or reducing crime should be a community-based, largely informal system that uses traditional process and punishment as a last resort. Such an approach has come to be known in recent years as **restorative justice**. Box 14.1 provides some information on restorative justice practices that are consistent with Braithwaite's theory.

Expanding on the policy implications of the theory, Braithwaite and Pettit (1990) advocate a "republican" approach to criminal justice in which formal interventions are minimized and in which subjective assurances of liberty, equality, fraternity, and dialogue are guaranteed all citizens (also see Braithwaite 1991). The reintegrative prospects of

Box 14.1   RESTORATIVE JUSTICE

Restorative justice involves a holistic approach to criminal justice and crime prevention that promotes the healing of the victim, offender, and community. It is inspired by a genuine desire to right a wrong (crime), but in a fair and humane way. Restorative justice differs from traditional criminal justice in several ways. First, its focus is on the future. Healing requires an understanding of the past harm, but healing the injury, rebuilding the community, and forging interdependencies should be paramount. Second, the process by which justice is to be achieved is through dialogue, mediation, and negotiation, not through adversarial "war-like" techniques. Healing is the goal, not the amount of people who can be sent away to prison. Third, the offender takes responsibility for the crime and repentance is encouraged. This is crucial for reintegration, as traditional punishment and revenge philosophies generally do not facilitate healing. Fourth, restorative justice carries a concern not only for the victims of crime, but also a sincere concern for the well-being of the offender. Historically, offenders were considered violators of the abstracted "society" and unfit for membership in the community.

There are many types of restorative justice practices in Australia, New Zealand, and the United States. Here are some that are consistent with Braithwaite's shaming theory:

- Victim-offender, community accountability, and family group conferences where offenders, victims, and communities come together to reintegratively shame and restore community and victim health
- Community and neighborhood advisory boards, which offer input and advice for the handling of deviance and deviants in the community
- Peer mediation and conferencing, where the offender is shamed by peers and intimates and then reintegrated into the group
- Victim services and victim impact statements, where victims can be heard by state officials, special victims agents, and the offender
- Offender community service, in which the offender gives back to the community harmed
- Offender competency development, such as the teaching of life, civic, and parenting skills

Many county courts, prosecutor's offices, and probation departments in the United States have embraced the philosophy of restorative justice. To the many practitioners who have seen the failures of traditional justice, restorative justice is seen as an attractive approach, but it is still unclear whether the restorative justice movement will become the dominant form of doing justice in the years to come.

Sources: Minnesota Department of Corrections (1998a, 1998b) and The Restorative Justice Institute (1999).

community shaming in such a setting are enhanced and the likelihood is greater that the offender will recognize his offense and shame himself. In this manner, shaming becomes conscience-building, the essence of crime prevention in Braithwaite's view.

Despite its originality, broad scope, and impressive integration of existing theories, the theory of reintegrative shaming leaves at least one important issue unresolved. For example, Braithwaite (1989a, 13) claims his theory accommodates the existence of "multiple moralities" in modern societies whereas some others do not. He argues, "[a] severe limitation of theories that deny this, like Hirschi's control theory, is that they give no account of why some uncontrolled individuals become heroin users, some become hit men, and others price fixing conspirators." This is fair enough, but aside from identifying criminal subcultures as the milieu in which crime is learned and via which tastes may be indulged in illegitimate ways, it is by no means clear how one would derive predictions about variations in the prevalence and incidence of particular types of crime, or about crime selection by predisposed individuals. Braithwaite may wish to reconsider the contributions of the rationality-opportunity perspective we reviewed in Chapter 13.

Tittle's Control Balance Theory

Recall from Chapter 12 that Hirschi's social control theory holds that people who are not strongly bonded to conventional society are those most likely to commit crime. Hirschi's argument, then, is that this *lack of control* produces criminal outcomes. But what about people who have a lot of control or those who are over-controlled? Are they likely to commit crimes as well? Would they commit different types of crime from those who are under-controlled?

Charles Tittle (1995) has recently produced an integrative *control balance theory of deviance* that addresses these and other questions. First, Tittle intends his theory to explain deviance, not just crime. Deviance, according to Tittle (1995, 124), is "any behavior that the majority of a given group regards as unacceptable or that typically evokes a collective response of a negative type."

The central thesis of control balance theory is that the "amount of control to which people are subject relative to the amount of control they can exercise" affects the probability of deviance more generally, as well as the *type* of deviance (Tittle 1995, 142). Being controlled or experiencing control means that a person is subject to the will of others through, for example, rewards and punishments. If a teenager is not free to stay out all night, drink beer, choose her friends, or go to concerts, one might say she is experiencing control. When people *exercise* control, they have the ability to limit the options, choices, and behaviors of others. The parent who sets the limits in the earlier example is exercising control.

The relationship of control to deviance is found in the **control ratio**, which is the overall level of control people have in their lives. The ratio is calculated by weighing the total level of control a person exercises against the total level of control that the person is subject to. People who control more than they are controlled by others have a **control surplus**, while those who are controlled more than they control others have a **control deficit**. Tittle (1995, 266) provides the following example:

> [A] man may have a control surplus in the domestic realm but a control deficit in the work environment, a youth may have a control deficit in the society as a whole, but a control surplus in the recreational domain, and a woman may have a control surplus in the realm of interpersonal relations, but a control deficit with respect to the physical environment.

Another example is in order. Think of the class for which you are reading this book. How much control do you have over the course? How much control are you subject to in the course? You have probably been subject to control in the following ways: You must meet the class requirements, such as passing grades on papers and examinations; even the number, nature, and length of the papers and examinations is probably out of your control. You may also be required to attend lectures and participate in classroom discussions. You must also earn a certain number of points or a certain overall grade to have this class "count" for credit. You have probably had little if any control over the textbook used, whether class is canceled, or if it is dismissed early. Clearly you are subject to great amounts of control and regulation in a typical college classroom. Now, what kinds of things can you control in the course?

Unless the class is extremely unfair, most students have some control over their performance on exams and the relative content of their papers. You may also have some control in group discussions and by making observations or raising questions to the professor. You also, of course, have the ability to drop the course, be more or less interested in the course, and express your views about the course and instructor on teaching evaluations. All told, however, you can see how most students probably have a control deficit when it comes to the typical college course. Can you think of how this control deficit might lead to deviance in the form of cheating, plagiarism, and lying to the professor? How might the professor act deviantly as a result of his or her control surplus? Are there professors who sexually harass, discriminate, or use psychological "warfare" to intimidate students?

TYPES OF DEVIANCE   According to Tittle, those who have a **control balance** are least likely to engage in deviance, but the probability and seriousness of deviance rises with the degree of control deficit and surplus. This is straightforward enough, but Tittle goes one step further by theorizing that the *type* of resulting deviance will differ depending on whether one has a surplus or deficit

(see Figure 14.2). Those with a control deficit seek to escape or rectify their problem through deviance, while those with a surplus seek to extend their control. Therefore, those with a surplus are more likely to commit *autonomous* forms of deviance, which Tittle describes as deviant acts of exploitation (economic white-collar crimes), plunder (violent and unjust state and corporate crimes), and decadence (group sex with children and sadism). However, those with a control deficit are more likely to commit *repressive* forms of deviance, which are the deviant forms of predation (traditional forms of violent crime), defiance (representing contempt for authority), or submission (blind conformity) (Tittle 1995, 137–140).

What's more, the greater the control imbalance, the more extreme the deviance is likely to be. This means, as Figure 14.2 shows, that small control deficits prompt predation, intermediate levels prompt defiance, and extreme control deficits are likely to cause submissive deviance. Likewise, a minimal level of control surplus is related to acts of exploitation, while intermediate amounts prompt plunder, and extreme control surpluses are likely to produce decadent deviance. Simply stated, these differing deviant manifestations are caused by the attempt to either rectify or balance the control ratio

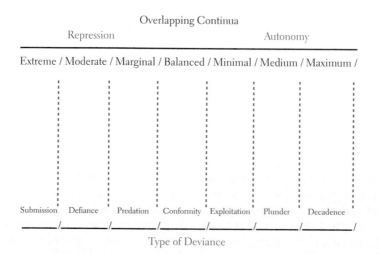

▲ FIGURE 14.2

Tittle's Control Balance Theory: The Types and Levels of Deviance

Source: Charles Tittle, *Control Balance: Toward a General Theory of Deviance* (Boulder, CO: Westview Press, 1995), 189. Reprinted with permission.

(in the case of a control deficit) or an attempt to *expand* control in the case of those with a control surplus.

CRITICAL VARIABLES   Surely a control imbalance is not by itself sufficient for the deviant act to take place. Tittle rightly acknowledges that other independent variables play a role in the genesis and persistence of deviant behavior:

1. The *predisposition* toward deviant motivation
2. The situational stimulation of deviance (*provocation*)
3. The likelihood of *constraint* in the face of deviance
4. The *opportunity* to commit deviance

Let us briefly review each of these variables. Tittle argues that the predisposition to deviance is rooted in a fundamental aspect of human nature: the desire for autonomy. This means that people generally want to escape the control of others as well, to extend their control over others. This universal drive for freedom and power is likely to result in deviance when control is imbalanced. Thus, while the theory is called control balance, a major *motivation* for deviance is the elimination of the control imbalance. Tittle also suggests that autonomy and control are embedded not only in the personal, individual context, but within organizational contexts, such as family and work.

While motivation is a necessary component of the deviant act, certain events and circumstances trigger the behavior. This is what Tittle (1995, 163) calls *provocation*, which includes "… contextual features that cause people to become keenly cognizant of their control ratios and the possibilities of altering them through deviant behavior…." Examples of provocation include being insulted, dismissed from employment, and any number of threats or challenges which can then trigger an attempt to balance the control ratio.

Constraint refers to the "probability or the perceived probability that control will actually be exercised" (Tittle 1995, 167). Constraint, then, could be manifested in the form of the probability that the deviant act would result in, for example, arrest or discovery by a significant other. It can also be generally understood to be a calculation of the *risk* associated with deviance.

The last major variable in control balance theory is opportunity. Like the rational-opportunity theories reviewed in Chapter 13, Tittle agrees that a situation or circumstance must be available for the performance of deviance. This means that there must be, for example, available victims, people to rob and assault, drugs to sell and use, and things to steal and destroy.

EVALUATION OF THE THEORY   There are many strengths of control balance theory. First, the theory is truly *general*. It provides us with sound ways of understanding both white-collar and traditional street crime and deviance. Unlike Gottfredson and Hirschi's theory, Tittle does a splendid job of dealing with the conceptually difficult issues that distinguish occupational from organizational crime. Indeed, Tittle understands that there is more to white-collar crime than simple embezzlement or fraud.

Second, Tittle's theory is intended to explain deviance, not just those things that legislators happen to define as crime. While Hirschi and Gottfredson claim they transcend a narrow definition of crime, it is still too limited. Tittle's sociological approach to crime and deviance provides a measure of breadth and depth not found in many other theories of crime.

Third, control balance theory weaves many of the most well-supported findings in criminological theory into the novel idea of control ratio. Tittle's specificity and attention to detail in these matters in many ways breaks the mold. While Braithwaite (1989a) also explains the relationship of his novel concept (shame) to other well-tested variables in criminology, Tittle does it more explicitly, with keen attention to how the theory may be empirically tested in the future.

It usually takes several years for a theory in criminology to undergo rigorous testing. Tittle's theory was subject to such a test in a recent study by Piquero and Hickman (1999). While overall support was found for the notion that control imbalance leads to deviance, the types of deviance predicted by Tittle were not supported. More specifically, it was found that predation and defiance were significantly related to those with a control surplus, not just a control deficit. This finding confirms the suspicion voiced by Braithwaite (1997) that it would be better to collapse the types of deviance categories into simpler, broader constructs (e.g., reducing the types of autonomous deviance into a larger "predation" category). Tittle (1997) has agreed with a few of Braithwaite's suggestions along these lines. Indeed, it seems to us that Tittle's theory explains deviant predation more completely than other forms of deviance. It also seems to us, as Braithwaite (1997) argues, that people quite plainly and universally seek more control, no matter what level of control they already believe they possess.

No doubt Tittle's control balance theory is a major contribution to theoretical criminology. However, the theory is still quite young and it should not surprise anyone if it undergoes modification in the years to come.

Katz's Seductions of Crime

A fascinating book hit the shelves in the late 1980s, Jack Katz's *Seductions of Crime: Moral and Sensual Attractions in Doing Evil*. In this book, Katz explores the relationship between doing crime and the emotional states of the offender. His focus is the foreground of crime as opposed to the background variables traditionally emphasized in positivistic criminology. It is an analysis of the seductions and compulsions that are felt by people as they engage in criminal activity and that draw them into and through criminal "projects." To understand (and explain) crime as action, it is first necessary to reconstruct criminal events as they are experienced by participants. Criminology, Katz argues, should move from the inside of crime outward, rather than the other way around.

For Katz (1988, 9), the commonality among such diverse crimes as pilfering, robbery, gang violence, and apparently senseless robbery-murders is the "family of moral emotions" that are subjectively experienced by offenders: "humiliation, righteousness, arrogance, ridicule, cynicism, defilement, and vengeance. In each [crime] the attraction that proves to be most fundamentally compelling is that of overcoming a personal challenge to moral—not material—existence." The following passage illustrates Katz's central argument:

> The closer one looks at crime, at least at the varieties examined here, the more vividly relevant become the moral emotions. Follow vandals and amateur shoplifters as they duck into alleys and dressing rooms and you will be moved by their delight in

deviance; observe them under arrest and you may be stunned by their shame. Watch their strutting street display and you will be struck by the awesome fascination that symbols of evil hold for the young men who are linked in the groups we often call gangs. If we specify the opening moves in muggings and stickups, we describe an array of "games" or tricks that turn victims into fools before their pockets are turned out. The careers of persistent robbers show us, not the increasingly precise calculations and hedged risks of "professionals," but men for whom gambling and other vices are a way of life, who are "wise" in the cynical sense of the term, and who take pride in a defiant reputation as "bad." And if we examine the lived sensuality behind events of cold-blooded "senseless" murder, we are compelled to acknowledge the power that may still be created in the modern world through the sensualities of defilement, spiritual chaos, and the apprehension of vengeance. Running across these experiences of criminality is a process juxtaposed in one manner or another against humiliation. In committing a righteous slaughter, the impassioned assailant takes humiliation and turns it into rage; through laying claim to a moral status of transcendent significance, he tries to burn humiliation up. The badass, with searing purposiveness, tries to scare humiliation off; as one ex-punk explained to me, after years of adolescent anxiety about the ugliness of his complexion and the stupidity of his every word, he found a wonderful calm in making "them" anxious about his perceptions and understandings. Young vandals and shoplifters innovate games with the risks of humiliation, running along the edge of shame for its exciting reverberations.... Against the historical background of a collective insistence on the moral nonexistence of their people, "bad niggers" exploit ethically unique possibilities for celebrating assertive conduct as "bad." (Katz 1988, 312–313)

Katz's "empirical" theory is, then, a theory of moral self-transcendence constructed through examination of the doing of crime as experienced and understood by its participants. Crime becomes a "project" through which offenders transcend the self that is caught up in the mundane routines of modern life. Crime embodies a creative exploration of emotional worlds beyond the realm of rational controls—it is spiritual, nonrational, self-fulfilling, and self-proclaiming. The lure of crime is, *inter alia*, its promise of providing "expanded possibilities of the self ... ways of behaving that previously seemed inaccessible" (Katz 1988, 73).

Katz (1988, 9) argues that there are three necessary and sufficient steps through which the construction of crime takes place: "(1) a path of action—distinctive practical requirements for successfully committing the crime; (2) a line of interpretation—unique ways of understanding how one is and will be seen by others; and (3) an emotional process—seductions and compulsions that have special dynamics."

If there is a link between the foreground and background in Katz's theory, the path of action is one obvious place to look:

> As a consequence of the inequality of resources in society, some of the ways of transcending mundane life are more open to some groups of people than to others. Sky diving, for example, may offer a transcendent experience, but it is unlikely to be available to many young black members of the urban under-class. Crack, on the other hand, may provide a similarly transcending experience ... but unlike sky diving is available to all, rich and poor. Moreover, the poor, perhaps more than any others in modernity, are faced with lives in which meaninglessness and the destruction of the self are ever present possibilities. (O'Malley and Mugford 1991, 16)

O'Malley and Mugford make this observation in the face of criticism that Katz cannot explain the shape of crime, that is, its distribution among social classes, between cities, or among racial or ethnic groups, because he rejects structural perspectives, particularly strain theory. Yet one strength of Katz's work lies precisely in the fact that it begins with no assumptions about how predispositions to crime might be distributed and concludes that only through examination of the experience of elite (or white-collar) crime can we construct the necessary comparative picture (Katz 1988, 313–324). However, Katz is not confident of criminology's ability to study the foreground of white-collar crime:

> Now, where would we get the data? With white-collar crime, we have a special problem in locating facts to demonstrate the lived experience of deviance. Despite their presumably superior capacity to write books and the healthy markets that await their publication efforts, we have virtually no "how-I-did-it-and-how-it-felt-doing-it" autobiographies by corrupted politicians, convicted tax frauds, and chief executive officers who have been deposed by scandals over inside trading. (Katz 1988, 319)

Katz goes on to suggest that what will turn out to be distinctive about elite crime is not its motivations or consequences but its emotional quality: Feelings of shame often attend its discovery. In contrast, "[s]tickup men, safecrackers, fences, and drug dealers often wear the criminal label with pride, apparently relishing the opportunity to tell their criminal histories in colorful, intimate detail" (Katz 1988, 319).

Bringing up the issue of shame returns us to the central element in Braithwaite's (1989a) theory of crime. We noted that Braithwaite is largely silent on the emotional process involved in shaming except to say that people find shaming a humiliating experience that provokes fear and anxiety and, consequently, avoidance behavior on the part of the person shamed. The avoidance may come in the form of conformity (most likely if the shamed also experience pangs of conscience), or it may come in the form of withdrawal from the group and participation in deviant subcultures—behavior that provoked shaming now becomes behavior that is rewarded. If the shaming is followed by forgiveness and other reintegrative processes, it becomes a particularly powerful mechanism for reinforcing cultural (group) values and identity.

Katz complements Braithwaite in his documentation of the emotions moving around the edge of shame. His analysis of the process of transcendence may help criminologists understand more completely the dynamics of shaming, especially when it fails. The humiliating subordination that shaming is (when there is no self-participation or reintegration) represents a moral affront that must be "put right" through a transcendent process of self-reaffirmation, of reconstruction that salvages honor, identity, and worth. The formation and persistence of criminal subcultures, crucial to understanding the forms that deviance takes, and an important criminogenic source in Braithwaite's model (see Figure 14.1), can be explored within the framework of foreground analysis of the kind Katz has demonstrated.

Importantly, Katz's (1988, 52–79) analysis of *sneaky thrills*—shoplifting, pilfering, vandalism, joyriding (some of which were discussed in Chapter 5)—also shows how shaming can act as a stimulus for crime as well as a reaction to be avoided. It is precisely the people who have some emotional investment in the conventional order (especially their standing in it) who are likely to be responsive to shaming—otherwise, who cares if a parent, teacher, police officer, or judge bawls you out? Yet the euphoria or thrill of sneaky theft—the seduction of the crime itself—lies precisely in the risk that one will be shamed if caught:

> Thus, the other side of the euphoria felt from being successful is the humiliation from being caught. What the sneak thieves are avoiding, or getting away with by not being caught, is the shame they would feel if they were caught.... The thrills of sneaky thefts are metaphysically complex matters. On the one hand, shoplifters and vandals know what they are doing is illegal; the deviant character of the practice is part of the appeal. On the other hand, they typically register a kind of metaphysical shock when an arrest induces a sense that what they are doing might be treated as real crime.... Once an arrest occurs, the shoplifting career typically ends in response to an awareness that persistence would now clearly signal a commitment to a deviant identity. (Katz 1988, 64–66)

CHAPTER SUMMARY

This brief excursion into general theories of crime brings the text to a close. Consistent with the goal of general theory, these works seek to identify the things diverse crimes have in common and to build explanations around them. Most of the theories are heavily indebted to existing ideas about crime, and what is new is more in the packaging than in the substance. On the other hand, Katz shows us a way of thinking about crime that departs significantly from the other approaches even as it complements Braithwaite's.

It is safe to say that criminologists will be examining these theories closely in the years ahead. Do not expect that one will emerge as *the* explanation of crime. For one thing, criminologists disagree on the definition of their subject matter. For another, the data and methodology for adequate tests of all theories do not yet exist. What is likely to happen is continued refinement and reshaping, so that the dominant theories a decade from now will show their indebtedness but will not be the same.

Remember, too, that the criminological enterprise is affected not only by the ideas and values of its participants but also by the ideology underlying public policy. That ideology affects the funding of research. Theories that challenge established paradigms tend in any case to be embraced with great caution, all the more so if they conflict with the funding priorities of governments and universities.

If the measure of criminology is its success at explaining crime, where do you think we stand? We certainly know a lot about the crime scene, and well we should after more than 100 years of research. We can also point to theories that have remained prominent for many, many years—differential association is perhaps the best example. Some of the general theories we have reviewed in this chapter address crime at both micro and macro levels of analysis, and some integrate theories that once appeared incompatible. Some also bring together behaviors that were once thought to be so different as to require different explanations—rape and shoplifting, for example. It is noteworthy, too, that an argument made long ago by French sociologist Emile Durkheim now seems more relevant than ever: that crime and punishment are two parts of an inseparable whole; that one cannot be explained without also explaining the other.

KEY TERMS

background factors (p. 304)

communitarianism (p. 313)

control balance (p. 316)

control deficit (p. 315)

control ratio (p. 315)

control surplus (p. 315)

criminality (p. 307)

disintegrative shaming (p. 312)

foreground factors (p. 304)

interdependency (p. 313)

low self-control (p. 307)

reintegrative shaming (p. 312)

restorative justice (p. 314)

versatility construct (p. 307)

RECOMMENDED READINGS

Braithwaite, John. 1989a. *Crime, Shame and Reintegration*. Cambridge, UK: Cambridge University Press.

Cohen, Lawrence E., and Richard Machalek. 1988. "A General Theory of Expropriative Crime: An Evolutionary Ecological Approach." *American Journal of Sociology* 94:465–501.

Gottfredson, Michael R., and Travis Hirschi. 1990. *A General Theory of Crime*. Stanford, CA: Stanford University Press.

Katz, Jack. 1988. *Seductions of Crime: Moral and Sensual Attractions in Doing Evil*. New York: Basic Books.

Tittle, Charles R. 1995. *Control Balance: Toward a General Theory of Deviance*. Boulder, CO: Westview.

Wilson, James Q., and Richard J. Herrnstein. 1985. *Crime and Human Nature*. New York: Simon & Schuster.

RECOMMENDED WEB SITES

Real Justice Organization

Information on research, programs, experiments, and policies aligned with many dimensions of Braithwaite's theory of reintegrative shaming.
http://www.realjustice.org

Journal of Criminal Justice and Popular Culture

A free-access electronic journal that publishes reviews and articles on most areas of crime and criminal justice.
http://www.albany.edu/scj/jcjpc/index.html

APPENDIX: OFFENSES IN UNIFORM CRIME REPORTING

The Uniform Crime Reporting Program classifies offenses into two groups, Part I and Part II. Each month contributing agencies submit information on the number of Part I (Crime Index) offenses known to law enforcement; those cleared by arrest or exceptional means; and the age, sex, and race of persons arrested. Contributors provide only arrest data for Part II offenses.

PART I OFFENSES

criminal homicide (a) Murder and nonnegligent manslaughter: the willful (nonnegligent) killing of one human being by another. Deaths caused by negligence, attempts to kill, assaults to kill, suicides, and accidental deaths are excluded. The Program classifies justifiable homicides separately and limits the definition to (1) the killing of a felon by a law enforcement officer in the line of duty; or (2) the killing of a felon, during the commission of a felony, by a private citizen. (b) Manslaughter by negligence: the killing of another person through gross negligence. Traffic fatalities are excluded. While manslaughter by negligence is a Part I crime, it is not included in the Crime Index.

forcible rape The carnal knowledge of a female forcibly and against her will. Rapes by force and attempts or assaults to rape regardless of the age of the victim are included. Statutory offenses (no force used, victim under age of consent) are excluded.

robbery The taking or attempting to take anything of value from the care, custody, or control of a person or persons by force or threat of force or violence and/or by putting the victim in fear.

aggravated assault An unlawful attack by one person upon another for the purpose of inflicting severe or aggravated bodily injury. This type of assault usually is accompanied by the use of a weapon or by means likely to produce death or great bodily harm. Simple assaults are excluded.

burglary (breaking or entering) The unlawful entry of a structure to commit a felony or theft. Attempted forcible entry is included.

larceny-theft (except motor vehicle theft) The unlawful taking, carrying, leading, or riding away of property from the possession or constructive possession of another. Examples are thefts of bicycles or automobile accessories, shoplifting, pocket-picking, or the stealing of any property or article which is not taken by force and violence or by fraud. Attempted larcenies are included. Embezzlement, confidence games, forgery, worthless checks, etc., are excluded.

motor vehicle theft The theft or attempted theft of a motor vehicle. A motor vehicle is self-propelled and runs on the surface and not on rails. Motorboats, construction equipment, airplanes, and farming equipment are specifically excluded from this category.

arson Any willful or malicious burning or attempt to burn, with or without intent to defraud, a dwelling house, public building, motor vehicle or aircraft, personal property of another, etc.

PART II OFFENSES

other assaults (simple) Assaults and attempted assaults where no weapons are used and which do not result in serious or aggravated injury to the victim.

forgery and counterfeiting Making altering, uttering, or possessing, with intent to defraud, anything false in the semblance of that which is true. Attempts are included.

fraud Fraudulent conversion and obtaining money or property by false pretenses. Confidence games and bad checks, except forgeries and counterfeiting, are included.

embezzlement Misappropriation or misapplication of money or property entrusted to one's care, custody, or control.

stolen property; buying, receiving, possessing Buying, receiving, and possessing stolen property, including attempts.

vandalism Willful or malicious destruction, injury, disfigurement, or defacement of any public or private property, real or personal, without consent of the owner or persons having custody or control. Attempts are included.

weapons; carrying, possessing, etc. All violations of regulations or statutes controlling the carrying, using, possessing, furnishing, and manufacturing of deadly weapons or silencers. Attempts are included.

prostitution and commercialized vice Sex offenses of a commercialized nature, such as prostitution, keeping a bawdy house, procuring, or transporting women for immoral purposes. Attempts are included.

sex offenses (except forcible rape, prostitution, and commercialized vice) Statutory rape and offenses against chastity, common decency, morals, and the like. Attempts are included.

drug abuse violations State and/or local offenses relating to the unlawful possession, sale, use, growing, and manufacturing of narcotic drugs. The following drug categories are specified: opium or cocaine and their derivatives (morphine, heroin, codeine); marijuana; synthetic narcotics—manufactured narcotics that can cause true addiction (demerol, methadone); and dangerous nonnarcotic drugs (barbiturates, benzedrine).

gambling Promoting, permitting, or engaging in illegal gambling.

offenses against the family and children Nonsupport, neglect, desertion, or abuse of family and children. Attempts are included.

driving under the influence Driving or operating any vehicle or common carrier while drunk or under the influence of liquor or narcotics.

liquor laws State and/or local liquor law violations except drunkenness and driving under the influence. Federal violations are excluded.

drunkenness offenses relating to drunkenness or intoxication. Driving under the influence is excluded.

disorderly conduct Breach of the peace.

vagrancy Begging, loitering, etc. Includes prosecutions under the charge of suspicious persons.

all other offenses All violations of state and/or local laws except those listed above and traffic offenses.

suspicion No specific offense; suspect released without formal charges being placed.

curfew and loitering laws (persons under age 18) Offenses relating to violations of local curfew or loitering ordinances where such laws exist.

runaways (persons under age 18) Limited to juveniles taken into protective custody under provisions of local statutes.

Source: Federal Bureau of Investigation, *Crime in the United States*. Washington, D.C.: Federal Bureau of Investigation (2000): 405–406.

Abadinsky, Howard. 1990. *Organized Crime*. 3d ed. Chicago, IL: Nelson-Hall.

Abdelrahman, A. I., Gloria Rodriguez, John A. Ryan, John F. French, and Donald Weinbaum. 1998. "The Epidemiology of Substance Abuse among Middle School Students: The Impact of School, Familial, Community, and Individual Risk Factors." *Journal of Child and Adolescent Substance Abuse* 8 (1): 55–75.

Adams, Mike S. 1996. "Labeling and Differential Association: Toward a General Social Learning Theory of Crime and Deviance." *American Journal of Criminal Justice* 20 (2): 147–164.

Adams, Mike S., and David T. Evans. 1996. "Teacher Disapproval, Delinquent Peers, and Self-Reported Delinquency: A Longitudinal Test of Labeling Theory." *Urban Review* 28 (3): 199–211.

Adler, Freda. 1975. *Sisters in Crime: The Rise of the New Female Criminal*. New York: McGraw-Hill.

Adler, Patricia A. 1985. *Wheeling and Dealing: An Ethnography of an Upper-Level Drug Dealing and Smuggling Community*. New York: Columbia University Press.

Adler, Patricia A. 1993. *Wheeling and Dealing: An Ethnography of an Upper-Level Drug Dealing and Smuggling Community*. 2d ed. New York: Columbia University Press.

Agnew, Robert. 1985. "Social Control Theory and Delinquency." *Criminology* 23:47–60.

Agnew, Robert. 1990. "Adolescent Resources and Delinquency." *Criminology* 28:535–566.

Agnew, Robert. 1992. "Foundation for a General Strain Theory of Crime and Delinquency." *Criminology* 30:47–87.

Agnew, Robert. 1994. "The Techniques of Neutralization and Violence." *Criminology* 32:555–580.

Agnew, Robert. 1999. "A General Strain Theory of Community Differences in Crime Rates." *The Journal of Research in Crime and Delinquency* 36 (2): 123–155.

Agnew, Robert, and Helene Raskin White. 1992. "An Empirical Test of General Strain Theory." *Criminology* 30 (4): 475–511.

Akers, Ronald L. 1973. *Deviant Behavior: A Social Learning Approach*. Belmont, CA: Wadsworth.

Akers, Ronald L. 1991. "Self-Control As a General Theory of Crime." *Journal of Quantitative Criminology* 7:201–211.

Akers, Ronald L. 1994. *Criminological Theories: Introduction and Evaluation*. Los Angeles, CA: Roxbury.

Akers, Ronald L., Robert L. Burgess, and Weldon I. Johnson. 1968. "Opiate Use, Addiction and Relapse." *Social Problems* 15:459–469.

Alarid, Leanne Fiftal, Velmer S. Burton, and Francis T. Cullen. 2000. *Journal of Research in Crime and Delinquency* 37, no. 2 (May): 171–199.

Alder, Christine. 1985. "Self-Reported Sexual Aggression." *Crime and Delinquency* 31:306–331.

Alder, Christine. 1986. "Unemployed Women Have Got It Heaps Worse: Exploring the Implications of Female Youth Unemployment." *Australian and New Zealand Journal of Criminology* 19:210–224.

Alexander, Reginald. 1994. "Confessions of a Drug Kingpin." *Prison Life* (January): 31–35.

Alix, Ernest K. 1969. "The Functional Interdependence of Crime and Community Social Structure." *Journal of Criminal Law, Criminology, and Police Science* 60:332–339.

Allen-Hagan, Barbara. 1991. "Children in Custody 1989." *OJJDP Update on Statistics* (January): l–10.

Allen, Francis A. 1959. "Criminal Justice, Legal Values, and the Rehabilitative Ideal." *Journal of Criminal Law, Criminology, and Police Science* 50:226–236.

Allen, Francis A. 1974. *The Crimes of Politics*. Cambridge, MA: Harvard University Press.

Allen, John. 1977. *Assault with a Deadly Weapon: The Autobiography of a Street Criminal*. New York: Pantheon Books.

Allison, Julie A., and Lawrence S. Wrightsman. 1993. *Rape: The Misunderstood Crime*. Newbury Park, CA: Sage.

Alschuler, Albert W. 1978. "Sentencing Reform and Prosecutorial Power: A Critique of Recent Proposals for 'Fixed' and 'Presumptive' Sentencing." In *Determinate Sentencing: Reform or Regression, Proceedings of the Special Conference on Determinate Sentencing*. University of California, Berkeley, CA, June 2–3, 1977.

Altman, Janet R., and Richard O. Cunningham. 1967. "Preventive Detention." *George Washington University Law Review* 6:178–189.

American Association for World Health. 1997. *Denial of Good and Medicine: The Impact of the U.S. Embargo on Health and Nutrition in Cuba*. Washington, D.C.: American Association for World Health.

American Bar Association. 1970. *Standards Relating to Probation*. New York: Institute of Judicial Administration.

American Society of Criminology. 1999. *Draft Code of Ethics*. Unpublished manuscript.

Amir, Menachim. 1971. *Patterns in Forcible Rape*. Chicago, IL: University of Chicago Press.

Anastasia, George. 1993. *Blood and Honor: Inside the Scarfo Mob*. New York: Morrow.

Andenaes, Johannes. 1966. "The General Preventive Effects of Punishment." *Pennsylvania Law Review* 114:949–983.

Andenaes, Johannes. 1974. *Punishment and Deterrence*. Ann Arbor, MI: University of Michigan Press.

Anderson, Elijah. 1990. *Streetwise: Race, Class, and Change in an Urban Community*. Chicago, IL: University of Chicago Press.

Anderson, Elijah. 1994. "The Code of the Streets." *The Atlantic Monthly* 273:81–94.

Anderson, Elijah. 1999. *Code of the Street*. New York: Norton.

Andrews, D. A. 1980. "Some Experimental Investigations of the Principles of Differential Association through Deliberate Manipulation of the Structure of Service Systems." *American Sociological Review* 45:448–462.

Andrews, D. A., Ivan Zinger, Robert D. Hoge, James Bonta, Paul Gendreau, and Francis T. Cullen. 1990. "Does Correctional Treatment Work? A Clinically Relevant and Psychologically Informed Meta-Analysis." *Criminology* 28:369–404.

Andrews, George. 1967. *The Book of Grass: An Anthology of Indian Hemp*. New York: Grove Press.

Angel, Arthur R. 1971. "Preventive Detention: An Empirical Analysis." *Harvard Civil Rights-Civil Liberties Law Review* 6:309–332.

Anglin, Douglas M., and George Speckart. 1988. "Narcotics Use and Crime: A Multisample, Multimethod Analysis." *Criminology* 26:197–233.

Anonymous. 1972. "Editorial." *Yale Law Journal* 81:1380.

Anti-Defamation League of the B'nai B'rith. 1987. *The Hate Movement Today: A Chronicle of Violence and Disarray*. New York: ADLBB.

Anti-Defamation League of the B'nai B'rith. 1988. *Hate Groups in America*. New York: ADLBB.

Archambeault, William G., and Charles R. Fenwick. 1983. "A Comparative Analysis of Japanese and American Police Organizational Models." *Police Studies* (fall): 3–12.

Archer, Dane, and Rosemary Gartner. 1984. *Violence and Crime in Cross-National Perspective*. New Haven, CT: Yale University Press.

Aronowitz, Alexis A. 1994. "Germany's Xenophobic Violence: Criminal Justice and Social Responses." In *Hate Crime: International Perspectives on Causes and Control*. Ed. Mark S. Hamm. Cincinnati, OH: Anderson.

Arrigo, Bruce. 1998. "Marxist Criminology and Lacanian Psychoanalysis: Outline for a General Constitutive Theory of Crime." Pp. 40–62 in *Cutting the Edge: Current Perspectives in Radical/Critical Criminology and Criminal Justice*. Ed. Jeffrey I. Ross. Westport, CT: Praeger.

Arrigo, Bruce. 1999. *Social Justice/Criminal Justice: The Maturation of Critical Theory in Law, Crime, and Deviance.* Belmont, CA: West/Wadsworth.

Ashley, Barbara Renchkovsky, and David Ashley. 1984. "Sex As Violence: The Body against Intimacy." *International Journal of Women's Studies* 7:352–371.

Association of Certified Fraud Examiners. 1999. *Report to the Nation.* Austin, TX: ACFE.

Attenborough, F. L. 1963. *The Laws of the Earliest English Kings.* New York: Russell and Russell.

Audett, Blackie. 1954. *Rap Sheet: My Life Story.* New York: William Sloane.

Aulette, Judy R., and Raymond J. Michalowski. 1993. "Fire in Hamlet: A Case Study of State-Corporate Crime." In *Political Crime in Contemporary America.* Ed. Kenneth Tunnell. New York: Garland.

Austin, James, Michael Jones, and Melissa Bolyard. 1993. "The Growing Use of Jail Boot Camps: The Current State of the Art." *NIJ Research in Brief* (October): 1–8.

Austin, William, and Thomas A. Williams III. 1977. "A Survey of Judges' Responses to Legal Cases: Research Notes on Sentencing Disparity." *Journal of Criminal Law and Criminology* 68:306–310.

Ayres, Ian, and John Braithwaite. 1992. *Responsive Regulation: Transcending the Deregulation Debate.* New York: Oxford University Press.

Babbington, Anthony. 1968. *The Power to Silence.* London, UK: Robert Maxwell.

Bachman, Ronet. 1994. *Violence against Women.* Washington, D.C.: U.S. Department of Justice.

Bacon, Sheldon. 1935. *The Early Development of American Municipal Police.* Ph.D. diss., Yale University.

Badillo, Herman, and Milton Haynes. 1972. *A Bill of No Rights: Attica and the American Prison System.* New York: Auterbridge and Lazard.

Bailey, Ronald H. 1976. *Violence and Aggression.* New York: Time Life Books.

Bailey, William C. 1998. "Deterrence, Brutalization, and the Death Penalty: Another Examination of Oklahoma's Return to Capital Punishment." *Criminology* 36:711–733.

Baird, Robert M., and Stuart Rosenbaum. 1998. *Pornography: Private Right or Public Menace?* New York: Prometheus.

Baker, Michael A., and Alan F. Westin. 1987. *Employer Perceptions of Workplace Crime.* Washington, D.C.: U.S. Department of Justice.

Baldus, David, Charles Pulaski, and George Woodworth. 1983. "Comparative Review of Death Sentences: An Empirical Review of the Georgia Experience." *Journal of Criminal Law and Criminology* 74:661–753.

Baldus, David C., George Woodworth, and C. A. Pulaski. 1985. "Monitoring and Evaluating Contemporary Death Sentencing Systems: Lessons from Georgia." *University of California Davis Law Review* 18, no. 4 (summer): 1375–1407.

Ball, J. C. 1982. "Lifetime Criminality of Heroin Addicts in the United States." *Journal of Drug Issues* 12:225–239.

Ball, J. C., J. W. Shaffer, and D. N. Nurco. 1983. "Day-to-Day Criminality of Heroin Addicts in Baltimore—A Study of the Continuity of Offense Rates." *Drug and Alcohol Dependence* 12:119–142.

Ball, J., L. Chester, and R. Perrott. 1978. *Cops and Robbers: An Investigation into Armed Bank Robbery.* London, UK: Andre Deutsch.

Bandura, Albert. 1973. *Aggression: A Social Learning Analysis.* Englewood Cliffs, NJ: Prentice Hall.

Banton, Michael. 1973. *Police Community Relations.* London, UK: William Collins.

Barak, Gregg. 1994. *Media, Process, and the Social Construction of Crime: Studies in Newsmaking Criminology.* New York: Garland.

Barak, Gregg. 1998. *Integrating Criminologies.* Boston, MA: Allyn and Bacon.

Barak, Gregg. 2000. *Crime and Crime Control: A Global View.* Westport, CT: Greenwood Press.

Barak-Glantz, Israel L., and Elmer H. Johnson. 1983. *Comparative Criminology.* Beverly Hills, CA: Sage.

Barker, Thomas, and David L. Carter, eds. 1994a. *Police Deviance.* 3d ed. Cincinnati, OH: Anderson.

Barker, Thomas, and David L. Carter. 1994b. "A Typology of Police Deviance." In *Police Deviance.* 3d ed. Ed. Thomas Barker and David L. Carter. Cincinnati, OH: Anderson.

Barlow, David E., and Melissa Hickman Barlow. 2000. *Police in a Multicultural Society: An American Story.* Prospect Heights, IL: Waveland.

Barlow, Hugh D. 1983. "Factors Affecting the Lethality of Criminal Assaults." Presented at the annual meeting of the American Society of Criminology, Denver, CO.

Barlow, Hugh D. 1985a. "The Medical Factor in Homicide Victimization." Presented at the Fifth International Symposium on Victimology, Zagreb, Yugoslavia.

Barlow, Hugh D. 1985b. "Victim Injuries and the Prosecution of Violent Offenders." Presented at the annual meeting of the Academy of Criminal Justice Sciences, Las Vegas, NV.

Barlow, Hugh D. 1987. "Of Secrets and Visions: Stanley Cohen on Crime Control." *Journal of Criminal Law and Criminology* 78:430–441.

Barlow, Hugh D. 1991. "Explaining Crimes and Analogous Acts, or the Unrestrained Will Grab at Pleasure Whenever They Can." *Journal of Criminal Law and Criminology* 82:229–242.

Barlow, Hugh D. 1993. "From Fiddle Factors to Networks of Collusion: Charting the Waters of Small Business Crime." *Crime, Law and Social Change* 20:319–337.

Barlow, Hugh D. 1994. "The Labeling Perspective Is Far from Abandoned in Modern Criminology: Reply to Richard Wright." *Teaching Sociology* 23 (January): 55–57.

Barlow, Hugh D. 1995. *Crime and Public Policy: Putting Theory to Work.* Boulder, CO: Westview.

Barlow, Hugh D. 1996. *Introduction to Criminology.* 6th ed. New York: HarperCollins.

Barlow, Hugh D. 2000. *Criminal Justice in America.* Upper Saddle River, NJ: Prentice Hall.

Barlow, Hugh D., and Lynne Schmidt Barlow. 1988. "More on the Role of Weapons in Homicidal Violence." *Medicine and Law* 7:347–358.

Barlow, Hugh D., and Theodore N. Ferdinand. 1992. *Understanding Delinquency.* New York: HarperCollins.

Barlow, Melissa Hickman, David E. Barlow, and Theodore G. Chiricos. 1995a. "Economic Conditions and Ideologies of Crime in the Media: A Content Analysis of Crime News." *Crime and Delinquency* 41:3–19.

Barlow, Melissa Hickman, David E. Barlow, and Theodore G. Chiricos. 1995b. "Mobilizing Support for Social Control in a Declining Economy: Exploring Ideologies of Crime within Crime News." *Crime and Delinquency* 41 (2): 191–202.

Barnard, Herbert P. 2000. "The Netherlands: Let's Be Realistic." Pp. 186–188 in *Annual Editions: Drugs, Society, and Behavior.* Ed. Hugh T. Wilson. Sluice Dock, CT: Dushkin/McGraw-Hill.

Barnes, Carole Wolf, and Rodney Kingsnorth. 1996. "Race, Drugs, and Criminal Sentencing: Hidden Effects of the Criminal Law." *Journal of Criminal Justice* 24:39–55.

Barnett, Arnold. 1985. "Some Distribution Patterns for the Georgia Death Sentence." *University of California-Davis Law Review* 18:1327–1374.

Barnett, Harold. 1981. "Corporate Capitalism, Corporate Crime." *Crime and Delinquency* 27:4–23

Baron, Larry, and Murray A. Straus. 1990. *Four Theories of Rape in American Society.* New Haven, CT: Yale University Press.

Barr, Kellie E. M., Michael P. Farrell, Grace M. Barnes, and John W. Welte. 1993. "Race, Class, and Gender Differences in Substance Abuse: Evidence of Middle Class/Underclass Polarization among Black Males." *Social Problems* 40:314–327.

Bartol, Curt R. 1995. *Criminal Behavior: A Psychological Approach.* Englewood Cliffs, NJ: Prentice Hall.

Barton, David. 2000. "Pain Breakers." Pp. 113–115 in *Annual Editions: Drugs, Society, and Behavior.* Ed. Hugh T. Wilson. Sluice Dock, CT: Dushkin/McGraw-Hill.

Bastion, Lisa. 1995. "Criminal Victimization, 1993." *BJS Bulletin* (May): 1–6.

Bastion, Lisa D., and Bruce M. Taylor. 1991. *School Crime: A National Crime Survey Report.* Washington, D.C.: U.S. Department of Justice.

Baum, Rudy M. 1985. "New Variety of Street Drug Poses Growing Problem." *Chemical and Engineering News* (September 9): 7–16.

Baumer, Terry L., and Dennis P. Rosenbaum. 1984. *Combatting Retail Theft: Programs and Strategies.* Boston, MA: Butterworths.

Bayley, David H. 1988. "The Management of Violence by Police Patrol Officers." *Criminology* 27:1–25.

Bayley, David H., and Egon Bittner. 1989. "Learning the Skills of Policing." *Law and Contemporary Problems* 47:35–59.

Bayley, David H., and Harold Mendelsohn. 1968. *Minorities and the Police: Confrontation in America.* New York: Free Press.

Bazelon, David L. 1981. "Foreword, the Morality of Criminal Law: The Rights of the Accused." *Journal of Criminal Law and Criminology* 72:1143–1170.

Beare, Margaret E. 1998. "Corruption and Organized Crime: Lessons from History." *Crime, Law, and Social Change* 28 (2): 155–172.

Beccaria, Cesare. 1963. *Essay on Crimes and Punishments.* Trans. Henry Paolucci. Indianapolis, IN: Bobbs-Merrill.

Beck, Allen J., Thomas P. Bonczar, and Darrell K. Gilliard. 1993. "Jail Inmates, 1992." *BJS Bulletin* (August): 1–10.

Becker, Gary S. 1968. "Crime and Punishment: An Economic Approach." *Journal of Political Economy* 76:493–517.

Becker, Howard S. 1963. *Outsiders: Studies in the Sociology of Deviance*. New York: Free Press.

Becker, Howard S., ed. 1964. *The Other Side: Perspectives on Deviance*. New York: Free Press.

Beirne, Piers. 1983. "Generalization and Its Discontents: The Comparative Study of Crime." In *Comparative Criminology*. Ed. Israel L. Barak-Glantz and Elmer H. Johnson. Beverly Hills, CA: Sage.

Beirne, Piers, and James Messerschmidt. 2000. *Criminology*. 3d ed. Boulder, CO: Westview.

Bell, Daniel, ed. 1965. "Crime As an American Way of Life: A Queer Ladder of Social Mobility." In *The End of Ideology*. Rev. ed. New York: Free Press.

Bennett, Georgette. 1987. *Crimewarps: The Future of Crime in America*. New York: Anchor Books.

Bennett, James. 1981. *Oral History and Delinquency*. Chicago, IL: University of Chicago Press.

Bennett, Trevor. 1985. "A Decision-Making Approach to Opioid Addiction." Presented at the Home Office Conference on Criminal Decision Making, Cambridge, UK.

Bennett, Trevor, and Richard Wright. 1981. "Burglars' Choice of Targets: The Use of Situational Cues in Offender Decision Making." Presented at the annual meeting of the American Society of Criminology, Washington, D.C.

Bennett, Trevor, and Richard Wright. 1984. *Burglars on Burglary*. Aldershot, UK: Gower.

Bensing, Robert G., and Oliver Schroeder. 1960. *Homicide in an Urban Community*. Springfield, IL: Thomas.

Benson, Allen L. 1927. "The Propaganda against Prohibition." In *Prohibition: Modification of the Volstead Law*. Ed. Lamar T. Beman. New York: H. W. Wilson.

Benson, Michael L. 1985. "Denying the Guilty Mind: Accounting for Involvement in White-Collar Crime." *Criminology* 23:583–607.

Benson, Michael L. 1989. "The Influence of Class Position on the Formal and Informal Sanctioning of White-Collar Offenders." *Sociological Quarterly* 30:465–479.

Benson, Michael L., and Francis T. Cullen. 1998. *Combating Corporate Crime: Local Prosecutors at Work*. Boston, MA: Northeastern University Press.

Benson, Michael L., and Esteban Walker. 1988. "Sentencing the White-Collar Offender." *American Sociological Review* 53:294–302.

Benson, Michael L., William J. Maakestad, Francis T. Cullen, and Gilbert Geis. 1988. "District Attorneys and Corporate Crime: Surveying the Prosecutorial Gatekeepers." *Criminology* 26:505–516.

Bent, Alan Edward. 1974. *The Politics of Law Enforcement*. Lexington, MA: D. C. Heath.

Bentham, Jeremy. 1948. *The Principles of Morals and Legislation*. New York: Hofner Publishing.

Bequai, August. 1978. *White-Collar Crime: A Twentieth Century Crisis*. Lexington, MA: Lexington Books.

Berk, Richard A., Jack Boyer, and Robert Weiss. 1993. "Chance and the Death Penalty." *Law and Society Review* 27:89–110.

Berk, Richard A., Kenneth J. Lenihan, and Peter H. Rossi. 1980. "Crime and Poverty: Some Experimental Evidence from Ex-Offenders." *American Sociological Review* 45:766–786.

Berkowitz, Leonard. 1962. *Aggression: A Social Psychological Analysis*. New York: McGraw-Hill.

Berlin, Peter. 1996. *National Report on Shoplifting*. Jericho, NJ: Shoplifters Anonymous.

Berton, Margaret, and Sally D. Stabb. 1996. "Exposure to Violence and Post-Traumatic Stress Disorder in Urban Adolescents." *Adolescence* 31:489–498.

Beschner, George M., and William Brower. 1985. "The Scene." In *Life with Heroin*. Ed. Bill Hanson, George Beschner, James M. Walters, and Elliott Bovelle. Lexington, MA: Lexington Books.

Best, Joel. 1999. *Random Violence: How We Talk about New Crimes and New Victims*. Berkeley and Los Angeles, CA: University of California Press.

Beyleveld, Deryck. 1980. *A Bibliography on General Deterrence*. London, UK: Saxon House.

Bickle, Gayle S., and Ruth D. Peterson. 1991. "The Impact of Gender-Based Family Roles on Criminal Sentencing." *Social Problems* 38:372–394.

Biderman, Albert. 1967. *Report on a Pilot Study in the District of Columbia on Victimization and Attitudes toward Law Enforcement, Field Survey 1*. Washington, D.C.: U.S. Government Printing Office.

Binder, Arnold, and Gilbert Geis. 1983. *Methods of Research in Criminology and Criminal Justice.* New York: McGraw-Hill.

Bishop, Donna. 1984. "Deterrence: A Panel Analysis." *Justice Quarterly* 1:311–328.

Bittner, Egon, and Anthony M. Platt. 1966. "The Meaning of Punishment." *Issues in Criminology* 2:81–105.

Black, Donald J. 1970. "Production of Crime Rates." *American Sociological Review* 35:733–748.

Black, Donald J. 1980. *The Manners and Customs of the Police.* New York: Academic Press.

Blackstone, Sir William. 1962. *Commentaries on the Laws of England.* Vol. 4. Boston, MA: Beacon Press.

Blanchard, W. H. 1959. "The Group Process in Gang Rape." *Journal of Social Psychology* 49: 259–266.

Blankenship, Michael B., ed. 1993. *Understanding Corporate Criminality.* New York: Garland.

Blankenship, Ralph L. 1974. "Toward a Sociolinguistic Perspective on Deviance Labeling." *Sociology and Social Research* 58:253–261.

Blau, Judith, and Peter M. Blau. 1982. "The Cost of Inequality: Metropolitan Structure and Crime." *American Sociological Review* 47:114–129.

Bleich, Jeff. 1989. "The Politics of Prison Crowding." *California Law Review* 77:5–35.

Bloch, Herbert A., and Gilbert Geis. 1970. *Man, Crime, and Society.* 2d ed. New York: Random House.

Bloch, Peter B., and Deborah Anderson. 1974. *Policewomen on Patrol: Final Report.* Washington, D.C.: The Police Foundation.

Block, Alan A. 1991. *The Business of Crime: A Documentary Study of Organized Crime in the American Economy.* Boulder, CO: Westview Press.

Block, Alan A., and Frank Scarpitti. 1986. "Casinos and Banking: Organized Crime in the Bahamas." *Deviant Behavior* 7:301–312.

Block, Anton. 1974. *The Mafia of a Sicilian Village.* New York: Harper Torchbooks.

Block, Carolyn Rebecca. 1987. *Homicide in Chicago.* Chicago, IL: Loyola University of Chicago Urban Insight Series.

Block, Carolyn Rebecca. 1991. "Trends in Homicide Syndromes and Economic Cycles in Chicago over 25 Years." Presented at the annual meeting of the American Society of Criminology, November 18–23, San Francisco, CA.

Block, Carolyn Rebecca. 1993. "Lethal Violence in the Chicago Latino Community." In *Homicide: The Victim/Offender Connection.* Ed. Anna Victoria Wilson. Cincinnati, OH: Anderson.

Block, Carolyn Rebecca. 1995. *Major Trends in Chicago Homicide: 1965–1994.* Chicago, IL: Criminal Justice Information Authority.

Block, Carolyn Rebecca, and Richard Block. 1993. "Street Gang Crime in Chicago." *NIJ Research in Brief* (December): 1–11.

Block, Richard. 1976. "Homicide in Chicago: A Nine Year Study (1965–1973)." *Journal of Criminal Law and Criminology* 66:496–510.

Block, Richard, and Carolyn Rebecca Block. 1991. "Beginning with Wolfgang: An Agenda for Homicide Research." Presented at the annual meeting of the American Society of Criminology, November 18–23, San Francisco, CA.

Block, Richard, and Franklin E. Zimring. 1973. "Homicide in Chicago: 1965–1970." *Journal of Research in Crime and Delinquency* 10:1–12.

Blum, Richard, and Associates. 1972. *The Dream Sellers.* San Francisco, CA: Jossey-Bass.

Blumberg, Abraham S. 1967. "The Practice of Law as a Confidence Game: Organizational Cooptation of a Profession." *Law and Society Review* 1:15–39.

Blumenthal, Monica, Robert L. Kahn, Frank M. Andrews, and Kendra B. Head. 1972. *Justifying Violence: Attitudes of American Men.* Ann Arbor, MI: Institute for Social Research.

Blumer, Herbert. 1969. *Symbolic Interactionism: Perspective and Method.* Upper Saddle River, NJ: Prentice Hall.

Blumstein, Alfred. 1993. "Making Rationality Relevant." *Criminology* 31:1–16.

Blumstein, Alfred, Jacqueline Cohen, and David P. Farrington. 1988a. "Criminal Career Research: Its Value for Criminology." *Criminology* 26:1–35.

Blumstein, Alfred, Jacqueline Cohen, and Daniel Nagin, eds. 1978. *Deterrence and Incapacitation: Estimating the Effects of Criminal Sanctions on Crime Rates.* Washington, D.C.: National Academy of Science.

Blumstein, Alfred, Jacqueline Cohen, Jeffrey Roth, and Christy A. Visher, eds. 1986. *Criminal Careers and Career Criminals.* Vol. 1. Washington, D.C.: National Academy Press.

Blumstein, Alfred, Jacqueline Cohen, and David P. Farrington. 1988b. "Longitudinal and Criminal

Career Research: Further Clarifications." *Criminology* 26:57–74.

Boggs, Sarah Lee. 1964. "The Ecology of Crime Occurrence in St. Louis: A Reconceptualization. Ph.D. diss., Washington University, St. Louis, MO.

Bohannan, Paul. 1960. *African Homicide and Suicide*. Princeton, NJ: Princeton University Press.

Bohm, Carol. 1974. "Judicial Attitudes toward Rape Victims." *Judicature* (spring): 303–307.

Bohm, Robert M. 1982. "Radical Criminology: An Explication." *Criminology* 19:565–589.

Bohm, Robert M. 1998. "Understanding Crime and Social Control in Market Economies: Looking Back and Moving Forward." In *Cutting the Edge: Current Perspectives in Radical/Critical Criminology*. Ed. Jeffrey Ian Ross. Westport, CT: Praeger.

Bohm, Robert M., Ronald E. Vogel, and Albert A. Maisto. 1993. "Knowledge and Death Penalty Opinion: A Panel Study." *Journal of Criminal Justice* 21:29–45.

Bonger, Willem. 1916. *Criminality and Economic Conditions*. Boston, MA: Little, Brown.

Bonger, Willem. 1969. Criminality and Economic Conditions, abridged version. Bloomington, IN: Indiana University Press.

Booth, Alan. 1981. "The Built Environment as a Crime Deterrent: A Reexamination of Defensible Space." *Criminology* 18:557–570.

Bordua, David J., ed. 1967. *The Police: Six Sociological Essays*. New York: Wiley.

Boris, Steven Barnet. 1979. "Stereotypes and Dispositions for Criminal Homicide." *Criminology* 17:139–158.

Boritch, Helen, and John Hagan. 1990. "A Century of Crime in Toronto: Gender, Class, and Patterns of Social Control, 1859–1955." *Criminology* 28:567–600.

Bottomley, A. Keith. 1970. *Prison before Trial*. London, UK: G. Bells and Sons.

Bottomley, A. Keith. 1973a. *Decisions in the Penal Process*. London, UK: Martin Robinson.

Bottomley, A. Keith. 1973b. "Parole Decisions in a Long-Term Closed Prison." *British Journal of Criminology* 13:26–40.

Bottomley, A. Keith, and C. Coleman. 1981. *Understanding Crime Rates*. Farnborough, UK: Gower.

Bourgois, P. 1995. *In Search of Respect: Selling Crack in El Barrio*. Cambridge, UK: Cambridge University Press.

Bowers, William J. 1974. *Executions in America*. Lexington, MA: D.C. Heath.

Bowker, Lee H. 1977. *Prisoner Subcultures*. Lexington, MA: D. C. Heath.

Bowker, Lee H. 1978. "Victimization in Correctional Institutions: An Interdisciplinary Analysis." Presented at the annual meeting of the Academy of Criminal Justice Sciences, March, New Orleans, LA.

Bowman, Phillip J. 1980. "Toward a Dual Labor-Market Approach to Black-on-Black Homicide." *Public Health Reports* 95:555–556.

Box-Grainger, Jill. 1986. "Sentencing Rapists." In *Confronting Crime*. Ed. Roger Matthews and Jock Young. Beverly Hills, CA: Sage.

Box, Steven. 1981. *Deviance, Reality, and Society*. 2d ed. London, UK: Holt, Rinehart, and Winston.

Box, Steven. 1983. *Power, Crime, and Mystification*. London, UK: Tavistock.

Box, Steven, and Chris Hale. 1986. "Unemployment, Crime and Imprisonment, and the Enduring Problem of Prison Overcrowding." In *Confronting Crime*. Ed. Roger Matthews and Jock Young. Beverly Hills, CA: Sage.

Boyd, Neil, and John Lowman. 1991. "The Politics of Prostitution and Drug Control." In *The Politics of Crime Control*. Ed. Kevin Stenson and David Cowell. Newbury Park, CA: Sage.

Boyle, Kathleen, and M. Douglas Anglin. 1994. "To the Curb: Sex Bartering and Drug Use among Homeless Crack Users in Los Angeles." Pp. 159–186 in *Crack Pipe As Pimp: An Ethnographic Investigation of Sex-for-Crack Exchanges*. Ed. Mitchell S. Ratner. New York: Lexington Books.

Bradley, Robert J. 1984. "Trends in State Crime-Control Legislation." In *Information Policy and Crime Control Strategies*, Search Group, Inc. Washington, D.C.: U.S. Department of Justice.

Bradshaw, Tausha L., and Alan E. Marks. 1990. "Beyond a Reasonable Doubt: Factors That Influence the Legal Disposition of Child Sexual Abuse Cases." *Crime and Delinquency* 36:276–285.

Braithwaite, John. 1978. "An Exploratory Study of Used Car Fraud." In *Two Kinds of Deviance: Crimes of the Powerless and Powerful*. Ed. P. R. Wilson and J. B. Braithwaite. Brisbane, Australia: University of Queensland Press.

Braithwaite, John. 1982. "Challenging Just Desserts: Punishing White-Collar Criminals." *Journal of Criminal Law and Criminology* 73:723–763.

Braithwaite, John. 1985. *To Punish or Persuade: Enforcement of Coal Mine Safety*. Albany, NY: State University of New York Press.

Braithwaite, John. 1988. "White-Collar Crime, Competition, and Capitalism." *American Journal of Sociology* 94:627–632.

Braithwaite, John. 1989a. *Crime, Shame and Reintegration*. Cambridge, UK: Cambridge University Press.

Braithwaite, John. 1989b. "Organizational Theory and Organizational Shame." *Justice Quarterly* 6:401–426.

Braithwaite, John. 1991. "Inequality and Republican Criminology." Presented at the annual meeting of the American Society of Criminology, November 18–23, San Francisco, CA.

Braithwaite, John. 1997. "Charles Tittle's Control Balance and Criminological Theory." *Theoretical Criminology* 1 (1) (February): 77–97.

Braithwaite, John, and Philip Pettit. 1990. *Not Just Desserts: A Republican Theory of Criminal Justice*. Oxford, UK: Oxford University Press.

Brantingham, Paul J., and Patricia L. Brantingham. 1981. *Environmental Criminology*. Beverly Hills, CA: Sage.

Brecher, Edwin M. 1972. *Licit and Illicit Drugs*. Boston, MA: Little, Brown.

Bredemeier, Harry C., and Toby Jackson. 1961. *Social Problems in America*. New York: Wiley.

Bresler, Fenton. 1992. *Interpol*. London, UK: Penguin.

Brezina, Timothy. 1998. "Adolescent Maltreatment and Delinquency: The Question of Intervening Processes." *Journal of Research in Crime and Delinquency* 35 (1): 71–89.

Brockway, Zebulon R. [1912] 1969. *Fifty Years of Prison Service: An Autobiography*. Montclair, NJ: Patterson Smith.

Brodie, H. Keith. 1973. "The Effects of Ethyl Alcohol in Man." In *National Commission on Marijuana and Drug Abuse (1973), Patterns and Consequences of Drug Use*. Washington, D.C.: U.S. Government Printing Office.

Broidy, Lisa, and Robert Agnew. 1997. "Gender and Crime: A General Strain Theory Perspective." *Journal of Research in Crime and Delinquency* 34:275–306.

Brooks, Laura Weber. 1989. "Police Discretionary Behavior: A Study of Style." In *Critical Issues in Policing*. Ed. Roger G. Durham and Geoffrey P. Alpert. Prospect Heights, IL: Waveland Press.

Brosi, Kathleen B. 1979. *A Cross-City Comparison of Felony Case Processing*. Washington, D.C.: U.S. Government Printing Office.

Brown, Brenda A. 1974. "Crime against Women Alone." Mimeograph. Memphis, TN: Memphis Police Department.

Brown, David, Tom Ellis, and Karen Larcombe. 1992. *Changing the Code: Police Detention under the Revised PACE Codes of Practice*. London, UK: H.M.S.O.

Brown, Jodi M., and Patrick A. Langan. 1998. *State Court Sentencing of Convicted Felons, 1994*. Washington, D.C.: U.S. Department of Justice.

Brown, Michael. 1988. *Working the Streets: Police Discretion and Dilemmas of Reform*. New York: Russell Sage.

Brown, Richard Maxwell. 1969. "Violence in America." In *Crimes of Violence*. Ed. Donald J. Mulvihill, Melvin Tumin, and Lynn Curtis. Washington, D.C.: U.S. Government Printing Office.

Browne, Angela. 1987. *When Battered Women Kill*. New York: Macmillan.

Browne, Angela, and Kirk R. Williams. 1987. "Gender Specific Effects on Patterns of Homicide Perpetration." Presented to the American Psychological Association.

Browne, Angela, Kirk R. Williams, and Donald G. Dutton. 1999. "Homicide between Intimate Partners: A 20-Year Review." In *Homicide: A Sourcebook of Social Research*. Ed. M. D. Smith and M. Zahn. Thousands Oaks, CA: Sage.

Brownmiller, Susan. 1975. *Against Our Will*. New York: Simon & Schuster.

Bruinsma, Gerben. 1992. "Differential Association Theory Reconsidered: An Extension and Its Empirical Test." *Journal of Quantitative Criminology* 8 (1): 29–49.

Bryan, James H. 1965. "Apprenticeships in Prostitution." *Social Problems* 12:287–297.

Bryan, James H. 1966. "Occupational Ideologies and Individual Attitudes of Call Girls." *Social Problems* 13:441–450.

Bryant, Clifton D., and C. Eddie Palmer. 1975. "Massage Parlors and 'Hand Whores': Some Sociological Observations." *Journal of Sex Research* 11:227–241.

Bucke, Tom. 1997. "Ethnicity and Contacts with the Police: Latest Findings from the British Crime Survey." *Research Findings*, UK Home Office Research and Statistics Directorate 59:1–4.

Buckle, Abigail, and David P. Farrington. 1984. "An Observational Study of Shoplifting." *British Journal of Criminology* 24:63–72.

Buikhuisen, Wouter. 1988. "Chronic Juvenile Delinquency: A Theory." In *Explaining Criminal Behavior*. Ed. Wouter Buikhuisen and Sarnoff A. Mednick. Linden, Netherlands: E. J. Brill.

Bullock, Henry Allen. 1961. "Significance of the Racial Factor in Length of Prison Sentences." *Journal of Criminal Law, Criminology and Police Science* 52:411–417.

Burchard, John D., and Sara N. Burchard, eds. 1987. *Prevention of Delinquent Behavior*. Beverly Hills, CA: Sage.

Bureau of Alcohol, Tobacco and Firearms. 2000. *Commerce in Firearms in the United States*. Washington, D.C.: U.S. Department of Treasury.

Bureau of the Census. 2000. *National Crime Victimization Survey: NCUS-1 Basic Screen Questionnaire*. Washington, D.C.: U.S. Department of Commerce.

Bureau of Justice Assistance. 1993. *Problem-Oriented Drug Enforcement*. Washington, D.C.: U.S. Department of Justice.

Bureau of Justice Assistance. 1997. *A Policymaker's Guide to Hate Crimes*. Washington, D.C.: U.S. Department of Justice.

Bureau of Justice Statistics. 1983. *Special Report: Career Patterns in Crime*. Washington, D.C.: U.S. Department of Justice.

Bureau of Justice Statistics. 1984a. *Special Report: Electronic Fund Transfer and Crime*. Washington, D.C.: U.S. Department of Justice.

Bureau of Justice Statistics. 1984b. *Special Report: Family Violence*. Washington, D.C.: U.S. Department of Justice.

Bureau of Justice Statistics. 1984c. *Tracking Offenders: The Child Victim*. Washington, D.C.: U.S. Department of Justice.

Bureau of Justice Statistics. 1984d. *Special Report: Time Served in Prison*. Washington, D.C.: U.S. Department of Justice.

Bureau of Justice Statistics. 1984e. *Prison Admissions and Releases, 1981*. Washington, D.C.: U.S. Department of Justice.

Bureau of Justice Statistics. 1985a. *Special Report: Reporting Crimes to the Police*. Washington, D.C.: U.S. Department of Justice.

Bureau of Justice Statistics. 1985b. *The Crime of Rape*. Washington, D.C.: U.S. Department of Justice.

Bureau of Justice Statistics. 1985c. *Special Report: Examining Recidivism*. Washington, D.C.: U.S. Department of Justice.

Bureau of Justice Statistics. 1985d. *Household Burglary*. Washington, D.C.: U.S. Department of Justice.

Bureau of Justice Statistics. 1985e. *The Growth of Appeals*. Washington, D.C.: U.S. Department of Justice.

Bureau of Justice Statistics. 1985f. *Pretrial Release and Misconduct*. Washington, D.C.: U.S. Department of Justice.

Bureau of Justice Statistics. 1985g. *Capital Punishment, 1984*. Washington, D.C.: U.S. Department of Justice.

Bureau of Justice Statistics. 1985h. *Special Report: Felony Sentencing in 18 Local Jurisdictions*. Washington, D.C.: U.S. Department of Justice.

Bureau of Justice Statistics. 1985i. *Prisoners in 1984*. Washington, D.C.: U.S. Department of Justice.

Bureau of Justice Statistics. 1985j. *Special Report: The Prevalence of Imprisonment*. Washington, D.C.: U.S. Department of Justice.

Bureau of Justice Statistics. 1987. *Special Report: Robbery Victims*. Washington, D.C.: U.S. Department of Justice.

Bureau of Justice Statistics. 1988a. *Crime and Justice in America*. 2d ed. Washington, D.C.: U.S. Department of Justice.

Bureau of Justice Statistics. 1988b. *BJS Data Report, 1987*. Washington, D.C.: U.S. Department of Justice.

Bureau of Justice Statistics. 1988c. *Criminal Victimization in the United States, 1986*. Washington, D.C.: U.S. Department of Justice.

Bureau of Justice Statistics. 1988d. *Bulletin: Households Touched by Crime, 1987*. Washington, D.C.: U.S. Department of Justice.

Bureau of Justice Statistics. 1988e. *Special Report: International Crime Rates*. Washington, D.C.: U.S. Department of Justice.

Bureau of Justice Statistics. 1988f. *Jail Inmates in 1987*. Washington, D.C.: U.S. Department of Justice.

Bureau of Justice Statistics. 1990a. *Black Victims*. Washington, D.C.: U.S. Department of Justice.

Bureau of Justice Statistics. 1990b. *Criminal Victimization, 1989*. Washington, D.C.: U.S. Department of Justice.

Bureau of Justice Statistics. 1990c. *Special Report: Handgun Crime Victims*. Washington, D.C.: U.S. Department of Justice.

Bureau of Justice Statistics. 1990d. *Prison Time*. Washington, D.C.: U.S. Department of Justice.

Bureau of Justice Statistics. 1991a. *Crime and the Nation's Households, 1990*. Washington, D.C.: U.S. Department of Justice.

Bureau of Justice Statistics. 1991b. *Criminal Victimization in the United States: 1973–1988 Trends*. Washington, D.C.: U.S. Department of Justice.

Bureau of Justice Statistics. 1991c. *Drug Crime Facts, 1990*. Washington, D.C.: U.S. Department of Justice.

Bureau of Justice Statistics. 1991d. *National Update*. Washington, D.C.: U.S. Department of Justice.

Bureau of Justice Statistics. 1991e. *Profile of Jail Inmates*. Washington, D.C.: U.S. Department of Justice.

Bureau of Justice Statistics. 1991f. *Bulletin: Capital Punishment, 1990*. Washington, D.C.: U.S. Department of Justice.

Bureau of Justice Statistics. 1991g. *Pretrial Release of Felony Defendants, 1988: National Pretrial Reporting Program*. Washington, D.C.: U.S. Department of Justice.

Bureau of Justice Statistics. 1991h. *Jail Inmates, 1990*. Washington, D.C.: U.S. Department of Justice.

Bureau of Justice Statistics. 1991i. *Special Report: Women in Prison*. Washington, D.C.: U.S. Department of Justice.

Bureau of Justice Statistics. 1991j. *Bulletin: Prisoners in 1990*. Washington, D.C.: U.S. Department of Justice.

Bureau of Justice Statistics. 1992. *National Update*. Vol. 2. Washington, D.C.: U.S. Department of Justice.

Bureau of Justice Statistics. 1993a. *National Update*. Vol. 3. Washington, D.C.: U.S. Department of Justice.

Bureau of Justice Statistics. 1993b. *Highlights from 20 Years of Surveying Crime Victims*. Washington, D.C.: U.S. Department of Justice.

Bureau of Justice Statistics. 1993c. *Census of State and Local Law Enforcement Agencies, 1992*. Washington, D.C.: U.S. Department of Justice.

Bureau of Justice Statistics. 1993d. *Survey of State Prison Inmates, 1991*. Washington, D.C.: U.S. Department of Justice.

Bureau of Justice Statistics. 1994a. *Criminal Victimization in the United States: 1973–1992 Trends*. Washington, D.C.: U.S. Department of Justice.

Bureau of Justice Statistics. 1994b. *Demonstrating the Operational Utility of Incident-Based Data for Local Crime Analysis*. Washington, D.C.: U.S. Department of Justice.

Bureau of Justice Statistics. 1994c. "Fact Sheet: Drug Use Trends." *BJS Drugs and Crime Data* (February): 1–6.

Bureau of Justice Statistics. 1994d. "Fact Sheet: Drug Data Summary." *BJS Drugs and Crime Data* (July): 1–5.

Bureau of Justice Statistics. 1996. *Compendium of Federal Justice Statistics*. Washington D.C.: U.S. Department of Justice.

Bureau of Justice Statistics. 1997. *Sex Offenses and Offenders*. Washington, D.C.: U.S. Department of Justice.

Bureau of Justice Statistics. 1998. At <www.ojp.usdoj.gov/bjs>.

Bureau of Justice Statistics. 1999. *Criminal Victimization in the United States, 1998*. Washington, D.C.: U.S. Department of Justice.

Bureau of Justice Statistics. 1999. At <www.ojp.usdoj.gov/bjs>.

Bureau of Justice Statistics. 2000. *Criminal Victimization 1999: Changes 1998–99 with Trends 1993–99*. Washington, D.C.: U.S. Department of Justice.

Bureau of the Census. 1985. *Statistical Abstract of the United States*. Washington, D.C.: U.S. Government Printing Office.

Bureau of the Census. 1990. *Statistical Abstract of the United States, 1990*. Washington, D.C.: U.S. Department of Commerce.

Burgess, Robert L. 1979. "Family Violence: Some Implications from Evolutionary Biology." Presented to the annual meeting of the American Society of Criminology, San Francisco, California.

Burgess, Robert L., and Ronald L. Akers. 1966. "A Differential Association-Reinforcement Theory of Criminal Behavior." *Social Problems* 14:128–147.

Burgess, Robert L., and Patricia Draper. 1989. "The Explanation of Family Violence: The Role of Biological, Behavioral, and Cultural Selection." In *Family Violence*. Ed. Lloyd Ohlin and Michael Tonry. Chicago, IL: University of Chicago Press.

Burrows, John N., and Kevin Heal. 1980. "Police Car Security Campaigns." In *Designing Out Crime*.

Ed. Ronald V. Clarke and Pat Mayhew. London, UK: H.M.S.O.

Bursik, Robert J., Jr. 1980. "The Dynamics of Specialization in Juvenile Offenses." *Social Forces* 59:851–864.

Bursik, Robert J., Jr. 1988. "Social Disorganization and Theories of Crime and Delinquency: Problems and Prospects." *Criminology* 26:519–551.

Bursik, Robert J., Jr. 2000. "The Systematic Theory of Neighborhood Crime Rates." In *Of Crime and Criminality: The Use of Theory in Everyday Life*. Ed. Sally S. Simpson. Thousand Oaks, CA: Pine Forge Press.

Bursik, Robert J., and Harold G. Grasmick. 1993. *Neighborhoods and Crime: The Dimensions of Effective Community Control*. Lexington, MA: Lexington Books.

Bursik, Robert J., and Harold G. Grasmick. 1995. "Neighborhood-Based Networks and the Control of Crime and Delinquency." In *Crime and Public Policy: Putting Theory to Work*. Ed. Hugh D. Barlow. Boulder, CO: Westview.

Bush, Tracey, and John Hood-Williams. 1995. "Domestic Violence on a London Housing Estate." *Home Office Research Bulletin* 37:11–18.

Butts, Jeffrey A. 1997. "Delinquency Cases Waived to Criminal Courts, 1985–1994." *OJJDP Fact Sheet* 52:1–2

CNN. 2000. Interview with Emmanuel Goldstein. At >www.cnn.com/TECH/specials/hackers/qandas/goldstein.html>.

Calavita, Kitty, and Henry N. Pontell. 1990. "Heads I Win, Tails You Lose: Deregulation, Crime, and Crisis in the Savings and Loan Industry." *Crime and Delinquency* 36:309–341.

Calavita, Kitty, and Henry N. Pontell. 1991. "Other People's Money Revisited: Collective Embezzlement in the Savings and Loan and Insurance Industries." *Social Problems* 38:94–112.

Calavita, Kitty, and Henry N. Pontell. 1993. "Savings and Loan Fraud As Organized Crime: Toward a Conceptual Typology of Corporate Criminality." *Criminology* 31:519–548.

Calder, James D., and John F. Bauer. 1992. "Convenience Store Robberies: Security Measures and Store Robbery Incidents." *Journal of Criminal Justice* 20:553–566.

Calhoun, George. 1927. *The Growth of Criminal Law in Ancient Greece*. Berkeley, CA: University of California Press.

Callahan, Charles M., and Frederick P. Rivara. 1992. "Urban High School Youth and Handguns." *JAMA* 267:3038–3042.

Calvert, E. Roy. Repr. 1971. *Capital Punishment in the Twentieth Century*. New York: Kennikat Press.

Calvin, Allen D. 1981. "Unemployment among Black Youths, Demographics and Crime." *Crime and Delinquency* 27:234–244.

Cameron, Mary Owen. 1964. *The Booster and the Snitch*. New York: Free Press.

Campbell, Ann. 1984. *Girls in the Gang*. Oxford, UK: Basil Blackwell.

Cannavale, Frank J. 1976. *Witness Cooperation*. Lexington, MA: D.C. Heath.

Carey, James T. 1968. *The College Drug Scene*. Englewood Cliffs, NJ: Prentice Hall.

Caringella-MacDonald, Susan. 1991. "An Assessment of Rape Reform: Victim and Case Treatment under Michigan's Model." *International Review of Victimology* 1:347–361.

Carlin, Jerome E. 1968. *Lawyer's Ethics*. New York: Russell Sage.

Carlson, Kenneth. 1993. "Prosecuting Criminal Enterprises." *BJS Special Report* (November): 1–7.

Carroll, Leo. 1974. *Hacks, Blacks, and Cons: Race Relations in a Maximum Security Prison*. Lexington, MA: D.C. Heath.

Carter, Robert M. 1965. "The Johnny Cain Story: A Composite of Men Executed in California." *Issues in Criminology* 1:66–76.

Carter, Robert M., and Leslie T. Wilkins. 1967. "Some Factors in Sentencing Policy." *Journal of Criminal Law, Criminology, and Police Science* 58:503–514.

Carter, Robert M., and Leslie T. Wilkins, eds. 1976. *Probation, Parole, and Community Corrections*. 2d ed. New York: Wiley.

Carter, Ronald L., and Kim Q. Hill. 1979. *The Criminal's Image of the City*. New York: Pergamon.

Casper, Jonathan D. 1971. "Did You Have a Lawyer When You Went to Court? No I Had a Public Defender." *Yale Review of Law and Social Action* 1:4–9.

Casper, Jonathan D. 1972. *American Criminal Justice: The Defendant's Perspective*. Englewood Cliffs, NJ: Prentice Hall.

Caspi, Avshalom, Terrie E. Moffit, Phil A. Silva, Magda Stouthamer-Loeber, Robert F. Krueger, and Pamela S. Schmutte. 1994. "Are Some

People Crime-Prone? Replications of the Personality-Crime Relationship across Countries, Genders, Races, and Methods." *Criminology* 32:163–195.

Caulfield, Susan L. 1991. "The Perpetuation of Violence through Criminological Theory: The Ideological Role of Subculture Theory." Pp. 228–238 in *Criminology as Peacemaking*. Ed. H. E. Pepinsky and R. Quinney. Bloomington, IN: Indiana University Press.

Caulfield, Susan L., and Nancy A. Wonders. 1993. "Personal and Political: Violence against Women and the Role of the State." In *Political Crime in Contemporary America: A Critical Approach*. Ed. Kenneth D. Tunnell. New York: Garland.

Cavadino, Michael, and James Dignan. 1992. *The Penal System*. Newbury Park, CA: Sage.

Cavan, Sherri. 1966. *Liquor License: An Ethnography of Bar Behavior*. Chicago, IL: Aldine.

Caywood, Tom. 1998. "Routine Activities and Urban Homicides: A Tale of Two Cities." *Homicide Studies* 2, no. 1 (February): 64–82.

Center for Research on Criminal Justice. 1975. *The Iron Fist and the Velvet Glove*. Berkeley, CA: Center for Research on Criminal Justice.

Centers for Disease Control. 1985. *Morbidity and Mortality, Weekly Report* (October 11): 613–618.

Cernkovich, Stephen A., and Peggy C. Giordano. 1987. "Family Relationships and Delinquency." *Criminology* 25:295–319.

Cernkovich, Stephen A., Peggy C. Giordano, and Meredith D. Pugh. 1985. "Chronic Offenders: The Missing Cases in Self-Report Delinquency Research." *Journal of Criminal Law and Criminology* 76:705–732.

Chaiken, Marcia R. 1993. "The Rise of Crack and Ice: Experiences in Three Locales." *NIJ Research in Brief* (March): 1–8.

Chaiken, Marcia R., and Jan M. Chaiken. 1991. "Priority Prosecution of High Rate Dangerous Offenders." *NIJ Research in Action* (March): 1–8.

Chambers, Carl D. 1971. *An Assessment of Drug Use in the General Population*. New York: Narcotics Addiction Control Commission.

Chambliss, William J. 1967. "Types of Deviance and the Effectiveness of Legal Sanctions." *Wisconsin Law Review* (summer): 703–719.

Chambliss, William J. 1971. "Vice, Corruption, Bureaucracy, and Power." *Wisconsin Law Review* (fall): 1150–1173.

Chambliss, William J., ed. 1972. *Box Man: A Professional Thief's Journey*. New York: Harper & Row.

Chambliss, William J. 1973. "The Saints and the Roughnecks." *Society* 11:24–31.

Chambliss, William J. 1975a. "The Political Economy of Crime: A Comparative Study of Nigeria and the U.S.A.." In *Critical Criminology*. Ed. Ian Taylor, Paul Walton, and Jock Young. London, UK: Routledge and Kegan Paul.

Chambliss, William J. 1975b. *Criminal Law in Action*. Santa Barbara, CA: Hamilton.

Chambliss, William J. 1978. *On the Take: From Petty Crooks to Presidents*. Bloomington, IN: Indiana University Press.

Chambliss, William J. 1988a. *Exploring Crime*. New York: Macmillan.

Chambliss, William J. 1988b. *On the Take: From Petty Crooks to Presidents*. 2d ed. Bloomington, IN: Indiana University Press.

Chambliss, William J. 1999. *Power, Politics, and Crime*. Boulder, CO: Westview.

Chambliss, William J., and John T. Liell. 1966). "The Legal Process in the Community Setting." *Crime and Delinquency* 12:310–317.

Chambliss, William J., and Robert B. Siedman. 1971. *Law and Order*. Reading, MA: Addison-Wesley.

Chambliss, William J., and Robert Seidman. 1982. *Law, Order, Power*. Reading, MA: Addison-Wesley.

Chambliss, William J., and Marjorie Zatz. 1993. *Making Law: The State, the Law, and Structural Contradictions*. Bloomington, IN: Indiana University Press.

Chamlin, Mitchell B., and John K. Cochran. 1997. "Social Altruism and Crime." *Criminology* 35 (2): 203–227.

Champion, Dean. 2000. *Research Methods for Criminal Justice and Criminology*. Upper Saddle River, NJ: Prentice Hall.

Champion, Jane Dimmitt. 1999. "Life Histories of Rural Mexican American Adolescents Experiencing Abuse." *Western Journal of Nursing Research* 21 (5): 699–717.

Chancer, Lynn S. 1987. "New Bedford, Massachusetts, March 6, 1983–March 22, 1984: The 'Before and After' of a Group Rape." *Gender and Society* 1:239–260.

Chapman, Dennis. 1968. *Sociology and the Stereotype of the Criminal*. London, UK: Tavistock.

Chapman, William R. 1986. "The Role of Peers in Strain Models of Delinquency." Presented to annual meeting of the American Society of Criminology, Atlanta, GA.

Chappell, Duncan. 1989. "Violence, Crime and Australian Society." *National Committee on Violence, Violence Today Series* (December): 1–8.

Chappell, Duncan, Robley Geis, and Gilbert Geis. 1977. *Forcible Rape: The Crime, the Victim, and the Offender.* New York: Columbia University Press.

Cheatwood, Darrell. 1988. "Is There a Season for Homicide?" *Criminology* 26:287–306.

Chermak, Steven. 1994. "Crime in the New Media: A Refined Understanding of How Crimes Become News." In *Media, Process, and the Social Construction of Crime: Studies in Newsmaking Criminology.* Ed. Gregg Barak. New York: Garland.

Chesney-Lind, Meda. 1987a. *Girls' Crime and Women's Place: Toward a Feminist Model of Female Delinquency.* Honolulu, HI: University of Hawaii Youth Development and Research Center.

Chesney-Lind, Meda. 1987b. "Female Status Offenders and the Double Standard of Juvenile Justice: An International Problem." Presented at the annual meeting of the American Society of Criminology, November 11–14, Montreal, Canada.

Chesney-Lind, Meda. 1988. "Girls in Jail." *Crime and Delinquency* 34:150–168.

Chesney-Lind, Meda, and Randall G. Shelden. 1992. *Girls, Delinquency, and Juvenile Justice.* Pacific Grove, CA: Brooks/Cole.

Chimbos, P. D. 1978a. *Marital Violence: A Study of Interspouse Homicide.* San Francisco, CA: R and E Research Associates.

Chiricos, Ted, Kathy Padgett, and Marc Gertz. 2000. "Fear, TV News, and the Reality of Crime." *Criminology* 38 (3): 755–786.

Chodorkoff, Bernard, and Seymour Baxter. 1969. "Psychiatric and Psychoanalytic Theories of Violence and Its Origins." In *Crimes of Violence.* Ed. Donald J. Mulvihill, Melvin Tumin, and Lynn Curtis. Washington, D.C.: U.S. Government Printing Office.

Christiansen, Harold T., and Christina Gregg. 1970. "Changing Sex Norms in America and Scandinavia." *Journal of Marriage and the Family* 32:625–626.

Christiansen, K. O. 1977a. "A Preliminary Study of Criminality among Twins." In *Biosocial Basis of Criminal Behavior.* Ed. Sarnoff A. Mednick and K. O. Christiansen. New York: Wiley.

Christiansen, K. O. 1977b. "A Review of Studies of Criminality among Twins." In *Biosocial Basis of Criminal Behavior.* Ed. Sarnoff A. Mednick and K. O. Christiansen. New York: Wiley.

Churchill, W., and J. Vander Wall. 1990. *The Cointelpro Papers.* Boston, MA: South End Press.

Cicourel, Aaron V. 1968. *The Social Organization of Juvenile Justice.* New York: Wiley.

Clark, Alexander L., and Jack P. Gibbs. 1965. "Social Control: A Reformulation." *Social Problems* 12:398–415.

Clarke, Ronald V. 1997. *Situational Crime Prevention: Successful Case Studies.* 2d ed. New York: Harrow and Heston.

Clarke, Ronald V., and Patricia Mayhew, eds. 1980. *Designing Out Crime.* London, UK: H.M.S.O.

Clarke, Ronald V., and Patricia M. Harris. 1992a. "Auto Theft and Its Prevention." In *Crime and Justice: A Review of Research.* Vol. 16. Ed. Michael Tonry. Chicago, IL: University of Chicago Press.

Clarke, Ronald V., and Patricia Mayhew. 1988. "The British Gas Suicide Story and Its Criminological Implications." In *Crime and Justice: A Review of Research.* Vol. 10. Ed. Michael N. Tonry and Norval K. Morris. Chicago, IL: University of Chicago Press.

Clarke, Ronald V., and Patricia M. Harris. 1992b. "A Rational Choice Perspective on the Targets of Automobile Theft." *Criminal Behavior and Mental Health* 2:25–42

Clarke, R. V., and R. Homel. 1997. "A Revised Classification of Situational Crime Prevention Techniques." In *Crime Prevention at a Crossroads.* Ed. Steven P. Lab. Cincinnati, OH: Anderson.

Claster, Daniel. 1992. *Bad Guys and Good Guys: Moral Polarization and Crime.* New York: Greenwood.

Clear, Todd R., John D. Hewitt, and Robert M. Regoli. 1978. "Discretion and the Determinate Sentence: Its Distribution, Control, and Effect on Time Served." *Crime and Delinquency* 24:428–445.

Clifford, Nancy. 1998. *Environmental Crime: Enforcement, Policy, and Social Responsibility.* Gaithersburg, MD: Aspen.

Clinard, Marshall B. 1983. *Corporate Ethics and Crime: The Role of Middle Management.* Beverly Hills, CA: Sage.

Clinard, Marshall B. 1989. "Reflections of a Typologic, Corporate, Comparative Criminologist." *The Criminologist* 14:1, 6, 11, 14–15.

Clinard, Marshall B., and Daniel J. Abbot. 1973. *Crime in Developing Countries*. New York: Wiley.

Clinard, Marshall B., and Richard Quinney, eds. 1967. *Criminal Behavior Systems: A Typology*. New York: Holt, Rinehart, & Winston.

Clinard, M., and R. Quinney. 1973. *Criminal Behavior Systems: A Typology*. New York: Holt, Rinehart, & Winston.

Clinard, Marshall B., Peter C. Yeager, Jeanne Brissette, David Petrashek, and Elizabeth Hames. 1979. *Illegal Corporate Behavior*. Washington, D.C.: LEAA.

Cloward, Richard A., and Lloyd E. Ohlin. 1960. *Delinquency and Opportunity: A Theory of Delinquent Gangs*. New York: Free Press.

Cochran, John K., Mitchell B. Chamlin, and Mark Seth. 1994. "Deterrence or Brutalization: An Impact Assessment of Oklahoma's Return to Capital Punishment." *Criminology* 32:107–134.

Cohen, Albert K. 1951. *Juvenile Delinquency and the Social Structure*. Cambridge, MA: Harvard University Press.

Cohen, Albert K. 1955. *Delinquent Boys: The Culture of the Gang*. New York: Free Press.

Cohen, Albert K. 1977. "The Concept of Criminal Organization." *The British Journal of Criminology* 17:97–111.

Cohen, Jacqueline. 1983. *Incapacitating Criminals: Recent Research Findings, NIJ Reports*. Washington, D.C.: National Institute of Justice.

Cohen, Lawrence E., and Marcus Felson. 1979. "Social Change and Crime Rate Trends: A Routine Activity Approach." *American Sociological Review* 44:588–608.

Cohen, Lawrence E., and Richard Machalek. 1988. "A General Theory of Expropriative Crime: An Evolutionary Ecological Approach." *American Journal of Sociology* 94:465–501.

Cohen, Lawrence E., David Cantor, and James R. Klugel. 1981. "Robbery Victimization in the United States: Analysis of a Nonrandom Event. *Social Science Quarterly* 62:644–657.

Cohen, Lawrence E., Marcus Felson, and Kenneth C. Land. 1980. "Property Crime Rates in the United States: A Macrodynamic Analysis, 1947–1977, with Ex-Ante Forecasts for the Mid-1980s." *American Journal of Sociology* 86:90–118.

Cohen, Mark A. 1998. "Sentencing the Environmental Criminal." In *Environmental Crime: Enforcement, Policy, and Social Responsibility*. Ed. Nancy Clifford. Gaithersburg, MD: Aspen.

Cohen, Stanley, ed. 1971. *Images of Deviance*. Harmondsworth, UK: Penguin Books.

Cohen, Stanley. 1985. *Visions of Social Control: Crime, Punishment and Classification*. New York: Polity Press.

Cohen, Stanley. 1988. *Against Criminology*. New Brunswick, NJ: Transaction Books.

Cohen, Stanley. 1993. "Human Rights and Crimes of the State: The Culture of Denial." *Australian and New Zealand Journal of Criminology* 26:97–115.

Cohn, Steven F., Steven E. Barkan, and William A. Halteman. 1991. "Punitive Attitudes toward Criminals: Racial Consensus or Racial Conflict?" *Social Problems* 38:287–294.

Cole, George F. 1970. "The Decision to Prosecute." *Law and Society Review* 4:331–343.

Cole, George F. 1989. *The American System of Criminal Justice*. 5th ed. Pacific Grove, CA: Brooks/Cole.

Coleman, James W. 1989. *The Criminal Elite*. 2d ed. New York: St. Martin's Press.

Collins, James T., Robert L. Hubbard, and J. Valley Rachel. 1985. "Expensive Drug Use and Illegal Income: A Test of Explanatory Hypotheses." *Criminology* 23:743–763.

Colvin, Mark, and John Pauly. 1983. "An Integrated Structural-Marxist Theory of Delinquency." *American Journal of Sociology* 89 (3): 513–551.

Conklin, John E. 1972. *Robbery and the Criminal Justice System*. Philadelphia, PA: Lippincott.

Conklin, John E., ed. 1973. *The Crime Establishment: Organized Crime and American Society*. Englewood Cliffs, NJ: Prentice Hall.

Conklin, John E., and Egon Bittner. 1973. "Burglary in a Suburb." *Criminology* 11:206–232.

Conrad, John P. 1975. "We Should Never Have Promised a Hospital." *Federal Probation* 39:1–12.

Cook, Philip J. 1982. "The Role of Firearms in Violent Crime." In *Criminal Violence*. Ed. Marvin E. Wolfgang. Beverly Hills, CA: Sage.

Cook, Philip J. 1987. "Robbery Violence." *Journal of Criminal Law and Criminology* 78:357–376.

Cook, Phillip J., and M. H. Moore. 1999. "Guns, Gun Control and Homicide: A Review of Research and Public Policy." In *Homicide: A Sourcebook of Social Research*. Ed. M. Dwayne Smith and Margaret A. Zahn. Thousand Oaks, CA: Sage.

Cordes, Helen. 2000. "Generation Wired: Caffeine is the New Drug of Choice for Kids." Pp. 79–83 in *Annual Editions: Drugs, Society, and Behavior*. Ed.

Hugh T. Wilson. Sluice Dock, CT: Dushkin/McGraw-Hill.

Cornish, Derek B., and Ronald V. Clarke. 1986a. "Situational Prevention, Displacement of Crime and Rational Choice Theory." In *Situational Crime Prevention*. Ed. Kevin Heal and Gloria Laycock. London, UK: H.M.S.O.

Cornish, Derek B., and Ronald V. Clarke. 1986b. *The Reasoning Criminal: Rational Choice Perspectives on Offending*. New York: Springer-Verlag.

Cornish, Derek B., and Ronald V. Clarke. 1987. "Understanding Crime Displacement: An Application of Rational Choice Theory." *Criminology* 25:933–947.

Costello, Barbara J., and Paul R. Vowell. 1999. "Testing Control Theory and Differential Association: A Reanalysis of the Richmond Youth Project Data." *Criminology* 37 (4): 815–842.

Cramer, James A., ed. 1978a. *Preventing Crime*. Beverly Hills, CA: Sage.

Crank, John P. 1998. *Understanding Police Culture*. Cincinnati, OH: Anderson.

Crawford, Charles. 2000. "Gender, Race, and Habitual Offender Sentencing in Florida." *Criminology* 38 (1): 263–280.

Crawford, Charles, Theodore Chiricos, and Gary Kleck. 1998. "Race, Racial Threat, and Sentencing Habitual Offenders." *Criminology* 36: 481–511.

Cressey, Donald R. 1953. *Other People's Money: A Study in the Social Psychology of Embezzlement*. New York: Free Press.

Cressey, Donald R. 1965. "The Respectable Criminal." *Transaction* 3:12–15.

Cressey, Donald R. 1969. *Theft of the Nation: The Structure and Operations of Organized Crime in America*. New York: Harper & Row.

Crew, B. Keith. 1991. "Race Differences in Felony Charging and Sentencing: Toward an Integration of Decision-Making and Negotiation Models." *Journal of Crime and Justice* 14 (1): 99–122.

Criminal Justice Collective of Northern Arizona University. 2000. *Investigating Difference: Human and Cultural Relations in Criminal Justice*. Boston, MA: Allyn and Bacon.

Critchley, T. A. 1972. *A History of Police in England and Wales*. 2d ed. Montclair, NJ: Patterson Smith.

Croall, Hazel. 1989. "Who Is the White-Collar Criminal?" *British Journal of Criminology* 29:157–174.

Cromwell, Paul F., ed. 1996. *In Their Own Words: Criminals on Crime*. Los Angeles, CA: Roxbury.

Cromwell, Paul F., ed. 1999. *In Their Own Words: Criminals on Crime*. 2d ed. Los Angeles, CA: Roxbury.

Cromwell, Paul F., Lee Parker, and Shawna Mobley. 1999. "The Five-Finger Discount: An Analysis of Motivations for Shoplifting." In *In Their Own Words: Criminals on Crime*. 2d ed. Ed. Paul F. Cromwell. Los Angeles, CA: Roxbury.

Cromwell, Paul F., J. Olson, and D. Avary. 1991. *Breaking and Entering: An Ethnographic Analysis of Burglary*. Newbury Park, CA: Sage.

Crowell, Nancy, and Ann W. Burgess. 1996. *Understanding Violence against Women*. Washington, D.C.: National Academy Press.

Cullen, Francis T. 1983a. "Paradox in Policing: A Note on Perceptions of Danger." *Journal of Police Science and Administration* 11:457–462.

Cullen, Francis T. 1983b. *Rethinking Crime and Deviance Theory: The Emergence of a Structuring Tradition*. Totowa, NJ: Rowman and Allanheld.

Cullen, Francis T. 1994. "Social Support As an Organizing Concept for Criminology: Presidential Address to the Academy of Criminal Justice Sciences." *Justice Quarterly* 11:527–559.

Cullen, Francis T., Bruce G. Link, Lawrence F. Travis III, and John F. Wozniack. 1985b. "Consensus of Crime Seriousness: Empirical Reality or Methodological Artifact?" *Criminology* 23:99–118.

Cullen, Francis T., Gregory A. Clark, John R. Cullen, and Richard A. Matthews. 1985a. "Attribution, Salience, and Attitudes toward Criminal Sanctioning." *Criminal Justice and Behavior* 12:305–331.

Cullen, Francis T., Kathryn M. Golden and John B. Cullen. 1975. "Sex and Delinquency: A Partial Test of the Masculinity Hypothesis." *Criminology* 17:302–310.

Cullen, Francis T., William J. Maakestad, and Gary Cavender. 1987. *Corporate Crime under Attack: The Ford Pinto Case*. Cincinnati, OH: Anderson.

Cumming, Elaine, Ian Cumming, and Laura Edell. 1965. "Policeman As Philosopher, Guide and Friend." *Social Problems* 12:276–286.

Cunningham, William C., and Todd Taylor. 1985. *The Hallcrest Report: Private Security and Police in America*. Portland, OR: Chancellor Press.

Cunningham, William C., John T. Strauchs, and Clifford M. Van Meter. 1991. *Private Security: Patterns and Trends*. Washington, D.C.: U.S. Department of Justice.

Cupples, Thomas, and David Kauzlarich. 1997. "La Cosa Nostra in Philadelphia: A Functionalist Perspective." *Criminal Organizations* 11 (1–2): 17–24.

Curran, Daniel J., and Claire M. Renzetti. 1994. *Theories of Crime*. Boston, MA: Allyn and Bacon.

Currie, Elliott. 1985. *Confronting Crime: An American Challenge*. New York: Pantheon.

Currie, Elliott. 1997. "Market, Crime, and Community: Toward a Mid-Range Theory of Post-Industrial Violence." *Theoretical Criminology* 1 (2): 147–172.

Currie, Elliott. 1998. *Crime and Punishment in America*. New York: Henry Holt and Company.

Cusson, Maurice, and Pierre Pinsonneault. 1986. "The Decision to Give Up Crime." In *The Reasoning Criminal*. Ed. Derek B. Cornish and Ronald V. Clarke. New York: Springer-Verlag.

Czajkoski, Eugene H. 1973. "Exposing the Quasi-Judicial Role of the Prosecutor's Office." *Federal Probation* 37:9–13.

Dale, Robert. 1974. *Memoirs of a Contemporary Cutpurse*. Cambridge, MA: Schenkman.

D'Alessio, Stewart J., and Lisa Stolzenberg. 1999. "Crime, Arrests, and Pretrial Jail Detention: An Examination of the Deterrence Thesis." *Criminology* 36 (4): 735–761.

Daly, Kathleen. 1987a. "Structure and Practice of Familial-Based Justice in a Criminal Court." *Law and Society Review* 21:267–290.

Daly, Kathleen. 1987b. "Gender and White-Collar Crime." Revised version of a paper presented to the annual meeting of the American Society of Criminology, Montreal, Canada.

Daly, Kathleen. 1988. "The Social Control of Sexuality: A Case Study of the Criminalization of Prostitution in the Progressive Era." *Research in Law, Deviance and Social Control* 9:171–206.

Daly, Kathleen. 1989. "Neither Conflict nor Labeling nor Paternalism Will Suffice: Intersections of Race, Ethnicity, Gender and Family in Criminal Court Decisions." *Crime and Delinquency* 35:136–168.

Daly, Kathleen, and Meda Chesney-Lind. 1988. "Feminism and Criminology." *Justice Quarterly* 5:101–143.

Daly, Martin, and Margo Wilson. 1988a. "Evolutionary Social Psychology and Family Homicide." *Science* 242:519–524.

Daly, Martin, and Margo Wilson. 1988b. *Homicide*. New York: Aldine DeGruyter.

Damaska, Mirjam R. 1968. "Adverse Legal Consequences of Conviction and Their Removal: A Comparative Study." *Journal of Criminal Law, Criminology, and Police Science* 59:347–360, 542–568.

Daniel, A. E., and P. W. Harris. 1982. "Female Homicide Offenders Referred for Pre-Trial Psychiatric Examination: A Descriptive Study." *Bulletin of the American Academy of Psychiatry and Law* 10:261–269.

Darrow, W., H. Jaffee, and J. Curran. 1983. "Passive Anal Intercourse As a Risk Factor for AIDS in Homosexual Men." *Lancet* 2:309–313.

Datesman, Susan K., and Frank R. Scarpitti. 1980. *Women, Crime and Justice*. New York: Oxford University Press.

Daudistel, Howard C., William B. Sanders, and David F. Luckenbill. 1979. *Criminal Justice: Situations and Decisions*. New York: Holt, Rinehart, and Winston.

Davidson, Ralph. 1965. "The Promiscuous Fine." *Criminal Law Quarterly* 8:74–76.

Davis, Alan J. 1968. "Sexual Assaults in the Philadelphia Prison System and Sheriffs' Vans." *Transaction* 6:9–16.

Davis, F. James. 1962. *Law As a Type of Social Control*. New York: Free Press.

Davis, J. K. 1992. *Spying on America*. Westport, CT: Praeger.

Davis, Robert C., and Barbara Smith. 1995. "Domestic Violence Reforms: Empty Promises or Fulfilled Expectations?" *Crime and Delinquency* 41:522–541.

Dawley, David. 1992. *A Nation of Lords: The Autobiography of the Vice Lords*. 2d ed. Prospect Heights, IL: Waveland Press.

Dawson, John M. 1992. "Prosecutions in State Courts, 1990." *BJS Bulletin* (March): 1–9.

Dawson, John M. 1993. *Murder in Large Urban Counties, 1988*. Washington, D.C.: U.S. Department of Justice.

Dawson, John M., and Patrick A. Langan. 1994. "Murder in Families." *BJS Special Report* (July): 1–13.

Dawson, John M., Steven K. Smith, and Carol J. DeFrances. 1993. "Prosecutors in State Courts, 1992." *BJS Bulletin* (December): 1–8.

Decker, Scott H. 2000. "Legitimating Drug Use: A Note on the Impact of Gang Membership and Drug Sales on the Use of Illicit Drugs." *Justice Quarterly* 17 (2): 393–410.

DeFrancis, Vincent. 1969. *Protecting the Child Victims of Sex Crimes Committed by Adults*. Denver, CO: American Humane Society.

DeKeseredy, Walter S., and Martin D. Schwartz. 1998. *Woman Abuse on Campus: Results from the Canadian National Survey*. Thousand Oaks, CA: Sage Publications.

DeMause. 1998. "The history of child abuse." *The Journal of Psychohistory* 25 (3): 216–236.

Denno, Deborah W. 1985. "Sociological and Human Developmental Explanations of Crime." *Criminology* 23:711–741.

Denno, Deborah W. 1990. *Biology and Violence from Birth to Adulthood*. Cambridge, UK: Cambridge University Press.

Dershowitz, Allen M. 1961. "Increasing Control over Corporate Crime: A Problem in the Law of Sanctions." *Yale Law Journal* 71:291.

De Stefano, George. 2000. "Ungood Fellas." *The Nation* 270 (5): 31–33.

Dible, Debra A., and Raymond H. C. Teske Jr. 1993. "An Analysis of the Prosecutory Effects of a Child Sexual Abuse Victim-Witness Program." *Journal of Criminal Justice* 21:79–85.

Dighton, Daniel. 1998. "Isolation and Limited Resources Create Challenges for Rural Law Enforcement." *The Compiler* (spring): 4–5.

Doerner, William G. 1983. "Why Does Johnny Reb Die When Shot? The Impact of Medical Resources upon Lethality." *Sociological Inquiry* 53:1–12.

Doerner, William G. 1998. *Introduction to Law Enforcement: An Insider's View*. Boston, MA: Butterworth-Heinemann.

Doleisch, Wolfgang. 1960. "Theft in Department Stores." *Proceedings of Fourth International Criminological Congress, The Hague*, 2, sec. 2:4–7.

Dollard, John, N. Miller, L. Doob, O. H. Mowrer, and R. R. Sears. 1939. *Frustration and Aggression*. New Haven, CT: Yale University Press.

Donnelly, Patrick G., and Charles E. Kimble. 1997. "Community Organizing, Environmental Change, and Neighborhood Crime." *Crime and Delinquency* 43 (4): 493–511.

Donziger, Steven. 1996. *The Real War on Crime*. New York: HarperPerennial.

Dorman, Michael. 1972. *Payoff: The Role of Organized Crime*. New York: David McKay.

Douglas, Jack D., ed. 1970. *Observations of Deviance*. New York: Random House.

Downie, Leonard, Jr. 1972. *Justice Denied*. Baltimore, MD: Penguin Books.

Downs, William R., Joan F. Robertson, and Larry R. Harrison. 1997. "Control Theory, Labeling Theory, and the Delivery of Service for Drug Abuse to Adolescents." *Adolescence* 32:1–24.

Doyle, James C. 1953. "Unnecessary Hysterectomies." *American Medical Association Journal* 151:360–365.

Drug Enforcement Agency. 2001. "Marijuana." At <www.usdoj.gov/dea/concern/marijuana.htm>.

Dukes, Richard L., Judith A. Stein, and Jodie B. Ullman. 1997. "Long-Term Impact of DARE: Results of a 6-Year Follow-Up." *Evaluation Review* 21 (4): 483–500.

Dunford, Franklyn W., and Delbert S. Elliott. 1984. "Identifying Career Offenders Using Self-Reported Data." *Journal of Research in Crime and Delinquency* 21:57–86.

Dunford, Franklyn W., David Huizinga, and Delbert S. Elliott. 1990. "The Role of Arrest in Domestic Assault: The Omaha Police Experiment." *Criminology* 28:183–206.

Dunham, Roger G., and Geoffrey P. Alpert. 1989. *Critical Issues in Policing*. Prospect Heights, IL: Waveland Press.

Dunlap, Eloise, Bruce D. Johnson, and Ali Manwar. 1997. "A Successful Female Crack Dealer: Case Study of a Deviant Career." In *Drugs, Crime, and Justice: Contemporary Perspectives*. Ed. Larry K. Gaines and Peter B. Kraska. Prospect Heights, IL: Waveland Press.

Durkheim, Emile. 1893. *De la Division du Travail Social*. Paris, France: Alcan.

Durkheim, Emile. 1900. "Deux lois de l'évolution pénale." *l'Annee Sociologique* 4:65–93.

Durkheim, Emile. 1950. *The Rules of the Sociological Method*. Glenroe, IL: Free Press.

Durkheim, Emile. 1952. *Suicide*. London, UK: Routledge and Kegan Paul.

Durkheim, Emile. 1964a. *The Division of Labor in Society*. New York: Free Press.

Durkheim, Emile. 1964b. *The Rules of Sociological Method*. New York: Free Press.

Durkheim, Emile. 1999. "The Normal and the Pathological." In *Social Deviance: Readings in Theory and*

Research. Ed. Henry N. Pontell. Upper Saddle River, NJ: Prentice Hall.

Dworkin, Andrea. 1981. *Pornography: Men Possessing Women*. New York: Putnam.

Earle, Alice M. 1969. *Curious Punishments of By-Gone Days*. Montclair, NJ: Patterson Smith.

Edelhertz, Herbert. 1970. *The Nature, Impact, and Prosecution of White-Collar Crime*. Washington, D.C.: U.S. Government Printing Office.

Edelhertz, Herbert, and Marilyn Walsh. 1978. *The White-Collar Challenge to Nuclear Safeguards*. Lexington, MA: Lexington Books.

Edwards, John N. 1972. *Sex and Society*. Chicago, IL: Markham.

Edwards, Loren E. 1958. *Shoplifting and Shrinkage Protection for Stores*. Springfield, IL: Charles C. Thomas.

Edwards, S. S. M. 1986. *The Police Response to Domestic Violence in London*. London, UK: Central London Polytechnic.

Edwards, Willie J. 1993. "Constructing and Testing a Multiple-Theory Integrated Model of Juvenile Delinquency." *Mid-American Review of Sociology* 17 (1): 31–43.

Egger, Steven A. 1990. *Serial Murder: An Elusive Phenomenon*. New York: Praeger.

Egger, Steven A. 1998. *The Killers among Us: An Examination of Serial Murder and Its Investigation*. Upper Saddle River, NJ: Prentice Hall.

Einstadter, Werner J. 1969. "The Social Organization of Armed Robbery." *Social Problems* 17:64–83.

Ekland-Olson, Sheldon, John Lieb, and Louis Zurcher. 1984. "The Paradoxical Impact of Criminal Sanctions: Some Microstructural Findings." *Law and Society Review* 18:159–178.

Elias, Robert. 1986. *The Politics of Victimization*. New York: Oxford University Press.

Elias, Robert. 1993. *Victims Still*. Newbury Park, CA: Sage.

Elliott, Delbert S., Beatrix A. Hamburg, and Kirk R. Williams. 1998. *Violence in American Schools*. Cambridge, UK: Cambridge University Press.

Elliott, Delbert S. 1994. "Serious Violent Offenders: Onset, Developmental Course, and Termination." *Criminology* 32:1–21.

Elliott, Delbert S., David Huizinga, and Suzanne S. Ageton. 1985. *Explaining Delinquency and Drug Use*. Beverly Hills, CA: Sage.

Ellis, Albert, and Ralph Brancale. 1965. *The Psychology of Sex Offenders*. Springfield, IL: Thomas.

Ellis, Lee. 1991. "Monoamine Oxidase and Criminality: Identifying an Apparent Biological Marker for Antisocial Behavior." *Journal of Research in Crime and Delinquency* 28:227–251.

Ellis, Lee, and Harry Hoffman, eds. 1990. *Crime: Biological, Social, and Moral Contexts*. New York: Praeger.

Ellis, Lee, and Anthony Walsh. 1997. "Gene-Based Evolutionary Theories in Criminology." *Criminology* 35 (2): 229–276.

Empey, LaMar T., and Maynard L. Erickson. 1972. *The Provo Experiment: Evaluating Community Control of Delinquency*. Lexington, MA: Lexington Books.

Enker, Arnold. 1967. "Perspectives on Plea Bargaining." In *President's Commission on Law Enforcement and the Administration of Justice, Task Force Report: The Courts*. Washington, D.C.: U.S. Government Printing Office.

Erickson, Maynard L., Jack P. Gibbs, and Gary L. Jensen. 1977. "The Deterrence Doctrine and Perceived Certainty of Legal Punishments." *American Sociological Review* 42:305–317.

Erickson, Rosemary J., Waymon J. Crow, Louis A. Zurcher, and Archie V. Connett. 1973. *Paroled but Not Free*. New York: Behavioral Publications.

Erikson, Kai T. 1962. "Notes on the Sociology of Deviance." *Social Problems* 9:307–314.

Erikson, Kai T. 1966. *Wayward Puritans: A Study in the Sociology of Deviance*. New York: Wiley.

Erikson, Kai T. 1976. *Everything in Its Path: Destruction of Community in the Buffalo Creek Flood*. New York: Simon & Schuster.

Erikson, Richard V. 1990. "Review." *Policing and Society* 1:77–89.

Ermann, David M., and Richard J. Lundman. 1982. *Corporate Deviance*. New York: Holt, Rinehart and Winston.

Ermann, M., and R. J. Lundman. 1978. *Corporate and Governmental Deviance: Problems of Organizational Behavior in Contemporary Society*. New York: Oxford University Press.

Esbensen, Finn, and Scott Menard. 1990. "Is Longitudinal Research Worth the Price?" *The Criminologist* 15:1, 3, 5, 6.

Eskridge, Chris. 1989. "College and the Police: A Review of Issues." In *Police and Policing: Contemporary Issues*. Ed. Dennis Jay Kenney. New York: Praeger.

Esselzstyn, C. 1968. "Prostitution in the United States." *The Annals* 376:126–143.

Evans, T. David, Francis T. Cullen, and Paula J. Dubeck. 1993. "Public Perceptions of Corporate Crime." In *Understanding Corporate Criminality*. Ed. Michael B. Blankenship. New York: Garland.

Evans, T. David, Francis T. Cullen, Velmer S. Burton Jr., R. Gregory Dunaway, and Michael L. Benson. 1997. "The Social Consequences of Self-Control: Testing the General Theory of Crime." *Criminology* 35, no. 3 (August): 475–504.

Evans-Pritchard, E. E. 1940. *The Nuer*. Oxford, UK: Clarendon Press.

Ewing, Charles Patrick. 1990. *Kids Who Kill*. New York: Avon Books.

Exxon Valdez Oil Spill Trustee Council. 2000. At <www.oilspill.state.ak.us>.

Fagan, Jeffrey. 1990. "Intoxification and Aggression." In *Drugs and Crime*. Vol. 13, *Crime and Justice: A Review of Research*. Ed. Michael Tonry and James Q. Wilson. Chicago, IL: University of Chicago Press.

Fagan, Jeffrey. 1996. *The Criminalization of Domestic Violence: Promises and Limits*. Washington, D.C.: U.S. Department of Justice.

Farley, John E. 1988. *Majority-Minority Relations*. 2d ed. Englewood Cliffs, NJ: Prentice Hall.

Farley, John E. 1998. *Introduction to Sociology*. 4th ed. Englewood Cliffs, NJ: Prentice Hall.

Farley, Melissa, Isin Baral, Merab Kiremire, and Ufuk Sezgin. 1998. "Prostitution in Five Countries: Violence and Post-Traumatic Stress Disorder." *Feminism & Psychology* 8 (4): 405–426.

Farley, Reynolds. 1980. "Homicide Trends in the United States." *Demography* 17:177–188.

Farrington, David P. 1988. "Social, Psychological and Biological Influences on Juvenile Delinquency and Adult Crime." In *Explaining Criminal Behaviour*. Ed. Wouter Buikhuisen and Sarnoff A. Mednick. Leiden, Netherlands: E. J. Brill.

Farrington, David P., Lloyd Ohlin, and James Q. Wilson. 1986. *Understanding and Controlling Crime: Toward a New Research Strategy*. New York: Springer-Verlag.

Farrington, Jan. 2000. "Resisting Cocaine's Tragic Lure." Pp. 66–69 in *Annual Editions: Drugs, Society, and Behavior*. Ed. Hugh T. Wilson. Sluice Dock, CT: Dushkin/McGraw-Hill.

Faupel, Charles E. 1999. "The Drugs-Crime Connection among Stable Addicts." Pp. 198–206 in *In Their Own Words: Criminals on Crime*. 2d ed. Edited by Paul F. Cromwell. Los Angeles, CA: Roxbury.

Faupel, Charles E. 1991. *Shooting Dope: Career Patterns of Hard-Core Heroin Users*. Gainesville, FL: University of Florida Press.

Faupel, Charles E., and Carl B. Klockars. 1987. "Drugs-Crime Connections: Elaborations from the Life Histories of Hard-Core Heroin Addicts." *Social Problems* 34:54–68.

Federal Bureau of Investigation. 1965. "Profile of a Robber." *Law Enforcement Bulletin* 34:21.

Federal Bureau of Investigation. 1988a. *Crime in the United States, 1987*. Washington, D.C.: U.S. Department of Justice.

Federal Bureau of Investigation. 1988b. *Population-at-Risk Rates and Selected Crime Indicators*. Washington, D.C.: U.S. Department of Justice.

Federal Bureau of Investigation. 1988c. *Age-Specific Arrest Rates and Race-Specific Arrest Rates for Selected Offenses*. Washington, D.C.: U.S. Department of Justice.

Federal Bureau of Investigation. 1990. *Hate Crime Data Collection Guidelines*. Washington, D.C.: U.S. Department of Justice.

Federal Bureau of Investigation. 1991. *Crime in the United States, 1990*. Washington, D.C.: U.S. Department of Justice.

Federal Bureau of Investigation. 1997. *Crime in the United States, 1996*. Washington, D.C.: U.S. Department of Justice.

Federal Bureau of Investigation. 1998. *Crime in the United States, 1997*. Washington, D.C.: U.S. Department of Justice.

Federal Bureau of Investigation. 1999. *Crime in the United States, 1998*. Washington, D.C.: U.S. Department of Justice.

Federal Bureau of Investigation. 2000. *Crime in the United States, 1999*. Washington, D.C.: U.S. Department of Justice.

Federal Bureau of Prisons. 1986. *1985 Annual Report*. Washington, D.C.: U.S. Department of Justice.

Federal Bureau of Prisons. 1991. *State of the Bureau, 1990*. Washington, D.C.: U.S. Department of Justice.

Feeney, Floyd. 1999. "Robbers As Decision Makers." In *In Their Own Words: Criminals on Crime*. 2d ed. Edited by Paul Cromwell. Los Angeles, CA: Roxbury.

Felson, Marcus. 1994. *Crime and Everyday Life.* Thousand Oaks, CA: Pine Forge.

Felson, Marcus. 1998. *Crime and Everyday Life.* 2d ed. Thousand Oaks, CA: Pine Forge.

Felson, Marcus, and Ronald V. Clarke. 1998. "Opportunity Makes the Thief: Practical Theory for Crime Prevention." *Policing on Reducing Crime Unit.* UK Home Office. At <www.home office.gov.uk/prgpubs/fprs98.pdf>.

Feltey, Kathryn. 1991. "Sexual Coercion Attitudes among High School Students: The Influence of Gender and Rape Education." *Youth and Society* 23:229–250.

Ferdinand, Theodore N. 1968. "Sex Behaviors and the American Class Structure: A Mosaic." *The Annals* 376:82–84.

Ferguson, Florence S. 1987. "Sentencing Guidelines: Are (Black) Offenders Given Just Treatment?" Presented at the annual meeting of the American Society of Criminology, Montreal, Canada.

Ferrell, Jeff. 1993. *Crimes of Style: Urban Graffiti and the Politics of Criminality.* New York: Garland.

Ferrell, Jeff, and Mark S. Hamm. 1998. *Ethnography at the Edge.* Boston, MA: Northeastern University Press.

Feucht, Thomas E. 1997. "Prostitutes on Crack Cocaine: Addition, Utility, and Marketplace Economics." Pp. 131–146 in *Drugs, Crime, and Justice: Contemporary Perspectives.* Ed. Larry K. Gaines and Peter B. Kraska. Prospect Heights, IL: Waveland.

Field, Simon. 1990. *Trends in Crime and Their Interpretation. Home Office Research Study*, no. 119. London, UK: H.M.S.O.

Fields, Allen, and James M. Walters. 1985. "Hustling: Supporting a Heroin Habit." In *Life with Heroin.* Ed. Bill Hanson et al. Lexington, MA: Lexington Books.

Figueira-McDonough, Josefina. 1986. "School Context, Gender, and Delinquency." *Journal of Youth and Adolescence* 15:79–97.

Finch, Robert Thorne. 1992. *Ending the Silence.* Toronto, Ontario: University of Toronto Press.

Finkelhor, David. 1984. *Child Abuse: New Theory and Research.* New York: Free Press.

Finkelhor, David, and Kersti Yllo. 1985. *License to Rape: Sexual Abuse of Wives.* New York: Free Press.

Finkelhor, David, L. M. Williams, and N. Burns. 1988. *Nursery Crimes.* Newbury Park, CA: Sage.

Finn, Peter, and Andrea K. Newlyn. 1993. "Miami Drug Court Gives Drug Defendants a Second Chance." *NIJ Research in Action* (November): 13–20.

Finney, H. C., and H. R. Lesieur. 1982. "A Contingency Theory of Organizational Crime." In *Research in the Sociology of Organizations.* Ed. S. B. Bacharach. New York: Random House.

Fishbein, Diana H. 1990. "Biological Perspectives in Criminology." *Criminology* 28:27–72.

Fisher, Bonnie S., Francis T. Cullen, and Michael G. Turner. 2000. *The Sexual Victimization of College Women.* National Institute of Justice. At <www.ncjrs.org>.

Fisher, Bonnie S., John J. Sloan, Francis T. Cullen, and Chunmeng Lu. 1998. "Crime in the Ivory Tower: The Level and Sources of Student Victimization." *Criminology* 36 (3): 671–710.

Fisher, Dawn, Anthony Beech, and Kevin Browne. 1999. "Comparisons of Sex Offenders to Nonoffenders on Selected Psychological Measures." *International Journal of Offender Therapy and Comparative Criminology* 43 (4): 473–491.

Fisher, Joseph C. 1976. "Homicides in Detroit: The Role of Firearms." *Criminology* 14:387–400.

Fishman, Laura. 1998. "The Black Bogeyman and White Self-Righteousness." In *Images of Color, Images of Crime.* Ed. Coramae Richey Mann and Marjorie S. Zatz. Los Angeles, CA: Roxbury.

Fisse, Brent. 1985. "Sanctions against Corporations: The Limitations of Fines and the Enterprise of Creating Alternatives." In *Corrigible Corporations and Unruly Law.* Ed. Brent Fisse and Peter A. Finch. San Antonio, TX: Trinity University Press.

Fisse, Brent, and John Braithwaite. 1988. "The Allocation of Responsibility for Corporate Crime: Individualism, Collectivism and Accountability." *Sydney Law Review* 11:468–513.

Fitch, J. H. 1952. "Men Convicted of Sex Offenses against Children: A Follow-Up Study." *British Journal of Sociology* 13:18–37.

Flanagan, Timothy J., and Katherine M. Jamieson, eds. 1988. *Sourcebook of Criminal Justice Statistics.* Washington, D.C.: U.S. Department of Justice.

Flanagan, Timothy J., and Dennis R. Longmire. 1996. *Americans View Crime and Justice: A National Public Opinion Survey.* Thousands Oaks, CA: Sage.

Flavin, Jeanne. 1998. "Razing the Wall: A Feminist Critique of Sentencing Theory, Research, and Policy." Pp. 145–164 in *Cutting the Edge: Current*

Perspectives in Radical/Critical Criminology and Criminal Justice. Ed. Jeffrey I. Ross. Westport, CT: Praeger.

Fleming, Zachary. 1999. "The Thrill of It All: Youthful Offenders and Auto Theft." In *In Their Own Words: Criminal on Crime*. Ed. Paul Cromwell. Los Angeles, CA: Roxbury.

Fletcher, Connie. 1990. *What Cops Know*. New York: Pocket Books.

Fletcher, Connie. 1991. *Pure Cop*. New York: Pocket Books.

Fleury, R. E., C. M. Sullivan, D. I. Bybee, and W. S. Davidson. 1998. "Why Don't They Just Call the Cops?: Reasons for Differential Police Contact among Women with Abusive Partners." *Violence and Victims* 13 (4): 333–346.

Foldessy, Edward P. 1971. *The Paper Hangers*. Princeton, NJ: Dow Jones Books.

Food Safety and Inspection Service. 2000. News Release: "Grand Rapids Firm Guilty of Selling Adulterated Meat and Poultry." Washington, D.C.: USDA.

Foote, Caleb. 1958. "A Study of the Administration of Bail in New York City." *University of Pennsylvania Law Review* 106:633–658.

Foote, Caleb. 1978. "Deceptive Determinate Sentencing." In proceedings of the Special Conference on Determinate Sentencing, University of California, Berkeley, June 2–3.

Ford, Daniel, and Amesley K. Schmidt. 1985. "Electronically Monitored Home Confinement." *NIJ Reports* (November). Washington, D.C.: U.S. Department of Justice.

Forst, Brian E., and Jolene C. Hernon. 1985. "The Criminal Justice Response to Victim Harm." *NIJ Research in Brief*. Washington, D.C.: U.S. Department of Justice.

Fort, Joel. 1973. *Alcohol: Our Biggest Drug Problem*. New York: McGraw-Hill.

Fox, James Alan, and Jack Levin. 1999. "Serial Murder: Popular Myths and Empirical Realities." In *Homicide: A Sourcebook of Social Research*. Ed. M. Dwayne Smith and Margaret A. Zahn. Thousand Oaks, CA: Sage.

Fox, James Alan, and Jack Levin. 2000. *The Will to Kill: Making Sense of Senseless Murder*. Boston, MA: Allyn and Bacon.

Fox, James G., and Elizabeth Szockyj. 1996. *Corporate Victimization of Women*. Boston, MA: Northeastern University Press.

Fox, James Alan, and Marianne W. Zawitz. 1999. *Homicide Trends in the United States*. Washington, D.C.: Bureau of Justice Statistics.

Fraad, Harriet. 1997. "At Home with Incest." *Rethinking Marxism* 9 (4): 16–39.

Frazier, Charles E., and E. Wilbur Bock. 1982. "Effects of Court Officials on Sentence Severity." *Criminology* 20:257–272.

Freeman, Kenneth R., and Terry Estrada-Mullaney. 1988. "Using Dolls to Interview Child Victims: Legal Concerns and Interview Procedures." *NIJ Reports*, no. 207:2–6.

French, John F. 1994. "Pipe Dreams: Crack and the Life in Philadelphia and Newark." In *Crack Pipe As Pimp: An Ethnographic Investigation of Sex-for-Crack Exchanges*. Ed. Mitchell S. Ratner. New York: Lexington Books.

Friday, Paul C. 1977. "Changing Theory and Research in Criminology." *International Journal of Criminology and Penology* 5:159–170.

Friedland, Martin. 1965. *Detention before Trial*. Toronto, Ontario: University of Toronto Press.

Friedman, Monroe. 1992. "Confidence Swindles of Older Consumers." *Journal of Consumer Affairs* 26:20–46.

Friedman, Robert I. 2000. *Red Mafia: How the Russian Mob Has Invaded America*. Boston, MA: Little, Brown.

Friedrichs, David O. 1980. "The Legitimacy Crisis: A Conceptual Analysis." *Social Problems* 27 (5): 540–555.

Friedrichs, David O. 1982. "Weberian Conceptions of Rationality and Legitimacy: Transcending Parochialism in Criminological Theory." Pp. 35–60 in *Rethinking Criminology*. Ed. Harold Pepinsky. Beverly Hills, CA: Sage.

Friedrichs, David O. 1995. "State Crime or Governmental Crime: Making Sense of the Conceptual Confusion." In *Controlling State Crime*. Ed. Jeffrey Ian Ross. New York: Garland.

Friedrichs, David O. 1996. *Trusted Criminals: White-Collar Crime in Contemporary Society*. New York: Wadsworth.

Friedrichs, David O. 1998a. "New Directions in Critical Criminology and White-Collar Crime." Pp. 77–94 in *Cutting the Edge: Current Perspectives in Radical/Critical Criminology and Criminal Justice*. Ed. Jeffrey I. Ross. Westport, CT: Praeger.

Friedrichs, David O. 1998b. *State Crime*. Vol. 1 and 2. Aldershot, U.K.: Dartmouth.

Fukauri, Hiroshi, E. Butler, and R. Krooth. 1993. *Race and the Jury: Racial Disenfranchisement and the Search for Justice*. New York: Plenum.

Fyfe, James J. 1982. "Blind Justice: Police Shootings in Memphis." *Journal of Criminal Law and Criminology* 73:707–722.

Fyfe, James J. 1987. *Police Personnel Practices, 1986*. Washington, D.C.: International City Management Association.

Fyfe, James J. 1989. "Police/Citizen Violence Reduction Project." *FBI Law Enforcement Bulletin*, 58–59.

Fyfe, James J., David A. Klinger, and Jeanne M. Flavin. 1997. "Differential Police Treatment of Male-on-Female Spousal Violence." *Criminology* 35:455–473.

Gabor, Thomas, Micheline Baril, Maurice Cusson, Daniel Elie, Marc LeBlanc, and André Normandeau. 1988. *Armed Robbery: Cops, Robbers, and Victims*. Springfield, IL: Thomas.

Gaes, Gerald G. 1991. "Challenging Beliefs about Prison Crowding." *Federal Prisons Journal* 2:19–23.

Gager, Nancy, and Cathleen Schurr. 1976. *Sexual Assault: Confronting Rape in America*. New York: Grosset and Dunlap.

Gaines, Larry K., and Peter B. Kraska. 1997. *Drugs, Crime, and Justice: Contemporary Perspectives*. Prospect Heights, IL: Waveland Press.

Gallo, Jon J. 1966. "The Consenting Adult Homosexual and the Law: An Empirical Study of Enforcement and Administration in Los Angeles County." *UCLA Law Review* 13:647–832.

Gallup Organization. 1999. *Questions on Crime*. At <www.gallup.com/poll/releases/pr990406.asp>.

Gallup Organization. 2000. At <www.gallup.com/poll/indicators/indcrime.asp>.

Garfinkel, Harold. 1949. "Research Note on Inter- and Intra-Racial Homicides." *Social Forces* 27:369–381.

Garland, David. 1985a. *Punishment and Welfare: A History of Penal Strategies*. London, UK: Gower.

Garland, David. 1985b. "The Criminal and His Science." *British Journal of Criminology* 28:109–137.

Garner, Joel H. 1987. "Delay Reduction in the Federal Courts: Rule 50(b) and the Federal Speedy Trial Act of 1974." *Journal of Quantitative Criminology* 3:229–250.

Garner, Joel H., and Elizabeth Clemer. 1986. "Danger to Police in Domestic Disturbances—A New Look." *NIJ Research in Brief* (November): 1–18.

Gartner, Michael, ed. 1971. *Crime As Business*. Princeton, NJ: Dow Jones Books.

Gartner, Rosemary. 1990. "The Victims of Homicide: A Temporal and Cross-National Comparison." *American Sociological Review* 55:92–106.

Gasser, Robert Louis. 1963. "The Confidence Game." *Federal Probation* 27:47–54.

Gastil, Raymond. 1971. "Homicide and a Regional Culture of Violence." *American Sociological Review* 36:412–427.

Gebhard, Paul, John H. Gagnon, Wardell B. Pomeroy, and Cornelia V. Christiansen. 1965. *Sex Offenders: An Analysis of Types*. New York: Harper & Row.

Gegax, T. Trent, and Sarah Van Boven. 2000. "Heroin High." In *Annual Editions: Drugs, Society and Behavior*. Ed. Hugh T. Wilson. Sluice Dock, CT: Dushkin/McGraw-Hill.

Geis, Gilbert. 1967. "The Heavy Electrical Equipment Antitrust Cases of 1961." In *Criminal Behavior Systems*. Ed. M. Clinard and R. Quinnet. New York: Holt, Rinehart, and Winston.

Geis, Gilbert. 1978a. "Rape-in-Marriage: Law and Law Reform in England, the United States, and Sweden." *Adelaide Law Review* 6:284–303.

Geis, Gilbert. 1978b. "Lord Hale, Witches, and Rape." *British Journal of Law and Society* 5:26–44.

Geis, Gilbert. 1978c. "Deterring Corporate Crime." In *Corporate and Governmental Deviance*. Ed. M. David Ermann and Richard J. Lundman. New York: Oxford University Press.

Geis, Gilbert. 1988. "From Deuteronomy to Deniability: A Historical Perlustration on White-Collar Crime." *Justice Quarterly* 5:7–32.

Geis, Gilbert. 1997–98. "Crime and the Czech Republic: Summary Observations." *Crime, Law, and Social Change* 28 (3–4): 311–323.

Geis, Gilbert, and Robley Geis. 1979. "Rape in Stockholm." *Criminology* 17:311–322.

Geis, Gilbert, Paul Jesilow, and Henry N. Pontell. 1982. "Policing Physicians: Practitioner Fraud and Abuse in a Government Medicaid Program." *Social Problems* 30:117–125.

Geis, Gilbert, Paul Jesilow, and Henry N. Pontell. 1985. "Fraud and Abuse of Government Medicaid Benefits by Psychiatrists." *American Journal of Psychiatry* (February): 117–125.

Geis, Gilbert, and Robert Meier. 1977. *White-Collar Crime: Offenses in Business, Politics, and the Professions*. New York: Free Press.

Geller, William A., and Kevin J. Karales. 1981. "Shooting of and by Chicago Police: Uncommon Crises, Part I: Shootings by Chicago Police." *Journal of Criminal Law and Criminology* 72:1813–1866.

Geller, William A., and Kevin J. Karales. 1982. "Shootings of and by Chicago Police: Uncommon Crises, Part II: Shootings of Police, Shooting Correlates, and Control Strategies." *Journal of Criminal Law and Criminology* 73:331–378.

Gelles, Richard J. 1978. "Violence toward Children in the United States." *American Journal of Orthopsychiatry* 48:580–592.

Gelles, Richard J., and Murray A. Straus. 1979. "Violence in the American Family." *Journal of Social Issues* 35:15–39.

Gelsthorpe, Loraine. 1992. "Social Inquiry Reports: Race and Gender Considerations." *Home Office Research Bulletin* 32:17–22.

General Accounting Office. 1990. *Death Penalty Sentencing*. Washington, D.C.: U.S. Government Printing Office.

Giacopassi, David J., Jerry R. Sparger, and Preston M. Stein. 1992. "The Effects of Emergency Medical Care on the Homicide Rate: Some Additional Evidence." *Journal of Criminal Justice* 20:249–259.

Gibbons, Don C. 1973. *Society, Crime, and Criminal Careers*. 2d ed. Englewood Cliffs, NJ: Prentice Hall.

Gibbons, Don C. 1994. *Talking about Crime and Criminals: Problems and Issues in Theory Development in Criminology*. Englewood Cliffs, NJ: Prentice Hall.

Gibbons, Don C., and Peter Garabedian. 1974. "Conservative, Liberal and Radical Criminology: Some Trends and Observations." In *The Criminologist: Crime and the Criminal*. Ed. Charles E. Reasons. Pacific Palisades, CA: Goodyear.

Gibbs, Jack P. 1966. "Crime and the Sociology of Law." *Sociology and Social Research* 51:23–38.

Gibbs, Jack P. 1975. *Crime, Punishment and Deterrence*. New York: Elsevier.

Gibbs, Jack P. 1985. "Review Essay." *Criminology* 23:381–388.

Gibbs, Jack P. 1987. "An Incorrigible Positivist." *The Criminologist* 12 (4): 1, 4.

Gibbs, Jack P. 1988. "Reply to Michalowski." *The Criminologist* 13 (4): 4–5.

Gibbs, Jack P., and Glenn Firebaugh. 1990. "The Artifact Issue in Deterrence Research." *Criminology* 28:347–367.

Gibbs, Jack P., and James F. Short. 1974. "Criminal Differentiation and Occupational Differentiation." *Journal of Research in Crime and Delinquency* 11:89–100.

Gibbs, John J., Dennis Giever, and Jamie S. Martin. 1998. "Parental Management and Self-Control: An Empirical Test of Gottfredson and Hirschi's General Theory." *Journal of Research in Crime and Delinquency* 35, no. 1 (February): 40–70.

Gigeroff, Alex K. 1968. *Sexual Deviation and the Criminal Law*. Toronto, Ontario: University of Toronto Press.

Giles, Jean Sims. 1983. *Wife Battering: A Systems Theory Approach*. New York: Gilford Press.

Gillespie, Robert W. 1980. "Fines As an Alternative to Incarceration: The German Experience." *Federal Probation* 44:20–26.

Gilliard, Darrell K., and Allen J. Beck. 1994. "Prisoners in 1993." *BJS Bulletin* (June): 1–11.

Gilligan, James. 1996. *Violence: Our Deadly Epidemic and Its Causes*. New York: Grosset/Putnam.

Giordano, Peggy C., and Stephen A. Cernkovich. 1979. "On Complicating the Relationship between Liberation and Delinquency." *Social Problems* 26:467–481.

Giordano, Peggy C., and Sharon Mohler Rockwell. 2000. "Differential Association Theory and Female Crime." In *Of Crime and Criminality: The Use of Theory in Everyday Life*. Ed. Sally S. Simpson. Thousand Oaks, CA: Pine Forge Press.

Giordano, Peggy C., Toni J. Millhollin, Stephen A. Cernkovich, M. D. Pugh, and Jennifer L. Rudolph. 1999. "Delinquency, Identity, and Women's Involvement in Relationship Violence." *Criminology* 37 (1): 17–40.

Gitchoff, Thomas G. 1988. "Privatization and the Criminologist: Some First-Hand Observations." *The Criminologist* 13:14–15, 17.

Glaser, Daniel. 1956. "Criminality Theories and Behavioral Images." *American Journal of Sociology* 61:433–444.

Glaser, Daniel. 1971. *Social Deviance*. Chicago, IL: Markham.

Glass, Stephen. 1997. "Don't You D.A.R.E." *The New Republic* (March 3): 18–28

Glueck, Sheldon, and Eleanor Glueck. 1950. *Unraveling Juvenile Delinquency*. New York: Commonwealth Fund.

Goffman, Erving. 1952. "On Cooling the Mark Out: Some Aspects of Adaptation to Failure." *Psychiatry* 15:451–463.

Goldcamp, John. 1979. *The Classes of Accused: A Study of Bail and Detention in American Justice.* Cambridge, MA: Ballinger.

Goldfarb, Ronald L., and Linda R. Singer. 1973. *After Conviction.* New York: Simon & Schuster.

Goldkamp, John S., and Doris Weiland. 1993. "Assessing the Impact of Dade County's Felony Drug Court." *NIJ Research in Brief* (December): 1–11.

Goldstein, Herman. 1990. *Problem-Oriented Policing.* New York: McGraw-Hill.

Goldstein, Joseph. 1960. "Police Discretion Not to Invoke the Criminal Process: Low Visibility Decisions in the Administration of Justice." *Yale Law Journal* 69:543–570.

Goldstein, Paul J. 1993. "Drugs and Violence." In *Questions and Answers in Lethal and Non-Lethal Violence.* Ed. Carolyn Rebecca Block and Richard L. Block. Washington, D.C.: U.S. Department of Justice.

Goode, Erich. 1972. *Drugs in American Society.* New York: Knopf.

Goode, Erich. 1993. *Drugs in American Society.* 4th ed. New York: McGraw-Hill.

Goode, William. 1973. *Explorations in Social Theory.* New York: Oxford University Press.

Gordon, Cyrus H. 1957. *The Code of Hammurabi: Quaint or Forward Looking?* New York: Holt, Rinehart & Winston.

Gordon, David M. 1971. "Class and the Economics of Crime." *Review of Radical Economics* 3:51–75.

Gordon, David M. 1973. "Capitalism, Class and Crime in America." *Crime and Delinquency* 19:163–186.

Gordon, Judy G. 1991. "The Female Offender: ACA's Look to the Future." *Federal Prisons Journal* 2:3–5.

Gordon, Margaret A., and Daniel Glaser. 1991. "The Use and Effects of Financial Penalties in Municipal Courts." *Criminology* 29:651–676.

Gordon, Robert A. 1987. "SES versus IQ in the Race-IQ-Delinquency Model." *International Journal of Sociology and Social Policy* 7:30–88.

Gorman, D. M., and Helene Raskin White. 1995. "You Can Choose Your Friends, but Do They Choose Crime? Implication of Differential Association Theories for Crime Prevention Policy."

Pp. 131–156 in *Crime and Public Policy: Putting Theory to Work.* Ed. Hugh D. Barlow. Boulder, CO: Westview.

Gottfredson, Michael R., and Don M. Gottfredson. 1988. *Decision-Making in Criminal Justice.* 2d ed. New York: Plenum.

Gottfredson, Michael R., and Travis Hirschi. 1987. "The Methodological Adequacy of Longitudinal Research on Crime." *Criminology* 26:581–614.

Gottfredson, Michael R., and Travis Hirschi. 1988. "Science, Public Policy, and the Career Paradigm." *Criminology* 26:37–55.

Gottfredson, Michael R., and Travis Hirschi. 1990. *A General Theory of Crime.* Stanford, CA: Stanford University Press.

Gottman, Jon. 1989. "Decriminalizing Marijuana." *American Behavioral Scientist* 32:243–248.

Gould, Leroy C. 1969. "The Changing Structure of Property Crime in an Affluent Society." *Social Forces* 48:50–59.

Gove, Walter R., Michael Hughes, and Michael Geerken. 1985. "Are Uniform Crime Reports a Valid Indicator of Index Crime? An Affirmative Answer with Minor Qualifications." *Criminology* 23:451–501.

Gowdy, Voncile B. nd. "Intermediate Sanctions." *NIJ Research in Brief* (nd): 1–10.

Grabowski, John. 1984. *Cocaine: Pharmacology, Effects and Treatment of Abuse.* Washington, D.C.: National Institute of Drug Abuse.

Grace, Sharon. 1993. "Resisting Sexual Assault: A Review of the Literature." *Home Office Research Bulletin* 34:18–25.

Grace, Sharon. 1995. *Policing Domestic Violence in the 1990s.* London, UK: H.M.S.O.

Graham, Dee L. R., Edna I. Rawlings, and Roberta K. Rigsby. 1994. *Loving to Survive: Sexual Terror, Men's Violence, and Women's Lives.* New York: New York University Press.

Green, Edward. 1993. *The Intent to Kill.* Baltimore, MD: Clevedon Books.

Green, Gary S. 1990. *Occupational Crime.* Chicago, IL: Nelson-Hall.

Green, Mark J., with Beverly C. Moore and Bruce Wasserstein. 1976. "Criminal Law and Corporate Disorder." In *Crisis in American Institutions.* 3d ed. Edited by Jerome Skolnick and Elliott Currie. Boston, MA: Little, Brown.

Green, Sherry. 1993. "Preventing Illegal Diversion

of Chemicals: A Model Statute." *NIJ Research in Brief* (November): 1–7.

Greenberg, David F. 1975. "The Incapacitative Effect of Imprisonment: Some Estimates." *Law and Society Review* 9:541–580.

Greenberg, David F. 1977. "Crime and Deterrence Research and Social Policy." In *Modeling the Criminal Justice System.* Ed. Stuart S. Nagel. Beverly Hills, CA: Sage.

Greenberg, David F., ed. 1981. *Crime and Capitalism.* Palo Alto, CA: Mayfield.

Greenberg, David F. 1985. "Age, Crime, and Social Explanation." *American Journal of Sociology* 91:1–21.

Greenberg, David F. 1999. "The Weak Strength of Social Control Theory." *Crime and Delinquency* 45 (1): 66–81.

Greenberg, Martin S., Chauncey E. Wilson, and Michael K. Mills. 1982. "Victim Decision-Making: An Experimental Approach." In *The Criminal Justice System and Social Psychological Analysis.* Ed. Vladimir J. Konecni and Ebbe B. Ebbesen. San Francisco, CA: W. H. Freeman.

Greene, Jack R. 1989. "Police and Community Relations: Where Have We Been and Where Are We Going?" In *Critical Issues in Policing.* Ed. Roger G. Dunham and Geoffrey P. Alpert. Prospect Heights, IL: Waveland Press.

Greene, Michael B. 1993. "Chronic Exposure to Violence and Poverty: Interventions That Work for Youth." *Crime and Delinquency* 39:106–124.

Greenfeld, Lawrence A., and Stephanie Minor-Harper. 1991. "Women in Prison." *BJS Special Report* (March): 1–8.

Greenfeld, Lawrence A., and James J. Stephan. 1993. "Capital Punishment 1992." *BJS Bulletin* (December): 1–13.

Greenleaf, Richard G., and Lonn Lanza-Kaduce. 1995. "Sophistication, Organization, and Authority-Subject Conflict: Rediscovering and Unraveling Turk's Theory of Norm Resistance." *Criminology* 33 (4): 565–573.

Greenwood, Peter W. 1984. "Selective Incapacitation: A Method of Using Our Prisons More Effectively." *NIJ Reports.* Washington, D.C.: National Institute of Justice.

Greenwood, Peter W. 1992. "Substance Abuse Problems among High-Risk Youth and Potential Interventions." *Crime and Delinquency* 38:444–458.

Greenwood, Peter W., and Allan Abrahamse. 1982. *Selective Incapacitation.* Santa Monica, CA: Rand.

Greenwood, Peter W., Jan Chaiken, and Joan R. Petersilia. 1977. *The Criminal Investigation.* Lexington, MA: D. C. Heath.

Griffin, Susan. 1971. "Rape: The All-American Crime." *Ramparts* 10:34–35.

Griffiths, John. 1970. "Ideology in Criminal Procedure, or a Third 'Model' of the Criminal Process." *Yale Law Journal* 79:359–417.

Gross, Edward. 1978. "Organizational Crime: A Theoretical Perspective." In *Studies in Symbolic Interaction.* Ed. N. Denzin. Greenwich, CT: JAI Press.

Gross, Samuel R., and Robert Mauro. 1989. *Death and Discrimination: Racial Disparities in Capital Sentencing.* Boston, MA: Northeastern University Press.

Grossman, Brian. 1974. "The Discretionary Enforcement of Law." In *Politics and Crime.* Ed. Sawyer F. Sylvester and Edward Sagarin. New York: Praeger.

Groth, Nicholas. 1979. *Men Who Rape: The Psychology of the Offender.* New York: Plenum.

Guenther, Anthony L. 1975. "Compensations in a Total Institution: The Forms and Functions of Contraband." *Crime and Delinquency*, 243–254.

Guerry, André Michel. 1833. *Essai sur la Statistique Morale.* Paris, France: P. Renovard.

Haass, R. 1998. *Economic Sanctions and American Diplomacy.* New York: Council on Foreign Relations.

Hackney, Sheldon. 1969. "Southern Violence." In *Violence in America.* Ed. Hugh D. Graham and Robert T. Gurr. Washington, D.C.: U.S. Government Printing Office.

Hagan, Frank E. 1982. *Research Methods in Criminal Justice and Criminology.* New York: Macmillan.

Hagan, Frank, and Peter Benekos. 1992. "What Charles Keating and 'Murph the Surf' Have in Common: A Symbiosis of Professional and Occupational and Corporate Crime." *Criminal Organizations* 7:3–13, 24.

Hagan, John. 1974. "Extra-Legal Attributes and Criminal Sentencing: An Assessment of a Sociological Viewpoint." *Law and Society Review* 8:357–383.

Hagan, John. 1982. "The Corporate Advantage: The Involvement of Individual and Organizational Victims in the Criminal Justice Process." *Social Forces* 60:993–1022.

Hagan, John. 1985. *Modern Criminology: Crime, Criminal Behavior and Its Control*. New York: McGraw-Hill.

Hagan, John. 1988. *Structural Criminology*. New Brunswick, NJ: Rutgers University Press.

Hagan, John. 1994. *Crime and Disrepute*. Thousand Oaks, CA: Pine Forge Press.

Hagan, John, and Alberto Palloni. 1988. "Crimes As Social Events in the Life Course: Reconceiving a Criminological Controversy." *Criminology* 26:87–100.

Hagan, John, A. R. Gillis, and J. Chan. 1978. "Explaining Official Delinquency: A Spatial Study of Class, Conflict and Control." *Sociological Quarterly* 19:386–398.

Hagan, John, A. R. Gillis, and John Simpson. 1985. "The Class Structure, Gender and Delinquency: Toward a Power-Control Theory of Common Delinquent Behavior." *American Journal of Sociology* 90:1151–1175.

Hagan, John, A. R. Gillis, and John Simpson. 1990. "Clarifying and Extending Power-Control Theory." *American Journal of Sociology* 95:1024–1037.

Hagan, Michael P., and Karen L. Gust-Brey. 1999. "A Ten Year Longitudinal Study of Adolescent Rapists upon Return to the Community." *International Journal of Offender Therapy and Comparative Criminology* 43:448–458.

Hagarth, John. 1971. *Sentencing As a Human Process*. Toronto, Ontario: Toronto University Press.

Hagedorn, John. 1988. *People and Folks*. Chicago, IL: Lake View Press.

Hagedorn, John. 1991. "Gang Neighborhoods and Public Policy." *Social Problems* 38:529–540.

Hagedorn, John. 1994. "Homeboys, Dope Fiends, Legits, and New Jacks." *Criminology* 32:197–219.

Haghighi, Bahram, and Jon Sorensen. 1996. "America's Fear of Crime." In *Americans View Crime and Justice: A National Public Opinion Survey*. Ed. Timothy J. Flanagan and Dennis R. Longmire. Thousands Oaks, CA: Sage.

Haines, Herb. 1992. "Flawed Execution, the Anti-Death Penalty Movement, and the Politics of Capital Punishment." *Social Problems* 39:125–138.

Hakim, Simon, and George F. Rengert, eds. 1981. *Crime Spillover*. Beverly Hills, CA: Sage.

Hale, Robert. 1997. "Motives of Reward among Men Who Rape." *American Journal of Criminal Justice* 22:101–120.

Hall, Jerome. 1952. *Theft, Law, and Society*. Rev. ed. Indianapolis, IN: Bobbs-Merrill.

Hall, Jerome. 1960. *General Principles of Criminal Law*. Indianapolis, IN: Bobbs-Merrill.

Hall, Richard. 1987. "Organizational Behavior: A Sociological Perspective." In *Handbook of Organizational Behavior*. Ed. J. W. Lorsch. Englewood Cliffs, NJ: Prentice Hall.

Haller, Mark H. 1976. "Historical Roots of Police Behavior: Chicago, 1890–1925." *Law and Society Review* 10:303–324.

Haller, Mark H. 1990. "Illegal Enterprise: A Theoretical and Historical Interpretation." *Criminology* 28:207–235.

Haller, Mark H. 1991. *Life under Bruno: The Economics of an Organized Crime Family*. Philadelphia, PA: Pennsylvania Crime Commission.

Hamlin, John E. 1988. "The Misplaced Role of Rational Choice in Neutralization Theory." *Criminology* 23:223–240.

Hamm, Mark S. 1993. *American Skinheads: The Criminology and Control of Hate Crime*. Westport, CT: Praeger.

Hamm, Mark S. 1994. *Hate Crime: International Perspectives on Causes and Control*. Cincinnati, OH: Anderson.

Hammett, Theodore M., and Joel Epstein. 1993. "Prosecuting Environmental Crime: Los Angeles County." *NIJ Program Focus* (August): 1–16.

Hammett, Theodore M., Lynne Harold, Michael Gross, and Joel Epstein. 1993. *1992 Update: HIV/AIDS in Correctional Facilities*. Washington, D.C.: U.S. Department of Justice.

Hans, Valerie P., and David M. Ermann. 1989. "Responses to Corporate versus Individual Wrongdoing." *Law and Human Behavior* 13:151–166.

Hanson, Bill, George Beschner, James M. Walters, and Elliott Bovelle. 1985. *Life with Heroin*. Lexington, MA: Lexington Books.

Hanson, R. Karl, Otto Cadsky, Andrew Harris, and Coralie Lalonde. 1997. "Correlates of Battering among 997 Men: Family History, Adjustment, and Attitudinal Differences." *Violence and Victims* 12 (3): 191–208.

Harland, Alan T. 1981. *Restitution to Victims of Personal and Household Crimes*. Analytic Report VAD-9. Washington, D.C.: U.S. Department of Justice.

Harlow, Caroline Wolf. 1991a. *Female Victims of Violent Crime*. Washington, D.C.: U.S. Department of Justice.

Harlow, Caroline Wolf. 1991b. *Drugs and Jail Inmates*. Washington, D.C.: U.S. Department of Justice.

Harlow, Caroline Wolf. 1993. *BJS Special Report: HIV in U.S. Prisons and Jails*. Washington, D.C.: National Institute of Justice.

Harries, Keith D. 1989. "Homicide and Assault: A Comparative Analysis of Attributes in Dallas Neighborhoods, 1981–1985." *The Professional Geographer* 41:29–38.

Harris, David A. 1999. "Driving While Black. An American Civil Liberties Special Report." At <www.aclu.org>.

Harris, Judith A. 1994. "Review." *Teaching Sociology* 22:125–126.

Harris, Richard N. 1973. *The Police Academy: An Inside View*. New York: Wiley.

Harrison, Lana D. 1992. "The Drug-Crime Nexus in the USA." *Contemporary Drug Problems* 19 (2): 203–245.

Harrison, Lana, and Joseph Gfroerer. 1992. "The Intersection of Drug Use and Criminal Behavior: Results from the National Household Survey on Drug Abuse." *Crime and Delinquency* 38:422–443.

Hartjen, Clayton. 1974. *Crime and Criminalization*. New York: Praeger.

Hartogs, Renatus, and Eric Artzt. 1970. *Violence: Causes and Solutions*. New York: Dell.

Hartstone, Eliot, and Karen V. Hansen. 1984. "The Violent Juvenile Offender." In *Violent Juvenile Offenders: An Anthology*. Ed. Robert A. Mathias, Paul DeMuro, and Richard S. Allinson. San Francisco, CA: National Council on Crime and Delinquency.

Hassine, Victor. 1996. *Life without Parole*. Los Angeles, CA: Roxbury.

Hawkins, Darnell F. 1999. "What Can We Learn from Data Disaggregation?: The Case of Homicide and African Americans." In *Homicide: A Sourcebook of Social Research*. Ed. M. Dwayne Smith and Margaret A. Zahn. Thousand Oaks, CA: Sage.

Hawkins, Gordon. 1976. *The Prison: Policy and Practice*. Chicago, IL: University of Chicago Press.

Hay, Carter. 2001. "An Exploratory Test of Braithwaite's Reintegrative Shaming Theory." *Journal of Research in Crime and Delinquency* 38 (2): 132–153.

Hay, Douglas. 1975. *Albion's Fatal Tree: Crime and Society in Eighteenth Century England*. London, UK: Allen Lowe.

Healy, William. 1915. *The Individual Delinquent: A Textbook and Prognosis for All Concerned in Understanding Offenders*. Boston, MA: Little, Brown.

Hedderman, Carol, and Loraine Gelsthorpe. 1997. *Understanding the Sentencing of Women*. London, UK: H.M.S.O.

Heimer, Karen. 1997. "Socioeconomic Status, Subcultural Definitions, and Violent Delinquency." *Social Forces* 75:799–833.

Heimer, Karen, and Stacy De Coster. 1999. "The Gendering of Violent Delinquency." *Criminology* 37 (2): 277–318.

Heiner, Robert. 1996. *Criminology: A Cross-Cultural Perspective*. New York: West.

Heis, Lori L. 1998. "Violence against Women: An Integrated, Ecological Framework." *Violence against Women* 3 (3): 262–290.

Henry, Stuart. 1978. *The Hidden Economy*. Oxford, UK: Martin Robinson.

Henry, Stuart, and Dragan Milovanovic. 1991. "Constitutive Criminology: The Maturation of Critical Criminology." *Criminology* 29:293–315.

Henry, Stuart, and Dragan Milovanovic. 1996. *Constitutive Criminology: beyond Postmodernism*. Thousands Oaks, CA: Sage.

Henry, Stuart, and Dragan Milovanovic. 1999. *Constitutive Criminology at Work: Applications to Crime and Justice*. Albany, NY: State University of New York Press.

Hepburn, John R. 1985. "The Exercise of Power in Coercive Organizations: A Study of Prison Guards." *Criminology* 23:145–164.

Herek, G., and K. Berrill. 1992. *Hate Crimes: Confronting Violence against Lesbians and Gay Men*. Newbury Park, CA: Sage.

Heyl, Barbara Sherman. 1979. *The Madam As Entrepreneur: Career Management in House Prostitution*. New York: Transaction Books.

Hickey, Eric W. 1991. *Serial Murderers and Their Victims*. Pacific Grove, CA: Brooks/Cole.

Hickey, Eric W. 1997. *Serial Murderers and Their Victims*. 2d ed. Pacific Grove, CA: Brooks/Cole.

Hill, Gary D., and Elizabeth M. Crawford. 1990. "Women, Race, and Crime." *Criminology* 28:601–626.

Hills, Stuart L. 1971. *Crime, Power, and Morality*. Scranton, PA: Chandler.

Hills, Stuart L., and Ron Santiago. 1992. *Tragic Magic: The Life and Crimes of a Heroin Addict*. Chicago, IL: Nelson-Hall.

Hill, Susan, and Bob Edelman. 1972. *Gentleman of Leisure*. New York: New American Library.

Hillsman, Sally T., Barry Mahoney, George F. Cole,

and Bernard Auchter. 1987. "Fines As Criminal Sanctions." *Research in Brief*. Washington, D.C.: U.S. Department of Justice.

Hindelang, Michael J. 1974. "Decisions of Shoplifting Victims to Invoke the Criminal Justice Process." *Social Problems* 21:580–593.

Hindelang, Michael J. 1978. "Race and Involvement in Common Law Personal Crimes." *American Sociological Review* 43:93–109.

Hindelang, Michael J., Travis Hirschi, and Joseph G. Weiss. 1979. "Correlates of Delinquency: The Illusion of Discrepancy between Self-Report and Official Measures." *American Sociological Review* 44:995–1014.

Hinkle, William G., and Stuart Henry. 2000. "Preface." *Annals of the American Academy of Political and Social Science* 567:8.

Hirschi, Travis. 1971. *Causes of Delinquency*. Berkeley, CA: University of California Press.

Hirschi, Travis. 1983. "Crime and the Family." In *Crime and Public Policy*. Ed. James Q. Wilson. San Francisco, CA: Institute for Contemporary Studies.

Hirschi, Travis. 1986. "On the Compatibility of Rational Choice and Social Control Theories of Crime." In *The Reasoning Criminal*. Ed. Derek B. Cornish and Ronald V. Clarke. New York: Springer-Verlag.

Hirschi, Travis, and Michael R. Gottfredson. 1983. "Age and the Explanation of Crime." *American Journal of Sociology* 89:552–584.

Hirschi, Travis, and Michael R. Gottfredson. 1987. "Causes of White-Collar Crime." *Criminology* 25:949–974.

Hirschi, Travis, and Michael R. Gottfredson. 1988. "Toward a General Theory of Crime." In *Explaining Criminal Behavior: Interdisciplinary Approaches*. Ed. Walter Buikhuisen and Sarnoff A. Mednick. Linden, Netherlands: E. J. Brill.

Hirschi, Travis, and Michael J. Hindelang. 1977. "Intelligence and Delinquency: A Revisionist View." *American Sociological Review* 42:572–587.

Hochstedler, Ellen, ed. 1984. *Corporations As Criminals*. Beverly Hills, CA: Sage.

Hoebel, E. Adamson. 1941. *The Cheyenne Way*. Norman, OK: University of Oklahoma Press.

Hoebel, E. Adamson. 1954. *The Law of Primitive Man*. Cambridge, MA: Harvard University Press.

Hogarth, John. 1971. *Sentencing As a Human Process*. Toronto, Ontario: Toronto University Press.

Hollinger, Richard C. 1991. "Neutralization in the Workplace: An Empirical Analysis of Property Theft and Production Deviance." *Deviant Behavior* 12:169–202.

Holmes, Ronald M., and Stephen T. Holmes. 1992. "Understanding Mass Murder: A Starting Point." *Federal Probation* (March): 53–61.

Holmes, Ronald M., and Stephen T. Holmes. 1994. *Murder in America*. Thousand Oaks, CA: Sage.

Homer, Marjorie, A. Leonard, and P. Taylor. 1985. "The Burden of Dependency." *Sociological Review Monograph* 31:77–93.

Hood, Roger. 1962. *Sentencing in Magistrates' Courts*. London, UK: Stevens.

Hood, Roger. 1972. *Sentencing the Motoring Offender*. London, UK: Heinemann.

Hood, Roger. 1992. *Race and Sentencing*. Oxford, UK: Clarendon.

Hooton, Earnest A. 1939. *Crime and the Man*. Cambridge, MA: Harvard University Press.

Horney, Julie, and Ineke Haen Marshall. 1992. "Risk Perceptions among Serious Offenders: The Role of Crime and Punishment." *Criminology* 30:575–592.

Horning, Donald N. M. 1970. "Blue-Collar Theft: Conceptions of Property, Attitudes toward Pilfering, and Work Group Norms in a Modern Industrial Plant." In *Crimes against Bureaucracy*. Ed. Erwin O. Smigel and H. Laurence Ross. New York: Van Nostrand.

Horowitz, Ruth. 1987. "Community Tolerance of Group Violence." *Social Problems* 34:437–449.

Horowitz, R., and A. E. Pottieger. 1991. "Gender Bias in Juvenile Justice Handling of Seriously Crime-Involved Youth." *Journal of Research in Crime and Delinquency* 28:75–100.

Hotchkiss, Susan. 1978. "Realities of Rape." *Human Behavior* (December): 18–23.

Hough, Michael J., and Pat Mayhew. 1983. *The British Crime Survey*. London, UK: H.M.S.O.

Hough, Michael J., Ronald V. Clarke, and Pat Mayhew. 1980. "Introduction." In *Designing Out Crime*. Ed. Ronald V. Clarke and Pat Mayhew. London, UK: H.M.S.O.

Hudson, Joe, and Burt Galoway. 1975. *Restitution in Criminal Justice*. Lexington, MA: Lexington Press.

Hufbauer, G., J. Schott, and A. Elliot. 1990. *Economic Sanctions Reconsidered*. 2d ed. Washington, D.C.: Institute for International Economics.

Huff-Corzine, Lin, Jay Corzine, and David C. Moore. 1986. "Southern Exposure: Deciphering the South's Influence on Homicide Rates." *Social Forces* 24:906–924.

Hughes, Everett C. 1964. "Good People and Dirty Work." In *The Other Side: Perspectives on Deviance.* Ed. Howard S. Becker. New York: Free Press.

Hughes, Helen MacGill. 1961. *The Fantastic Lodge: The Autobiography of a Girl Drug Addict.* New York: Houghton Mifflin.

Huizinga, David, and Delbert S. Elliott. 1987. "Juvenile Offenders: Prevalence, Incidence, and Arrest Rates by Race." *Crime and Delinquency* 33:206–223.

Humphreys, Laud. 1970. *Tearoom Trade.* Chicago, IL: Aldine.

Hunt, Dana F. 1990. "Drugs and Consensual Crime." In *Drugs and Crime.* Vol. 13, *Crime and Justice: A Review of Research.* Ed. Michael Tonry and James Q. Wilson. Chicago, IL: University of Chicago Press.

Hunt, Geoffrey, Stephanie Riegel, Tomas Morales, and Dan Waldorf. 1993. "Changes in Prison Culture: Prison Gangs and the Case of the 'Pepsi Generation.'" *Social Problems* 40:398–409,

Hunt, Jennifer. 1991. "Police Accounts of Normal Force." In *Down to Earth Sociology.* 6th ed. Ed. James M. Henslin. New York: Free Press.

Hunt, Raymond G., and John M. Magenau. 1993. *Power and the Police Chief: An Institutional and Organizational Analysis.* Newbury Park, CA: Sage.

Hutchinson, John. 1969. "The Anatomy of Corruption in the Trade Unions." *Industrial Relations* 8:135–137.

Iadicola, Peter, and Anson Shupe. 1998. *Violence, Inequality, and Human Freedom.* Dix Hills, NY: General Hall, Inc.

Ianni, Francis A. J. 1974. "New Mafia: Black, Hispanic and Italian Styles." *Society* 11:30–36.

Ianni, Francis A. J. 1975. *Black Mafia: Ethnic Succession in Organized Crime.* New York: Pocket Books.

Ianni, Francis A. J. 1998. "New Mafia: Black, Hispanic, and Italian Styles." *Society* 35 (2): 115–129.

Ianni, Francis A. J., and Elizabeth Reuss-Ianni. 1973. *A Family Business: Kinship and Control in Organized Crime.* New York: Russell Sage.

Illinois Criminal Justice Information Authority. 1985. *The Compiler.* Vol. 6. Chicago, IL: ICJIA.

Illinois Motor Vehicle Theft Prevention Council. 1993. *Statewide Motor Vehicle Theft Prevention Strategy.* Chicago, IL: Illinois Criminal Justice Information Authority.

Illinois Task Force on Crime and Corrections. 1993. *Final Report.* Springfield, IL: Illinois State Police.

Imlay, Carl H., and Charles R. Glasheen. 1971. "See What Conditions Your Conditions Are in." *Federal Probation* 35:3–11.

Inciardi, James A. 1975. *Careers in Crime.* Chicago, IL: Rand McNally.

Inciardi, James A. 1979. "Heroin Use and Street Crime." *Crime and Delinquency* 25:335–346.

Inciardi, James A. 1986. *The War on Drugs.* Palo Alto, CA: Mayfield.

Inciardi, James A. 1987. "Beyond Cocaine: Basuco, Crack and Other Coca Products." Presented to the annual meeting of the Academy of Criminal Justice Sciences, St. Louis, MO.

Inciardi, James I., and L. D. Harrison. 1998. *Heroin in the Age of Crack Cocaine.* Thousand Oaks, CA: Sage.

Innes, Christopher A. 1988. *Special Report: Drug Use and Crime.* Washington, D.C.: U.S. Department of Justice.

International Court of Justice. 1996. *The Legality of the Threat or Use of Nuclear Weapons.* Advisory Opinion Request. General List, no. 95, 8 July.

Inwald, Robin, and Dennis Jay Kenney. 1989. "Psychological Testing of Police Candidates." In *Police and Policing: Contemporary Issues.* Ed. Dennis Jay Kenney. New York: Praeger.

Irwin, John. 1970. *The Felon.* Englewood Cliffs, NJ: Prentice Hall.

Irwin, John. 1980. *Prisons in Turmoil.* Boston, MA: Little, Brown.

Irwin, John, and James Austin. 1994. *It's about Time: America's Imprisonment Binge.* Belmont, CA: Wadsworth.

Irwin, John, and Donald R. Cressey. 1962. "Thieves, Convicts and the Inmate Culture." *Social Problems* 10:142–155.

Ito, Koichiro. 1993. "Research on Fear of Crime: Perceptions and Realities of Crime in Japan." *Crime and Delinquency* 39:385–392.

Jackall, Robert. 1988. *Moral Mazes: The World of Corporate Managers.* New York: Oxford University Press.

Jackman, Norman R., Richard O'Toole, and Gilbert Geis. 1963. "The Self-Image of the Prostitute." *Sociological Quarterly* 4:150–161.

Jackson, Bruce. 1969a. *A Thief's Primer*. New York: Macmillan.

Jackson, Bruce. 1969b. "Exile from the American Dream: The Junkie and the Cop." *Atlantic Monthly* 219:44–51.

Jacobs, Bruce A. 1999a. "Crack to Heroin?: Drug Markets and Transition." *The British Journal of Criminology* 39 (4): 555–574.

Jacobs, Bruce A. 1999b. *Selling Crack: The Social World of Streetcorner Selling*. Boston, MA: Northeastern University Press.

Jacobs, Bruce A., Volkan Topalli, and Richard T. Wright. 2000. "Managing Retaliation: Drug Robbery and Informal Sanction Threats." *Criminology* 38:171–198.

Jacobs, James B. 1974. "Street Gangs behind Bars." *Social Problems* 21:395–409.

Jacobs, James B. 1976. "Stratification and Conflict among Prison Inmates." *Journal of Criminal Law and Criminology* 66:476–482.

Jacobs, James B. 1977. *Stateville: The Penitentiary in Mass Society*. Chicago, IL: University of Chicago Press.

Jacobs, James B., and Harold G. Retsky. 1975. "Prison Guard." *Urban Life and Culture* 4:5–29.

Jaffee, Harold W., William W. Darrow, and Dean F. Echenberg et al. 1985. "The Acquired Immunodeficiency Syndrome in a Cohort of Homosexual Men: A Six-Year Follow-Up Study." *Annals of Internal Medicine* 103:210–214.

James, Jennifer, and William Thornton. 1980. "Women's Liberation and the Female Delinquent." *Journal of Research in Crime and Delinquency* 17:230–244.

James, J. T. 1817. *Journal of a Tour*. London, UK: John Murray.

Jane's Intelligence Review. 2000. "Heroin and Cocaine—A Global Threat." Pp. 72–73 in *Annual Editions: Drugs, Society, and Behavior*. Ed. Hugh T. Wilson. Sluice Dock, CT: Dushkin/McGraw-Hill.

Jang, Sung Joon. 1999. "Age-Varying Effects of Family, School, and Peers on Delinquency: A Multilevel Modeling Test of Interactional Theory." *Criminology* 37 (3): 643–686.

Jankowski, Martin Sanchez. 1991. *Islands in the Street: Gangs and American Urban Society*. Berkeley, CA: University of California Press.

Jaspan, Norman, and Hillel Black. 1960. *The Thief in the White Collar*. New York: Lippincott.

Jefferson, T., and J. Clarke. 1973. "Down These Mean Streets: The Meaning of Mugging." *Stencilled occasional paper, the Centre for Contemporary Cultural Studies*, The University of Birmingham, England.

Jefferson, T., and J. Clarke. 1975. "Mugging and Law 'n Order." *Stencilled occasional paper, Centre for Contemporary Cultural Studies*, University of Birmingham, England.

Jeffery, C. Ray. 1957. "The Development of Crime in Early English Society." *Journal of Criminal Law, Criminology, and Police Science* 47:533–552.

Jeffery, C. Ray. 1959. "An Integrated Theory of Crime and Criminal Behavior." *Journal of Criminal Law, Criminology, and Police Science* 49:533–552.

Jeffery, C. Ray. 1977. *Crime Prevention through Environmental Design*. Beverly Hills, CA: Sage.

Jeffery, C. Ray. 1994. "Biological and Neuropsychiatric Approaches to Criminal Behavior." Pp. 15–28 in *Varieties of Criminology*. Ed. Gregg Barak. Westport, CT: Praeger.

Jenkins, Philip. 1988. "Myth and Murder: The Serial Killer Panic of 1983–85." *Criminal Justice Research Bulletin* 3:1–7.

Jenkins, Philip. 1993. "African Americans and Serial Homicide." *American Journal of Criminal Justice* 17 (2): 47–60.

Jenkins, Philip. 1994. *Using Murder: The Social Construction of Serial Homicide*. New York: Aldine De Gruyter.

Jenness, Valerie. 1990. "From Sex As Sin to Sex As Work: COYOTE and the Reorganization of Prostitution As a Social Problem." *Social Problems* 37:403–420.

Jensen, A. R. 1969. "How Much Can We Boost IQ and Scholastic Achievement?" *Harvard Educational Review* 39:1–123.

Jensen, Gary F., and Kevin Thompson. 1990. "What's Class Got to Do With It: A Further Examination of Power-Control Theory." *American Journal of Sociology* 95:1009–1023.

Jerin, Robert A., and Charles B. Fields. 1994. "Murder and Mayhem in USA Today: A Quantitative Analysis of the National Reporting of States' News." In *Media, Process, and the Social Construction of Crime: Studies in Newsmaking Criminology*. Ed. G. Barak. New York: Garland.

Jesilow, Paul, Henry N. Pontell, and Gilbert Geis. 1993. *Prescription for Profit*. Los Angeles, CA: University of California Press.

Johnson, Barbara E., Douglas L. Kuck, and Patricia R. Schander. 1997. "Rape Myth Acceptance and Sociodemographic Characteristics: A Multidimensional Analysis." *Sex Roles* 36:693–707.

Johnson, B., P. Goldstein, E. Preble, J. Schmeidler, D. Lipton, B. Spunt, and T. Miller. 1985. *Taking Care of Business*. Lexington, MA: Lexington Books.

Johnson, David R., and Laurie K. Scheuble. 1991. "Gender Bias in the Disposition of Juvenile Court Referrals: The Effects of Time and Location." *Criminology* 29:677–699.

Johnson, Guy B. 1941. "The Negro and Crime." *The Annals* 277:93–104.

Johnson, Richard E. 1986. "Family Structure and Delinquency: General Patterns and Gender Differences." *Criminology* 24:65–84.

Johnson, Robert. 1987. *Hard Time: Understanding and Reforming the Prison*. Monterey, CA: Brooks/Cole.

Johnson, Robert. 1990. *Death Work: A Study of the Modern Execution Process*. Pacific Grove, CA: Brooks/Cole.

Jones, David P. H., and J. Melbourne McGraw. 1987. "Reliable and Fictitious Accounts of Sexual Abuse to Children." *Journal of Interpersonal Violence* 2:1–6.

Jordon, Philip D. 1970. *Frontier Law and Order*. Lincoln, NE: University of Nebraska Press.

Joyce, Nola M. 1992. "A View of the Future: The Effect of Policy on Prison Population Growth." *Crime and Delinquency* 38:357–368.

Kadish, Mortimer R., and Sanford H. Kadish. 1973. *Discretion to Disobey*. Palo Alto, CA: Stanford University Press.

Kandel, Denise, and Mark Davies. 1991. "Friendship Networks, Intimacy, and Illicit Drug Use in Young Adulthood: A Comparison of Two Competing Theories." *Criminology* 29:441–469.

Kandel, Elizabeth, and Sarnoff A. Mednick. 1991. "Perinatal Complications Predict Violent Offending." *Criminology* 29:519–529.

Kanin, Eugene J. 1967. "Reference Groups and Sex Conduct Norms Violation." *Sociological Quarterly* 8:495–504.

Kantor, Glenda Kaufman, and Murray A. Straus. 1987. "The 'Drunken Bum' Theory of Wife Beating." *Social Problems* 34:214–230.

Kappeler, Victor E., Richard D. Sluder, and Geoffrey P. Alpert. 1994. *Forces of Deviance: Understanding the Dark Side of Policing*. Prospect Heights, IL: Waveland Press.

Kappeler, Victor E., Mark Blumberg, and Gary W. Potter. 2000. *The Mythology of Crime and Justice*. 3d ed. Prospect Heights, IL: Waveland Press.

Katz, Jack. 1988. *Seductions of Crime: Moral and Sensual Attractions of Doing Evil*. New York: Basic Books.

Kauzlarich, David. 1995. "A Criminology of the Nuclear State." *Humanity and Society* 19 (3): 37–57.

Kauzlarich, David. 1997. "Nuclear Weapons on Trial: The Battle at the International Court of Justice." *Social Pathology* 3 (3): 157–164.

Kauzlarich, David, and David O. Friedrichs. 2001. "Crimes of the State." In *Controversial Issues in Criminology: Critical Criminology*. Ed. Martin D. Schwartz and Suzanne Hatty. Cincinnati, OH: Anderson.

Kauzlarich, David, and Ronald C. Kramer. 1993. "State-Corporate Crime in the U.S. Nuclear Weapons Production Complex." *The Journal of Human Justice* 5 (1): 4–28.

Kauzlarich, David, and Ronald C. Kramer. 1998. *Crimes of the American Nuclear State: At Home and Abroad*. Boston, MA: Northeastern University Press.

Kauzlarich, David, Ronald C. Kramer, and Brian Smith. 1992. "Toward the Study of Governmental Crime: Nuclear Weapons, Foreign Intervention, and International Law." *Humanity and Society* 16 (4): 543–563.

Kauzlarich, David, Rick A. Matthews, and William Miller. 2000. "A Victimology of State Crime." *American Behavioral Scientist*. In press.

Keane, Carl, Paul S. Maxim, and James J. Teevan. 1993. "Drinking and Driving, Self Control, and Gender: Testing a General Theory of Crime." *Journal of Research in Crime and Delinquency* 30:30–46.

Keil, Thomas J., and Gennaro F. Vito. 1989. "Race, Homicide Severity, and the Application of the Death Penalty: A Consideration of the Barnett Scale." *Criminology* 27:511–535.

Kelling, George L. 1988. *Police and Communities: The Quiet Revolution*. Washington, D.C.: National Institute of Justice.

Kelling, George L., and William J. Bratton. 1993. "Implementing Community Policing: The Administrative Problem." *NIJ Perspectives on Policing* (July): 1–11.

Kelly, Robert J. 1991. "AIDS and the Societal Reaction." In *Perspectives on Deviance: Domination,*

Degradation and Denigration. Ed. Robert J. Kelly and Donal E. J. MacNamara. Cincinnati, OH: Anderson.

Kempf, Kimberly L., ed. 1990. *Measurement Issues in Criminology.* New York: Springer-Verlag.

Kennedy, Leslie W., and David R. Forde. 1990. "Routine Activities and Crime: An Analysis of Victimization in Canada." *Criminology* 28:137–152.

Kennedy, Leslie W., Robert A. Silverman, and David R. Forde. 1991. "Homicide in Urban Canada: Testing the Impact of Income Inequality and Social Disorganization." *Canadian Journal of Sociology* 16:397–410.

Kennedy Bergen, Raquel. 1996. *Wife Rape.* Thousand Oaks, CA: Sage.

Kennedy Bergen, Raquel. 1998. *Issues in Intimate Violence.* Thousand Oaks, CA: Sage.

King, Harry. 1972. *Boxman: A Professional Thief's Journey.* Ed. William Chambliss. New York: Harper & Row.

Kinkade, Patrick J., and Matthew C. Leone. 1992. "The Effects of 'Tough' Drunk Driving Laws on Policing: A Case Study." *Crime and Delinquency* 38:239–254.

Kinsey, Richard, John Lea, and Jack Young. 1986. *Losing the Fight against Crime.* Oxford, UK: Basil Blackwell.

Kirkpatrick, Clifford, and Eugene J. Kanin. 1957. "Male Sex Aggression on a University Campus." *American Sociological Review* 22:53–62.

Kitsuse, John I. 1962. "Societal Reactions to Deviant Behavior: Problems of Theory and Method." *Social Problems* 9:247–256.

Kittrie, Nicholas N. 1973. *The Right to Be Different: Deviance and Enforced Therapy.* Baltimore, MD: Penguin Books.

Klebba, Joan A. 1975. "Homicide Trends in the United States, 1900–1974." *Public Health Reports* 90:195–204.

Kleck, Gary. 1981. "Racial Discrimination in Criminal Sentencing: A Critical Evaluation of the Evidence with Additional Evidence on the Death Penalty." *American Sociological Review* 46:783–805.

Kleck, Gary, and Susan Sayles. 1990. "Rape and Resistance." *Social Problems* 37:149–162.

Kleiman, Mark A. R., and Kerry D. Smith. 1990. "State and Local Drug Enforcement: In Search of a Strategy." In *Drugs and Crime.* Vol. 13, *Crime and Justice: A Review of Research.* Ed. Michael Tonry and James Q. Wilson. Chicago, IL: University of Chicago Press.

Klein, Malcom W. 1971. *Street Gangs and Street Workers.* Englewood Cliffs, NJ: Prentice Hall.

Klein, Malcom W. 1989. *Cross-National Research in Self-Reported Crime and Delinquency.* Dordrecht, Netherlands: Kluwer.

Klein, Malcolm W., and Cheryl L. Maxson. 1989. "Street Gang Violence." In *Violent Crime, Violent Criminals.* Ed. Neil Weiner and Marvin Wolfgang. Newbury Park, CA: Sage.

Klein, Malcom W., Cheryl L. Maxson, and Lea C. Cunningham. 1991. "'Crack,' Street Gangs, and Violence." *Criminology* 29:623–650.

Kleinknecht, William. 1996. *The New Ethnic Mobs: The Changing Face of Organized Crime in America.* New York: The Free Press.

Klemke, Lloyd. 1992. *The Sociology of Shoplifting: Boosters and Snitches Today.* New York: Praeger.

Klinger, David A. 1994. "Demeanor or Crime? Why 'Hostile' Citizens are More Likely to be Arrested." *Criminology* 32:475–493.

Klockars, Carl B. 1974. *The Professional Fence.* New York: Free Press.

Klofas, John M. 1993. "Drugs and Justice: The Impact of Drugs on Criminal Justice in a Metropolitan Community." *Crime and Delinquency* 39:204–224.

Knapp Commission Report on Police Corruption. 1972. New York: George Braziller.

Knight, B. J., and D. J. West. 1975. "Temporary and Continuing Delinquency." *British Journal of Criminology* 15:43–50.

Knoohuizen, Ralph, Richard P. Fahey, and Deborah J. Palmer. 1972. *The Police and Their Use of Fatal Force in Chicago.* Evanston, IL: Chicago Law Enforcement Study Group.

Kobetz, Richard W. 1978. *Criminal Justice Education Directory, 1978–1980.* Gaithersburg, MD: International Association of Chiefs of Police.

Koch, Brigitte, and Trevor Bennett. 1993. "Community Policing in Canada and Britain." *Home Office Research Bulletin* (summer): 36–42.

Kolata, Gina. 1982. "When Criminals Turn to Computers, Is Anything Safe?" *Smithsonian* 13:117–126.

Kooistra, Paul. 1990. "Criminals As Heroes: Linking Symbol to Structure." *Symbolic Interaction* 13:217–239.

Kovandzic, Tomislav V., Lynne M. Vieraitis, and

Mark R. Yeisley. 1998. "The Structural Covariates of Urban Homicide: Reassessing the Impact of Income Inequality and Poverty in the Post-Reagan Era." *Criminology* 36:569–599.

Kowalski, Gregory S., and Thomas A. Petee. 1991. "Sunbelt Effects on Homicide Rates." *Sociology and Social Research* 75:73–79.

Kramer, John H., and Robin L. Lubitz. 1985. "Pennsylvania's Sentencing Reform: The Impact of Commission-Established Guidelines." *Crime and Delinquency* 31:481–500.

Kramer, Ronald C. 1984. "Corporate Criminality: The Development of an Idea." In *Corporations As Criminals.* Ed. Ellen Hochstedler. Beverly Hills, CA: Sage.

Kramer, Ronald C. 1992. "The Space-Shuttle Challenger Explosion: A Case Study of State-Corporate Crime." In *White-Collar Crime Reconsidered.* Ed. Kip Schlegel and David O. Weisburd. Boston, MA: Northeastern University Press.

Kramer, Ronald C. 2000. "Poverty, Inequality, and Youth Violence." *Annals of the American Academy of Political and Social Science* 567:123–139.

Kramer, Ronald C., and David Kauzlarich. 1999. "The Opinion of the International Court of Justice on the Use of Nuclear Weapons: Implications for Criminology." *Contemporary Justice Review* 2 (4): 395–413.

Kramer, Ronald C., and Raymond J. Michalowski. 1987. "The Space between the Laws: The Problem of Crime in a Transnational Context." *Social Problems* 34:34–53.

Kramer, Ronald C., and Raymond J. Michalowski. 1990. "State-Corporate Crime." Paper presented at the annual meeting of the American Society of Criminology, Baltimore, MD.

Kramer, Ronald C., and Raymond J. Michalowski. 1991. "State-Corporate Crime." Paper based on the 1990 presentation at the annual meeting of the American Society of Criminology, Baltimore, MD.

Kramer, Ronald C., and Raymond J. Michalowski. 1995. "The Iron Fist and the Velvet Tongue: Crime Control Policies in the Clinton Administration." *Social Justice* 22 (2): 87–97.

Kramer, Ronald C., and Raymond J. Michalowski. 1999. "The Changing Nature of State Crime in an Era of Globalization." Paper presented at the annual meeting of the American Society of Criminology, Toronto, Ontario.

Kraska, Peter B. 1993. *Altered States of Mind: Critical Observations of the Drug War.* New York: Garland.

Kraska, Peter B., and Louis J. Cubellis. 1997. "Militarizing Mayberry and Beyond: Making Sense of American Paramilitary Policing." *Justice Quarterly* 14:607–629.

Krinsky, M., and D. Golove. 1993. *U.S. Economic Measures against Cuba: Proceedings in the United Nations and International Law Issues.* Northhampton, MA: Aletheia Press.

Kurz, D. 1998. "Old Problems and New Directions in the Study of Violence against Women." In *Issues in Intimate Violence.* Ed. Raquel Kennedy Bergen. Thousand Oaks, CA: Sage.

Kuykendall, Jack, and David Burns. 1980. "The Black Police Officer: An Historical Perspective." *Journal of Contemporary Criminal Justice* 4:103–113.

Lab, Steven P., and J. T. Whitehead. 1990. "From 'Nothing Works' to 'the Appropriate Works': The Latest Stop on the Search for the Secular Grail." *Criminology* 28:405–417.

LaFree, Gary D. 1989. *Rape and Criminal Justice: The Social Construction of Sexual Assault.* Belmont, CA: Wadsworth.

LaFree, Gary D., Barbara F. Reskin, and Christy Visher. 1991. "Jurors' Responses to Victims' Behavior and Legal Issues in Sexual Assault Trials." *Social Problems* 32:389–407.

LaGrange, Randy L., Kenneth F. Ferraro, and Michael Supancic. 1992. "Perceived Risk and Fear of Crime: Role of Social and Physical Incivilities." *Journal of Research in Crime and Delinquency* 29:311–332.

LaGrange, Teresa C. 1999. "The Impact of Neighborhoods, Schools, and Malls on the Spatial Distribution of Property Damage." *Journal of Research on Crime and Delinquency* 36 (4): 393–422.

LaGrange, Teresa C., and Robert A. Silverman. 1999. "Low Self-Control and Opportunity: Testing the General Theory of Crime As an Explanation for Gender Differences in Delinquency." *Criminology* 37 (1): 41–72.

Lamberth, John. 1998. "Driving While Black: A Statistician Proves That Prejudice Still Rules the Road." *Washington Post,* 16 August.

Lane, Roger. 1967. *Policing the City: Boston, 1821–1885.* Cambridge, MA: Harvard University Press.

Lane, Roger. 1992. "Urban Police and Crime in

Nineteenth-Century America." In *Modern Policing*. Ed. Michael Tonry and Norval Morris. Chicago, IL: University of Chicago Press.

Langan, Patrick A. 1991. *Race of Prisoners Admitted to State and Federal Institutions, 1926–1986*. Washington, D.C.: U.S. Department of Justice.

Lanza-Kaduce, Lonn. 1988. "Perceptual Deterrence and Drinking and Driving among College Students." *Criminology* 26:321–334.

Lasley, Jim. 1988. "Toward a Control Theory of White-Collar Offending." *Journal of Quantitative Criminology* 4:347–362.

Laub, John H., and Robert J. Sampson. 1988. "Unraveling Families and Delinquency: A Reanalysis of the Gluecks' Data." *Criminology* 26:355–380.

Laub, John H., Robert J. Sampson, Ronald P. Corbett Jr., and Jinnie S. Smith. 1995. "The Public Policy Implications of a Life-Course Perspective on Crime." In *Crime and Public Policy: Putting Theory to Work*. Ed. Hugh D. Barlow. Boulder, CO: Westview Press.

Law Enforcement Assistance Administration. 1970. *National Jail Census, 1970: A Report on the Nation's Local Jails and Types of Inmates*. Washington, D.C.: U.S. Government Printing Office.

Law Enforcement Assistance Administration. 1975a. *Census of State Correctional Facilities, 1974, Advance Report*. Washington, D.C.: U.S. Government Printing Office.

Law Enforcement Assistance Administration. 1975b. *The Nation's Jails*. Washington, D.C.: U.S. Government Printing Office.

Law Enforcement Assistance Administration. 1977. *Forcible Rape: A National Survey of Response by Prosecutors*. Washington, D.C.: U.S. Department of Justice.

Lawrence, Richard A. 1997. *School Crime and Juvenile Justice*. New York: Oxford University Press.

LeBeau, James L. 1988. "Is Interracial Rape Different?" *Sociology and Social Research* 73:43–46.

Lederer, Laura, ed. 1980. *Take Back the Night*. New York: Bantam Books.

Lee, Matthew R. 2000. "Concentrated Poverty, Race, and Homicide." *The Sociological Quarterly* 41 (2): 189–206.

Lein, Laura, Robert Richard, and Tony Fabelo. 1992. "The Attitudes of Criminal Justice Practitioners toward Sentencing Issues." *Crime and Delinquency* 38:189–203.

Leiser, Burton M. 1973. *Liberty, Justice and Morals*. New York: Macmillan.

Lejeune, Robert. 1977. "The Management of a Mugging." *Urban Life* 6:123–148.

Lemert, Edwin M. 1951. *Social Pathology*. New York: McGraw-Hill.

Lemert, Edwin M. 1972. *Human Deviance, Social Problems and Social Control*. 2d ed. Englewood Cliffs, NJ: Prentice Hall.

Lemert, Edwin M. 1974. "Beyond Mead: The Societal Reaction to Deviance." *Social Problems* 21:457–468.

Leonard, Eileen B. 1982. *Women, Crime and Society*. New York: Longman.

Leonard, Kimberly Kempf, Carl E. Pope, and William H. Feyerherm. 1995. *Minorities in Juvenile Justice*. Thousand Oaks, CA: Sage.

Leonard, William N., and Marvin Glenn Weber. 1970. "Automakers and Dealers: A Study of Crimogenic Market Forces." *Law and Society Review* 4:408–422.

Letkemann, Peter. 1973. *Crime As Work*. Englewood Cliffs, NJ: Prentice Hall.

Levi, Michael. 1987. *Regulating Fraud: White-Collar Crime and the Criminal Process*. London, UK: Tavistock.

Levi, Michael, and S. Jones. 1985. "Public and Police Perceptions of Crime Seriousness in England and Wales." *British Journal of Criminology* 25:234–250.

Levin, Jack, and James Alan Fox. 1985. *Mass Murder: America's Growing Menace*. New York: Plenum.

Levin, Jack, and Jack McDevitt. 1993. *Hate Crimes: The Rising Tide of Bigotry and Bloodshed*. New York: Plenum Press.

Lichter, Linda S., and S. Robert Lichter. 1983. *Prime Time Crime: Criminals and Law Enforcement in TV Entertainment*. Washington, D.C.: Media Institute.

Light, Roy, Claire Nee, and Helen Ingham. 1993. *Car Theft: The Offender's Perspective*. London, UK: H.M.S.O.

Lilly, J. Robert, Richard A. Ball, and Jennifer Wright. 1987. "Home Incarceration with Electronic Monitoring in Kenton County, Kentucky: An Evaluation." In *Intermediate Punishments: Intensive Supervision, Home Confinement, and Electronic Monitoring*. Ed. Belinda R. McCarthy. Monsey, NY: Criminal Justice Press.

Lilly, Robert J., Francis T. Cullen, and Richard A. Ball. 1989. *Criminological Theory: Context and Consequences.* Newbury Park, CA: Sage.

Lincoln, Alan J., and Murray A. Straus. 1985. *Crime and the Family.* Springfield, IL: Thomas.

Linden, E., and J. C. Hackler. 1973. "Affective Ties and Delinquency." *Pacific Sociological Review* 16:27–47.

Lindesmith, Alfred R. 1967. *The Addict and the Law.* New York: Random House.

Link, Bruce, and Francis T. Cullen. 1983. "Reconsidering the Social Rejection of Ex-Mental Patients: Levels of Attitudinal Response." *American Journal of Community Psychology* 11:261–273.

Linsky, Arnold S., Jr., John P. Colby, and Murray Straus. 1986. "Drinking Norms and Alcohol-Related Problems in the United States." *Journal of Studies on Alcohol* 47:384–393.

Lintott, A. W. 1968. *Violence in Republican Rome.* Oxford, UK: Clarendon Press.

Lippmann, Walter. 1931. "The Underworld As Servant." In *Organized Crime in America.* Ed. Gus Tyler. Ann Arbor, MI: University of Michigan Press.

Lipsky, Michael, ed. 1970. *Law and Order: Police Encounters.* Chicago, IL: Aldine.

Liska, Allen E., and William Baccaglini. 1990. "Feeling Safe by Comparison: Crime in the Newspapers." *Social Problems* 37:360–372.

Lizotte, Alan J. 1985. "The Uniqueness of Rape: Reporting Assaultive Violence to the Police." *Crime and Delinquency* 31:169–190.

Lizotte, Alan J., and David J. Bordua. 1980. "Firearms Ownership for Sport and Protection: Two Divergent Models." *American Sociological Review* 45:229–244.

Lloyd, Charles, and Roy Walmsley. 1989. *Changes in Rape Offences and Sentencing.* London, UK: H.M.S.O.

Loeber, Rolph, and Thomas J. Dishion. 1983. "Early Predictors of Male Delinquency." *Psychological Bulletin* 94:68–99.

Lofland, John. 1977. *The Dramaturgy of State Executions.* Montclair, NJ: Patterson Smith.

Loftin, Colin, and Robert H. Hill. 1974. "Regional Subculture and Homicide: An Examination of the Gastil-Hackney Thesis." *American Sociological Review* 39:714–724.

Lombroso, Cesare. 1911. *Crime, Its Causes and Remedies.* Boston, MA: Little, Brown.

Long-Onnen, Jami, and Derral Cheatwood. 1992. "Hospitals and Homicide: An Expansion of Current Theoretical Paradigms." *American Journal of Criminal Justice* 16 (2): 57–74.

Lorenz, Konrad. 1971. *On Aggression.* New York: Bantam Books.

Lovald, Keith, and Helger R. Stub. 1968. "The Revolving Door: Reactions of Chronic Drunkenness to Court Sanctions." *Journal of Criminal Law, Criminology and Police Science* 59:525–530.

Loves, Mark F. 1992. "Organized Crime on Wheels: The Evolution of the Outlaw Motorcycle Gangs in the United States and Canada." *Criminal Organizations* 6:9, 13.

Luckenbill, David F. 1977. "Criminal Homicide As a Situated Transaction." *Social Problems* 25:176–186.

Luckenbill, David F. 1980. "Patterns of Force in Robbery." *Deviant Behavior* 1:361–378.

Luckenbill, David F., and Daniel P. Doyle. 1989. "Structural Position and Violence: Developing a Cultural Explanation." *Criminology* 27:419–436.

Luconi, Stefano. 1999. "Mafia-Related Prejudice and the Rise of Italian American in the United States." *Patterns of Prejudice* 33 (1): 43–57.

Lunde, Donald T. 1970. *Murder and Madness.* San Francisco, CA: San Francisco Book Co.

Lundesgaarde, Henry P. 1977. *Murder in Space City.* New York: Oxford University Press.

Lundman, Richard J. 1980. *Police and Policing.* New York: Holt, Rinehart & Winston.

Lundman, Richard J. 1984. *Prevention and Control of Juvenile Delinquency.* New York: Oxford University Press.

Lundman, Richard J. 1991. "Police and Drunk Driving: Baseline Data and DUI Arrests, 1960–1989." Presented at the annual meeting of the American Sociological Association, August 22–26, Cincinnati, OH.

Lupsha, Peter A. 1981. "Individual Choice, Material Culture, and Organized Crime." *Criminology* 19:3–24.

Luttwak, Edward N. 1995. "Going Dutch: The Unending Cost of the Drugs War." *Times Literary Supplement* 1 (September): 4–5.

Lyman, Stanford M., and Marvin B. Scott. 1975. *The Drama of Social Reality.* New York: Oxford University Press.

Lynch, Michael J., Raymond Michalowski, and W. Byron Groves. 2000. *The New Primer in Radical*

Criminology: Critical Perspectives on Crime, Power and Identity. Monsey, NY: Criminal Justice Press.

Lynch, Michael J. 1997. *Radical Criminology.* Aldershot, UK: Dartmouth.

Lynch, Michael J., and W. Byron Groves. 1989. *A Primer in Radical Criminology.* 2d ed. New York: Harrow and Heston.

Maas, Peter. 1968. *The Valachi Papers.* New York: Putnam.

MacDonald, John M. 1971. *Rape: Offenders and Their Victims.* Springfield, IL: Thomas.

Machalek, Richard, and Lawrence E. Cohen. 1991. "The Nature of Crime: Is Cheating Necessary for Cooperation?" *Human Nature* 2:215–233.

Mack, J. A. 1964. "The Able Criminal." *British Journal of Criminology* 12:45–55.

Mack, J. A. 1975. *The Crime Industry.* London, UK: Saxon House.

MacKenzie, Doris Layton, James W. Shaw, and Voncile B. Gowdy. 1993. "An Evaluation of Shock Incarceration in Louisiana." *NIJ Research in Brief* (June): 1–7.

MacKinnon, C. 1989. *Toward a Feminist Theory of the State.* Cambridge, MA: Harvard University Press.

MacNamara, Donal E. J. 1968. "Sex Offenses and Sex Offenders." *The Annals* 376:153–162.

Maguire, Kathleen, and Timothy Flanagan. 1991. *Sourcebook of Criminal Justice Statistics.* Washington, D.C.: U.S. Department of Justice.

Maguire, Kathleen, and Ann L. Pastore, eds. 1996. *Sourcebook of Criminal Justice Statistics, 1995.* Washington, D.C.: U.S. Department of Justice.

Maguire, Kathleen, and Ann L. Pastore, eds. 1997. *Sourcebook of Criminal Justice Statistics, 1996.* Washington, D.C.: U.S. Department of Justice.

Maguire, Kathleen, and Ann L. Pastore, eds. 1998. *Sourcebook of Criminal Justice Statistics, 1997.* Washington, D.C.: U.S. Department of Justice.

Maguire, Kathleen, and Ann L. Pastore, eds. 1999. *Sourcebook of Criminal Justice Statistics, 1998.* Washington, D.C.: U.S. Department of Justice.

Maguire, Kathleen, and Ann L. Pastore, eds. 2000. *Sourcebook of Criminal Justice Statistics, 1999.* Washington, D.C.: U.S. Department of Justice.

Maguire, Kathleen, Ann L. Pastore, and Timothy J. Flanagan. 1993. *Sourcebook of Criminal Justice Statistics.* Washington, D.C.: U.S. Department of Justice.

Maher, Lisa. 1997. *Sexed Work: Gender, Race, and Resistance in a Brooklyn Drug Market.* Oxford, UK: Clarendon Press.

Maher, Lisa, and Kathleen Daly. 1998 *Criminology at the Crossroads: Feminist Readings in Crime and Justice.* New York: Oxford University Press.

Maine, Sir Henry Sumner. 1905. *Ancient Law.* 10th ed. London, UK: John Murray.

Mair, George. 1991. "What Works: Nothing or Everything?" *Home Office Research Bulletin,* no. 30. London, UK: H.M.S.O.

Makkai, Toni, and John Braithwaite. 1991. "Criminological Theories and Regulatory Compliance." *Criminology* 29:191–217.

Makkai, Toni, and John Braithwaite. 1994. "Reintegrative Shaming and Compliance with Regulatory Standards." *Criminology* 32:361–383.

Malamud-Goti, Jaime. 1992. *Smoke and Mirrors: The Paradox of the Drug Wars.* Boulder, CO: Westview Press.

Malinowski, Bronislaw. 1926. *Crime and Custom in Savage Society.* New York: Harcourt Brace, Jovanovich.

Mann, Coramae Richey. 1993. *Unequal Justice: A Question of Color.* Bloomington, IN: Indiana University Press.

Mann, Coramae Richey. 1996. *When Women Kill.* Albany, NY: SUNY Press.

Mannheim, Hermann. 1946. *Criminal Justice and Social Reconstruction.* London, UK: Routledge and Kegan Paul.

Manning, Peter K. 1977. *Police Work: The Social Organization of Policing.* Cambridge, MA: MIT Press.

Manning, Peter K. 1988. *Symbolic Communication: Signifying Calls and the Police Response.* Cambridge, MA: MIT Press.

Manning, Peter K. 1989. "Community Policing." In *Critical Issues in Policing.* Ed. Roger G. Dunham and Geoffrey P. Alpert. Prospect Heights, IL: Waveland Press.

Manning, Peter K. 1994. "The Police, Symbolic Capital, Class, and Control." In *Inequality, Crime, and Social Control.* Ed. George Bridges and Martha A. Myers. Boulder, CO: Westview Press.

Mark, H. Moore. 1994. "Research Synthesis and Policy Implications." In *The Challenge of Community Policing.* Ed. Dennis P. Rosenbaum. Thousand Oaks, CA: Sage.

Marquart, James W., Sheldon Ekland-Olson, and Jonathan Sorensen. 1993. *The Rope, the Chair, and the Needle.* Austin, TX: University of Texas Press.

Mars, Gerald. 1982. *Cheats at Work! An Anthropology of Workplace Crime.* London, UK: George Allen and Unwin.

Mars, Gerald. 1983. *Cheats at Work: An Anthropology of Workplace Crime*. London, UK: Unwin Paperbacks.

Martin, J. B. 1952. *My Life in Crime*. New York: Harper & Row.

Martin, Susan E. 1989. "Female Officers on the Move? A Status Report on Women in Policing." In *Critical Issues in Policing*. Ed. Roger G. Dunham and Geoffrey P. Alpert. Prospect Heights, IL: Waveland Press.

Martinez, Orlando. 1987. "Minority Youth and Crime." *Crime and Delinquency* 33:325–328.

Martinson, Robert. 1974. "What Works? Questions and Answers about Prison Reform." *The Public Interest* 35:22–54.

Marx, Gary T. 1988. *Undercover: Police Surveillance in America*. Berkeley, CA: University of California at Berkeley Press.

Marx, Karl. [1859] 1971. *A Contribution to the Critique of Political Economy*. London, UK: Lawrence and Wishart.

Marx, Karl. [1862] 1969. *Theories of Surplus Value*. Vol. 1. Moscow, USSR: Foreign Languages Publishing House.

Marx, Karl, and Frederick Engels. [1846] 1947. *The German Ideology*. New York: International Publishers.

Matoesian, Gregory. 1993. *Reproducing Rape: Domination through Talk in the Courtroom*. London, UK: Polity Press.

Matsueda, Ross L. 1982. "Testing Control Theory and Differential Association: A Causal Modeling Approach." *American Sociological Review* 47:489–504.

Matsueda, Ross L., and Karen Heimer. 1987. "Race, Family Structure, and Delinquency: A Test of Differential Association and Social Control Theories." *American Sociological Review* 52:826–840.

Matsueda, Ross L., and Kathleen Anderson. 1998. "The Dynamics of Delinquent Peers and Delinquent Behavior." *Criminology* 36 (2): 269–308.

Matthews, Rick A. 2001. "Marxist Criminology." In *Controversial Issues in Criminology: Critical Criminology*. Ed. Martin D. Schwartz and Suzanne Hatty. Cincinnati, OH: Anderson.

Matthews, Rick A., and David Kauzlarich. 2000. "The Crash of Valujet Flight 592: A Case Study in State-Corporate Crime." *Sociological Focus* 3:281–298.

Matthews, Roger. 1986. "Policing Prostitution." In *Confronting Crime*. Ed. Roger Matthews and Jock Young. Beverly Hills, CA: Sage.

Matthews, Roger. 1987. "Taking Realist Criminology Seriously." Presented to the annual meeting of the American Society of Criminology, November, Montreal, Canada.

Matthews, Roger, and Jock Young, eds. 1986. *Confronting Crime*. Beverly Hills, CA: Sage.

Matza, David. 1964. *Delinquency and Drift*. New York: Wiley.

Mauer, Marc. 2000. "The Racial Dynamics of Imprisonment." In *Building Violence: How America's Rush to Incarcerate Creates More Violence*. Ed. John P. May. Thousand Oaks, CA: Sage.

Maurer, D. W. 1940. *The Big Con*. Indianapolis, IN: Bobbs-Merrill.

Maurer, D. W. 1964. *Whiz Mob*. New Haven, CT: College and University Press.

Mawby, R. I., and S. Walklate. 1994. *Critical Victimology*. Thousand Oaks, CA: Sage.

Maxfield, Michael A., Dan A. Lewis, and Ron Szoc. 1980. "Producing Official Crimes: Verified Crime Reports As Measures of Police Output." *Social Science Quarterly* 61:221–236.

May, John P. 2000. *Building Violence: How America's Rush to Incarcerate Creates More Violence*. Thousand Oaks, CA: Sage.

Mayhew, Patricia, Ronald V. Clarke, and David Elliott. 1989. "Motorcycle Theft, Helmet Legislation and Displacement." *The Howard Journal* 28:1–8.

Mayhew, Patricia, Ronald V. Clarke, and J. M. Hough. 1992. "Steering Column Locks and Car Theft." In *Situational Crime Prevention: Successful Case Studies*. New York: Harrow and Heston.

Mayhew, P., R. V. G. Clark, J. N. Burrows, J. M. Hough, and S. W. Winchester. 1979. "Crime in Public Places." *Home Office Research Study*, no. 49. London, UK: H.M.S.O.

Mayhew, Patricia, Natalie Aye Maung, and Catriona Mirrlees-Black. 1993. *The 1992 British Crime Survey*. London, UK: H.M.S.O.

Maynard, Douglas W. 1982. "Defendant Attributes in Plea Bargaining: Notes on the Modeling of Sentencing Decisions." *Social Problems* 29:347–360.

Maynard, Douglas W. 1984. *Inside Plea Bargaining*. New York: Plenum Press.

Mayor of New York's Committee on Marijuana. 1944. *The Marijuana Problem in the City of New York*. New York: Cattell.

Mazerolle, Paul. 1998. "Gender, General Strain, and Delinquency: Empirical Examination." *Justice Quarterly* 15:65–91.

McCaghy, Charles H. 1967. "Child Molesters: A Study of Their Careers As Deviants." In *Criminal Behavior Systems: A Typology*. Ed. Marshall B. Clinard and Richard Quinney. New York: Holt, Rinehart & Winston.

McCaghy, Charles H. 1976. *Deviant Behavior: Crime, Conflict and Interest Groups*. New York: Macmillan.

McCaghy, Charles H., and Timothy A. Capron. 1994. *Deviant Behavior: Crime, Conflict, and Interest Groups*. 3d ed. New York: Macmillan.

McCarthy, Belinda Rodgers, and Charles A. Lindquist. 1988. "The Impact of Guilty Pleas on the Sentencing Process: A Crime-Specific Analysis of Prosecutorial, Defendant, and Judicial Behavior." Presented to the annual meeting of the Academy of Criminal Justice Sciences, Chicago, IL.

McCarthy, Bill, John Hagan, and Todd S. Woodward. 1999. "In the Company of Women: Structure and Agency in a Revised Power-Control Theory of Gender and Delinquency." *Criminology* 37 (4): 761–788.

McCartt, John M., and Thomas J. Mangogna. 1976a. "The History of Halfway Houses in the United States." In *Probation, Parole, and Community Corrections*. 2d ed. Edited by Robert M. Carter and Leslie T. Wilkins. New York: Wiley.

McCartt, John M., and Thomas J. Mangogna. 1976b. "Overview of Issues Relating to Halfway Houses and Community Treatment Centers." In *Probation, Parole, and Community Corrections*. Ed. Robert M. Carter and Leslie T. Wilkins. New York: Wiley.

McCord, Joan. 1978. "A Thirty-Year Follow-Up of Treatment Effects." *American Psychologist* 33:284–289.

McCord, Joan. 1980. "The Treatment That Did Not Help." *Social Action and Law* 5:85–87.

McCord, Joan. 1986. "Instigation and Insulation: How Families Affect Antisocial Behavior." In *Development of Antisocial and Prosocial Behavior*. Ed. D. Olweus, J. Block, and M. Radke-Yarrow. Orlando, FL: Academic Press.

McCord, Joan. 1991. "Family Relationships, Juvenile Delinquency, and Adult Criminality." *Criminology* 29:397–417.

McCord, William, and Joan McCord. 1959. *Origins of Crime: A New Evaluation of the Cambridge-Somerville Youth Study*. New York: Columbia University Press.

McCorkle, Richard C. 1993. "Research Note: Punish and Rehabilitate? Public Attitudes toward Six Common Crimes." *Crime and Delinquency* 39:240–252.

McDermott, M. Joan. 1979. *Rape Victimization in 26 American Cities*. Washington, D.C.: U.S. Department of Justice.

McDonald, Douglas C., and Kenneth E. Carlson. 1993. *Sentencing in the Federal Courts: Does Race Matter?* Washington, D.C.: U.S. Department of Justice.

McDonald, William F., ed. 1976. *Criminal Justice and the Victim*. Beverly Hills, CA: Sage.

McDonald, William F. 1985. *Plea Bargaining: Critical Issues and Common Practices*. Washington, D.C.: U.S. Department of Justice.

McEwen, Thomas J.. 1989. *Dedicated Computer Crime Units*. Washington, D.C.: U.S. Department of Justice.

McEwen, Thomas J. 1991. "Computer Ethics." *NIJ Research in Action* (January/February): 8–12.

McGarrell, Edmund F. 1993. "Trends in Racial Disproportionality in Juvenile Court Processing: 1985–1989." *Crime and Delinquency* 39:29–48.

McGarrell, Edmund F., and Timothy J. Flanagan, eds. 1985. *Sourcebook of Criminal Justice Statistics*. Washington, D.C.: U.S. Government Printing Office.

McIntosh, Mary. 1971. "Changes in the Organization of Thievery." In *Images of Deviance*. Ed. Stanley Cohen. Hammondsworth, UK: Penguin Books.

McIntyre, Donald M., and David Lippman. 1970. "Prosecutors and Early Disposition of Felony Cases." *American Bar Association Law Journal* 56:1154–1159.

McIntyre, Jennie J., and Thelma Myint. 1979. "Sexual Assault Outcomes: Completed and Attempted Rapes." Presented at the annual meeting of the American Sociological Association, August, Boston, MA.

McIver, John P. 1981. "Criminal Mobility: A Review of Empirical Studies." In *Crime Spillover*. Ed. Simon Hakim and George F. Rengert. Beverly Hills, CA: Sage.

McKusick, Leon, William Horstman, and Thomas J. Coates. 1985. "AIDS and Sexual Behavior Reported by Gay Men in San Francisco." *American Journal of Public Health* 75:493–496.

McNamara, John H. 1967. "Uncertainties of Police Work: Recruits' Background and Training." In *The Police: Six Sociological Essays*. Ed. David Bordua. New York: Wiley.

McNeely, R. L., and Carl E. Pope. 1981. *Race, Crime, and Criminal Justice*. Beverly Hills, CA: Sage.

McNulty, Elizabeth W. 1994. "Generating Common-Sense Knowledge among Police Officers." *Symbolic Interaction* 17:281–294.

Mednick, Sarnoff A., Jr., and K. O. Christiansen. 1977. *Biosocial Basis of Criminal Behavior*. New York: Wiley.

Mednick, Sarnoff A., Jr., W. F. Garbrielli, and B. Huthings. 1984. "Genetic Influences in Criminal Convictions: Evidence from an Adoption Cohort." *Science* 224:891–895.

Mendelsohn, Alan J. 1956. "The Influence of Defendants' Plea on Judicial Determination of Sentence." *Yale Law Journal* 66:204–222.

Merrill, Gregory S. 1998. "Understanding Domestic Violence among Gay and Bisexual Men." In *Issues in Intimate Violence*. Ed. Raquel Kennedy Bergen. Thousand Oaks, CA: Sage.

Merry, Sally Engle. 1981. *Urban Danger: Life in a Neighborhood of Strangers*. Philadelphia, PA: Temple University Press.

Merton, Robert K. 1938. "Social Structure and Anomie." *American Sociological Review* 3:672–682.

Merton, Robert K. 1957. *Social Theory and Social Structure*. New York: Free Press.

Messerschmidt, James W. 1986. *Capitalism, Patriarchy, and Crime*. Totowa, NJ: Rowman and Littlefield.

Messerschmidt, James W. 1994. *Masculinities and Crime*. Totowa, NJ: Rowman and Littlefield.

Messerschmidt, James W. 1997. "From Patriarchy to Gender: Feminist Theory, Criminology, and the Challenge of Diversity." Pp. 176–188 in *International Feminist Perspectives in Criminology: Engendering a Discipline*. Ed. Nicole Hahn Rafter and Frances Heidensohn. Buckingham, UK: Open University Press.

Messerschmidt, James W. 2000. *Nine Lives: Adolescent Masculinities, the Body, and Violence*. Boulder, CO: Westview.

Messner, Steven F. 1983. "Regional and Racial Effects on the Urban Homicide Rate: The Subculture of Violence Revisited." *American Journal of Sociology* 88:997–1007.

Messner, Steven F. 1989. "Economic Discrimination and Homicide Rates: Further Evidence on the Cost of Inequality." *American Sociological Review* 54:597–611.

Messner, Steven F., and Reid M. Golden. 1992. "Racial Inequality and Racially Disaggregated Homicide Rates: An Assessment of Alternative Theoretical Explanations." *Criminology* 30:421–445.

Messner, Steven F., and Richard Rosenfeld. 1994. *Crime and the American Dream*. Belmont, CA: Wadsworth.

Messner, Steven F., and Richard Rosenfeld. 1996. *Crime and the American Dream*. 2d ed. Belmont, CA: Wadsworth.

Messner Steven F., and Richard Rosenfeld. 2000. *Crime and the American Dream*. 3d ed. Belmont, CA: Wadsworth.

Metz, Tim. 1971. "Hot Stocks." In *Crime As Business*. Ed. Michael Gartner. New York: Dow Jones Books.

Meyers, Martha A. 1988. "Social Background and the Sentencing Behavior of Judges." *Criminology* 26:649–675.

Michalowski, Raymond J. 1985. *Order, Law, and Crime*. New York: Random House.

Michalowski, Raymond J. 1987. "Reply to Gibbs." *The Criminologist* 12 (6): 12, 18.

Michalowski, Raymond J. 1988. "Response to Nettler." *The Criminologist* 13 (4): 4.

Michalowski, Raymond J., and Susan Carlson. 1999. "Unemployment, Imprisonment and Social Structures of Accumulation: Historical Contingency in the Ruschh-Kircheimer Hypothesis." *Criminology* 37 (2): 217–250.

Michalowski, Raymond J., and Ronald C. Kramer. 1987. "The Space between the Laws: The Problem of Corporate Crime in a Transnational Context." *Social Problems* 34:34–53.

Michalowski, Raymond, and Erdwin H. Pfuhl. 1991. "Technology, Property, and Law." *Crime, Law and Social Change* 15:255–275.

Miethe, Terance D. 1982. "Public Consensus on Crime Seriousness: Normative Structure or Methodological Artifact?" *Criminology* 20: 513–526.

Miethe, Terance D., and Richard McCorkle. 1998. *Crime Profiles: The Anatomy of Dangerous Persons, Places, and Situations.* Los Angeles, CA: Roxbury.

Mihalic, S. W., and D. Elliott. 1997. "If Violence Is Domestic, Does It Really Count?" *Journal of Family Violence* 12 (3): 293–311.

Miller, Eleanor M. 1986. *Street Women.* Philadelphia, PA: Temple University Press.

Miller, Jody. 1998a. "Gender and Victimization Risk among Young Women in Gangs." *The Journal of Research in Crime and Delinquency* 35 (4): 429–453.

Miller, Jody. 1998b. "Up It Up: Gender and the Accomplishment of Street Robbery." *Criminology* 36 (1): 37–65.

Miller, Jody. 2001. *One of the Guys: Girls, Gangs, and Gender.* New York: Oxford University Press.

Miller, Ted R., Mark A. Cohen, and Brian Wiersema. 1996. *Victim Costs and Consequences: A New Look.* National Institute of Justice Report. Washington, D.C.: NIJ.

Miller, Walter B. 1958. "Lower Class Culture As a Generating Milieu of Gang Delinquency." *Journal of Social Issues* 14:5–19.

Miller, Walter B. 1966. "Violent Crimes in City Gangs." *The Annals* 364:109–112.

Miller, Walter B. 1973. "Ideological and Criminal Justice Policy: Some Current Issues." *Journal of Criminal Law and Criminology* 64:141–162.

Mills, C. Wright. 1956. *White Collar.* New York: Galaxie Books.

Millspaugh, Arthur G. [1937] 1972. *Crime Control by the National Government.* New York: Da Capo Press.

Milner, Christina, and Richard Milner. 1972. *Black Players: The Secret World of Black Pimps.* Boston, MA: Little, Brown.

Milovanovic, Dragan. 1997. *Postmodern Criminology.* New York: Garland Publishing.

Milton, C. 1972. *Women in Policing.* Washington, D.C.: Police Foundation.

Minichiello, Victor, Rodrigo Marino, Jan Browne, and Maggie Jamieson. 1999. "A Profile of the Clients of Male Sex Workers in Three Australian Cities." *Australian and New Zealand Journal of Public Health* 23 (5): 511–518.

Minor, W. William. 1975. "Political Crime, Political Justice, and Political Prisoners." *Criminology* 12:385–397.

Minor, W. William. 1978. "Deterrence Research: Problems of Theory and Method." In *Preventing Crime.* Ed. James A. Cramer. Beverly Hills, CA: Sage.

Minor, W. William. 1980. "The Neutralization of Criminal Offense." *Criminology* 18:103–120.

Minor, W. William. 1981. "Techniques of Neutralization: A Reconceptualization and Empirical Examination." *Journal of Research in Crime and Delinquency* 18:295–318.

Mintz, Morton. 1965. *The Therapeutic Nightmare: A Report on Prescription Drugs, the Men Who Take Them, and the Agency That Controls Them.* Boston, MA: Houghton Mifflin.

Mintz, Morton. 1970. *The Therapeutic Nightmare: A Report on Prescription Drugs, the Men Who Take Them, and the Agency That Controls Them.* 2d ed. Boston, MA: Houghton Mifflin.

Mirrlees-Black, Catriona. 1995. "Estimating the Extent of Domestic Violence: Findings from the 1992 BCS." *Home Office Research Bulletin* 37:1–9.

Mirrlees-Black, Catriona, and Natalie Aye Maung. 1994. "Fear of Crime: Findings from the 1992 British Crime Survey." *Home Office RPU Research Findings* no. 9 (April): 1–6.

Mirrlees-Black, Catriona, Pat Mayhew, and Andrew Percy. 1996. "The 1996 British Crime Survey." *Home Office Statistical Bulletin* (September): 1–78.

Mokhiber, Russell. 1988. *Corporate Crime and Corporate Violence.* San Francisco, CA: Sierra Club.

Mokhiber, Russell. 1999. "The Decade's Worst Corporate Criminals." At <www.corporatepredators.org/top100.html>.

Mokhiber, Russell, and Robert Weissman. 1999. *Corporate Predators: The Hunt for Mega-Profits and the Attack on Democracy.* Monroe, ME: Common Courage Press.

Monahan, John. 1981. *Predicting Violent Behavior: An Assessment of Clinical Techniques.* Beverly Hills, CA: Sage.

Monahan, John, and Henry J. Steadman. 1983. "Crime and Mental Disorder: An Epidemiological Approach." In *Crime and Justice: An Annual Review.* Ed. Michael Tonry and Norval K. Morris. Chicago, IL: University of Chicago Press.

Moore, Joan. 1998. "Understanding Youth Street Gangs: Economic Restructuring and the Urban Underclass." In *Cross-Cultural Perspectives on Youth and Violence.* Ed. Meredith W. Watts. Stamford, CT: JAI Press.

Moore, Mark H. 1986. "Organized Crime As a Business Enterprise." Presented to the annual meeting of the American Society of Criminology, November, Atlanta, GA.

Moore, Mark H. 1990. "Supply Reduction and Drug Law Enforcement." In *Drugs and Crime*. Vol. 13, *Crime and Justice: A Review of Research*. Ed. Michael Tonry and James Q. Wilson. Chicago, IL: University of Chicago Press.

Moore, Mark H. 1992. "Problem-Solving and Community Policing." In *Modern Policing*. Ed. Michael Tonry and Norval Morris. Chicago, IL: University of Chicago Press.

Moore, Mark H., and Robert C. Trojanowicz. 1988. *Policing and the Fear of Crime*. Washington, D.C.: National Institute of Justice.

Moore, Mark H., Robert C. Trojanowicz, and George Kelling. 1988. *Crime and Policing*. Washington, D.C.: National Institute of Justice.

Moore, Wilbert E. 1964. *Social Aspects of Economic Development*. Chicago, IL: Rand McNally.

Morash, Merry. 1986. "Understanding the Contribution of Women to Police Work." In *The Police and the Community*. 4th ed. Edited by Louis A. Radalet. New York: Macmillan.

Morash, Merry, and Jack R. Greene. 1986. "Evaluating Women on Patrol: A Critique of Contemporary Wisdom." *Evaluation Review* 10:230–255.

Morris, Allison. 1987. *Women, Crime and Criminal Justice*. Oxford, UK: Basil Blackwell.

Morris, Norval. 1991. "The Case for Intermediate Punishments." *Federal Prison Journal* 2:11–14.

Morris, Terrence. 1958. *The Criminal Area*. New York: Humanities Press.

Mullins, Christopher W., and David Kauzlarich. 2000. "The Ghost Dance and Wounded Knee: A Criminological Examination." *Social Pathology* 6 (4).

Mulvihill, Donald J., Melvin Tumin, and Lynn Curtis. 1969. *Crimes of Violence*. Washington, D.C.: U.S. Government Printing Office.

Munford, Robert S., Ross J. Kazer, Roger A. Feldman, and Robert R. Strivers. 1976. "Homicide Trends in Atlanta." *Criminology* 14:213–232.

Murphy, J. E. 1984. "Date Abuse and Forced Intercourse among College Students." Presented to the National Conference for Family Violence Researchers, University of New Hampshire.

Murton, Tom, and Joe Hyams. 1969. *Accomplices to the Crime: The Arkansas Prison Scandal*. New York: Grove Press.

Mustaine, Elizabeth E. 1997. "Victimization Risks and Routine Activities: A Theoretical Examination Using a Gender-Specific and Domain-Specific Model." *American Journal of Criminal Justice* 22, no. 1 (fall): 41–70.

Muzzatti, Stephen L. 2000. "Crotch Rocket Heroes: Reflections on Speed, Youth Identity and Delinquency through Consumerism." Paper presented at the annual meeting of the Midwest Sociological Society, Chicago, IL.

Nader, Ralph. 1967. "We're Still in the Jungle." *The New Republic* 161:11–12.

Nader, Ralph, and Mark Green. 1972. "Coddling the Corporations: Crime in the Suites." *The New Republic* 166:18–24.

Nagel, Stuart S. 1967. "Disparities in Criminal Procedures." *UCLA Law Review* 14:1296.

Nagel, Stuart S., ed. 1977. *Modelling the Criminal Justice System*. Beverly Hills, CA: Sage.

Nagel, William G. 1973. *The New Red Barn: A Critical Look at the Modern American Prison*. New York: Walker.

Nagin, Daniel S., and Raymond Paternoster. 1991. "The Preventive Effects of the Perceived Risk of Arrest: Testing an Expanded Conception of Deterrence." *Criminology* 29:561–587.

Nagin, Daniel S., and Raymond Paternoster. 1993. "Enduring Individual Differences and Rational Choice Theories of Crime." *Law and Society Review* 27:467–496.

Natarajan, Mangai, and Mathieu Belanger. 1998. "Varieties of Drug Trafficking Organizations: A Typology of Cases Prosecuted in New York City." *Journal of Drug Issues* 28 (4): 1005–1025.

Nathan, Robert Stuart. 1980. "Corporate Criminals Who Kept Their Jobs." *Business and Social Review* 33:19–20.

National Center for Education Statistics. 1999. *Violence and Discipline Problems in U.S. Public Schools: 1996–97*. Washington, D.C.: NCES.

National Center for Victims of Crime. 1996. "Crime Victims Sourcebook." At <www.nvc.org/index.html>.

National Coffee Association. 2000. At <www.ncausa.org>.

National Commission on Marijuana and Drug Abuse. 1973. *Patterns and Consequences of Drug Use*. Washington, D.C.: U.S. Government Printing Office.

National Committee on Violence [Australia]. 1989. "Racist Violence." *Violence Today* 8:1–7.

National Council on Crime and Delinquency. 2000. *And Justice for Some*. Washington, D.C.

National Crime and Justice Learning Center. 2000. At <www.crimeand punishment.net>.

National Infrastructure Protection Center. 2000. At <http://sun00781.dn.net/irp/agency/doj/fbi/nipc>.

National Institute of Justice. 1991a. *Drug Use Forecasting*. Washington, D.C.: U.S. Department of Justice.

National Institute of Justice. 1991b. *Research in Brief*. Washington, D.C.: U.S. Department of Justice.

National Institute of Justice. 1992a. "New Approach to Interviewing Children: A Test of Its Effectiveness." *NIJ Research in Brief* (May): 1–6.

National Institute of Justice. 1992b. *Making the Offender Foot the Bill: A Texas Program*. Washington, D.C.: U.S. Department of Justice.

National Institute of Justice. 1993. *Drug Use Forecasting: 1992 Annual Report*. Washington, D.C.: U.S. Department of Justice.

National Institute of Justice. 1996. *The Extent and Costs of Crime Victimization: A New Look*. Research Preview. Washington, D.C.: NIJ.

National Institute on Drug Abuse. 1985. *Highlights from Drugs and American High School Students, 1975–1983*. Washington, D.C.: U.S. Government Printing Office.

National Institute on Drug Abuse. 2000. At <www.nida.nih.gov>.

National Insurance Crime Bureau. 1999. "Mini Vans, SUVs and Pick-Ups at Top of Vehicle Thieves Shopping List." At <www.nicb.com/minivan2.html>.

National Narcotics Intelligence Consumers Committee. 1993. *The NNICC Report 1992*. Washington, D.C.: U.S. Drug Enforcement Administration.

National Retail Security Survey. 1999. University of Florida.

Nee, Claire. 1993. "Car Theft: The Offender's Perspective." *Home Office Research Findings* (February): 1–4.

Nelson, Candace, and Lin Huff-Corzine. 1998. "Strangers in the Night: An Application of the Lifestyle-Rating Activities Approach to Elderly Homicide Victimization." *Homicide Studies* 2, no. 2 (May): 130–159.

Nelson, Candice, Jay Corzine, and Lin Huff-Corzine. 1994. "The Violent West Reexamined: A Research Note on Regional Homicide Rates." *Criminology* 32:149–161.

Nelson, Stephen. 1988. "To Catch a Thief." *INC* (January): 89–90.

Nettler, Gwynne. 1974. "Embezzlement without Problems." *British Journal of Criminology* 14:70–77.

Nettler, Gwynne. 1988. "Christian Science vs. Social Science: Michalowski vs. Gibbs." *The Criminologist* 13 (2): 4–5.

Newburn, Tim. 1993. "The Long-Term Impact of Criminal Victimization." *Home Office Research Bulletin* 33:30–34.

Newman, Donald J. 1958. "White-Collar Crime." *Law and Contemporary Problems* 283:735–753.

Newman, Graeme R. 1978. *The Punishment Response*. Philadelphia, PA: Lippincott.

Newman, Graeme R. 1979. *Understanding Violence*. Philadelphia, PA: Lippincott.

Newman, Graeme, Ronald V. Clarke, and S. Giora Shoham, eds. 1997. *Rational Choice and Situational Crime Prevention: Theoretical Foundations* Aldershot, UK: Dartmouth; Brookfield, CT: Ashgate.

Newman, Graeme R., Jean C. Jester, and Donald J. Articolo. 1981. "A Structural Analysis of Fraud." In *The New and the Old Criminology*. Ed. Edith Flynn and John P. Conrad. New York: Praeger.

Newman, Graeme R., and Pietro Marongiu. 1990. "Penological Reform and the Myth of Beccaria." *Criminology* 28:325–346.

Newman, Graeme R., Ronald V. Clarke, and S. Shoham. 1997. *Rational Choice and Situational Crime Prevention: Theoretical Foundations*. Aldershot, UK: Ashgate.

Newman, Oscar. 1972. *Defensible Space: Crime Prevention through Urban Design*. New York: Macmillan.

Newton, George D., and Franklin E. Zimring. 1969. *Firearms and Violence in America*. Washington, D.C.: U.S. Government Printing Office.

Niederhoffer, Arthur J. 1967. *Behind the Shield: The Police in Urban Society*. New York: Anchor.

Nielsen, Marianne O. 2000. "Stolen Lands, Stolen Lives: Native Americans and Criminal Justice." In *Investigating Difference: Human and Cultural Difference in Criminal Justice*. Ed. The Criminal Justice Collective of Northern Arizona University. Boston, MA: Allyn and Bacon.

Nielsen, Marianne O., and Robert A. Silverman. 1996. *Native Americans, Crime, and Justice*. Boulder, CO: Westview.

Nobile, Philip, and Eric Nadler. 1986. *United States of America vs. Sex*. New York: Minotaur Press.

Normandeau, Andre. 1968. *Trends and Patterns in Crimes of Robbery*. Ph.D. diss., University of Pennsylvania.

Nurco, David N., Thomas E. Hanlon, Timothy W. Kinlock, and Karen R. Duszynski. 1988. "Differential Crime Patterns of Narcotic Addicts over an Addictive Career." *Criminology* 26:407–423.

O'Brien, Robert M. 1991. "Sex Ratios and Rape Rates: A Power Control Theory." *Criminology* 29:99–114.

O'Brien, Robert M. 1996. "Police Productivity and Crime Rates: 1973–1992." *Criminology* 34: 183–207.

Occupational Safety and Health Administration. 2000a. *OSHA Facts*. Washington, D.C.: U.S. Department of Labor. At <www.osha.gov>.

Occupational Safety and Health Administration. 2000b. "OSHA Cites Four Contractors in Connection with Double Fatality in Boston Harbor Tunnel." Press Release, January 19. Washington, D.C.: U.S. Department of Labor. At <www.osha.gov>.

Occupational Safety and Health Administration. 2000c. "Companies Fined in Miller Park Worker Deaths." Press Release. Washington, D.C.: U.S. Department of Labor. At <www.osha.gov>.

Occupational Safety and Health Administration. 2000d. "Big Dig Contractor Cited by OSHA for Alleged Workplace Safety Violation in Fatal Fall of Worker." Press Release, October 5. Washington, D.C.: U.S. Department of Labor. At <www.osha.gov>.

Occupational Safety and Health Administration. 2000e. "OSHA Fines Dublin, GA, Company Following Worker Fall." Press Release, October 6. Washington, D.C.: U.S. Department of Labor. At <www.osha.gov>.

O'Conner, Thomas. 1998. "The Contributions of Marx, Weber, and Simmel." In *Cutting the Edge*. Ed. Jeffrey Ian Ross. New York: Garland.

Odem, Mary E., and Jody Clay-Warner. 1998. *Confronting Rape and Sexual Assault*. Wilmington, DE: SR Books.

Office of Justice Programs. 1996. At <www.ojp.usdoj.gov>.

Office of Justice Programs. 1997. At <www.ojp.usdoj.gov>.

Office of Justice Programs. 1998. At <www.ojp.usdoj.gov>.

Office of Justice Programs. 1999. At <www.ojp.usdoj.gov>.

Office of Juvenile Justice and Delinquency Prevention. 1999. *Violence after School*. Washington, D.C.: U.S. Department of Justice.

O'Keefe, Maura, and Michal Sela-Amit. 1997. "An Examination of the Effects of Race/Ethnicity and Social Class on Adolescents' Exposure to Violence." *Journal of Social Service Research* 22 (3): 53–71.

O'Leary, Vincent, and Kathleen Hanrahan. 1977. "Law and Practice in Parole Proceedings: A National survey." *Criminal Law Bulletin* 13:205–211.

O'Malley, Pat, and Stephen Mugford. 1991. "Crime, Excitement and Modernity." Presented at the annual meeting of the American Society of Criminology, November 18–23, San Francisco, CA.

Orchowsky, S. 1998. *Unique Nature of Domestic Violence in Rural Areas*. Justice Research and Statistics Association. Washington, D.C.: U.S. Dept of Justice, Bureau of Justice Statistics.

Orsagh, Thomas. 1980. "Unemployment and Crime." *Journal of Criminal Law and Criminology* 71:181–183.

Osgood, D. Wayne, Martin Gold, and Carolyn Miller. 1986. "For Better or Worse?: Peer Attachment and Peer Influence among Incarcerated Adults. A Paper presented at the annual meeting of the American Society of Criminology, Atlanta, GA.

Pace, Denny F., and Jimmie Y. Styles. 1983. *Organized Crime: Concepts and Control*. Englewood Cliffs, NJ: Prentice Hall.

Packer, Herbert L. 1964. "The Crime Tariff." *American Scholar* 33:551–557.

Packer, Herbert L. 1968. *The Limits of the Criminal Sanction*. Stanford, CA: Stanford University Press.

Palley, Howard A., and Dana A. Robinson. 1988. "Black on Black Crime." *Society* 25:59–62.

Palmer, Stuart. 1968. "Murder and Suicide in Forty Non-Literate Societies." *Journal of Criminal Law, Criminology, and Police Science* 56:320–324.

Parent, Dale G. 1989. *Shock Incarceration: An Overview of Existing Programs*. Washington, D.C.: U.S. Department of Justice.

Parker, Howard J. 1974. *View from the Boys*. London, UK: David and Charles.

Paschall, Mallie J., Robert L. Flewelling, and Susan T. Ennett. 1998. "Racial Differences in Violent Behavior among Young Adults: Moderating and Confounding Effects." *The Journal of Research in Crime and Delinquency* 35:148–185.

Passas, Nikos. 1993. "Structural Sources of International Crime: Policy Lessons from the BCCI Affair." *Crime, Law and Social Change* 20:293–309.

Passes, Nikos. 1995. *Organized Crime*. Aldershot, UK: Ashgate.

Passas, Nikos. 1999. *Transnational Crime*. Aldershot, UK: Ashgate.

Passas, Nikos, and Robert Agnew. 1997. *The Future of Anomie Theory*. Boston, MA: Northeastern University Press.

Paternoster, Raymond. 1983. "The Decision to Seek the Death Penalty in South Carolina." *Journal of Criminal Law and Criminology* 74:754–787.

Paternoster, Raymond. 1987. "The Deterrent Effect of the Perceived Certainty and Severity of Punishment: A Review of the Evidence and Issues." *Justice Quarterly* 4:173–217.

Paternoster, Raymond, and Robert Brame. 1998. "The Structural Similarity of Processes Generating Criminal and Analogous Behaviors." *Criminology* 36, no. 3 (August): 633–669.

Paternoster, Raymond, and Paul Mazerolle. 1994. "General Strain Theory and Delinquency: A Replication and Extension." *Journal of Research in Crime and Delinquency* 31:235–263.

Paternoster, Raymond, and Ruth Triplett. 1988. "Disaggregating Self Reported Delinquency and Its Implications for Theory." *Criminology* 26:591–620.

Paternoster, Raymond, Linda E. Saltzman, Gordon P. Waldo, and Theodore G. Chiricos. 1983. "Perceived Risk of Social Control: Do Sanctions Really Deter?" *Law and Society Review* 17:457–479.

Paternoster, Raymond, Linda E. Saltzman, Gordon P. Waldo, and Theodore G. Chiricos. 1985. "Assessments of Risk and Behavioral Experience: An Exploratory Study of Change." *Criminology* 23:417–433.

Patterson, E. Britt. 1991. "Poverty, Income Inequality and Community Crime Rates." *Criminology* 29:755–773.

Pearl, Michael. 1974. *The Confessions of a Master Fence*. Cambridge, MA: Schenkman.

Peircey, Marge. 1998. "Rape Poem." In *Confronting Rape and Sexual Assault*. Ed. Mary E. Odem and Jody Clay-Warner. Wilmington, DE: SR Books.

Pennsylvania Crime Commission. 1989. (Untitled). Conshohocken, PA.

Pepinsky, Hal. 1999. "Peacemaking Criminology and Social Justice." In *Social Justice/Criminal Justice: The Maturation of Critical Theory in Law, Crime, and Deviance*. Ed. Bruce A. Arrigo. Belmont, CA: West/Wadsworth.

Pepinsky, Hal. 2000. "Shame and Punishment, Democracy and Anger." *The Red Feather Journal of Postmodern Criminology: An International Journal* 8. At <www.tryoung.com/journal-pomo crim/vol-8-shaming/content.html>.

Pérez, Cynthia. 1991. "United States v. Jacobson: Are Child Pornography Stings Creative Law Enforcement or Entrapment?" *University of Miami Law Review* 46:235–261.

Petersilia, Joan. 1985a. "Racial Disparities in the Criminal Justice System: A Summary." *Crime and Delinquency* 31:15–34.

Petersilia, Joan. 1985b. *Granting Felons Probation: Public Risks and Alternatives*. Santa Monica, CA: Rand Corp.

Petersilia, Joan. 1985c. *Probation and Felony Offenders, NIJ Reports*. Washington, D.C.: National Institute of Justice.

Petersilia, Joan. 1987. *Expanding Options for Criminal Sentencing*. Santa Monica, CA: Rand Corp.

Petersilia, Joan, and S. Turner. 1985. *Guidelines-Based Justice: The Implications for Racial Minorities*. Santa Monica, CA: Rand Corp.

Petersilia, Joan, Allan Abrahamse, and James Q. Wilson. 1990. "The Relationship between Police Practice, Community Characteristics, and Case Attrition." *Policing and Society* 1:23–38.

Peterson, David M., and Paul C. Friday. 1975. "Early Release from Incarceration: Race As a Factor in the Use of 'Shock Probation.'" *Journal of Criminal Law and Criminology* 66:79–87.

Peterson, Mark A., Harriett B. Braiker, and Suzanne M. Polich. 1980. *Doing Crime: A Survey of California Prison Inmates*. Santa Monica, CA: Rand Corp.

Peterson, Ruth D., and William C. Bailey. 1991. "Felony Murder and Capital Punishment: An Examination of the Deterrence Question." *Criminology* 29:367–395.

Petras, James, and Christian Davenport. 1991. "Crime and the Transformation of Capitalism." *Crime, Law, and Social Change* 16:155–175.

Pfohl, Stephen J. 1985. *Images of Deviance and Social Control*. New York: McGraw-Hill.

Phillips, David P. 1983. "The Impact of Mass Media Violence on Homicide." *American Sociological Review* 48:560–568.

Pike, Luke Owen. 1968. *A History of Crime in England*. Vol. 2. Montclair, NJ: Patterson Smith.

Pileggi, Nicholas. 1968. "1968 Has Been the Year of the Burglar." *New York Times Magazine*, 17 November.

Piliavin, Irving, and Scott Briar. 1964. "Police Encounters with Juveniles." *American Journal of Sociology* 70:206–214.

Piliavin, Irving, Rosemary Gartner, Craig Thornton, and Ross L. Matsueda. 1986. "Crime, Deterrence, and Rational Choice." *American Sociological Review* 51:101–119.

Piquero, Alex R., and Matthew Hickman. 1999. "An Empirical Test of Tittle's Control Balance Theory." *Criminology* 37, no. 2 (May): 319–341.

Piquero, Alex, and Raymond Paternoster. 1998. "An Application of Stafford and Warr's Reconceptualization of Deterrence to Drunk Driving." *Journal of Research in Crime and Delinquency* 35 (1): 3–39.

Pittman, David J., and William Handy. 1964. "Patterns in Criminal Aggravated Assault." *Journal of Criminal Law, Criminology, and Police Science* 55:462–470.

Platt, Anthony M. 1971. *The Politics of Riot Commissions*. New York: Macmillan.

Platt, Anthony M. 1974. "Prospects for a Radical Criminology in the United States." *Crime and Social Justice* 1:3–10.

Ploscowe, Morris. 1951. *Sex and the Law*. Englewood Cliffs, NJ: Prentice Hall.

Plucknett, Theodore F. T. 1948. *A Concise History of Common Law*. London, UK: Butterworth.

Pogrebin, Mark R., and Eric D. Poole. 1991. "Police and Tragic Events: The Management of Emotions." *Journal of Criminal Justice* 19:395–403.

Pogrebin, Mark R., and Eric D. Poole. 1993. "Vice Isn't Nice: A Look at Working Undercover." *Journal of Criminal Justice* 21:383–394.

Polk, Kenneth. 1991. "Male-to-Male Homicides: Scenarios of Masculine Violence." Presented at annual meeting of the American Society of Criminology, November 18–23, San Francisco, CA.

Polk, Kenneth. 1998. "Violence, Masculinity, and Evolution: A Comment on Wilson and Daly." *Theoretical Criminology* 2, no. 4 (November): 461–469.

Pollock-Byrne, Joycelyn M. 1990. *Women, Prison and Crime*. Pacific Grove, CA: Brooks/Cole.

Pollock, Sir Frederick, and Frederick William Maitland. 1968. *The History of English Law*. Vol. 2. 2d ed. Cambridge, UK: Cambridge University Press.

Polsky, Howard W. 1962. *Cottage Six*. New York: Wiley.

Polsky, Ned. 1967. *Hustlers, Beats, and Others*. Chicago, IL: Aldine.

Pontell, Henry N. 1984. *A Capacity to Punish*. Bloomington, IN: Indiana University Press.

Pontell, Henry N., and Kitty Calavita. 1993. "The Savings and Loan Industry." In *Beyond the Law: Crime in Complex Organizations*. Ed. Michael Tonry and Albert J. Reiss Jr. Chicago, IL: University of Chicago Press.

Pope, Carl C., and William Feyerherm. 1991. "Minority Status and Juvenile Justice Processing." *Criminal Justice Abstracts* 22:327–336 (Part 1); 22:527–542 (Part 2).

Porcer, Anthony C. 1993. "Supreme Court Review." *Journal of Criminal Law and Criminology* 83:868–892.

Porkorny, Alex D. 1965. "Human Violence: A Comparison of Homicide, Aggravated Assault, and Attempted Suicide." *Journal of Criminal Law, Criminology, and Police Science* 56:488–497.

Pornfeld, Mayde, and Candace Kruttschnitt. 1992. "Do the Stereotypes Fit? Mapping of Gender-Specific Outcomes and Risk Factors." *Criminology* 30:397–419.

Post, James E., and Edwin Baer. 1978. "Demarketing Infant Formula: Consumer Products for the Developing World." *Journal of Contemporary Business* 7:17–37.

Pound, Roscoe. 1923. *Interpretations of Legal History*. New York: Macmillan.

Pound, Roscoe. 1943. "A Survey of Social Interests." *Harvard Law Review* 57:1–39.

Powers, Edwin, and Helen L. Witmer. 1951. *An Experiment in the Prevention of Delinquency: The Cambridge-Somerville Study*. New York: Columbia University Press.

Pratt, Michael. 1980. *Mugging As a Social Problem*. London, UK: Routledge and Kegan Paul.

Pratt, Travis C., and Francis T. Cullen. 2000. "The Empirical Status of Gottfredson and Hirschi's General Theory of Crime: A Meta-Analysis." *Criminology* 38 (3): 931–964.

Preble, Edward A., and John J. Casey. 1969. "Taking Care of Business—The Heroin User's Life on the Street." *International Journal of the Addictions* 4:8–12.

President's Commission on Law Enforcement and the Administration of Justice. 1967a. *Task Force Report: Organized Crime*. Washington, D.C.: U.S. Government Printing Office.

President's Commission on Law Enforcement and the Administration of Justice. 1967b. *Task Force Report: The Courts*. Washington, D.C.: U.S. Government Printing Office.

President's Commission on Law Enforcement and the Administration of Justice. 1969. *Task Force Report: Crime and Its Impact*. Washington, D.C.: U.S. Government Printing Office.

Pringle, Patrick. n.d. *Stand and Deliver: The Story of the Highwayman*. New York: Norton.

Prothrow-Stith, Deborah. 1991. *Deadly Consequences*. New York: HarperCollins.

Pyle, Gerald F. 1976. "Spatial and Temporal Aspects of Crime in Cleveland, Ohio." *American Behavioral Scientist* 20:175–178.

Quetelet, Adolphe. 1835. *Sur l'Homme et le Développment de Ses Facultés; un Essai de Physique Sociale*. Paris, France.

Quina, Kathryn, and N. Carlson. 1989. *Rape, Incest, and Sexual Harassment*. New York: Praeger.

Quinney, Richard. 1963. "Occupational Structure and Criminal Behavior: Prescription Violations by Retail Pharmacists." *Social Problems* 2:179–183.

Quinney, Richard. 1970. *The Problem of Crime*. New York: Dodd, Mead.

Quinney, Richard. 1974. *Critique of Legal Order: Crime Control in Capitalistic Society*. Boston, MA: Little, Brown.

Quinney, Richard. 1975. *Criminology: Analysis and Critique of Crime in America*. Boston, MA: Little, Brown.

Quinney, Richard. 1977. *Class, State, and Crime*. New York: Longman.

Quinney, Richard. 1979. *Criminology*. 2d ed. Boston, MA: Little, Brown.

Quinney, Richard, and Hal Pepinsky. 1991. *Criminology As Peacemaking*. Bloomington, IN: Indiana University Press.

Rada, Richard. 1975. "Alcohol and Rape." *Medical Aspects of Human Sexuality* 9:48–65.

Rada, Richard. 1976. "Testosterone Levels in the Rapist." *Psychosomatic Medicine* 38:257–268.

Radcliffe-Brown, A. R. 1948. *The Andaman Islanders*. New York: Free Press.

Radelet, Michael L. 1990. "Post-Furman Botched Executions." *Lifelines* (September/October): 7.

Radzinowicz, Leon. 1966. *Ideology and Crime*. New York: Columbia University Press.

Rafter, Nicole Hahn, and Frances Heidensohn. 1997. *International Feminist Perspectives in Criminology: Engendering a Discipline*. Buckingham, UK: Open University Press.

Ragonese, Paul. 1991. *The Soul of a Cop*. New York: St. Martin's Press.

Rand, Michael. 1990. *Handgun Crime Victims*. Washington, D.C.: U.S. Department of Justice.

Rand, Michael R. 1994a. "Carjacking." *BJS Crime Data Brief* (March): 1–2.

Rand, Michael R. 1994b. "Guns and Crime." *Crime Data Brief* (April): 1–2.

Rankin, Joseph. 1979. "Changing Attitudes toward Capital Punishment." *Social Forces* 58:194–211.

Rasche, Christine E. 1993. "'Given' Reasons for Violence in Intimate Relationships." In *Homicide: The Victim/Offender Connection*. Ed. Anna Victoria Wilson. Cincinnati, OH: Anderson.

Ratner, Mitchell S. 1994. *Crack Pipe As Pimp: An Ethnographic Investigation of Sex-for-Crack Exchanges*. New York: Lexington Books.

Rau, Richard M. 1991. "Forensic Science and Criminal Justice Technology: High Tech Tools for the 90s." *NIJ Research in Action* (June): 1–10.

Rawlinson, Patricia. 1998. "Mafia, Media, and Myth: Representations of Russian Organized Crime." *Howard Journal of Criminal Justice* 37 (4): 346–358.

Reasons, Charles E. 1974. *The Criminologist: Crime and the Criminal*. Pacific Palisades, CA: Goodyear Publishing.

Reasons, Charles E., and Russell L. Kaplan. 1975. "Tear Down the Walls?—Some Functions of Prisons." *Crime and Delinquency* 21:360–372.

Reaves, Brian. 1992. "Pretrial Release of Felony Defendants, 1990." *BJS Bulletin* (November): 1–14.

Reaves, Brian. 1993. "Pretrial Release of Felony Defendants." *BJS Bulletin* (November): 1–17.

Reckless, Walter. 1973. *The Crime Problem*. 5th ed. Englewood Cliffs, NJ: Prentice Hall.

Reckless, Walter C., and Simon Dinitz. 1967. "Pioneering with Self-Concept As a Vulnerability Factor in Delinquency." *Journal of Criminal Law, Criminology, and Police Science* 58:515–523.

Reed, Gary E., and Peter Cleary Yeager. 1996. "Organizational Offending and Neoclassical Criminology: Challenging the Reach of a General

Theory of Crime." *Criminology* 34, no. 3 (August): 357–382.

Reed, John Shelton. 1971. "To Live … and die … in Dixie: A Contribution to the Study of Southern Violence." *Political Science Quarterly* 86:424–443.

Reed, John Shelton. 1977. "Below the Smith and Wesson Line: Reflections on Southern Violence." Lecture to the second annual Hugo Black Symposium, Birmingham, AL.

Reichman, Nancy. 1993. "Insider Trading." In *Beyond the Law: Crime in Complex Organizations*. Ed. Michael Tonry and Albert J. Reiss Jr. Chicago, IL: University of Chicago Press.

Reid, Sue Titus. 1989. *Criminal Law*. New York: Macmillan.

Reilly, Michael J. 1992. "Racketeering and Organized Crime in the Bingo Industry." *Criminal Organizations* 7:8–11.

Reiman, Jeffrey. 1984. *The Rich Get Richer and the Poor Get Prison*. 2d ed. New York: Wiley.

Reiman, Jeffrey. 1997. *The Rich Get Richer and the Poor Get Prison*. 5th ed. Boston, MA: Allyn and Bacon.

Reiman, Jeffrey. 2001. *The Rich Get Richer and the Poor Get Prison: Ideology, Class, and Criminal Justice*. 6th ed. Boston, MA: Allyn and Bacon.

Reiss, Albert J., Jr. 1970. "Police Brutality: Answers to Key Questions." In *Law and Order: Police Encounters*. Ed. Michael Lipsky. Chicago, IL: Aldine.

Reiss, Albert J., Jr. 1971. *The Police and the Public*. New Haven, CT: Yale University Press.

Reiss, Albert J., Jr. 1988. "Private Employment of Public Police." *NIJ Research in Brief* (December): 1–6.

Reiss, Albert J., Jr., and Jeffrey A. Roth, eds. 1993. *Understanding and Preventing Violence*. Washington, D.C.: National Academy Press.

Reiss, Albert J., Jr., and Michael Tonry, eds. 1986. *Communities and Crime*. Chicago, IL: University of Chicago Press.

Remington, Frank J., Donald J. Newman, Edward L. Kimball, Marygold Melli, and Herman Goldstein. 1969. *Criminal Justice Administration*. Indianapolis, IN: Bobbs-Merrill.

Rengert, George F., Alex R. Piquero, and Peter R. Jones. 1999. "Distance Decay Reexamined." *Criminology* 37, no. 2 (May): 427–445.

Rennison, Callie Marie. 2000. *Criminal Victimization 1999: Changes 1998–99 with Trends 1993–99*. Washington, D.C.: Bureau of Justice Statistics.

Renzetti, Claire M. 1992. *Violent Betrayal: Partner Abuse in Lesbian Relationships*. Thousand Oaks, CA: Sage.

Renzetti, Claire M. 1998. "Violence and Abuse in Lesbian Relationships: Theoretical and Empirical Issues." In *Issues in Intimate Violence*. Ed. Raquel Kennedy Bergen. Thousand Oaks, CA: Sage.

Renzetti, Claire M., and Lynne Goodstein. 2001. *Women, Crime, and Criminal Justice: Original Feminist Readings*. Los Angeles, CA: Roxbury.

Reppetto, Thomas A. 1974. *Residential Crime*. Cambridge, MA: Ballinger.

Reuter, Peter. 1983. *Disorganized Crime: Illegal Markets and the Mafia*. Cambridge, MA: MIT Press.

Reuter, Peter, and Mark Kleiman. 1986. "Risks and Prices: An Economic Analysis of Drug Enforcement." In *Crime and Justice: An Annual Review of Research*. Vol. 7. Ed. Michael Tonry and Norval Morris. Chicago, IL: University of Chicago Press.

Reuter, Peter, Jonathon Rubinstein, and Simon Winn. 1983. *Racketeering in Legitimate Industries: Two Case Studies*. Washington, D.C.: U.S. Department of Justice.

Rideau, Wilbert, and Ron Wikberg. 1992. *Life Sentences: Rage and Survival behind Bars*. New York: New York Times Books.

Riedel, Marc. 1993. *Stranger Violence*. New York: Garland.

Riedel, Marc, and Margaret A. Zahn. 1985. *The Nature and Patterns of American Homicide*. Washington, D.C.: National Institute of Justice.

Riis, Roger, and John Patric. 1942. *The Repairman Will Get You If You Don't Watch Out*. New York: Doubleday.

Riley, D. 1980. "An Evaluation of a Campaign to Reduce Vandalism." In *Designing Out Crime*. Ed. Ronald V. Clarke and Pat Mayhew. London, UK: H.M.S.O.

Ritzer, George. 1990. *Frontiers of Social Theory: The New Synthesis*. New York: Columbia University Press.

Roberts, Julian V., and Loretta J. Stalans. 1997. *Public Opinion, Crime, and Criminal Justice*. Boulder, CO: Westview.

Robin, Gerald D. 1967. "The Corporate and Judicial Disposition of Employee Thieves." *Wisconsin Law Review* (summer): 635–702.

Robin, Gerald D. 1987. *Introduction to the Criminal Justice System*. 3d ed. New York: Harper & Row.

Robin, Gerald D. 1991. *Violent Crime and Gun Control*. Cincinnati, OH: Anderson.

Robinson, Matthew B., and Barbara H. Zaitow. 1999. "Criminologists: Are We What We Study?" *The Criminologist* 24 (2): 1, 4, 17–19.

Rock, Paul. 1973. "Feature Review Symposium." *Sociological Quarterly* 14:595.

Rockwell, Robin. 1990. "The Advent of Computer Related Crimes." *Secured Lender* (July/August): 40–42.

Roebuck, Julian B., and Thomas Barker. 1974. "A Typology of Police Corruption." In *Crime Prevention and Social Control*. Ed. Ronald L. Akers and Edward Sagarin. New York: Praeger.

Roebuck, Julian B., and Ronald C. Johnson. 1964. "The 'Short Con' Man." *Crime and Delinquency* 10:235–248.

Rolph, C. H. 1955. *Women of the Streets*. London, UK: Secker and Warburg.

Romenesko, Kim, and Eleanor M. Miller. 1989. "The Second Step in Double Jeopardy: Appropriating the Labor of Female Street Hustlers." *Crime and Delinquency* 35:109–135.

Roncek, Dennis W. 1981. "Dangerous Places: Crime and Residential Environment." *Social Forces* 60:74–96.

Roncek, Dennis W., and Pamela A. Maier. 1991. "Bars, Blocks, and Crimes Revisited: Linking the Theory of Routine Activities to the Empiricism of 'Hot Spots.'" *Criminology* 29: 725–753.

Rose, Dina R., and Todd R. Clear. 1998. "Incarceration, Social Capital, and Crime: Implications for Social Disorganization Theory." *Criminology* 36 (3): 441–480.

Rose, Harold M., and Paula McClain. 1981. *Black Homicide and the Urban Environment*. Rockville, MD: National Institute of Mental Health.

Rosefsky, Robert S. 1973. *Frauds, Swindles, and Rackets*. Chicago, IL: Follett.

Rosenbaum, Dennis P., ed. 1994. *The Challenge of Community Policing*. Thousand Oaks, CA: Sage.

Rosenbaum, Dennis P., and Gordon S. Hanson. 1998. "Assessing Effects of School-Based Drug Education: A Six-Year Multilevel Analysis of Project DARE." *Journal of Research in Crime and Delinquency* 35 (4): 381–412.

Rosenfeld, Richard. 1996. "Gun Buy-Backs: Crime Control or Community Mobilization?" In *Under Fire: Gun Buy-Backs, Exchanges, and Amnesty Programs*. Ed. M. Plotkin. Washington, D.C.: Police Executive Research Forum.

Rosett, Arthur, and Donald R. Cressey. 1976. *Justice by Consent*. Philadelphia, PA: Lippincott.

Rosoff, Stephen M., Henry N. Pentell, and Robert Tillman. 1994. *Profit without Honor: White-Collar Crime and the Looting of America*. Upper Saddle River, NJ: Prentice Hall.

Ross, H. Laurence. 1982. "Interrupted Time Series Studies of Deterrence of Drinking and Driving." In *Deterrence Reconsidered: Methodological Innovations*. Ed. John Hagan. Beverly Hills, CA: Sage.

Ross, Jeffrey Ian. 1995. *Controlling State Crime: An Introduction*. New York: Garland.

Ross, Jeffrey Ian. 2000. *Varieties of State Crime and Its Control*. Monsey, NY: Criminal Justice Press.

Rossi, Peter H., Emily Waite, Christine E. Bose, and Richard E. Berk. 1974. "The Seriousness of Crimes: Normative Structure and Individual Differences." *American Sociological Review* 39: 224–237.

Roth, Jeffrey A. 1994. "Psychoactive Substances and Violence." *NIJ Research in Brief* (February): 1–8.

Roth, Jeffrey A. 1994a. "Understanding and Preventing Violence." *NIJ Research in Brief* (February): 1–11

Roth, Jeffrey A. 1994b. "Firearms and Violence." *NIJ Research in Brief* (February): 1–7.

Rothman, David J. 1994. "The Crime of Punishment." *The New York Review of Books* 41:34–38.

Rountree, Pamela Wilcox, Kenneth C. Land, and Terrence C. Miethe. 1994. "Macro-Micro in the Study of Victimization: A Hierarchical Logistic Model Analysis across Seattle Neighborhoods." *Criminology* 32 (3): 387–409.

Rowe, Alan, John H. Lindquist, and O. Z. White. 1989. "A Note on the Family and Crime in the United States." *Psychological Reports* 65: 1001–1002.

Rowe, David C. 1986. "Genetic and Environmental Components of Antisocial Behavior: A Study of 265 Twin Pairs." *Criminology* 23:223–240.

Rowe, David C., and W. D. Osgood. 1984. "Heredity and Sociological Theories of Delinquency: A Reconsideration." *American Sociological Review* 49:526–540.

Rowe, David C., and Joseph L. Rodgers. 1988. "The Etiology of Deviance: Sibling Mutual Influence, Heredity, and 'D.'" Presented to the Society for Research on Adolescence, March.

Rowe, David C., Wayne D. Osgood, and Alan D. Nicewander. 1990. "A Latent Trait Approach to Unifying Criminal Careers." *Criminology* 28:230–237.

Rubin, Sol. 1965. "Cops, Guns, and Homicides." *The Nation* (December 27): 527–531.

Rubinstein, Jonathan. 1973. *City Police*. New York: Farrar, Straus & Giroux.

Rubinstein, Michael L., Stevens H. Clarke, and Teresa J. White. 1980. *Alaska Bans Plea Bargaining*. Washington, D.C.: U.S. Department of Justice.

Runkle, Gerald. 1976. "Is Violence Always Wrong?" *Journal of Politics* 38:367–389.

Russell, Diana E. H. 1983. *Rape in Marriage*. New York: Collier.

Rynbrandt, Linda J., and Ronald C. Kramer. 1995. "Hybrid Nonwomen and Corporate Violence: The Silicone Breast Implant Case." *Violence against Women* 1 (3): 206–227.

Rynbrandt, Linda J., and Ronald C. Kramer. 2001. "Corporate Violence against Women." In *Women, Crime, and Criminal Justice: Original Feminist Readings*. Ed. Claire M. Renzetti and Lynne Goodstein. Los Angeles, CA: Roxbury.

Sagalyn, Arnold. 1971. *The Crime of Robbery in the U.S.* Washington, D.C.: National Institute of Law Enforcement and Administration Justice.

Sagarin, Edward. 1974. "Sexual Criminality." In *Current Perspectives on Criminal Behavior*. Ed. Abraham S. Blumberg. New York: Knopf.

Sagarin, Edward. 1979. *Criminology: New Concerns*. Beverly Hills, CA: Sage.

Salerno, Ralph, and John S. Tompkins. 1969. *The Crime Confederation*. Garden City, NY: Doubleday.

Sampson, Robert J. 1985. "Race and Criminal Violence: A Demographically Disaggregated Analysis of Urban Homicide." *Crime and Delinquency* 31:47–82.

Sampson, Robert J. 1986. "Crime in Cities: The Effects of Formal and Informal Social Control." In *Communities and Crime*. Ed. Albert J. Reiss and Michael Tonry. Chicago, IL: University of Chicago Press.

Sampson, Robert J. 1987a. "Communities and Crime." In *Positive Criminology*. Ed. Michael R. Gottfredson and Travis Hirschi. Beverly Hills, CA: Sage.

Sampson, Robert J. 1987b. "Urban Black Violence: The Effect of Male Joblessness and Family Disruption." *American Journal of Sociology* 93: 348–382.

Sampson, Robert J., and Jacqueline Cohen. 1988. "Deterrent Effects of the Police on Crime: A Replication and Theoretical Extension." *Law and Society Review* 22:163–189.

Sampson, Robert J., and John Laub. 1990. "Crime and Deviance over the Life Course: The Salience of Adult Social Bonds." *American Sociological Review* 55:609–627.

Sampson, Robert J., and John Laub. 1992. "Crime and Deviance in the Life Course." *Annual Review of Sociology* 18:63–84.

Sampson, Robert J., and John Laub. 1993a. "Structural Variations in Juvenile Court Processing: Inequality, the Underclass and Social Control." *Law and Society Review* 27:285–312.

Sampson, Robert J., and John Laub. 1993b. *Crime in the Making*. Cambridge, MA: Harvard University Press.

Sampson, Robert J., and William Julius Wilson. 1991. "Toward a Theory of Race, Crime, and Urban Inequality." Paper presented to the annual meeting of the American Society of Criminology, November 21, San Francisco, CA.

Sampson, Robert J., Stephen W. Raudenbush, and Felton Earls. 1997. "Neighborhoods and Violent Crime: A Multilevel Study of Collective Efficacy." *Science* 277, no. 5328 (August): 918–924.

San Marco, Louise R. 1979. "Differential Sentencing Patterns among Criminal Homicide Offenders in Harris County, Texas." Ph.D. diss., Sam Houston State University.

Sanchez Jankowski, Martin. 1991. *Islands in the Street: Gangs and American Urban Society*. Berkeley, CA: University of California Press.

Sanday, Peggy Reeves. 1996. *A Woman Scorned: Acquaintance Rape on Trial*. New York: Doubleday.

Sanders, William B. 1977. *Detective Work: A Study of Criminal Investigations*. New York: Free Press.

Sanders, William B. 1983. *Criminology*. Reading, MA: Addison-Wesley.

Sanders, William B. 1994. *Gangbangs and Drive-bys*. New York: Aldine de Gruyter.

San Francisco Task Force on Prostitution. 2000. At <www.bayswan.org/1TF.html>.

Saunders, Edward J. 1986. "Judicial Attitudes toward Child Sexual Abuse: A Preliminary Examination." *Judicature* 70:95–98.

Schafer, Stephen. 1969. *Theories in Criminology*. New York: Random House.

Schafer, Stephen. 1971. "The Concept of the Political Criminal." *Journal of Criminal Law, Criminology, and Police Science* 62:380–387.

Schelling, Thomas D. 1967. "Economic Analysis of Organized Crime." In *Task Force Report: Organized Crime*. President's Commission on Law Enforcement and the Administration of Justice. Washington, D.C.: U.S. Government Printing Office.

Schlegel, Kip, and David Weisburd. 1992. *White-Collar Crime Reconsidered*. Boston, MA: Northeastern University Press.

Schlosser, Eric. 1994. "Reefer Madness." *Atlantic Monthly* (August): 45–63.

Schmidt, Amesley K. 1985. "Deaths in the Line of Duty." *NIJ Reports* (January): 6.

Schneider, Anne L. 1977. *The Portland Forward Check of Crime Victims: Final Report*. Eugene, OR: Oregon Research Institute.

Schneider, Hans Joachim. 1997. "Sexual Abuse of Children: Strengths and Weaknesses of Current Criminology." *International Journal of Offender Therapy and Comparative Criminology* 41:310–324.

Schrager, Laura. S., and James F. Short. 1978. "Toward a Sociology of Organizational Crime." *Social Problems* 25:407–419.

Schuessler, Karl. 1954. "Review." *American Journal of Sociology* 49:604–610.

Schwartz, Martin D., and Walter S. DeKesseredy. 1997. *Sexual Assault on the College Campus: The Role of Male Peer Support*. Thousand Oaks, CA: Sage.

Schwartz, Martin D., and David O. Friedrichs. 1994. "Postmodern Thought and Criminological Discontent: New Metaphors for Understanding Violence." *Criminology* 32:221–246.

Schwartz, Michael, and Sandra S. Tangri. 1965. "A Note on Self-Concept As an Insulator against Delinquency." *American Sociological Review* 30:922–926.

Schwendinger, Herman, and Julia Schwendinger. 1970. "Defenders of Order or Guardians of Human Rights?" *Issues in Criminology* 5 (2): 123–157.

Schwendinger, Herman, and Julia Siegel Schwendinger. 1985. *Adolescent Subcultures and Delinquency*. New York: Praeger.

Schwendinger, Julia Siegel, and Herman Schwendinger. 1983. *Rape and Inequality*. Newbury Park, CA: Sage Publications.

Scraton, Phil, Joe Sim, and Paula Skidmore. 1991. *Prisons under Protest*. Milton Keynes, UK: Open University Press.

Scull, Andrew T. 1977. *Decarceration: Community Treatment and the Deviant—A Radical View*. Englewood Cliffs, NJ: Prentice Hall.

Scully, Diana, and Joseph Marolla. 1985. "Riding the Bull at Gilley's: Convicted Rapists Describe the Rewards of Rape." *Social Problems* 32:251–263.

Searles, Patricia, and Ronald J. Berger. 1995. *Rape and Society: Readings in the Problem of Sexual Assault*. Boulder, CO: Westview.

Sellin, Thorsten. 1935. "Race Prejudice in the Administration of Justice." *American Journal of Sociology* 41:212–217.

Sellin, Thorsten. 1937. "The Lombrosian Myth in Criminology." *American Journal of Sociology* 42:898–899.

Sellin, Thorsten. 1938. *Culture Conflict and Crime*. New York: Social Science Research Council.

Sellin, Thorsten, and Marvin E. Wolfgang. 1964. *The Measurement of Delinquency*. New York: Wiley.

Shaffer, Howard J., and Stephanie B. Jones. 1989. *Quitting Cocaine*. Lexington, MA: Lexington Books.

Shannon, Lyle W. 1982. *Assessing the Relationship of Adult Criminal Careers to Juvenile Careers: A Summary*. Washington, D.C.: U.S. Department of Justice.

Shannon, Lyle W. 1991. *Changing Patterns of Delinquency and Crime*. Boulder, CO: Westview Press.

Shapiro, Susan. 1990. "Collaring the Crime, Not the Criminal: Reconsidering the Concept of White-Collar Crime." *American Sociological Review* 55:346–365.

Shaw, Clifford R. 1930. *The Jack-Roller: A Delinquent Boy's Own Story*. Chicago, IL: University of Chicago Press.

Shaw, Clifford R. 1931a. *Delinquency Areas*. Chicago, IL: University of Chicago Press.

Shaw, Clifford R. 1931b. *The Natural History of a Delinquent Career*. Chicago, IL: University of Chicago Press.

Shaw, Clifford R., and Henry D. McKay. 1942. *Juvenile Delinquency and Urban Areas*. Chicago, IL: University of Chicago Press.

Shaw, Clifford R., Henry D. McKay, and James F. McDonald. 1938. *Brothers in Crime*. Chicago, IL: University of Chicago Press.

Shearing, Clifford D. 1979. "Subterranean Processes, the Maintenance of Power: An Examination of the Mechanisms Coordinating Police Action." Presented to the annual meeting of the American Sociological Association, August 17–21.

Sheehy, Gail. 1973. *Hustling: Prostitution in Our Wide-Open Society*. New York: Delacorte.

Shelley, Louise. 1981. *Crime and Modernization*. Edwardsville and Carbondale, IL: Southern Illinois University Press.

Sherman, Lawrence W. 1992. "Attacking Crime: Police and Crime Control." In *Modern Policing*. Ed. Michael Tonry and Norval Morris. Chicago, IL: University of Chicago Press.

Sherman, Lawrence W. 1993. "Defiance, Deterrence, and Irrelevance: A Theory of the Criminal Sanction." *Journal of Research in Crime and Delinquency* 30:445–471.

Sherman, Lawrence W., and Richard Berk. 1984. "Specific Deterrent Effects of Arrest for Domestic Assault." *American Sociological Review* 49:261–272.

Sherman, Lawrence W., and Dennis P. Rogan. 1995. "Effects of Gun Seizures on Gun Violence: 'Hot Spots' Patrol in Kansas City." *Justice Quarterly* 12:673–693.

Sherman, Lawrence W., Patrick R. Gartin, and Michael Buerger. 1989. "Hot Spots of Predatory Crime: Routine Activities and the Criminology of Place." *Criminology* 27:27–55.

Sherman, Lawrence W., James W. Shaw, and Dennis P. Rogan. 1995. "The Kansas City Gun Experiment." *NIJ Research in Brief* (January): 1–11.

Sherman, Lawrence W., Janell D. Schmidt, Dennis P. Rogan, Patrick R. Gartin, Ellen G. Cohn, Dean J. Collins, and Anthony R. Bacich. 1991. "From Initial Deterrence to Long-Term Escalation: Short-Custody Arrest for Poverty Ghetto Domestic Violence." *Criminology* 29:821–850.

Shihadeh, Edwards S., and Graham C. Ousey. 1998. "Industrial Restructuring and Violence: The Link between Entry-Level Jobs, Economic Deprivation and Black and White Homicide." *Social Forces* 77:185–206.

Shoham, Shlomo. 1970. *The Mark of Cain*. Dobbs Ferry, NY: Citadel.

Short, James F. 1990. "Cities, Gangs, and Delinquency." *Sociological Forum* 5 (4): 657–668.

Shover, Neal. 1973. "The Social Organization of Burglary." *Social Problems* 20:499–514.

Shover, Neal. 1983. "The Later Stages of Ordinary Property Offender Careers." *Social Problems* 31:208–218.

Shover, Neal. 1985. *Aging Criminals*. Beverly Hills, CA: Sage.

Shover, Neal. 1991. "Burglary." In *Crime and Justice: A Review of Research*. Vol. 14. Ed. Michael Tonry and James Q. Wilson. Chicago, IL: University of Chicago Press.

Shover, Neal, and Belinda Henderson. 1995. "Repressive Crime Control and Male Persistent Thieves." In *Crime and Public Policy: Putting Theory to Work*. Ed. Hugh D. Barlow. New York: Westview.

Shover, Neal, and David Honaker. 1992. "The Socially Bounded Decision Making of Persistent Property Offenders." In *In Their Own Words: Criminals on Crime*. Ed. Paul Cromwell. Los Angeles, CA: Roxbury.

Shover, Neal, and David Honaker. 1992. "The Socially Bounded Decision Making of Persistent Property Offenders." *The Howard Journal of Criminal Justice* 31:276–293.

Shover, Neal, and David Honaker. 1999. "The Socially Bounded Decision Making of Persistent Property Offenders." Pp. 10–22 in *In Their Own Words: Criminals on Crime*. Ed. Paul E. Cromwell. Los Angeles, CA: Roxbury.

Shover, Neal, and Carol Y. Thompson. 1992. "Age, Differential Expectations, and Crime Desistance." *Criminology* 30:601–616.

Shover, Neal, and John Paul Wright. 2001. *Crimes of Privilege: Readings in White-Collar Crime*. New York: Oxford University Press.

Shover, Neal, Greer Littonfox, and Michael Mills. 1991. "Victimization by White-Collar Crime and Institutional Delegitimation." Unpublished paper, University of Tennessee, Knoxville, TN.

Sieh, Edward W. 1987. "Garment Workers: Perceptions of Inequity and Employee Theft." *British Journal of Criminology* 27:174–190.

Silver, Allan. 1967. "The Demand for Order in Civil Society." In *The Police: Six Sociological Essays*. Ed. David Bordua. New York: Wiley.

Silverman, Robert A., and Leslie W. Kennedy. 1987. "The Female Perpetrator of Homicide in Canada." *Discussion Paper II, Center for Criminological Research*. University of Alberta, Calgary, Alberta: Center for Criminological Research,

Silverman, Robert A., and Leslie W. Kennedy. 1988.

"Women Who Kill Their Children." *Violence and Victims* 3:113–127.

Silverstein, Lee. 1966. "Bail in the State Courts—A Field Study and Report." *Minnesota Law Review* 50:621–631.

Simon, David R. 1999. *Elite Deviance*. 6th ed. Boston, MA: Allyn and Bacon.

Simon, David R., and D. Stanley Eitzen. 1993. *Elite Deviance*. 4th ed. Boston, MA: Allyn and Bacon.

Simon, David R., and Frank E. Hagan. 1999. *White-Collar Deviance*. Boston, MA: Allyn and Bacon.

Simon, Rita J. 1975. *Women and Crime*. Lexington, MA: Lexington Books.

Simpson, Sally. 1990. "Corporate Crime Deterrence and Corporate Control Policies: Views from the Inside." Presented at the Edwin Sutherland Conference on White-Collar Crime: 50 Years of Research and Beyond, May 12–15, Indiana University.

Simpson, Sally S., and Christopher S. Koper. 1992. "Deterring Corporate Crime." *Criminology* 30:347–375.

Simpson, Sally S., M. Lyn Exum, and N. Craig Smith. 2000. "The Social Control of Corporate Criminals: Shame and Informal Sanction Threats." In *Of Crime and Criminality: The Use of Theory in Everyday Life*. Ed. Sally S. Simpson. Thousand Oaks, CA: Pine Forge Press.

Sinclair, Andrew. 1964. *Era of Excess: A Social History of the Prohibition Movement*. New York: Harper & Row.

Singer, Neil M. 1973. *The Value of Inmate Manpower*. Washington, D.C.: American Bar Association.

Singer, Simon I. 1993. "The Automatic Waiver of Juveniles and Substantive Justice." *Crime and Delinquency* 39:253–261.

Skogan, Wesley G. 1977. "Dimensions of the Dark Figure of Unreported Crime." *Crime and Delinquency* 23:41–50.

Skogan, Wesley G. 1986. "Fear of Crime and Neighborhood Change." In *Communities and Crime; Crime and Justice: A Review of Research*. Vol. 8. Ed. Albert J. Reiss Jr. and Michael Tonry. Chicago, IL: University of Chicago Press.

Skogan, Wesley. 1990. *Disorder and Decline*. Los Angeles, CA: University of California Press.

Skogan, Wesley G., and Michael G. Maxfield. 1981. *Coping with Crime: Individual and Neighborhood Reactions*. Beverly Hills, CA: Sage.

Skolnick, Jerome H. 1966. *Justice without Trial*. New York: Wiley.

Skolnick, Jerome H. 1975. *Justice without Trial*. 2d ed. New York: Wiley.

Skolnick, Jerome H., and Elliott P. Currie. 1976. *Crisis in American Institutions*. 3d ed. Boston, MA: Little, Brown.

Sloan, John Henry, Arthur L. Kellerman, and Donald T. Reay. 1988. "Handgun Regulations, Crime, Assaults, and Homicide." *New England Journal of Medicine* 319:1256–1262.

Smart, Carol. 1979. "The New Female Criminal: Reality or Myth?" *British Journal of Criminology* 19:50–59.

Smigel, Erwin O. 1956. "Public Attitudes toward Stealing As Related to the Size of the Victim Organization." *American Sociological Review* 21:320–327.

Smigel, Erwin O., and Ross H. Lawrence, eds. 1970. *Crimes against Bureaucracy*. New York: Van Nostrand.

Smith, Alexander B., and Harriett Pollack. 1975. *Some Sins Are Not Crimes*. New York: Franklin Watts.

Smith, Douglas A. 1986. "The Neighborhood Context of Police Behavior." In *Communities and Crime*. Ed. Albert J. Reiss Jr. and Michael Tonry. Chicago, IL: University of Chicago Press.

Smith, Dwight C. 1980. "Paragons, Pariahs, and Pirates: A Spectrum-Based Theory of Enterprise." *Crime and Delinquency* 26:358–386.

Smith, Lorna J. F. 1989. *Concerns about Rape*. London, UK: H.M.S.O.

Smith, M. Dwayne. 1987. "Patterns of Discrimination in Assessments of the Death penalty: The Case of Louisiana." *Journal of Criminal Justice* 15:279–286.

Smith, M. Dwayne, and Margaret A. Zahn. 1999. *Homicide: A Sourcebook of Social Research*. Thousand Oaks, CA: Sage.

Smolowe, Jill. 1994. "Sleeping with the Enemy." *Time* (July 4): 18–25

Snodgrass, Jon. 1982. *The Jack-Roller at Seventy*. Lexington, MA: Lexington Books.

Snyder, Howard N. 1990. "Growth in Minority Detentions Attributed to Drug Law Violators." *Juvenile Justice Bulletin*.

Snyder, Howard N., and Terrence A. Finnegan. 1987. *Delinquency in the United States, 1983*. Washington, D.C.: U.S. Department of Justice.

Sourcebook of Criminal Justice Statistics. 1999. At <www.albany.edu/sourcebook>.

Sourcebook of Criminal Justice Statistics. 2000. At <www.albany.edu/sourcebook>.

Sowle, Claude R., ed. 1962. *Police Power and Individual Freedom*. Chicago, IL: Aldine.

Sparks, Richard F. 1980. "Criminal Opportunities and Crime Rates." In *Indicators of Crime and Criminal Justice: Quantitative Studies*. Ed. Stephen F. Feinberg and Albert J. Reiss. Washington, D.C.: U.S. Government Printing Office.

Spector, Malcolm, and John I. Kitsuse. 1987. *Constructing Social Problems*. New York: Aldine de Gruyter.

Speiglman, Richard. 1976. "Building the Walls Inside Medicine, Corrections and the State Apparatus for Repression." Ph.D. diss., University of California, Berkeley, CA.

Spergel, Irving. 1964. *Racketville, Slumtown, Haulberg: An Exploratory Study of Delinquent Subcultures*. Chicago, IL: University of Chicago Press.

Spitzer, Steven. 1975. "Toward a Marxian Theory of Deviance." *Social Problems* 22:638–651.

Spohn, Cassia. 1994. "Crime and the Social Control of Blacks: Offender/Victim Race and the Sentencing of Violent Offenders." In *Inequality, Crime, and Social Control*. Ed. George S. Bridges and Martha Myers. Boulder, CO: Westview Press.

Spohn, Cassia, and David Holleran. 2000. "The Imprisonment Penalty Paid by Young, Unemployed Black and Hispanic Male Offenders." *Criminology* 38:281–306.

Stafford, Mark C., and Mark Warr. 1993. "A Reconceptualization of General and Specific Deterrence." *Journal of Research in Crime and Delinquency* 30:123–135.

Stanko, Elizabeth. 1990. *Everyday Violence*. London, UK: Pandora.

Stanko, Elizabeth. 1995. "Gendered Criminological Policies: Femininity, Masculinity, and Violence." Pp. 207–226 in *Crime and Public Policy: Putting Theory to Work*. Ed. Hugh D. Barlow. Boulder, CO: Westview.

Stark, Rodney. 1987. "Deviant Places: A Theory of the Ecology of Crime." *Criminology* 25:893–909.

State of Texas. 1998. Indictment of the Accused Murderer of James Byrd.

State of Wyoming. 1998. Indictment of the Accused Murderers of Matthew Shepard.

Steffensmeier, Darrell J. 1986. *The Fence: In the Shadow of Two Worlds*. Totowa, NJ: Rowman and Littlefield.

Steffensmeier, Darrell J. 1995. "A Public Policy Agenda for Combating Organized Crime." In *Crime and Public Policy: Putting Theory to Work*. Ed. Hugh D. Barlow. Boulder, CO: Westview.

Steffensmeier, Darrell J., and Emilie Anderson Allan. 1988. "Sex Disparities in Arrests by Residence, Job and Age: An Assessment of the Gender Convergence Hypothesis." *Justice Quarterly* 5:53–80.

Steffensmeier, Darrell J., and Robert M. Terry. 1986. "Institutional Sexism in the Underworld: A View from the Inside." *Sociological Inquiry* 56:305–323.

Steffensmeier, Darrell J., John Kramer, and Cathy Streifel. 1993. "Gender and Imprisonment Decisions." *Criminology* 31:411–446.

Steffensmeier, Darrell J., Jeffrey Ulmer, and John Kramer. 1998. "The Interaction of Race, Gender, and Age in Criminal Sentencing: The Punishment Cost of Being Young, Black, and Male." *Criminology* 36:763–797.

Steinman, Michael. 1991. *Woman Battering: Policy Responses*. Cincinnati, OH: Anderson.

Stellwagen, Lindsey P. 1985. *Use of Forfeiture Sanctions in Drug Cases*. Washington, D.C.: National Institute of Justice.

Stevens, Dennis J. 1992. "Research Note: The Death Sentence and Inmate Attitudes." *Crime and Delinquency* 38:272–279.

Stewart, J. 1987. *The Prosecutors*. New York: Touchstone.

Stoddard, Ellwyn R. 1968. "The Informal 'Code' of Police Deviancy: A Group Approach to 'Blue Coat Crime.'" *Journal of Criminal Law, Criminology, and Police Science* 59:201–213.

Straus, Murray A. 1986. "Domestic Violence and Homicide Antecedents." *Bulletin of New York Academy of Medicine* 62:446–465.

Straus, Murray A., and Richard J. Gelles. 1986. "Societal Change and Change in Family Violence from 1975 to 1985 As Revealed by Two National Surveys." *Journal of Marriage and the Family* 48:465–479.

Straus, Murray A., Richard J. Gelles, and Suzanne K. Steinmetz. 1980. *Behind Closed Doors: Violence in the American Family*. New York: Anchor Books.

Sullivan, Peggy S. 1989. "Minority Officers: Current Issues." In *Critical Issues in Policing*. Ed. Roger

G. Dunham and Geoffrey P. Alpert. Prospect Heights, IL: Waveland Press.

Sullivan, Peggy S., Roger G. Dunham, and Geoffrey Alpert. 1987. "Attitude Structures of Different Ethnic and Age Groups Concerning Police." *Journal of Criminal Law and Criminology* 78:177–193.

Sutherland, Edwin H. 1937a. *Criminology*. New York: Lippincott.

Sutherland, Edwin H. 1937b. *The Professional Thief.* Chicago, IL: University of Chicago Press.

Sutherland, Edwin H. 1939. *Criminology*. Philadelphia, PA: J. B. Lippincott.

Sutherland, Edwin H. 1945. "Is 'White-Collar Crime' Crime?" *American Sociological Review* 10:132–139.

Sutherland, Edwin H. 1949. *White-Collar Crime*. New York: Dryden Press.

Sutherland, Edwin H., and Donald R. Cressey. 1974. *Criminology*. 9th ed. Philadelphia, PA: Lippincott.

Sutton, Mike. 1993. "From Receiving to Thieving: The Market for Stolen Goods and the Incidence of Theft." *Home Office Research Bulletin* 34:3–8.

Sykes, Gresham M. 1958. *The Society of Captives*. Princeton, NJ: Princeton University Press.

Sykes, Gresham M. 1972. "The Future of Criminality." *American Behavioral Scientist* 15:409–419.

Sykes, Gresham M. 1978. *Criminology*. New York: Harcourt Brace Jovanovich.

Sykes, Gresham M., and David Matza. 1957. "Techniques of Neutralization: A Theory of Delinquency." *American Sociological Review* 22:664–670.

Sylvester, Sawyer F., and Edward Sagarin, eds. 1974. *Politics and Crime*. New York: Praeger.

Takagi, Paul. 1979. "Death by 'Police Intervention.'" In *A Community Concern: Police Use of Deadly Force*. U.S. Department of Justice. Washington, D.C.: U.S. Government Printing Office.

Takaki, Ronald T. 1993. *A Different Mirror: A History of Multicultural America*. Boston, MA: Little, Brown.

Tangri, Sandra S., and Michael Schwartz. 1967. "Delinquency Research and the Self-Concept Variable." *Journal of Criminal Law, Criminology, and Police Science* 58:182–190.

Tannenbaum, Frank. 1938. *Crime and the Community*. New York: Columbia University.

Tappan, Paul W. 1947. "Who Is the Criminal?" *American Sociological Review* 12:96–102.

Taylor, Bruce M. 1989. *New Directions for the National Crime Survey*. Washington, D.C.: U.S. Department of Justice.

Taylor, G. Rattray. 1965. *Sex in History*. London, UK: Panther.

Taylor, Ian, Paul Walton, and Jock Young, eds. 1975. *Critical Criminology*. London, UK: Routledge and Kegan Paul.

Temple, Mark, and Patricia Ladoucer. 1986. "The Alcohol-Crime Relationship as an Age-Specific Phenomenon: A Longitudinal Study." *Contemporary Drug Problems* 86:89–115.

Terry, C. E., and Mildred Pellens. [1928] 1970. *The Opium Problem*. Montclair, NJ: Patterson Smith.

Thomas, D. A. 1967. "Sentencing: The Basic Principles." *Criminal Law Review*, 514–520.

Thomas, Jim. 1982. "New Directions in Deviance Research." Pp. 288–318 in *The Sociology of Deviance*. Ed. M. Michael Rosenberg, Robert A. Stebbins, and Allan Turowetz. New York: St. Martins.

Thompson, Margaret E., Steven H. Chaffee, and Hayg H. Oshagan. 1990. "Regulating Pornography: A Public Dilemma." *Journal of Communications* 40:73–83.

Thornberry, Terence P. 1973. "Race, Socioeconomic Status, and Sentencing in the Juvenile Justice System." *Journal of Criminal Law and Criminology* 64:90–98.

Thornberry, Terence P. 1987. "Toward an Interactional Theory of Delinquency." *Criminology* 25:863–891.

Thornberry, Terence P., and R. L. Christenson. 1984. "Unemployment and Criminal Involvement: An Investigation of Reciprocal Causal Structures." *American Sociological Review* 49:398–411.

Thornhill, Randy, and Craig T. Palmer. 2000. *A Natural History of Rape: Biological Bases of Sexual Coercion*. Boston, MA: MIT Press.

Thornton, William E., and Jennifer James. 1980. "Masculinity and Delinquency Revisited." *British Journal of Criminology* 19:225–241.

Thrasher, Frederick M. 1929. *The Gang*. Chicago, IL: University of Chicago Press.

Tifft, Larry, and Lynn Markham. 1991. "Battering Women and Battering Central Americans: A Peacemaking Synthesis." In *Criminology as Peacemaking*. Ed. Richard Quinney and Hal Pepinsky. Bloomington, IN: Indiana University Press.

Tifft, Larry, and Dennis Sullivan. 1980. *The Struggle*

to Be Human: Crime, Criminology, and Anarchism. Sanday, Orkney, UK: Cienfuegos Press.

Tillmanane, Robert, and Henry N. Pontell. 1992. "Is Justice Collar-Blind?: Punishing Medicaid Provider Fraud." *Criminology* 30:547–574.

Tittle, Charles R. 1980. *Sanctions and Deterrence.* New York: Praeger.

Tittle, Charles R. 1988. "Two Empirical Regularities (Maybe) in Search of an Explanation: Commentary on the Age/Crime Debate." *Criminology* 26:75–85.

Tittle, Charles R. 1995. *Control Balance: Toward a General Theory of Deviance.* Boulder, CO: Westview.

Tittle, Charles R. 1997. "Thoughts Stimulated by Braithwaite's Analysis of Control Balance Theory." *Theoretical Criminology* 1, no. 1 (February): 99–110.

Toch, Hans. 1977. *Police, Prisons, and the Problem of Violence.* Rockville, MD: National Institute of Mental Health.

Tonry, Michael. 1994. "Racial Disproportion in U.S. Prisons." *British Journal of Criminology.*

Tonry, Michael N., and Norval K. Morris, eds. 1983. *Crime and Justice: An Annual Review of Research.* Vol. 4. Chicago, IL: University of Chicago Press.

Tonry, Michael N., and Norval K. Morris, eds. 1988. *Crime and Justice: An Annual Review of Research.* Vol. 10. Chicago, IL: University of Chicago Press.

Toro-Calder, Jaime. 1950. "Personal Crimes in Puerto Rico." Master's thesis, University of Wisconsin.

Tracy, Paul E., Marvin E. Wolfgang, and Robert M. Figlio. 1990. *Delinquency Careers in Two Birth Cohorts.* New York: Plenum Press.

Trasler, Gordon. 1986. "Situational Crime Control and Rational Choice." In *Situational Crime Prevention: From Theory into Practice.* Ed. Kevin Heal and Gloria Laycock. London, UK: H.M.S.O.

Trebach, Arnold S., and James A. Inciardi. 1993. *Legalize It? Debating American Drug Policy.* New York: The American University Press.

Triplett, Ruth. 2000. "The Dramatization of Evil: Reacting to Juvenile Delinquency during the 1990s. In *Of Crime and Criminality: The Use of Theory in Everyday Life.* Ed. Sally S. Simpson. Thousand Oaks, CA: Pine Forge Press.

Trivizas, Eugene, and Philip T. Smith. n.d. "The Deterrent Effect of Terrorist Incidents on the Rates of Luggage Theft in Railway and Underground Stations." *The British Journal of Criminology* 37 (1): 63–75.

Trotter, R. T. 1972. "Clockwork Orange in a California Prison." *Science News* 101:174–175.

Tucker, James. 1989. "Employee Theft as Social Control." *Deviant Behavior* 10:319–334.

Tucker, Robert C. 1978. *The Marx-Engels Reader.* 2d ed. New York: W. W. Norton Company.

Tuel, Beverly D., and Richard K. Russell. 1998. "Self-Esteem and Depression in Battered Women: A Comparison of Lesbian and Heterosexual Survivors." *Violence against Women* 4 (3): 344–362.

Tunnell, Kenneth D. 1990. "Choosing Crime: Close Your Eyes and Take Your Chances." *Justice Quarterly* 7:4.

Tunnell, Kenneth D. 1992. *Choosing Crime: The Criminal Calculus of Property Offenders.* Chicago, IL: Nelson-Hall.

Tunnell, Kenneth D. 2000. *Living Off Crime.* Chicago, IL: Burnham.

Turk, Austin T. 1966. "Conflict and Criminality." *American Sociological Review* 31:338–352.

Turk, Austin T. 1969. *Criminality and Legal Order.* Chicago, IL: Rand McNally.

Turner, J. W. Cecil, ed. 1966. *Kenney's Outlines of Criminal Law.* 19th ed. Cambridge, UK: Cambridge University Press.

Tyler, Gus, ed. 1962. *Organized Crime in America.* Ann Arbor, MI: University of Michigan Press.

U.S. Bureau of the Census. 1993. *Statistical Abstract of the United States, 1993.* Washington, D.C.: U.S. Department of Commerce.

U.S. Census Bureau. 2000. NCVS Questionnaire. At <www.census.gov>.

U.S. Center for Women Policy Studies. 1979. *Violence in the Home Is a Crime against the Whole Family.* Washington, D.C.: U.S. Government Printing Office.

U.S. Department of Agriculture. 2000. At <www.usda.gov>.

U.S. Department of Education. 1999. At <www.ed.gov>.

U.S. Department of Education. 2000. *1999 Annual Report on School Safety.* Washington, D.C.: U.S. Department of Education.

U.S. Department of Health and Human Services. 2000. "Annual National Household Survey Results Released." Press Release. Washington, D.C.

U.S. Department of Health and Human Services. 1997. *National Center on Child Abuse and Neglect, Study on Incidence and Prevalence.* Washington, D.C.

U.S. Department of Justice. 1976. *The LEAA: A Partnership for Crime Control.* Washington, D.C.: U.S. Government Printing Office.

U.S. Department of Justice. 1979. *A Community Concern: Police Use of Deadly Force.* Washington, D.C.: U.S. Government Printing Office.

U.S. Department of Justice. 1999. *American Indians and Crime.* Washington, D.C.: U.S. Department of Justice.

Uchida, Craig D., Brian Forst, and Sampson O. Annan. 1992. *Modern Policing and the Control of Illegal Drugs.* Washington, D.C.: U.S. Department of Justice.

Uncapher, Willard. 1991. "Trouble in Cyberspace." *The Humanist* (Sept/Oct): 5–34.

United Nations. 1999. Ad Hoc on the Elaboration of a Convention against Transnational Organized Crime. At <www/un.org>.

Vadas, Melinda. 1992. "The Pornography/Civil Rights Ordinance v. the BOG: And the Winner Is ...?" *Hypatia* 7:94–109.

Vagg, Jon. 1998. "Delinquency and Shame: Data from Hong Kong." *Criminology* 35, no. 2 (May): 203–227.

Valentine, Alan. 1956. *Vigilante Justice.* New York: Reynal.

van den Berghe, Pierre L. 1974. "Bringing Beasts Back in: Toward a Biosocial Theory of Aggression." *American Sociological Review* 39:777–778.

van Wormer, Katherine Stuart, and Clemens Bartollas. 2000. *Women and the Criminal Justice System.* Boston, MA: Allyn and Bacon.

Vander-May, Brenda J., and Donald L. Neff. 1984. "Adult-Child Incest: A Sample of Substantiated Cases." *Family Relations* 33:549–557.

Vaughan, Diane. 1996. *The Challenger Launch Decision: Risky Technology, Culture, and Deviance at NASA.* Chicago, IL: University of Chicago Press.

Vaughan, Diane. 1998. "Rational Choice, Situated Action, and the Social Control of Organizations." *Law and Society Review* 32 (1): 23–61.

Vega, William A., and Andres G. Gil. 1999. "A Model for Explaining Drug Use Behavior among Hispanic Adolescents." *Drugs and Society* 14 (1–2): 57–74.

Velarde, Albert J., and Mark Warlick. 1973. "Massage Parlors: The Sensuality Business." *Society* 11:63–74.

Venkatesh, Sudhir-Alladi. 1998. "African American Organized Crime: A Social History." *American Journal of Sociology* 103 (6): 1747–1749.

Vetri, Dominick R. 1964. "Guilty-Plea Bargaining: Compromise by Prosecutors to Secure Guilty Pleas." *University of Pennsylvania Law Review* 112:896–908.

Vila, Bryan J. 1994. "A General Paradigm for Understanding Criminal Behavior: Extending Evolutionary Ecological Theory." *Criminology* 32:311–359.

Vila, Bryan J., and Lawrence E. Cohen. 1993. "Crime As Strategy: Testing an Evolutionary Ecological Theory of Expropriative Crime." *American Journal of Sociology* 98:873–912.

Vold, George B. 1958. *Theoretical Criminology.* New York: Oxford University Press.

Vold, George B. 1979. *Theoretical Criminology.* 2d ed. Prepared by Thomas J. Bernard. New York: Oxford University Press.

Vold, George B., and Thomas J. Bernard. 1986. *Theoretical Criminology.* New York: Oxford University Press.

von Hentig, Hans. 1948. *The Criminal and His Victim.* New Haven, CT: Yale University Press.

von Hirsch, Andrew. 1984. "Selective Incapacitation: A Critique." *NIJ Reports.* Washington, D.C.: National Institute of Justice.

Waegel, William B. 1989. "The Use of Lethal Force by Police: The Effect of Statutory Change." *Crime and Delinquency* 30:121–140.

Wagstaff, Alan, and Alan Maynard. 1988. *Economic Aspects of the Illicit Drug Market and Drug Enforcement Policies in the United Kingdom.* London, UK: H.M.S.O.

Walker, Lenore E. 1989. *Terrifying Love.* New York: Harper & Row.

Walker, Samuel. 1989. "Broken Windows and Fractured History: The Use and Misuse of History in Recent Police Patrol Analysis." In *Critical Issues in Policing.* Ed. Roger G. Dunham and Geoffrey P. Alpert. Prospect Heights, IL: Waveland Press.

Walker, Samuel. 1992. *The Police in America: An Introduction.* 2d ed. New York: McGraw-Hill.

Walker, Samuel. 1998. *Sense and Nonsense about Crime and Drugs: A Policy Guide.* 4th ed. New York: West/Wadsworth.

Walker, Samuel. 2001. *Sense and Nonsense about Crime and Drugs: A Policy Guide.* 5th ed. Belmont, CA: Wadsworth.

Walsh, Anthony, and Lee Ellis. 1999. "Political Ideology and American Criminologists' Explanations for Criminal Behavior." *The Criminologist* 24, no. 6 (November/December): 1, 14.

Walsh, Dermot. 1980. *Break-ins: Burglary from Private Houses*. London, UK: Constable.

Walsh, Marilyn. 1977. *The Fence*. Westport, CT: Greenwood Press.

Walters, James M. 1985. "'Taking Care of Business' Updated: A Fresh Look at the Daily Routine of the Heroin User." In *Life with Heroin*. Ed. Bill Hanson, George Beschner, James M. Walters, and Elliott Bovelle. Lexington, MA: Lexington Books.

Walton, Robert P. 1938. *America's New Drug Problem*. Philadelphia, PA: Lippincott.

Waltz, Jon R. 1953. "Shoplifting and the Law of Arrest." *Yale Law Journal* 62:788–805.

Warchol, Greg. 1998. *Workplace Violence, 1992–96*. Washington, D.C.: U.S. Department of Justice.

Ward, David A., Maurice Jackson, and Renee E. Ward. 1969. "Crimes of Violence by Women." In *Crimes of Violence*. Ed. Donald J. Mulvihill, Melvin Tumin, and Lynn Curtis. Washington, D.C.: U.S. Government Printing Office.

Warr, Mark, and Mark Stafford. 1991. "The Influences of Delinquent Peers: What They Think or What They Do?" *Criminology* 29:851–866.

Warren, E. H., Jr. 1978. "The Economic Approach to Crime." *Canadian Journal of Criminology* 10:437–449.

Warshaw, R. 1989. *I Never Called It Rape*. New York: Harper & Row.

Watkins, B., and A. Bentovim. 1992. "The Sexual Abuse of Male Children and Adolescents: A Review of Current Research." *Journal of Child Psychology and Psychiatry* 33:197–248.

Webb, Barry. 1994. "Steering Column Locks and Motor Vehicle Theft: Evaluation from Three Countries." In *Crime Prevention Studies*. Vol. 2. Ed. Ronald V. Clarke. Monsey, NY: Criminal Justice Press.

Weber, Max. 1954. *Law in Economy and Society*. Cambridge, MA: Harvard University Press.

Webster, Barbara, and Edward F. Connors. 1992. "The Police, Drugs, and Public Housing." *NIJ Research in Brief* (June): 1–6.

Webster, Barbara, and Michael S. McCampbell. 1992. "International Money Laundering: Research and Investigation Join Forces." *NIJ Research in Brief* (September): 1–8.

Weinberg, Martin S., and Colin J. Williams. 1975. *Male Homosexuals: Their Problems and Adaptations*. Baltimore, MD: Penguin Books.

Weinberg, Martin S., Frances Shaver, and Colin J. Williams. 1999. "Gendered Sex Work in the San Francisco Tenderloin." *Archives of Sexual Behavior* 28 (6): 503–521.

Weiner, Norman. 1974. "The Effect of Education on Police Attitudes." *Journal of Criminal Justice* 2:323–330.

Weis, Kurt, and Sandra S. Borges. 1973. "Victimology and Rape: The Case of the Legitimate Victim." *Issues in Criminology* 8:85–89.

Weisburd, David, and Lorraine Green. 1995. "Policing Drug Hot Spots: The Jersey City Drug Market Analysis Experiment." *Justice Quarterly* 12:711–735.

Weiss, T. G. 1997. *Political Gain and Civilian Pain: Humanitarian Impacts of Economic Sanctions*. Lanham, MD: Rowman and Littlefield.

Weitzer, Ronald. 1991. "Prostitutes' Rights in the United States: The Failure of a Movement." *Sociological Quarterly* 32:23–41.

Wellford, Charles. 1975. "Labeling Theory and Criminology: An Assessment." *Social Problems* 22:332–345.

Welsh, Brandon C., and David P. Farrington. 1999. "Value for Money? A Review of the Costs and Benefits of Situational Crime Prevention." *The British Journal of Criminology* 39 (3): 345–369.

Welsh, Wayne N., Jack R. Greene, and Patricia H. Jenkins. 1999. "School Disorder: The Influence of Individual, Institutional, and Community Factors." *Criminology* 37 (1): 73–116.

Werner, Emmy E. 1987. "Vulnerability and Resiliency in Children at Risk for Delinquency: A Longitudinal Study from Birth to Young Adulthood." In *Prevention of Delinquent Behavior*. Ed. John D. Buchard and Sara N. Buchard. Beverly Hills, CA: Sage.

Werner, E. E., and R. S. Smith. 1977. *Kauai's Children Come of Age*. Honolulu, HI: University of Hawaii Press.

Werner, E. E., J. M. Bierman, and F. E. French. 1971. *The Children of Kauai: A Longitudinal Study from the Prenatal Period to Age Ten*. Honolulu, HI: University of Hawaii Press.

Werthman, Carl. 1967. "The Function of Social Definitions in the Development of Delinquent Careers." In *Task Force Report: A Report of the President's Commission on Law Enforcement and the*

Administration of Justice. Washington, D.C.: U.S. Government Printing Office.

Werthman, Carl, and Irving Piliavin. 1967. "Gang Members and the Police." In *The Police: Six Sociological Essays*. Ed. David Bordua. New York: Wiley.

West, Donald J. 1967. *The Young Offender*. Harmondsworth, UK: Penguin Books.

West, Donald J. 1982. *Delinquency: Its Roots, Careers, and Prospects*. London, UK: Heinemann.

West, Donald J., and David P. Farrington. 1973. *Who Becomes Delinquent?* London, UK: Heinemann.

West, Donald J., and David P. Farrington. 1977. *The Delinquent Way of Life*. London, UK: Heinemann.

Westerman, Ted D., and James W. Burfeind. 1991. *Crime and Justice in Two Societies: Japan and the United States*. Pacific Grove, CA: Brooks/Cole.

Westley, William A. 1970. *Violence and the Police: A Sociological Study of Law, Custom and Morality*. Cambridge, MA: MIT Press.

Weston, Paul B., and Kenneth M. Wells. 1972. *Law Enforcement and Criminal Justice*. Pacific Palisades, CA: Goodyear.

Whitaker, Catherine J. 1989. *The Redesigned National Crime Survey: Selected New Data*. Washington, D.C.: U.S. Department of Justice.

Whitaker, Catherine J., and Lisa D. Bastian. 1991. *Teenage Victims: A National Crime Survey Report*. Washington, D.C.: U.S. Department of Justice.

Whitcomb, Debra. 1985. "Prevention of Child Sexual Abuse: Innovations in Practice." *NIJ Research in Brief* (November): l–7.

Whitcomb, Debra, Gail S. Goodman, Desmond K. Runyan, and Shirley Hook. 1994. "The Emotional Effects of Testifying on Sexually Abused Children." *NIJ Research in Brief* (April): 1–7.

White, Leslie T. 1972. "The Definitions and Prohibitions of Incest." In *Sex and Society*. Ed. John N. Edwards. Chicago, IL: Markham.

White, Mel. 1994. *Stranger at the Gate*. New York: Simon & Schuster.

Whitehead, J. T., and Steven P. Lab. 1989. "A Meta-Analysis of Juvenile Correctional Treatment." *Journal of Research in Crime and Delinquency* 26:276–295.

Whitehead, Tony L. 2000. "The 'Epidemic' and 'Cultural Legends' of Black Male Incarceration: The Socialization of African American Children

to a Life of Incarceration." In *Building Violence: How America's Rush to Incarcerate Creates More Violence*. Ed. John P. May. Thousands Oaks, CA: Sage.

Whitman, Howard. 1951. *Terror in the Streets*. New York: Dial Press.

Whyte, William Foote. 1943. *Streetcorner Society*. Chicago, IL: University of Chicago Press.

Widom, Cathy Spatz. 1992. "The Cycle of Violence." *NIJ Research In Brief* (October): 1–6.

Wilbanks, William. 1984. *Murder in Miami*. New York: University of America Press.

Wilbanks, William. 1985. "Is Violent Crime Intraracial?" *Crime and Delinquency* 31:117–128.

Wilkins, Leslie T., Jack M. Kress, Don M. Gottfredson, Joseph C. Calpin, and Arthur M. Gelman. 1978. *Sentencing Guidelines: Structuring Judicial Discretion*. Washington, D.C.: U.S. Government Printing Office.

Williams, Frank P., III, and Marilyn D. McShane. 1988. *Criminological Theory*. Englewood Cliffs, NJ: Prentice Hall.

Williams, Hubert, and Patrick V. Murphy. 1990. "The Evolving Strategy of Police: A Minority View." In *Perspectives on Policing*. Vol. 13. Washington, D.C.: National Institute of Justice.

Williams, Joyce E., and Karen Holmes. 1981. *The Second Assault: Rape and Public Attitudes*. Westport, CT: Greenwood Press.

Williams, Kirk R. 1984. "Economic Sources of Homicide: Re-Estimating the Effects of Poverty and Inequality." *American Sociological Review* 49:283–289.

Williams, Kirk R., and Robert L. Flewelling. 1988. "The Social Production of Criminal Homicide: A Comparative Study of Disaggregated Rates in American Cities." *American Sociological Review* 53:421–431.

Williams, Kristen M. 1976. "The Effects of Victim Characteristics on the Disposition of Violent Crimes." In *Criminal Justice and the Victim*. Ed. William McDonald. Beverly Hills, CA: Sage.

Williams, Kristen M. 1978. *The Role of Victims in the Prosecution of Violent Crime*. Washington, D.C.: Institute for Law and Social Policy.

Williams, Linda. 1984. "Sex, Race, and Rape: An Analysis of Interracial Sexual Violence." Presented to the annual meeting of the American Society of Criminology, Cincinnati, OH.

Wilson, Hugh T. 2000. *Annual Editions: Drugs, Society, and Behavior*. Sluice Dock, CT: Dushkin/McGraw-Hill. Pp. 186–188.

Wilson, James Q. 1975. *Thinking about Crime*. New York: Basic Books.

Wilson, James Q. 1984. "Problems in the Creation of Adequate Criminal Justice Information Systems." In *Information Policy and Crime Control Strategies*. Search Group, Inc. Washington, D.C.: U.S. Department of Justice.

Wilson, James Q. 1988. "Entering Criminology through the Back Door." *The Criminologist* 13(6): 4, 7–8.

Wilson, James Q., and Barbara Boland. 1978. "The Effect of the Police on Crime." *Law and Society Review* 12:367–390.

Wilson, James Q., and Richard J. Herrnstein. 1985. *Crime and Human Nature*. New York: Simon & Schuster.

Wilson, Margo, and Martin Daly. 1998. "Sexual Rivalry and Sexual Conduct: Recurring Themes in Fatal Conflicts." *Theoretical Criminology* 2 (3): 291–310.

Wilson, Nanci Koser. 1993. "Gendered Interaction in Criminal Homicide." In *Homicide: The Victim/Offender Connection*. Ed. Anna Victoria Wilson. Cincinnati, OH: Anderson.

Wilson, Sheena. 1980. "Vandalism and Defensible Space in London Housing Estates." In *Designing Out Crime*. Ed. R. V. G. Clarke and P. Mayhew. London, UK: H.M.S.O.

Wilson, William Julius. 1987. *The Truly Disadvantaged: The Inner City, the Underclass, and Public Policy*. Chicago, IL: University of Chicago Press.

Wiltz, Christine. 1999. *The Last Madam: A Life in the New Orleans Underworld*. New York: Faber and Faber.

Winick, Charles. 1962. "Maturing Out of Narcotic Addiction." *Bulletin on Narcotics* 14:1–7.

Winick, Charles, and Paul M. Kinsie. 1971. *The Lively Commerce: Prostitution in the United States*. Chicago, IL: Quadrangle Books.

Winterfield, Laura A., and Sally T. Hillsman. 1993. "The Staten Island Day-Fine Project." *NIJ Research in Brief* (January): 1–7.

Wiseman, Jacqueline P. 1970. *Stations of the Lost: The Treatment of Skid Row Alcoholics*. Englewood Cliffs, NJ: Prentice Hall.

Wittebrood, Karin, and Paul Nieuwbeerta. 2000. "Criminal Victimization during One's Life Course: The Effects of Previous Victimization and Patterns of Routine Activities." *Journal of Research in Crime and Delinquency* 37, no. 1 (February): 91–122.

Wolf, Daniel R. 1991. *The Rebels: A Brotherhood of Outlaw Bikers*. Toronto, Ontario: University of Toronto Press.

Wolfgang, Marvin E. 1958. *Patterns in Criminal Homicide*. Philadelphia, PA: University of Pennsylvania Press.

Wolfgang, Marvin E. 1961. "Pioneers in Criminology: Cesare Lombroso (1835–1909)." *Journal of Criminal Law, Criminology, and Police Science* 52:361–391.

Wolfgang, Marvin E. 1967. *Crimes of Violence: A Report to the President's Commission on Law Enforcement and the Administration of Justice*. Washington, D.C.: U.S. Government Printing Office.

Wolfgang, Marvin E., and Bernard Cohen. 1970. *Crime and Race*. New York: Institute of Human Relations Press.

Wolfgang, Marvin E., and Franco Ferracuti. 1967. *The Subculture of Violence*. London, UK: Tavistock.

Wolfgang, Marvin E., and Marc Riedel. 1973. "Law, Judicial Discretion, and the Death Penalty." *The Annals* 407:119–133.

Wolfgang, Marvin E., Robert M. Figlio, and Thorsten Sellin. 1972. *Delinquency in a Birth Cohort*. Chicago, IL: University of Chicago Press.

Wolin, Sheldon S. 1970. "Violence and the Western Political Tradition." In *Violence: Causes and Solutions*. Ed. Renatus Hartogs and Eric Artzt. New York: Dell.

Woodrum, Eric. 1992. "Pornography and Moral Attitudes." *Sociological Spectrum* 13:329–347.

Wright, Helena. 1968. *Sex and Society*. London, UK: Allen and Unwin.

Wright, James D., and Peter H. Rossi. 1981. *Weapons, Crime, and Violence in America*. Washington, D.C.: National Institute of Justice.

Wright, James D., and Peter H. Rossi. 1986. *Armed and Considered Dangerous: A Survey of Felons and Their Firearms*. New York: Aldine de Gruyter.

Wright, James D., Joseph F. Sheley, and M. Dwayne Smith. 1992. "Kids, Guns, and Killing Fields." *Society* 30:84–89.

Wright, Kevin N., and Karen E. Wright. 1994. *Family Life, Delinquency, and Crime: A Policymaker's Guide*. Washington, D.C.: Office of Juvenile Justice and Delinquency Prevention.

Wright, Richard A. 1994. "Twenty Recent Criminology Textbooks: Continued Diversity without Currency or Quality." *Teaching Sociology* 22:87–104.

Wright, Richard T. 2000. Comments made at a presentation at Southern Illinois University Edwardsville, March.

Wright, Richard T., and Scott H. Decker. 1994. *Burglars on the Job: Streetlife and Residential Break-ins*. Boston, MA: Northeastern University Press.

Wright, Richard T., and Scott H. Decker. 1997. *Armed Robbers in Action*. Boston, MA: Northeastern University Press.

Yablonsky, Lewis. 1966. *The Violent Gang*. New York: Penguin Books.

Yeager, Peter Cleary, and Gary E. Reed. 1998. "Of Corporate Persons and Straw Men: A Reply to Herbert, Green, and Larragoite." *Criminology* 36, no. 4 (November): 885–897.

Yin, Robert. 1994. *Case Study Research: Design and Methods*. 2d ed. Thousands Oaks, CA: Sage.

Yochelson, Samuel, and Stanton E. Samenow. 1976, 1977. *The Criminal Personality*. Vol. 1 and 2. New York: Jason Aronson.

Yogan, Lissa J. 2000. "School Tracking and Student Violence." *The Annals of the American Academy of Political and Social Science* 567:108–122.

Young, James H. 1967. *The Medical Messiahs*. Princeton, NJ: Princeton University Press.

Young, Jock. 1986. "The Failure of Criminology: The Need of Radical Realism." In *Confronting Crime*. Ed. Roger Matthews and Jock Young. Beverly Hills, CA: Sage.

Young, Jock. 1997. "Left Realism: The Basics." In *Thinking Critically about Crime*. Ed. Brian MacLean and Dragan Milovanovic. Vancouver, BC: The Collective Press.

Young, Jock. 2000. *The Exclusive Society*. London, UK: Sage.

Zahn, Margaret A., and Philip C. Sagi. 1987. "Stranger Homicide in Nine American Cities." *Journal of Criminal Law and Criminology* 78:377–397.

Zatz, Marjorie S., and Edwardo L. Portillos. 2000. "Voices from the Barrio: Chicano/a Gangs, Families, and Communities." *Criminology* 38 (2): 369–402.

ZDNET. 2000. "Are They Hackers or Crackers?" At <www.zdnet.com/special/stories/defense/0,104 59,2504308,00.html>.

Zeitz, Dorothy. 1981. *Women Who Embezzle or Defraud: A Study of Convicted Felons*. New York: Praeger.

Zimbardo, Philip G. 1972. "The Pathology of Imprisonment." Society 9:4–8.

Zimring, Franklin E. 1972. "The Medium Is the Message: Firearm Caliber as a Determinant of Death from Assault." *Journal of Legal Studies* 15:97–123.

Zimring, Franklin E., and Gordon J. Hawkins. 1973. *Deterrence: The Legal Threat in Crime Control*. Chicago, IL: University of Chicago Press.

Zinn, Howard. 1999. *A People's History of the United States: 1492–Present*. 20th Anniversary ed. New York: HarperCollins.

Zupan, Linda L. 1992. "Men Guarding Women: An Analysis of the Employment of Male Correction Officers in Prisons for Women." *Journal of Criminal Justice* 20:297–309.

PHOTO CREDITS

Chapter 1

Page 1: Geoff Hansen/Valley News/Impact Visuals Photo & Graphics, Inc.; **page 5:** Richard Choy/Peter Arnold, Inc.; **page 12:** Stele of Hammurabi—detail of upper part: The sun god dictating his laws to King Hammurabi; Babylonian relief from Susa, c. 1760 B.C. (diorite, height of stele c. 2.1 m, height of relief 71 cm); Louvre, Paris, France; Giraudon/Art Resource, N.Y.; **page 14:** J. Scott Applewhite/AP/Wide World Photos.

Chapter 2

Page 22: Joel Gordon Photography; **page 24:** AP/Wide World Photos; **page 34:** Michael Newman/PhotoEdit; **page 37:** C. H. Simonpietre/Corbis/Sygma.

Chapter 3

Page 41: IT International Ltd./eStock Photography LLC; **page 53:** Courtesy of Jefferson County SO/Kevin Moloney for the NYT/Liaison Agency, Inc.; **page 58:** Max Whittaker/Liaison Agency, Inc.; **page 61:** Deborah Copaken/Liaison Agency, Inc.

Chapter 4

Page 68: Michael Newman/PhotoEdit; **page 70:** David De Lossy/The Image Bank; **page 71:** Barbara Peacock/FPG International LLC; **page 87:** © Bettman/Corbis; **page 88:** James Carroll/Stock Boston.

Chapter 5

Page 91: Barbara Alper/Stock Boston; **page 98:** Jeff Greenberg/Peter Arnold, Inc.; **page 109:** SuperStock, Inc.

Chapter 6

Page 115: Michael J. Philippot/Corbis/Sygma; **page 123:** Michael Newman/PhotoEdit; **page 134:** Telegraph Colour Library/FPG International LLC; **page 136:** Zoran Milich/Liaison Agency, Inc.; **page 137:** AP/Wide World Photos.

Chapter 7

Page 142: © Bettman/Corbis; **page 145, left:** J. Markowitz/Corbis/Sygma; **page 145, right:** Mark Lennihan/AP/Wide World Photos; **page 154:** Kobal Collection.

Chapter 8

Page 168: Sean Murphy/Stone; **page 172:** © Owen Franken/Corbis; **page 181:** Bonnie Kamin/PhotoEdit; **page 189:** Timothy Healy/Design Conceptions; **page 191:** Michael Siluk.

Chapter 9

Page 194: © Joel Gordon 2000; **page 203:** Kent Meireis/The Image Works; **page 214:** Frank Pedrick/The Image Works; **page 216:** © Bettman/Corbis.

Chapter 10

Page 222: Ken Whitmore/Stone; **page 231:** © Bettman/Corbis; **page 232:** © Bettman/Corbis; **page 236:** © Bettman/Corbis.

Chapter 11

Page 240: Liaison Agency, Inc.; **page 242:** © Bettman/Corbis; **page 247:** Eric Gay/AP/Wide World Photos; **page 250:** Mark Ludak/The Image Works; **page 253:** Photo Researchers, Inc.

Chapter 12

Page 263: Telegraph Colour Library/FPG International LLC; **page 265:** SuperStock, Inc.; **page 273:** E. Crews/The Image Works; **page 274:** Bruce Ayres/Stone.

Chapter 13

Page 283: Mark Antman/The Image Works; **page 288:** Joel Gordon Photography; **page 289:** Earl Dotter/Impact Visuals Photo & Graphics, Inc.; **page 293:** Peter Cade/Stone; **page 299:** Stephen Shames/Matrix International, Inc.

Chapter 14

Page 302: Joel Gordon Photography; **page 310:** David Young-Wolff/PhotoEdit; **page 312:** Mary Evans Picture Library.

AUTHOR INDEX

SUBJECT INDEX

An *f* or *t* following the page number indicates a figure or table, respectively.